500

places for **food** & **wine** lovers

1st Edition

by Holly Hughes

with Charlie O'Malley

WILEY

Wiley Publishing, Inc.

Contents

Published by:

Wiley Publishing, Inc.

111 River St.
Hoboken, NJ 07030-5774

ISBN 978-0-470-28775-0

Editor: Maureen Clarke
Production Editor: Michael Brumitt
Photo Editor: Cherie Cincilla
Interior book design: Melissa Auciello-Brogan
Production by Wiley Indianapolis Composition Services

Front cover photo: Jim Denevan and his moveable feast, Outstanding in the Field, outside Seattle.
Back cover photo: Istanbul, Turkey: Spice Bazaar; Miami, Florida: Basil Panna Cotta at Michael's Genuine Food & Drink; Dallas, Texas: Sonny Bryan's Smokehouse; traditional soft French cheeses
For information on our other products and services or to obtain technical support, please contact our Customer Care Department within the U.S. at 877/762-2974, outside the U.S. at 317/572-3993 or fax 317/572-4002.

Wiley also publishes its books in a variety of electronic formats. Some content that appears in print may not be available in electronic formats.

Manufactured in the United States of America

5 4 3 2 1

About the Author

Holly Hughes has traveled the globe as an editor and writer. A former executive editor of Fodor's Travel Publications, she edits the annual *Best Food Writing* anthology and is the author of the bestselling *500 Places to Take Your Kids Before They Grow Up, 500 Places to See Before They Disappear,* and *Frommer's New York City with Kids.* She has also written fiction for middle graders. New York City makes a convenient jumping-off place for her travels with her three children and husband.

About the Co-Author

Charlie O'Malley lives in South America's wine capital—Mendoza in Argentina—where he runs a magazine called *Wine Republic* and a wine tour company called Trout & Wine. He has contributed to several Frommer's travel guides covering Argentina, Uruguay, Bolivia, Nicaragua, and El Salvador.

An Invitation to the Reader

In researching this book, we discovered many wonderful places. We're sure you'll find others. Please tell us about them, so we can share the information with your fellow travelers in upcoming editions. If you were disappointed with a recommendation, we'd love to know that, too. Please write to:

Frommer's 500 Places for Food & Wine Lovers, 1st Edition
Wiley Publishing, Inc. • 111 River St. • Hoboken, NJ 07030-5774

An Additional Note

Please be advised that travel information is subject to change at any time—and this is especially true of prices. We therefore suggest that you write or call ahead for confirmation when making your travel plans. The authors, editors, and publisher cannot be held responsible for the experiences of readers while traveling. Your safety is important to us, however, so we encourage you to stay alert and be aware of your surroundings. Keep a close eye on cameras, purses, and wallets, all favorite targets of thieves and pickpockets.

Frommer's Icons

We use four feature icons to help you quickly find the information you're looking for. At the end of each review, look for:

ⓘ   Where to get more information

✈   Nearest airport

🚆   Nearest train station

🛏   Recommended kid-friendly hotels

Frommers.com

Now that you have this guidebook to help you plan a great trip, visit our website at **www.frommers.com** for additional travel information on more than 4,000 destinations. We update features regularly to give you instant access to the most current trip-planning information available. At Frommers.com, you'll find scoops on the best airfares, lodging rates, and car rental bargains. You can even book your travel online through our reliable travel booking partners. Other popular features include:

- Online updates of our most popular guidebooks
- Vacation sweepstakes and contest giveaways
- Newsletters highlighting the hottest travel trends
- Podcasts, interactive maps, and up-to-the-minute events listings
- Opinionated blog entries by Arthur Frommer himself
- Online travel message boards with featured travel discussions

Why These 500 Places?

Maybe you don't call yourself a "foodie"—that's such a worn-out label by now. Neverthe-less, for a lot of us travelers, half the joy of going on vacation lies in scoring that prize reservation at the best restaurant in town, or discovering the most authentic little road-side inn, or getting up early to browse through the open-air markets with the locals to sample the region's signature flavors—from fresh-off-the-boat Maine lobsters to Spain's finest Iberico ham, from gleaming handmade raw-milk cheese to peaty aged single-malt whiskey.

Along with these pleasures, we also know the frustration of hearing afterwards from some know-it-all friend, "You mean you went all the way to _____ and you didn't eat at _____?"

Well, I'll admit, I can't promise to make those know-it-all friends go away. When it comes to food and wine, there will always be that element of one-upmanship. But never fear— among the 500 places I've written about in these pages, you're bound to find several that will make your next trip deliciously memorable—and maybe some that even enlighten the know-it-alls.

Granted, selecting only 500 destinations to profile turned out to be a daunting task. I could just as easily have covered 5,000 such places, and they'd all be wonderful. But because this is above all a travel guide, not just a restaurant list, I've tried to balance my choices to make as diverse a guide as possible. Here you'll find a broad range of sites scattered around the globe, from organic farms to gourmet food emporiums, from down-home diners to exquisite white tablecloth restaurants, with a fair number of baker ies and coffee bars and brewpubs thrown in for good measure. My colleague Charlie O'Malley added a sampling of vineyards around the world—with an emphasis on places that are the most fun to visit. The geographic index in the back will help you match nearby destinations, so that you can take in a whole cluster of sights on one vacation.

The food scene, of course, is so dynamic that many of these destinations will have changed by the time you get there. Chefs—especially the rising stars—are always mov-ing around; menus change seasonally or even day by day; and the life span of a "hot" restaurant is often disgracefully short. (Though the food may still be brilliant even after the restless scenesters have moved on.) That's why I've tried to choose restaurants with enough of a track record that I feel confident they'll still be serving great food by the time you read this. I should also note that in order to cover the map as widely as possible, I've listed a number of restaurants I haven't yet eaten at, on the basis of strong recommenda-tions by my fellow Frommer's writers, or by food writer friends around the world. They're all on my short list of places to try out the next time I'm lucky enough to be in that part of the world.

A Note on Hotels

I wish I'd had space to give you full-blown hotel reviews, but you can rely on the options we list as some of the area's most dependable lodgings, well-located and offering good value for money. In many cases, they also have their own notable restaurants, or at least provide excellent breakfasts. I tend to recommend moderately priced hotels more than the swanky luxury spots, and favor independents over chain hotels (you don't need my help in finding those). **Price ranges** are relative—I have noted three price ranges, $$$ (expensive), $$ (moderate), and $ (inexpensive), but they conform to the local market, not any across-the-board equivalents. (For example, a $125-per-night motel room along Route 66 or in rural Mexico would seem expensive, but if you can find something clean and safe at that price in London or Paris, snap it up.) For fuller descriptions and other useful travel advice, please consult the corresponding Frommer's guides for these destinations. Note that **phone numbers** listed begin with international country codes—if you're dialing from within the country, drop the first set of numbers and add 0 before the regional dialing code. U.S. and Canadian numbers, however, do not have the international prefixes listed.

Acknowledgments

From Holly Hughes

I'm endlessly grateful for all the tips and advice that poured in from Frommer's writers all over the world—you guys are the best! I'd also like to add special thanks to Charlie O'Malley, Julie Duchaine, Hugh Ward, Elizabeth Brannan-Williams, Iñaki Garcia-Galera, Matthew Amster-Burton, Laura Taxel, Mary Tilghman, Jane Yager, and Tania Kollia. Most of all, thanks to my wonderful, patient editor Maureen Clarke—I owe you dinner!

From Charlie O'Malley

Many thanks to all my friends who tolerated my selfish, obsessive behavior while completing this book: In particular Jason and Mariela Mabbett and Sooty, who lent me their lovely home when the deadline loomed. I am very grateful to my collaborator Holly Hughes and editor Maureen Clarke for being so understanding and encouraging. Last but not least, I must thank my wife Ana for her incredible patience and support.

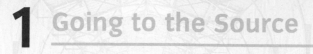

1 Going to the Source

Under the skylit arched nave of San Francisco's Ferry Plaza Market.

Ostermalms Saluhall

Smorgasbord Chic

Stockholm, Sweden

Stockholm has emerged as a culinary hot spot only in the past few years, but its top gourmet market—perhaps Scandinavia's best indoor food market—has been around since 1888. Behind the fortresslike presence of this neo-Gothic red-brick building, today the Saluhall has an air of epicurean chic that's well suited to the tony Old Town neighborhood in which it's located.

Enter through the main tower and you'll reach the large, light-filled hall, with cast-iron struts supporting a glass ceiling and stalls handsomely framed with carved wood pillars and fretwork canopies. Originally there were 153 small stalls, but today about 20 upscale merchants set up shop, each spreading out over a number of booths; several also operate as restaurants or cafes.

Vendors earn their places through a competitive process, so the quality is quite high. Fish and game—cornerstones of Swedish cuisine—are prominently displayed; if you've ever hankered to try reindeer meat, now's your chance. Between the piled-high Swedish pastries, braided loaves of bread, hanging joints of meat, silvery mounds of fish, and brilliant baskets of berries, it's like one still life after another. Among the longest established tenants are **Lisa Elmqvist** (© 46/8/553-404-00) for fish and delicatessen products, **Gerdas Fisk & Skaldjursrestaurang** (© 46/8/553-404-40) a seafood restaurant, **J. E. Olsson & Söner** (© 46/8/661-31-42) for fruits and vegetables, and **Betsy Sandberg Choklad** (© 46/8/663-63-05) for handmade chocolates. Expect stiff prices—this isn't a spot where you'd do your weekly shopping on a regular basis—but it's worth the splurge for the luxe experience.

While you're in the neighborhood, head up Nybrogatan to no. 55, where a stand named **Bruno's** serves the city's best Swedish hot dogs, or *korvs*—a variety of sausages grilled to tooth-snapping perfection and stuffed in a French bread roll.

ⓘ Nybrogatan 31 (no phone; www.saluhallen.com).

✈ Stockholm Arlanda Airport (41km/25 miles).

🛏 $$$ **Victory Hotel,** Lilla Nygatan 5 (© 46/8/506-400-00; www.victory-hotel.se). $$ **Clas på Hörnet,** Surbrunnsgatan 20 (© 46/8/16-51-30; www.claspahornet.se).

Old English Market
The Market Craic in Cork
Cork, Ireland

Though today it's a sophisticated university town with a burgeoning restaurant scene, in centuries past Cork was one of the Irish cities most oppressed by English rule, a prized harbor town kept firmly within the British grasp. There's a bittersweet irony, then, in the fact that its central city market—founded with a charter from James I in 1610, and housed in a stately Georgian building dating from 1786—is still called the Old English Market. Originally, only loyal English settlers could shop here. Nowadays it has developed into Ireland's best retail food market, especially after a 1980 fire led to a top-to-toe refurbishment—preserving, of course, the gleaming woodwork and an elegant polychrome fountain near the entrance. Once considered a workaday place to shop for produce, it has gone upscale since the mid-1990s, with the addition of several gourmet stalls alongside businesses owned by the same families for generations.

Located in the flat center of hilly Cork city, the English Market (nobody in Cork adds the "old") announces its main entrance with an ornate iron gate on the Grand Parade, though you can also duck in through side gates from atmospheric adjacent lanes lined with small shops. Food stands inside the vaulted two-story arcade brim with meats, fish, vegetables, fruit, and baked goods; among the newer arrivals are stalls that sell exotic imported goods (handmade pastas, chocolates, and pastries) or specialize in organic produce. Silvery fish gleam on beds of ice at O'Connell's fish stall, and haunches and joints of freshly slaughtered animals are

The Old English Market in Cork, Ireland, has been in business for nearly 400 years.

3

hung on display at various traditional meat and poultry stalls. But the chief attraction is the traditional Irish food products—tripe (animal stomach), smoked eel, black pudding, soda bread, and Cork specialties such as hot buttered eggs, *crubeens* (pigs' feet), and *drisheens* (local blood sausage). Though there are a few delis and takeout sandwich stands, you could also put together a lunch from ripe French cheeses and pâtés at the **Pig's Back** or Irish farmhouse cheeses from Iago, accompanied by crusty oven-fresh bread from the **Arbutus Bakery.**

Closed on Sundays, the English Market doesn't open at dawn like some wholesale markets do. Business begins at a reasonable 9am and closes at 5:30pm. The **Farmgate Restaurant** gives you a panoramic view of the market from an open balcony one floor above the bustle.

ⓘ Grand Parade, between Patrick and Oliver Plunkett streets (no phone).

✈ Cork Airport (122km/76 miles south of Shannon International).

🛏 $$$ **Hayfield Manor Hotel,** Perrott Ave. (🕾 **800/525-4800** or 353/21/431-5600; www.hayfieldmanor.ie). $$ **The Gresham Metropole,** MacCurtain St., Tivoli (🕾 **353/ 21/450-8122**).

Borough Market
Whole-Food Haven
London, England

If appearing in a Harry Potter movie means you've made it, then London's Borough Market finally hit the big time in 2004. This bustling covered market—London's oldest and biggest—seems like a natural film location, a jumble of stalls along a maze of lanes snuggled under the green girders of a railway bridge. London's late-20th-century culinary renaissance has certainly helped to raise Borough Market's profile as the place to go in the capital for top-quality food shopping.

But it wasn't always that way. Though Borough Market occupied the south end of London Bridge for centuries—some claim it was already an established site in Roman times—by the 13th century it was considered a nuisance because the food stalls blocked traffic across the bridge. The south side of the river was always more disreputable than the north bank, a neighborhood of taverns and inns (Chaucer's pilgrims started their trip to Canterbury nearby) and playhouses (including Shakespeare's Globe Theatre). Various

monarchs over the years tried in vain to control the market's chaos and congestion. For the past 250 years, however, it has been respectably settled on its current site, just south of Southwark Cathedral, as a wholesale fruit-and-vegetable market run as a charity by a board of trustees whose members must live in the neighborhood.

Conveniently close to the river's wharves, and later London Bridge railway station, Borough Market never was just about local produce; purveyors from all over the U.K.—and several from Europe—ship their goods here. **Orkney Rose,** for example, features fresh salmon, heather-fed lamb, Angus beef, and seafood from the Orkney Islands—products from small rural producers who individually could never afford to sell in London. The wholesale market is open 2am to 8am nightly except Saturday, and a retail arm of the market was launched with instant success in 1999 (only open Thurs 11am–5pm; Fri noon–6pm; and Sat 9am–4pm), as things got trendier south of the river. These retailers sell not only produce but meat, fish, baked goods, and gourmet delicacies such as chocolates, coffee, tea, and olive oil. Among the cafes, restaurants, and pubs in the Market area are **Roast,** known for its hearty breakfasts, and **The Rake,** a pub whose name recalls William Hogarth's famous 18th-century engravings of the raffish Borough Market scene.

Unfortunately, several buildings on the surrounding streets may be demolished by the construction of a major train viaduct; what this will do to the market's character remains to be seen. The main market buildings date from the mid–19th century; the Borough High Street entrance is an Art Deco addition from 1932, and the South Portico of the Floral Hall was moved here in 2004 from the Royal Opera House at Covent Garden—an area also known for its street vendors (think Eliza Doolittle from *My Fair Lady*). It's a bit of a hodgepodge, all right—but then, that's what Borough Market has been all along.

Borough Market under the girders of the London Bridge railway station.

ⓘ 8 Southwark St. (✆ **44/20-7407-1002;** www.boroughmarket.org.uk).

✈ Heathrow (24km/15 miles) or Gatwick (40km/25 miles).

🛏 $$$ **Covent Garden Hotel,** 10 Monmouth St., Covent Garden (✆ **800/553-6674** in the U.S., or 44/20/7806-1000; www.firmdale.com). $$ **B + B Belgravia,** 64–66 Ebury St., Belgravia (✆ **800/682-7808** in the U.S., or 44/20/7734-2353; www.bb-belgravia.com).

Marché d'Aligre
A Touch of the Souk
Paris, France

While most markets are shut tight on Sunday morning, that is the very best time of the week to visit Paris's Marché d'Aligre. Set in the outlying 12th *arrondissement,* the market has a distinctly North African flavor (where else in town could you pick up henna, rosewater, or spicy harissa paste?). Though this east Paris neighborhood itself isn't chic, the hipsters are out in full force on Sunday mornings, scouring the market stalls for bargains.

In the heart of the square are the permanent stalls of Marché Couvert Beauvau-St-Antoine, built in 1779 and one of the last remaining covered markets in Paris. By the 1800s, it had expanded to include a farmer's market in the open square around it and was second only to Les Halles as Paris's most important market. By the early 1970s, however, the atmospheric Les Halles had closed its stalls, moving its wholesale operations out to much less colorful digs in the suburb of Rungis—which left Marche d'Aligre as a lone survivor of Paris's great market tradition. (There are still a number of less permanent open-air street markets, of course, including the stalls along Marché Buci, on rue Mouffetard in the 5th arrondissement; and on rue Montorgueil, behind the St-Eustache church in the 1st arrondissement.)

The shopping inside the covered market itself is decidedly high end, with fresh poultry, charcuterie, butchers, excellent fish, luxury fruits, and imported foodstuffs for sale by long-established merchants in smartly outfitted stalls. If you ever doubted that France produces more than 1,000 varieties of cheese, you'll be convinced by the amazing selections in the *fromageries* here.

The scene surrounding the covered market has an entirely different character—more multicultural, more for bargain-hunters, and more vibrant. Prices are often low, and a spirit of hawking and haggling keeps things lively. Many Algerian, Moroccan, and Tunisian vendors operate here, selling fruits and vegetables they bought earlier in the morning out in Rungis at the wholesale market. Generally, they've sold out their stock and packed up by lunchtime, while the indoor stalls maintain regular store hours.

Thanks to those grazing hipsters, several excellent small shops and cafes ringing the square have their own following. Don't miss the flaky French pastries at **Ble du Sucre** (7 rue Antoine Vollon), the organic breads at **Moisan** (5 rue d'Aligre), or the fresh-roasted coffee at **Cafe Aouba** (rue d'Aligre).

ⓘ Between le faubourg St-Antoine and la rue de Charenton, 12th arrondissement (http://marchedaligre.free.fr).

✈ De Gaulle (23km/14 miles). Orly (14km/8²/₃ miles).

🛏 $$ **La Tour Notre Dame,** 20 rue du Sommerard, 5e (☏ **33/1/43-54-47-60;** www.la-tour-notre-dame.com). $ **Hotel de la Place des Vosges,** 12 rue de Birague, 4e (☏ **33/1/42-72-60-46;** www.hotelplacedesvosges.com).

KaDeWe Food Halls

Into the West

Berlin, Germany

To the epicures of Berlin, the fall of the Berlin Wall meant one thing—the food halls at KaDeWe could recapture their status as a luxury mecca for international delicacies. New owners even built an entire new floor atop this century-old giant of a department store, where dazzling imported foods are curated and displayed like works of art.

Though KaDeWe's official name is Kaufhaus Des Westerns (Department Store of the West), since its 1907 opening it has been known as KaDeWe (pronounced *kah-day-vay*). The "West" referred to its location in a residential neighborhood of West Berlin, though it doesn't look very residential anymore. KaDeWe was nearly gutted after a U.S. plane flew into it during World War II. When it reopened in the 1950s, its new food halls were its greatest attraction in a divided, war-torn city. After the Wall went up in 1961, the "west" in the name became even more significant—KaDeWe was off-limits to East Germans, now cut off from the gourmet delights of the Free World.

Since reunification, the remodeled seventh-floor food department more than ever celebrates world foods—no locavorism here. The cheese counters, for example, may stock 200 different kinds of German cheese, but there are twice as many from France, as well as hundreds from Italy, Switzerland, and many other nations. Other departments offer 120 exotic cooking oils, or 120 global varieties of vinegar. The produce section plies exotic fruits such as mangosteen, cherimoya, dragon fruit, rambutan, tamarillo, uglifruit, kaki, and cassava. The meat hall has an emphasis on free-range meats, as well as game meats such as moose, venison, and wild boar in season. Sure, they sell hearty German sausages, but an inventory of more than 1,200 types of sausage inevitably goes much farther afield. Fish are flown in from Hawaii, the Seychelles, and Mozambique. There's a definite French bias evident—witness the Brittany oysters, the Bresse chickens, the breads and pastries from Lenôtre, the renowned Parisian baker. Granted, the chocolates in the confectionery department are locally made—you can even watch the candy makers at work—but the chocolates they use are sourced worldwide. After all those years of Iron Curtain isolation, Berliners can't really be blamed for embracing the global cornucopia.

When hunger sets in, shoppers repair to a cafe serving coffees, teas, and sweets or to the counter stools at more than 30 "gourmet bars" scattered around the selling floor, featuring delicacies such as lobster, caviar, champagne, oysters, and sushi. The classic KaDeWe dining experience is on the floor below, the **Restaurant Silberstrasse,** with its vintage Art Nouveau interior under an elegant glass dome.

ⓘ Tauentzienstrasse 21 (U-bahn Wittenbergplatz) (☎ **49/30/21210;** www.kadewe-berlin.de). Closed Sunday.

✈ Berlin-Tagel (14km/8¾ miles).

🛏 $$ **Hotel Hackescher Markt,** Grosse Präsidentenstrasse 8 (☎ **49/30/280030;** www.loock-hotels.com). $$ **Myers Hotel Berlin**, Betzer Strasse 26 (☎ **49/30/440140;** www.myershotel.de).

---

6 Open-Air Markets

Victualienmarkt

Robust Bavarian

Munich, Germany

While tourists throng into the Marienplatz to gawk at the town hall's quaint glockenspiel, you'll get a richer glimpse of Munich's daily life a few minutes' walk southeast, just off Tal, at the city's top street market. With the copper-spired tower of St. Peter's church rising over its shade trees and umbrellas, the Victualienmarkt (*victualen* being the German word for "food") expresses the easygoing Bavarian sensibility. The market sprawls over a wide stone-paved area, its tented open-air stalls run by some 150 independent merchants who maintain whatever hours they want, often packing up as soon as the day's inventory sells out. And of course there's a popular Bavarian-style beer garden set up right in the middle, under spreading chestnut trees.

Though this is chiefly a retail market (most restaurants buy their provisions at the wholesale Grossmarkthalle, out in the industrial southern suburb of Thalkirchen), serious household shoppers show up around 8am, toting capacious shopping baskets, to stock their larders. By 5pm, only the die-hard merchants are still open. Yet while the scene resembles the sort of weekly farmer's market you'd find in any German town, these are permanent vendors, offering not only fresh produce but wine, meats, cheeses, freshly squeezed juices, herbs, and spices, as well as flowers and some craft items. Seek out Bavarian specialties such as Schweinshax'n, Speck, and Weisswurst.

The Victualienmarkt has been in place here in the Altstadt for 2 centuries, originally founded as an herb market in 1807. Over the years, it has become not just a shopping place but also a public gathering spot, where street musicians frequently play (look for a handful of statues and fountains commemorating local singers and folk actors). Plenty of food stands sell bratwurst, fish, and other takeout meals, and small cafes and beerhouses are sprinkled around the periphery. A rather startling new element now lies at the far end: the **Schrannenhalle,** an indoor marketplace with shops and restaurants, built on the site of the city's old grain market, which burned down in 1932. Though it was constructed using the original iron frames, the new building is aggressively modern architecture, an odd backdrop to this most traditional Bavarian market scene.

ⓘ Munich town center, behind the old Town Hall (no phone).

✈ Franz-Josef-Strauss International (29km/ 18 miles).

🛏 $$ **Hotel St. Paul,** St-Paul-Strasse 7 (✆ **49/89/5440-7800;** www.hotel-stpaul. de). $ **Am Markt,** Heiliggeistrasse 6 (✆ **49/ 89/22-50-14;** www.hotelinmunich.de).

Open-Air Markets 7

Mercat de La Boqueria

Catalan Cornucopia

Barcelona, Spain

Just off the picturesque flower market of La Rambla, a wide pedestrian boulevard rolling downhill from Barcelona's downtown to the harbor, La Boqueria seems tucked into a sliver of space between colonnaded buildings. But walk under its elegant wrought-iron entrance arch, with its colorful coat-of-arms, and you'll step into a lofty, immense cavern of a market—a vibrant expression of Barcelona's buzzing culinary culture.

The sheer number of vendors—hardly any of them with much space for their wares—is astounding. Each tidy little stall is piled high with the best Catalonian food products: pyramids of citrus fruit, crisp green vegetables, garlands of bright chili peppers, red-marbled beef, hefty smoked hams, garlicky sausages, soft white cheeses, darkly gleaming offal. A distinctly fishy aroma leads you to the heart of the market, a large oval section full of fishmongers displaying the catch of the day; local specialties such as olives, legumes, mushrooms, and dried fruits have their own vendors. There are a few stands selling imported goods and one organic specialist, but by and large this is still a working farmer's market, where local householders—and chefs from Barcelona's top restaurants—pick up their daily ingredients.

In typically exuberant Catalonian manner, stall holders are known for chatting up their customers, so don't expect briskly efficient service; on the other hand, you won't have to fend off aggressive hard-sell tactics. You'll find a few small and intensely popular tapas bars and takeout kiosks (worth hunting for: **Pinoxto** and **El Quim de la Boquería**) scattered around the market, but it's overwhelmingly a place for food shopping, and customers often wait two or three deep at the most popular stalls.

La Boquería is named after the old city gate that once stood here, when local farmers set up outside the city walls to sell their produce. In the 1840s, permanent market structures began to take shape, though the overarching steel roof wasn't installed until 1914—the heyday of Catalonian architecture, as it happens, which explains the panache of that colorful, modernistic entrance arch. Closed Sundays.

(i) La Rambla 91 (✆ **34/93/318-20-17;** www.boqueria.info).

✈ El Prat (13km/8 miles).

⊨ $$$ **Montecarlo,** Les Ramblas 124 (✆ **34/93-412-04-04;** www.montercarlo bcn.com). $$ **Duques de Bergara,** Bergara 11 (✆ **34/93-301-51-51;** www.hoteles-catalonia.com).

The landmark entrance of La Boquería market near the Rambla in Barcelona.

Naschmarkt
Bazaar for Noshing
Vienna, Austria

Inside the Ring, Vienna often seems like a city drenched in late-19th-century nostalgia—a slow-moving dream of Viennese waltzes and Germanic stodginess set in massive gray stone. But just outside the Ring, a more dynamic, multicultural Vienna emerges. While Vienna has two dozen permanent open-air markets, the hustle and bustle is palpable at the Naschmarkt, a picturesque collection of stalls strung along several city blocks, just off Mariahilferstrasse in the 6th district.

The name sounds like a place for noshing, or snacking (in German, *naschen* means specifically to nibble sweets), and

there's no question that Naschmarket is a superb spot for hungry grazing. Historians, however, insist that the name was originally "Aschmarkt," either because it was located by an old ash dump or because milk was sold here from ashwood buckets. (Perhaps it's no accident that locals gradually let the name morph into something more appetizing.) Whatever the origins of the name, there's been some sort of market here since the 16th century; it has officially been a fruit-and-vegetable market since 1793, migrating from nearby Karlsplatz to the present location in the late 19th century when the

Wien River was roofed over and renamed Wienzeile.

There's a real bazaarlike feel to this open-air market, with its narrow main street lined with awninged shops, their bins spilling out on the street. Vendors ply the usual fresh produce and local specialties, such as Wiener schnitzel, strudel, and barrelfuls of sauerkraut, but shelves are also stocked with bottled vinegars, neatly labeled cellophane packets of imported spices and herbs, cases full of seafood, prepared salads, and even sushi. As you browse along the stalls, you may notice how many vendors hail from Turkey or the former Yugoslavia, a reminder of Vienna's historic role as central Europe's cultural melting pot. A caveat: Shoppers don't come here for bargains, but for hard-to-find goods and very fresh produce, it can't be beat.

Along a side lane a string of *beisls* (small cafes) features an international range of cuisines, from kebabs to Chinese food to traditional Viennese dishes such as *Kaiserschmarrn* or *Palatschinken*. A smattering of hip late-night bars suggest how the Naschmarkt has been embraced by the trendy set as well as tourists looking for local color. Be sure to stroll around the surrounding neighborhood, which has some fine examples of Jugendstil architecture. The market is closed Sundays; check out the neighboring flea market on Saturdays.

ⓘ Between Linke and Rechte Wienzeile from Kettenbrückengasse to Getreidemark. (U-Bahn: Karlsplatz) (no phone).

✈ Vienna International (23km/14 miles).

🛏 $$$ **Hotel Römischer Kaiser**, Annagasse 16 (ⓒ **800/528-1234** or 43/1/512775113; www.bestwestern.com). $$ **Hotel am Schubertring,** Schubertring 11 (ⓒ **43/1/717020;** www.schubertring.at).

Open-Air Markets   9

Központi Vásárcsarnok
Hungry in Hungary
Budapest, Hungary

Cavernous as a train station, Budapest's biggest indoor market is the sort of place where you can wander for hours, until sensory overload kicks in. Though it's a popular tourist stop—and there are a raft of stalls selling Hungarian dolls, embroidered linens, glassware, and other souvenirs—plenty of locals do their regular food shopping here as well. The ground floor in particular offers an overwhelming bounty of fresh produce, locally made cheese, and meats, not to mention ropes of garlic, spicy salami, velvety foie gras, ground red paprika and yellow saffron, Tokay wine, and caviar.

Set on the Pest side of the Danube River, conveniently close to the famous Chain Bridge, the Vasarcsarnok was first built in 1897 when the rival cities of Buda and Pest were being combined into one great metropolis. With its magnificent tiled roof, patterned orange brick facade, cathedral-like portal, and soaring glass roof, this vast hall was intended as an expression of civic opulence. It was even designed with a canal running down the center, so that vendors could float in their produce. Significantly damaged in World War II, the hall limped along for decades during the Communist regime, until it had to be closed down in the early 1990s; an extensive restoration in 1994, however, has returned the hall to its former magnificence.

The canal is long gone, replaced with a broad tiled corridor, flanked by two other aisles running the length of the ground floor hall, where most of the food vendors are. Look especially for unique Hungarian produce such as parsley root and sweet white peppers, and don't miss the glorious peaches in summer. Things are a little cooler on the basement floor, where you'll find fish merchants, purveyors of pickled vegetables (another Hungarian specialty), and a conventional grocery store. There are also a number of food stands on the mezzanine, along with the **Fakanál Étterem** restaurant, which serves traditional Hungarian specialties like goulash and chicken paprikash; Fakanál Étterem even offers 1-day cooking classes, where you can learn how to use all those exotic ingredients displayed in the stalls below. The market is closed Sundays and terrifically crowded on Saturdays; come here earlier in the week for a more relaxed shopping experience.

ⓘ IX. Vámház körút 1–3 (℈ **36/1/366-3300;** www.csapi.hu; Metro station Kálvin tér [Blue line]).

✈ Budapest (20km/12 miles).

⊨ **$$ Hotel Erzsébet,** V. Károlyi Mihály u. 11-15, Budapest (℈ **36/1/889-3700;** www.danubiusgroup.com). $$ **Hotel Papillon,** II. Rózsahegy u. 3/b (℈ **36/1/212-4750**).

⑩ Open-Air Markets

Khari Baoli
The Spice of Life
Old Delhi, India

The western end of Old Delhi's most atmospheric quarter—Shahjahanabad, a labyrinth of tiny lanes near the Red Fort, lined with crumbling 17th-century mansions—seems an appropriate place to find Asia's biggest spice market, Khari Baoli. It has been here since the time of the Mughal emperor Shah Jahan, when there was still a fortified gate at this end of Chandni Chowk. Colors, textures, and aromas literally spill out into the street from the cramped shops lining the wide thoroughfare, but you'll want to duck inside to get the full heady effect—an only-in-India sort of experience.

Spices, nuts, dried fruits, rice, beans, and herbs are sold here in wholesale quantities—workers busily trundle huge sacks of these commodities through the crowds on hand carts, so watch your back—but individual customers can also buy smaller amounts. Black peppercorns, pale green cardamom pods, bright yellow turmeric root, red chilies, cumin—all the flavors of Indian cooking are laid out on display, some in metal bowls, some in burlap sacks. Jars of pungent Indian pickles are stacked on the shelves of other shops. Prices are reasonable, though you'll see plenty of haggling going on for large purchases. Chaotic and bustling, best reached by rickshaw, it's a popular tourist stop just for the intoxicating aromas and the vibrant street life.

When you're done with Khari Baoli, there's still more shopping to do along Chandni Chowk, Shahjahanabad's principal commercial street (the name means "Moonlight Avenue," referring to the nighttime reflection off its canal). A number of colorful markets branch off Chandni Chowk: **Chawri Bazaar** for brass and copper icons and other souvenirs, **Churiwali Galli** for bangles, **Nai Sarak** for fine stationery, **Kinari Bazaar** for cheap gold and silver trinkets and accessories, and **Dariba Kalan** for more valuable jewelry. Make a final stop at **Karim's** (Jama Masjid; ℈ **91/11/23269880**), a century-old restaurant/hotel tucked away in a small courtyard, famous for its authentic Mughlai tandoori dishes, spicy mutton stews, and spit-roasted kebabs.

ⓘ Near Turkman Gate, Khari Baoli Road (no phone).

✈ Indira Gandhi International (20km/12 miles).

🛏 $$$ **The Imperial,** 1 Janpath (℗ **011/ 2334-1234;** www.theimperialindia.com). $$ **Oberoi Maidens,** 7 Sham Nath Marg, North Delhi (℗ **011/2397-5464,** or central reservations 1 600 11 7070; www.maidens hotel.com).

Tsukiji Fish Market
Seafood at Sunrise
Tokyo, Japan

It should come as no surprise that the world's largest and most famous seafood market is in Japan's capital, Tokyo—the heart of an island nation whose people have always lived off the sea. Be prepared to rise before dawn to visit it, however; the action starts at about 3am, and it's all over by 9am or so.

All through the night, boats, trains, and trucks converge at this immense, hangar-like facility to unload their catch, not just locally caught but imported from some 60 other countries, including Africa and the Americas. Under the harsh glare of electric light, a bewildering variety of fish—hundreds of types, from tiny sardines to hulking tuna, slithery eels to gangly octopi and spiky sea urchins—are laid out on wooden pallets for licensed wholesalers to inspect. Fast-paced auctions finally take place from about 4:40 to 6:30am (tuna auctions have been closed to spectators since 2005, but you can still see those gigantic fish laid out for their once-over).

The wholesale fishmongers then haul what they've bought to their own stalls in the inner section of the market (*jonai shijo*), where they sell to buyers from retail stores and restaurants. (Almost all the seafood consumed in Tokyo—around 2,000 tons a day—passes through this one market.) As the day slowly dawns outside, it's a scene of controlled chaos, with men tromping around the wet floors in black rubber boots, trundling wheelbarrows and dollies through the aisles. It's fascinating, if gruesome, to watch the vendors cutting up the fish they've bought—a ballet performed to the tune of buzzing band-saws and cleavers clanging on chopping blocks. It seems all the more surreal if you don't understand Japanese or can't read the scrawled characters on the handwritten signs at each stall, yet it's a very popular visit for foreign tourists (very few Japanese make it here). While you're not allowed to photograph the auctions, feel free to snap photos of the wholesalers at work; workers burst with pride if you single them out for a photograph.

The outer sections of the market (*jogai shijo*) are rows of barracklike buildings divided into sushi restaurants and shops related to the fish trade. The immediate neighborhood is also crammed with tiny retail shops and stalls where you can buy the freshest seafood in town, as well as dried fish, seaweed, vegetables, knives, and other cooking utensils.

(i) 5-2-1 Tsukiji, Chuo-ku (© **03/3542-1111;** www.tsukiji-market.or.jp/tukiji_e.htm).

✈ Narita International (66km/40 miles).

🛏 $$$ **Capitol Tokyu Hotel,** 2-10-3 Nagata-cho, Chiyoda-ku (© **800/888-4747**

in the U.S. and Canada, or 03/3581-4511; www.capitoltokyu.com). $$ **Park Hotel Tokyo,** 1-7-1 Higashi Shimbashi, Minato-ku, Ginza (© **03/6252-1111;** www.park hoteltokyo.com).

12 Open-Air Markets

Queen Victoria Market

Oz Classic

Melbourne, Australia

The name may sound all starchy and tea-party prim, but although this Melbourne institution was named after the British monarch when it was built in 1878, the place has been improvising and re-inventing itself Aussie-style ever since. It now sprawls over several blocks at the northern edge of the city center, a 7-hectare (17-acre) spread with hundreds of stalls. Despite a neoclassical main entrance with a bas-relief of farm animals over the door, most of the market is a rough-and-ready open-sided setup (shopping here can get chilly in winter), with a completely eclectic range of goods, from live rabbits to bargain clothes.

Food lovers, however, will be happy to note that more than 50% of the market is still dedicated to food stalls, clustered in the older market buildings east of Queen Street. Vendors are assigned locations according to food groups—the fish and meat are in one "hall," fruits and vegetables in another, dairy products in a third—which encourages brisk competition between neighboring stall holders. Within each section, merchants have carved out their own specialties—one meat seller focusing on sausages and another on pork, for example. The fish area is definitely Melbourne's Seafood Central, with a wide assortment of absolutely fresh whole fish, filets, and shellfish. Fruit dealers compete to import the most unusual specimens from Asia and around the Pacific; an

entire shed is devoted to organic and bio-dynamic produce.

Perhaps the most impressive area is the dairy hall, built in 1929 at the height of Art Deco design. It's basically a massive deli-catessen, where expanses of cool marble counters (installed to keep food cold in those prerefrigeration days) display a beguiling selection of imported foods. There's far more than just dairy products here these days; some 17 merchants sell everything from olive oil and handmade pasta to crocodile and kangaroo meat. Several inexpensive cafes are scattered around the premises, and the large enclosed food court offers an international range of cuisine, but the best place in the market to eat just may be the seating at the side of the deli hall, where you can assemble your own picnic-style lunch. Note that the food stalls generally close down midafternoon. The market in general is closed Mondays, Wednesdays, and public holidays.

In the full entrepreneurial spirit, the Queen Victoria Market hosts a constant stream of entertainment events to bring locals into the market; there's a 2-hour **Foodies Tour** most mornings (© **03/9320 5835**), and well-known chefs give cooking classes upstairs at the **Electrolux Cooking School** (© **03/9320 5830;** call for reservations).

(i) Corner Elizabeth and Victoria streets (🕾 **03/9320 5822;** www.qvm.com.au).

✈ Melbourne (21km/13 miles).

🛏 $$$ **The Como Melbourne,** 630 Chapel St., South Yarra (🕾 **1800/033 400**

in Australia, or 800/552-6844 in the U.S. and Canada; www.mirvachotels.com.au). $$ **Fountain Terrace,** 28 Mary St., St. Kilda (🕾 **03/9593 8123;** www.fountainterrace. com.au).

Open-Air Markets

13

Mercado Central
School of Fish
Santiago, Chile

Seafood, seafood, seafood—the long, skinny country of Chile is practically nothing but coastline; you'd expect the local cuisine to center around seafood. And that's what this covered market in Chile's capital is all about. A distinctly fishy aroma prevails as you wander around fishmongers' stalls piled high with the fruits of the sea, accompanied by a crowd of seafood restaurants where the prices are moderate and the servings huge.

Built in 1872, the market's pale yellow arcaded exterior is a graceful example of neoclassical colonial architecture, but inside is an Art Nouveau–style cast-iron interior that looks more like a train station than a covered market, with a soaring steel roof imported from England. For years this was Santiago's main wholesale food market, but in recent years the fishmongers have been squeezing out the produce vendors (they now sell fruits and vegetables across the river at the colorful La Vega market), and now the restaurants are beginning to overrun the retail operations.

Touristy it may be, but it's quite a vibrant scene—stroll around and watch the vendors deftly gutting and filleting their fish at lighting speed, while waiters shill vociferously to lure prospective diners into their restaurants. Look especially

for massive Chilean sea bass, salmon, and king crabs; salt-crusted oysters, still alive, are piled in buckets, alongside heaps of mussels, razor clams, and sea urchins on beds of shaved ice.

Come at lunchtime, when you can follow up your shopping with a stop at a restaurant for a freshly made ceviche or perhaps the local *caldillo de congrio* (conger eel soup). Ignore the aggressive advances of the waiters at the larger, more commercial restaurants and head to the back corners of the market to get better value for your money (**Tío Lucha** and **Donde Blanca** are two good choices); the fish should be plenty fresh, so opt for the simplest preparations. The market is open daily, but closes around 4pm—by which time what's left of that morning's catch is past its prime anyway.

(i) Ismael Valdes Vergara and Av. 21 de Mayo (🕾 **56/2/696-8327**).

✈ Comodoro Arturo Merino Benítez Airport (14km/9 miles).

🛏 $$$ **Plaza El Bosque,** Ebro 2828 (🕾 **56/2/498-1800;** www.plazaelbosque. cl). $ **Vilafranca Petit Hotel,** Perez Valenzuela 1650 (🕾 **56/2/232-1413;** www.vila franca.cl).

Reading Terminal Market/Italian Market
City of Brotherly Markets
Philadelphia, Pennsylvania

In a city so conscious of its history, it's no surprise that not one but two traditional markets have survived for more than a century. Between the bustling Reading Terminal Market downtown and the Italian Market in South Philly, a food shopper in Philadelphia could eat happily for weeks without ever going near a supermarket.

The older and more classic covered market is the indoor Reading Terminal Market, opened in 1892 in the train shed beneath the Reading Railroad, which conveniently delivered food orders directly to suburban matrons. The Market hung tough through the Depression and two world wars, eventually even outlasting the Reading Railroad, which became defunct in the early 1970s. Extensively renovated in the early 1990s as a gateway to Philly's convention center, the Market today is definitely a tourist destination—it's where visitors head once they've finished with the Liberty Bell and Independence Hall—and a number of its 80-plus merchants cater to the general shopper with crafts, books, and gift items. But the Reading Terminal Market still has an authentic atmosphere, with small local vendors rather than chains. Most striking is the number of Amish businesses, among them Beiler's Bakery, Fisher's Soft Pretzels, the Hatville Deli, AJ Pickle Patch, the Lancaster Co. Dairy, and the L. Halteman Family for meat and poultry products; hearty home-style breakfasts at the Amish-run Dutch Eating Place are justly famous. You'll also find organic and artisanal products from the local region sold at Livengood's, Kauffman's, and the Fair Food Farmstand. Many stall owners have a long history: Termini Bros Bakery has been here since 1921, Harry G. Ochs & Sons butchers since 1906, and Bassett's Ice Cream has been on this site since 1861, pre-dating the market itself.

If it's local color you're after, though, you may prefer the immigrant street-market vibe of the Italian Market over on 9th Street—a 10-block-long row house strip where the proprietors of ground-floor shops set out their wares on the sidewalks under colorful metal awnings. The market still carries the slightly gritty stamp of this South Philly neighborhood's traditional Italian-American residents, though later Hispanic and Asian arrivals have added their flavors as well (there are some great *taquerias* and pho shops in the area). A classic Italian Market shopping spree might include cannolis from Isgro Pastries, Sicilian-style bread from Ianelli's Bakery, fresh ravioli from Talluto's, mozzarella from Claudio's, imported cheese from DiBruno's, clams and fresh fish from Anastasi Seafood, sausage and venison from D'Angelo Brothers, fresh chicken and eggs from Carl's Vineland, or delicate veal and pork from Esposito Meats. A wide range of cafes and restaurants are tucked in around the shops, including **Pat's** and **Geno's**—two rival shrines for Philly cheese steak (see 200). The market is closed Mondays.

ⓘ **Reading Terminal Market:** 12th and Arch streets (✆ **215/922-2317;** www.readingterminalmarket.org).

Italian Market: 9th Street from Wharton to Fitzwater streets (no phone; www.phillyitalianmarket.com).

✈ Philadelphia International (19km/12 miles).

🛏 $$$ **Rittenhouse 1715,** 1715 Rittenhouse Sq. (✆ **877/791-6500** or 215/546-6500; www.rittenhouse1715.com). $$ **Penn's View Hotel,** 14 N. Front St. (✆ **800/331-7634** or 215/922-7600; www.pennsviewhotel.com).

Pike Place Market
Stocking Up Seattle
Seattle, Washington

As Seattle's reputation as a foodie mecca has mushroomed, the Pike Place Market has accrued enormous gourmet cachet—these days it's nearly as essential a tourist stop as the Space Needle. Don't let the throngs deter you, however; a visit to Pike Place is still the best way to deconstruct Seattle's glorious local food culture.

Running along the waterfront at the western edge of Seattle's downtown, the Pike Place Market isn't hard to find, not with that classic red neon "Public Market" sign on top of the long shedlike main arcade, which was built in 1908. It's de rigueur, of course, to check out Pike Place Fish at the southern end—you'll know it by its trademark brass pig—where the staff flings immense salmon through the air to be picked up by customers. At Beecher's Handmade Cheese, you can watch an artisanal cheese maker at work through a wall of glass windows. You'll also find traditional butchers like Don & Joe's Meats, and a range of bakeries from the French patisserie Le Panier to the homier Three Girls Bakery. But as it has grown over the years, the market has evolved into a maze-like warren of little shops, and they're by no means all food oriented—you can now buy antiques, clothing, ceramics, candles, toys, fine art, leather goods, and lots of unique crafts here. Even among the food shops, these days the focus is generally high-end gourmet stuff: smoked salmon from the Totem Smokehouse, chocolate-covered dried cherries at Chukar Cherries, truffle oils at La Buona Tavola, teas and spices at Market Spice, and all sorts of blueberry products from Canter-Berry, just to name a few.

The north arcade, however, has more of a farmer's market air, with plenty of wonderful locally grown fruit and vegetables—go especially for berries and apples in season. As you'd expect in the eco-conscious Northwest, a fair amount of the produce sold here is organic. And as Pike Place has become more and more of a tourist destination, its roster of cafes and restaurants has expanded, some in the main market buildings and several others in the streets surrounding the market. Check the market's website for various special events throughout the year, including chef demonstrations and tours of the market led by local chefs.

While you're in town, it would be a shame to miss another Seattle foodie landmark: **Uwajimaya** at 600 5th Ave. South

Fresh halibut cheeks and other fruits of the sea at Seattle's Pike Place Market.

(☎ **206/624-6248**), an amazing supermarket in the International District crammed with products imported from Asia. The ramen aisle alone is mind-bogglingly extensive.

ⓘ Pike St. and First Ave. (☎ **206/682-7453;** www.pikeplacemarket.org).

✈ Seattle-Tacoma International (14 miles/23km).

🛏 $$$ **Inn at the Market,** 86 Pine St. (☎ **800/446-4484** or 206/443-3600; www.innatthemarket/com). $$ **Bacon Mansion Bed & Breakfast,** 959 Broadway E (☎ **800/240-1864** or 206/329-1864; www.baconmansion.com).

16 Open-Air Markets

Ferry Plaza Market
Going Gourmet by the Bay
San Francisco, California

For San Francisco locavores, aiming to eat within a 100-mile radius is no hardship, given northern California's superlative network of farmers and food artisans. And you can't go wrong if you measure those 100 miles from the Ferry Plaza Market.

Beneath its iconic 240-ft. (72m) Spanish-style clock tower, the historic 1898 Ferry Building's indoor market contains such topnotch local retailers as the Acme Bread Company, Scharffen Berger Chocolate, Recchiuti Confections, and the Cowgirl Creamery Cheese Shop, set around a three-story-high arched nave punctuated with skylights. The indoor market has no fewer than three stores specializing in designer olive oil, another just for mushrooms, another for herbs, and one for caviar, plus high-end fishmongers and butchers, a select few bakeries, and a chic flower shop.

The impetus for a food market stemmed from a 1992 event—a one-time-only farmer's market held on the plaza outside the building's exterior arcades. An overwhelming success, it returned as a year-round market in May 1993; the justly famous **Ferry Plaza Farmers Market** (☎ **415/291-3276**) is now held every Tuesday (10am–2pm) and Saturday (8am–2pm). In the sometimes overheated Bay Area food scene, shopping days at the farmer's market can

get frenzied, with well over 10,000 shoppers competing to snap up prime produce from small regional farmers and ranchers, the majority of them certified organic. Various artisanal specialties are also sold—including breads, cheeses, jams—and weekly cooking demonstrations and interviews with farmers are mounted by the market's organizers. A couple of the permanent shops inside the building began as wildly popular stalls in the farmer's market—the Frog Hollow Farm store now sells famous Frog Hollow peaches and other fruit and preserves 7 days a week; the Farm Fresh to You store sells freshly harvested seasonal produce from Capay Organic Farm and other local organic growers.

Set right on the Bay, on the embarcadero, the Ferry Plaza—accessible by MUNI, BART, ferry boats, and the Market Street trolley cars—was once the main entry point for travelers and commuters coming into the city. Ferry service became obsolete, however, after the Golden Gate and Bay Bridges were built in the 1930s, and from the 1950s on it was more or less a white elephant, hacked up into office space and blighted by an elevated freeway blocking its face. But as Marin ferry service came back into vogue in the 1980s, this elegant building begged for renovation;

On the Embarcadero, the Ferry Plaza Market building dates to 1898.

when the freeway was dismantled in 1991, the way was clear for the Ferry Building to be reborn.

ⓘ Ferry Building Plaza (at the foot of Market St. at The Embarcadero) (✆ **415/693-0996;** www.ferrybuildingmarketplace.com).

✈ San Francisco International (14 miles/ 23km).

🛏 $$$ **Hotel Adagio,** 550 Geary St. (✆ **800/228-8830** or 415/775-5000; www. thehoteladagion.com). $ **Hotel des Arts,** 447 Bush St. (✆ **800/956-4322** or 415/956-3232; www.sfhoteldesarts.com).

Open-Air Markets 17

L.A. Farmer's Market
The Hollywood Version
Los Angeles, California

There's a bit of huckster atmosphere about the L.A. Farmer's Market. A private enterprise rather than a public facility, it has been tarted up with on-site entertainment, busloads of tourists, a host of restaurants (more than half of the vendors now are eateries), and shops selling gift items such as candles, souvenirs, clothing, and greeting cards. But that has been true ever since this market was born, back in the Depression era, when it began as a series of canvas-roofed wooden sheds provided to farmers who'd been selling their produce from truck tailgates in the dirt lot at Third and Fairfax.

The Farmer's Market has undergone its own version of SoCal sprawl ever since; for years its owners also operated a stadium and racetrack on an adjoining lot, and more recently a massive shopping mall went up at its eastern end—a Vegas-style architectural pastiche called The Grove, with a faux-village layout and electric trolleys to and from the Market. In contrast to that, the claustrophobic aisles and crowded patios of the Farmer's Market look plenty old-fashioned—a little slice of old Los Angeles (around here, the 1930s are ancient history).

Angelenos don't need to buy their fresh fruit and vegetables here anymore, given the well-developed network of once-a-week farmer's markets throughout the Los Angeles area. Yet the Farmer's Market retains authentic features and remains an outpost of traditional butchers (Huntingdon's Meat & Sausage, Marconda's Meats), fishmongers (Tusquella's), poultry dealers (Farmers Market Poultry, Puritan Poultry), high-end produce hawkers (Farm Fresh Produce, The Fruit Company), and bakers (the Russian pastries at T & Y, and the famous pies of DuPar's Pie Shop). To draw in the browsing tourists, they often lay on a little razzle-dazzle too—with the candy man who makes his own confections in his window of Littlejohn's English Toffee House, the ice-cream makers behind the window at Bennett's Ice Cream, or the baker decorating cakes in the window of Thee's Continental Pastries.

Though it's not where local residents do their grocery shopping, there are still plenty of reasons to join the office workers from the nearby CBS studios who come here to grab lunch. The Farmer's Market's delightful array of food stands are mostly still mom-and-pop affairs, with hand-painted signs and counter stools (very few food-court chains have penetrated here). The range of food includes oysters, hot doughnuts, fresh-squeezed orange juice, corned beef sandwiches, fresh-pressed peanut butter, and all kinds of international foods. For a full sit-down meal, the Cajun seafood gumbo at the **Gumbo Pot** is popular, as is the *churrascaria* at **Pampas Grill** and the *teppan*-style Japanese food at **Kado**.

ⓘ 6333 W. 3rd St., Los Angeles (✆ **323/933-9211;** www.farmersmarketla.com).

✈ Los Angeles International (12 miles/19km).

🛏 $$ **Roosevelt Hotel, Hollywood,** 7000 Hollywood Blvd. (✆ **800/950-7667** or 323/466-7000; www.hollywoodroosevelt.com). $$ **Beverly Garland's Holiday Inn,** 4222 Vineland Ave., North Hollywood (✆ **800/BEVERLY** or 818/980-8000; www.beverlygarland.com).

18 Open-Air Markets

St. Lawrence Market

Canadian Casual

Toronto, Ontario

Toronto's premier food market is the antithesis of the glossy, chain store–friendly Eaton Center, the city's best-known shopping mall. In a cavernous red-brick building in the heart of old Toronto, you'll find two rambling levels of food stalls selling fresh produce, meats, and artisanal food products. There's little gourmet pretension here, despite the availability of imported cheeses and teas, caviar, smoked salmon, lobsters, and exotic tropical fruits. The iconic specialty of the St. Lawrence Market? It's pea-meal bacon on a bun, a hearty and thoroughly Ontarian sandwich.

These are mom-and-pop businesses in the best sense of the term. Most are family run, or are being carried on by former employees of the original owners, whose immigrant backgrounds (Ukrainian, Italian, Greek, Korean) are proof positive of Toronto's ethnic diversity. Signs are hand painted, and regular customers are known by name. And talk about longevity: Of the more than 50 vendors keeping shop in the South Market hall, several—Wittevein Meats, Scheffler's Deli & Cheese, Olympic Cheese Mart, Kozlik's Canadian Mustard—have been there since the 1950s. Ponesse Foods has been selling fresh produce since 1900, and Brown Brothers Butchers predates the market, having been in business since 1895. Locals sometimes scoff at the St. Lawrence Market as a yuppie hangout (especially now that the surrounding neighborhood's vacant warehouses have been transformed by urban chic), and it may be, compared to the cacophony of the Kensington Market street market, Toronto's other chief food shopping resource. (The number of organic vendors is steadily increasing, a sure sign of yuppification.) But the vibe here is still casual and laid back.

Since 1803, some sort of weekly farmer's market has taken place here at Front and Jarvis streets; the permanent covered market building came into being in 1899, when a former City Hall was converted into its current train shedlike form. The North Market building is still the site of a Saturday's farmer's market, which gets going at 5am (that's when the farmers arrive) and draws food shoppers from quite a distance. The market is closed Sunday and Monday.

There are a handful of cafes and take-out stands at the South Market but only one full-service restaurant, Paddington's Pump—and even that is a casual sort of joint. Plans are afoot to open a kitchen/demonstration area on the west mezzanine for cooking classes.

ⓘ 92 Front St. E (☏ **416/392-7219;** www.stlawrencemarket.com).

✈ Toronto International (29km/18 miles).

🛏 $$$ **Le Royal Meridien King Edward,** 37 King St. E (☏ **800/543-4300** or 416/863-9700; www.starwoodhotels.com). $$ **The Drake Hotel,** 1150 Queen St. W (☏ **416/531-5042;** www.thedrakehotel.ca).

Gourmet Emporiums & Specialty Shops

19

Harrods Food Halls
Food, Glorious Food
London, England

London's world-famous luxury department store in Knightsbridge actually had its origins in 1849 as a high-end grocery store, so it's only fitting that its centerpiece should still be the food halls. A lavish series of ballroom-sized salons, the food halls sell everything from dressed pheasant, legs of Iberico ham, and whole smoked salmon to exquisite chocolates, teas, and cheese biscuits; it's like a *Masterpiece Theatre* fantasy of country-house weekends and shooting-party picnic hampers, cunningly packaged for aspiring middle-class punters.

Not only are the high-ceilinged halls superbly outfitted, with marble counters, mahogany shelving, sparkling glass cases, and richly tiled walls, the food displays themselves are artful as still lifes. Cuts of Scotch beef, Dutch veal, and streaky bacon in the butcher section have been trimmed with almost surgical precision. The dairy department offers raw-milk cheeses, high-fat butters, and a number of other products that Americans can't get at home. Increasingly Harrods has developed its own store brands—stacks of handsomely packaged jams, cookies, and confectionery and tins of tea, perfect for souvenirs. Even if you don't buy anything (and at these prices, you'll be calculating every purchase), it's a visual experience not to be missed. If you're feeling peckish—or simply overwhelmed by the opulence and profusion—take advantage of the counters around the halls where you can sit down and enjoy small servings of sushi, oysters, charcuterie, tapas, pizza, or pastries.

Strung up with white lights at night, like a Pearly Queen, Harrods is a blaring tourist magnet, no question about it. And it's no longer an official royal provisioner—not since owner Mohamed Al Fayed's public denunciation of the royal family, following the death of his son Dodi alongside Princess Diana. Service is coolly professional, and because the place is generally thronged (must pick up those souvenirs before getting on the plane!), it can take ages to get served; it's not a place you just dash into to pick up a quick nibble. But add the entertainment value of shopping here

The food displays and the setting are equally lavish at Harrods in Knightsbridge.

into the price of these comestibles, and its value for money.

ⓘ 87–135 Brompton Rd. (✆ **44/20/7730 1234;** www.harrods.com).

✈ Heathrow (24km/15 miles) or Gatwick (40km/25 miles).

🛏 $$$ **22 Jermyn St.,** 22 Jermyn St., St. James (✆ **800/682-7808** in the U.S., or 44/20/7734-2353; www.22jermyn.com). $$ **Vicarage Private Hotel,** 10 Vicarage Gate, South Kensington (✆ **44/20/7229-4030;** www.londonvicaragehotel.com).

Paxton & Whitfield/Neal's Yard Dairy

A Spot of Cheese, Please

London, England

Forty years ago, Monty Python made hilarious comedy with a sketch set in a completely clueless English cheese shop. These days, however, Great Britain's great cheese-making tradition has bounced back from near-extinction—and that renaissance has at least in part been spurred on by London's two finest cheese purveyors, Paxton & Whitfield and Neal's Yard Dairy.

Neal's Yard in Covent Garden sells artisanal cheeses from throughout the UK and Ireland.

There's no question which of the two has the more venerable pedigree—**Paxton & Whitfield,** at 93 Jermyn St. (© **44/ 20/7930 0259;** www.paxtonandwhitifled. co.uk) has been around since 1797, and in its current premises for more than a century. The gold-lettered black storefront looks like something out of Dickens, or a Beatrix Potter watercolor, with its large-paned vitrine stacked high with substantial cheeses and hams. On prominent display is the crest of its Royal Warrant as cheesemonger to the queen; Winston Churchill himself praised this refined little venue in St. James as the only place where a gentleman (or his gentleman's gentleman) should buy his cheese, although its proximity to Jermyn Street haberdashers may have swung Churchill's vote. But there's no disputing the store's depth in both English and French cheeses—ask the knowledgeable counterman to cut you a wedge of well-aged Stilton, creamy Brie des Meaux, a supple Camembert, or a hearty farmhouse Cheddar, accompanied perhaps by oatcakes and a bottle of P&W's own real ale. P&W also has suitably discreet-looking branches in Stratford-Upon-Avon (13 Wood St.) and in Bath (1 John St.)—not coincidentally two other towns with plenty of Ye Olde England tourist appeal.

By comparison, **Neal's Yard Dairy,** at 17 Shorts Garden, Covent Garden (© **44/ 20/7240 5700;** www.nealsyarddairy.co.uk) is an upstart, and yet many British foodies would give it the nod as London's best cheese shop. Founded in 1979, it quickly became a player in Britain's nascent whole foods movement, and was a catalyst in transforming the gritty Covent Garden area into a retail hotspot. The Neal's Yard guys made their own cheeses as well as sourcing artisanal products directly from small cheese makers around the United Kingdom and Ireland. Although the operation has grown into a major business, the original passion for British cheese (some would say obsession) is still apparent. The store has a sort of scrubbed-deal honesty that's very appealing, with immense wheels and wedges of cheese jumbled everywhere—not only double and single Gloucester, but more unusual varieties such as Irish Gubbeen and Cornish Yarg and Welsh Caerphilly, not to mention Stinking Bishop. Though the selection is smaller than P&W's, the focus on flavor and quality comes through; they also offer several unpasteurized cheeses. Neal's Yard has an outlet at Borough Market as well.

Cheese lovers, be forewarned: Choosing between the two stores is nearly impossible. The only solution is to visit both.

✈ Heathrow (24km/15 miles) or Gatwick (40km/25 miles).

🛏 $$$ **22 Jermyn St.,** 22 Jermyn St., St. James (© **800/682-7808** in the U.S., 44/20/7734-2353; www.22jermyn.com). $$$ **Covent Garden Hotel,** 10 Monmouth St., Covent Garden (© **800/553-6674** in the U.S., 44/20/7806-1000; www.firmdale.com).

Gourmet Emporiums & Specialty Shops

21

Valvona & Crolla
Beyond Haggis
Edinburgh, Scotland

Back in 1934, when the Italian wine merchants Valvona & Crolla opened their new shop in the gray precincts of Edinburgh's New Town, there were no other delicatessens in the Scots capital. In fact, most Edinburghers probably didn't even know what a delicatessen was. But these enterprising shop owners quickly filled the gap, providing local Italian immigrants with all the foodstuffs they so sorely missed from the old country. In just a few years, the shop's expanding gourmet food selection had outstripped the wine shop, with imported cheeses, cured meats, pastas, vinegars, and luxury tinned goods shipped in exclusively from Milan. It didn't take long before the market's fame spread beyond the immigrant community, introducing haggis-loving Scotsmen to the wonders of salami and prosciutto. (Just to be safe, though, V&C made plenty of room for a wide-ranging whiskey selection alongside the wine offerings.)

Still run by descendants of Raffaele Valvona and Alfonso Crolla, the shop maintains an air of epicurean dignity behind its sober white-and-green façade, discreetly emblazoned nowadays with the crest of a royal warrant as cheese mongers to the queen. In today's globalized food culture, the goods at Valvona & Crolla may not be as exclusive as they once were, but the shop's longstanding gourmet reputation has taken it beyond mere retail. Besides operating its own in-house bakery and stocking fresh fruits and vegetables, Valvona & Crolla has an excellent kitchenware and cookbook section, and presents a continual line-up of events—from cheese tastings, cooking demonstrations, and wine tastings to the ever popular Fungi Forays, field trips to forage for the many edible mushrooms found in the nearby countryside. The Caffè Bar tucked behind the main shop is also a popular place to stop in for breakfast or lunch (the toasted paninis come highly recommended); a branch nearby in Multrees Walk also has a full-service Italian restaurant, **VinCaffè** (℮ **44/131/557-0088**).

ⓘ 19 Elm Row (℮ **44/131/556-6066;** www.valvonacrolla.co.uk).

✈ Edinburgh (10km/6mi).

🛏 $$$ **Holyrood Hotel,** 81 Holyrood Rd. (℮ **44/870/194-2106;** www.macdonald hotels.co.uk). $$ **The Bank Hotel,** 1 South Bridge St. (℮ **44/131/622-6800;** www. festival-inns.co.uk).

Fauchon

Epicurean Epicenter

Paris, France

If ever you're tempted to doubt that Paris is the epicenter of the gastronomic world, one visit to Fauchon should set you straight. Everything in this luxury food shop on the place de la Madeleine is absolutely *comme il faut,* and yet perfectly delicious. Is it food or fashion? If you have to ask, do you deserve to shop here?

Founded in 1886 by Auguste Fauchon, the store has recently expanded worldwide, but the undeniable chic of the Paris flagship makes it feel like anything but a chain. The heart of the business may be its patisserie, where even the simplest croissants, macaroons, and madeleines evoke a Proustian response in some jaded Parisians (others simply marvel at the sculptural perfection of its decorated cakes). The confectionery section's chocolates are also justly famous, as is its wine shop. The *traiteur* division is where you'll find the best of French cheeses, terrines, foie gras, and pâtés, as well as a select range of caviars. Fresh pastas, conserves, spices, teas, and jams fill the *epicerie* section. None of this comes cheap, of course, but the selection is impeccable, not to mention

the elegant pink-and-black packaging. In typically Parisian style, the baroque rituals of selecting your food, visiting the cash register, and claiming your purchases are anything but efficient, but then nothing this good should come easy, right? Along with shopping, you may want to dine at the on-site restaurant, **Brasserie Fauchon,** or the tea salon, where you can consume those trademark pastries. Fauchon is closed Sundays.

Well before Fauchon set up shop on place de la Madeleine, the elegant **Hédiard,** at 21 place de la Madeleine (℮ **01-43-12-88-88**), was already peddling fine coffees, teas, spices, and jams; its salons were recently refurbished to look as they did a century ago, in a clear attempt to eat into Fauchon's franchise. You may also want to check out **Maison de la Truffe,** at 19 place de la Madeleine (℮ **01-42-65-53-22**), a convivially cramped fantasy of an old-fashioned butcher shop selling all the essentials of Parisian cookery—foie gras, caviar, and truffles. What else does a Parisian epicure need?

(i) 26 place de la Madeleine, 8e (Métro: Madeleine; (C) **01-47-42-91-10;** www.fauchon.fr).

✈ De Gaulle (23km/14 miles), Orly (14km/8²/₃ miles).

🛏 $$$ **Hôtel Luxembourg Parc,** 42 rue de Vaugirard, 6e ((C) **33/1/53-10-36-50;** www.luxembourg-paris-hotel.com). $$ **Hôtel Saintonge,** 16 rue Saintonge, 3e ((C) **44/1/42-77-91-13;** www.saintonge marais.com).

Gourmet Emporiums & Specialty Shops

23

Poilâne
Daily Bread
Paris, France

Everyone knows what French bread is: It's a long, slender white-bread baguette, with a fragile crisp brown crust. But ubiquitous as baguettes may be on the streets of Paris, what's generally accepted as Paris's best bread is something completely different—the peasanty sourdough loaves sold at this shop in Saint-Germain des Près.

Poilâne, which is still family-owned, hasn't changed much since it opened in 1932 (though recent expansion, including a shop at 49 bd. de Grenelle and another in—mon Dieu!—London, at 46 Elizabeth St., has raised a few eyebrows). Bread is still baked here following Pierre Poilâne's time-tested techniques, using stone-ground flour and sea salt, shaping loaves by hand, and baking them in a wood-fired oven. Pierre's gregarious son Lionel—perhaps the world's first celebrity baker—found ways to update the business, however, without sacrificing the bread's artisanal quality.

These larger, denser loaves, which weigh as much as 4 pounds apiece, don't get stale as quickly as baguettes do, and they're easier to slice. They've become so famous that the generic name for this type of loaf is now *pain poilâne;* Poilâne's bakers distinguish the genuine loaf by decorating it with a big cursive P. They also turn out delectable apple tarts, delicate butter cookies, gingerbreads, and other pastries,

but the bread is the main attraction. The tiny shop opens early, at 7:15am (closed Sun), and there's usually a line out the door. Thousands of loaves are also baked

Monogrammed sourdough loaves fresh from Poilâne's wood-firing oven.

daily and shipped worldwide from a commercial bakery outside of town (with small wood-fired ovens, of course). Buying a loaf from the original Latin Quarter shop, however, is the essential Parisian experience. If the shop's not too busy, you may be able to persuade a baker to take you down into the stone cellar to see the wood-fired ovens at work.

This being Paris, of course, there are plenty of dissenters who insist on the superiority of their own favorite *boulangerie*. Some insist that the secret Poilâne family recipe comes out better when it's baked by Lionel's brother Max, at 87 rue Brancion (☎ **44/1/48-28-45-90**), who split from the family business many years ago. Two organic bread makers also give the Poilânes a run for their money: **Moisan,** in the 12th arrondissement at 5 place d'Aligre by the Marche d'Aligre, and several other locations (☎ **44/1/43-45-46-60**), and **Le Boulangerie de Monge,** in the 5th arrondissement at 123 rue Monge (☎ **44/1/43-37-54-20**). Both shops sell baguettes (and *ficelles*) as well.

ⓘ **Poilâne,** 8 rue du Cherche-Midi, 6e (Métro: St-Sulpice); ☎ **39/1/45-48-42-59**; www.poilane.fr).

✈ De Gaulle (23km/14 miles), Orly (14km/$8^2/_3$ miles).

🛏 $$$ **Hôtel Luxembourg Parc,** 42 rue de Vaugirard, 6e (☎ **33/1/53-10-36-50**; www.luxembourg-paris-hotel.com). $$ **Hôtel Saintonge,** 16 rue Saintonge, 3e (☎ **44/1/42-77-91-13**; www.saintongemarais.com).

Gourmet Emporiums & Specialty Shops

24

Dallmayr

Feeding the Crowned Heads

Munich, Germany

At the turn of the last century, most of the crowned heads of Europe had accounts at Dallmayr—one can easily imagine Mad King Ludwig ordering up a hamper of oysters and champagne to Neuschwanstein from this dignified luxury grocery near the Rathaus. Even today, gastronomes from Hamburg or Berlin phone in their orders for exotica not readily available anywhere else; its list of VIP clients reads like a who's who of German industry and letters.

Here you'll find Munich's upper crust browsing for Scottish salmon, foie gras, English cookies, rare brandies, out-of-season asparagus, and white raspberries. An almost bewildering variety of luxe items are displayed in these marble salons: Over 6,000 food products range from chocolates, jams, honey, smoked fish, and caviar to meat, sausage, chicken, and fresh seafood; there's also fresh pasta, fancy pastries, and prepared salads as well as a substantial line of wines and spirits.

The business dates back as far as the 17th century, though the present-day store with its ornate neoclassical façade was only built in 1950, replicating an earlier store destroyed during World War II. The tone of the place is definitely upscale and lavish, with counter clerks garbed in distinctive blue blouses with crisp white aprons, and an indoor fountain stocked with live crayfish.

Attention to quality has always been a Dallmayr hallmark, but its owners (Dallmayr is still a family-run business) have stayed ahead of the game through entrepreneurial innovation as well. Dallmayr was one of the first firms to import tropical fruits for sale back in the 19th century, and originated the idea of a cold buffet selling prepared salads. Its line of exotic coffee beans has been a specialty since the 1930s, with beans stored in huge porcelain urns of painted Nymphenburg china. Dallmayr has an extensive Internet business, shipping many delicacies around the world, but a visit to the Munich store reveals hundreds of other specialty items too perishable to be shipped abroad. The fine-dining restaurant upstairs (© **49/89/2-13-51-00**) has won acclaim for its Mediterranean-inspired menu under chef Diethard Urbansky. The market is closed Sundays.

ⓘ Dienerstrasse 14–15 (© **49/89/2-13-50;** www.dallmayr.de).

✈ Franz-Josef-Strauss International (29km/18 miles).

🛏 $$ **Hotel St. Paul,** St-Paul-Strasse 7 (© **49/89/5440-7800;** www.hotel-stpaul.de). $ **Am Markt,** Heiliggeiststrasse 6 (© **49/89/22-50-14;** www.hotelinmunich.de).

Peck

The Italian Job

Milan, Italy

Take Italy's fervent food culture and marry it to Milan's exquisite fashion and design aesthetic and presto!, you've got the world's most upscale delicatessen. Actually, "delicatessen" is a pretty feeble term to apply to this four-story food showcase, on a side street quite close to the Duomo. Though it was founded way back in 1883 by a charcutier from Prague named Francesco Peck, Milan's famous food emporium has evolved over the years into a sleekly stylish and pricey showcase devoted to the foods of Italy.

Apparently it's no hard task to fill four stories with top-grade olive oils, balsamic vinegars, freshly made pastas in all shapes and sizes, porcini mushrooms, and truffles (where else would you pick up those essential Piedmont white truffles?). The cool cellar full of Italian wines is an amazing cave in and of itself. The cheese counter is a marvel, featuring pale glistening globes of buffalo mozzarella, enormous wheels of Parmesan, creamy Gorgonzolas, and luscious mascarpone. And given Peck's origins, it's no surprise that the

Founded by a Czech charcutier, Milan's Peck Market is now an Italian landmark.

salumeria is outstanding, with a stunning array of prosciuttos, salamis, mortadellas, cotechinos, Parma hams, and stuffed pigs' feet. The artfully decorated little cakes in the pastry shop can be taken right to the upstairs cafe, where freshly roasted coffee is also sold. The service is generally haughty and even rude, and don't attempt to comparison shop—of course you can buy the same products elsewhere for less. But somehow this place makes you feel as if it's worth paying extra just for the Peck experience.

Naturally, the store has spun off a couple of eateries—there's the sleek Italian Bar around the corner, which offers a selection of roast veal, risottos, porchetta, salads, aspics, cheeses, and pastries, and then there's the full-fledged restaurant **Cracco-Peck,** at Via Victor Hugò 4 (© **02-876-774**). Like the store, they're both absurdly high priced, but for stylish, creative cuisine, they deliver the goods.

ⓘ Via Spadari 9 (© **39/2/802-3161;** www.peck.it; closed Mon).

✈ Milan's **Aeroporto di Linate** (internal European flights; 16km/10 miles) and **Aeroporto Malpensa** (transatlantic flights; 48km/30 miles).

🛏 $$$ **Four Seasons Hotel Milano,** Via Gesú 8 (© **39/2/77088;** www.fourseasons.com). $$ **Antica Locanda Leonardo,** Corso Magenta 78 (© **39/2/463317;** www.leoloc.com).

Salumeria Garibaldi
The Prosciutto Pros
Parma, Italy

It's hard not to eat well in Italy—but even in context, the city of Parma is a standout. Parmesan cheese, Parma ham, sparkling red Lambrusco wine, the balsamic vinegar of nearby Modena—the list of regional specialties goes on and on. Eating locally here is dead easy: Corn grown in the Po Valley feeds the region's heirloom-bred dairy cows, whose milk is turned into Parmigiano-Reggiano cheese; local pigs are fed on the whey cast off during the cheese-making process, and then slaughtered to make the region's famous pork products. (Parma even hosts a prosciutto festival every Sept.) Po Valley corn also feeds the local chickens, whose eggs are combined with Po Valley wheat flour to make such fresh pasta as *tortelli,* Parma's characteristic stuffed pasta.

For one-stop shopping for all these local specialties, you can't do better than Salumeria Garibaldi, a sleekly handsome large shop conveniently located near the train station. **Salumeria Garibaldi** has been in business for over 50 years and in this location since 1986. The shop's core business, of course, is its cured pork products, which include *culatello* (pig's buttock cured in a pig's bladder, but delicious), *cotechino* (coarse pork sausage), *fiochetto,* raw prosciutto, salami, mortadella, and copa di Parma (cured shoulder of pork). The shop touts the sources of its pork products as only the best and most traditional local artisans, and their production processes are carefully monitored at every step in order to qualify for controlled appellation status. Huge pale-yellow wheels of granular

Parmigiano-Reggiano cheese are another essential, which customers buy in hefty chunks to be grated later (though with Parmesan this fresh, it's hard to resist paring off little slices to pop straight into your mouth).

Salumeria Garibaldi supplements those basics with bountiful glass cases full of prepared foods, from stuffed artichokes to stuffed rabbit, ham wrapped in cabbage to roasted chicken, fritto misto and torta fritta (deep-fried yeast wafers), and a table laden with cakes and flaky pastries. Upscale as the shop looks, it has a friendly staff, happy to share their appreciation of their hometown's gustatory delights. Consider it Parma's equivalent of a takeout fast-food joint—and wish you lived in Parma full time.

ⓘ Via Garibaldi 42 (✆ **39/521/235606;** www.specialitadiparma.it/default2.asp).

🚄 Parma (1 hr. from Bologna, 1½ hr. from Milan, 2 hr. from Florence).

🛏 $$$ **Palace Hotel Maria Luigia,** Viale Mentana 140 (✆ **39/521/281032;** www.sinahotels.it). $$ **Hotel Button,** Strada San Vitale Borgo Salina 7 (✆ **39/521/ 208039**).

Gourmet Emporiums & Specialty Shops

27

Yeliseyevsky Gastronom
Temple of the Gluttons
Moscow, Russia

Its nickname was once "Temple of the Gluttons," a cutting reference to the czars who used to patronize this landmark 1901 emporium. But in the new capitalist Russia, gluttony is no longer frowned upon—in fact, Russians spend more of their income on food than any other European nation. And $3 million has been lavished on restoring the original crystal chandeliers, neobaroque carved ceilings, and Art Nouveau stained glass of this 19th-century Moscow mansion, with a sister store in St. Petersburg, at 56 Nevsky Prospect.

Taken over by the Bolsheviks in 1917 and converted to an employee-owned enterprise in the early 1990s, Yeliseyevsky Gastronom stocks a mix of Russian delicacies and imported luxury foods, catering to the culinary whims of newly affluent Muscovites. The centerpiece of the ornate ground floor is a stunning array of perishables in glass cases—fresh seafood and meat, cheeses, produce, and prepared foods (including regional specialties like Siberian meat dumplings and Georgia cheese pies). There's also a large section in the back for wines and liquors, including flavored vodkas and Armenian brandies. As you'd expect, the caviar section displays more varieties of caviar than you'd think possible. It's certainly not a place where locals do their shopping unless they're out to make a splash with a special dinner party. But despite the high prices, Russians come here for imported novelties like Italian wines and American soda, while tourists lay down rubles for souvenir items like wooden boxes of chocolates, charmingly lacquered and painted in folk-art style.

Yeliseyevsky Gastronom has been getting some competition lately from **Gastronom No. 1,** which enjoys the advantage of a choice location in the GUM shopping center on Red Square. A re-creation of a historic market, with marble floors and Art Deco fixtures, Gastronom No. 1 certainly offers the expected gourmet treats such as fresh seafood, sushi, tropical fruits, coffee beans, and runny French cheeses, but it also goes for a Disney-esque packaged nostalgia, stocking Soviet-era treats such as canned sprats, smoked beef, and pickled mushrooms—there's even a retro soda fountain serving the sparkling flavored soda called *gazirovky,* popular in the Communist era.

(i) 14 Tverskaya Ulitsa (metro: Teatralnaya or Chekhovskaya; *7/95/209-0760*).

✈ Sheremetyevo International Airport (34km/21 miles).

|=== $$$ **Sheraton Palace,** 19 1st Tverskaya-Yamskaya Ulitsa (*7/95/931-9700;* http://eng.sheratonpalace.ru). $$ **East-West Hotel,** 14 Tverskoi Bulvar, building 4 (*7/95/290-0404;* www.eastwesthotel.ru).

Gourmet Emporiums & Specialty Shops

28

Zabar's

Hello, Deli!

New York, New York

In old Europe, the word "delicatessen" just meant any sort of luxury edibles. When 19th-century Jewish immigrants came to America, though, something got lost in translation. Their "appetizing" stores, selling kosher delicatessen goods, were promptly misnamed delicatessens by hungry Gentile customers, who then proceeded to shorten the word to deli—and a whole new category of food store was born.

When it comes to American deli stores—as opposed to deli restaurants (see chapter 4)—few have the cachet of Zabar's. Though it was only founded in the 1930s, as a smoked fish counter in a larger market, Zabar's has become an institution on Manhattan's Upper West Side, which for many years was a predominantly middle-class Jewish neighborhood. In a maze-like series of low-ceilinged, fluorescent-lit rooms, Zabar's still has the sawdust floors, white tile walls, and wooden barrels of an old-fashioned immigrant appetizing store, though the goods are crammed in so abundantly you can barely see the decor.

Wide selection, top quality, and competitive prices are the cornerstones of Zabar's success. Besides the classic gefilte fish, lox, and smoked herring, Zabar's offers all sorts of salami and pastrami, not to mention a full range of cold cuts, pâtés, and a mind-boggling international array of cheeses. There are cases packed with prepared salads in plastic tubs with the trademark orange Zabar's logo; nearby are racks stacked high with jars and tins of imported foods from around the world (including some very well-priced tins of caviar), as well as an impressive selection of coffee beans and excellent fresh breads. Upstairs is an excellent collection of housewares and restaurant-quality cookware. Prepare yourself for exasperating crowds and sometimes brusque counter service; it's all part of the patented Zabar's experience.

While the Upper West Side Zabar's is operated by brothers Saul and Stanley Zabar, sons of founder Louis Zabar, their brother Eli runs two rival gourmet groceries on the Upper East Side, the **Vinegar Factory,** at 431 E. 91st St. (*212/369-5700*), and **Eli's Manhattan,** at 1411 Third Ave. (*212/717-8100*). Both have extensive deli counters and prepared food sections, as well as on-site restaurants and all the fresh fruits and vegetables that the original Zabar's doesn't carry. East Side shoppers have become just as addicted to Eli's interpretation of the Zabar formula as West Siders are to the Broadway original. Gourmet stores they may be, but these are gourmet stores where the neighborhood regularly shops too.

ⓘ 2245 Broadway (☎ **212/787-2000;** www.zabars.com).

✈ John F. Kennedy Intl (15 miles/24km); Newark Liberty Intl (16 miles/27km); LaGuardia (8 miles/13km).

🛏 $$ **The Lucerne,** 201 W. 79th St. (☎ **800/492-8122** or 212/875-1000; www.thelucernehotel.com). $ **Belleclaire Hotel,** 250 W. 77th St. (☎ **877/HOTEL-BC** or 212/362-7700; www.hotelbelleclaire.com).

Gourmet Emporiums & Specialty Shops

29

Zingerman's Deli
Deconstructing the Deli
Ann Arbor, Michigan

There's no reason why a New York–style deli should have taken off in the middle of Michigan, even given the college-town sophistication of Ann Arbor. But take off Zingerman's did—and how.

Founded in 1982 by two University of Michigan grads, Paul Saginaw and Ari Weinzweig, Zingerman's doesn't look like much. It's still just a two-story brick storefront, a 1902-vintage former grocery on a street in the historic Kerrytown district, near the Ann Arbor Farmer's Market. There's usually a line out the door, and crowds mill around the narrow aisles inside.

But the business has been a rousing success almost from the start, and it wasn't just because you couldn't get Jewish specialties anywhere else in Ann Arbor. Zingerman's was shrewdly designed to cover all bases. On one hand, the deli serves outstanding examples of the traditional Jewish dishes that Saginaw and Weinzweig had grown up with in their respective hometowns of Detroit and Chicago—corned beef, pastrami, chopped liver, and smoked fish. But alongside that, they peddle trendier gourmet offerings such as farmhouse cheeses, estate-bottled olive oils, varietal

vinegars, and single-origin chocolates—but never in snooty, museum-like displays. (Not that there'd be room for such a thing in Zingerman's cramped quarters.) Sandwiches are notoriously huge and messy, though they're not bargains; Zingerman's mantra is high quality, not low prices. Counter staff freely offers samples, believing that a fine food's taste will sell it better than anything else. And on the theory that an educated customer will spend more money, Zingerman's friendly, enthusiastic workers hand out chatty flyers to customers and slap wordy, colorful handmade posters on the walls.

Though Zingerman's has steadfastly resisted the urge to clone itself in other cities, Saginaw and Weinzweig have extended their brand with their own bread bakery and cheese-making operation, as well as a popular casual restaurant next door and a phenomenally vigorous mail-order business. Weinzweig also publishes a remarkably knowledgeable food newsletter and food guide, incidentally positioning the Zingerman's guys as food experts—which, of course, they are.

Long lines and boisterous activity rarely let up at Zingerman's Deli in Ann Arbor.

(i) 422 Detroit St. (© **734/663-DELI;** www.zingermansdeli.com).

✈ Detroit Metropolitan International (20 miles/32km).

🛏 $$$ **The Burnt Toast Inn,** 415 W. William St. (© **734/662-6685;** www.burnt toastinn.com). $$ **Library Bed and Breakfast,** 808 Mary St. (© **734/668-6815**).

Gourmet Emporiums & Specialty Shops **30**

Salumi

Finding the Cure

Seattle, Washington

It would make a much better story if celebrity chef Mario Batali had become a great restaurateur because he grew up helping mind the store at his father's old-fashioned salumeria. In fact, this unprepossessing beige-tiled storefront in Seattle's historic Pioneer Square district didn't open until Mario had already left home, when his father, Armandino, decided to retire from Boeing Aircraft and devote himself to the food traditions of his Italian forebears (Armandino's grandfather, it's true, operated Seattle's first Italian grocery over a century ago).

But the Batali obsessiveness is apparently a genetic trait. Though he'd cooked seriously for years, Armandino spent 2 years learning the meat-curing process from the ground up before he and his wife, Marilyn, opened this small deli in the late 1990s to sell his handmade Italian-style cured meats. Rave reviews poured in, many of them from people who had no idea that the owners' son was on his way to becoming one of America's top chefs.

The charcuterie is all handmade from traditional methods, though the curing facility uses plenty of state-of-the-art equipment (there's the mark of the Boeing ex-engineer) to control the curing climate more rigorously than any old-country manufactory could. The silken textures and melting tenderness of Batali's meats are transcendental, the peppers and spices sounding a sharp, clear note, and they're much in demand with Seattle chefs and a growing online retail business.

Salumi sells not only the traditional specialty meats—*culatello, dario, finocchiona, coppa, pancetta, guanciale, sopressata*—but also experiments with things like lamb prosciutto, smoked paprika sausage, a mole-flavored salami, and citrus-and-cardamom-flavored *agrumi*. Two communal tables at the back of the store enable customers to eat right on the premises (sandwiches, breads, cheeses, and various cooked daily specials are also served), though you can also buy meats at the counter to take away. When you plan your visit, keep in mind that Salumi is only open Tuesday through Friday, starting at a leisurely 11am and closing at 4pm. Hey, the guy's supposed to be retired; he has a right to keep whatever hours he wants.

ⓘ 309 Third Ave. South (📞 **206/621 8772;** www.salumicuredmeats.com).

✈ Seattle-Tacoma International (14 miles/ 23km).

🛏 $$$ **Inn at the Market,** 86 Pine St. (📞 **800/446-4484** or 206/443-3600; www.innatthemarket/com). $$ **Bacon Mansion Bed & Breakfast,** 959 Broadway E (📞 **800/ 240-1864** or 206/329-1864; www.bacon mansion.com).

Gourmet Emporiums & Specialty Shops

31

Acme Bread Company
Let Them Eat Bread
Berkeley, California

As is so often the case in the Bay Area, the Acme Bread Company story starts with Chez Panisse. In 1978 Berkeley undergrad Steve Sullivan returned to his job as a busboy at Alice Waters's groundbreaking restaurant, rhapsodizing over the handmade, crusty bread he'd eaten on his summer vacation in Europe. With Waters's encouragement, Sullivan taught himself breadmaking and became Chez Panisse's in-house bread baker. In 1983, by the time he moved the baking operations out of the crowded Chez Panisse kitchen, he'd won enough of a following among Berkeley food lovers to launch Acme in a tiny shop in Berkeley, a stone's throw away from Alice's restaurant.

By now Acme has added a branch at the Ferry Plaza Market and commercial bakeries for its growing retail business, but shoppers still line up outside the miniscule Berkeley shop, where the simple wooden racks behind the counter are piled high with whole, unsliced loaves baked in a large brick oven right on the premises. Special steam humidifiers in the ovens create the characteristic crust for Acme's hallmark breads, the *pain au levain* (a hearty large-crumbed bread from a long-fermented dough) and the walnut *pain au levain,* as well as a perfectly chewy white bread, pumpernickel rye, tangy olive bread, cinnamon currant loaf, baguettes, and croissants (chocolate, plain, and ham-and-cheese). The flours used are all organic, and there are no preservatives—though very few customers can resist eating their purchases long before they'd go stale. Bread is baked three times a day, but get here early to score a flaky apple turnover (regulars insist that the pumpkin rolls and cheese rolls make up for it just fine). Take your purchases next door to Café Fanny to enjoy them right away with an appropriate cup of café au lait.

Thankfully, Acme has resisted the temptation to open dozens of branches or to raise its prices sky-high (though the Ferry Plaza outpost does command slightly higher prices, no doubt to offset the rent for this posh address). Is it the best bread in San Francisco? That's your call. San Francisco has been a bread-baker's capital ever since the Gold Rush, when miners zealously hoarded their sourdough starters. The standard-bearer for San Francisco sourdoughs for years has been Boudin Bakery, founded in 1849 (their breads are still widely available around the Bay Area). While the rest of the United States was seduced by spongy factory-made white breads in the 1950s and 1960s, artisanal breads survived here in the Bay Area, ready for the culinary revolution to come. You may want to sample several different brands while you're here—all in the name of research, of course.

ⓘ 1601 San Pablo Ave. (☏ **510/524-1327;** www.ferrybuildingmarketplace.com).

✈ San Francisco International (14 miles/ 23km).

🛏 $$$ **Hotel Adagio,** 550 Geary St. (☏ **800/228-8830** or 415/775-5000; www. thehoteladagion.com). $ **Hotel des Arts,** 447 Bush St. (☏ **800/956-4322** or 415/956-3232; www.sfhoteldesarts.com).

Street Eats 32

Doner Kebab
Shawarma Crawl
Berlin, Germany

The Turkish vendors call it doner kebab, while others—Lebanese, Syrian, or Arabs—call it shawarma. No matter; shawarma and doner are virtually the same thing, and they've become the iconic cheap eats of Berlin, found at hundreds of *imbisse,* or takeout stands, all over town.

Oddly enough, this fast food—a compounded mix of seasoned meats roasted on a vertical spit, then shaved off in thin strips and served in pita bread with shredded lettuce and tangy white sauce—may be based on Middle Eastern kebabs and Greek gyros, but its present form developed in Berlin's Turkish immigrant neighborhood, Kreuzberg, in the 1970s. While its popularity has boomed all over Germany, Berlin remains the center of the doner kebab universe, with an estimated 1,500 doner outlets.

The man who claims to have "invented" doner kebab operates a small chain of casual sit-down restaurants called **Hasir** (try the one in Kreuzberg at Adalbertstr. 10; ☏ **49/30/614 2373;** www.hasir.de). It's a little pricier than the typical street doner, but the ingredients are higher quality—plus it's open 24 hours, making it popular with club-hopping night owls. For the classic walk-up doner stand experience in Kreuzberg, check out **Mustafas Gemüse Kebab** (Mehringdamm 32), which does a great chicken doner laced with potatoes, fried veggies, and sheep's cheese. On the shawarma side of the equation, **Restaurant Rissani** (Spreewaldplatz 4–6; ✆ **49/30/6162 9433**) is a Lebanese favorite in Kreuzberg for its shawarma, falafel, hummus, couscous, and (best of all) bargain prices. Upon request, they can perk up your food with spicy *scharfe sauce,* though they've toned down the spiciness for the typical German palate.

You'll find plenty of excellent stands outside of Kreuzberg as well. Try the classic stand **Kaplan Doner** (Müllerstr. 150) on Leopoldplatz in Wedding, or the casual sit-down joint **Babel** (Kastanienallee 33; ✆ **49/30/4403 1318**) in trendy Prenzlauerberg, a laid-back eatery that also offers falafel, halloumi sandwiches, and complimentary tea.

✈ Berlin-Tagel (11km/7 miles).

🛏 $$ **Hotel Hackescher Markt,** Grosse Präsidentenstrasse 8 (✆ **49/30/280030;** www.loock-hotels.com). $$ **Myers Hotel Berlin,** Belzer Strasse 26 (✆ **49/30/440140;** www.myershotel.de).

33 Street Eats

Hawker Stalls

Asian Melting Pot

Singapore

Sure, Singapore is aggressively tidy, thronged with skyscrapers, and stripped of local color in the name of modernization. But for exotic street food, Singapore beats any other Asian city, no contest. Best of all, you don't have to scour the streets to find it: Since the 1950s and 1960s, the government has herded independent street vendors into giant food centers all over town. Under one roof, as many as 100 stalls, most selling only one specialty item, surround a group of tables; diners can hop from stall to stall, sampling their wares. These bustling hawker centers, filled with the clang of woks, the hiss of escaping steam, the sizzle of hot oil, the smell of ginger and curry, and the shouted come-ons of competing food sellers, are a Singapore experience not to be missed.

Singaporean food is a polyglot mix of Chinese, Malay, Indian, and Thai cuisines, blended into several dishes you'll find only here. Dishes to sample include spicy chili crab (and its cousin pepper crab); *laksa,* seafood and rice noodles in a hot coconut chili soup; *bak kut teh,* a savory soup filled with pork ribs; *chwee kueh,* rice cakes topped with fried radish; fish ball noodle soup, with balls made from pounded fish and rice flour; *char kway teow,* flat rice noodles fried with seafood; samosa-like *curry puffs; popiah,* a deep-fried roll stuffed with turnip, egg, pork, prawn, and sweet chili sauce; *rojak,* a sort of salad of fried dough, tofu, cucumber, pineapple, and whatever the chef has handy, mixed with thick peanut-shrimp paste sauce; and all manner of dumplings, stuffed breads, and *satays,* grilled skewers of meat and seafood served with peanut sauce. Each dish will cost only a couple of dollars.

The bible of every Singapore foodie is the guidebook *Makansutra* by K. F. Seetoh (Makansutra Publishing), which will tell you which stalls at which hawker center have the best examples of each food. As soon as you walk into a center, claim a seat at a communal table (local trick: put a tissue packet down on the table to indicate that the spot is taken). Then cruise the stalls, checking out each one's specialty. Most vendors display a photo or a sample dish to advertise their wares. When you order food, tell the vendor your table number, and your food will be delivered to you; you pay upon delivery.

These cheap-eats havens are found more in residential districts than in the center of town. Some of the best are the **Maxwell Road Food Centre** at the corner of Maxwell and South Bridge roads; **Lau Pa Sat,** at the corner of Raffles Way and Boon Tat Street; **Chinatown Complex,** at 335 Smith St.; the **East Coast**

Lagoon Food Centre, at 1220 East Coast Parkway; the **Golden Mile Food Centre,** at 505 Beach Rd.; and the **Old Airport Cooked Food Centre** on Airport Road.

✈ Changi International Airport, Singapore (19km/12 miles).

🛏 $$ **The Inn at Temple Street,** 36 Temple St. (© **65/6221-5333;** www.theinn. com.sg). $$ **Traders Hotel Singapore,** 1A Cuscaden Rd. (© **800/942-5050** in the U.S. and Canada, 800/222-448 in Australia, or 0800/442-179 in New Zealand; www. shangri-la.com).

Street Eats 34

Neapolitan Pizza Pilgrimage
That's Amore!
Naples, Italy

In the 16th century, most Europeans considered tomatoes poisonous (tomatoes are, after all, in the deadly nightshade family). The working folk of Naples, however, knew better—they ate tomatoes all the time, layered atop yeasty flat bread.

From such humble beginnings, pizza has spread around the world, giving rise to so many variations that Naples's pizza makers formed an association zealously guarding the tradition of pizza Napolitano. Naples's classic pizzerias serve only two kinds of pizza—marinara (named after the fishermen who traditionally ate it topped with tomatoes, oregano, garlic, olive oil, and salt) and Margherita (named after the queen of Italy, with mozzarella and basil added to give pizza the colors of the Italian flag). Crusts are invariably lumpy, soft, hand-kneaded, and baked in wood-fired beehive ovens; the real purists use only local San Marzano canned plum tomatoes and always drizzle the olive oil in a clockwise spiral.

Pizza had always been a street-vendor snack until 1830, when the first pizzeria,

Antica Pizzeria Port D'Alba (via Port'Alba 18; © **39/81/45-97-13**) set up a few tables to serve customers. Port d'Alba still features fine pies on its varied menu, though many pizza hounds prefer the more casual **Trianon da Ciro** (via Pietro Colletta 46; © **39/81/55-39-426**), also in the city's historic center, Spaccanapoli. Nearby family-run **Da Michele** (Via Cesare Sersale 1; © **39/81/55-39-204;** www.damichele.net) has a history stretching from 1870; some say its springy crust is the best in town. If the lines there are too long, head a few blocks north to Spaccanapoli's narrow main street via dei Tribunale, where you can compare the pizzas of neighboring archrivals **Di Matteo** (via dei Tribunali 94; © **39/81/45-52-62**), or **Il Pizzaiolo del Presidente** (via dei Tribunali 120/121; © **39/81/21-90-03**).

In the via Chiaia shopping district, **Pizzeria Brandi** (Salita Santa Anna di Palazzo 2; © **39/81/41-69-2**), founded in 1889, invented the Margherita pizza. But locals claim the pies are better at nearby **Pizzeria Umberto** (via Alabardieri 30; 39/81/41-85-55; www.umberto.it), family-owned since 1916 and run today by no less than the vice-president of the Assoiciazione Verace Pizza Napoletana, Massimo Di Porzio. If he can't turn out an authentic Neapolitan pizza, no one can.

Naples' Aeroporto Capodochino (7.8km/4³/₄ miles).

$$$ **Hotel Excelsior,** Via Partenope 48, Naples (39/81-7640111; www.excelsior.it). $$ **Hotel Britannique,** Corso Vittorio Emanuele 133 (39/81-7614145; www.hotelbritannique.it).

35 Street Eats

Filling Up on Pho
Oodles of Noodles
Hanoi, Vietnam

Eating outdoors in Hanoi isn't just a special-occasion option; it's where you get the most authentic local cooking, in small open-air street-side joints that often serve only one local specialty. There's no more iconic Vietnamese dish, of course, than the ubiquitous *pho* noodle soup, born in Hanoi. The formula is simple: delicious cured beef *(bo)*, fresh noodles, and spices—done the same way, over and over, for years.

All around town, you'll find branches of the national chain **Pho 24**—try the one at the south end of Hoam Kien Lake (1 Hang Kay St.; 84/4/936-5259). Brighter and cleaner than most independent pho shops, it's a good starting point for visitors; you can tick boxes off a list of ingredients to customize your own bowl of soup. Tourists can also get a taste of *pho* at one of the replica street stalls surrounding the central garden of **Brother's Café** (26 Nguyen Thai Hoc; 84/4/733-3866; www.brothercafe.com).

If you're ready to be more adventurous, however, head for the *pho* shops where the locals eat, no-name places where you order your soup on the way in the door, claim a spot at one of the communal tables, and wait for your bowl to be deposited in front of you. A line out the door is your clue to where the best food is. Needless to say, they don't take plastic and you

don't need reservations—most don't even list a phone number. On the west side of the Old Quarter, near the old citadel wall, **Gia Thuyen Pho** (49 Bat Dan St.) looks like a grimy hole-in-the-wall, but it's acknowledged as one of the most serious *pho* shops in Hanoi, and it's exceedingly popular. Unlike most *pho* joints, this one is self-service—carry your own bowl to an open slot at a crowded table, whip out your chopsticks, and dig in. Things are brighter and cleaner at the shop at **10 Ly Quoc Su Street,** where the broth is robust and the beef good quality; another one of the more refined places is **Pho Tu Lun** on Au Trieu Street near St. Joseph's Cathedral. Family-run **Pho Thin** (13 Lo Duc St.) is widely admired for its no-nonsense bowls of flavorful beef noodle soup in the Hai Ba Trung district. If you prefer chicken *(ga)* in your soup, try the tiny *pho ga* shop at **18 Lan Ong,** where the chicken is tender and noodles plentiful.

Noi Bai International, Hanoi (38km/24 miles).

$$$ **Sofitel Metropole Hanoi,** 15 Ngo Quyen St. (800/221-4542 or 84/4/826-6919; www.accor.com). $$ **Zephyr Hotel,** 4–6 Ba Trieu St. (84/4/934-1256; www.zephyrhotel.com.vn).

On the Tapas Trail

Quite a Mouthful

Barcelona, Spain

Technically, tapas—the tasty bar snacks first served in Jerez, Andalusia, to keep sherry drinkers from getting tipsy—could be anything: toasted almonds, olives, a slice of chorizo laid over a wineglass (the word tapa means "lid" in Spanish). But as the tapas custom spread around Spain, then around the world, bars began creating increasingly elaborate tapas: snails, shrimp, stuffed peppers, saucy eel or octopus, dabs of seafood salad, even bull testicles, until a *tapeo*, or tapas crawl, could supplant dinner entirely. And thanks to Catalonian culinary creativity, the most intriguing tapas scene these days is in Barcelona.

A great place to start is in the heart of the Old City, at **Taller de Tapas** (Calle de l'Argenteria 51; ✆ **34/93/268-85-59**), a pleasant exposed-brick eatery that's a virtual tapas classroom, with table service, a trilingual menu (Catalan, Spanish, and English), and an open kitchen turning out classic Spanish tapas—marinated anchovies from the Costa Brava, Palamós prawns with scrambled eggs, grilled duck foie, or sizzling chorizo cooked in cider. Within a few streets' radius of Taller de Tapas, a number of bars take tapas in other intriguing directions. To the north, **Mosquito** (Calle Carders 46; ✆ **34/93/268-75-69**) goes international with Indian, Thai, and Malaysian-style tapas. To the east, **Santa María** (Calle Comerç 17; ✆ **34/93/315-12-27**) serves Spanish-Asian fusion tapas, such as local fruits stuffed with Thai-spiced peanuts, suckling pig with wasabi and soy, or raw sea bass marinated in passion fruit, tomato, and lime vinaigrettes. To the west, convivial **Cal Pep** (Plaça de les Olles 8; ✆ **34/93/310-79-61**) offers a 50-strong list

Classic Spanish bar snacks at Taller de Tapas.

of snacks with lots of fresh-off-the-boat seafood, like tiny clams in spicy broth or tuna with sesame sauce. Just south, **Bar Celta** (Calle Mercè 16; ✆ **34/93/315-00-06**) works wonders with novelties such as octopus tentacles, pigs' lips and ears, and delightful green peppers known as *pimientos del padrón*.

Heading uptown, veer off touristy Passeig de Gràcia to find busy **Ciudad Condal** (Rambla de Catalunya 18; ✆ **34/93/318-19-97**), beloved for its *patatas bravas*, fried fish, and anchovies. Then, push on up the road to **Cervecería Catalana** (Carrer Majorca 236; ✆ **34/93/216-03-68**), for juicy slices of filet beef skewered with peppers, and giant prawn brochettes.

Taller de Tapas in the heart of Barcelona's Gothic quarter.

 El Prat (13km/8 miles)

🛏 $$$ **Montecarlo,** Les Ramblas 124 (☎ **34/93-412-04-04;** www.montercarlo

bcn.com). $$ **Duques de Bergara,** Bergara 11 (☎ **34/93-301-51-51;** www.hoteles-catalonia.com).

Searching for Souvlaki
Succulent Shish Kebab
Athens, Greece

Chunks of well-seasoned meat, grilled on skewers to succulent perfection—that's souvlaki at its simple best, found all over Greece. Things get a little more confusing in cosmopolitan Athens, where the term souvlaki is also used to refer to gyros, sandwiches made from thin slabs of meat shaved off of those roasting hunks of meat on vertical spits in shop windows (which can also be delicious, there's no denying).

But if it's the shish kebab kind of souvlaki you want, you'll be gratified to find it served at stands and in casual cafes all over town. (You've got to love a city whose

chief fast food is something this honest and delicious.) One standout in the bustling commercial center of town is **Ta Souvlakis tou Hasapi** (1 Apollonos St.; ☎ **30/210/322-0459**), which is basically a butcher's outlet, fast, cheap, and incredibly popular at lunchtime. Though traditionally Greek souvlaki is made from pork, you can order your skewer with pork, chicken, or ground beef here. Another option lies on Mitropoleos Street, 1 block north but several streets west, toward the Plaka. The pedestrianized section at the end, by Monastiraki Square, is known as "kebab street," with a handful of excellent souvlaki places. The top choice is **Thanasis** (69 Mitropoleos St.; ☏ **30/210/324-4705**), which sells great minced-meat souvlaki in a pita to go. Or you can always follow the locals off the beaten path to the nameless souvlaki joint at 7A Petraki St. (a short lane btw. Ermou and Mitropoleos sts.), under a Coke-ad awning just down from the Subway chain sandwich shop.

Just off Omonia Square, near the National Archaeological Museum, **Taygetos** (4 Satovriandou; ☏ **30/210/523-5352**) serves quick and casual cheap meals, including some excellent souvlaki. If hunger strikes while you're browsing around the Central Market or visiting the beautiful Byzantine church of Agii Theodori, stop off in Klafthmonos Square at **Alpeis** (7 Palaion Patron Germanou St.; ☏ **30/210/331-0384**), where you can pick up a flavorful souvlaki in a pita or a full meal.

✈ Athens International Airport Eleftherios Venizelos.

🛏 $$ **Athens Art Hotel,** 27 Marni (☏ **30/210/524-0501;** www.arthotelathens.gr). $$ **Hermes Hotel,** 19 Appollonos St. (☏ **30/210/323-5514;** www.hermes-athens.com).

Street Eats **38**

Bagels to Go
The Holy Grail
New York, New York

Why don't bagels in other cities taste as good as New York bagels do? There can't be such a mystery, after all, to baking what's essentially a chewy bread doughnut. Yet somehow the bagel—brought to the U.S. by German and Polish Jewish immigrants, for whom the quick-to-bake circle of boiled dough was a handy way to break the Sabbath—reached its quintessential form in Manhattan. Other cities' versions lack that same chewy softness and slightly sweet, yeasty flavor.

For New Yorkers, bagels aren't just for breakfast. They also make great sandwiches, and can be found in almost any deli in town (though most delis run out of bagels later in the day and order new ones fresh every morning). New Yorkers prefer them untoasted (the toasting habit got started with Lender's frozen bagels) and topped with a "schmear" of cream cheese and/or smoked salmon, or else chopped liver or egg salad. Traditionally they're coated with either poppy seeds or sesame seeds, though varieties flavored with onion flakes, garlic, or cinnamon and raisins are also popular. Variations such as blueberry bagels and jalapeño pepper bagels are considered bastardizations.

Upper West Siders get their bagel fix at **H&H Bagels** (2239 Broadway; ☏ **212/595-8000**), a strictly bare-bones takeout joint where bagels come fresh from the oven. Many delis around town buy their bagels from H&H; there's also an outlet at 639 W. 46th St. (☏ **212/765-7200**), handily close to the West Side Highway. **H&H Bagels East** (1551 Second Ave.; ☏ **212/734-7441**) is a former branch that sued the original for the right to use the name; it has a full deli along with the bagel counter. Then there are the sit-down **Ess-A-Bagel** delis in the Gramercy area (359 First Ave.; ☏ **212/260-2252**) and in east Midtown (831 Third Ave.; ☏ **212/980-1010**). All of these peddle superbly chewy, fresh-baked boiled bagels, puffy with a moist outside. But if you really want to get authentic, journey down to the Lower East Side to try the bagels at **Kossar's Bialys** (367 Grand

St.; ☎ **212/473-4810**). And while you're at it, sample the bagel's first cousin, a bialy, as well.

✈ John F. Kennedy International (15 miles/24km); Newark Liberty International (16 miles/27km); LaGuardia (8 miles/13km).

🛏 $$ **The Lucerne,** 201 W. 79th St. (☎ **800/492-8122** or 212/875-1000; www.thelucernehotel.com). $ **Milburn Hotel,** 242 W. 76th St. (☎ **800/833-9622** or 212/362-1006; www.milburnhotel.com).

Windy City Wieners

Show Stealing Hot Dogs

Chicago, Illinois

Hot dogs, frankfurters, wieners—whatever you call them—they're a handy street food in many cities (not to mention ballparks) around the U.S. But no town appreciates the hot dog's star qualities like Chicago does. Starting out with a top-quality frankfurter made by revered local supplier Vienna Beef, a classic Chicago hot dog is then heaped with a very specific list of condiments—chopped onions, green relish, a slather of yellow mustard, pickle spears, fresh tomato wedges, a dash of celery salt, and a couple of hot peppers. That incredible combination of crunch, juice, acidic bite, and fiery spice sets off the salty, savory meat of the hot dog perfectly.

No matter where you are in town, you can get a classic Chicago dog. In the Loop? Try **Gold Coast Dogs** (159 N. Wabash Ave.; ☎ **312/917-1677**). Shopping the Magnificent Mile? There's **Fluky's**, in The Shops at North Bridge mall (520 N. Michigan Ave.; ☎312/245-0702), part of a local chain that has been serving great hot dogs since the Depression. Cruising around River North? **Portillo's** (100 W. Ontario St.; ☎ **312/587-8930**) is another local chain that specializes in hot dogs, along with pastas and salads. In the Lincoln Park neighborhood, **The Wieners Circle** (2622 N. Clark St.; ☎ **773/477-7444**), is a late-night favorite where rude order-takers are part of the shtick. Up near Wrigley Field, **Murphy's Red Hots** (1211 W. Belmont Ave.; ☎ **773/935-2882**) is a popular neighborhood spot.

Two Chicago hot-doggeries are well worth a little extra travel. The first is **Superdawg Drive-In,** on the northwest side of the city

The same family has run Superdawg in Chicago for three generations.

(6363 N. Milwaukee Ave.; © **773/763-0660**), a 1950s-style flashback distinguished by giant hot dogs dressed as Tarzan and Jane dancing on the roof. Run by the same family for three generations, Superdawg still has carhops who bring out your order. And if you think the terms "gourmet" and "hot dog" don't belong together, then you've never been to **Hot Doug's,** in the Roscoe Park area (3324 N. California Ave.; © **773/279-9550**), which takes encased meats to a new level. The menu includes corn dogs, veggie dogs, hot andouille sausages, a whole range of European sausages, and rotating special game sausages made from pheasant, antelope, and kangaroo.

✈ O'Hare International (18 miles/29km).

🛏 $$ **Homewood Suites,** 40 E. Grand St., Chicago (© **800/CALL-HOME** or 312/644-2222; www.homewoodsuiteschicago.com). $$ **Hotel Allegro Chicago,** 171 N. Randolph St., Chicago (© **800/643-1500** or 312/236-0123; www.allegrochicago.com).

Cookbooks & Kitchenware 40

Books for Cooks

Cooking on Premises
London, England

This cheery little red-awninged shop in Notting Hill is a bit off London's beaten tourist paths, but that's all the more reason why cooks should make the pilgrimage. With more than 8,000 titles in stock, the international selection of cookbooks is impressive, and the staff is known for being able to track down any book they don't have. But what really distinguishes Books for Cooks is the user-friendly ambience, right down to the cluttered cozy nooks and a well-worn sofa where you can curl up while paging through a volume you might like to buy. On Saturdays, when the nearby Portobello Market draws swarms of shoppers to the neighborhood, it can get a little overrun, but come here on a weekday (it's closed Sun) and you'll be able to browse to your heart's content.

Since it opened in 1983—back when London's culinary scene was distinctly stodgy, even before the River Café opened—Books for Cooks has gradually evolved to become more than a bookshop: There's a cafe at the back where recipes from the various cookbooks are

Customers can browse in comfort among the 8,000 titles in stock at Books for Cooks.

road-tested, so to speak, every lunchtime (get here early if you want to get a seat); and cookery classes are led by well-known chefs in the upstairs demonstration kitchen.

Cooks may also want to make a stop in nearby Holland Park to check out the sophisticated kitchenware at **Summerill & Bishop,** at 100 Portland Rd. (📞**44/20/7221-4566;** www.summerillandbishop.com), from Japanese knives to Italian steel pots to Belgian glassware.

ⓘ 4 Blenheim Crescent (Tube: Ladbroke Grove; 📞 **44/20/7221-1992;** www.books forcooks.com).

✈ Heathrow (24km/15 miles) or Gatwick (40km/25 miles).

🛏 $$$ **22 Jermyn St.,** 22 Jermyn St., St. James (📞 **800/682-7808** in the U.S., or 44/20/7734-2353; www.22jermyn.com). $$ **Vicarage Private Hotel,** 10 Vicarage Gate, South Kensington (📞 **44/20/7229-4030;** www.londonvicaragehotel.com).

Librairie Gourmande

In the Shadow of Les Halles

Paris, France

The great Les Halles food market may have decamped from this Parisian neighborhood many years ago, but the culinary spirit lives on in this wonderful two-story bookshop, its shelves laden with books on food and wine. Quintessentially French as that may seem, Librairie Gourmande is much more international than you'd expect, stocking books in several languages, including a sizeable English-language section.

Librairie Gourmande began as an open-air book stall along the Seine in the mid-1980s. It then occupied a tiny shop on the rue Dante for years before moving to this neighborhood under new ownership in 2007. Oddly enough, considering how important food and wine are to Parisians, it's the city's only culinary book specialist. Alongside cookbooks, biographies, and food history, you'll find a number of scholarly titles and reference works. Most titles are new, although there are some secondhand copies of classic books as well. The customers are an eclectic mix of professional chefs, home cooks, and food enthusiasts.

Inspired by the cookbooks you've found at Librairie Gourmande, you may want to acquire exotic equipment for all the new French techniques you will be trying out. *Naturellement,* Paris has several excellent kitchenware sources, all close to Librairie Gourmande. Right down the street you'll find **A. Simon,** at 48 and 52 rue Montmartre, 2e (📞 **33/1/42-33-71-65**), which has been supplying professional cooks since 1884. That makes it a newcomer, however, compared to nearby **E. Dehillerin,** at 18 rue Coquillière, 1er (📞 **33/1/42-36-53-13**), founded in 1820. These large shops go well beyond pots and pans, offering implements and accessories you never dreamed existed.

ⓘ 90 rue Montmartre, 2e (Métro: Sentier; 📞 **33/1/43-54-37-27;** www.libraire gourmande.fr).

✈ De Gaulle, 23km/14 miles). Orly (14km/8²/₃ miles).

🛏 $$ **La Tour Notre Dame,** 20 rue du Sommerard, 5e (📞 **33/1/43-54-47-60;** www.la-tour-notre-dame.com). $ **Hotel de la Place des Vosges,** 12 rue de Birague, 4e (📞 **33/1/42-72-60-46;** www.hotelplacedes vosges.com).

Books to Cooks

In-Store Cooking

Vancouver, Canada

Former restaurateur and cookbook writer Barbara-Jo McIntosh runs this handsome, stylish Vancouver bookshop, which sells mostly new food and wine titles, a few well-chosen out-of-print volumes, periodicals, and a few unusual kitchen accessories.

The store's greatest strength is definitely its culinary events, which go well beyond the occasional cookbook signing—there's a full schedule of demonstrations and tastings in the on-premises demonstration kitchen, and an intriguing series of food culture classes taught by local food gurus. McIntosh's connections in the Vancouver restaurant community make this Yaletown shop a nexus for the foodie community. Check ahead to book a space at any of these popular classes or demonstrations.

Books to Cooks also has a small branch store in the Net Loft retail complex on Granville Island, a natural destination for food lovers with the Granville Island Public Market nearby. Also in Net Loft, there's one-stop shopping for gourmet kitchen equipment at the **Market Kitchen Store,** at 2-1666 Johnston (© **604/681-7399**).

ⓘ 1740 W. 2nd Ave. (© **604-688-6755;** www.bookstocooks.com).

✈ Vancouver (12km/7¹/₂ miles).

🛏 $$$ **Pan Pacific Hotel Vancouver,** 300-999 Canada Place (© **800/937-1515** in the U.S., or 604/662-8111; www.panpacific. com). $$ **Camelot Inn,** 2212 Larch St. (© **604/ 739-6941;** www.camelotinnvancouver.com).

Culinary classes and events take place regularly at Books to Cooks' demonstration table.

Kitchen Arts & Letters
Well-Connected Cookbooks
New York, New York

There's very little happening in the world of culinary publishing that the guys at Kitchen Arts & Letters don't know about. In this laid-back, book-crammed shop in a relaxed part of the Upper East Side, you can browse for hours, discovering all sorts of imports, finds from small regional publishers, and out-of-print titles on its tightly packed shelves. Best of all, just ask owner Nach Waxman or manager Matt Sartwell for recommendations—they're incredibly knowledgeable, and they certainly aren't shy with their opinions. With nearly 12,000 titles in stock at any given time, it's amazing how they seem to know every book on their shelves. The usual glossy cookbooks by celebrity chefs are available, but they're overshadowed by the generous piles of reference books, scholarly compendiums, food histories, biographies, memoirs, food-themed travel books, and culinary essays displayed invitingly on the store's tables. An important new book that hasn't been released yet? Nach or Matt has probably already reviewed it in galley proof, sent straight from the publisher. (They even publish a newsletter, bringing their customers up to date on all the new arrivals.) The store is closed Sundays.

For long-out-of-print editions, you may have to travel down to Greenwich Village to **Bonnie Slotnick Cookbooks,** at 163 W. 10th St. (212/989-8962), a tiny shop in a century-old brownstone that holds a treasure trove of vintage cookbooks, mostly American and English, as well as recipe pamphlets, kitchen gadgets, and other charming bits of culinary nostalgia. Phone ahead for hours, as they vary from week to week.

From there it's only a couple of blocks to one of New York's prime sources for knives, pans, and bake ware, the **Broadway Panhandler,** at 65 E. 8th St. (**212/966-3434**). To outfit a kitchen in professional style, you may also want to travel up to Chelsea, where the large **Bowery Kitchen Supplies** store, at 460 W. 16th St. (**212/376-4982**), moved uptown from its original Bowery location. It's now located in the **Chelsea Market,** a sleek indoor arcade of specialty food shops in a

New York chefs and foodies often seek advice from Kitchen Arts & Letters owner Nach Waxman.

7 Places to Eat in . . . Vancouver, British Columbia

Country paté at Pied-A-Terre.

Blessed with a coastal bounty of seafood, a rich mélange of Pacific Rim cultures, and superb microclimate for local farmers, Vancouver couldn't help but become a fine-dining capital. This vibrant, cosmopolitan city, cupped around a sparkling harbor with a backdrop of snow-capped mountains, already had a wealth of museums, gardens, and other attractions; add all the fantastic restaurants in town, not to mention the divine public food market on Granville Island, and it's almost too good to be true.

If seafood's your pleasure, head out to Yaletown for two winning fish restaurants. The constant buzz swirling around the handsome brick-and-beam ④ Blue Water Café (1095 Hamilton St.; ☏ **604/688-8078;** www.bluewatercafe.net) comes from its fresh seafood, culled from sustainable and wild fisheries only, and assembled in memorable dishes such as baked Galliano Island swimming scallops with tomatoes, lemons, and capers; pumpernickel-crusted white sturgeon with beets and cauliflower puree; or B.C. sablefish caramelized with soy and sake. Blue Water also has a fantastic raw bar. The seafood and the people-watching are equally excellent down the street at sleek, contemporary ④ Coast (1257 Hamilton St.; ☏ **604/685-5010;** www.coastrestaurant.ca). If you're lucky, you may be able to score a seat at the "community table" for a close-up of chef Josh Wolfe at work. An evening at Coast can seem like a trip around the world—starting with a Dungeness crab cake, then going on to the giant Baja sea scallop and sea tiger prawns with Thai coconut risotto, Alaskan king crab gnocchi, or Liverpool-style fish and chips.

Multicultural Vancouver has some of the continent's best Asian restaurants as well, including the stunning (and pricey) ④ Tojo's Restaurant (1133 W. Broadway; ☏ **604/872-8050;** www.tojos.com), where Chef Hidekazu Tojo and his sushi chefs display their knife skills at a gleaming maple-countered sushi bar. Order the *omakase,* or chef's tasting menu, to get the full spectrum of Tojo's brilliance. Reservations are essential. You can't even make a reservation, however, for an Indian feast at cozy ④ Vij (1480 W. 11th Ave.; ☏ **604/736-6664;** www.vijs.ca). Be prepared to queue up outside for a table, where patient patrons are treated to tea and *papadums* while they wait. While the menu changes monthly to make the most of local ingredients, its constants are hand-ground and roasted seasonings and dishes that honor the entire breadth of Indian regional cooking, such as halibut in ground fennel and fenugreek seed curry, beef short ribs in a cinnamon and red-wine curry, or B.C. spot prawns marinated in ghee, jalapeño peppers, and cumin seed.

For distinctively Canadian cuisine, try 48 Raincity Grill (1193 Denman St.; ✆ **604/685-7337;** www.raincitygrill.com), a long, low, intimate room overlooking English Bay in the West End. Raincity's farm-to-table cuisine focuses on seafood, game, poultry, organic vegetables, and wines exclusively from British Columbia and the Pacific Northwest. Meticulous preparations transform those ingredients into some spectacular dishes, such as rare albacore tuna loin with green pea risotto and honey-roasted carrots, or seared duck breast with braised black lentils and root vegetables. If classic French bistro cuisine is more your fancy, you may want to head to the West Side and the intimate, low-key 49 Pied-A-Terre (3369 Cambie St., ✆ **604/873-3131;** www.pied-a-terre-bistro.ca), where chef Andrey Durbach's old-school menu features timeless favor-

Chef Hidekazu Tojo.

ites like Alsatian onion pie, a hearty salade frisee, Dijon mustard rabbit, a fine hanger steak, and tarte tatin.

Perhaps the finest regional restaurant in town is 50 West (2881 Granville St.; ✆ **604/738-8938;** www.westrestaurant.com), a warm, streamlined space with leather-paneled walls and rice-paper lampshades. The menu changes several times a month, but first courses might include cured coho salmon with grilled fennel coleslaw or a ravioli of quail. For a main course you might find grilled lobster with citrus-glazed squash and caramelized sweet corn puree; honey-and-clove-braised pork cheeks; or lamb with a ballotine of leeks, onion rings, and mint polenta. If you can, reserve one of the two "chef tables" adjacent to the kitchen—it will be an experience you won't forget.

✈ Vancouver International.

🛏 $$$ **Wedgewood Hotel,** 845 Hornby St. (✆ **800/663-0666** or 604/689-7777; www.wedgewoodhotel.com). $$ **Granville Island Hotel,** 1253 Johnston St. (✆ **800/663-1840** or 604/683-7373; www.granvilleislandhotel.com).

renovated 1890s-era Nabisco factory between Ninth and Tenth avenues (Chelsea Market is also home to the Food Network).

ⓘ 1435 Lexington Ave. (ⓒ **212/876-5550;** www.kitchenartsandletters.com).

✈ John F. Kennedy Intl (15 miles/24km); Newark Liberty International (16 miles/27km); LaGuardia (8 miles/13km).

🛏 $$$ **Carlton Hotel on Madison Avenue,** 88 Madison Ave. (ⓒ **212/532-4100;** www.carltonhotelny.com). $$ **Washington Square Hotel,** 103 Waverly Place (ⓒ **800/222-0418** or 212/777-9515; www. washingtonsquarehotel.com).

Cookin'

From Hard-to-Find to One-of-a-Kind

San Francisco, California

It's definitely got the kind of character you won't find at a mall franchise. Owner Judith Kaminsky's secondhand cookware shop goes way beyond cluttered, and at first glance, it may not seem all that impressive. But for quality vintage pots and pans, uniquely shaped baking pans, and one-of-a-kind cooking gadgets, Cookin' has no rival. Hard-core cooks can easily get lost here, hunting for that culinary Holy Grail amid the small shop's constantly changing selection. Though the staff occasionally can be cranky, there are real gems to be found among the merchandise if you're patient, from old-fashioned food mills to original Osterizer blenders, from garlic presses to cookie guns, from shiny copper sauté pans to cast-iron enameled Dutch ovens, all in perfect working order. (It's definitely a store for working cooks, not an antiques shop for culinary kitsch.) There's also a small cookbook section at the back. Despite the thrift-store look of the place, don't expect thrift-store prices—Kaminsky sells only top-grade items, and she knows their value indeed. Closed Mondays.

For brand-new luxury kitchenware, your best stop may be just off Union Square at this two-story outlet of glossy **Sur La Table,** at 77 Maiden Lane (ⓒ **415/732-7900**). For a little more San Francisco local color, head up Grant Avenue toward Chinatown to find a delightfully esoteric array of equipment specifically for Asian cooking—everything from sashimi knives to a yin yang pot to a Thai rice steamer—at the bustling **Wok Shop,** at 718 Grant St. (ⓒ **415/989-3797**).

ⓘ 339 Divisadero (btw. Oak and Page sts.; ⓒ **415/861-1854**).

✈ San Francisco International (14 miles/23km).

🛏 $$$ **Hotel Adagio,** 550 Geary St. (ⓒ **800/228-8830** or 415/775-5000; www. thehoteladagion.com). $ **Hotel des Arts,** 447 Bush St. (ⓒ **800/956-4322** or 415/956-3232; www.sfhoteldesarts.com).

The Cook's Library/Cook Books
Where SoCal Cooks Hang Out
Los Angeles/Pasadena, California

The Cook's Library looks just like what it is—a smart, sophisticated hangout for Los Angeles chefs, both amateur and professional. With almost 8,000 titles in stock, tea and nibbles offered to afternoon browsers, and a frequent roster of authors doing in-store appearances, the Cook's Library has been fostering a community of local foodophiles since owner Ellen Rose opened it in 1989. Many of the knowledgeable staffers are trained chefs themselves, and eager to chat about not only books but the food scene in general; check out the bulletin board near the door for cooking classes and other chef news. The summertime used book sale is definitely worth marking your calendar for. The store is handily situated on a thriving Westside retail strip between the Farmer's Market and the Beverly Center. (Another of our favorite shops, the **Traveler's Bookcase,** is right next door, at 8375 W. 3rd St.)

If what you're seeking is something out of print and rare, head north to Pasadena, where Janet Jarvis's **Cook Books** crams an extraordinary inventory of over 30,000 secondhand cookery books into one tiny out-of-the-way shop. With all those one-of-a-kind items shelved floor to ceiling, it's for bibliophiles as well as cooks—a prism of American history viewed from the kitchen perspective. Jarvis's selection is more than comprehensive, it's almost compulsive—entire sets of Time-Life food books, for example, or every known edition of the *Betty Crocker Cookbook*. Things look

Many of the Cook's Library's knowledgeable staffers are trained chefs.

disorganized, but just ask the staff and they'll help you locate the book you need—as well as others you never knew you needed. Prices can be high, but not prohibitive when you know you'll never find that particular rare book anywhere else ever again.

ⓘ **The Cook's Library,** 8373 W. Third St., West Hollywood (☏ **323/655-3141;** www.cookslibrary.com; closed Sun). **Cook Books,** 1388 E. Washington Blvd., Pasadena

(☏ **626/296-1638;** www.cookbooksjj.com; closed Sun–Mon).

✈ Los Angeles International (11 miles/ 17km).

🛏 $$ **Artists' Inn & Cottage Bed & Breakfast,** 1038 Magnolia St,. South Pasadena (☏ **888/799-5668** or 626/799-5668; www.artistsinns.com). $ **Saga Motor Hotel,** 1633 E. Colorado Blvd., Pasadena (☏ **800/793-7242** or 626/795-0431; www. thesagamotorhotel.com).

Cookbook Store

Northern Star

Toronto, Ontario

Since the Cookbook Store first opened in 1983, this spunky independent bookstore downtown has become a de rigueur stop for culinary luminaries visiting Canada—everyone from Martha Stewart to Jamie Oliver, from Gordon Ramsay to Nigella Lawson—as well as local food and wine experts. Besides book signings, the shop hosts regular wine tastings and other foodie events, such as an evening where customers can bring in their old cookbooks and find out if they're valuable.

The Cookbook Store definitely functions as home base for local foodies, and the engaging staff seems to know everything about the Toronto food scene. (Chat long enough and you may get some great restaurant recommendations from them.) Though the store is fairly small, it has up to 6,000 titles in stock, including both British editions of cookbooks that haven't been Americanized and U.S. books that aren't readily available in overseas markets.

While you're here, it's only a block's walk to the nearest branch of **Kitchen Stuff Plus,** at 703 Yonge St. (☏ **416/944-2718**), which sells quality bake ware, pots and pans, knives, and kitchen gadgets at discount prices.

ⓘ 850 Yonge St. (☏ **416/920-2665;** www. cook-book.com).

✈ Toronto International (28km/17 miles).

🛏 $$$ **Le Royal Meridien King Edward,** 37 King St. E (☏ **800/543-4300** or 416/863-9700; www.starwoodhotels. com). $$ **The Drake Hotel,** 1150 Queen St. W (☏ **416/531-5042;** www.thedrake hotel.ca).

Books for Cooks
Turning the Pages
Melbourne, Australia

While Sydney and Melbourne run neck-and-neck when it comes to the liveliness of their food scenes, Melbourne's got one thing Sydney hasn't: Books for Cooks. Tucked away in the suburb of Fitzroy, this culinary bookstore is a rare find, with an amazingly extensive stock—somewhere around 22,000 volumes at any one time—of books about food and wine, both new and secondhand (including many rare vintage books and even a number of titles in languages other than English). Spread across a double-wide storefront, it's the sort of clean, well-lighted place where you could browse for hours.

While the London shop of the same name (4 Blenheim Cres; ✆ **44 20 72211992;** www.booksforcooks.com) has come to be known for its cooking classes and recipe testing, its Australian counterpart remains squarely a bookseller, taking distinctive pride in tracking down any title a customer might want. The selection is constantly changing as the staff acquires books from an ingenious variety of sources. It's not just cookbooks; they also offer scholarly food history, food science books, wine guidebooks, and other essential reference works.

ⓘ 233 Gertrude St, Fitzroy (✆ **61/3/8415 1415;** www.booksforcooks.com.au).

✈ Melbourne (24km/15 miles).

🛏 $$$ **The Como Melbourne,** 630 Chapel St., South Yarra (✆ **1800/033 400** in Australia, or 800/552-6844 in the U.S. and Canada; www.mirvachotels.com.au). $$ **Fountain Terrace,** 28 Mary St., St. Kilda (✆ **03/9593 8123;** www.fountain terrace.com.au).

The Food Museums of Parma
The Treasures of Food Valley
Parma, Italy

It's known as Food Valley—the scenic province of Parma, long hailed for its world-famous luscious ham, tomatoes, and, of course, its hard, pungent, delicious Parmesan cheese. Parma's Musei del Cibo—the Museums of Food—had an intriguing idea: Instead of stuffing food exhibits together in one central museum, why not spin off three small museums throughout the region, each one devoted to another of Parma's signature foods?

The first to open was in the medieval town of Soragna, with its 15th-century castle. Here, in a gated courtyard just outside the castle walls, the **Parmesan Cheese Museum** (Via Volta 5; ✆ **39/521/ 596-129**) opened in 2003 in a round whitewashed building, originally built in 1848 as a cheese factory. (It looks almost like a big wheel of cheese itself.) Five different provinces of the Emilia region are officially allowed to call their cheese "Parmigiano";

all five of them have donated artifacts to be exhibited here. The museum's first room features an extensive collection of ancient dairy tools and utensils, including an 18th-century copper cauldron and a hand-pulled milk wagon; the second room details the history of curing; the third is the aging room, where various rounds of cheese are labeled according to how long they have been sitting to mature. It could be a cruelly tantalizing display, were it not for the free samples. Everyone has tasted something called Parmesan cheese, but you can be guaranteed that the Parmesan you taste here will be nothing like the bland imitations sold in most American supermarkets.

Next came the **Museum of Prosciutto and Cured Pork Products** in Langhirano (Via Bocchialini 7; ✆ **39/521/864-324**), an unwieldy name that shows just how seriously those distinctions are taken here. Its setting is the early-20th-century brick sheds of the cattle market between the town center and the river, close to the town's traditional ham curing plants. The beginning section begins where all pork begins—with the pig itself—while successive rooms explain in fine detail the various stages of slaughtering, salting, curing, and drying that produce all the meats of Parma's *salumeria:* Prosciutto and coppa from Parma, culatello from Zibello, salame

from Felino, and shoulder of ham from San Secondo. (Already plans are in the works to give salame its own separate museum.) And just in case you don't know your cula-tello from your coppa, a tasting room at the end will allow you to sample these silky, salty, deeply flavorful meats for yourself.

Occupying a fine old medieval monastic farmstead, the **Corte di Giarola (Tomato Museum)** in Collechio (Strada Giarola; ✆ **39/521/228152**) completes the set, with exhibits that solve the mystery: Why was this region of Italy the only one that persisted in cultivating tomatoes in the 19th century, when they were considered poisonous everywhere else (they are, after all, related to deadly nightshade)? Parma's leadership in developing the canning industry in the 1920s is also explored in artwork, maps, and artifacts.

ⓘ **Musei del Cibo de Parma** (✆ **39/521/228-152;** www.museidelcibo.it).

🚆 Parma (1 hr. from Bologna, 1½ hr. from Milan, 2 hr. from Florence).

🛏 $$$ **Palace Hotel Maria Luigia,** Viale Mentana 140, Parma (✆ **39/521/281032;** www.sinahotels.it). $$ **Hotel Button,** Strada San Vitale Borgo Salina 7, Parma (✆ **39/521/208039**).

Food Museums **56**

Shin-Yokohama Ramen Museum

Noodling Around

Yokohama, Japan

A museum doesn't have to be a dull repository of artifacts. A case in point is the Shin-Yokohama Ramen Museum, an exhilarating multimedia monument to the Japanese love of noodles. Everywhere you turn, there's a fascinating exhibit—displays of cooking implements, walls decorated with noodle packets from around the globe, TV monitors playing a continuous loop of ramen commercials, life-size

dioramas depicting the inner workings of an instant ramen factory. There are even whimsical ramen-themed video games (just try pulling your kids away from those).

This hip approach to noodle education seems entirely appropriate, given the international attention recently focused on Momofuku Ando, the inventor of the ramen noodle. Though Ando was born in

Taiwan into a Chinese family, after World War II he moved to Osaka and became a Japanese citizen. He introduced the first packet of instant noodles, called Chikin Ramen, in 1958, to a postwar Japan eager to turn traditional noodles into a convenience food. He further revolutionized the industry by introducing Cup Noodles in 1971. Not only is David Chang's hot New York restaurant named after him (see ❹❸), Elvis Costello also named his latest CD *Momofuku* in tribute to Ando's meal-in-a-minute invention.

Adding to the museum's delicious chaos is "Ramen Town," a small theme park on two underground floors. The park itself is a re-creation of 1950s Tokyo, a period when Japan had not yet become the modern juggernaut it is today. This affectionately nostalgic re-creation depicts vendors hawking sweets and pastries, replicas of period billboards and storefronts, an old game store, and a fortune-teller's corner. And at the center of it all there are eight noodle shops, each one representing one of the best ramen

restaurants in Japan. A visit wouldn't be complete without a bowl of noodles washed down with a cup of sake. Bowls on offer range from noodles in a salty broth to miso soup and other soy-based soups; different shops, of course, serve distinctly different noodles, so sample several. The restaurants are enormously popular; expect them to be very crowded during the noon hour. Before you leave, you'll want to visit the gift shop for some takeout packages of noodles and perhaps a set of chopsticks.

ⓘ 2-14-21 Shin-Yokohama, Kohoku-ku, Yokohama 222 (✆ **81/45/471-0503**).

🚆 Shin-Yokohama (30–40 min. from Tokyo).

🛏 $$$ **Capitol Tokyu Hotel,** 2-10-3 Nagata-cho, Chiyoda-ku, Tokyo (✆ **800/888-4747** in the U.S. and Canada, or 03/3581-4511; www.capitoltokyu.com). $$ **Park Hotel Tokyo,** 1-7-1 Higashi Shimbashi, Minato-ku, Ginza, Tokyo (✆ **03/6252-1111;** www.parkhoteltokyo.com).

57 Food Museums

Holland Kaas Museum
Smile and Say "Cheese"
Alkmaar, Netherlands

The lovely village of Alkmaar in North Holland dates from the 10th century; it's an idyllic town of picturesque canals, drawbridges, churches, merchant houses, and ramparts. Alkmaar's greatest moment in history came during the Eighty Years War, in 1573, when people of Alkmaar fought back against the invading Spanish army with boiling tar and burning branches.

But that long-ago moment of heroism aside, Alkmaar is essentially a market town in the middle of dairy land, and that is reflected in its two most famous attractions—its historic Cheese Market and the Holland Kaas Museum, both located in the heart of Alkmaar. The cheese museum (*kaas* is the Dutch word for "cheese") is located in

a traditional weighing house dating back to 1390; in fact, the ground floor is still used as a weighhouse on market days, every Friday morning April through September. Exhibits on the upper floors, however, make it a great place to learn about dairy production throughout the centuries, and how it evolved from farmhouses to factories. The collection includes old churns, presses, molds, and other implements, as well as a series of 24 portraits from the 16th century depicting women in period costumes, all painted in fastidious detail on wood panels. Children can participate in a treasure hunt (successful completion earns them a "diploma" as professors in the history of cheese), and there is, of course, a cheese tasting.

Try to time your trip for a Friday between early April and late September so that you can also enjoy the spectacle of the Alkmaar Cheese Market, one of the country's biggest tourist attractions. Taking place in Alkmaar's cobbled main square, it features a group of men known as "cheese porters," dressed in white uniforms and straw hats with colorful ribbons. These members of various guilds carry about enormous orange wheels of cheese on wooden barrows balanced on their shoulders. Traditionally, the porter's role was to bring buyers and sellers together, but today the whole affair is just for show, as Dutch cheese-making has been mass-marketed since the 1960s. It takes place at 10am; get there early to beat the tour groups to the good spots.

ⓘ **Holland Kass Museum,** Waagplein 2 (✆ **31/72/515-5516;** www.cheesemuseum.com).

✈ Amsterdam Schiphol Airport (25km/16 miles).

🛏 $$$ **Golden Tulip Hotel,** Arcadialaan 6 (✆ **31/72/540-1414;** www.goldentulipalkmaar.com). $$ **Amrâth Hotel Alkmaar,** Geestersingel 15 (✆ **31/72/518-6186;** www.amrathhotels.nl).

Food Museums

58

Alimentarium
Food for Thought
Vevy, Switzerland

Known as one of the "Pearls of the Swiss Rivera," Vevy has an enviable location, with stunning views of Lake Geneva, vineyards, and brilliant flower beds encouraged by a lovely, mild climate. The panorama looks like something pictured on the wrapper of a bar of Swiss chocolate—so perhaps it's appropriate that Vevy is also home to the Vevy Alimentarium, a museum set up by the Nestle Foundation.

Far from a self-serving corporate showcase, the Alimentarium takes on the ambitious subject of food in all its facets—history, methods of preparation, eating, and even digesting. The approach is sometimes scholarly, sometimes cultural and social-historical, but the lively interactive exhibits keep it from ever seeming dull. The cooking exhibit, for example, features a large kitchen where visitors can watch and discuss the techniques being demonstrated by professional chefs. You may also roll up your sleeves and take part in a cooking workshop. The eating section of the museum thoughtfully examines the symbols and status associated with different types of food; it also offers examples of mealtimes in various parts of the world, including a history of tableware. The last section, "Digesting," gives you the opportunity to gauge your metabolism while learning about diet and its connection to well-being. Food history is explored in special theme exhibits like the one on the history of the potato. And yes, there is one room that throws the spotlight on the Nestle Company, which paid for all this. This tribute to the company's founder, Henri Nestle, is filled with packaging and advertisements delineating the evolution of the business that is now the world's largest food company.

School-age kids can take advantage of The Alimentarium Junior, an interactive space designed for school groups as well as individual children; it has its own kitchen, a video game, and a giant walk through a model of the digestive tract (perfect for the "yuck" factor). Hands-on exhibits let young visitors push buttons that release food aromas, light up dioramas, and launch film clips.

Rotating menus in the cafeteria are tailored to feature whatever foods the current exhibits celebrate (in the case of the potato exhibit, for instance, you could fill your plate with tasty tubers prepared in the manner of several different cultures). Outside, you'll find a lovely garden facing Lake Geneva, landscaped with plants reflecting the season. It's a great place to sit and digest all the food lore you've just learned.

ⓘ Quai Perdonnet, Vevy (ⓒ **021/924-41-11**).

✈ Geneva Airport (trains leave from the airport to Montreux/Vevyon the hour).

🛏 $$$ **Hotel du Lac,** 1 rue d' Italie (ⓒ **800/780-7234** in the U.S., or 021/925-06-06).

The Southern Food & Beverage Museum
Deep South Down-Home Lowdown
New Orleans, Louisiana

They say that the way to a man's heart is through his stomach, but the founders of the Southern Food and Beverage Museum take it one step further. They believe that the way to the heart of a culture is through its food. What's equally important, they also are convinced that it can be a dynamic and entertaining journey.

The Southern Food and Beverage Museum opened its doors on June 7, 2008, in a sleek modern space on the second floor of the Riverwalk Market development, right by the city's convention center. Although it is located in New Orleans, its mission is to showcase the food and drink of the entire American South—and what a fascinating patchwork that is. Various parts of the museum are devoted to celebrating the melting pot of ethnic groups that have brought their cuisines to the region; examining the various trades responsible for gathering food (from fishermen to farmers to hunters); and deconstructing the wide range of restaurants and stores that offer the food for sale. Visitors can tour imaginative exhibits that showcase the menus, tableware, and eating customs of both the humble and celebrated; there are several short films to take in, and collections of postcards, photos, books, and manuscripts are on display.

The history of southern beverages is not overlooked, either, with a special museum-within-the-museum titled Museum of the American Cocktail. While cocktails and other alcoholic drinks play a large role, there is more to the South than mint juleps and Sazeracs—it is a region that wakes up to strong hickory coffee and then slakes its thirst throughout the day with pitchers of Luzianne iced tea or glasses of root beer and Coca-Cola. The history of southern breweries get its due as well, with brands like Dixie, Crescent City, and Abita.

The museum takes its role as cultural history resource quite seriously. For example, its ongoing Menu Project actively roots out old menus—whether they come from honky-tonks or from fine dining establishments—and donates them to the University of New Orleans for researchers and historians. It also has a library on the premises with cookbooks and manuscripts devoted to Southern cuisine and drink.

ⓘ Riverwalk, 1 Poydras St. #169 (ⓒ **504/569-0405;** www.southernfood.org).

✈ Louis Armstrong International Airport (15 miles/24km).

🛏 $$$ **Omni Royal Orleans,** 621 St. Louis St. (ⓒ **800/THE-OMNI** or 504/529-5333; www.omniroyalorleans.com). $$ **Hotel Monteleone** (ⓒ **800/535-9595** or 504/523-3341; www.hotelmonteleone.com).

7 Places to Eat in . . . New Orleans, Louisiana

Like most visitors to New Orleans, you've probably come here eager to eat, and eat well you shall. Naturally, you should make the requisite French Quarter stops—have a café au lait and beignet for breakfast from Café du Monde in Jackson Square, get a stuffed-thick muffaletta from Central Grocery on Decatur Street, and pick up a po' boy sandwich from Johnny's Po' Boys on St. Louis Street. For tradition's sake, you may want to experience one of the classic Creole institutions too—Galatoire's, Antoine's, Arnaud's, Brennan's, Commander's Palace—where the food and service haven't changed in years.

The James Beard Association deemed Willie Mae's fried chicken an American classic.

But what makes New Orleans a great culinary capital is the depth of its pool of fantastic restaurants—a depth that can only be sounded by venturing beyond the French Quarter. Cross Canal Street to the Central Business District, for instance, to find ⓿ Café Adelaide (300 Poydras St.; ℂ 504/595-3305; www.cafeadelaide.com), a pale, sleek, contemporary spot where a younger generation of Brennans are coming into their own. Chef Danny Trace, the former sous chef at Commander's Palace, puts fresh spins on classic Creole dishes; try his Tabasco soy-glazed redfish, the Louisiana *boucherie* (pork tenderloin with blackberry honey, tasso-braised cabbage, and *boudin* crepinette), or the rhubarb-glazed duck breast with sweet-and-sour pepper jelly. Just off Lafayette Square, chef Donald Link dazzles diners at warm, wood-paneled ⓿ Herbsaint (701 St. Charles Ave.; ℂ 504/524-4114; www.herbsaint.com), featuring regional delicacies like fried frog's legs, smothered pork belly, duck confit with dirty rice, and a spectacular bisque made of shrimp, tomato, and the local pastis Herbsaint (best known as the starring ingredient of a Sazerac cocktail).

Take the St. Charles streetcar out toward Audubon Park to find ⓿ Upperline (1413 Upperline St.; ℂ 504/891-9822; www.upperline.com), a moderately priced, friendly, art-filled cafe in residential Uptown. Upperline's chef Ken Smith can hold his own against celebrity chefs like Paul Prudhomme and Emeril Lagasse; try the roast duck, the lamb shank, the cane river country shrimp, or the fried green tomatoes appetizer with shrimp rémoulade sauce (invented here and now copied all over town). Also Uptown, you'll see lines outside waiting for a table at funky, colorful 63 Jacques Imo (8324 Oak St.; 504/861-0886; www.jacques imoscafe.com), a great place to try Big Easy dishes like shrimp Creole, catfish stuffed with crabmeat, or fried chicken (from a recipe by

Herbsaint takes its name from a locally made pastis.

the late Austin Leslie). Way out at the end of St. Charles, the 64 Camellia Grill (626 S. Carrollton Ave.; 504/309-2679) has been around since 1946, save for 18 anxious months after Hurricane Katrina struck; you may have to wait for a stool at the counter, especially at breakfast—Camellia's immense, luscious omelets and pecan waffles are beloved. At lunchtime, their big, sloppy burgers are wonderful (especially the patty melt), followed by the celebrated chocolate pecan pie.

Or head out Canal Street to Mid-City for two neighborhood favorites whose post-Katrina rising from the ashes became symbols of New Orleans's recovery. Reborn in the same pink-frame house it has been in for 50 years, congenial 65 Mandina's (3800 Canal St.; 504/482-9179; www.mandinasrestaurant.com) serves an Italian-Creole menu starring classics such as shrimp rémoulade, trout *meunière,* and the best turtle soup in town; come here Monday for traditional red-beans-and-rice dinner. Though it's only open 11am to 3pm, 66 Willie Mae's Scotch House (2401 Saint Ann St.; 504/822-9503) is worth a daytime trip; this humble white-clapboard corner cafe is a showcase for Southern comfort foods, including a secret-recipe fried chicken certified as an American classic by the James Beard Association.

✈ Louis Armstrong New Orleans Intl (15 miles/24km).

⇌ **Omni Royal Orleans,** 621 St. Louis St. (**800/THE-OMNI** [800/843-6664] or 504/529-5333; www.omniroyalorleans.com). **Hotel Monteleone** (**800/535-9595** or 504/523-3341; www.hotelmonteleone.com).

67

Jell-O Gallery

Wiggly and Wobbly in New York

LeRoy, New York

When Bill Cosby visited the Jell-O Gallery in 2004, he was met with a hero's welcome by staff members marking his 30th year as a Jell-O pitchman. It's fitting that they should fete their spokesman, since canny marketing has been such a big part of Jell-O history. Cosby follows in the footsteps of a century's worth of show-biz luminaries who have advanced the cause of Jell-O over the years, from Kate Smith, Jack Benny, and Lucille Ball on the radio, to Andy Griffith on TV.

The story began in 1897, when local LeRoy carpenter Pearle Wait made the first batch of flavored gelatin while he was preparing a home-remedy cough syrup. (His wife, May, came up with the catchy name.) He didn't have the business acumen to market his discovery, however; so after 2 years, the business changed hands and was eventually bought by the Genesee Pure Food Company. Genesee shrewdly employed noted artists such as Maxfield Parish and Norman Rockwell to produce striking images for their print ads. By 1902, sales had rocketed to a whopping $250,000. Two years later came the Jell-O Girl, a 4-year-old spokesperson who held a teakettle in one hand and a packet of powdered gelatin in the other. By 1923, the booming Jell-O Company had the assets to outright purchase its own parent company, Genesee Pure Food (eventually

the product came to be manufactured by Kraft/General Foods). Throughout the many changes in ownership, the public remained steadfast in its affection for the product once advertised as "Delicate, delightful and dainty."

This surprisingly entertaining museum, just an hour's drive east of Niagara Falls and Buffalo, and run by the LeRoy Historical Society, celebrates the history of both the product and the advertising that has made this wiggly treat a household word. After the tour, you'll be able to identify which fruits float and which ones don't, and astonish your friends with trivia like the fact that a wobbling bowl of Jell-O has the same frequency as adult human brain waves.

The gift shop is a testament to Jell-O's tradition of clever marketing. There, you'll find Jell-O branded thimbles, clocks, postcards, doormats—and that's just a start. Suffice to say that there is something to please every Jell-O enthusiast.

ⓘ 23 East Main St. (☏ **585/768-7433;** www.jellogallery.org).

🛏 $$ **Edson House Bed and Breakfast,** Route 19, LeRoy (☏ **585/768-8579;** www.edsonhousebb.com). $$ **The Fox & the Grapes Bed & Breakfast,** 9496 State Rte. 414, Lodi (☏ **607/582-7528;** www.thefoxandthegrapes.com).

Mount Horeb Mustard Museum

Fun with Colonel Mustard

Mount Horeb, Wisconsin

A sense of fun and impish good humor pervades the Mount Horeb Mustard Museum, a cheerfully wacky storefront museum on this small Wisconsin town's Main Street (just look for the hanging sign—bright yellow, of course). With more than 5,000 different mustards on display, it's got to be the world's most comprehensive condiment collection.

Who knew there was so much to say about mustard? Exhibits in this quirky museum cover the history of mustard from A to Z, along with displays of antique mustard pots, mustard tins, vintage advertisements, and assorted memorabilia and educational films. For those who want to delve even more deeply, degrees are available from the museum's Poupon U, which has its own highly silly fight song. (One becomes a student by purchasing Poupon U T-shirts, sweatshirts, mugs, toilet seats, and all sort of other paraphernalia that will make you the envy of your friends and neighbors.)

Courses such as "The Ecodynamics of Mustard Management" are taught by museum founder and curator Barry Levenson. According to Levenson, he began collecting mustards to assuage the depression he felt after the Red Sox lost the World Series in 1986. In 1991, he left his job as assistant attorney general for the state of Wisconsin to pursue his passion for mustard full time. In 1992, the museum opened its doors. Today, besides hosting regular visitors, it sponsors National Mustard Day, held every year on the first Saturday in August (the event includes music, games, and free Oscar Mayer hot dogs, slathered with you-know-what), as well as publishing *The Proper Mustard*, a monthly newsletter, available online at www.mustardweb.com.

While much of the museum has a tongue-in-cheek approach, you can't help but become fascinated with all the gourmet variations on the mustard theme it reveals. In the shop, mustards from all across the United States share shelf space with those from 60 different countries. On hand are sweet hot mustards, fruit mustards, hot pepper mustards, horseradish mustards, and even spirit mustards. Museum employees (dubbed "Confidential Condiment Counselors") can help you choose from a dizzying array of packages perfect for gift giving.

And while you're here, stroll up and down Main Street, admiring the number of carved wooden trolls set along the street, earning Mount Horeb the title Troll Capital of the World. You have to admit, the Mustard Museum fits right in.

ⓘ 100 W. Main St. (✆ **608/437-3986;** www.mustardweb.com).

✈ Milwaukee International (108 miles/ 174km).

🛏 $ **Village Inn Motel,** 701 Springdale St. (✆ **608/437-3350**). $$ **Holiday Inn Express Hotel & Suites,** Verona (✆ **877/ 270-6397;** www.holiday-inn.com).

2 Food Vacations

Students learn to master complicated techniques in no time through the Culinary Institute's Bootcamp courses.

Inn at Little Washington
The Little Inn That Could
Washington, Virginia

Set tantalizingly close to Washington, D.C., in the foothills of the Blue Ridge Mountains, the Inn at Little Washington is one of the East Coast's most coveted places for a romantic special occasion dinner. Almost since the day Patrick O'Connell started serving food here in 1978, this intimate 30-table restaurant has been the sort of reservation you scheme to get. (Although you can book up to a year in advance for weeknights, the mad scramble for Sat and Sun officially opens only 30 days in advance.) If you're able to snag a table, the 67-mile (108km) drive from the nation's capital will seem like nothing.

O'Connell's cooking goes by all the buzzwords—regional products, farm-fresh produce, classical French techniques—but those don't adequately convey the brilliance of what his kitchen can do. Each dish is designed so that a few clear flavors play off each other, often recombining classics in subtle, revelatory new ways. You might start, for example, with something as deeply American as macaroni and cheese with Virginia country ham, aged Gouda, and shaved black summer truffle; the next course might be a witty reinvention of veal Parmesan, a prosciutto-wrapped pan-roasted loin of veal with tiny spinach ravioli dunked in an intensely cheesy Parmesan broth. Dessert might contrast the textures of three different chocolate puddings, or the summery sweetness of three different fruit cobblers. The fixed-price menu changes daily; you simply sit back and let the courses keep on arriving at your table. The wine list is beyond impressive, from a 14,000-bottle wine cellar. For a real treat, reserve one of

The food and decor are sumptuous at the Inn at Little Washington.

The Inn at Little Washington, at the base of the Blue Ridge Mountains.

From the outside, this colonial-style white inn with its double verandas is unassuming—it doesn't even have a sign. But within, the decor is a heady onslaught of art, swagged draperies, antiques, huge floral arrangements, dainty rose-colored lampshades, sparkling crystal and china. And for guests who want to keep the pampered glow going, O'Connell and his co-owner Reinhold Lynch offer 18 equally plush accommodations, decorated in lavish English country-house style. These luxurious digs range from double rooms to two-story suites to separate cottages (the President's Retreat is 17 miles [27km] away, but the cost includes a butler who will drive you back and forth from the inn and serve breakfast the next morning). Even the most modest rooms cost over $400 a night, and charges go up considerably on weekends. Still, rates include breakfast and afternoon tea and, best of all, guarantee your dinner reservation. Of course, the rooms book up a year in advance too. But who ever said that perfect luxury should come easy?

the two fireside tables back in the kitchen, where you can watch the master and his crew at work.

(i) Middle and Main Sts., Washington (© **540/675-3800;** www.theinnatlittle washington.com).

✈ Reagan Washington National (61 miles/98km).

Gourmet Inns & Resorts 70

Auberge de Soleil
Wine Country Pioneer
Napa Valley, California

The name means "Inn of the Sun," and when this Provençal-inspired restaurant opened in a Napa Valley olive grove in 1981, it was an immediate hit—just the sort of upscale place that Napa's burgeoning wine tourism needed. Despite its Mediterranean accents, the restaurant made local produce and food producers its stars—a relatively fresh idea in 1981, when California cuisine had already taken a detour into fussy fusionism. By transforming French cuisine into something robustly Californian, Auberge du Soleil helped to signal Napa Valley's coming of age as a wine region.

In 1985, the inn added luxury accommodations in a series of small buildings terraced down the hillside. Every room has a view of the valley, the inn's gardens, or a hillside of olive trees, and huge windows and roomy private terraces make the most of those views. The low-key contemporary decor—all white walls, burnished brown woods, tiled floors, and earth-toned fabrics—complements the views as well. Somehow each room has the feeling of a rustic French farmhouse despite a full array of modern amenities. Picking up another Napa theme, the resort added a spa as well, with a menu of massages and soaks and steams that strikes a fine balance between back-to-nature holistic therapy and pampering luxury.

In the 20-plus years since Auberge du Soleil opened, Napa Valley has become one of North America's prime tourism destinations, and several other superb restaurants and resorts have come onto the scene. But Auberge remains at the forefront, a destination resort in its own right; visitors who sleep elsewhere still make a meal at Auberge a high point of their trip, while some well-heeled repeat guests relax here for days without ever feeling compelled to "do Napa."

The restaurant's current chef, Robert Curry, has all the right California credentials—he studied under Wolfgang Puck and formerly cooked down the road at Domaine du Chandon and Greystone—but he has also trained with French star chefs like Alain Ducasse, Michel Richard, and Michel Rostang. (There's that France-California melding again.) As you'd expect, the wine list is outstanding—they claim it's the most extensive in the Valley—and wine pairings are a focal element of the six-course tasting menu. In keeping with the times, Auberge the restaurant seeks out organic local produce, with its own vegetable and herb garden outside the kitchen door, and guestroom amenities are organic and sustainable as well. That's only fitting, because getting in touch with the earth—or maybe we should say *terroir*—is what Auberge du Soleil is all about.

(i) 180 Rutherford Hill Rd., Rutherford (C **800/348-5406** or 707/963-1211; www.aubergedusoleil.com).

✈ San Francisco International (76 miles/122km); Oakland International Airport (69 miles/111km).

The Broadmoor
Rocky Mountain High
Colorado Springs, Colorado

Even if you weren't interested in dining well, you'd have plenty of compelling reasons to stay at the Broadmoor—the three golf courses, the tennis courts, the riding stables, the fly-fishing school, the state-of-the-art fitness center and spa, the great swimming complex that seems to spring like magic out of Cheyenne Lake. Then there's the massive grandeur of the pink Italian Renaissance–style main building, with its marble floors and staircase, ponderous chandeliers, hand-painted beamed ceilings, ornate furnishings, and baroque entrance fountain. The 700 guest rooms are spacious and opulently decorated; service is attentive and polished. One of the first guests when it opened in 1918 was John D. Rockefeller, and the resort has treated guests like Rockefellers ever since.

Superb dining has always been a cornerstone of the Broadmoor experience, however. From the outset, founder Spencer Penrose—eager to lure titans of Gilded Age industry out west to his new resort—demanded that the hotel introduce fine European-style dining to rough-and-tumble Colorado, and that tradition lives on. A dozen different restaurants are scattered around the 3,000-acre (1,215-hectare) property, including Colorado's only AAA five-diamond restaurant, the rooftop **Penrose Room,** a glossy formal dining room with panoramic mountain views and a refined Continental menu. The **Charles Court** restaurant, with its English country-house decor and picture-window views of Cheyenne Lake, heads into more contemporary territory with a creative American menu skewed toward Rocky Mountain ingredients—things like a carpaccio of Colorado beef with smoked sweet-potato hash and a quail egg, or a duet of brook trout and Wagyu beef short ribs, served with crimson lentils and a sauce Romanesco. The most adventurous cuisine of all is across the street at the stand-alone **Summit** restaurant (19 Lake Circle; ⓒ **719/577-5896**), with its sleek earth-toned Adam Tihany–designed decor and an ever-changing menu of eclectic brasserie fare—anything from monkfish "osso buco" to frisée salad with smoked bacon, from raw oysters to roasted beets, depending on what's seasonally available. Both the

Penrose Room and Summit have small private dining rooms for tastings and cooking demos; the Charles Court has a chef's table in the kitchen.

Don't feel like dressing up for dinner? Then settle into the pine-paneled **Tavern,** first opened in 1939 (check out the authentic Toulouse-Lautrec lithographs on the walls). On an open stone grill, they fire up excellent steaks, burgers, and fish (try the Colorado brown trout). Or indulge your Anglophilia at the **Golden Bee,** an actual English pub that was packed up and shipped over to Colorado; it features steak-and-mushroom pie, fish and chips, trifle, real ale, and even pub singalongs. Even at the casual golf course and poolside restaurants, the food is executed with flair. You don't have to be a titan of industry to eat well at the Broadmoor—though you may end up feeling like one.

ⓘ Lake Circle, at Lake Ave., Colorado Springs (ⓒ **800/634-7711** or 719/634-7711; www.broadmoor.com).

✈ Colorado Springs (10 miles/16km).

Tendrils/Cave B Inn at SageCliffe

The Gorge Rises

Quincy, Washington

The "cliffe" part of the name is no mere poetic detail—not with that setting on sheer basalt cliffs 900 feet (270m) above the Columbia River. It's a stunning place to find an intimate little luxury inn, and the Cave B Inn at SageCliffe (named after the surrounding Cave B Estate Winery) never lets you forget that breathtaking location, with huge walls of glass in the lobby and dining room and floor-to-ceiling windows in the 30 guest rooms.

And then there's the "sage" part of the name, which references the 30-odd varieties of sage growing wild on this

scrubby, semi-arid edge of the Columbia Plateau. Hosts of restaurants talk about using local ingredients, but Tendrils, the inn's acclaimed restaurant, depends on them, going so far as to forage for wild sage. Chef Shauna Scriver culls daily produce from an on-site organic chef's kitchen and orchard—including heirloom foods such as amaranth, quinoa, orach (mountain spinach), farro wheat, and Ozette potatoes. The entire SageCliffe property is committed to being green (look down and you'll notice that the floor of the restaurant is made of recycled railroad ties), so it's no surprise that the kitchen follows a Slow Food aesthetic as well. Tendrils presents itself as a casual wine country bistro, but don't be fooled by that: Scriver's cooking is sophisticated, indeed. Local king salmon may be served with fiddlehead ferns and wild rice; braised lamb chops come with yellow corn cake and wilted greens; goat cheese is flavored with the garden's herbs and roasted garlic, along with hummus made from local chestnut beans; and a white onion and potato soup is topped with, of course, blue sage. Scriver also collaborates with Cave B's winemaker Freddy Arredondo to create food-wine pairings that showcase the winery's esteemed estate wines, which include an award-winning *Cuvée du Soleil* Bordeaux blend and a full-bodied Syrah.

With vineyards all around, the inn itself looks like a series of upended wine barrels, with low curved corrugated-metal roofs arched over rough-cut stone walls quarried right on the property—they almost seem to merge into the cliff-top terrain. The richly appointed guest rooms range from large rooms in the main lodge (where the restaurant is located) to spacious one- and two-bedroom "cliffhouses." Besides touring the winery, you can relax in the spa or beside the swimming pool; the Cellar music club on site and the next door Gorge Amphitheatre host a number of concerts as well (REM, Sting, and Bob Dylan are among the artists who've recently played the Gorge). The inn, which opened in 2005, is just the first stage of a much more extensive resort to be built over the next several years. SageCliffe is certainly off to a remarkable start.

ⓘ 344 Silica Rd. NW, Quincy (✆ **888/785-2283** or 509/785-2283; www.cavebinn.com).

✈ Pangborn Memorial Airport, Wenatchee (29 miles/47km).

Sooke Harbour House

Where the Gardens Meet the Sea

Sooke, British Columbia

Set at the very tip of Vancouver Island, with jaw-dropping views over the Strait of Juan de Fuca toward Washington's rugged Olympic Mountains, this small country inn casts a much bigger shadow than you'd expect. It's known worldwide for its quirky art-filled decor, splendid gardens, naturewatching (you can spot seals, otters, and seabirds right from your bedroom deck), and above all fine dining, with one of Canada's most acclaimed restaurants.

Walking into the lobby, you may be excused for thinking you've entered an art gallery instead—in fact Sooke Harbour House is a de facto art gallery, featuring bold original artwork by up-and-coming local artists, all of it for sale. Each of the rambling white inn's 28 suites is individually decorated by the inn's French co-owner, Frederique Philip, with antiques, polished wood floors, fresh flowers, striking artworks, and witty handcrafted furnishings, all set off by gallery-white walls and drapes. Every suite has its own fireplace and (except for one room) outdoor deck; many also have Jacuzzis or Japanese soaking tubs. A simple room-service breakfast is included in the room rate; a full range of spa services is also available.

Even guests who aren't staying in the inn come here to dine at the inn's renowned restaurant. Its emphasis is on Pacific Northwest ingredients, including vegetables, herbs, and edible flowers from

Skate wing with tuberous nasturtium at Sooke Harbour House in British Columbia.

Tuson's network of local suppliers provide wild mushrooms and berries, organic chicken, wild duck and rabbit, and tender suckled lamb, pork, and veal. The menu changes every day, but you may find entrees like herb-roasted lamb leg with a nectarine-oxeye-daisy salsa on potato corn cakes with braised fennel and purple cabbage, or a baked Pacific halibut filet with trout roe, served with cabbage-fennel ravioli, broccoli, and banana squash.

During the week, dining is all prix-fixe, though some a la carte selections are available on weekends. Book in advance if you want the seven- or nine-course tasting menu, which also includes a wine-pairing option. (*Wine Spectator* places Sooke Harbour House's wine list in its elite "best in the world" category.) Various special packages nab you with special perks like a tour of the inn's wine cellars, a guided tour of the gardens, or an afternoon spent with the chef. Note that the inn closes for 2 weeks in January, and on Tuesday and Wednesday in winter, except for the December holiday season. Sooke Harbour House has the courage to be a little different—that's all part of its ineffable charm.

the inn's own gardens—everything from rosemary and thyme to kiwis, plums, nasturtiums, and passionflowers. Seafood also features prominently, including Dungeness crab, salmon, black cod, mussels, and oysters, much of it caught in the waters right outside the inn. Chef Edward

(i) 1528 Whiffen Spit Rd., Sooke Harbour (✆ **800/889-9688** or 250/642-3421; www.sookeharbourhouse.com).

✈ Victoria (30km/19 miles).

Gourmet Inns & Resorts 74

Three Chimneys & the House Over-By

Skye High

Isle of Skye, Scotland

A century-old stone crofter's house on a remote loch on this windswept Hebridean island—it's a most unlikely setting for one of the world's top restaurants. And yet here is where you'll find the award-wining Three Chimneys, which proudly declares its

Scottish heritage with menu items such as Aberdeen Angus beef with potatoes Dauphinoise; pan-fried Scottish salmon with asparagus and lemon sauce; roast loin of Glenhinnisdal lamb with kidney, heart, and liver, *neep purry* (mashed rutabagas), and *colcannon* (mashed cabbage and potatoes); or a dessert of hot marmalade pudding with Drambuie custard. Robert Burns would no doubt approve.

With only four small dining areas, the Three Chimneys is an intimate sort of place, with candlelight flickering off its rustic stone walls and low beamed ceilings. Nevertheless, the tables are set with crisp white linen, crystal, and china, and the service is faultlessly attentive. Specialties are fresh seafood, Skye-grazed lamb and beef, and Highland game, accompanied by handmade cheeses, free-range eggs, and fresh local produce; breads, oatcakes, and traditional pastries are baked fresh every day in the kitchen. Founding chef Shirley Speare, who launched the restaurant in 1985 and garnered its first accolades, has taken a back seat since 2005, working behind the scenes with her successor, Michael Smith, who carries on the torch splendidly. The restaurant also has a distinguished wine list, developed by Shirley's husband and co owner, Eddie Spear.

Describing itself as a "restaurant with rooms," the Three Chimneys just happens to have six suites for overnight guests in a modern house across the courtyard. And they all just happen to be luxuriously appointed, with modern amenities such as a TV, VCR, CD player, and minibar, not to mention panoramic seacoast views. Rooms are spacious, with a striking simple decor, bold splashes of color, roomy tiled bathrooms, and doors opening onto a private garden with its own chattering brook (or "burn," to use the Scottish term). Opened in 1999, the House-Over-By perfectly complements the Three Chimneys experience (not least of all because there are so few other lodging options in the immediate area). Three Chimney's stunning remote location has always been part of its attraction—the B&B turns it into one of the most memorable getaway spots in the world.

ⓘ Hwy. B884, Colbost, Isle of Skye (℘ **44/ 1470/511-258;** www.threechimneys.co.uk).

✈ Inverness (129km/80 miles).

Three Chimneys & the House Over-By on the Isle of Skye in Scotland.

Le Manoir aux Quat' Saisons

A Manor for All Seasons

Oxford, England

A Norman nobleman first built this gray-and honey-colored stone manor house, back in the early 1300s. So there's a peculiar justice in the fact that Le Manoir aux Quat' Saisons should have been brought to its greatest glory by a Frenchman—in this case, Raymond Blanc, the inn's owner and top chef of its world-famous restaurant.

When Blanc opened the Manoir in 1984, he named it after the award-winning restaurant where he'd first established his reputation in England, in the north Oxford suburb of Summertown. Blanc had always yearned to preside over a country-house hotel, something along the lines of the provincial restaurant-inns where great French chefs like Fernand Point, Pierre and Jean Troisgros, Paul Bocuse, and Bernard Loiseau had made their names. The idyllic Oxfordshire village of Great Milton had just the right ambience, with its stone-and-stucco cottages and ancient church, and when the manor house became available, after the death of its then-owner Lord Cromwell, Blanc seized the opportunity and transplanted the Quat' Saisons restaurant. Ever since 1990, Le Manoir aux Quat' Saisons has held two coveted Michelin stars, the only English country-house hotel to win such accolades.

As the name promises, Quat' Saisons has always been all about seasonal menus. Even though Blanc has yielded day-to-day cooking responsibilities to his protégé, executive chef Gary Jones, the kitchen is still devoted to promoting whatever's fresh and local. The Manoir's splendid two-acre kitchen garden grows over 90 different vegetables and 70 types of herbs, providing much of the produce used in the kitchens (it's all organic, of course—Blanc has been on the organic bandwagon since the late 1980s). The menu is constantly changing, but expect a definite French bias, in dishes like confit of foie gras, a ceviche of Scottish sea scallops and tuna, or the assiette of suckling pig roasted in its own juices. While rugged stone walls, lead-paned casement windows, wood-paneled salons, and roaring fireplaces remind you of the manor's heritage, everything is furnished in up-to-date comfort. Diners can enjoy a three-course luncheon menu, a five-course prix fixe menu, or a 10-course tasting menu.

The hotel itself has 32 rooms. Individually decorated by well-known designers like Michael Priest, Emily Todhunter, and Trevillon, each is a dazzling showpiece of styles from frilly Victorian to rustic French provincial to scarlet opium den. Luxurious to the max, they're also pricey, best saved for a special romantic indulgence.

Since 1997, the Manoir has also included an on-site cooking school, where members of Blanc's team teach a full roster of 1-, 2-, or 4-day cooking courses. Classes cover a range of topics, including fusion cuisine, bread baking, fish and shellfish, dinner parties, and—*naturellement*—garden-to-table cookery.

ⓘ Great Milton, Oxfordshire (✆ **800/845-4274** in the U.S., or 44/1844/278881; www.manoir.com).

✈ London Heathrow (61km/38 miles).

🚃 Oxford (19km/12 miles).

Hôtel-Restaurant Troisgros
All in the Family
Loire Valley, France

Once upon a time, this was a run-of-the-mill small-town hotel, the sort of place that depended on the nearby train station for most of its business. But that was before Jean-Baptiste Troisgros and his wife, Marie, bought the place in 1930. Situated on the N7 highway, Hôtel-Restaurant Troisgros lay right on the path of French "gastronomads" touring the provinces in search of great meals, and they soon found them at Troisgros's restaurant. With Jean-Baptiste running the dining room and Marie at the stove, the hotel's reputation spread like wildfire.

In the 1950s, a postwar travel boom brought an international clientele to the area around Lyon, and sons Pierre and Jean—who had taken over the kitchen after Papa made sure they trained with all the best chefs in France—won their first Michelin star in 1954. By 1968 they had three stars, and the restaurant has hung on to them for 40 years and counting.

Under Pierre's son Michel, who is now running the kitchen, the restaurant is reaching new heights. Staying current with an ever-more-competitive gastronomic universe, Michel has opened up the classical French menu to influences from Asia (Michel lived in Japan as a child when his father was chef at Maxim's in Tokyo) and California (under mentor Michel Guérard, Michel traveled to America), while still hewing to the Troisgros tradition of using fresh regional ingredients and cooking with an almost breathtaking simplicity. Don't expect foams and fusion here, but honest, flavorful dishes such as fried foie gras served with marinated eggplant, chestnut soup flavored with Granny Smith apple, rouget with fennel and kumquats, salmon with sage sauce, or beef served with Fleurie wine and bone marrow. For dessert, ask to see one of the best assortments of esoteric cheeses in the region, or perhaps enjoy a praline soufflé.

Decorated in neutral colors and lined with contemporary artwork, the restaurant features superb cuisine and impeccably tailored service—and of course, astronomical prices. Though the attached hotel has never garnered as much attention as the restaurant, it is definitely more than just "a restaurant with rooms"; Michel's wife, Marie-Pierre, has decorated the 16 guest rooms in a stunning minimalist contemporary style that matches the restaurant's sleek neutral-toned decor.

Confections from the Hôtel-Restaurant Troisgros.

69

They also operate the casual cafe Le Central down the street, with its attached gourmet food shop. Ever in search of new horizons, Michel also has a restaurant at the Hyatt Regency Tokyo (there's the Japanese note again) and is developing an inn farther out in the Roanne countryside. You can't blame a chef this talented for wanting to do more than just take over the family business—even when the family business is something as remarkable as the Hôtel-Restaurant Troisgros.

(i) Place Jean Troisgros, Roanne (**33/4/ 77-71-66-97;** www.troisgros.com).

✈ Lyon (118km/73 miles).

Château Les Crayères

Champagne Tastes

Reims, France

Champagne is more than just a fizzy drink—the very name epitomizes an upper-crust lifestyle, and a way of doing things with sybaritic panache. Perhaps the ultimate expression of that Champagne mindset is this country-manor hotel-restaurant just outside of the regional capital of Reims. The cuisine here has always been a magnet for the champagne barons of the area, but these days the luxury accommodations are an even greater draw, earning Les Crayères a place on several magazines' lists of "best hotel in the world" over the past decade. It's an essential stop for well-heeled wine tourists from around the world.

The setting is drop-dead gorgeous, an upscale *maison bourgeoise* (actually a mini-château) dating from 1903, surrounded by a 5.6-hectare (14-acre) park. It's a showpiece indeed, full of soaring ceilings, chandeliers, elaborate moldings and wood paneling, gilt-framed oil paintings and tapestries, marble floors and pilasters, Art Nouveau wrought iron, and richly patterned carpets, upholstery, and draperies. Originally built for the Marquis and Marchioness of Polignac and associated with the Pommery champagne estate, the chateau became a luxury hotel in 1983. Renowned local chef Gérard Boyer was persuaded to transfer his esteemed restaurant La Chaumière onto the site as well, and Relais & Châteaux soon snapped up the property.

Les Crayères's 16 guest rooms, some in the château and others in cottages around the lushly landscaped grounds, are individually decorated in lavish French provincial style—expect lots of toile-patterned fabrics and brocades, eclectic artwork, and overstuffed armchairs and sofas. Spacious and crammed with all modern amenities (including air-conditioning, not always a given in France), they're top-of-the-line lodgings indeed.

The dining salon's Belle Epoque elegance perfectly matches the classical French cuisine. Current chef Didier Elena, an Alain Ducasse protégé, has been working wonders here. Launch your meal with ravioli stuffed with escargots or sample an appetizer of three different preparations of foie gras. A Bresse chicken breast comes delicately interlarded with ham and black truffles; the spring lamb is accompanied by a luscious eggplant-Parmesan persillade. The wild turbot and the grilled lobster are ineffably delicate, and the roast duck with honey vinegar sauce is an earthy regional delight. Among the prix-fixe menus you'll find a special Tradition De Champagne seven-course tasting menu featuring wine pairings—it's a great way to explore a variety of local wines, which include far more than just the effervescent méthode *Champenoise* wines.

Traveling around the Champagne region, you'll wander through wineries in several grand châteaux. Here's your chance to stay in one yourself, and feel like a champagne baron at least for a night.

ⓘ 64 bd. Henri-Vasnier (℗ **33/3/26-82-80-80**; www.lescrayeres.com).

✈🚗 Reims (2.2km/1⅓ miles).

Locanda dell'Amorosa

Back to the Farm

Sinalunga, Italy

In the Chiana valley, just east of Siena and south of Arezzo, an arrow-straight country lane lined with slim dark cypresses leads away from modern-day Sinalunga to a charming relic of Italy's rich agrarian past. Spend a few days at Locanda dell'Amorosa and you'll find the ideals of the Slow Food movement making more sense to you than ever.

In medieval times, Amorosa was a bustling, self-sufficient feudal farm complex, attached to a manor house owned by the powerful Piccolominis of Pienza. The villagers lived in an arcaded building of rough-cast fieldstone and bricks, its shallow red-tiled roofs fending off the Tuscan sun, right across the courtyard from the cattle barns and other farm buildings. Back in the 14th century, such farming communes peppered the Italian countryside; Amorosa is one of the few that have survived. It's still a working farm, although today its surrounding fields grow gourmet crops like grapes, olives, and sunflowers; the manor is decked out with upscale guest rooms, and the old stone stables house one of Tuscany's most atmospheric restaurants.

The estate's current owners turned it into a country restaurant, Le Coccole, in 1971, with the idea of bringing the farm's products directly to the public in fine-dining form. In the wake of the restaurant's success, the owners added 27 guest rooms as well, decorated in an eclectic mix of country antiques and rustic handmade furniture, with wood-beamed ceilings, whitewashed plaster walls, and large casement windows looking out across the farmlands. Though fully outfitted with modern amenities, they still exude a wonderful peasant sturdiness and simplicity that's ideally suited to the site.

Locanda dell'Amorosa is still a working farm.

There are actually two restaurants on site—a casual enoteca where you can sample a full range of local wines accompanied by regional dishes, and the upscale gourmet restaurant. It still looks a bit like a cow barn, with low whitewashed brick arches, tiled floors, and handmade iron fixtures, though add enough white napery and crystal and candlelight, and it's romantically transformed. Chef Giancarlo Propedo's refined cooking pays tribute to Tuscan flavors: dishes are based on the celebrated Chianina beef and Cinta Senese pork, barnyard poultry, produce from the farm or neighboring farms, *salame* from Trequanda, cheeses from Pienza and Montalcino, white truffles from San Giovanni d'Asso, Tuscan extra-virgin olive oil, and homemade pastas.

Locanda dell'Amorosa makes a fine base for daily excursions around the Tuscan countryside, though you may also want simply to lounge by the small swimming pool and bask in relaxing peace, perhaps with a bottle of the estate's wine. Stay for a few days and you may forget the notion of hurrying altogether.

ⓘ Off the SS326 (Sinalunga-Torrita di Siena Rd.), Chiusi/Chianciano (✆ **39/577/ 677-211;** www.amorosa.it).

✈ Perugia/Sant'Egidio (73km/45 miles).

Mount Nelson Hotel
Whoa, Nellie!
Cape Town, South Africa

Affectionately nicknamed "the Nellie," the Mount Nelson is a grand old colonial institution, a sort of Merchant-Ivory British Empire fantasy set amid 3.6 hectares (9 acres) of palm-dotted gardens, seemingly a world away from the rest of bustling Cape Town. Opened in 1899 as a first-class railroad hotel, this sprawling pink Victorian grande dame naturally had become a little creaky and fusty over the years. Yet much as South Africa—once a pariah among nations—reinvented itself as a hot ecotourist and wine tourist destination, so has the Nellie recently been brightly refurbished for the 21st century.

Like any large-scale hotel, the Mount Nelson offers a variety of dining venues. The open terrace of casual Oasis takes advantage of South Africa's abundant sunshine for al fresco lunches and buffet breakfasts. While the sleek and trendy bar Planet draws every visiting celebrity to Cape Town, those who want to revel in British tradition head for the prodigious afternoon tea served in the white wedding-cake main lounge, by the Lord Kitchener Fountain. For one of Cape Town's most serious gourmet experiences, however, you can't miss dining at the Cape Colony restaurant, which has been rated one of the top 10 hotel restaurants in the world. The old-world elegance of this dining room—with its vaulted ceilings, fluted columns, potted palms, swagged draperies, and tiny glowing table lamps—belies the inventive cooking of executive chef Ian Mancais. Yes, half of his menu gives a nod to the Nellie's old-guard clientele with perfectly executed classic dishes like lobster bisque, duck terrine, and beef

Cape Colony restaurant, widely considered one of the world's best hotel restaurants, in Cape Town's Mount Nelson Hotel.

Wellington in puff pastry, but he really takes off with the contemporary side of the menu, where you'll find intriguing dishes like ostrich tartare with poached quail egg, braised bitter-chocolate-flavored oxtail stuffed in agnolotti pasta, Vietnamese black-lacquered lamb, or grilled tuna on pineapple carpaccio. A chef's table for 6 to 10 diners has been set up in the heart of Mancais's sparkling kitchen, and special food-and-wine evenings are offered regularly, to showcase the products of South Africa's buzzing wine industry.

Given the stately profile of the Mount Nelson's exterior, it's surprising to see how crisp and clean-lined the guest room decor is, incorporating traditional elements—antique reproductions, vintage-print fabrics, and plump upholstered seating—into a muted, refined look that's utterly contemporary. With two pristine outdoor swimming pools, an extensive fitness center, a holistic spa, tennis courts, and access to several golf courses, the Nellie's as close to a resort as you can get within the city limits. It's a great second chapter for this vintage old lady.

(i) 76 Orange St. (✆ **27/21/483-1000;** www.mountnelson.co.za).

✈ Cape Town Airport (8.4km/5¼ miles).

Michel Bras

The Mountain Climber

Laguiole, France

A country inn in the south of France, the home base for a celebrated French chef—you'd expect it to be rustic, quaint, and historic, right? But Michel Bras's restaurant-hotel in the Auvergne is nothing like that. This strikingly spare contemporary structure thrusts from its isolated hillside like a rugged granite outcrop or a lonely alien spaceship, crash-landed on Earth.

Once inside, you'll immediately see what Bras is getting at. The elegantly stripped-down style of the dining room and guest rooms—bare floors and empty walls, widely spaced tables, a muted palette of solid colors—focuses your attention outward, through wraparound walls of glass, to focus on a breathtaking panorama of brilliant green grass, jagged granite, and a dramatic cloud-streaked sky. It's an ideal complement to Bras's self-taught style of cooking, which is equally minimalist and focused on his native Aubrac countryside. Beef dishes are made from the unique local breed of cattle; cheeses are made locally from unpasteurized cows' milk (try the divine *aligot,* potatoes mashed with that local cheese). The menu changes with the seasons, but vegetables figure prominently, from the spring delicacy of asparagus and green beans to the juicy meatiness of a grilled eggplant to the deep savor of roasted onions. Bras's most famous dish, *gargouillou de jeunes légumes,* is a salad of some 40 native vegetables, flowers, herbs, and seeds, many of them gathered from the hillsides just that morning.

When you look at a Michel Bras dish arranged on its simple white plate, it seems straightforward enough—meticulously arranged, true, but with just a few fairly familiar ingredients, left in their natural forms. It's the fresh purity of these ingredients, and Bras's brilliant seasonings, that have earned this place a reputation as one of the world's great restaurants.

Bras and his wife moved their famous restaurant from the village to this mountaintop site in 1992 and added accommodations for overnight guests (a smart move, considering how far Laguiole is from any major towns). It's a bona fide family affair. Sebastien Bras assists his father in the kitchen, overseeing the pastry creation, including Bras's most famous dessert, a warm chocolate cookie with a pool of liquid chocolate inside. Even Michel's mother—from whom he learned all his cooking, he insists—still lends a hand. In rhythm with the seasons, the property is only open April through October—the most beautiful times of year for this harsh, spectacular landscape. Reservations are notoriously hard to get, so start planning your trip now.

ⓘ Route de l'Aubrac (☏ **33/5/6551-1820;** www.michel-bras.com).

✈ Rodez-Marcillac (63km/39 miles); Auvergne (156km/97 miles).

Crystal Food & Wine Festival
Living Large
Crystal Cruises

Cruise ship passengers are a captive audience—and when you have nowhere else to go during long days at sea, meals become the highlight of your day. Even if you're on a big boat, like Crystal Cruises' 1,080-passenger *Crystal Serenity* and the 940-passenger *Crystal Symphony*, with their endless stream of shore excursions, films, lectures, and other activities, you'll probably find yourself awaiting the next meal with an extraordinary level of interest.

Japanese-owned Crystal Cruises has been an industry leader on this front, offering food-themed cruises for more than a decade. Even on its standard cruises, Crystal puts a lot of emphasis on its food and wine service and succeeds remarkably well—especially considering how many mouths their kitchens have to feed. Besides the excellent dining room, there are two specialty restaurants, Prego, which serves a menu developed by Piero Selvaggio of L.A.'s Valentino restaurants, and the Silk Road/The Sushi Bar, which serves Asian food conceived by Nobu Matsuhisa. (Don't expect to see Nobu on board greeting guests, but still.) As soon as you embark, make reservations for meals there at least 1 or 2 nights of your cruise. Both ships also feature a private dining room, The Vintage Room, where for an extra fee about a dozen guests can partake of a meal tailored to complement certain premium wines (again, book as soon as possible if you're interested). Crystal prides itself on its wine profile, with master sommeliers on board, its own wine label, and well-stocked cellars with some 25,000 bottles. Service is attentive and polished as well—there's no cattle-car atmosphere whatsoever, which is amazing for ships this size.

But Crystal's annual food-themed cruises, under the banner Food and Wine Festival, raise the bar even further. Itineraries include Mediterranean and Far East options, a Panama Canal cruise, a New England shore cruise from Montreal to New York, and a Pacific cruise from Sydney to Singapore. On-board programs always feature a celebrity chef and a leading wine expert; guest chefs in the past have included Michelle Bernstein of Michy's, Henry Brosi of the Dorchester in London, and the legendary Andre Soltner of the late Lutece. Shore excursions may include winery visits, gourmet lunches, cooking lessons, or a lobster bake, as well as the usual roster of sightseeing and outdoor adventures. Overnight stops center on foodie-meccas such as Bordeaux and Barcelona.

Booking a foodie cruise also guarantees you'll meet some like-minded gourmands among your fellow passengers. And who knows what tasty shipboard friendships you'll strike up?

ⓘ Crystal Cruises, 2049 Century Park East, Suite 1400, Los Angeles, CA 90067 (✆ **888/722-0021;** www.crystalcruises.com).

Regent Food Cruises

What's Cooking?

Regent Seven Seas

Luxury is the name of the game for Regent Seven Seas, which operates an upscale trio of all-suite cruise ships circling the globe. And when you're going for the luxury market, it's not enough just to leave chocolate on the pillow. That's why Regent offers food-and-wine-themed cruises with guest chefs and tailors certain cruises for aspiring chefs and chocoholics.

Regent's on-board cooking classes are serious—three intensive 2-hour workshops during the course of a cruise, limited to only 10 participants, and taught by visiting chefs from no less an institution than Paris's Le Cordon Bleu cooking school. You may not be able to snag a sous-chef job at The French Laundry after this, but you'll certainly hone your skills, learn some new tricks, and gain insight into haute cuisine. The partnership with Cordon Bleu is a natural outgrowth of Cordon Bleu's involvement in developing menus for the ships' Signatures restaurants (reserve a table for dinner to sample the classic French menu—you may be cooking the same dishes in class). Regent offers these Cordon Bleu classes on several cruises throughout the year, which run anywhere from 8 to 20 nights, visiting ports as far flung as Buenos Aires, Istanbul, Osaka, Sydney, or Reykjavik. (Regent's home base is in Fort Lauderdale, but not all cruises begin or end there.) Participants pay an extra program fee for the course.

Mastering complicated French cooking techniques requires hard work and discipline, of course; cruisers who are less Type A may want instead to book Regent's lively Spotlight on Chocolate cruises. Visiting pastry chefs or chocolate experts lecture and do cooking demonstrations on board, while the ship wends it way from port to port through the Caribbean.

Regent is known for good dining. Its two large 700-passenger ships, the *Regent Mariner* and the *Regent Voyager,* have four restaurants: a main dining room serving Continental cuisine; the Cordon Bleu Signatures restaurants where the Cordon Bleu classes take place; a smaller restaurant serving Indochinese specialties; and a casual bistro-style restaurant. The smaller 490-passenger *Regent Navigator* has the main dining room and an Italian specialty restaurant. On the food-and-wine-themed cruises, Regent also sets up some fascinating shore excursions, such as vineyard visits, cooking classes, sessions at local food markets, and meals at the finest local restaurants, often hosted personally by their chefs.

ⓘ **Regent Seven Seas Cruises,** 1000 Corporate Dr., Suite 500, Fort Lauderdale, Florida 33334 (✆ **800/477-7500;** www.rssc. com).

Silversea Gourmet Tours
Exploring the Exotic
Silversea Cruises

Italian flair is evident everywhere on the cruise ships of Silversea—in the tastefully appointed all-suite cabins, most of which have oceanview balconies; in the charming service provided by an Italian-officered crew; in the excellent wine cellar; in the small alternative dining room that features special wine pairings; in the Relais & Châteaux–approved chefs in the kitchen. Even the specialty restaurants on board feature an Italian menu. And because these sleek white vessels carry only 300 to 400 passengers, the service on board is highly individualized. You'll still have your casino, your show lounge, your spa, your on-deck pool, and your state-of-the-art gym, but they'll be a little more intimate in scale.

Silversea's interest in gourmet travel doesn't stop at getting the basic food and beverages right. Several itineraries on their schedule are earmarked for special interests, including wine cruises (lectures by wine experts, shore excursions to visit vineyards) and gourmet cruises (lectures and excursions to dine at various top restaurants onshore). Other special cruises offer Viking Cooking School activities—cooking demos by Relais & Châteaux chefs, market tours on shore, an *Iron Chef*–style cook-off between several of the ships' sous chefs, and special lunches that may focus on wine pairing or on regional cuisine.

What really makes these cruises special is often the destinations they visit en route. Smaller ships like the *Silver Cloud, Silver Wind, Silver Shadow,* and *Silver Whisper* can visit a wider variety of exotic ports around the globe that larger ships can't visit—places like Phuket, Grenada, Dakar, Saõ Tomé, the Cape Verde Islands, the Whitsunday Islands. Cruising through Polynesia, the Panama Canal, the Indian Ocean, the Atlantic islands of Europe, or along the African coast exposes gourmets to interesting new foods, and Silversea's chefs play into that by featuring regional specialties in the ship restaurants.

These are great trips for experienced cruise travelers who have already covered the Caribbean and Mediterranean routes and want to broaden their horizons. These aren't budget cruises by any means—with their ultraluxurious amenities covered by an all-inclusive pricing plan. On the other hand, you won't get hit up with extra fees every time you order a glass of wine or take advantage of an activity. For the affluent, older, sophisticated passengers who tend to cruise with Silversea, a chef's tasting menu is preferable to a la carte fare—and worth the price.

ⓘ Silversea Cruises, 110 East Broward Blvd., Fort Lauderdale, FL 33301 (✆ **800/ 722-9955,** 844/770-9030 in the U.K., or 61/2/9255-0600 in Australia; www.silver sea.com).

Windstar Food & Wine Series

Taking the Yacht for a Spin

Windstar Cruises

Heads turn in every port as Windstar's ships sail in, with their majestic masts spreading dazzling white sails, which the crew furls and unfurls with the push of a button. Technically, these clever little hybrid ships are called M.S.Y.'s, or motor-sail-yachts. Powered by motor and wind, as suggested by their name, they're not little sloops; 150 passengers fit comfortably on board—300 if you're on the five-masted *Wind Spirit*. No one's going to make you hoist a jib or man the capstan, though you certainly can visit the open bridge and watch the sailing officers at the helm. Still, you cannot deny the romance of standing on deck with those immense white sails snapping in the sea wind above you.

Serving a younger, more outdoorsy market niche, Seattle-based Windstar visits the standard sun-kissed cruise regions—the Mediterranean, the Greek Isles, the Panama Canal, Costa Rica, the Caribbean. But passengers are likely to spend their shore visits kayaking, sailing, or exploring the shoreline on an inflatable—rather than sightseeing by bus, as cruise passengers often do onshore. An on-board naturalist makes Windstar's Costa Rica cruises particularly appealing for ecotourists who still want a bit of luxury. With such small ships, Windstar can visit ports that aren't inundated with cruise-ship crowds, such as Corsica; Tarragona, Spain; St. Tropez, France; Portferraio, Italy; and Split, Croatia. Except for the 2-week transatlantic itineraries, Windstar cruises generally last 7 days, a bonus for cruise passengers with shorter attention spans, limited vacation time, and less-than-inexhaustible bank accounts.

This casual, youthful approach carries through to Windstar's food and beverages as well. Shipboard dining includes lots of light cuisine and vegetarian options rather than standard Continental-style cruise cuisine. California superchef Joachim Splichal developed recipes for the line, showcased in *Wind Spirit*'s specialty restaurant Degrees. Several cruises have a gourmet slant—prominent winemakers or chefs are available throughout the cruise to discuss the food and wine served—as part of Windstar's Signature Host series.

The fleet's ships definitely feel like yachts, with teak decks and fitted wood interiors; cabins are snug, with porthole windows (when you wake in the morning, you'll remember instantly that you're on a boat). Without big-ship amenities such as movie theaters or show lounges, Windstar passengers tend to spend more time on deck, lounging by the pool or just gazing at the horizon. Imagine sipping a fine Chardonnay while you sail into the sunset—how cool is that?

(i) Windstar Cruises, 2101 Fourth Ave., Suite 1150, Seattle, WA 98121 (**800/258-7245;**www.windstarcruises.com).

West Coast Wine Country Cruises

Rivers of Wine

Cruise West

If American wine is your thing, these cruises are for you. Cruise West's small excursion ships spend their summers in Alaska and their winters down on the Mexican Riviera and Panama Canal routes. But in between they sandwich in some excellent river tours of the West Coast's premier wine regions. While you sleep and dine aboard the boat, your days are filled with vineyard tours, gourmet luncheons, and meetings with noted vintners and chefs.

In the autumn, the 138-passenger *Spirit of Yorktown* does 4- or 5-day roundtrips from San Francisco through Napa and Sonoma. Vessels slip up the Napa River, dock at St. Helena for a number of winery visits via motorcoach, then navigate back to the bay and up the Sonoma River to dock at Sonoma for another round of vineyards. Optional excursions include hot-air balloon rides, tours of an olive oil grove, and a cooking demonstration at Napa's branch of the Culinary Institute of America. Given Napa's congested traffic, particularly during the autumn harvest season, gliding past it all on a boat is a brilliant stress-free alternative. Another bonus: You don't have to worry about driving after too many tasting sessions.

In fall and spring, the 84-passenger *Spirit of Discovery* steams up the Columbia River as it twists and turns from Portland, Oregon, north into Washington State. These Pacific Northwest Tasting Tours visit a number of wineries en route in Walla Walla, Red Mountain, and Horse Heaven Hill. The Hood River region's fine pear and apple orchards are also on this 8-day itinerary, along with a tour and tasting of seafood fisheries back on the coast in Astoria, Oregon.

Cruise West is a solid cruise industry veteran, in operation for more than 60 years. Its small, agile, shallow-draft ships are designed for intimate encounters with nature. Lots of outdoor deck space and large picture windows afford great views of the countryside, whether it be Napa's rolling vineyard-pleated hills or the breathtaking drama of the Columbia River Gorge. The shipboard vibe is casual and outdoorsy rather than luxurious; the streamlined modern cabins, with their blond-wood accents, reflect this. Fine dining isn't Cruise West's raison d'être, but the onboard meals are perfectly competent, with a vegetarian option every night. Knowing that wine-cruise passengers are likely to be gourmands as well, they've upped the ante on the shore-excursion meals.

(i) Cruise West, 2301 Fifth Ave., Suite 401, Seattle, WA 98121-1856 (© **888/851-8133;** www.cruisewest.com).

French Country Waterways

Premier Cru Canal Cruising

Burgundy/Champagne/Alsace, France

Here's one way to get off the beaten track—travel via barge, on the intricate network of canals that thread through the heart of France. The wine regions of Burgundy, Champagne, and Alsace-Lorraine are all interlaced with charming waterways, and you can cruise them in luxury aboard the hotel barges of French Country Waterways.

Most European barge travel involves hiring a whole barge and organizing a group of friends to share cabins—sometimes even operating the barge yourself and doing your own cooking. Hotel barges like American-owned French County Waterway's allow individual passengers (usually couples) to book a single stateroom on a barge with a skilled English-speaking crew. The barges run in size from six passengers up to a grand 18-passenger vessel, all richly appointed in French provincial style. It's an intimate shipboard experience like staying in an exclusive B&B. With no phones, TVs, or Internet connections, it's more likely you'll get to know your fellow travelers during the course of your week on board.

These 6-night cruises cover five different routes: one in Champagne, one in the Germanic Alsace-Lorraine region, and three in different parts of ever-popular Burgundy. Bicycles are available if you want to pedal around the leafy lanes and quaint villages you're passing, and a motorcoach follows the barge's route to whisk guests off on daytime tours. You'll visit wineries and historic towns like Reims, Dijon, and Strasbourg, as well as the grandest local châteaux, abbeys, and cathedrals. One night per cruise, passengers dine at a Michelin-starred restaurant onshore.

Meals on board are something to look forward to as well, with nightly four-course dinners served by romantic candlelight. Because you're on canals and rivers instead of at sea, the chef has daily access to fresh produce and breads warm from the village bakery. The cuisine is iconically French—escargots, foie gras, truffles, soufflés, the whole Julia Child bit. Wines are high quality as well, usually estate bottled from grand cru and premier cru vineyards. You may find yourself drinking rare vintages from wonderful little family vineyards that don't produce enough wine to export—now there's an experience you can't duplicate at home.

French Country Waterways' cruise staff.

(i) French Country Waterways, P.O. Box 2195, Duxbury, MA 02331-2195 (© **800/ 222-1236** or 781/934-2454; www.fcwl.com).

Ballymaloe Cookery School

Irish Idyll

Shanagarry, Ireland

The word "idyllic" comes to mind upon sight of this cozy farmstead. Just outside a small fishing village in county Cork, it's surrounded by 4 hectares (10 acres) of parterred gardens and mossy orchards and, surrounding that, a flourishing 41-hectare (100-acre) organic farm. You could easily stop by on a day trip from Cork city to visit the fragrant rambling gardens, which are open to the public. But how much better to stay for a spell, living in one of the whitewashed 18th-century cottages tucked around the courtyard while taking a cooking course?

As rustic as the buildings look from the outside, once you step inside you'll find a smartly equipped culinary classroom with large windows, a phalanx of counters and chopping blocks, and cooktops ready for action. Ballymaloe offers serious 12-week courses for those looking for a culinary career, but a long roster of shorter courses are available year-round. They might be anything from a 3-hour introduction to the art of sushi or tapas or charcuterie, to a full-day crash course in butter making, beekeeping, or making jams and preserves from the bounty of Ballymaloe's own hives, dairy, and orchards. Even if you're just touring the gardens, you're likely to see students in their chef's whites out in the garden plucking herbs for the morning's cooking class. Essential techniques are taught in 2½-day and 5-day courses, which may focus on baking, for example, or entertaining or cooking family meals.

Students at the Ballymaloe Cookery School in Shanagarry, County Cork, Ireland.

Several of these are conceived as a series, so returning students can hone their skills on successive visits to Ballymaloe. All this activity requires input from several teachers in residence, but Ballymaloe's fame attracts lots of excellent guest teachers as well (Richard Corrigan and Claudia Roden are among the visiting experts in 2009).

Afternoon demonstrations, which you can book just a few days ahead of time, home in on a single skill such as how to fillet a fish or how to make a perfect omelet or loaf of bread. The longer classes fill up early, however, so reserve your spot well in advance, at least 6 weeks if possible. The school's own cottages generally book up with guests taking the longer courses, but there are several other places to stay in the neighborhood, including the luxurious Ballymaloe House, an acclaimed upscale country-house hotel up the road.

The school's director, Darina Allen, was once chef at Ballymaloe House. Her husband Tim Allen's family owns the place; Tim runs the farm; and Darina's brother and daughter are now teachers in the school as well. That's the sort of homey place Ballymaloe remains, despite its international acclaim. In the silence of a misty morning, as butterflies flit through the gardens and sheep baa in nearby pastures, it's hard to imagine how anyone could ever move away from such a place. Idyllic, indeed.

ⓘ (✆ **353/21/464-6785;** www.cookingis fun.ie).

✈ Cork City (32km/20 miles).

🛏 $$$ **Ballymaloe House,** Ballycotton Rd., Shanagarry (✆ **353/21/465-2531;** www. ballymaloe.ie). $$ **The Garryvoe Hotel,** Ballycotton Bay, Castlemartyr (✆ **353/21/ 464-6718;** www.garryvoehotel.com).

Cooking Schools for Travelers **88**

On Rue Tatin

Tasting France

Normandy, France

When American cookbook writer Susan Herrman Loomis first moved to Normandy with her husband and toddler son in the 1980s, intent on restoring a crumbling old convent across the street from a Gothic church, she didn't envision that the property would become a popular cooking school. (Read her engaging memoir *On Rue Tatin* to get the full story.) Nowadays, however, her On Rue Tatin programs are much in demand; limited to eight participants per 5-day session, they book up well in advance, so plan ahead for your trip to France.

The idea behind On Rue Tatin workshops is that they don't just teach you French cuisine, they use food as a pathway to immerse you in French culture. For 6 days, participants not only cook, they take time to savor the meals they've prepared, either outdoors in the graveled courtyard or in the wood-beamed dining room of Loomis's half-timbered 15th-century house. Course participants also sample wines from throughout France; shop at local markets; meet artisan bakers, cheese makers, and butchers; visit local farms; and hang out in atmospheric cafes, soaking up the ambience of small-town Normandy. A few of the courses center around special themes—the seafood of Normandy, for example, or apples (Loomis has her own small orchard), or the ever-popular Chocolate Indulgence workshop. Classes are conducted in English; recipes are geared to the home cook rather than the restaurant kitchen. (Many are drawn from Loomis's popular cookbooks such as *The French Farmhouse Cookbook* or *Cooking at Home*.) Students get hands-on practical experience in the thoroughly up-to-date teaching kitchen that Loomis has installed within her historic house. Students must book their own accommodation in the area.

For guests who don't have time for the full 6-day course, Loomis also offers a few 3-day programs throughout the year, as well as gracious multicourse Sunday lunches, which are entirely doable as a day trip from Paris. And speaking of Paris, a few times a year Loomis relocates there, where she conducts a combination of week-long and 1-day classes, using the Left Bank cooking studio of her noted friend Patricia Wells. If you can't make it all the way to rue Tatin, Paris isn't a bad consolation.

ⓘ 1 Rue Tatin, Louviers (✆ **866/369-8073,** or 214/306-8734 in the U.S.; www.onruetatin.com).

✈ Paris Charles de Gaulle (123km/76 miles).

🚃 Val de Reuil (1½ hr. from Paris).

🛏 $$ **Le Pré St. Germain,** 7 rue St. Germain, Louviers (✆ **33/2/32-40-48-48;** le.pre.saint.germain@wanadoo.fr).

A Week in Provence

The Warmth of the Sun

Condorcet, France

Summers are a glorious time of year to be in sunny Provence. The air is heavily scented with wild lavender and thyme, and endless blue skies arch over olive groves and stony hillside pastures. Beautiful as this landscape is, it would be a shame to rush through it on your way to somewhere else; how much better to settle in for a week and learn the secrets of robust, earthy Provençal cooking.

The cornerstone foods of Provence—olives, garlic, bell peppers, lamb, goat, and fragrant sun-dried herbs like rosemary and thyme—add up to a quintessentially rustic cuisine, so it's especially fitting that this cooking program should be based in an 18th-century farmhouse nestled in the hills outside the village of Condorcet. It's a rural, isolated haven in the mountainous Haute-Provence region, known for its sun-drenched days and clear, starry nights; only 32km (20 miles) away lies Nyons, regarded as the olive capital of France.

Classes are held in June and September, and limited to 10 students maximum. Participants live right in the farmhouse, eating most meals together, enjoying a hillside panorama from the terrace, and swimming in a small stone-rimmed spring-fed swimming pool.

Each day includes 3 to 5 hours of hands-on instruction in the cheery teaching kitchen, taught in English by classically trained French chef Daniel Bonnot, who made his name at his New Orleans restaurants Chez Daniel and Bizou. With such small classes, the level of instruction is, naturally, tailored to the skill levels of the various people in the class. Optimally, the class themselves will prepare all the meals they eat at the farmhouse.

Outside of class, hosts Anne and David Reinauer also organize daily expeditions around the area, which may include wine tastings, market outings, tours of olive oil factories, or visits to local farms to see goat cheese being made or ducks being fattened up for foie gras.

Since there are only four sessions a year, be sure to book your spot several months in advance. A week in Provence is as much an intoxicating vacation experience as it is a culinary training course—what you get out of it may surprise you.

ⓘ Moutas, Condorcet (☏ **337/436-4422** in the U.S., or 33/4/75-27-73-47 in France; www.frenchcookingclasses.com).

✈ Marseilles (2-hr. drive).

🚃 Montelimar (1-hr. drive).

🛏 on site.

Finca Buenvino

Andalucian Illusion

Aracena, Spain

Many European cooking schools are in session only during the high tourist season of summer. Not so Finca Buenvino. The cooking classes in this charming hilltop villa, in a remote village near the Portuguese border, are held during the winter months, when the weather in the Andalucian Sierra can get nippy—a good time to hunker down in the kitchen, turn up the stove, and get cooking.

There's a method to Finca Buenvino's madness, of course. It's also a working farm, and things get too busy in the summer to teach cookery. The rosy pink villa is set amid 70 hectares (28 acres) of chestnut and cork-oak forest; a herd of free-range black Iberian pigs roots around the forest, fattening up on chestnuts. (Later in the season, owners Sam and Jeannie Chesterton slaughter the pigs and cure their own *jamon Serrano,* as well as *salchichón* and *chorizo.*) Fruit orchards and olive groves also need to be tended and harvested, as do the large garden plots that grow most of the organic vegetables used on site. The main house is grander than a mere farmhouse, but with its cozy cluttered decor of deep Mediterranean colors, it feels wonderfully homey.

The Chestertons' farm-to-table approach deeply informs the cooking classes. Jeannie's an expert in southern Spanish recipes, which often have a North African accent, especially in the use of nuts and spices; fruits (lemons, apricots, quinces) are often incorporated into roasts and stews as well. You'll learn to make a classic paella, perhaps, or *arroz negro,* black rice with squid ink. Of course, hearty wintertime favorites like roasts and game dishes are particularly popular, but as always, things depend on what's available in the local markets or in the farm's own storehouse. The weeklong courses also include a visit to a sherry producer and a sightseeing trip into beautiful historic Seville. Classes are limited to 12 students, which is all the villa can accommodate.

You can visit the finca in summer as well, when it operates as a bed-and-breakfast inn with five double rooms in the villa and three separate self-catering cottages. (Note that in July–Aug, the small villa is often booked up by private parties.) Dinner is served every evening. The rocky hillsides are clad in heather, and meadows fill with wildflowers; you can lounge by the swimming pool and drink in lovely mountain views. But Jeannie's cooking classes make the winter experience at Finca Buenvino just as special—that and the divine homemade Ibérico ham.

ⓘ Los Marines, Aracena (☏ **34/959/12-40-34;** www.fincabuenvino.com).

✈ Seville (90 min.).

International Cooking School of Italian Food & Wine

La Cucina Italiana, Demystified

Bologna, Italy

If you're going to run a cooking school in Italy, Bologna's the place to do it. Acknowledged as the gastronomic capital of Italy, it's one of the most fascinating cities in the world for food shopping, cooking, and eating. In 1987, the Italian government invited American food writer Mary Beth Clark to launch these English-language culinary workshops based in Bologna; the author of *Trattoria* and *Essentials of the Italian Kitchen,* she runs six programs a year in May, September, and October.

Cooking classes take place in an authentic 16th-century Renaissance palazzo. Amid the warm sienna-colored stone arcades of the city's historic heart, it's conveniently close to the food markets that are such a part of cooking in Italy—the Pescherie Vecchie, the Mercato delle Erbe, and the food shops of Via Drapperie. (The first thing the class does is head for the market, before they even begin to think about cooking.) A fully outfitted teaching kitchen in the high-ceilinged palazzo serves as classroom, with a charming baroque salon attached where the class and any friends who've paid a fee to join as "tasters" can dine on what they've cooked. Though guests don't stay in the palazzo itself, accommodations in nearby hotels are included in the course package.

Students gather for a meal at the International Cooking School of Italian Food & Wine in Bologna.

The core course, offered twice a year, teaches about a dozen students to cook 40 or so Italian recipes. Participants venture into the countryside to meet artisans who produce Emilia-Romagna's traditional specialties such as Parmesan cheese and balsamic vinegar. They also pay a visit behind the scenes to a Michelin-starred local restaurant. A 4-day version of that basic course is also offered twice a year. Two other courses explore farther afield. One rounds out the Bologna experience with a couple of days in Tuscany, in Siena, Florence, and Greve in Chianti. Another combines the Bologna portion of the class with a trip to the Piedmont, just in time for the annual truffle festival in Alba (a truffle hunt is included); the class stops along the way in Torino to participate in the Slow Food organization's international meeting, Terra Madre.

The Slow Food connection is telling. Clark's approach—spending time in local markets, cooking according to what's fresh today, and honoring food artisans—is consistent with the Slow Food philosophy, which first took root in Italy. It's a vital aspect of appreciating Italian food and, in turn, discovering what Italian culture is all about.

ⓘ U.S. office: 201 E. 28th St., #15B, New York, NY 10016-8538 (✆ **212/779-1921;** www.internationalcookingschool.com).

✈ **Aeroporto Guglielmo Marconi** (6km/ 3³/₄ miles).

Cooking Schools for Travelers 92

Cooking with Giuliano Hazan

All in the Family

Verona, Italy

Being Marcella Hazan's son certainly gave Giuliano Hazan a head start on becoming a food expert, though anyone who has read his books, *How to Cook Italian* and *The Classic Pasta Cookbook,* knows that he brings plenty of his own talent to the table. For Marilisa Allegrini, growing up in the wine business—her family is renowned for its superb Amarone di Valpolicella—also bequeathed her with a wealth of oenophilic knowledge. Since 2000, these two scions of food and wine have joined forces to transmit their epicurean heritage to a select group of students. Best of all, they're doing it at one of the loveliest estates in Italy, gracious Villa Giona.

Set in the Veneto, just a few minutes' drive from romantic Verona and, in the other direction, beautiful Lake Garda, Villa Giona is a fine example of Renaissance harmony. Its symmetrical façade of pale arched stone faces onto a velvety green lawn dotted with classical sculpture; 4.8 hectares (12 acres) of lush private park and vineyards surround the house. Those recently planted vineyards are now producing grapes for a special Villa Giona wine, a full-bodied Bordeaux-style red made by Allegrini.

Classes, conducted in English, consist of 5 hours of intensive hands-on instruction with Giuliano. You'll learn how to make your own pasta, execute a silky risotto, and whip up all sorts of other Italian dishes. Marilisa takes care of the wine classes, presenting a thorough overview of Italy's many wine regions, discussing the intricacies of wine production (Allegrini has been at the forefront of revolutionizing viticulture in the Veneto), and leading tasting sessions. The class also takes a number of field trips around the Veneto, visiting a 17th-century rice mill, an olive-oil *frantoio,* a seafood restaurant on Lake Garda, and the nearby Allegrini winery; there's even a day trip to Emilia-Romagna to learn about Parmigiano-Reggiano cheese and the rare culatello air-dried ham.

Students get to stay in one of Villa Giona's 10 bedchambers, restored to deluxe international standards. Only four to six classes take place per year, in late spring and early fall—the loveliest seasons in the Veneto. Classes are small, with only 12 participants at a time, allowing for a lot of one-on-one interaction with Giuliano and Marilisa. The course has been so popular, Giuliano and Marilisa now offer a couple of classes each year designed for repeat students who want to expand their territory. We can't all be born into famous gourmet families, but a week at Villa Giona gets you close.

(i) Cooking with Giuliano Hazan at Villa Giona, 4471 S. Shade Ave., Sarasota, FL 34231 (✆ **941/923-1333;** www.giulianohazan.com/school).

✈ Valerio Catullo Airport Verona (14km/ 8¾ miles).

🚆 Verona (9.1km/5¾ miles).

🛏 **Villa Giona Azienda Agricola,** Via Cengia 8, San Pietro in Cariano (✆ **39 045 77 250 68;** www.villagiona.it).

93 Cooking Schools for Travelers

Seasons of My Heart

Back to the Land

Oaxaca, Mexico

For many fans of PBS television, Mexican food is practically synonymous with Susana Trilling. *"Seasons of My Heart,"* the TV series based on her 1999 book of the same name, introduced American food lovers to the deeply traditional foods of Oaxaca, Mexico, otherwise known as the "Land of the Seven Moles." Since 1993, Trilling has conducted cooking classes in her adopted home in Oaxaca, Rancho Aurora, on a panoramic hillside between two small villages, San Lorenzo Cacaotepec and San Felipe Tejalapan, 16km (10 miles) northeast of Oaxaca City.

Seasons of My Heart now offers a mix-and-match variety of cooking classes and culinary tours, anything from an afternoon's cooking demonstration to a 10- or 11-day regional food tour, often with a focus on specific foods such as mushrooms, chilies, or vanilla. One-day classes are usually held on Wednesdays and begin with a trip to the outdoor market in nearby Etla, after which students create a five-course meal based on those ingredients; afternoon classes do just the cooking without the market excursion. As you're planning a trip to Mexico, check the schedule to see what's happening while you're in Oaxaca, or perhaps plan your entire trip around one of Trilling's long weekend or weeklong workshops.

What makes these classes special is Trilling's interest in age-old cooking techniques, recipes, and ingredients. When she teaches the art of hand making tortillas, for example,

Susan Trilling's Seasons of My Heart cooking school in Oaxaca, "Land of the Seven *Moles*."

she's describing methods that have been handed down from generation to generation in Zapotec villages like San Felipe Tejalapan. As you learn to make mole, you may first visit a village home where chocolate is ground on an ancient stone *mecate*. For each meat or vegetable cooked in class, she knows the specific matching sauce that traditional cooks have always used. Herbs are studied not just for their culinary flavoring but for their medicinal and spiritual properties as well. Students may visit local artisans to see how they produce food "the old-fashioned way"; several of the tours and longer programs are built around important festivals and whatever foods local custom dictates for those festivals.

The cooking school's adobe home, with its red-domed roof and surrounding terraces, is a wonderful place to drink in the beauty of the Etla valley. Most course participants find accommodations elsewhere, but if you book early you can snag a charming bed-and-breakfast cottage just above the hill from the school.

ⓘ Rancho Aurora, AP #42, Admon 3, Oaxaca (✆ 52/951/508-0469; www.seasons ofmyheart.com).

✈ Oaxaca City.

🛏 $$$ **Camino Real Oaxaca,** 5 de Mayo 300, Oaxaca (✆ **800/722-6466** in the U.S. and Canada, or 52/951/501-6100; www.caminoreal.com/oaxaca). $ **Las Golondrinas,** Tinoco y Palacios 411, Oaxaca (✆ **52/951/514-3298** or 52/951/514-2126; lasgolon@prodigy.net.mx).

Chiang Mai Thai Cookery School
The King of Siam
Chiang Mai, Thailand

Sompon Nabnian has become a local celebrity since 1993, when he and his English wife, Elizabeth, first launched this cooking school in northern Thailand's capital, Chiang Mai. He has appeared on several international television shows, including his own U.K. series, *Thai Way II;* he has developed the Jasmine Rice Village Boutique Resort and Spa, where many cooking class participants stay; and he has opened a new restaurant in the historic heart of Chiang Mai—The Wok, a peaceful garden restaurant in an old wooden house, which also serves as an alternative venue for cooking classes. Not bad for the son of a village butcher.

Culinary tourism has lately become the hottest sector of Thailand's tourism industry, and the Nabnians' school is right at the forefront. Chiang Mai's distinctive regional cuisine incorporates accents from the southern Chinese who settled here centuries ago and the Burmese who ruled the region until 1775. Students try their hands at cooking classic Northern Thai dishes like sticky rice and *plaah goong* (a spicy prawn salad) as well as pad Thai noodles, chicken in coconut milk soup, Penang curry with pork, and steamed fish in banana leaves. The class schedule is supremely flexible; students take one class a day, choosing from among five different daylong programs, which can be

Outdoor classes at the Chiang Mai Thai Cookery School.

Places to Eat in . . . Miami, Florida

With more than 6,000 restaurants, the Miami metro area tends to stump diners—it isn't a question of where so much as which. It's a supercharged culinary scene, and everyone wants a piece of it—Emeril Lagasse, Nobu Matsuhisa, Cindy Hutson, Christian Delouvrier, and Govind Armstrong are among the

Grilled swordfish at Chef Allen's.

nationally known chefs who've opened branches here. Even after you've weeded out all those South Beach beauties where the celebrity action is more important than the food, you're still faced with a plethora of high-end choices. Where to begin?

For an authentic taste of Miami, gravitate to the local stars who've fused California-Asian with Caribbean and Latin elements to create a world-class flavor all its own—call it *Floribbean*. Exhibit A would be Allen Susser's New World cuisine at 95 Chef Allen's (19088 NE 29th Ave., Aventura; 305/935-2900; www.chefallens.com).

Though it's tucked in the back of a strip mall in the northern reaches of Miami Beach, since it opened in 1986 Susser has had no trouble packing this discreetly elegant space with customers eager to sample his inventive Caribbean-inspired dishes: grilled meats and seafood accented by jerk and curry and coconut-milk spices, harmonized by chutneys and salsas and ceviches made of mangoes, papayas, pineapple, and Key limes. The aptly named 96 Michael's Genuine Food & Drink in the Design District (130 NE 40th St.; 305/573-5550; www.michaelsgenuine.com) looks like just another neighborhood hangout, with its high ceilings and industrial-chic decor, but Michael Schwartz's simple-seeming menu items are a symphony of flavors, and each ingredient is allowed to sing. (Try the roasted Vidalia onion stuffed with ground lamb and apricots, or the grilled skirt steak with fennel-asparagus hash and black olive aioli.)

Then there's 97 Talula (210 E. 23rd St.; 305/672-0768; www.talulaonline.com), owned by the talented husband-and-wife team Frank Randazzo and Andrea Curto-Randazzo, who imaginatively mix up meticulously sourced ingredients in signature dishes like the grilled foie gras with caramelized figs, blue corn cakes, chili syrup, and candied walnuts, or the marinated hanger steak with horseradish whipped potatoes. Book a seat in the exhibition kitchen for an even more special experience. Curto-Randazzo used to cook at another well-regarded South Beach hotspot, 98 Wish (801 Collins Ave.; 305/531-2222; www.wishrestaurant.com), where Marco Ferraro now presides; in that snazzy lemon-lime-colored dining room, his Franco-Floribbean approach produces winning dishes like a chilled tomato-lime soup with lobster, or diver scallops encrusted with Serrano ham, served with fingerling potatoes, artichokes, piquillo peppers, and horseradish foam. In Coral Gables, at ⑨ Pascal's On Ponce (2611 Ponce de León Blvd.; ℂ 305/444-2024; www.pascalmiami.com), chef Pascal Oudin, who trained under Alain Ducasse, reimagines French cuisine with New World ingredients. Try his blue crab cake with tomato gazpacho, twice-baked Gruyère cheese soufflé, or roasted duck breast with savoy cabbage and sautéed pears.

Behind the scenes at Talula.

This being Florida, of course, at some point most folks expect to have ocean-fresh seafood. Though the obvious choice is the tried-and-true Miami institution Joe's Stone Crab, for something more sophisticated, head down to Coconut Grove and ⑩ Baleen (4 Grove Isle Dr.; ℂ 305/858-8300; www.groveisle.com/groveisle_dining.aspx) for spectacular griddled crab cakes, lobster bisque, or wood-roasted diver scallops, served on a romantically tented seaside terrace. To get your requisite taste of Cuban food, go west to Doral to ⑩ Chispa (11500 NW 41st St.; ℂ 305/591-7166; www.chisparestaurant.com), a stylish, pulsating place where Adam Votaw produces gourmet versions of Cuban classics like a shrimp-and-black-eyed-pea *croquetta* or slow-roasted glazed short rib filet.

Basil panna cotta at Michael's.

✈ Miami Intl (6¼ miles/10km).

🛏 $$$ **The Ritz-Carlton South Beach,** 1 Lincoln Rd. (ℂ **800/241-3333** or 786/276-4000; www.ritzcarlton.com). $$ **The Kent,** 1131 Collins Ave. (ℂ **866/826-KENT** or 305/604-5068; www.thekenthotel.com).

taken in any order. Each class explores a different vein of culinary skills—learning how to shop in the market one day, the next learning to identify the full range of exotic Thai spices, or making spicy pastes with a mortar and pestle, or carving fruits and vegetables. Not only that, you have two different choices of location, either in the Nabnians' pleasant home just outside Chiang Mai in Doi Saket, or in town at **The Wok** (44 Ratchamanka Rd.; © **66/53/208287**).

Nabnian and his assistant teachers are all fluent in English and offer lots of hands-on assistance. Every student is given his or her own workstation and equipment; they cook four dishes in the morning and two in the afternoon, and later eat the fruits of their labors. Culinary professionals and students who complete all 5 days of the course are also welcome to take master classes with Nabnian after 4pm.

Even if you're not taking a class, you can stay at the Jasmine Rice Village, with a cluster of private poolside villas that evoke the village life of northern Thailand. Set amid green rice paddies, the peaceful property even has an herb and vegetable garden that provides produce for the cooking classes, a short walk away. Rooms have a minimalist simplicity, trimmed in teak. The resort's restaurant, Fragrant Rice, showcases some of Nabnian's more ambitious cooking—a reminder that, no matter how much you've learned, you still haven't exhausted the wonders of Thai food.

ⓘ 47/2 Moon Muang Rd., Chiang Mai 50200 (© **66/53/206 388;** www.thaicookery school.com).

✈ Chiang Mai (14km/8½ miles).

🛏 $$ **Jasmine Rice Village,** 91 Moo 3 Soi 3, T. Luang Nua A. Doi Saket (© **66/ 53/206 3151;** www.jasminericevillage. com). $$ **Tamarind Village,** 50/1 Rathcadamnoen Rd., Chiang Mai (© **66/53/418 896**).

Cooking Schools for Travelers **102**

Ritz-Carlton Amelia Island Cooking School

Salts of the Earth

Amelia Island, Florida

Competition is fierce among the various resorts on Amelia Island, a beautiful Atlantic barrier island just off the north Florida coast, rich in white sand beaches and imposing stands of live oak trees. The Ritz-Carlton Amelia Island's 13-acre (5 hectare) beachfront wasn't enough to compete against the long-established Amelia Island Plantation next door. So the Ritz-Carlton hit one out of the ballpark with its elegant wood-paneled restaurant **Salt, The Grill,** where the exceptional seasonal American regional menu is matched by a stunning ocean view. It's now considered one of the top restaurants throughout the Southeast.

The Ritz-Carlton makes the most of this gastronomic jewel. Salt offers daily four- and seven-course chef's tasting menus, which of course include a sampling of different salts (you'll be surprised how distinct their tastes are). There's a four-person chef's table in the kitchen for interested gourmets; there are special monthly wine dinners; at 4pm every Saturday you can drop by for a "culinary preview" of that evening's menu. Luckily for Ritz Carlton guests, Salt's chef de cuisine, Richard Gras, is also interested in teaching. He takes time out of his cooking duties to lead a 2-day hands-on cooking seminar at the resort every couple of months, designed around intriguing themes such as Aphrodisiac Cooking, Nutritional Cooking, or Barbecue Around the World; they're well worth planning a vacation around.

The cooking classes include a tour behind the scenes of the resort's kitchens, a fascinating experience if you've never seen what it takes to service three restaurants plus room service for a 444-room resort. The class then produces its own four-course luncheon, working with chef Gras and his team. The second day builds on techniques taught the day before, and students prepare another, even more elaborate, gourmet meal. Gras's attention to seasonal flavors—not to mention seasonings—can be illuminating.

The course accepts both novice and experienced cooks; class sizes are limited to allow for personalized instruction. You can book a slot in the Cooking School even if you aren't staying at the Ritz Carlton, though packages that bundle accommodations and classes are a surprisingly good deal. Between the salty sea air on the beach and the salt tastings in the restaurant, you may never think of salt in the same way again.

✈ Jacksonville (43 miles/69km).

🛏 $$$ **Ritz-Carlton Amelia Island,** 4750 Amelia Island Pkwy., Amelia Island, FL (✆ **800/241-3333** or 904/277-1100; www.ritzcarlton.com).

CIA Boot Camps
Going Undercover with the Other CIA
Hyde Park, New York

With such culinary luminaries as Charlie Palmer, Todd English, Larry Forgione, Alfred Portale, and Anthony Bourdain among its alumni, the Culinary Institute of America is rightly proud of its rigorous degree program. You have to be dead serious about a food career before enrolling here. But even if cooking is just an avocational passion for you, these regularly scheduled intensive multiday workshops will kick your kitchen skills up a notch.

CIA's main campus in Hyde Park, New York, is a real campus, a lovely set of red-brick academic buildings and dorms on a green bluff above the Hudson River. Not that you'll see much of that when you're in boot camp—class begins at 7am and goes full-out until you've plated your final dish at 4pm. A variety of 1-day courses take place on Saturdays in the state-of-the-art CIA teaching kitchens. While they're great teasers, the real action occurs weekdays in the 4- and 5-day boot camps. The name's no

accident—chef-instructors push the students to master complicated Escoffier-level techniques. It may not be *Hell's Kitchen,* but there's no mollycoddling—expect a tongue-lashing if your soufflé falls or your sauce separates. Your fellow students will most likely be highly accomplished amateurs (who else devotes an entire week to a grueling cooking course?), so you'll bypass the basics and get right into sophisticated technique. Course offerings include specialized boot camps on baking, pastry-making, Italian cuisine, French cuisine, Asian cuisine, bistro recipes, healthy cooking, and the Gourmet Meals in Minutes workshop. Students wear chef's whites throughout the class and, by the end, feel they've earned them.

The CIA runs similar courses on its other campuses as well, for those who can't get up to Hyde Park—there are a number of single-day classes in New York City's Astor Center (23 E. 4th St., second floor) and at Napa Valley's Greystone campus (2555

Training sessions are intense during the Culinary Institute's Boot Camp courses.

Main St., St. Helena, California). Greystone also conducts 4- and 5-day Career Development courses that are a kinder, gentler version of the boot camps, including wine education. In San Antonio, Texas, the CIA opened a new campus for training Latino food professionals (312 Pearl Pkwy., Bldg. #3; © **210/222-1113**). Two and three-day courses focus on Mexican food and tapas. All told, it gives you a lot of options if you want to get serious about your cooking.

ⓘ Culinary Institute of America, 1946 Campus Dr. (Rte. 9), Hyde Park (© **800/888-7250** or 845/471-6608; www.ciachef. edu).

✈ John F. Kennedy International; Newark Liberty International; LaGuardia (approx. 2 hr.). Albany Airport (approx. 2 hr.).

🛏 $$$ **Inn at the Falls,** 50 Red Oaks Mill Rd., Poughkeepsie (© **800/344-1466** or 845/462-5770; www.innatthefalls.com).

Cooking Schools for Travelers

The Inn at Essex

Getting Inn with the Chefs

Essex Junction, Vermont

The New England Culinary Institute doesn't know what an ivory tower is. Since the school was founded in 1980, the cornerstone of its degree program has been to provide a load of real-world restaurants where its students can work on the front lines. One of their finest "labs" is the Inn at Essex. At this colonial-style white-clapboard resort on 20 acres (8 hectares) in the Green Mountains of Vermont, not far from the mellow shores of Lake Champlain, NECI students run two acclaimed restaurants: the fine-dining Butler's Restaurant and the casual Tavern. For the inn's guests, there's another draw—NECI chef-instructors lead a host of cooking demonstrations and hands-on classes on site.

Sure, the resort also offers golf, tennis, a swimming pool, and other resort amenities, but the specially outfitted demonstration theater (a 10-person private dining room) signals how important these culinary classes are to the resort. Their on-site gift shop sells professional kitchen tools alongside the usual maple sugar candies and other Vermont souvenirs, and the resort's gardens showcase fresh herbs and vegetables. It fully earns its marketing tag line, "Vermont's Culinary Resort."

Wednesdays through Sundays, they almost always offer at least one class, from 1 to 2 hours in length. These aren't just cutesy frippery but serious small-group classes that range from a knife skills primer to a sushi-making lesson, a seasonal soup workshop, a lecture on healthy eating, a crash course in sauces, or special holiday-oriented recipe bashes. Even better is the Chef "Inn" Training concept, where you get to help cook your own three-course dinner with a skilled chef-instructor. Best of all are the 3-day Culinary Boot Camps, with an intensive 5½-hour class each day; it's limited to six participants and held only a few times a year, so scope it out and book in advance.

All of these culinary activities require a separate fee. Like the two restaurants, they are open as well to visitors who aren't staying at the inn. Prebooking is highly advisable, as some of the classes do sell out.

ⓘ 70 Essex Way, Essex Junction (✆ **800/ 727-4295** or 802/878-1100; www.vtculinary resort.com).

✈ Burlington International (7 miles/ 11km).

🛏 $$ **The Inn at Essex,** 70 Essex Way, Essex Junction (✆ **800/727-4295** or 802/878-1100; www.theinnatessex.com). $$ **The Willard Street Inn,** 349 S. Willard St., Burlington (✆ **800/577-8712** or 802/ 651-8710; www.willardstreetinn.com).

The Greenbrier Culinary Arts Center

Resorting to the Kitchen

White Sulphur Springs, West Virginia

In 1778, when the Greenbrier first opened as a spa resort in the mountains of West Virginia, its upper-class guests weren't interested in cooking—they had servants to do that sort of thing (mostly slaves, in fact, this being the antebellum South). It took 2 centuries of changing times and tastes before the Greenbrier—now a 6,500-acre (2,632-hectare) National Historic Landmark—added cooking classes into the rich mix of recreational activities for guests. That mix today includes an almost bewildering array of golf (three courses), tennis, fishing, shooting, rafting, kayaking, horseback riding, swimming, hiking, bowling, movies, billiards, horseshoes, falconry, and croquet, but the cooking classes are nevertheless more popular than ever.

Launching this program in 1977 was a prescient move; someone at the Greenbrier must have guessed that cooking would develop into a serious hobby for many folk among the resort's well-heeled clientele. With a huge brigade of skilled chefs already on site to run the Greenbrier's three cafes and elegant main dining room, all the talent required is right on hand. Held in an up-to-date professional kitchen, an ongoing series of hands-on classes is scheduled 3 or 4 days a week from late May through November. Class time is from 9:30am to 1:30 pm, which of course leaves time for dining on what you've just cooked. With only 12 students per class, there's plenty of one-on-one instruction. Different classes cover topics such as baking and pastry, hors d'oeuvres, dinner parties, family suppers, or cooking with fresh ingredients. Greenbrier conducts 2-hour afternoon classes for children throughout the summer as well.

A few times a year, the Greenbrier invites celebrity chefs to conduct more intensive 3-day workshops. Anne Willan, for example, who founded the renowned La Varenne cooking school in France, has come to run a 3-day class on classical French techniques; Louisiana Cajun chef John Folse of Lafitte's Landing taught a workshop on how to cook with cast iron; there's also a popular barbecue workshop led by barbecue notables such as Steve Raichlen or Ray Lampe ("Dr. BBQ"). Greenbrier chefs also lead a multiday cooking course called Greenbrier Gourmet, which focuses on signature dishes from the Greenbrier's classically inspired main dining room menu. The course fee is separate from the cost of accommodations at the resort.

ⓘ Greenbrier Culinary Arts Center (✆ **800/ 228-5049**).

✈ Greenbrier Valley Airport (scheduled service from Atlanta and Cleveland; 7 miles/11km).

🚂 White Sulphur Springs (21 miles/ 33km).

🛏 $$$ **The Greenbrier,** 300 W. Main St. (✆ **800/453-4858;** www.greenbrier.com).

Strewn Winery Cooking School
The Food-Wine Connection
Niagara-on-the-Lake, Ontario

In Ontario's premier wine region, just north of Niagara Falls, vineyard touring and gourmet restaurants make a natural pairing. But the Strewn Winery—known for its flavorful Merlots, Cabernet Sauvignons, Rieslings, Chardonnays, Gewürztraminers, and ice wines—is further distinguished by its excellent Provençal-style restaurant, Terroir La Cachette, and the Strewn Winery Cooking School.

As you might suspect, the school's director, Jane Langdon, is married to the winery's winemaker, Joe Will. Naturally the program focuses on the relationship between food and wine, from finding appropriate wine pairings or cooking recipes using wine. The Strewn school advocates the use of local ingredients in season, from the summer's first tender strawberries to the ripe peaches of summer to the apples of autumn. (You can even pick herbs for cooking in the school's on-site herb garden.) Classes run from January through November, and the course recipes reflect the season. Students work in teams of two in a fully outfitted teaching

The Strewn Winery Cooking School in Niagara-on-the-Lake.

kitchen, then move to the attached dining room to savor their creations. The classroom and dining room both have large windows to let in floods of sunlight and wide views of the surrounding green vineyards—you'll never forget you're in the heart of wine country.

One-day classes are held most Saturdays; several of these are designated for "couples," which doesn't necessarily mean romantic partners (it's a fun mother-daughter activity or a great way for college roommates to reconnect). Once a month, the school operates a 2-day culinary weekend, which includes visits to local farmers and a wine tasting at Strewn. Then, starting in late May, monthly 5-day cooking workshops include the hands-on cooking classes supplemented by visits to food markets and artisanal food producers, wine tastings, breakfasts and lunches, and a Wednesday-night dinner at a top local restaurant (these are also bundled into a package with accommodations at the Harbour House Hotel; see below) Given that the winery schedules its own tours and tastings too, there's something happening here just about all the time. For a wine lover who's eager to cook, or a cook who is curious about wine, it's a heavenly match.

ⓘ 1339 Lakeshore Rd., RR3, Niagara-on-the-Lake (© **905/468-1229;** www.winecountrycooking.com).

🛏 $$$ **Harbour House Hotel,** 85 Melville St. (© **866/277-6677** or 905/468-4683; www.harbourhousehotel.ca). $$ **Riverbend Inn,** 16104 Niagara River Pkwy. (© **888/955-5553** or 905/468-8866; www.riverbendinn.ca).

7 Places to Eat in . . . Santa Fe, New Mexico

Remember all the foodie buzz this city generated in the late 1980s and early 1990s, when creative southwestern cuisine was the Next Big Thing? Well, things have finally simmered down, which means that Santa Fe's chefs are now able to break out of lockstep and branch out in new directions. The adobe precincts around the Plaza in downtown Santa Fe may look quaintly historic, but its dining scene is anything but stuck in the past.

Among the most romantic spots in town is adobe-arched, tin-ceilinged 107 **Trattoria Nostrani** (304 Johnson St.; © **505/983-3800;** www.trattoria nostrani.com), where Nelli Maltezos and Eric Stapelman honor northern Italian culinary traditions with specialties such as pumpkin ravioli, roasted quail with sweet Italian sausage and soft polenta, or a grilled rack of lamb with potatoes and artichokes and a black truffle reduction. At 108 **Anasazi Restaurant** (113 Washington Ave.; © **505/988-3236;** www.innoftheanasazi.com), the pueblo-esque contemporary wood-floored dining room of downtown's renowned Inn of the Anasazi, chef Oliver Ridgeway focuses on seasonal ingredients, coming up with imaginative combinations such as Hawaiian tuna with a wasabi-nut crust, or veal medallions glazed in mole sauce with asparagus, morels, and elephant garlic. Local sourcing is a passion for chef Brian Knox, at 109 **Aqua Santa** (51 W. Alameda St.; © **505/982-6297**). Working out of an open kitchen in this tiny, sought-after spot, the gregarious Knox changes his menu continually, bringing out the deepest flavors in dishes like Tuscan bean soup with white-truffle oil, or a slow-braised lamb ragout flavored with hazelnuts and pecorino. A little farther southeast of the Plaza, the restored Borrego House, a low-slung ranch house built in 1756, is the setting for elegant 110 **Geronimo** (724 Canyon Rd.; © **505/982-1500;** www.geronimo

Behind the scenes at Trattoria Nostrani.

restaurant.com), which still defines the casual sophistication of Santa Fe–style cuisine at its height. The menu here puts a southwestern spin on dishes like grilled mahimahi pineapple salad, the peppery elk tenderloin, or mesquite-grilled lobster tails.

At jovial 111 Café Pasqual's (121 Don Gaspar St.; © **505/983-9340;** www.pasquals.com), diners tuck into dishes like grilled chipotle prawn tostadas, Thai green curry, or grilled lamb chop with pomegranate molasses, all made with organic ingredients. Colorful folkloric Mexican murals set the festive mood; there's a communal table for those who'd like to meet new people over a meal. Run by the same family since 1953, the 112 Shed (113½ E. Palace Ave.; © **505/982-9030;** www.sfshed.com) occupies nine tiny rooms around a vine-shaded courtyard; it's famous for its spicy chilies, locally grown exclusively for the Shed. Sample the heat in dishes like chili verde con papas, green chili chicken corn chowder, or the red chili enchilada plate topped with a fried egg.

And when you've had your fill of high-end dining rooms, hike over to Guadalupe Street to the roadside stand 113 Bert's Burger Bowl (235 N. Guadalupe St.; © **505/982-0215**), in business since 1954. Bert's lays claim to having invented the green chili cheeseburger; they serve a powerfully meaty slab of burger, topped with all the right fresh fixings and delicately golden onion rings on the side. Bert's also does a pretty good job with Santa Fe's other beloved road food, the Fritos pie: a mound of chili with cheese, sour cream, and jalapeños, loaded on top of a bagful of Fritos corn chips.

The scene at Trattoria Nostrani.

✈ Albuquerque (60 miles/96km).

🛏 $$ **Hacienda Nicholas,** 320 E. Marcy St. (© **888/284-3170** or 505/992-8385; www.haciendanicholas.com). $ **Santa Fe Motel and Inn,** 510 Cerrillos Rd. (© **800/930-5002** or 505/982-1039; www.santafemotel.com).

Santa Fe School of Cooking
Doing the Taco-Tamale Two-Step
Santa Fe, New Mexico

Given Santa Fe's reputation as a foodie mecca, somebody was bound to launch a cooking school here sooner or later; that constant stream of gastro-tourists was too perfect a market niche to pass up. It was hardly the first city with a recreational cooking school, opposed to college-level culinary arts degree programs, but the folks who run the Santa Fe School of Cooking made sure they tapped into the city's enormous pool of culinary talent. Several top local chefs have done a turn as guest instructors, and the school also runs frequent gourmet walking tours around town, to help visitors sample a number of restaurants in a short time. It's a natural symbiosis that works well.

The SFSC's classes are generally single-session events that last 2 to 3 hours. They take place in the mornings and afternoons, leaving your nights free for dining around town. Most days of the week there's something on tap, so even if you're only in town for a couple of days, you should be able to fit one in. As you'd expect, the emphasis is very much on Southwestern food. Various classes focus on special regional dishes such as chili, salsa, tamales, fajitas, tapas, or mole sauces; there's a class on Native American foods, one on the wines of New Mexico, another on cooking light Mexican food, another on contemporary Southwest Cuisine. One of the most fun classes

is Farm Fresh and Local, where each participant is challenged to cook with a "mystery box" of seasonal produce from a local organic farm, Los Poblanos Organics. The school is handily located in the heart of Santa Fe's historic downtown, just steps off the Plaza.

Plan ahead and you may also be able to take advantage of the school's periodic weeklong courses. The New Mexico Culture and Cuisine Tour, for example, takes place during harvest season. Students spend a day on a farm, helping to harvest produce that they will later turn into a meal. The Outdoor Lover's Culinary Adventure Week combines outdoor sports with classes that focus on healthy cooking strategies. Packages are offered in conjunction with leading local hotels such as the Inn on the Alameda and La Posada de Santa Fe (see below)—another example of symbiosis at work.

ⓘ 116 W. San Francisco St. (ⓒ **800/982-4688** or 505/983-4511; www.santafeschool ofcooking.com).

🛏 $$$ **Inn on the Alameda,** 303 E. Alameda St., Santa Fe (ⓒ **800/289-2122** or 505/984-2121; www.innonthealameda. com). $$$ **La Posada de Santa Fe Resort & Spa,** 330 E. Palace Ave. (ⓒ **800/727-5276** or 505/986-0000; www.rockresorts. com).

Maverick Farms

Back to the Land

Valle Crucis, North Carolina

This small upland vegetable farm in the Blue Ridge Mountains of North Carolina began supplying produce to local restaurants in the mid-1970s, during the earliest days of the back-to-the-land movement. Several decades later, however, the operation faced encroaching real estate and the same economic uncertainties as many other small family farms—until the owner's daughters Hillary and Alice Brooke Wilson came to the rescue in 2004. Enlisting like-minded food fanatics Tom Philpotts, Sara Safransky, and Leo Gaev, they dedicated their new enterprise to ideals like "experimenting with human-scale farming techniques," "transforming food and farming practices," and "reclaiming the pleasures of eating and sharing meals in a culture overrun by industrial agriculture and flavorless food." Registering themselves as a nonprofit educational enterprise, they wanted a fresh brand to suit their new lofty purpose and renamed their cooperative Maverick Farms.

Maverick still sells vegetables to local restaurants. But now they also run a local CSA (community supported agriculture) program; mentor young farmers; set up camps to introduce teenagers to farming; build a passive solar greenhouse; offer occasional three-course organic farm dinners; and run a small bed-and-breakfast operation from the three bedrooms of their two-story, 125-year-old gray frame farmhouse. Guests are welcome to lounge on the wraparound porch or in hammocks down by the creek, but they can also help in the gardens or the orchard, weeding or gathering eggs or harvesting herbs, fruit, and vegetables. (You can use your farm labor to pay for part of your room or arrange other kinds of barter as well.) Paying guests help underwrite the farm's activities, but they also allow the Maverick mavericks to share their vision with curious visitors.

The farm dinners, served in the roomy large-windowed dining room, are wonderful events with live music, linen tablecloths, and candlelight. Menus feature the best organic ingredients, either from the farm itself or from neighboring growers. Some past dinners have had a Tuscan theme, with rosemary focaccia and rabbit pâté or butternut ravioli with sage-butter sauce; a Mexican theme, including tacos with braised chard and avocado salsa or grilled steak with chili salsa; or a harvest-time theme, featuring cider-glazed pork roast with pear chutney or sweet potato flan. If a farm dinner isn't scheduled during your stay, the Maverick folks will happily steer you toward some excellent local restaurants that serve Maverick produce, where you can experience the same interwoven web of food and farm.

ⓘ 410 Justus Rd., Valle Crucis (☏ **828/963-4656;** www.maverickfarm.com).

✈ Asheville (95 miles/153km).

Blackberry Farm

Cream of the Crop

Walland, Tennessee

Luxury resort or farm stay? It's up to you. On the one hand, you can visit Blackberry Farm to be pampered in its luxurious estate guest rooms, suites, and cottages; eat your meals in either of two acclaimed onsite restaurants; lounge in the spa; or fly-fish, horseback ride, or sail in a hot-air balloon over the dreamy Smoky Mountain landscape. On the other hand, you can time your visit to coincide with demonstrations by guest chefs such as Grant Achatz, Nancy Silverton, or David Chang; take cooking classes; spend the day with the on-site cheese maker or head gardener; stroll around the fruit and nut orchards; forage for mushrooms, berries, paw paws, and wild greens; or visit pastures full of sheep, poultry, and honeybee hives.

This upscale 4,200-acre (1,701-hectare) Smoky Mountain estate includes a serious sustainable farm, where the symbiosis of livestock, crops, insects, and soil has been conceived in the most organic ways. Notice, for example, how they rotate the sheep from pasture to pasture, and move the chickens about in rolling henhouses, to aid fertilization and pest control. On-site artisanal workshops include a butcher, bakery, creamery, jam kitchen, and salumeria where the farm's products are processed, along with meats and produce from neighboring farms. A significant portion of the food in the restaurants comes right from the farm, from handmade ewes-milk cheeses to golden-yolked eggs, from exquisite honey to apple cider, from crisp radishes and tender collard greens to hazelnuts—even black truffles that have begun to grow on the roots of the orchard's hazelnut trees.

For an intense agricultural experience, book a room in the Farmhouse, a white-washed frame house (new, but made with wood reclaimed from older farm structures), across the road from the fieldstone Main House. Here you'll also find The Barn, an adventurous fine-dining restaurant in a relocated 18th-century Amish barn, where chef Peter Glander creates multicourse set menus from the farm's bounty. Glander's cooking has been dubbed Foothills Cuisine, for the way it blends country traditions and farm-fresh produce with sophisticated culinary techniques. The Barn also contains the demonstration kitchen where cooking classes, farm demonstrations, and other culinary events take place; many of the on-site food artisans set up shop in the nearby Larder. Of course, while you're here, you'll also want to try out a meal in the relaxed Main House dining room.

The resort's owner, Sam Beall, is a trained chef, which no doubt explains the resort's emphasis on food. But Blackberry has also been his family's farm since 1976, and his stewardship of the landscape shines through everywhere. He could have made Blackberry just another luxury resort. Instead he has let the farm flourish around it—and that's what makes his place so special.

ⓘ 1471 West Millers Cove Rd., Walland (☏ **800/648-4242** or 865/984-8166; www.blackberryfarm.com).

✈ Knoxville (18 miles/29km).

117 Farm Stays

Fairburn Farm Culinary Retreat & Guesthouse

Slow Fooding the Valley

Duncan, British Columbia

If Slow Foodists ran the world, every resort would be like Fairburn Farm—a rambling farmhouse B&B set on a bountiful 53-hectare (130-acre) farm. Instead of golf, tennis, and a spa, Fairburn offers its guests cooking classes, mushroom-foraging expeditions, bread-making seminars, and tours of the cheese-making facility, where artisans create fresh mozzarella using milk from the farm's Italian water buffaloes. You'll participate in tastings at local vineyards or cideries, visit the Duncan farmers' market to buy ingredients for tonight's dinner. You'll roam around the garden, gathering herbs and vegetables, or wander through the old apple orchard where San Clemente goats and Navajo Churro sheep graze. By the time you leave, you'll have explored the Cowichan Valley *terroir* in every dimension.

The center of energy around here is the superbly outfitted kitchen, the domain of cooking teacher Mara Jernigan, who's also one of British Columbia's leading culinary activists. Here she conducts weekly cooking classes and invites guest chefs in to do demonstrations; in the summer especially there's a full program of food-related events, timed to the cycles of the season and harvest. (Call

Fairburn Farm Culinary Retreat & Guesthouse in British Columbia.

The grounds at Fairburn Farm sprawl across 130 acres.

ahead or check the website to book a visit to coincide with special events.)

The white clapboard farmhouse itself is a beautifully preserved example of a frontier homestead. Founded in 1884, the farm has high ceilings, antique moldings, tiled fireplaces, and a broad porch that affords sweeping valley views. Each room is individually decorated in lovely, almost Quaker-inspired simplicity; all have modern en suite bathrooms, and some even have Jacuzzi tubs. A hearty breakfast is included in the room rates; overnight guests can also dine here Thursday through Saturday nights, with four- or seven-course menus focused on local and regional organic foods. The six-course Sunday lunches served in summer out on the veranda are leisurely relaxed affairs reminiscent of a weekly family feast on a traditional Italian farm.

You're welcome to stay here simply as a guest, without dining in; you can dine and stay overnight without availing yourself of the cooking program. But it's the cooking program that really makes this such a special place; it's a way of connecting all the dots from farm to table, one thoughtful dot at a time.

ⓘ 3310 Jackson Rd., Duncan (✆ **250/746-4637**; www.fairburnfarm.bc.ca).

✈ Victoria (57km/35 miles).

Philipkutty's Farm

The Real Coconut Grove

Kerala, India

Staying at Philipkutty's Farm is a luxuriously exotic yet rustic experience. You'll eat sumptuous Indian feasts in a thatched-roof pavilion. You'll sleep in a waterfront villa on a peaceful backwater island, cooled only by the breezes off the lake, with bananas, mangoes, nutmeg, coconut, vanilla, and pepper growing around you. At the same time, you'll be poling in simple *vallam* country boats around the calm silvery waters of Vembanad Lake with a local farming family as hosts—Ana and Vinod Mathew, his mother, Aniamma, and their son, Philip. You'll walk the raised stone dikes by which they've reclaimed this 18-hectare (45-acre) organic farm from the palm-fringed lake, and eat hearty home-cooked meals with the family. You can even organize a culinary vacation that includes daily cooking classes. It's great exposure into the heart of southern Indian culture.

Aniamma's cooking is one of the main attractions here. She happily invites guests into the family's kitchen to watch her and Anu cook. The Mathews follow a Syrian Christian diet, featuring a lot of fish, farm vegetables and fruits, rice, duck, chicken, rice-based breads (*appams* and *iddis*), and chutneys. Some of her specialties include fried *karimeen* (pearlspot fish), fish molee, grilled freshwater prawns taken from the farm's own canals, roasted duck, curd curries, and red-hot Kerala fish curry. And you simply must try toddy, a unique local liquor made right on the farm from the fermented sap of coconut trees.

The farm has only five villas, so guests get a lot of personal attention and interaction from the family if they want it. The furnishings are gracious antiques, yet the bathrooms are completely modern. You'll even have a small refrigerator in your villa to keep cold drinks handy. Clay-tiled floors and varnished wooden ceilings give guest quarters the rustic look of a typical Keralan backwater bungalow; each villa is ringed by its own small veranda—its "sit-out"—painted in a traditional crimson color. There's no television, no room service, no in-room phones—but then, those would only disrupt the homey, tranquil experience of staying at Philipkutty's Farm.

ⓘ Puthankayal Island, Pallivathukal, Ambika Market, Veechor (✆ **91/482/927-6529** or 91/482/927-6530; www.philipkuttysfarm. com).

✈ Kochi International Airport (75km/47 miles).

🚂 Kottayam (20km/12 miles).

3 Meals to Remember

Chef Josh Wolfe's "community table" at Coast in Vancouver (see 45).

El Bulli

We're Off to See the Wizard

Roses, Spain

In 1964, it was a casual Costa Brava beach bar run by a German doctor and his wife, named after their pet bulldogs. By 1997, it was one of the few non-French restaurants in the world to earn three Michelin stars. In 2002 it was anointed the best restaurant in the world by *Restaurant* magazine, an honor repeated in 2006, 2007, and 2008.

What happened in the intervening years was a mop haired Catalonian named Ferran Adrià, who showed up in 1983 to cook during his month's leave from military service and never really left. Adrià—who became chef de cuisine in 1987 and co-owner in 1990—didn't exactly spring up out of nowhere, of course. El Bulli had one Michelin star already before he arrived, for the German owners were serious gastronomes. During their annual 2-month winter closure (back then there wasn't enough low-season business to justify staying open), Dr. Schilling urged his young chefs to do stages in the best restaurants; Adrià's mentors included Joël Robuchon, Michel Bras, and Pierre Gagnaire.

But what elevated El Bulli to the culinary stratosphere was Ferran Adrià's restless curiosity and eagerness to experiment, not only with new ingredients but with new technologies. It's often referred to as "that place that does the foam," but Adrià's innovations include much more than just transforming food into beads and foams and powders and nectars. The winter closure (now 6 months long) gives Adrià and his "development team" time to retreat to a special workshop in Barcelona where they experiment with new tastes and textures and shapes, as well as a chance to visit other great restaurants, a luxury few working chefs get. It also gives Adrià freedom to write cookbooks and

schmooze with celebrities during the off-season, so when you eat at El Bulli, the star chef himself will actually be in attendance.

El Bulli fields over half a million requests a year for reservations, but only some 8,000 lucky diners snag a table. E-mail the restaurant in October (don't telephone) to request a specific date and number of diners for the coming season, and then be patient—you may have to wait weeks for a reply, whether positive or negative. As you can imagine, there are few last-minute cancellations. Open April through early October, El Bulli only serves one meal a day, usually dinner (in spring there are Sun lunches instead), and they're typically closed Monday and Tuesday. Check the website for specifics. *Tip:* If you can't get a table, head instead for Seville, where El Bulli's "greatest hits" are served in the hotel restaurant at **Adrià's Hacienda Benazuza** (Calle Virgen de las Nieves s/n, Sanlúcar la Mayor; ✆ **34/95/570-3344;** www.elbullihotel.com).

For a restaurant this celebrated, El Bulli's wood-beamed, rustic-looking dining room is surprisingly casual and relaxed; of course, every diner there seems completely focused on the food. Each season's menu is different, and shifts daily according to what produce is at its peak. Your best bet is the 30-course tasting menu, a succession of culinary surprises served on eccentric plates and utensils, their crumpled and scooped-out contours designed specifically for each recipe. You'll begin your meal on the terrace with a number of intriguing *amuse-bouches*, then move to your table, where attentive waiters instruct you on how to eat each tiny course—whether to sip it, nibble it, lick it, bite into a gushing center for an explosion of flavor, or simply let it melt dreamily on your tongue. Ever had a cappuccino made of guacamole? Tomato couscous with basil sorbet? A frozen raspberry topped with wasabi? A gelatin of rabbit broth? Calamari lasagna? Fruit pasta? Escargot caviar? Whatever you can imagine, Ferran Adrià has probably created it.

ⓘ Cala Montjoi, Roses, north of Girona (✆ **34/97/215-0 457;** www.elbulli.com).

✈ Barcelona (95 miles/153km).

🛏 $$ **Hotel Historic,** Carrer Bellmirall 4A, Girona (✆ **34/97/222-3583;** www. hotelhistoric.com). $$$ **Mas de Torrent,** Afueras de Torrent, Torrent (✆ **34/97/230-3292;** www.mastorrent.com).

The Fat Duck
The Food Geek
Bray, England

Heston Blumenthal wasn't the first teenager to be gobsmacked by the wonderful food on a family vacation in France. But Blumenthal took that gastro-epiphany to the level of obsession, hunkering down over French cookery books for endless hours. This was in the early 1980s, when Britain was still hung up on the idea that all great chefs came from across the Channel; it was an uphill struggle for a home-schooled cook. Still, he persisted, opening his own restaurant in 1995 in the Berkshire countryside where he'd grown up. In only 5 years, he bagged three Michelin stars; in 2006, he briefly stole the crown of best restaurant in the world from Ferran Adrià.

Being a rank outsider actually may have helped Blumenthal doff Escoffier orthodoxy. Instead he found his personal guru in Harold McGee, whose *On Food and Cooking* excited the novice chef with culinary science. As molecular gastronomy took off, no one was better equipped to ride the bandwagon than Blumenthal. Continually experimenting with freezing, blow-torching, injecting, dehydrating, slow-cooking, what have you, he's still fascinated with manipulating the entire sensory experience of eating—aroma, taste, mouth feel, texture, even sounds (getting just the right brittle crunch in a homemade potato chip, for example).

Set in a plain tan brick building opening straight off the village high street, The Fat Duck is an unpretentious looking place—no faux old English clutter or haute French frippery, just an honest square white room, with rough wooden beams and a bare floor; the only colors are the lemon-yellow chairs and one long yellow oil painting. Clearly, diners come here to focus on the food, not glamorous accoutrements. Whether you order from the three-course prix fixe or the tasting menu (warning: both are pricey), you'll be treated to an ever-changing roster of marvels.

For starters, there might be the intense taste-texture contrast of a Pommery mustard ice-cream accompanied by red

A bill, a plume, and a webbed foot mark the entrance to The Fat Duck.

cabbage gazpacho, or Blumenthal's famous snail porridge, a witty updating of classic French escargots. A roast scallop dish runs the full scale of textures from silky scallop tartare to caviar to white chocolate velouté. Salmon might come poached in licorice gel; a pork loin pot roast with a gratin of truffled macaroni; a filet of beef with pan-fried foie gras, wild mushroom flan, and beet balsamic *jus*. Reserve 2 months in advance. The restaurant is closed Sunday evenings and Mondays.

ⓘ 1 High St., Bray (near Maidenhead; Ⓒ **44/1628/580-333;** www.fatduck.co.uk).

✈ Heathrow (26km/16 miles).

🛏 $ **Langton House,** 46 Alma Rd., Windsor (Ⓒ **44/1753/858299;** www.langtonhouse.uk). $$$ **Oakley Court Hotel,** Windsor Rd., Water Oakley (Ⓒ **44/1753/609988;** www.moathousehotels.com).

St. John

The Offal Truth

London, England

Fergus Henderson is the opposite of a molecular gastronomist—he doesn't make food delicate and tiny, he makes it big and sloppy. Market-fresh produce? He'd rather serve you a slab of freshly slaughtered meat. Reducing foods to their essence? Well, certainly—that is, if you consider internal organs the most essential part of an animal.

And yet cutting-edge food it is, or rather cleaver's-edge food. St. John's chef-owner Henderson is known for what he calls "nose-to-tail" cookery, which finds a way to use all of an animal—neck, feet, tail, liver, heart, the works. His location is spot-on appropriate, in a long-abandoned smokehouse just north of the old meat market at Smithfield. Henderson and his partner Trevor Gulliver didn't do much to tart it up—slap a coat of white paint onto the brick walls, punch a few skylights into the ceiling, install a bar and kitchen appliances, and cart in some square brown wood tables. But somehow, that bare-bones decor is just right for the earthy simplicity of Henderson's cooking.

This nose-to-tail notion would never have caught on, of course, if Henderson wasn't so skilled. For starters, you might have a salad of brawn (boar's flesh) and chicory, of roast bone marrow and parsley, or of cold Middlewhite ham (a Yorkshire breed of swine) with celeriac rémoulade. (For the faint of heart, there are also plain oysters or a smoked mackerel and potato salad.) Then it's on to hearty main courses like roast beef with sea beet and mustard; ox hearts with beets and picked walnut; chitterlings and dandelions; a pheasant and trotter pie (dig the bone sticking out of the crust); or smoked eel, bacon, and clam stew. (Again, there are less daring choices like lemon sole or girolle mushrooms on toast.) With advance order, a private party can even have a roast suckling pig. With delicious simple bread baked in its own bakery, and desserts like Eccles cake, bread pudding, spotted dick, and plum jelly, it's one of the most deeply British menus in town—and at the same time almost dangerously radical. Tasting menu? That's way too effete for St. John, although they do offer a "feasting menu" for larger groups.

There's also an excellent wine list, though it mostly features French wines—you'd expect the bar here to have a substantial selection of real ales, but it's surprisingly limited. The bar is, however, a great place to get a quicker, cheaper sampling of Henderson's cooking, with a blackboard menu that offers several appetizers

Places to Eat in . . . San Sebastian, Spain

Truth to tell, it's barely in Spain at all, but nestled between two green mountains, with a spectacular view of the Bay of Biscay, on the edge of maverick Basque country. Yet this refined Spanish resort—the 19th-century summer home of the Spanish court— has become a destination of choice for European foodies, who flock here to sample an extraordinary cluster of superlative restaurants. It's impossible to account for the concatenation of culinary talent in this relatively small city—even the local version of tapas, *pinxtos,* is executed with flair in every casual bar in town.

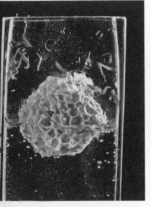
Arzak enlivens traditional Basque cuisine with molecular gastronomy techniques.

The two grand old men of the scene are Juan Mari Arzak at Arzak (Avda. Alcalde Jose Elosegui 273; ✆ **34/943/ 28-55-93;** www.arzak.es), an elegantly modern renovation of his family's century-old tavern, and Pedro Subijana at Akelare (Paseo del Padre Orkolaga 56; ✆ **34/943/21-20- 52;** www.akelare.net), a seaside hexagonal villa on the western edge of San Sebastián. Arzak pays tribute to Basque tradition, but his willingness to experiment, with techniques like quick-freezing ingredients in liquid nitrogen or vaporizing liquids into a powder, inspired his protégé Ferran Adrià of El Bulli fame (see); Arzak set up his own food "laboratory" to explore new techniques long before Adrià did. While the ingredients on Arzak's menu may be familiar—oysters, foie gras, crayfish, squid, pheasant—what Arzak (and now his daughter Elena) does with them continues to amaze diners. Subijana's preparations, on the other hand, define *la nueva cocina vasca* (modern Basque cuisine), a sublime mix of traditional farmstead preparations (beans with bacon, chorizo, and pork ribs or a special *marmitako* fisherman's stew) with innovative dishes like boiled cabbage stuffed with duck and served with purée of celery.

Most Spaniards would consider Juan Iturralde of Juanito Kojua (Puerto 14; ✆ **34/94/342-01-80;** www.juanitokojua.com) as the third pillar of San Sebastian's gastronomic culture. Though Michelin stardom has somehow escaped this snug seafood restaurant in Old Town, with its unpretentious 1950s-vintage pine-paneled decor, it's famous throughout Spain for the reliable excellence of its fresh fish and shellfish, prepared with robust Basque recipes.

As the next generation has come into its own, they've taken those influences in surprising new directions. Chef Andoni Luis Aduriz carries on the high-tech torch at his countryside restaurant  Mugaritz (Aldura Aldea 20, Errenteria; 34/943/52 24 55; www.mugaritz. com), 20 minutes southeast of town. *Restaurant* magazine named it the fourth best restaurant in the world in 2008. His gastronomic flights of fancy can be anything from vacuum-poached baby carrots, baby squid, and carrot blossoms floating in squid broth, to tiny purple Basque potatoes transformed into hard-shelled "pebbles" that melt in your mouth. On the outskirts of town, Martín Berasategui (Loidi Kalea 4; 34/94/336-64-71; www.martinberasat egui.com) learned his craft from his mother, but what has won him three Michelin stars is a fanatical attention to detail: For a *porrusalda* (eel soup), for example, he collects

Juan Mari and Elena Arzak.

the moisture eels give off when smoked and mixes it back into the savory broth. Berastegui's protégé Raúl Cabrera has caught his first Michelin star at Kursaal (Zurriola Pasealekua 1; 34/94/300 31 62; www.restaurantêkursaal. com), a starkly modern light-filled restaurant overlooking the beach in the Kursaal Convention Centre. Cabrera's recipes playfully explore the deep flavors of his locally grown products. Simplicity seems to have been what scored the star for chef Daniel Lopez at Kokotxa (Campanario 11; 34/94/342 19 04; www.restaurantekokotxa.com), in the Old Town—from the minimalist white decor of his airy dining room, to attentive service, to meticulously cooked small portions of fresh seafood served on stark white plates.

The San Sebastian experience is very much tied to the personalities of these individual chefs, who preside over their small kitchens day after day instead of jetting off to film TV shows or oversee spinoffs. (Many places are closed on Mon, to give the chefs a much-needed day of rest.) Menus change often, according not only to the chefs' inventiveness but also to the seasonality of ingredients, especially seafood.

Note: Reservations, made well in advance, are absolutely essential for all of these restaurants. If you've come this far, you don't want to miss out.

✈ Fuenterrabía (20km/12 miles).

🛏 $$$ **Hotel María Cristina,** Calle Oquendo 1 (34/943/43-76-76; www.westin. com). $$ **Anoeta Hotel,** Paseo de Anoeta 30 (34/943/45-14-99; www.hotelanoeta. com).

In this spare setting, Chef Fergus Henderson gets to the heart, liver, feet, and tail of the matter.

and side dishes (anchovy toast, Welsh rarebit) from the dining room menu.

ⓘ 26 St. John St. (✆ **44/20/7251-0848;** www.stjohnrestaurant.co.uk).

✈ Heathrow (24km/15 miles) or Gatwick (40km/25 miles).

🛏 $$$ **Covent Garden Hotel,** 10 Monmouth St., Covent Garden (✆ **800/553-6674** in the U.S., or 44/20/7806-1000; www.firmdale.com). $$ **B + B Belgravia,** 64-66 Ebury St., Belgravia (✆ **800/682-7808** in the U.S., or 44/20/7734-2353; www.bb-belgravia.com).

Cutting-Edge Kitchens 129

Amador
Kitchen Magician
Langen, Germany

You'd hardly expect to find such an accomplished restaurant in a small town just south of Frankfurt. And judging from that half-timbered 18th-century exterior, you wouldn't expect it to serve such dazzlingly modern food, exquisite tiny sculptures of foam, ice, smoke, and edible lace. But then you might think that Amador—with that Spanish name—must be another Adrià acolyte from Catalonia. Yet even there your expectations would be turned around. Chef-owner Juan Amador was born and raised in Germany (although his parents were Spanish) and trained in German restaurants, including Albert Bouley's much-admired Hotel Waldhorn in Ravensburg.

And talk about fast learners—Amador only opened his eponymous restaurant in 2004, but 3¹/₂ years later he had three Michelin stars to show for his efforts.

Once you get inside that historic building, you find a lovely small dining room (it only seats 36) with mellow golden stone walls and matching butter-yellow table linens and armchairs. Diners can choose between two tasting menus, one of three courses and one of seven courses, but if you order the shorter one, you may end up looking wistfully at the strange and wonderful things being brought to your neighbors' tables. Amador's cooking falls at the gimmicky end of molecular gastronomy—there's the apple-wasabi cream you squeeze out of a toothpaste tube onto beet macaroons, the poached quail egg impaled on a metal rod, the glass jar containing a prawn marinated in barbecue sauce that releases a whoosh of smoke when you lift the lid, the test tube of lobster bisque set alongside the lobster entree, the iced duck liver sprinkled with "space dust." Amador even re-imagines the classic German ham-and-egg sandwich known as *strammer Max*, with tiny toasty roll-ups of egg-filled bread accompanied by glass straws through which you sip an intense shot of bacon-flavored oil. But Amador got his three stars not for magic tricks, but for the vivid flavors that his preparations call forth—as in more straightforward entrees like a robust Aragon lamb cooked with coffee, celeriac, and walnuts, or the tender pigeon breast served with coconut milk, mango, and purple curry spices.

Restaurant Amador's extensive wine list concentrates on Spanish and German wines—not surprising, given the chef's polyglot heritage. In the end, though, Amador isn't Spanish or German, or Asian or Italian or haute French—it is a planet unto itself.

ⓘ Vierhäusergasse 1, Langen (✆ **49/6103/50 27 14;** www.restaurant-amador.de).

✈ Frankfurt (10km/6¹/₄ miles).

🛏 $$$ **Villa Kennedy,** Kennedy Allee 70, Frankfurt (✆ **49/69/717120;** www.villa kennedy.com). $$ **Hotel Robert Mayer,** Robert-Mayer-Strasse 44, Frankfurt (✆ **49/ 69/9709101;** www.arthotel-frankfurt.de).

⟨130⟩ Cutting-Edge Kitchens

WD-50

Lift-Off on the Lower East Side

New York, New York

In 1999, a young chef named Wylie Dufresne started cooking at an edgy little joint called 71 Clinton Fresh Foods on Manhattan's Lower East Side. Seemingly overnight, the gritty, down-at-heel neighborhood became a magnet for Upper East Side diners as well as young hipsters. In 2003, Dufresne moved down the street into his own restaurant, WD-50 (a name concocted from Dufresne's initials plus the restaurant's street address), and awards have been flowing in ever since.

Wylie Dufresne—who first rose through the ranks in Jean-George Vongerichten's restaurant empire (see ⟨405⟩)—may not have been solely responsible for the sudden gentrification of the neighborhood, but his innovative cooking sure helped to define it as a place of fresh ideas and casual sophistication. Occupying what was once a grubby bodega, WD-50 is a stylish space filled with blond wood, whiskey-colored leather, black iron, abstract white-glass-and-copper light fixtures, and a dramatic

113

deep-blue backdrop. The real art, though, is on the plates—tiny, meticulously arranged assemblages that make you rethink all your notions about food.

Although Dufresne is often lumped in with the molecular gastronomists—and he does employ their whole battery of techno-methods—what's really intriguing here is how his dishes deconstruct classic preparations from around the world. Instead of a corned beef on rye sandwich, for example, he wraps a strip of corned duck meat around purple mustard and horseradish cream and sets it atop a rye-crisp flatbread. His "pizza pebbles" consist of freeze-dried spheres of Parmesan, tomato, and olive oil alternating with blobs of pepperoni sauce and frills of shiitake mushroom. Eggs Benedict sets cubes of hollandaise sauce, battered and deep-fried, alongside cylinders of custardy gelled egg yolk topped by paper-thin fans of dried ham. His riff on Jamaican jerked pork is a pork rib served with sweet fried plantain, tart rhubarb, and a dribble of savory jerk consommé. His "cyber-egg" is a yolklike pool of carrot-cardamom puree sitting atop a white puddle of firm-set coconut milk—though it looks just like a fried egg, the deep sweetness floods you with surprise. Dufresne's approach is often sculptural—a slender ribbon of foie gras tied in a knot and studded with toasted sesame seeds and dots of sauce—but it's also about finding harmonies between contrasting flavors, as in the briny filet of turbot topped with smoky barbecued lentils, sun-sweetened dried apricots, and thin crisp curls of cauliflower.

Dufresne's reach sometimes exceeds his grasp; occasionally a dish will miss its mark (and doesn't last long on the menu). Still, a meal at WD-50 is always fascinating, and the tasting menu is the way to go (though it's priced around $150—that's when you know you're not in the "old"

One of Wylie Dufresne's many winsome concoctions at WD-50.

Lower East Side). Be sure to save room for dessert, because pastry chef Alex Stupak's brilliant confections are just as inventive and stunningly presented—some diners rave that they're the best part of the meal.

ⓘ 50 Clinton St. (✆ **212/477-2900;** www. wd-50.com).

✈ John F. Kennedy International (15 miles/24km); Newark Liberty International (16 miles/27km); LaGuardia (8 miles/13km).

🛏 $$$ **Carlton Hotel on Madison Avenue,** 88 Madison Ave. (✆ **212/532-4100;** www.carltonhotelny.com). $$ **Washington Square Hotel,** 103 Waverly Place (✆ **800/222-0418** or 212/777-9515; www.washingtonsquarehotel.com).

Alinea

Molecular Gastronomy in Chicago #1

Chicago, Illinois

Why Chicago? Well, why *not* Chicago? This great midwestern metropolis seems to have become the capital of molecular gastronomy these days—who would have expected Carl Sandburg's "City of the Big Shoulders" to go so mad over tiny portions of foam, jelly, and smoke?

The leader of the pack is Grant Achatz, who opened his dazzling restaurant Alinea in May 2004 up in Lincoln Park. The accolades haven't stopped since—he's become a fixture on every magazine's best chef list, and Alinea's been called the best restaurant in the country. With its top-ticket tasting menu, the Grand Tour, priced at $225 without wines, it has also been ranked as the most expensive restaurant in the country.

Before opening Alinea, Achatz—who was previously the chef at Chicago's acclaimed Trio—spent a year honing his craft with culinary innovators like Ferran Adrià (see ⑲) and Thomas Keller (see ㉑), and their influence is clear in the wizardry of his tiny, cunningly composed courses. Achatz gives his menu items the simplest possible one-word names—bean, crab, oyster, guava, tomato, chocolate—but what you get may not even have the same color as that familiar food, let alone the same shape or consistency. "Rhubarb" is a series of tiny pink sculptures that are rhubarb in various forms—liquid, puff, cube, roll, curl, gel. "Tomato" is a long tomato-red squiggle topped with half a dozen different pinwheels and flowers and frills and globules. Morsels of intensely flavored food are delivered on white ceramic pedestals, or impaled on long metal pins, or cradled on frosted glass, or nestled into a scoop of black pottery, or perched on lavender-scented pillows. The menu changes constantly, but you're guaranteed to taste something new here, whether it's ravioli that gushes forth a liquid-truffle filling, bites of tender bison tenderloin encased in crispy potatoes and seasoned with cinnamon, or suspended curls of dehydrated bacon cloaked in butterscotch glaze and apple shavings and sprigs of thyme. What really makes this all work is Achatz's perfectionism, his attention to aroma and texture as well as taste, which elevate it all way beyond mere gimmick.

The dining room perfectly complements the futuristic food—it's a sharply contemporary space in taupe and black, with lots of space between tables, a few dramatic pieces of contemporary art, and large gauze-shaded windows. Service is crisply polished and attentive; a hushed air of awe and wonder pervades the place. Dinner's the only meal served, and it's only served Wednesday through Sunday; phone for reservations, as far ahead as possible.

ⓘ 1723 N. Halsted St. (✆ **312/867-0110;** www.alinea-restaurant.com).

✈ O'Hare International (25 miles/16km).

🛏 $$ **Homewood Suites,** 40 E. Grand St., Chicago (✆ **800/CALL-HOME** [800/225-4663] or 312/644-2222; www.homewoodsuiteschicago.com). $$ **Hotel Allegro Chicago,** 171 N. Randolph St., Chicago (✆ **800/643-1500** or 312/236-0123; www.allegrochicago.com).

Moto

Molecular Gastronomy in Chicago #2

Chicago, Illinois

The paint was barely dry at Alinea before Homaro Cantu, a former sous-chef at Charlie Trotter's (see ⓐ), opened his own culinary laboratory, Moto, in late 2004, out west of the Loop in the Fulton River district. Cantu's Asian-inspired food is even more whacked-out high tech than Achatz's—he does stuff like pumping carbonation into fruit so that it bubbles in your mouth, twining herbs into special patented forks that infuse herbal tastes into the food while you're eating, and printing his menu with food-based inks on edible soy paper so you can eat it once you've ordered.

Cantu's culinary wit makes dining at Moto a mind game as well as a meal. You may start out with a bowl of hot miso soup filled with globules of liquid-nitrogen-frozen egg, which bubble and smoke in the soup. A hot black resin box set on your table contains a piece of sea bass that starts cooking, to be eaten two courses later on. Cantu's version of surf and turf is a sliver of smoked salmon resting on a puddle of sea-salt foam, next to a composed pile of duck breast, duck confit, and foie gras (accompanied by an edible print of M. C. Escher's design in which a sky full of birds morphs into an ocean of fish). Bread crumbs surround a blob of grape gelatin that sheathes a dollop of peanut-butter cream—a deconstructed peanut-butter-and-jelly sandwich. "Nachos and cheese" turns out to be a dessert, with sweet chips of Mexican corn and flan, chocolate granulated to look like ground beef, and grated mango sprinkled on top like Monterey jack cheese.

It's also an interactive experience— diners are instructed to mix and match bites with contrasting flavors, to squeeze a bulb of liquid into their mouths before eating another ingredient, or to pour hot liquid onto something to watch it melt. To get the full three-ring circus, you can order the 20-course Grand Tour (close to $200— but cheaper than Alinea's), though there are also five-course and 10-course options. The dining room's spare black-and-white decor is even more minimalist than Alinea's, but then who needs dramatic decor, with so much entertainment right there on your plate?

ⓘ 945 W. Fulton Market (ⓒ **312/491-0058;** www.motorestaurant.com).

✈ O'Hare International (17 miles/27km).

🛏 $$ **Homewood Suites,** 40 E. Grand St., Chicago (ⓒ **800/CALL-HOME** [800/ 225-4663] or 312/644-2222; www.home woodsuiteschicago.com). $$ **Hotel Allegro Chicago,** 171 N. Randolph St., Chicago (ⓒ **800/643-1500** or 312/236-0123; www. allegrochicago.com).

Schwa

Molecular Gastronomy in Chicago #3

Chicago, Illinois

If Alinea is the overachieving oldest brother and Moto the smart-alecky middle kid, then Schwa is the lovable baby of Chicago's new wave trio. Opened in 2006, this tiny storefront restaurant out in boho Wicker Park only seats 26 diners at a time. Pale green walls and simple black furniture is about it for decor—that and a window in the back wall that lets you look into the cramped kitchen. Sommelier? Wine pairings? Nope, this joint is strictly BYOB. And with a staff of only four, your server tonight will also be the guy who's cooking your meal. But hey, who better to explain what the heck it is you're eating?

Chef-owner Michael Carlson, who carries on a running conversation with diners in between flurries of cooking, makes no secret of his admiration for Grant Achatz, with whom he worked a few years ago at Trio. Though he doesn't have the same state-of-the-art kitchen as Achatz, Carlson employs a lot of the same innovative techniques—emulsifying gels, liquid nitrogen, cryovac, sous-vide. And while he doesn't have Alinea's dizzying assortment of special custom-designed plates, his menu items still look like miniature works of art, stunningly composed on their simple white plates.

The thing that really matters, of course, is that Carlson's food just plain tastes good. For a starter, you might have a teacup of vividly salty consommé made from prosciutto, with a tiny ball of melon bobbing in the bottom; or perhaps you'll get a rich soup of Belgian Chimay cheese, topped with a "head" of Chimay ale emulsion and a warm pretzel knot (there's even a dried sheet of solid mustard to add tang to the pretzel). A salad of divinely flavorful heirloom tomatoes comes topped not only with the tried-and-true tastes of balsamic vinegar and olive oil, but also with a scoop of perky tomato sorbet.

Carlson's sensory imagination sometimes rises to the level of sheer poetry. Cut into a delicate ravioli with your fork and the yolk of a lightly poached quail egg streams out, made even creamier by a touch of ricotta and Parmesan. Briny chunks of quick-pickled Jonah crab comes with alternating bites of earthy celery-root puree. Rare slices of antelope meat, with their juicy gaminess, are dusted with curry powder and then swirled through white chocolate pudding. A cube of toasted brioche oozes the essence of hot, concentrated banana puree.

Schwa (the name comes from a phonetic symbol for an unstressed vowel) has a three-course tasting menu and a nine-course tasting menu; even the nine-course one only costs about half of Alinea's grand tour. And you'll want the nine-course, not only to sample more of Carlson's creative dishes, but also to prolong your stay in this mellow, upbeat spot. Dinner is served Tuesday through Saturday; call for reservations. Just hope one of the guys in the kitchen picks up the phone.

ⓘ 1466 N. Ashland St. (☏ **773/252-1466;** http://schwarestaurant.com).

✈ O'Hare International (15 miles/24km).

🛏 $$ **Homewood Suites,** 40 E. Grand St., Chicago (☏ **800/CALL-HOME** [800/225-4663] or 312/644-2222; www.homewoodsuiteschicago.com). $$ **Hotel Allegro Chicago,** 171 N. Randolph St., Chicago (☏ **800/643-1500** or 312/236-0123; www.allegrochicago.com).

Taillevent

Why Break the Mold?

Paris, France

So what *is* the best restaurant in Paris? Poll 1,000 French gourmets and you'd get no consensus (in fact, you might get 1,000 different answers).

Nevertheless, if what you're looking for is the quintessential classic French dining experience—deeply steeped in the traditions of Escoffier and Brillat-Savarin—you can't beat Taillevent. This small, gracious Right Bank restaurant first opened in post-Occupation 1946, when Paris was intent on recapturing its old glory. Under three generations of the Vrinat family, it has maintained its position ever since at the pinnacle of haute cuisine.

For the price you'll pay at Taillevent (well into the hundreds, whether you're paying in dollars, pounds, or euros), every element of the dining experience should be superlative, and it is. The location is exquisite, an ornate 19th-century aristocratic town house just off the Champs-Elysées, with two dining salons—one oak-paneled with soft lighting and soothing brown upholstery, the other airy and bright with large windows looking onto a garden. Service is unfailingly correct, discreet, and attentive—better yet, warm and welcoming (a virtue all too rare in Parisian restaurants). The wine list is legendarily superb, one of the best in Paris, with a fine sommelier staff to match.

And the food, under chef Alain Solivérès, more than lives up to the setting. While you can still get classic dishes like cream of watercress soup with Sevruga caviar, coquilles St. Jacques, roast Bresse chicken breast, or a beef filet in reduced béarnaise sauce, Solivérès also draws inspiration from the Basque country, Bordeaux, and Languedoc for his daily changing menu. He might slip frogs' legs into a risotto, do a cassoulet with crayfish, or jazz up pan-fried duck liver with caramelized fruits and vegetables. It's by no means the most experimental food in Paris, but it gives that classic menu a healthy freshness and verve. And anyway, culinary innovation is not why you've come to Taillevent.

The death of Jean-Claude Vrinat in early 2008 saddened the gourmet community; his presence in the restaurant every night was one of the things in Paris you could always count on. However, diners report that under the direction of his daughter Valerie, the restaurant hasn't missed a beat; if anything, it has gotten a little sprightlier. Yes, the business expanded a few years ago to add a more casual (and relatively cheaper) alternative, **L'Angle du Faubourg** (193 rue de Faubourg Saint-Honoré; ☎ **33/1/40 74 20 20**), with a wine store **Les Caves Taillevent** next door. Yes, in 2007 Taillevent lost its third Michelin star, which it had held since 1973, a longer three-star run than any restaurant in the world. (They're determined to win it back, of course.) But in the fickle world of haute cuisine, fads come and go; stars rise and fall. Taillevent is a fixture you can count on.

ⓘ 15 rue Lamennais, 8e (☎ **33/1/4495 1501;** www.taillevent.com).

✈ De Gaulle (23km/14 miles); Orly (14km/8²⁄₃ miles).

🛏 $$ **La Tour Notre Dame,** 20 rue du Sommerard, 5e (☎ **33/1/43-54-47-60;** www.la-tour-notre-dame.com). $ **Hotel de la Place des Vosges,** 12 rue de Birague, 4e (☎ **33/1/42-72-60-46;** www.hotelplacedes vosges.com).

Guy Savoy

At the Top of His Game

Paris, France

The year 2002 was a banner year for Guy Savoy. His eponymous restaurant on the Right Bank, close to the Arc du Triomphe, finally won its third Michelin star, and his fellow chefs in Paris added the crowning touch of approval: They voted him chef of the year.

Savoy, who'd first opened the restaurant 15 years earlier, in 1987, had already garnered the French Legion d'Honneur for his culinary prowess; the fact that Michelin was so slow to confer the third star seems inexplicable. Guy Savoy may not be fussing around with foam and liquid nitrogen like the molecular gastronomy crew, but there's no question that his intricate, artfully composed small portions are just as innovative and exciting. He's intrigued by sensory contrasts (he even offers a set menu called Colours, Textures, and Savours), and can go off on delirious tangents, like during autumn mushroom season, when a dozen different types of fungi may crop up all at once on his menus. While he makes extravagant use of truffles, the ultimate luxury ingredient, he also seems fascinated by lentils, the earthiest of peasant food.

Savoy's signature dishes include the silky artichoke and black truffle soup, iced poached oysters, butter-roasted veal sweetbreads, a roast suckling lamb with a spinach-and-mushroom gratin, or delicately spiced crispy sea bass. His famous Colours of Caviar appetizer is a perfect example of how refined Savoy's culinary artistry can be: It's a layered parfait of caviar cream, caviar vinaigrette and green-bean puree with Sevruga caviar, and hot sabayon with Sevruga caviar.

The restaurant's decor reflects the subtlety of his cuisine—a tailored, deliberately understated study in sleek tonal woods, white stone, decorative leather wall insets, and frosted glass panels, with Japanese-like moving dividers to change the dining room layout. (The trademark design was closely replicated for Savoy's only non-Paris outpost, Restaurant Guy Savoy in Las Vegas's Caesar's Palace hotel.)

Like a handful of other top Parisian chefs, Savoy has spun off a number of less-expensive satellite bistros—**Les Boquinistes** near the Pont-Neuf (53 Quai des Grands Agustins; ✆ **33/1/43-25-45-94**), **Le Chiberta** off the Champs-Elysées (3 rue Arsène Houssaye; ✆ **33/1/53-53-42-00**), **La Buitte**

Guy Savoy has earned the French Legion d'Honneur and three Michelin stars.

Chaillot near the **Eiffel Tower** (110 bis, av. Kléber; © **33/1/47-27-88-88**), and the vintage-style rotisserie **L'Atelier Maître Albert** in the Latin Quarter (1 rue de Maître Albert; © **33/1/56-81-30-01**). But while Savoy helped develop the menus, in each place he has installed a young chef trained in his kitchen, whom he encourages to put his or her own stamp on the place. As for Savoy himself, he's not off jetting around the world and making TV shows; he's still in the kitchen on the rue Troyon, honing his craft. That third star *meant* something; he's not letting it slip away.

ⓘ 18 rue Troyon, 17e (© **33/1/4380-4061;** www.guysavoy.com).

✈ De Gaulle (23km/14 miles), Orly (14km/8²⁄₃ miles).

🛏 $$$ **Hôtel Luxembourg Parc,** 42 rue de Vaugirard, 6e (© **33/1/53-10-36-50;** www.luxembourg-paris-hotel.com). $$ **Hôtel Saintonge,** 16 rue Saintonge, 3e (© **44/1/42-77-91-13;** www.saintongemarais.com).

Temples of Gastronomy 136

Restaurant de l'Hôtel de Ville
The Swiss Diplomat
Crissier, Switzerland

In 1996, when the great Frédy Girardet retired, a lot was resting on the shoulders of his longtime assistant, Philippe Rochat. Could he maintain the exacting standards of his mentor? Could he keep all three Michelin stars for this legendary restaurant on the northern outskirts of Lausanne?

But of course, you don't rise to the pinnacle of the restaurant world by leaving anything to chance—Girardet groomed his successor with utmost care, and under Rochet the Restaurant de l'Hôtel de Ville carries on as one of the world's great classical French restaurants. There's no question it's a conservative, Swiss-banker sort of spot—set in a stout mansard-roofed stone building erected in 1929 as Crissier's town hall, and decorated with soft beige walls, thick carpets, and recessed lighting that swaddle you in first-class comfort. Service is seamlessly gracious, and the food is irreproachably marvelous.

With an institution this venerated, change can be risky. With infinite diplomacy, Rochet made a few discreet changes to brighten up the sober decor, and gradually eased new

dishes onto the menu, always following the classical traditions Girardet so fiercely defended against barbarians with blowtorches and canisters of liquid nitrogen. Specialties change frequently, but recent successes have included glazed sweetbreads with wild mushrooms, crawfish in caviar butter, turbot in creamy *vin jeune* sauce with crushed peppercorns, preserved duckling in lemon and spices, and a ragout of fresh quail with young vegetables. The cheese cart features a spectacular choice of cheeses, and the wine list is impeccable (featuring, of course, mostly French wines). One dish diners consistently rave about is a mousse of porcini mushrooms, surmounted by a fan of sliced porcinis, resting in their own cooking juices. When something so simple is so transcendently delicious, the chef has to be doing everything right.

Perhaps the Hôtel de Ville's continued excellence is only to be expected. At these prices, a restaurant should never have an off night (Michelin awards its stars on the basis of consistency as well as brilliance)—why should the departure of the founding chef disturb its well-honed brilliance? Even in 1996, the Restaurant de l'Hôtel de Ville was harkening back to timeless epicurean tradition. All Rochet had to do was step into the shoes of a master—and become a master in his own right.

ⓘ 1 rue d'Yverdon-Crissier (☎ **41/21/634 0505**; www.philippe-rochet.ch).

🚆 Lausanne (20 min. from Geneva).

🛏 $$$ **Hotel Angleterre** (☎ **41/21/ 613-34-34**; www.angleterre-residence.ch).

Le Gavroche

A Second Act

London, England

When the Roux brothers (Michel and Albert) first opened Le Gavroche in 1966, Swinging London was *the* place to be for rock music, fashion, and film—but it was a culinary wasteland. Just emerging from the food shortages of postwar austerity, the city seemed stuck between old-school hotel restaurants and fish-and-chips shops with a flood of cheap Italian, Chinese, and Indian restaurants filling in the gaps. Now here came suave Michel to preside over the clubby yet formal dining room, and brilliant Albert working wonders at the stove. Le Gavroche brought haute French cuisine at last to the British capital, and immediately became the *ne plus ultra* of London dining. When it won its third Michelin star in 1982, it was the first U.K. restaurant ever to hit that height.

Flash forward to the 1990s. A cheeky crop of British chefs—many of them trained under Albert Roux—were opening hot restaurants all over town, reclaiming London for British cookery. As Michel Roux, Jr., who had taken over the kitchen at Le Gavroche in 1991, began to introduce lighter, more modern dishes to uncle Albert's menu, the restaurant hit a bad patch (if you call being demoted from three Michelin stars to two "a bad patch"). Many critics wrote off Le Gavroche, saying it was past its prime.

But in the past few years, Michel's cooking has become a force to contend with, and Le Gavroche is sizzling again. With an ever-changing menu, reflecting the day's market produce, Michel finds cunning ways to preserve and yet update French culinary traditions. Signature dishes include warm foie gras with crispy, cinnamon-flavored crepes; the town's grandest cheese soufflé *(soufflé Suissesse);* and Scottish filet of beef with port wine sauce and truffled macaroni. Truly Gallic dishes include the langoustines and snails with hollandaise sauce, or the lobster mousse in champagne sauce. But after so many years in London, the menu can be forgiven for showing a British side as well, with items like stuffed pig's feet with roasted vegetables, or a roast suckling pig with a confit of golden raisins and shallots.

With so many other fantastic restaurants in London these days, why pay a fortune to dine at Le Gavroche? (At one time, the *Guinness Book of World Records* listed it as the world's most expensive restaurant, although the set lunch menu is surprisingly reasonable, at under £50/$31.) You come because this hushed and gracious dining room, with its green leather walls and tufted banquettes, still scintillates with old-world elegance. Service is faultless without being stuffy; men are required to wear jackets; only the host of the dining party gets a menu that lists prices. It's one of the last of a vanishing breed, but a dinosaur? No way.

ⓘ 43 Upper Brook St. (✆ **44/20/7408 0881;** www.le-gavroche.co.uk).

✈ Heathrow (24km/15 miles) or Gatwick (40km/25 miles).

🛏 $$$ **22 Jermyn St.**, 22 Jermyn St., St. James (✆ **800/682-7808** in the U.S., or

44/20/7734-2353; www.22jermyn.com). $$ **Vicarage Private Hotel,** 10 Vicarage Gate, South Kensington (✆ **44/20/7229-4030;** www.londonvicaragehotel.com).

The River Café
The Italian Job
London, England

The most memorable restaurant experiences are never just about the food. Part of the pleasure of dining at the River Café, still trendy decades after it opened in 1988, is seeing and being seen. Another part is simply being in such a beautiful place, either on the terrace overlooking the Thames or inside, where floods of light pour through huge windows into a streamlined steel-on-white design by co-owner

The food and the view are superb at the River Café, overlooking the Thames in London.

Ruth Rogers's husband, international architect Richard Rogers. Friendly, attentive, expert service adds even more to your sense of well-being, proving that a restaurant doesn't require you to put on a suit and tie to make you feel special.

But there's no question, the food must also be superlative. And on that score, the River Café delivers too, serving what most diners consider the best Italian cuisine in London. Why Italian? Because Ruth Rogers and her partner Rose Gray set out simply to re-create the kind of cuisine they'd enjoyed in the Italian countryside—divinely simple farmhouse meals with the freshest ingredients. Don't expect a locavore bias here: The River Café ships in ingredients from all over the world—first-spring asparagus harvested in Andalusia and arriving in London within the day, tiny bulbs of fennel zipped across the Channel from France, live scallops and langoustines taken by divers in the icy North Sea, and a daily shipment from Italy that may include anything from artichokes to zucchini, whatever's at its peak. Britain's own rich bounty appears on the menu as well, in the form of pheasant, grouse, and wild Scottish salmon. That's not to say it isn't seasonal—the *bufala mozzarella* starter, for example, may come with purslane and young English broad beans in summer, but shaved fennel and toasted pine nuts in autumn; the wood-roasted Dover sole comes with roasted carrots and plum tomatoes in July, but slow-cooked fennel and *cima du rape* in November. The River Café chefs (Jamie Oliver is one of many culinary stars who started out here) tend to do a lot of slow roasting or chargrilling to emphasize the deep flavors of those stellar ingredients. The cheese selection is outstanding, as is the wine list, which, except for its champagnes, is all Italian.

Nowadays, it's easy to forget what an influential institution the River Café has been; so many other restaurants have jumped on the Tuscan bandwagon since then, and Rogers and Gray's numerous cookbooks have also helped broadcast their recipes and techniques. Still, this is where it all started, and it still outshines all those lower-priced imitators. With food this deceptively simple, it's all about sourcing, and nobody does it better.

(i) **Thames Wharf,** Rainville Rd., W6, Hammersmith (© **44/20/7386-42001;** www.rivercafe.co.uk).

✈ Heathrow (24km/15 miles) or Gatwick (40km/25 miles).

🛏 $$$ **Covent Garden Hotel,** 10 Monmouth St., Covent Garden (© **800/ 553-6674** in the U.S., 44/20/7806-1000; www.firmdale.com). $$ **B+B Belgravia,** 64-66 Ebury St., Belgravia (© **800/682-7808** in the U.S., or 44/20/7734-2353; www.bb-belgravia.com).

---

139 Temples of Gastronomy

Le Bernardin

Fishing for Compliments

New York, New York

Most menus are divided into different sections for different courses—appetizers, fish, pasta, entrees, desserts, or something along those lines. But not Le Bernardin—Eric Ripert divides things into Almost Raw, Barely Touched, and Lightly Cooked. He doesn't have a fish course, because *every* course is a fish course. Oh, except for one more section, titled Upon Request, where Ripert sticks a few dishes for people who don't like seafood. He might as well have called it If You Must.

Even people who don't normally like seafood would be well advised to go with the fish at Le Bernardin, because Eric Ripert's fish cookery is a revelation. Part of this is a matter of sourcing—Ripert's famously skilled at buying the best and freshest seafood in Manhattan. (He does, however, make a point not to deal in endangered species—you'll find no Chilean sea bass, grouper, shark, swordfish, or wild bluefin tuna here.) But more than that, it's because Le Bernardin focuses on the fish. Ripert and his chefs know the various denizens of the sea so well, they have developed distinct methods of cooking to best enhance the essential flavors of each species, as well as a different list of suitable accompaniments for each. Sauces and sides never overwhelm the fish, only enhance it. You may get, for example, a spectrum of Kunamoto oysters, each one delicately calibrated to a different level of spiciness than one next to it. A thinly sliced geoduck comes marinated in smoky Peruvian-style spices, paired with dried sweet corn. Lightly sautéed calamari come stuffed with silky sweet prawns and shiitake mushrooms. Grilled salted cod salad is served with a piquant pesto of arugula and lemon confit. Crispy black bass comes with a velvety braised celery and parsnip custard and a vivid sauce of Iberico ham and green peppercorn.

Since the brother-and-sister team of Gilbert and Maguy le Coze moved their Parisian restaurant Le Bernardin to New York in 1987 (Gilbert was the chef, Maguy the restaurateur), it has been at the forefront of Manhattan dining. No other Manhattan restaurant has held onto its four-star rating from the *New York Times* as long as Le Bernardin has. The decor is professional and upscale, trimmed in glossy wood with a serious art collection and enormous floral arrangements—not stunning in its own right, but a sleek setting for stunning cooking. Maguy is still co-owner; when Gilbert died in 1995, it was she who hand-picked Ripert to carry on her brother's legacy. He's done more than that—he's made Le Bernardin possibly the best seafood restaurant in the world.

ⓘ 155 W. 51st St. (☎ **212/554-1515;** www.le-bernardin.com).

✈ John F. Kennedy International (24km/15 miles); Newark Liberty International (27km/16 miles); LaGuardia (13km/8 miles).

🛏 $$ **The Lucerne,** 201 W. 79th St. (☎ **800/492-8122** or 212/875-1000; www.thelucernehotel.com). $ **Milburn Hotel,** 242 W. 76th St. (☎ **800/833-9622** or 212/362-1006; www.milburnhotel.com).

Temples of Gastronomy 140

Nobu Fifty-Seven

Transcending Sushi

New York, New York

To call Nobu Matsuhisa a sushi chef is to miss the point. Yes, the dishes served at his Nobu restaurants—all 18 of them, in carefully chosen capitals of chic worldwide—have their grounding in Japanese cuisine. But ever since 1987, when he first wowed diners at his original restaurant in Beverly Hills, it became clear that he was operating in his own culinary universe.

New York's first **Nobu** down in Tribeca (105 Hudson St.; ☎ **212/219-0500**) quickly became Manhattan's most-impossible-to-get reservation after it opened in 1994. Frankly, the opening of the more casual **Nobu Next Door** (✆ **212/334-4445**) didn't make it much easier. But things are even more exclusive at this uptown version, which opened in 2005 in the Time-Warner Center alongside such other star restaurants as Thomas Keller's Per Se and Gray Kunz's Café Gray (which may make 57th St. the world's most concentrated block of culinary fabulousness). The multicourse *omakase,* or chef's choice, menus are like a joyride through chef Nobu's "new-style Japanese" cuisine, where the sushi tradition in which he was first trained meets and marries with the foods of Peru and Argentina, where he worked in his 20s.

Nobu's classic dishes include Tiradito Nobu-style, miso-glazed black cod, a golden-battered rock shrimp tempura, and a lobster ceviche spiked with cilantro; this disciplined kitchen executes the simplest dish with flair. But the place outshines its many imitators with its creative pairing of flavors—yellowtail sashimi may come with jalapeño pepper, halibut cheeks with wasabi pepper sauce, or Kumamoto oysters with a Maui onion salsa. And who ever tried avocado or pumpkin tempura before Nobu?

The heart of his cuisine is not just the raw fish bar but the wood-burning oven and the hibachi table, which call out deeper savory notes in the food. In fact, if you just want to focus on hibachi dining, there's an entire hibachi section on the menu, where instead of the full tasting menu you can choose a sampling of hibachi-grilled seafood. Another smart way to sample Nobu's cuisine for less is to eat in the lounge, where you can order most of the regular menu's hot and cold appetizers as bar food.

The design of this two-story restaurant definitely telegraphs Big Deal Restaurant, with sinuous curving walls, abalone-shell

The name Nobu is synonymous with superlative sushi.

chandeliers, sliced bamboo stalks in terrazzo tiles, scorched ash tables, Japanese quilt fabric, and a backdrop of stacked sake barrels over the ground-floor bar. You worked hard to get that reservation; you should feel the place is worth it from the minute you walk in—and you do. But just wait until the food arrives.

ⓘ 40 W. 57th St. (✆ **212/757-3000;** www. noburestaurants.com/fiftyseven).

✈ John F. Kennedy International (24km/ 15 miles); Newark Liberty International (27km/16 miles); LaGuardia (13km/8 miles).

🛏 $$$ **Carlton Hotel on Madison Avenue,** 88 Madison Ave. (✆ **212/532-4100;** www.carltonhotelny.com). $$ **Washington Square Hotel,** 103 Waverly Place (✆ **800/222-0418** or 212/777-9515; www. washingtonsquarehotel.com).

The French Laundry
Hold the Starch
Yountville, California

Mention that you've just come back from Napa Valley, and your foodie friends will ask breathlessly, "Did you eat at The French Laundry?" If you did, of course, you'll be expected to deliver a bite-by-bite account. They deserve a *little* vicarious pleasure.

Thomas Keller's cooking doesn't follow the orthodoxies of classical French haute cuisine, but that's irrelevant—this cuisine is as haute as you can get. Opened in 1994 in a 19th-century stone saloon (later used as a French-style steam laundry, hence the name), The French Laundry serves what Keller describes as American cuisine with French influences—American because of its love of local produce and its riffs on down-home classics, but French for its intricate preparations and dazzling plate presentations. (As a young chef, Keller trained at both Taillevent and Guy Savoy.) Keller's cuisine is ultimately unclassifiable,

though—which is to say, brilliant on its own terms.

When you come to The French Laundry, you put yourself in the chef's hands: The nine-course tasting menu is your only option, and it changes not just every day, but twice a day, with no ingredients repeated. There's also a separate tasting menu for vegetarians, and it's far more than a mere afterthought.

At first you may be surprised by how tiny each course looks as it is set in front of you—Keller wants you to long for "just one more bite of that"—but then the next course comes and wows you anew. It's all so deeply flavored, so rich and satisfying, you won't leave the table hungry. Although you can't count on any particular dish appearing when you're there, some of the dishes that have made Keller famous include "oysters and pearls" (pearl tapioca

Thomas Keller's signature "oysters and pearls" at The French Laundry.

with Island Creek oysters), "tongue in cheek" (a sliced round of braised lamb tongue and tender beef cheeks), and "macaroni and cheese" (butter-poached Maine lobster with creamy lobster broth and orzo with mascarpone cheese), as well as the wafer cone filled with salmon tartare that opens every meal.

The dining room has a romantic country inn look, with cream-colored wainscoting, wallpapers in muted sage and mustard tones, softly pleated table linens, fresh flowers everywhere, and French Empire chairs upholstered in deep royal blue. A meal here is expected to take hours—consider it dining as theater, with many courses finished table side, and laid in front of you on unique plates designed to show off each highly wrought portion. Your waiter becomes an usher, then an actor, and eventually your best friend for the duration of the meal.

Keller has branched out, opening two more casual outposts in Yountville

(**Bouchon,** 6534 Washington St.; ✆ **707/944-8037;** and **Ad Hoc,** 6476 Washington St.; ✆ **707/944-2487**) and in New York, their upscale urban sister **Per Se** (10 Columbus Circle; ✆ **212/823-9335**). But only The French Laundry is *The* French Laundry, and you have to give Keller credit—he's never tried to clone it. Reservations are accepted 2 months in advance of the date, starting at 10am California time. Get ready to hit the redial button.

ⓘ 6640 Washington St. (✆ **707/944-2380;** www.frenchlaundry.com).

✈ San Francisco International (68 miles/109km).

🛏 $$$ **Napa River Inn,** 500 Main St., Napa (✆ **877/251-8500** or 707/251-8500; www.napariverinn.com). $$$ **Yountville Inn,** 6462 Washington St., Yountville (✆ **707/944-5600;** www.yountvilleinn.com).

Charlie Trotter's

A Ringside Seat

Chicago, Illinois

In a world of superstar chefs who are forever shuttling back and forth between one high-profile side project and another, Charlie Trotter seems almost quaintly devoted to the high-end Chicago restaurant where he made his name. Yes, he has capitalized on his celebrity by doing TV shows and cookbooks (with almost impossible-to-follow recipes), and he has finally opened branches in Las Vegas and Los Cabos. The gourmet takeout shop in Lincoln Park, Trotter's To Go, was almost a no-brainer. Still, the place where you'll generally find Trotter is at this 20-year-old restaurant, which has won just about every honor the culinary world bestows.

Though Trotter's culinary style can be described as American food with French techniques and Asian influences, it's much more original than that would imply. Trotter doesn't believe in sauces loaded with butter and cream; he does believe in organic and free-range ingredients, which he feels have more vivid flavors than conventionally produced foods. And in general, he seems to get a kick out of surprising diners with new ingredients and arresting presentations. He offers just two options—a vegetable tasting menu and a grand tasting menu—so that he can lead folks through a carefully calibrated succession of flavors. They change daily, but sample

Chef Charlie Trotter presiding over his namesake restaurant in Chicago.

get a slightly different menu, a more free-form version of the fare served in the main dining room. The kitchen table is cramped and noisy, hardly as luxurious as the linen-draped tables in the thickly carpeted formal dining rooms; out there, amid pale walls and draperies and fresh flowers, you get the muffled clink of china and crystal and the low murmur of conversation, while the kitchen table is surrounded by the frenetic sizzle, clang, whack, and whoosh of a working kitchen. (Luckily for Trotter, his kitchen is relatively disciplined and smooth running—don't expect *Hell's Kitchen*–style tantrums.) Naturally, those are the most coveted seats in the house, typically booked up to 4 months in advance, the earliest you can book ahead.

Parties can also book a private dining room called the Studio Kitchen with its own cooking demonstration and a live camera feed into the kitchen. It's a cool experience—but hey, nothing matches the thrill of sitting at the kitchen table, catching the pulse of a genius chef and his brigade at work.

dishes from recent menus include steamed Casco Bay cod with cockles, picholine olives, artichokes, and stinging nettles; a poached Sonoma duck egg with Burgundy truffle, torpedo onion, and parsley; roasted veal loin with spiced pumpkin and juniper; and roasted saddle of rabbit with fingerling potatoes, turnips, and mustard greens.

To share his passionate opinions about food, years ago Trotter started allowing certain guests the privilege of dining in his kitchen, sitting at a four-to-six-person table shoved into the corner where they could watch him work. The kitchen guests even

ⓘ 816 West Armitage (✆ **773/248-6228;** www.charlietrotters.com/restaurant).

✈ O'Hare International (26km/16 miles).

🛏 $$ **Homewood Suites,** 40 E. Grand St., Chicago (✆ **800/CALL-HOME** [800/225-4663] or 312/644-2222; www.homewoodsuiteschicago.com). $$ **Hotel Allegro Chicago,** 171 N. Randolph St., Chicago (✆ **800/643-1500** or 312/236-0123; www.allegrochicago.com).

Chef's Tables **143**

Momofuku Ko

Rocking Out with the Anti-Chef

New York, New York

Like everything else in New York, culinary fashions come and go at the speed of light, but few chefs have blazed to stardom quite as quickly as David Chang. In some ways he's the Anti-Chef, still in his 30s with a buzz cut and profane language, committed to keeping his restaurants moderately priced and open to walk-in diners. Born in New Jersey, Chang fell into cooking almost by chance, and his inspirations come not from Escoffier and the great French chefs but from Momofuko Ando, the inventor of the instant ramen noodle. His two main restaurants—**Momofuku Noodle Bar** (171 First Ave.) and **Momofuku Ssäm Bar** (207 2nd Ave.), both on the slightly scruffy edge of the East Village—purport to be simple, earthy noodle shops. But alongside his trademark fare of steamed buns, smoked chicken wings, kimchi stew, and savory bowls of noodles, he also offers divinely nuanced dishes such as rabbit and pork terrine with fennel marmalade, bacon, and mustard; or a Niman Ranch tri-tip steak with nugget potatoes and kimchi butter. Even his beverage lists are contrarian, including more beers and sakes than wines.

For all his democratic impulses, Chang is a gifted chef, and Momofuku Ko is where he can give his avant-garde side free rein. It's basically nothing but a chef's table, an L-shaped blond wood counter with stools for 12 people. The chef—usually Chang's chef de cuisine Peter Serpico—cooks right in front of the diners, interacting with them, serving them directly from the stove and counter. There's one menu offering, a succession of small portions based on whatever the chef was inspired to cook that day—no a la carte, no substitutions, boom that's it. A dinner at Ko is expected to take around 2 hours; lunch on Friday, Saturday, and Sunday offers a more complex tasting menu that takes 3 hours and costs more. The soundtrack is rock music, played at a fair decibel level. You can only book online 7 days in advance starting at 10am (hope your computer is fast, because they book up in a nanosecond). You're explicitly not allowed to sell your reservation. You have to spell out things like this in New York, where any hot commodity has its buyers.

Every night the menu is wildly different. Chang and Serpico are partial to the smokiness of pork belly, the silkiness of scallops and flaked white fish, the tenderness of sous-vide cookery, the creaminess of custards and foie gras, the tang of pickled vegetables (a nod to Chang's Korean-American heritage). The cooking can be inconsistent, but it's always edgy, exciting, and deeply, deeply hip.

(i) 163 First Ave. (www.momofuku.com).

✈ John F. Kennedy International (15 miles/24km); Newark Liberty International (16 miles/27km); LaGuardia (8 miles/13km).

🛏 $$ **The Lucerne,** 201 W. 79th St. (✆ **800/492-8122** or 212/875-1000; www.thelucernehotel.com). $ **Milburn Hotel,** 242 W. 76th St. (✆ **800/833-9622** or 212/362-1006; www.milburnhotel.com).

Lacroix

From Lacrosse to Lacroix

Philadelphia, Pennsylvania

Interesting that a guy who attended college on a lacrosse scholarship should wind up as the executive chef at a restaurant called Lacroix. Of course, his lacrosse days at Syracuse were well over before Matthew Levin shifted lanes to attend the Culinary Institute of America. After apprenticing at restaurants such as Le Bec Fin, Aureole, and Charlie Trotter's, he finally took the reins of this top Philadelphia restaurant from esteemed French chef Jean-Marie Lacroix in 2006. When it opened in 2003, *Esquire* named Lacroix the country's best new restaurant; but since Levin took over day-to-day kitchen duties, Lacroix has won even more accolades.

It was an interesting move for chef Lacroix to cede his stove to the young American maverick. But Lacroix, despite his years of experience and his classical French training, had already been playing around with foam and a widening range of spices from Asia and North Africa, and Levin is happily heading even farther down that road (he even sells a six-pack of spice blends for diners to take home—Ras el Hanout, Smoked Honey Powder, Salty Apricot, Smokey Aromas, Chocolate Chimichurri, and Coconut Samsara).

Lacroix is still a hotel restaurant, with a brisk business in power lunches and client dinners; there's a conservative, tailored elegance to its soft yellow and olive-green decor, with big windows looking out over the treetops of posh Rittenhouse Square, and Levin's seasonally changing menu still provides the classic butter-poached lobsters and *jus*-dripping veal chops that Lacroix's regulars expect. But he pushes the envelope with other dishes, like his cauliflower tequila soup, the halibut in a warm egg-yolk sauce, or the Muscovy duck breast with parsnip-coconut. For those interested in his more daring experiments, he also offers a range of small-plate tasting menus (three, four, or five courses, all of them under $100—a bargain compared to some of the molecular gastronomy houses), which may feature things like tiger prawns with pine, wheat beer, and raspberry; Arctic char gussied up with white chocolate, artichoke, passion fruit, and udon noodles; or rabbit saddle with barbecue-flavored lentils, corn, and grapefruit. The bar menu is also a little-known secret, with several globally flavored morsels served as snacks (to call them "tapas" would be so yesterday), and regularly scheduled wine-pairing events with their own special tasting menus.

The ultimate tasting menu—which does cost a good deal more—is available only Mondays through Thursdays at the seven-seat table right in the kitchen, where Levin may set as many as 12 courses down in front of you. In a similar vein, you can periodically book a food shopping expedition with Levin, followed by a cooking demonstration and three-course lunch—yet another glimpse of a top chef at work behind the scenes.

ⓘ In the Rittenhouse Hotel, 210 W. Rittenhouse Sq. (✆ **215/790-2533;** www. lacroixrestaurant.com).

✈ Philadelphia International (9²/₃ miles/ 15km).

🛏 $$$ **Rittenhouse 1715,** 1715 Rittenhouse Sq. (✆ **877/791-6500** or 215/ 546-6500; www.rittenhouse1715.com). $$ **Penn's View Hotel,** 14 N. Front St. (✆ **800/ 331-7634** or 215/922-7600; www.penns viewhotel.com).

Chef's Tables **145**

Minibar
Boy Wonder
Washington, D.C.

Like many star chefs these days, José Andrés seems to be everywhere at once—accepting awards, promoting his cookbooks and television shows, working to feed the homeless, overseeing his seven (count 'em, seven) restaurants in the Washington area. Considering that he's still only in his thirties, it's pretty impressive. When does he even find time to sleep?

But when all is said and done, Spanish-born Andrés, like his mentor Ferran Adrià, doesn't want to stray too far from the stove. He may have stepped away from day-to-day cooking at his first smash-hit of

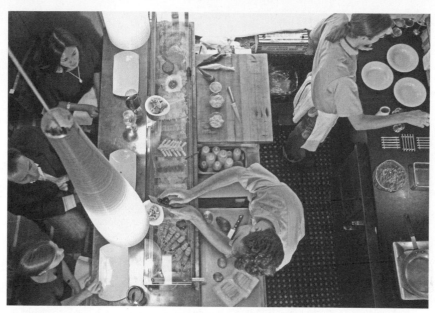

Chef José Andrés has seven restaurants, but you'll most likely find him at Minibar, which seats only 12 diners a night.

a restaurant, fiesta-like Café Atlantico, since he turned over the reins there to his talented chef de cuisine Katsuya Fukushima. But you can usually find him right upstairs at Minibar, a restaurant-within a-restaurant where he serves an incredible tasting menu of 25 to 30 small dishes for a single six-seat table 5 nights a week. There are two seatings per night, so do the math—only 60 people per week can have this insider experience, fewer than most restaurants serve in a single hour.

Counting on a self-selecting audience of curious gourmets, the Minibar goes for avant-garde cooking, the kind that may be a bit too daring for the three-level party that goes on every night in Café Atlantico and its super-popular spinoffs Oyamel and Zaytinya. Though Andrés describes his style as Nuevo Latino, the emphasis is way more on the "nuevo" up here on the second floor. It's full of head games like "bacon and eggs" (*kurobuta* pork belly confit with a soft egg, lentils, tamarind, and a puff of maple-flavored "air"); the "deconstructed glass of white wine" (a rectangular tile dotted with discreet flavor elements like grass, vanilla, and lemon); the huge transparent bubble called "light bulb of flavor"; a series of "meat and potatoes" ice cubes; foie gras in a coccoon of cotton candy; filaments of beet whipped into a tumbleweed. Items like seared *cigala* (prawn) with sea asparagus, a glass of vanilla and potato foam topped with caviar, or salmon-and-pineapple raviolis seem downright simple in comparison, though still delectable.

Reservations can be made (by phone only) a month in advance. The table fills up fast. You've been warned.

ⓘ 405 8th St. NW (☎ **202/393-0812;** www. cafeatlantico.com/minibar).

✈ Reagan National (3 miles/5km); Dulles International (26 miles/41km); Baltimore-Washington International (35 miles/56km).

🛏 $$ **Four Points by Sheraton,** 1201 K St. NW (☎ **202/289-7600;** www.fourpoints. com/washingtondcdowntown). $$ **George-town Suites,** 1111 30th St. NW (☎ **202/298-1600;** www.georgetownsuites.com).

Fearing's Restaurant
Kickin' Back in the Kitchen
Dallas, Texas

Who knows what the Ritz-Carlton did to woo Dean Fearing away from the Mansion on Turtle Creek, where for 20-plus years he'd been the dean (excuse the pun) of Dallas' fine-dining scene. Whatever it was, Fearing seems in his element at his new namesake restaurant in the swanky Ritz-Carlton. Getting instantly named Restaurant of the Year by *Esquire* magazine shortly after it opened in 2007 must have helped, and that was just the first of a flood of accolades.

Fearing pulls off a savvy blend of classical CIA training and southwestern regional tastes; the guy may wear chef's whites, but he wears them with jeans and custom-made cowboy boots. Many of the signature items on his menu—tortilla soup, jalapeño cornbread, prime rib, barbecued shrimp taco, and a mesquite-grilled rib-eye steak, are common enough on Tex-Mex menus, but Fearing's kitchen just plain does them better than your average cantina. And then he adds some of his own clever twists, as in the buffalo tenderloin marinated in maple and black peppercorn, served on a bed of jalapeño grits; *nilgai* antelope with wild boar sausage, toasted sage leaves, and chili-spiced fries; or coriander-crusted lamb chops with Texas smokehouse lamb chili. (Any chef who can dream up a dish like chicken-fried Maine lobster must be thinking out of the box.) Sourcing is a key element for Fearing, who's always on the lookout for the best Texas peppers, dried chilies, jicama, cilantro, tomatillos, Gulf seafood, and Hill Country wild game.

While Fearing's has seven different dining areas—including the gardenlike glass rotunda of the Sendero, the stone-vaulted Wine Cellar, the leather-and-onyx-accented Rattlesnake Bar, the high-ceilinged white-tablecloth dining salon the Gallery—the choicest spot of all is the chef's table. Limited to eight diners, it's set right inside Fearing's kitchen, where you can inhale the rich smoky aroma of grilling meats and watch the chefs at work. It's a fun way to hang out with Fearing himself—this down-to-earth Kentuckian may have trained with Wolfgang Puck, but he also plays a pretty mean Telecaster (he even recorded a CD with his all-chef alt-country band The Barbwires). Just like his music, Fearing's cooking is full of interesting riffs—and he hits all the high notes just right.

ⓘ 2121 McKinney Ave. (✆ **214/922-4848;** www.fearingsrestaurant.com).

✈ Dallas–Fort Worth International (85 miles/137km).

🛏 $$$ **The Melrose Hotel Dallas,** 3015 Oak Lawn Ave., Dallas (✆ **800/MELROSE** or 214/521-5151; www.melrose hoteldallas.com). $$ **Etta's Place,** 200 W. 3rd St., Fort Worth (✆ **866/355-5760** or 817/255-5760; www.ettas-place.com).

Colborne Lane

The Cosmopolitan Touch

Toronto, Canada

Colborne Lane has had Toronto diners buzzing ever since it opened in February 2007, in an historic part of downtown just a stone's throw from the St. Lawrence Market (see ⑱). Chef-owner Claudio Aprile—formerly the award-winning head chef at Senses—did a stint at El Bulli while Colborne Lane was under construction, and upon his return he shot out of the gate with wildly inventive cooking that took Toronto by storm. You can see his creativity unleashed in dishes like lemon custard pearls; a beef tartare kicked up with cornichon, roasted tomato, air-dried onion, and truffled soy; or a crispy wok-fried squid accented with caramelized peanut, green peppercorn, juicy Chinese sausage, and a trio of tropical fruits—Asian pear, pink grapefruit, and mango. At the same time, Aprile tempers his postmodern impulses with heartier dishes like the miso-glazed black cod with a sesame panna cotta and bok choy, or the tea-smoked squab breast with a croquette of squab confit and foie gras croquette, dribbled with date and chocolate sauces, or the braised beef rib with sunchoke risotto and glazed shallots. He *has* all the machines in his kitchen, he just doesn't feel he has to use them in every dish. The creativity, though, never stops flowing.

Born in Uruguay, Aprile also trained in Southeast Asia, and the Asian influence on his cooking is profound; more than that, however, it's cosmopolitan cooking, and it goes down well in this cosmopolitan city. The restaurant itself has a chic downtown vibe, with a soundtrack of mellow rock music instead of hushed Serious Dining silence. Shabby-chic architectural elements are set off by sleekly minimalist furniture, dramatic lighting, and stunningly simple table settings that let the artfully arranged food presentation take center stage.

From the very beginning, Aprile—who also apprenticed in Chicago at Charlie Trotter's and Alinea—knew he wanted to offer a chef's table, special front-row seating where the most curious gourmets could gather to focus on his food. Its six-person kitchen table is set in a private nook that offers an unobstructed view of the goings-on at the stove, and various members of the kitchen brigade stop by from time to time to chat with the guests. Kitchen table dining comes with its own special 15-course tasting menu showcasing the most daring items in his repertoire—when you're pushing the envelope, why not make the chef's table crowd your panel of taste testers?

ⓘ 45 Colborne St. (☎ **416/368-9009;** http://colbornelane.com).

✈ Toronto International (19km/12 miles).

🛏 $$$ **Le Royal Meridien King Edward,** 37 King St. E (☎ **800/543-4300** or 416/863-9700; www.starwoodhotels.com). $$ **The Drake Hotel,** 1150 Queen St. W (☎ **416/531-5042;** www.thedrakehotel.ca).

Gordon Ramsay at Claridge's

A London Blitz

London, England

Of course, you won't see Gordon Ramsay himself cooking here—he's too busy filming television shows, opening new outposts of his restaurant empire, and otherwise taking over the world. But after seeing a few episodes of the foul-mouthed blond Scot's antics on *Hell's Kitchen,* you might not need to see Ramsay himself in action.

You will see one of Ramsay's most trusted disciples, Mark Sargeant, who opened this hotel restaurant for Ramsay in 2001, promptly won a Michelin star, and helped develop Ramsay's growing chain of gastropubs. The sedate, creamy-toned Art Deco dining room is a good fit for the sophisticated cuisine that lifted Ramsay's flagship Chelsea restaurant, **Restaurant Gordon Ramsey** (68 Royal Hospital Rd.; 44/20/7352-4441) to the heights of culinary acclaim. Prices here are slightly less stratospheric—a six-course tasting menu (called a "Menu Prestige") is priced under £100, while the three-star Hospital Road mother ship charges over £125 for seven courses.

The six-person chef's table is right in Claridge's gleaming kitchen, at a marble-topped table overlooking the central pass; here you'll be served a special menu (more expensive than the restaurant's tasting menu) improvised from that day's market ingredients. With that front-row seat, you can observe different preparations, such as the bluefin tuna dish, which contrasts a tuna carpaccio with pickled white radish against a piece of tuna seared and marinated with black sesame seeds and soy dressing. Perhaps you'll be able to watch the chef rolling a piece of monkfish in Parma ham, or whipping up a watercress velouté with asparagus, or adding slivers of truffles to the pureed potatoes that accompany the roast Cornish lamb. Sargeant is cooking at a very high level here, and while the kitchen does have a corporate sort of slickness and efficiency, high-level kitchen action is always fascinating. The table can be reserved up to 6 months in advance.

There's also a chef's table at Ramsay's sleek contemporary Mayfair restaurant **Maze** (10–13 Grosvenor Sq.; 44/20/7107-0000), where Jason Atherton and his team create their Asian-accented tasting menus. Again, no Ramsay in evidence at the stove, but maybe that's just as well.

ⓘ **Claridge's Hotel,** Brook St. (44/20/7499-0099; www.gordonramsay.com).

✈ Heathrow (24km/15 miles) or Gatwick (40km/25 miles).

🛏 $$$ **22 Jermyn St.,** 22 Jermyn St., St. James (800/682-7808 in the U.S., or 44/20/7734-2353; www.22jermyn.com). $$ **Vicarage Private Hotel,** 10 Vicarage Gate, South Kensington (44/20/7229-4030; www.londonvicaragehotel.com).

Commerç 24

Foam, The Next Generation

Barcelona, Spain

The prime place to sit in this sleek, trendy Barcelona hot spot is at the high table right next to the brightly lit open kitchen, where you get a clear view of all the molecular gastronomy action. Plenty of creative young chefs have breezed through the El Bulli kitchen, hoping to pick Ferran Adrià's brain, but Carles Abellán worked there for nearly a decade, becoming one of Adrià's most trusted disciples. Now that he's got his own restaurant, it's fascinating to see how the master's ideas flower in Abellán's gifted hands.

Abellán describes his cooking as "glocal"—a hokey catchphrase, perhaps, but it's a winning marriage of global cuisines (Asian, Italian, and American figure prominently) with local Catalonian recipes and ingredients. The menu is designed to offer both small tastes—honoring the regional tapas tradition—and regular-sized a la carte portions, as well as larger dishes to be shared communally by the table. As at El Bulli, the tasting menus—here called "festival menus"—are the way to go, not least because menu descriptions can't possibly convey the full inventiveness of Abellán's cooking.

The menu is always changing, but signature dishes include lots of seafood—the tuna tartare in a pool of egg-yolk vinaigrette, the meticulous vanilla-scented salmon-on-salmon sashimi, a drinkable mousse of black cod brandade and artichokes, delicate ravioli of cuttlefish and morel mushrooms—and, for those who'd like a little heartier fare (something often lacking at El Bulli), a few surprisingly straightforward choices like grilled beef entrecote with potatoes, or a baked eggplant with Roquefort, pine nuts, and mushrooms. Perhaps his most iconic dish is a playful concoction called the Kinder Egg (*kinder* as in the German word for children)—an eggshell filled with soft egg, truffle, and potato foam, a molecular gastronomer's take on the classic Spanish potato omelet.

In complete contrast to the rustic look of El Bulli, Commerç 24 is an industrial-chic rehab of an old salting house, a modernist, minimalist vision of slate-gray floors and table tops, angular furniture, cast-iron columns, splashes of red and yellow, and dramatic spot lighting. If you can't book the kitchen-view table, try for a seat at the bar, where there's also a good view of the cooks at work.

ⓘ Carrer Comerç 24, Barcelona (✆ **34/93/319-2102;** www.commerc24.com).

✈ El Prat (13km/8 miles).

🛏 $$$ **Montecarlo,** Les Ramblas 124 (✆ **34/93-412-04-04;** www.montercarlo bcn.com). $$ **Duques de Bergara,** Bergara 11 (✆ **34/93-301-51-51;** www.hoteles-catalonia.com).

Millennium

High Minded, High End

San Francisco, California

At first glance it looks like any upscale bistro, with its zinc-topped bar, sponge-painted yellow walls, leather-upholstered banquettes, and burnished reddish-brown wood trim. But look closer and you'll find that the upholstery is faux leatherette, the lacy drapes over the ceiling fixtures are made from paper bags, and sheer curtains are woven from recycled plastic bags. (The zinc-topped bar, too, is recycled from a previous restaurant.) Sustainable design was a given, for Millennium is all about sustainable food. Sure, it's got a high-profile location on the outskirts of Union Square, but that doesn't mean Millennium is ever going to compromise its values.

Millennium's chef, Eric Tucker, is a man with a mission. He's determined to prove that traditional cooking techniques—including many taken from ethnic cuisines—don't have to include dairy products, eggs, oil, and other high-fat animal products in order to be delicious. Like many vegetarian chefs, Tucker makes use of Southeast Asian tastes in items like the Balinese-style salt-and-pepper-crusted oyster mushrooms with blood orange chili jam, but that's only the beginning. Borrowing from India, he does *masala dosa,* a lentil rice crepe with south Indian chickpea and red chard curry, sweet and spicy papaya chutney, and mint raita; with a nod to France, there's a stuffed roulade of roasted chestnuts and mushrooms and sautéed broccoli, cooked in black truffle butter, under a ragout of French lentils and black chanterelles. Italy inspires his edamame gnocchi (served with grilled oyster mushrooms, caramelized cippolini onions, and a coulis of miso and Jerusalem artichokes) and his carrot lasagnette (carrot pasta sheets layered with Meyer lemon, spring garlic, tahini cream, and roasted baby carrots, topped with pine nut gremolata). Caribbean influences run through his plantain torte with tropical fruit salsa and romesco sauce; Mexico lies behind his black bean torte, which layers a whole wheat tortilla, caramelized plantains, smoky black bean puree, pumpkin-habanero salsa verde, cashew sour cream, and strawberry-jicama salsa. And fine as the food is, you can still try a five-course tasting menu with wine pairings for under $100.

Millennium buys fresh produce every day, mostly from small farms that practice sustainable agriculture; if the produce is organic, even better. But Tucker and his crew know they're in the heart of a foodie city; their goal is to make vegetarian dining fun and exciting. Why should you have to sacrifice taste in order to feel environmentally conscious?

(i) 580 Geary St. ((C) **415/345-3900;** www.millenniumrestaurant.com).

✈ San Francisco International (14 miles/23km).

🛏 $$$ **Hotel Adagio,** 550 Geary St. ((C) **800/228-8830** or 415/775-5000; www.thehoteladagion.com). $ **Hotel des Arts,** 447 Bush St. ((C) **800/956-4322** or 415/956-3232; www.sfhoteldesarts.com).

Rover's

Tasting Your Veggies

Seattle, Washington

It may not be exclusively meat-free, but Rover's is where Seattle vegetarians tend to come when they really want to treat themselves. Chef Thierry Rautureau is in love with the local ingredients of the Northwest—that's part of what tempted him away from his native France to open this restaurant in 1987—and how better to show them off than with a five-course vegetarian tasting menu?

Though it's tucked away in a quaint clapboard house in the Madison Valley neighborhood east of downtown, Rover's is hardly a well-kept secret; it's one of Seattle's most acclaimed restaurants, and on the pricey end of the scale. Expect white tablecloths and crystal, candlelight and fresh flowers, formal dining room chairs and some neatly framed art on the golden walls of the dining room. Rover's consistently wins top awards for its service as well, although, this being the Northwest, it's more friendly and relaxed than stuffy.

Considering Rautureau's classical French training, all that is no surprise. What's intriguing, though, is how thoroughly Rautureau has gone native—he is known for wearing a straw fedora in the kitchen instead of a white toque—and there are American accents everywhere on his frequently changing menu. Having grown up himself on a farm in the Muscadet region of France, he's put together a vast network of local suppliers, including mushroom foragers, Washington State cheese makers, and area farmers, preferably those who run sustainable and organic operations. His various tasting menus—or *degustations*—allow him to introduce diners to as many of their products as possible, in artfully presented small portions.

While most celebrated chefs pay only lip service to the needs of vegetarians, Rautureau really does offer an impressive number of veggie options. There are all levels of vegetarianism, of course; Rover's menu items may not be suitable for strict vegans. (He does include some fish on the vegetarian selections, for example.) But among the choices are delectable things like scrambled eggs with lime crème fraîche and caviar; a spice-infused Pinot Noir sorbet; a lobster-mushroom bisque with marinated *cèpes* and Armagnac crème; a roasted pepper flan with grilled tomatillo, braised fennel and olive tapenade; or butternut squash with sweet corn, romano bean, and roasted garlic sauce. If your dining companions must

Chef Thierry Rautureau's Pacific Northwestern cuisine at Rover's.

137

have meat, they can find things like Wagyu beef with wild mushrooms and lentils, or Oregon rabbit with foie gras, to satisfy their carnivorous urges. Everybody can go home happy.

(i) 2808 E. Madison St. (© **206/325-7442;** www.rovers-seattle.com).

✈ Seattle-Tacoma International (14 miles/23km).

🛏 $$$ **Inn at the Market,** 86 Pine St. (© **800/446-4484** or 206/443-3600; www. innatthemarket.com). $$ **Bacon Mansion Bed & Breakfast,** 959 Broadway E (© **800/ 240-1864** or 206/329-1864; www.bacon-mansion.com).

Vegetarians **152**

Pure Food & Wine
The Raw Deal
New York, New York

While raw foodists can sometimes come off like a lunatic fringe, Pure Food & Wine presents its raw-food agenda with such elegant panache, you may forget that the menu contains no meat, dairy, wheat, soy, or refined sugars—and it's organic *and* vegan to boot. While the medical merits of a strictly raw diet are still under debate (studies show that over the long haul, human bodies need nutrients that raw food can't provide), a meal at Pure Food & Wine can be a wonderful tonic.

The theory of raw food is simple: No ingredient is ever raised to a temperature above 118°F, the magic point above which certain enzymes in food get destroyed. It's amazing, though, what a chef can do with just blenders, dehydrators, and a really good chopping knife. Fruits, vegetables, nuts, and seeds are the building blocks of raw food cuisine, so getting the best produce is essential. Of course, there's a side benefit: Although Pure Food is on the pricy end for veggie restaurants, even high-end raw food can be gratifyingly cheap compared to meals taken from higher up the food chain.

The menu at Pure Food & Wine goes well beyond health food salads and tofu burgers. Consider, for example, a starter of creamy cauliflower samosas with banana-tamarind sauce, or a heart-warming butternut squash soup, infused with rosemary and topped with pecans, medjoul dates, and a drizzle of miso coulis. A main course of wild mushroom and asparagus en papillote with celeriac cream is accented with truffle jus, endive, and wine-soaked figs; an

Food is never cooked above 118°F at Pure Food & Wine.

earthy tea-smoked portabella mushroom is paired with zingy caper potato salad. Not surprisingly, it's a menu full of global accents, especially from countries like India and Japan where the traditional cuisines use meat and dairy only sparingly, if at all.

Perhaps the most impressive part of the menu is the desserts, which are full of ice creams (how do they do that without dairy?) and chocolate cake (how do they do that without wheat?). To fulfill the second half of the restaurant's name, there's a full list of biodynamic wines offered, from top organic vineyards all over the world, although the wine list gets serious competition from the glorious menu of juices and smoothies.

There's a sort of Japanese look to the spare, sleek dining room, with red wall panels and upholstered chairs complementing the warm lacquered wood of

walls, tables, and bare floor. The glamour quotient among the clientele is fairly high—oh, if only raw food could make us all look this thin and beautiful! Located along a trendy strip of restaurants just south of Gramercy Park, it's definitely a hot spot. It just doesn't get any hotter than 118°F.

ⓘ 54 Irving Plaza (ⓒ **212/477-1010;** www.purefoodandwine.com).

✈ John F. Kennedy International (15 miles/24km); Newark Liberty International (16 miles/27km); LaGuardia (8 miles/13km).

🛏 $$$ **Carlton Hotel on Madison Avenue,** 88 Madison Ave. (ⓒ **212/532-4100;** www.carltonhotelny.com). $$ **Washington Square Hotel,** 103 Waverly Place (ⓒ **800/222-0418** or 212/777-9515; www.washingtonsquarehotel.com).

153 American Regional Stars

No. 9 Park Street

Boston Uncommon

Boston, Massachusetts

It's not all baked beans, lobster, and chowder in Boston anymore, and Barbara Lynch is one of the big reasons why. When she first opened this simple, chic restaurant in 1998 in a neoclassical 1803 Beacon Hill townhouse overlooking Boston Common, it promptly filled an important niche in Boston's dining scene. On the one end, there were upscale French restaurants like Jasper's (Jasper White) and L'Espalier (Frank McClelland); at the other were hearty casual bistros like Hamersley's Bistro (Gordon Hamersley) in the South End, and Olives (Todd English) out in Charlestown. Lynch's classy mix of Italian and French cuisine, featuring fresh local ingredients and regional boutique wines, slotted right in the middle and scored an immediate smash hit.

Although Lynch apprenticed with many of Boston's top cooks, including a stint under Todd English at Olives, a period of living in Italy was what really transformed her cooking. There she learned pasta-making firsthand from Italian farmhouse cooks, and developed a love of artisanal products. Luckily when she returned to New England the region's artisanal food producers were beginning to hit their stride, and Lynch herself has been a huge booster of her local suppliers.

Lynch's menus feature strong, distinct flavors, as in one of her signature dishes, the beet salad appetizer—an upended cylinder of shredded vegetables atop blue cheese, surrounded by mesclun greens. A vivid starter of heirloom tomatoes keeps the focus on the tomatoes themselves,

139

with simple accompaniments of feta cheese and house-cured prosciutto. Deeply savory prune-stuffed gnocchi (a house specialty) come with earthy foie gras and Vin Santo glaze; an organic *poussin* comes with bacon confit, dandelion greens, and a quail egg; crispy pork belly gets spiked up with braised Belgian endive, purslane, and jalapeño aioli; venison loin en croûte is complemented by shallot chutney.

Though No. 9 Park Street falls at the higher end of Boston's price scale, compared to other cities—and given the quality of the food—it's reasonable. (Even the seven-course chef's tasting menu is under $100.) Its aura is quietly chic, relaxed, and intimate, with a muted taupe palette and dark polished wood floors. If you want a lighter meal, try the cafe area near the front door, where you don't need a reservation to order items a la carte off the dinner menu.

ⓘ 9 Park St. (✆ **617/742-9991;** www.no9park.com).

✈ Boston Logan International (11 miles/18km).

🛏 $$ **Harborside Inn,** 185 State St., Boston (✆ **617/670-6015;** www.harborsideinnboston.com). $$$ **The Charles Hotel,** 1 Bennett St., Cambridge (✆ **800/882-1818** or 617/864-1200; www.charleshotel.com).

154

Lantern

The Global-Local Connection

Chapel Hill, North Carolina

If you hadn't already read about the place, you might not guess that this southern college-town restaurant is such a bright light. The decor resembles your classic strip-mall Chinese restaurant, only gone upscale: a muted ivory-and-green-tea palette accented with strokes of lacquer black and a profusion of parchment-colored hanging lanterns in a dizzying variety of shapes. You're primed for the food to taste Asian, and it does, although you can't quite pin it down—it flits all over the region, from China to Japan to Thailand to Vietnam to India.

So what makes the flavors in Andrea Reusing's fusion food brighter, more intense, more alive? Look closer at the menu and you'll have your answer: For all her global recipes, Reusing is a committed locavore, cooking as much as possible with produce, meat, and poultry from local organic farms. This New Jersey native's cooking is largely self-taught, gleaned from several years of living in New York City and exploring ethnic Asian restaurants in Chinatown and Flushing; it helps that she has been gifted with a great palate for the nuances of Asian cooking. Since she opened Lantern in 2002, she has risen brilliantly to the challenge of tailoring Asian recipes to what her vigorous network of local suppliers can provide.

The crackling calamari salad, for example, comes with a side of seasonal garden greens as well as a lime-miso vinaigrette; the fiery Bang Bang chicken with Szechuan peppers gets an extra oomph from being a free-range local bird. Even when she goes a little more down-country with North Carolina crab cakes, she spikes them up with vibrant Thai flavors such as lemon grass and mint. Similarly, a sweet-hot chili sauce puts the fire in a robust pork terrine that uses a head-to-tail sampling of parts from Fickle Creek Farm hogs (how thoroughly Chinese it is to use up all the "icky bits"). Pork is always popular, of course, in this great barbecue-centric state, but at Lantern you'll get a coconut-braised Niman Ranch shank, so tender it falls off the bone. Want a little seafood? Try Reusing's salt-and-pepper shrimp with fried jalapeños and coriander, or locally caught fried flounder with garlic, chilies, tamarind, fresh lime leaf, carrot salad, and jasmine rice. Her drunken chicken uses top-quality Rainbow Meadow Farm chicken, marinated in ginger, black vinegar, and sherry with a garden-fresh side of local greens and cucumbers. One of Reusing's signature dishes, her "tea and spice" smoked chicken with yang chow pork and shrimp fried rice, combines a whole host of North Carolina ingredients in new ways.

Don't worry about making your reservations in advance—they're not accepted. You'll just have to wait for a table like everybody else.

ⓘ 423 West Franklin Rd. (✆ **919/969-8846;** http://lanternrestaurant.com).

✈ Raleigh-Durham (18 miles/29km).

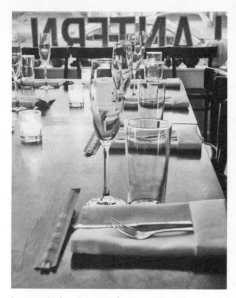

Lantern, Andrea Reusing's fusion cuisine restaurant in Chapel Hill.

🛏 $$$ **The Carolina Inn,** 211 Pittsboro St. (✆ **800/962-8519** or 919/933-2001; www.carolinainn.com). $$$ **Siena Hotel,** 1505 E. Franklin St. (✆ **800/223-7393** or 919/929-4000; www.sienahotel.com).

Lilly's

God Bless Our Local Farmers

Louisville, Kentucky

When Kathy Cary first opened her gourmet takeout shop and catering business in 1979, the idea of celebrating local farmers, fishermen, and food artisans was something you rarely heard in the middle of the U.S. In 1988, when she turned the catering business into a full-fledged restaurant, it was still a fresh concept here in Bluegrass Country.

But in Kathy Cary's kitchen, honoring farm produce and southern food was more than just a fad. Like the West Coast's Alice Waters, Cary gradually built a team of suppliers, encouraging them to pursue their own organic, sustainable, free-range convictions. She has even got her own organic garden now, where she can pick herbs and salad vegetables every morning in season.

Because Cary's recipes are based on local products—catfish, trout, country ham, sweet corn, wild greens, bourbon—she had to invent her own style of locavore cooking as she went along; the West Coast playbook just didn't apply. Her classical culinary training shows up in dishes like a garlic and leek soup with spinach flan, smoked trout, and white truffle oil; California bass and sautéed shrimp with saffron leek gnocchi; or seared duck breast and duck confit cabbage roulade in a port wine sauce. But she is just as likely to tuck local lake catfish into an Asian spring roll, mix spicy sautéed calamari with a local sausage-maker's chorizo, top corn cakes with barbecue pulled pork, or grill a pork chop with sweet potato hash, Brussels sprouts, a touch of ham, and red-eye gravy. And while all her desserts are uncommonly good (why is it that caterers always excel at desserts?), it's hard to pass up her homemade ice cream flavored with Woodford bourbon, served with chocolate shortbread.

The cheery, pleasant atmosphere of her storefront restaurant, in the mellow Cherokee Triangle residential neighborhood, accounts for a lot of Lilly's staying power too. Deep purples, reds, and yellows lend a sort of bohemian funkiness to the eclectic decor, accented by scattered oil paintings, gypsylike curtains, and a few Southern touches like ceiling fans and slatted blinds.

As the Midwest's dining scene has grown more sophisticated in the past few years, Cary is still ahead of the pack—one day schmoozing on TV with Martha Stewart or Rachael Ray, the next invited as a guest cook to the prestigious James Beard House in New York City. But Cary takes her local celebrity in stride, and on her menu she always gives credit where credit is due: "God Bless Our Local Farmers."

ⓘ 1147 Bardstown Rd. (© **502/451-0447;** www.lillyslapeche.com).

✈ Louisville (7 miles/11km).

🛏 $$ **21c Museum Hotel,** 700 W. Main St. (© **877/217-6400** or 502/217-6300; www.21cmuseumhotel.com). $$ **Camberley Brown,** 4th St. and West Broadway, Louisville (© **502/583-1234;** www.thebrownhotel.com).

American Regional Stars 156

T'Afia

Pope's Blessing

Houston, Texas

Being a locavore chef in Houston doesn't have to mean cranking out Tex-Mex tacos or chicken-fried steak. Just ask Monica Pope, one of the founders of the Saturday morning Midtown Farmer's Market and the chef-owner of T'afia (named after a Creole drinking toast, meaning "to your health!"). Winner of all sorts of national chef honors, Pope is keenly attuned to the central paradox of Texas cuisine—with its regional culinary tradition that grew from the hardships of cowboy life on the range, on the one hand; and, on the other, the modern reality of a bounteous year-round growing climate where farmers can cultivate anything from persimmons to Meyer lemons to Asian greens.

Like Alice Waters, to whom she's often compared, Pope's a bit of a culinary pioneer, single-handedly creating a market for organic farmers, small cheese makers, specialty ranchers, and chocolate makers, all within a 300-mile (483km) range of her Midtown Houston restaurant. (In sprawling Texas, that qualifies as a short drive.) Her nightly five-course tasting menus put Texas artisanal food products prominently in the spotlight—things like Pure Luck Hopelessly Bleu goat cheese with Joan's figs, poached in Texas Hills Merlot; a tempura of Gita's squash blossoms with saffron-sherry aioli; Lola's shell beans and farro with Texas tarragon; espresso-rubbed Katz cross quail with smoked pecan pilaf; or a chicken-fried Maverick Farms antelope cutlet with roasted okra and Wild Mustang grape jelly. Something as simple as summer pudding with local blueberries can be divine when the blueberries were handpicked that morning.

At less than $50 without wine, this tasting menu is a wonderful bargain, considering that you'll be sampling the best of Texas's organic boutique food products. The à la carte portion of the menu also includes an interesting mix-and-match option, where you choose your base entrée from a list of variously priced proteins and combine it with any one of 10 signature sauces, from port wine sauce to sweet-hot mustard to blossom butter.

Even the dining room of this scrubbed-down bistro, with its bare brick walls, blond woods, and plain white acrylic tables, features murals and paintings by local artists. It's a relatively small place, open only Tuesday through Saturday (the Fri lunch prix fixe is a well-kept local secret

T'afia is named after a Creole drinking toast meaning "to your health!"

worth seeking out). And here's another secret: Tuesday through Thursday, all the tasty snacks on the lounge menu—things like a pimiento mac-and-cheese, chickpea fries with red curry ketchup, and luscious little miniburgers—are free with drinks. It's an addictive deal.

ⓘ 3701 Travis St. (✆ **713/524-6922;** www.tafia.com).

✈ George Bush Intercontinental (37 miles/60km).

🛏 $$$ **Hilton University of Houston,** 4800 Calhoun Rd. (✆ **800/HOTELUH** [800/468-3584] or 713/741-2447; www.hilton.com). $$ **Best Western Downtown Inn and Suites,** 915 W. Dallas St. (✆ **800/780-7234** or 713/571-7733; www.bestwestern.com).

Janos

Blazing a Trail in Tucson

Tucson, Arizona

It's a good thing that the atmosphere at Janos is so affable and relaxed, because you may need to ask your server a *lot* of questions. (You may even get to ask chef Janos Wilder himself, as he regularly greets guests.) For instance, what is this spice called *piloncillo,* rubbed on the New York strip steak? What is an avocado serrano sorbet? An ancho–prickly pear vinaigrette? Piquillo peppers? Oaxacan *barbacoa?* That's before you even get around to asking how you make a popcorn bisque soup, or decipher the names of all the local orchardists and ranchers whose products are featured by name, items such as Fiore de Cabra chèvre cheese, Briggs and Eggers apples, or Tohono Old-ham squash.

This French-trained California chef has been opening locals' eyes to new flavors from their own southwestern backyard ever since he first opened his eponymous restaurant in 1983, in a historic adobe on the grounds of the Tucson Museum of Art. From the very start, he showcased exotic local ingredients such as mesquite flour and blue cornmeal, and not in humble Tex-Mex dishes but in sophisticated dishes executed with classical French flair. It was a radical approach indeed in 1983, when California Cuisine was the latest gourmet buzzword, and Santa Fe's New Southwest cooking wasn't even a dream.

With the passing years, despite count-less awards and honors, Wilder's enthusi-asm for local Arizona ingredients hasn't diminished. He has long kept his own gar-dens, where he plants ingredients that have captured his imagination, and a net-work of local farmers, fishermen, foragers, and ranchers vie to see their foods fea-tured on his menus. He's now located at the Westin La Paloma Resort, in a free-standing hacienda overlooking a sweep-ing view of the Tucson Valley. Decorated in deep desert colors, with Oriental rugs and chandeliers overlaying the adobe simplicity, it manages to be welcoming and luxurious. Whether you go for the five-course tasting menu or à la carte selection, you'll sample cooking of a very high order, where disparate elements like foie gras, truffles, figs, rabbit, salmon, corn, chipotle, and chilies somehow coex-ist in glorious harmony.

ⓘ 3770 East Sunrise Dr. (ⓒ **520/615-6100;** www.janos.com).

✈ Tucson International (16 miles/26km).

🛏 $$ **Catalina Park Inn,** 309 E. First St. (ⓒ **800/792-4885** or 520/792-4541; www.catalinaparkinn.com). $$$ **Westin La Paloma Resort & Spa,** 3800 E. Sunrise Dr. (ⓒ **800/WESTIN-1** [800/937-8461] or 520/742-6000; www.westinlapalomaresort. com).

Grace

Hollywood Star

Los Angeles, California

Nobody uses the term "California cuisine" anymore—it's too loaded with bad memories of the faddish excesses of the 1980s, the culinary equivalent of shoulder pads, aviator glasses, and permed shags. But call it New American with a California fusion focus, and you've got the essence of Neal Fraser's approach. Having trained in the kitchens of Wolfgang Puck, Thomas Keller, and Joachim Splichal, Fraser has no fear of creative combinations. (Locals still remember the all-hemp tasting menu he tried out years ago at Rix in Santa Monica.) With his new restaurant, Grace, which opened in Hollywood in 2003, he has hit his stride.

With its high ceilings, well-spaced tables, and soothing earth tones, Grace exemplifies its name. Indeed it's a gracious spot, relaxed and yet refined, in welcome contrast to the trendy buzz of so many other L.A. restaurants. Service is smooth, the wine list is knowledgeable, and the crowd is well-behaved, even on casual Sunday nights, when Fraser's wonderful gourmet burgers of prime dry-aged Highland beef are the focus, topped with buttermilk blue, Gruyère, or truffle cheese. Wednesday's Doughnut Night is another weekly highlight.

Fraser hasn't lost the exuberance of a kid in a candy store. Look especially at his daily specials, where seasonal ingredients spark his imagination to concoct dishes such as pumpkin risotto with sea urchin and sweet Maine shrimp, a carpaccio of tuna with fried green olives and pepper vinaigrette, or slow-braised pork shank with smoked shallots and cider-sage sauce. Lately he seems to be in love with game dishes; his special game tasting menu includes winning items like sautéed sweetbreads with sweet potato gnocchi, sage, and brown butter; wild Scottish hare sautéed with kabocha squash, beluga lentils, and guajillo chili sauce; wild-boar tenderloin with violet mustard sauce; and grilled antelope with Parmesan flan, *cavolo nero*, and huckleberry gastrique. But who knows, by the time you get here, he may be fired up about another family of tastes. That eagerness to try new things is what keeps his cooking fresh.

Grace's menu isn't extraordinarily long, but it's so eclectic, you may have trouble choosing. For starters, will it be the tangy soup of tomatoes and piquillo peppers, topped with a goat cheese monte cristo; a soothing savory roasted chestnut and squash soup with duck confit and toasted pistachios; or the vibrant Thai Lobster Soup? In Neal Fraser's capable

Neal Fraser's restaurant Grace serves New American cuisine with a California fusion focus.

kitchen, fusion is a delicious if confusing prospect.

(i) 7360 Beverly Blvd. (☏ **323/934-4400;** www.gracerestaurant.com).

✈ Los Angeles International (13 miles/ 20km).

🚄 $$$ **Peninsula Beverly Hills,** 9882 S. Santa Monica Blvd. (☏ **800/462-7899** or 310/551-2888; www.peninsula.com). $ **Best Western Marina Pacific Hotel,** 1697 Pacific Ave., Venice (☏ **800/786-7789** or 310/452-1111; www.mphotel. com).

American Regional Stars **159**

Restaurant Gary Danko
It's All in the Details
San Francisco, California

Poised at the end of the Hyde Street cable car line, Gary Danko's restaurant is an island of civilized elegance that seems worlds apart from the nearby scrum of Fisherman's Wharf tourist traps. It's still very Californian—don't expect stuffy formality—but meals here definitely feel like a special occasion, with impeccable service, a serene wood-paneled decor with spotlit modern art, and plenty of space between those linen-draped tables.

Chef-owner Gary Danko isn't out to be a trendsetter—his cooking is firmly rooted in classical French techniques, filtered through years of cooking and teaching at the best restaurants in San Francisco and the countrysides of New England and Napa Valley. One thing those country-inn experiences left him with was a keen appreciation for seasonal local ingredients, and so Danko set up a farm in Yountville to grow his own organic produce for the restaurant. The stint in Napa, where he ran Chateau Souverain's restaurant for the Beringer vineyards, also sharpened his interest in wines, and his restaurant has one of the city's best wine lists as a result.

Danko serves his signature dishes of roast lobster, foie gras, and lamb loin year-round, but he varies the accompaniments from season to season. He might pair seared foie gras, for example, with red onions and rhubarb in spring, but with roast figs in early fall. Earthy autumn sides of potato puree, corn, and chanterelles come with the roast lobster in fall, while in springtime he'll use morel mushrooms and asparagus instead. You need only look at another of Danko's trademark dishes— an appetizer of buttery-smooth glazed oysters with lettuce cream, zucchini pearls, and Osetra caviar—to remember how deeply his classical French training runs. And meticulous execution makes his cooking exquisite, more than just another by-the-book French knockoff.

You can choose between a three-, four- or five-course fixed-price menu, but within those parameters you're free to pick and choose. If you want just a sampling of appetizers or a flight of meat courses, you need only ask. Whatever you do, leave room for goodies from the extraordinary granite-topped cheese cart the servers wheel to your table at the end of the meal. It would be a shame to pass up one of the nation's best artisanal cheese arrays. Don't skip the flambéed desserts either; they're another Danko specialty. And it *is* a special occasion, after all.

Restaurant Gary Danko is a bastion of excellence on Fisherman's Wharf.

ⓘ 800 North Point St., Fisherman's Wharf (☏ **415/749-2060;** www.garydanko.com).

✈ San Francisco International (14 miles/23km).

🛏 $$$ **Hotel Adagio,** 550 Geary St. (☏ **800/228-8830** or 415/775-5000; www.thehoteladagio.com). $ **Hotel des Arts,** 447 Bush St. (☏ **800/956-4322** or 415/956-3232; www.sfhoteldesarts.com).

160 American Regional Stars

Canlis

You Don't Mess with Success

Seattle, Washington

It's easy to forget about Canlis. In a foodie city like Seattle, with great little restaurants popping up all over the place, why plunk down major bucks to eat at a formal restaurant that has been around since 1950?

The answer is, you don't stay in business that long without knowing what you're doing, and the Canlis family has a winning formula—a stunning dining room,

a superbly smooth team of waiters, top locally sourced ingredients, and a talent for hiring and retaining the best chefs. Most Seattleites concede that Canlis pretty much invented Northwest cuisine way back when, with its emphasis on the seafood, fruit, grains, greens, and wild game of Washington state. The third generation of Canlises now at the helm keeps honing the restaurant's edge and resisting stodgy complacency.

The current executive chef, Aaron Wright, has been at Canlis since 2000. Like his predecessors, he continues to burnish the Canlis tradition. There are certain menu items you don't mess with, like the Peter Canlis prawns (cooked in dry vermouth, garlic, red chilies, and lime), the creamy house seafood chowder (Dungeness crab, prawns, and Manila clams), steak tartare, escargot in puff pastry, raw oysters, Wagyu beef tenderloin, the twice-baked potato, the Grand Marnier soufflé. *Saveur* magazine has called Canlis's trademark salad—crisp romaine topped with bacon and Romano cheese and a special dressing of lemon, olive oil, and coddled egg—"one of the 100 best dishes in America." But Mark and Brian Canlis have clearly given Wright plenty of creative freedom to supplement the classics with items such as duck confit and plum salad with Oregon blue cheese and candied walnuts; sesame-crusted mahi-mahi with spiced mango coulis and smoked shiitake mushrooms; Australian lobster with wild mushroom gnocchi, dripping with yuzu butter and a soy truffle reduction; or delectable hand-cut french fries drizzled with white truffle oil. The five-course tasting menu is a sort of chef's prerogative, and it tends to favor Wright's more creative dishes, with the most seasonal ingredients front and center.

Set in an affluent Queen Anne neighborhood, Canlis looks like the 1950s landmark it is, a modernist beauty of massive cedar beams, rugged stone columns and fireplace, a copper charcoal broiler in the middle of the dining room, angled windows and a soaring glass wall open to the surrounding greenery (not to mention the dazzling view of downtown from the penthouse level). Canlis strikes a perfect balance between its cozy hunting-lodge aura and dressed-up fine-dining elegance—but after 50 years, that balancing act is blissfully assured.

(i) 2576 Aurora Ave. N (*206/283-3313;* www.canlis.com).

✈ Seattle-Tacoma International (14 miles/ 23km).

$$$ **Inn at the Market,** 86 Pine St. (*800/446-4484* or 206/443-3600; www.innatthemarket.com). $$ **Bacon Mansion Bed & Breakfast,** 959 Broadway E (*800/240-1864* or 206/329-1864; www.baconmansion.com).

American Regional Stars **161**

Merriman's

Hawaiian Punch

Waimea, Hawaii

Truthfully, there's not much else in Waimea besides Merriman's. Plunked down in the middle of the Big Island, in the heart of what used to be cattle ranch country, this low-slung, tin-roofed bungalow hardly looks like the culinary crossroads of Hawaii. But there's got to be some reason why every concierge at the luxe resorts on the Kohala and Kona coasts keeps a set of directions to Waimea at the front desk.

Ever since Peter Merriman and his wife Vicki opened their upcountry restaurant in 1988, it has been ground central for Hawaii Regional cuisine. After moving to Hawaii in 1983 to cook at the stellar Mauna Lani Bay Hotel, Merriman quickly figured out that creative sourcing was the way to suffuse his dishes with the spirit of this island paradise, and make them less dependent on imported foodstuffs. Seafood had always been a major feature of Hawaiian resort cuisine, but Merriman capitalized on the Big Island's cattle ranching history as well, to make use of local lamb, beef, and even pork—a staple of native Hawaiian food frequently overlooked by resort restaurants. As Merriman's flourished, he signed on local farmers to grow the other varieties of fruits and vegetables he wanted (you can't put coconut, pineapple, and coffee in every dish, after all). This support of local farmers has been a key factor in Merriman's success, right up there with his brilliant cooking and the consistently seamless service in the small but welcoming and ever-crowded dining room.

The lunch menu runs the gamut from Chinese short ribs (a Merriman's specialty, honoring the island's Asian immigrant heritage) to a goat-cheese-and-eggplant sandwich. Dinner is a little more upscale: Choose from the signature wok-charred ahi, ponzu-flavored mahimahi, kung pao shrimp, lamb from nearby Kahua Ranch, grass-fed beef filet with Maui onion jam, Pahoa corn and shrimp fritters, Kalua pig quesadillas, or the famous platters of seafood and meats. An heirloom tomato and beet salad, accented with asparagus, macadamia nuts, and local goat cheese exemplifies how Merriman has expanded the repertoire of local produce. Waimea spinach, sweet local corn, slender Nakano green beans—none of it comes from more than half an hour away, and Merriman never overdoes the preparations, which let the native flavors sing out.

Merriman has recently expanded to the **Kapalua Resort** on Maui (1 Bay Dr., Lahaina; 808/669-6400), which is good news for travelers who can't visit every

Peter Merriman has defined Hawaiian regional cuisine at his namesake restaurant in Waimea.

island during their Hawaiian vacation. Still, the homeyness of the original mid-island cottage is a big part of its appeal. You're in an island paradise—shouldn't you feel like you're eating its bounty?

ⓘ 65–1227 Opelo Rd. (Hwy. 19; 808/885-6822; www.merrimanshawaii.com).

✈ Kona (40 miles/64km).

⊨ $$$ **The Fairmont Orchid,** 1 N. Kaniku Dr. (800/845-9905 or 808/885-2000; www.fairmont.com/orchid). $$ **Areca Palms Estate Bed & Breakfast,** off Highway 11, South Kona (800/545-4390 or 808/323-2276; www.konabedandbreakfast.com).

Spoon

Ducasse Goes Global

Paris, France

Alain Ducasse is the greatest chef in the world—just ask him, he'll tell you himself. After wowing the world with his hyper-upscale restaurants in Paris (the **Plaza Athénée Restaurant,** 25 av. de Montaigne; ☎ **33/1/53-67-65-00**), Monaco (the **Louis XV,** place du Casino; ☎ **377/98-06-88-64),** and New York (**Adour Alain Ducasse,** 2 E. 55th St.; ☎ **212/710-2277**), what worlds were left for this enfant terrible to conquer?

Shrewdly, Ducasse realized that getting back to basics might be the answer, at least in terms of reaching a different market niche. By choosing the simplest of utensils—the spoon—as his symbol, he launched this trendy alternative venue in Paris in 1998; spinoffs in Mauritius, St-Tropez, and Hong Kong have followed. Though it's still upscale (and you may have to book your table weeks in advance), it's much more affordable that Ducasse's headline ventures, less pretentious, and definitely more hip. It has given Ducasse a place where he can cast off the classical French mold and go global, guest-starring a different country's cuisine each season of the year.

Naturally, when you're Alain Ducasse, even getting back to basics can take some crazy forms. The restaurant's cooks use old-fashioned mortars and pestles to grind condiments for their sauces; pastas are cooked in a specially designed Alessi pot that harks back to ancient Italian tradition.

While the rotating global focus ensures a constantly changing menu, signature staples include a citrusy sea bream ceviche, pan-seared tuna in satay sauce, spit-roasted lobster, pan-sautéed rabbit, wok-stirred vegetables, the caramelized apple *mille-feuille* dessert, or (a perennial favorite) bubble-gum ice cream. Mix-and-match salads based on fresh garden produce from the Ile de France are another innovation that should please vegetarians.

Spoon's dining room is sleeker and more contemporary looking than Ducasse's star spots as well, with a sort of Parisian-bistro-meets-California-cafe look. Tables are set closer together, and the room has a trendy buzz instead of hushed haute dignity. There are plenty of cheaper places to eat in Paris, but they don't have the imprimatur of the "world's greatest chef." One thing you've got to say about Alain Ducasse: He always delivers.

ⓘ 14 rue Marignan, 8e (☎ **33/1/40-76-34-44;** www.spoon.tm.fr; www.alain-ducasse.com/public/index.htm).

✈ De Gaulle, 23km/14 miles); Orly (14km/8²⁄₃ miles).

🛏 $$ **La Tour Notre Dame,** 20 rue du Sommerard, 5e (☎ **33/1/43-54-47-60;** www.la-tour-notre-dame.com). $ **Hotel de la Place des Vosges,** 12 rue de Birague, 4e (☎ **33/1/42-72-60-46;** www.hotelplacedesvosges.com).

L'Atelier de Joël Robuchon

Back in the Game

Paris, France

Joël Robuchon said he was done—after being hailed as the greatest chef in France (the Gault-Millau guide even named him "chef of the century" in 1989), he stunned the culinary world in 1996 by announcing he was hanging up his toque and packing away his knives for good. But once a chef always a chef, and eventually in 2003 Robuchon found himself back in the game, though in a different sort of place entirely.

In the swanky 7th arrondissement, L'Atelier de Joël Robuchon is like a chef's table on steroids: 36 seats are pulled up to a bar-style countertop that surrounds an open-to-view kitchen. To say that this is more casual than the haute restaurants where Robuchon made his name is not to say it's cheap or laid back. Instead of rococo glitz, you have an angular contemporary look with veneered woods, red leather, flat gray walls, stainless steel, and pools of downlighting. The dishes come in small tapas-like portions, but they still show a high degree of innovation and finesse. You might start with *foie gras en torchon* or eggplant confit in mille-feuille pastry, or morsels of spring lamb, pigeon, or suckling pig; there's even a pig's foot on a Parmesan tartine. Among the sublime main courses are caramelized quail glazed with shallot-perfumed sauce; buttery, tender langoustines in pastry; hanger steak with fries; or beef tournedos with black Malabar pepper. Duckling comes roasted, braised, and flavored with spices such as ginger, nutmeg, and cinnamon—and of course, Robuchon still makes the most divine mashed potatoes on the planet. Desserts include luscious things like a Chartreuse soufflé, coffee mousse flecked with crumbs of brownie, and chocolate "Sensation." Reservations are accepted for three seatings a day, at the very un-French hours of 11:30am, 2pm, and 6:30pm.

Once he was back in the game, Robuchon ended up franchising the L'Atelier concept all over the world—Hong Kong, Las Vegas, London, New York, Tokyo—as well as fine-dining restaurants in Monaco and Macao. At the moment his restaurants can claim a collective 17 Michelin stars, making his the most Michelin-honored restaurant empire in the world. He's like a culinary juggernaut that can't be stopped. But then, with food this good, who would want to stop him?

ⓘ 5-7 rue de Montalembert, 7e (© **33/1/42-22-56-56;** www.joel-robuchon.com).

✈ De Gaulle (23km/14 miles); Orly (14km/8²/₃ miles).

🛏 $$$ **Hôtel Luxembourg Parc,** 42 rue de Vaugirard, 6e (© **33/1/53-10-36-50;** www.luxembourg-paris-hotel. com). $$ **Hôtel Saintonge,** 16 rue Saintonge, 3e (© **33/1/42-77-91-13;** www. saintongemarais.com).

7 Places to Eat in . . . São Paolo, Brazil

The carioca culture of Rio de Janiero is great for music, barhopping, and beach-going, but when Brazilian gourmets want to indulge themselves, where do they head? São Paolo. In this affluent, booming, multicultural metropolis, restaurant-going is practically a religious pursuit. Paulistas deeply respect all the rituals of dining out—expect to dress up for dinner, to eat fashionably late (10pm is on the early side), and to wait for a table (most of São Paolo's best spots don't take reservations).

Navigating the São Paolo sprawl can be confounding, and the traffic is horrendous, so organize your time here by neighborhoods. Amid the skyscrapers of the Avenida Paulista district, the refined, sleek ⓵⓺⓸ **Antiquarius** (Alameda Lorena 1884; ☎ **55/11/3082-3015;** www.antiquarius.com.br) consistently wins raves for its classical Portuguese cuisine, including dishes rarely served outside Portugal—like *cataplana de peixes e frutos do mar,* a rich seafood stew with bacon and sausage, served in a traditional lidded pot; or *açorda,* a clay-pot casserole of crab, shrimp, and mussels—along with a definitive *bacalhau* (cod). Many of the city's best high-end restaurants are Italian; one standout is ⓵⓺⓹ **Massimo** (Alameda Santos 1826; ☎ **55/11/ 3284-0311**), with a menu that's practically a geography lesson in Italian regional cuisines: The changing menu may include oven-roasted lamb with vegetables, tomato, and white-wine sauce; trout filet served with olive oil and basil; or a lean suckling pig with roast potatoes; all with wine pairings to match.

A cassoulet at Figueira Rubaiyat.

It's hard not to fall in love with the lush green suburbs to the southwest, known collectively as *Jardins,* where you'll find the city's most stunning restaurant setting: ⓵⓺⓺ **Figueira Rubaiyat** (Rua Haddock Lobo 1738; ☎ **55/11/3063-3888;** www. rubaiyat.com.br), a glass-ceilinged beauty built around the gnarled trunk of a magnificent old fig tree. It's a perfect place to appreciate the Brazilian passion for meat: Most of the beef, chicken, and other meats served here come from the owners' own *fazenda* (cattle ranch), so the quality is always top-notch. (A more casual and cheaper spinoff, Baby Beef Rubaiyat, is a few blocks away at Av. Brigadeiro Faria Lima 2954.) For sheer star power, visit celebrity chef Alex Atala's ⓵⓺⓻ **D.O.M.** (R. Barão de Capanema 549; ☎ **55/11/3088 0761;** www.domrestaurante.com.br), a sleek, high-ceilinged, airy space with high gourmet buzz. Four- or eight-course set menus showcase Atala's classical French technique, imaginatively applied to native Brazilian ingredients like black beans, codfish, sardines, manioc, and hearts of palm. Atala is no lockstep locavore, though—he's just as likely to throw in imported delicacies like foie gras and truffles when the dish calls for it. This is one of the few São Paolo restaurants that does take reservations; you'll need one, at least a week in advance.

West of Centro, in leafy Higienópolis you'll find the casual-yet-chic whitewashed-brick bistro ⑯ Carlota (Rua Sergipe 753; ⓒ **55/11/3661-8670;** www.carlota.com.br). Owner-chef Carla Pernambuco blends the flavors of her own Italian heritage, the culinary style of her training in Manhattan, and fresh Brazilian ingredients; typical dishes include codfish and shiitake mushrooms with Indian curry sauce, a grilled duck magret with *jaboticaba* sauce and manioc puree, or huge ravioli stuffed with shrimp and asparagus.

In the old city center, Centro, stop by the Mercado Municipal (Rua da Cantareira 306), a glorious 1930s-vintage market hall with skylights and stained-glass windows; it bustles with meat, fish, and produce vendors every day except Sunday, from 5am to 4pm. Make a beeline for the ⑯ Bar do Mane food stand to sample São Paulo's classic street food, the overstuffed *mortadela* sandwich, a messy two-handed feast of smoked meat and sloppy melted cheese and shredded vegetables that's completely unhealthy and, fortunately, to-die-for. Fill up, because you'll have a long wait that evening for a table at ⑰ Famiglia Mancini (Rua Avanhandava 81; ⓒ **55/11/3256-4320**), a beloved checkered-tablecloth Italian restaurant with an enormous pasta menu—not only does it offer every shape of pasta imaginable, you can choose any of 30 different sauces to go on top.

✈ Guarulhos International (Sao Paulo; 27km/16 miles).

🛏 $$ **Quality Jardins,** Alameda Campinas 540 (ⓒ **0800/555-855** or 55/11/3147-0400; www.atlanticahotels.com.br). $$ **Tryp Higienópolis,** Rua Maranhão 371 (ⓒ **55/11/3665-8200;** www.solmelia.com).

The dining room at Figueira Rubaiyat is built around the trunk of an old fig tree.

Les Brasseries de Paul Bocuse
There's No Place Like Home
Lyon, France

The reality of the restaurant business is that it's very hard to get rich with a three-star restaurant, even if you're in the very top echelon of chefs. There's no question that **Paul Bocuse** is in that top echelon, and gourmet travelers are willing to make a special trip to Lyon to visit his main restaurant, Paul Bocuse (40 rue de la Plage; Collonges au Mont D'Or; ℭ **33/4/72-42-90-90;** www.bocuse.fr), acknowledged as a bastion of fine French cuisine. But even at the prices that a culinary genius like Bocuse can command, the profit margin on such labor-intensive cuisine can be surprisingly thin.

Perhaps it was nostalgia that first inspired Bocuse in 1994 to buy **Brasserie le Nord** (18 rue Neuve; ℭ **33/4/72-10-69-69**), the local restaurant near the city hall where he first started working as a teenager. With its speckled terrazzo floors and red leather booths, it's an exemplar of *cuisine bourgeois*—onion soup, snails, sausage in brioche, foie gras terrine, sole meunière, Bresse chicken in cream sauce, veal kidneys in mustard sauce, calf's head, tripe—and Bocuse had enough sense to preserve it just as it was. But once that took off, he began to see it as the business opportunity he'd been looking for. Next came **Brasserie le Sud** (place Antonin Poncet; ℭ **33/4/72-77-80-00**), a sunny cafe just off the quay of the Rhone river, where he painted the walls yellow and tilted the menu more toward Provence and Morocco, adding salade niçoise, pizza, osso buco, thyme-dusted lamb cutlets, tagines, and couscous. In 1997, he converted a lovely chrome-and-wood-trimmed Art Deco train station into **Brasserie de l'Est** (14 place Jules-Ferry; ℭ **33/4/37-24-25-26**), where there's a little more seafood on the menu; naturally, he had to round out the compass in 2003 with **La Brasserie de l'Ouest** (1 Quai du Commerce; ℭ **33/4/37-64-66-64**), a slick greenhouselike cafe in a modern office development, where the menu includes a few exotic extras like Caribbean-style cod fritters, tuna sashimi with wasabi, salmon tartare with Szechuan pepper, and prawns en brochette with Madras curry. Having exhausted all the compass points, Bocuse still had one more brasserie in him—the cozy wood-trimmed **Brasserie Argenson** out by the Gerland Olympic soccer stadium (40 allée Pierre de Coubertin; ℭ **33/4/72-73-72-73**).

With two- and three-course menus ranging between 20€ and 25€, Bocuse's bistros keep the locals happy and give visitors greater options for dining around Lyon. Let other star chefs replicate their flagships in far-flung cities—Bocuse has found a way to stay close to home and still be a restaurant mogul.

✈ Lyon (3.8km/2½ miles).

🛏 $$ **Grand Hotel-Boscolo Hotels,** rue Groleé 11, Lyon (ℭ **33/4/72-40-45-45;** www.boscolohotels.com). $$ **Campanile Lyon Centre Forum Part-Dieu,** 31 rue Maurice Flandin, Lyon (ℭ **33/4/72-36-31-00;** www.campanile.com).

Lupa
Batali Basic
New York, New York

There's nothing stuffy about Mario Batali or his farmhouse-inspired Italian cooking. Even his Michelin-starred flagships, **Babbo** (110 Waverly Place; © **212/777-0303;** www.babbonyc.com) and **Del Posto** (85 Tenth Ave.; © **212/497-8090**) are gracious, warm places, despite decidedly Manhattan-level prices. And except for his seafood trattoria **Esca** (402 W. 43rd St.; © **212/564-7272**), most of his New York City restaurant empire is scattered around the Greenwich Village area, where the atmosphere tends to be laid back and relaxed.

Still, whenever you see the affable red-haired Batali on television shows or in magazine interviews—and it seems you're always seeing him on TV or in magazines—the food he's raving about is simple, hearty Italian trattoria food. So if you can't get a reservation at Babbo (and often you can't) and you don't care to spend $300 on the wine-paired grand tasting menu at Del Posto, you can still get close to Batali's heart and soul at Lupa, in the heart of Greenwich Village between Bleecker and Houston streets. With its low ceilings, bare wood tables, white globe lights, and brick arches over the wine racks, this cheery, sometimes even raucous restaurant deftly captures the look of a vintage Roman trattoria. The menu follows suit, with appetizers like baccala, or tuna with cannellini beans; second courses like tripe, ricotta gnocchi with sausage and fennel, or *bucatini all' amatriciana;* and entrees like saltimbocca, pork shoulder with *treviso* and *aceto,* or *pollo alla diavola.* Regular patrons develop special favorites among the daily specials, like Monday's rabbit sausage or Sunday's *braciola alla cacciatoria.* And it should come as no surprise that the house-made cured meats are particularly luscious, since Batali's father, Armandino, runs Salumi, one of the country's best *salumerias,* out in Seattle (see ㉚).

For what's supposed to be a low-key neighborhood joint, Lupa can be awfully hard to get into on weekend nights, but with food this robust and satisfying, that was probably inevitable. Try it out for lunch, though, and you should have no problem. The same goes for Mario's rustic pizza restaurant, **OTTO Enoteca Pizzeria** (1 Fifth Ave.; © **212/995-9559;** www. ottopizzeria.com), a little farther north but still in the Village. Despite the pizzeria tag,

The bar at Babbo, Mario Batali's Michelin-starred flagship restaurant.

it's got lots of other things on the menu—pastas, antipasti, salads, a great cheese selection—and the salami is superb here as well. For all his jet-setting, Mario frequently pops into both Lupa and OTTO to make sure everybody's happy. Just look for the red ponytail.

(i) 170 Thompson St. (© **212/982-5089**).

✈ John F. Kennedy International (15 miles/24km); Newark Liberty International (16 miles/27km); LaGuardia (8 miles/13km).

🛏 $$$ **Carlton Hotel on Madison Avenue,** 88 Madison Ave. (© **212/532-4100;** www.carltonhotelny.com). $$ **Washington Square Hotel,** 103 Waverly Place (© **800/222-0418** or 212/777-9515; www.washingtonsquarehotel.com).

Where Star Chefs Go Casual 173

DB Bistro Moderne
Where Boulud Goes Mod
New York, New York

There's no question that Daniel Boulud is one of the world's most admired French chefs, even though he rose to culinary fame in New York. But let's say, just for the sake of argument, that you don't want to dine at his extraordinary haute cuisine palace **Restaurant Daniel** (60 E. 65th St.; © **212/288-0033**) in the toniest part of Manhattan's Upper East Side. If it's just the price tag that's stopping you ($100- plus for a three-course prix fixe), you could always slip uptown to its more casual sister **Café Boulud** (20 E. 76th St.; © **212/772-2600**). But what if you just don't want fancy French cuisine?

As it happens, Daniel Boulud knows where you're coming from—he hasn't been living in New York for over 25 years without picking up a few American tastes himself. That's why in 2001 he opened DB Bistro Moderne, his New York spin on the contemporary bistros that his Parisian peers had begun to open at the same time. Located in the nerve center of Midtown, just a couple of doors down from the Algonquin Hotel, it's a stunning, sophisticated space with deep-red walls, patterned stone floors, and huge riveting oil paintings. Cheap it's not, and there are still plenty of French items on the menu—old-school bistro classics such as foie gras

torchon, tomato *tarte tatin,* hanger steak, and *coq au vin.* But there's also a globe-hopping sensibility at work here—his escargot and chicken oyster fricassee comes with hazelnut spaetzle, the orrechette pasta with a Colorado lamb ragout, the *blanquette de veau* with basmati rice and a Riesling velouté. Hopping to North Africa, there's also a Moroccan tuna tartare and a completely traditional lamb couscous. Deeply familiar by now with American local ingredients, Boulud has sprinkled the menu with New American dishes like the refreshing peekytoe crab with frisée salad and green apple, while the dry-aged steak is a classic American steak house item, creamed spinach and all; the chicken breast with lettuce pomme puree and baby carrot is a far cry from your usual brasserie roast chicken.

Which brings us to the most famous thing on DB's menu—Boulud's over-the-top gourmet hamburger, a designer special of minced prime sirloin stuffed with *foie gras,* preserved black truffle, and braised short ribs, served on a Parmesan onion roll. It's the most expensive hamburger in the city, possibly in the world, and while some diners scoff at it as pretentious and extravagant, others rave about how delicious it tastes. One thing you've got to admit about Daniel Boulud—his cuisine is never boring.

ⓘ 55 W. 44th St. (☎ **212/391-2400;** www.danielnyc.com).

✈ John F. Kennedy International (15 miles/24km); Newark Liberty International (16 miles/27km); LaGuardia (8 miles/13km).

🛏 $$$ **Carlton Hotel on Madison Avenue,** 88 Madison Ave. (☎ **212/532-4100;** www.carltonhotelny.com). $$ **Washington Square Hotel,** 103 Waverly Place (☎ **800/222-0418** or 212/777-9515; www.washingtonsquarehotel.com).

Le Bar Lyonnais

A Pair of Perriers

Philadelphia, Pennsylvania

In 1970, when George Perrier opened Le Bec-Fin in Philadelphia, his classical French cooking was still considered an exotic luxury import. At a time when Julia Child had just awakened middle America's curiosity about French cuisine, nobody did it better than George—and nobody in Philadelphia came even close. Culinary fads might come and go, but Le Bec-Fin's signature Galette de Crabe and Quenelles de Brochet were dishes that every self-respecting gourmet had to sample at least once.

After 25 years at the top of the Philadelphia dining scene, however, George Perrier was shrewd enough to see that it was time for a fresh approach. While his "serious" restaurant, **Le Bec-Fin,** continued to roll smoothly along, Perrier began to extend his brand with several more casual ventures—Brasserie Perrier down the street (now closed); the sleek bistro **George's,** in the Main Line suburb of Wayne (503 W. Lancaster Ave.; ☎ 610/964-2588; www.georgesonthemainline.com); the power steakhouse **Table 31** in the Comcast Center (1701 JFK Blvd.; ☎ 215/567-7111; www.table31.com); and, in Atlantic City, **Mia** (Caesar's Palace, 2100 Pacific Ave.; ☎ 609/441-2345; www.miaac.com).

With much less fanfare, however, Perrier's fifth casual venture—serving brasserie-style fare in the bar downstairs from Le Bec-Fin's exquisite rococo dining rooms—may be the most satisfying of all. **Le Bar Lyonnais** evokes the traditional hotel restaurants of Perrier's native Lyons, France, with old-fashioned patterned wallpapers, carpets, and marled wood paneling. Serving lunch on Fridays and Saturdays and dinner Monday through Saturday, it offers classic brasserie food—robust favorites such as French onion soup, escargots, salad Lyonnais, steak tartare, sautéed foie gras, cassoulet, duck confit, lamb shank, and steak frites. Le Bar Lyonnais also serves burgers, or at least Perrier's haute version of a burger: grilled prime beef topped with caramelized onion puree and cherry tomato confiture on a brioche bun. Perrier himself, who has handed over Le Bec-Fin's day-to-day cooking to head chef Pierre Camels, hangs out here most often these days. Stop in and you'll understand why.

ⓘ 1523 Walnut St.; ☎ **215/567-1000;** www.lebecfin.com

✈ Philadelphia International (9¹/₂ miles/15km).

🛏 $$$ **Rittenhouse 1715,** 1715 Rittenhouse Sq. (☎ **877/791-6500** or 215/546-6500; www.rittenhouse1715.com). $$ **Penn's View Hotel,** 14 N. Front St. (☎ **800/331-7634** or 215/922-7600; www.pennsviewhotel.com).

Central Michel Richard

Happy in Both Kitchens

Washington, D.C.

For years, while all his French peers in other cities were expanding their empires, Michel Richard kept his head down, intently focused on cooking at his flagship restaurant, the superb **Citronelle** in upscale Georgetown (3000 M St. NW; ©**202/625-2150;** www.citronelledc.com). Citronelle continued to perform at such a high level, producing such light and creative French food, that some diners began to feel that Richard perhaps knew best—that they should take literally the title of his book *Happy in the Kitchen* and let the man be.

Yet while Michel Richard is indeed French—born in Brittany, trained in Paris under Gaston Lenôtre—after he first came to the United States in 1975, he fell so in love with American food, he never went back to France. That's why it makes sense that in 2007 he finally turned his full attention to American food by opening Central Michel Richard. This brasserie has a menu full of American classics, given a stylish French spin. The lobster burger comes layered with scallop mousse, the macaroni and cheese is dressed up with sour cream and tangy Gruyère, the fried chicken is bread-crumbed instead of battered. To maintain his edge over homegrown competition, Richard then throws in French classics such as hanger steak, onion soup, charcuterie, mussels with white wine and garlic, cassoulet, and french fries so definitive, no one in Washington would ever call them "freedom fries." A salad frisée appears on the menu next to a retro American salad of iceberg lettuce and blue cheese, braised beef cheeks next to a rib-eye steak, crème brûlée beside apple pan dowdy.

Richard's purpose in opening Central wasn't just to try different recipes; he also wanted to develop a younger audience—the congressional aides instead of the members of Congress themselves. Instead of a Georgetown location, he chose the District, between the White House and the Capitol, where there's plenty of lunchtime and happy hour business. The atmosphere here is much livelier than at Citronelle, with a large bar area (it even has a television) and an open kitchen; wine is stored in open racks that are themselves a design element, and you can look right into a corner meat locker. The decor is contemporary and angular, with soaring ceilings, warm golden colors, glossy blond wood, beige marble counters, and beige wall tiles. Perhaps the most striking detail of all is the big magenta silkscreened portrait of Michel Richard himself, his round bearded face casting an avuncular grin over the dining room. He's still happy in the kitchen—and he wants you to be happy too.

ⓘ 1001 Pennsylvania Ave. (© **202/626-0015;** www.centralmichelrichard.com).

✈ Reagan National (3 miles/5km); Dulles International (26 miles/41km); Baltimore-Washington International (35 miles/56km).

🛏 $$ **Four Points by Sheraton,** 1201 K St. NW (© **202/289-7600;** www.fourpoints.com/washingtondcdowntown). $$ **Georgetown Suites,** 1111 30th St. NW (© **202/298-1600;** www.georgetownsuites.com).

176

Lüke

Shelter from the Storm

New Orleans, Louisiana

Hurricane Katrina made a local hero out of John Besh. In those first dark days after the disaster, he could be found day after day, valiantly feeding scores of relief workers from huge vats of red beans and rice he'd set up in a Wal-Mart parking lot. His own restaurants were spared the worst of the flooding, so he devoted himself over the next few months to helping the rest of the restaurant community and their local suppliers get back on their feet.

Besh was in many ways transformed by the experience. When his renowned **Restaurant August** (301 Tchoupitoulas St.; © **504/299-9777;** www.restaurantaugust. com) reopened—one of the first New Orleans restaurants to rise from the flood—he fondly added red beans and rice to its haute French menu. He also rescued his former mentor's Provençal restaurant across Lake Pontchartrain, **La Provence** (25020 Hwy. 190, Lacombe; © **985/626-7662**). (He also operates **Besh Steak** in the Harrah's Casino; © **504/533-6111**). But having done the fussy upscale cuisine thing for a while, Besh's heart these days is in this cozy brasserie he opened in 2006 in the Central Business District.

With its dark wood trim, pressed-tin ceilings, fans, newspaper racks, blackboard specials, and paper cones of crusty french fries, Lüke has all the authentic flavor of the provincial German and French places where Besh first trained after graduating from the Culinary Institute of America. Besh digs deep into European bourgeois cuisine with pitch-perfect renderings of brasserie classics such as duck-and-white-bean cassoulet, roast suckling pig with cherry mustard and stewed greens, veal schnitzel with spatzle, herb-roasted chicken with mashed potatoes, *Flamen küche* (an Alsatian tort topped with chunks of bacon and caramelized onions), or the house sauerkraut, which comes laden with pork belly and pigs' knuckles. But this is no German theme restaurant: Lüke also turns out a big juicy cheeseburger with caramelized onions and thick-cut bacon, a satisfying seafood gumbo, and a remarkably luscious shrimp-and-grits. There's a great raw bar, too, supporting the local crabbers and oystermen that Besh got to know so well in the post-Katrina days.

Naturally, the imported beer selection is memorable, but Lüke also has its own three custom-brewed house ales on tap. Save room for the warm chocolate custard filled with mini-profiteroles.

ⓘ 333 St. Charles Ave. (© **504/378-2840;** www.lukeneworleans.com).

✈ Louis Armstrong New Orleans International (15 miles/24km).

🛏 **Omni Royal Orleans,** 621 St. Louis St. (© **800/THE-OMNI** [800/843-6664] or 504/529-5333; www.omniroyalorleans. com). **Hotel Monteleone,** 214 Rue Royale (© **800/535-9595** or 504/523-3341; www. hotelmonteleone.com).

Chez Panisse

Alice in Wonderland

Berkeley, California

It all started with Alice. The word "locavore" hadn't been coined when free-spirited Montessori teacher Alice Waters and French lit professor Paul Aratow opened this unassuming restaurant in countercultural Berkeley in 1971. Having just returned from a seminal year spent traveling around France, Waters was infused with passion about honest breads and market produce and handmade cheeses. Chez Panisse adopted a format that was radical for America then: two seatings a night, serving a four-course set menu written anew every morning according to what ingredients were best that day.

Over the next 30-plus years, Waters's ideals transformed American gastronomy. Any number of influential chefs—Jeremiah Tower, Mark Miller, Paul Bertolli, Judy Rodgers, Deborah Madison, Jonathan Waxman—started their careers in Waters's kitchen. What's more, by enthusiastically promoting her handpicked network of suppliers—mostly local farmers and ranchers dedicated to sustainable agriculture—Waters made concerns like Acme Bakery and Niman Ranch into culinary celebrities as well.

The restaurant is deliberately low key, a wood-trimmed Arts-and-Crafts-style dining

Chefs at work in the kitchen of Alice Water's Chez Panisse.

room with copper fixtures and framed French posters on the walls. Monday night menus are simpler and more rustic, while Fridays and Saturdays get a bit more elaborate (prices for the set menus are adjusted accordingly, though they're all under $100, a relative bargain for such a landmark restaurant). Monday night, for example, might feature a deeply rustic Sonoma Liberty duck leg braised in red wine with orange zest, little onions, and herb noodles; by Wednesday, a more refined dish of grilled Wolfe Ranch quail with wild mushroom risotto and wine grapes might take center stage; Saturday night might see an elegant rack, loin, and leg of Cattail Creek Ranch lamb, dressed up Provençal-style with green olives, green beans, and zucchini. Reservations can be made by phone only one calendar month ahead, and they're snapped up faster than the first strawberry of summer.

If you can't get a reservation downstairs, try the more informal **Café Panisse**

(☎ **510/548-5049**) upstairs, a congenial place with an open kitchen, charcoal grill, and a wood-burning oven for pizzas. The menu here is a la carte, with entrees in the $20 to $25 range; its laid-back vibe harks back to what Chez Panisse was originally intended to be, before it became such a gastronomic shrine. A few blocks away, **Café Fanny** (1603 San Pablo Ave.; ☎ **510/524-5447**), named after Waters' daughter, serves a takeout breakfast and lunch with a few cafe tables. It's all good—and good for you, in more ways than you can count.

ⓘ 1517 Shattuck Ave. (☎ **510/548-5525;** www.chezpanisse.com).

✈ Oakland International (15 miles/25km).

🛏 $$$ **Hotel Adagio,** 550 Geary St. (☎ **800/228-8830** or 415/775-5000; www.thehoteladagion.com). $ **Hotel des Arts,** 447 Bush St. (☎ **800/956-4322** or 415/956-3232; www.sfhoteldesarts.com).

178 Straight from the Farm

Herbfarm

Harvest Haute

Woodinville, Washington

Woodinville used to be a simple farming and logging community, just outside the Seattle sprawl—but that was before Bill and Lola Zimmerman began selling herbs from their roadside stand in 1974. With a growing cluster of boutique wineries nearby (see Chateau Ste. Michelle, ㉜), the Herbfarm was ideally located for snagging the new weekend gourmet trade. Then the Zimmermans' son Ron and daughter-in-law Carrie added a restaurant in a remodeled wing of the farmhouse in 1986, and suddenly the Herbfarm became much more than just a farm. Its fame spread like wildfire, even more so after Ron replaced himself in the kitchen with the enormously talented chef Jerry Traunfeld in 1990. (Traunfeld's bestselling *Herbfarm*

Cookbook spread the restaurant's name worldwide.)

Rebuilt on a new site after a disastrous 1996 fire, the Herbfarm transplanted all the fruit trees, berries, and herbs from the original farm, and added a few luxurious accommodations for overnight guests. (Come early and you can take a tour of the Herbfarm's extensive kitchen gardens, 1 mile/1.6km down the road.) The setting is a rambling timber-and-stucco house full of Victorian-style whimsy—baronial fireplaces, carved wood details, thick patterned rugs, floral-print upholstery and drapes and wallpaper, suffused with the yellow glow of small lamps and wall sconces. It's fussy and formal, but in a charmingly old-fashioned way.

Ron and Carrie are still very much at the heart of things here, though Traunfeld handed over the reins to young rising star chef Keith Luce in 2007, decamping to open his own restaurant in Seattle. Like Traunfeld, Luce—a former White House sous chef—serves a nine-course set menu every night, drawn from the morning's harvest as well as products from several other small local growers and food artisans. Menu items are full of specific place names and odd heirloom ingredients— things like Lummi Island sockeye salmon served in a squash blossom with lemon and thyme, stinging nettle soup with Puget Sound mussels, grilled squab on a pat of onion pudding with a rainbow of beets and fillet beans, or a braised shank of Anderson Ranch Oregon lamb served on emmer wheat. Luce's finely honed sense of contrasting flavors comes out in dishes like a trio of paddlefish caviar on crisped salmon skin, skewers of rosemary-mussels with cucumber kimchi, and Westcott Bay oysters with sorrel sauce. Wine pairings do a beautiful job of promoting the best Pacific Northwest wines.

Herbfarm is very much a Big Deal restaurant—a meal can last up to 5 hours and the price edges close to $200 with wines included. Single diners will be happy to know that there's a communal table every night where individuals can be seated. Check out the website for the frequent themed dinner evenings, which may focus on anything from mushrooms to wild game to truffles to exotic spices.

(i) 14590 NE 145th St. (© **425/485-5300;** www.theherbfarm.com).

✈ Seattle-Tacoma International (28 miles/45km).

🛏 $$$ **Willows Lodge,** 14580 NE 145th St., Woodinville (© **877/424-3930** or 425/424-3930; www.willowslodge. com).

Straight from the Farm 179

L'Etoile

The North Star

Madison, Wisconsin

Surely L'Etoile is the sort of place the Slow Food founders wanted to inspire—a French-style restaurant in the capital of a big farming state, where as many menu items as possible come from local, sustainable, organic farms.

Founded in 1976 by Odessa Piper, who had been both a chef and a farmer before opening her own place, L'Etoile was one of the very earliest restaurants in the Midwest to espouse Alice Waters's farm-to-table gospel. Piper had always cooked ambitious menus, which garnered her a 2001 James Beard award for the Midwest's best chef. New York–trained Tory Miller has done likewise since he took over the restaurant in 2005, after working as Piper's head chef for 2 years before she stepped aside. Look, for example, at his Tuscan-style bread soup: It's made with chicken, cheese, a sage-and-truffle meatball, and a mélange of vegetables including mushrooms, rutabaga, celery root, turnips, and radicchio—all of it except the truffle from nearby farms. Taking a local poultry farm's organic free-range chicken, Miller will cinnamon-smoke it, then serve it with creamy sage polenta, oyster and shiitake mushrooms, braised bok choy, and a Pinot Noir truffle sauce (there's that alien truffle again). A pan-roasted sturgeon may come from far away, but it's wonderfully savory accompaniment is locally raised braised short ribs, roasted beets, cabbage, and cauliflower purée. Cheese is a particular passion for Miller—a great passion to indulge in one of the nation's top dairy states—and he maintains a huge selection of artisanal Wisconsin cheeses, including a number of sheep's milk and goat cheese. You can order a complete tasting of the entire cheese board, but be warned, you'll be tasting upwards of 30 cheeses, all of them top notch.

Wisconsin is northern enough that it has a fairly short growing season, but that doesn't seem to faze the folks at L'Etoile—the restaurant's long list of suppliers includes several with extensive root cellars and environmentally correct unheated hoop houses to extend crops into the winter months. What's more, the restaurant follows the farm wives' strategy of "putting up" quantities of produce in season, so that preserves, jar-packed, and dried vegetables and fruits will be available for cooking year-round.

Wholesome as it all sounds, this is still a fine-dining restaurant: Most entrees cost over $25, and it's regularly voted Madison's top place for a special dinner. On the second floor of an older building on Capitol Square, it's a relatively small wood-beamed dining room with a lovely view of the state capitol dome. Downstairs, you can also pick up sandwiches and baked goods at Café Soleil, which—no surprise—serves only fair trade organic coffee.

ⓘ 25 North Pinckney St. (ⓒ **608/251-0500;** www.letoile-restaurant.com).

✈ Dane Regional Airport, Madison (7.2km/4¹/₂ miles).

🛏 $$$ **Mansion Hill Inn,** 424 N. Pinckney St. (ⓒ **800/798-9070** or 608/255-3999; www.mansionhillinn.com). $$ **The Edgewater,** 666 Wisconsin Ave. (ⓒ **800/922-5512** or 608/256-9071; www.thcedgewater.com.)

Patowmack Farm

Virtuous, with a View

Lovettsville, Virginia

Talk about transcendent experiences. You're sitting in a hilltop glass pavilion, looking out over the Loudon Valley, punctuated in the hazy blue distance by the Point of Rocks Bridge and the Potomac River. As night falls, crickets chirp in the nearby vegetable gardens; roosting chickens ruffle and sigh. You're feeling very good about yourself, because you know that the meal you're about to eat is completely organic and sustainable. Not only that, no carbon emissions were expended delivering produce, for it all comes right here from Patowmack Farm, from the spring's first tender shoots of asparagus to the last butternut squash of autumn.

Following sustainable farming methods that exceed the technical requirements for organic growing, Beverly Morton Billand and Chuck Billand began to cultivate fresh herbs and specialty vegetables in 1986 on this hilltop 50 miles (80km) from Washington, D.C. In 1998 they added a farm-to-table restaurant, where they showcase their harvest, complemented by natural meats, sustainable seafood, artisanal cheeses, and organic wines from other responsible suppliers.

Luckily, they found an ideal chef, Christian Evans, a self-taught cook who shares their love of fresh natural foods. Throughout the seasons, his ever-changing menu may include things like an heirloom tomato gazpacho; chilled truffle pea soup; "soup and sandwich" (an oniony duck broth with floating crouton of toast topped with goat cheese); puff pastry filled with a cream of elephant garlic, pimento, black olives, shallots, and Parmesan cheese; or chicken liver in a *vol-au-vent* pastry with caramelized onions, wild boar sausage, and truffle butter. Evans has developed a great network of artisanal suppliers, both from the area and from his native Vermont; their products reach the Patowmack table in dishes such as quail stuffed with wild game, accompanied by risotto *forestière* and braised collard greens; grilled hanger steak with vegetable-stuffed brown rice crepes; or roast Cornish game hen on a bed of creamy leeks.

What you don't expect—and what finally blows you away—is the intricate artistry of Evans's plate presentations. Sprigs of fresh herbs, edible flowers, and drizzles and droplets of gem-colored sauces set off his precisely arranged small portions, making you feel incredibly pampered as well as virtuous.

Dinner is served Thursday, Friday, and Saturday nights, either a la carte or in a five-course prix-fixe menu (also available with wine pairings); a vegetarian menu is always available as well. Saturday and Sunday brunches are an especially great time to visit, when you can tour the farm, walk the $1/2$-mile (.8km) nature trail, or just drink in those breathtaking views.

ⓘ 42461 Lovettsville Rd. (℘ **540/822-9017;** www.patowmackfarm.com).

✈ Washington Dulles International (15 miles/24km).

🛏 $$$ **Lansdowne Resort,** 44050 Woodridge Pkwy., Leesburg (℘ **800/541-4801** or 703/729-8400; www.lansdowneresort.com). $$ **Norris House Inn,** 108 Loudoun St. SW (℘ **703/771-8051;** www.norrishouse.com).

Straight from the Farm

181

L'Arpège
Passard's Passion
Paris, France

In 1986, when the gifted young chef Alain Passard bought the classy 7th arrondissement restaurant L'Archestrate from his mentor, Alain Senderens, he was stepping into the sort of haute cuisine restaurant for which Paris is renowned. Even when Passard renamed it L'Arpège, redecorated it in sinuous Deco-style wood, leather, and etched glass, and started to rack up the Michelin stars, it was still similar to others in its class. The telegenic Passard gained a worldwide audience in 1997 and 1999 with his performances on Japanese TV's *Iron Chef*—but he was still operating within classical French boundaries.

Then in 2001, Passard made a daring move: He banished red meat from his menu, dropping no less than 12 of his signature dishes, and focused fanatically on vegetables. For Passard, it wasn't necessarily about health and nutrition or even Slow Food politics; it was more of a been-there-done-that escape, the impulse of a restless genius looking for new trails to blaze. You can still order the occasional poultry dish, and there's plenty of seafood—shellfish, butter, and vegetables are the culinary cornerstones of Passard's native Brittany—but his stunning way with garden vegetables, cooked with painstaking gentleness to call out their deepest colors and aromas, has truly become his hallmark.

In 2002, Passard took the logical next step, planting a 2.5-hectare (6-acre) garden 220km (136 miles) southeast of Paris where all the produce for his restaurant is raised organically, without any machines (if you don't count a horse and plow). It's a complete ecosystem, with beehives, nesting boxes for birds, and a pond to attract slug-eating frogs. Each morning, workers load produce onto the 10am TGV train to Paris so it reaches the restaurant garden fresh. Garbage is then shipped back to the garden for composting.

The epicurean world was skeptical at first, but most diners have been won over by dishes such as a couscous of vegetables and shellfish, sage-filled ravioli, a fricassee of tiny peas with ginger and red grapefruit, lobster braised in the yellow wine of the Jura, braised monkfish in a mustard sauce, pigeon roasted with almonds and honey-flavored mead, or carpaccio of crayfish with caviar-flavored cream sauce. His signature dessert is a candied tomato stuffed with 12 kinds of dried and fresh fruit, served with anise-flavored ice cream.

If you have any doubt about Passard's passion, look at the spare, serene restaurant's decorative centerpieces—sculptural arrangements of vegetables rather than standard-issue fresh flowers. He's a true believer, that's for sure.

ⓘ 84 rue de Varenne, 7e (✆ **33/1/47-05-09-06;** www.alain-passard.com).

✈ De Gaulle (23km/14 miles); Orly (14km/8²/₃ miles).

🛏 $$$ **Hôtel Luxembourg Parc,** 42 rue de Vaugirard, 6e (✆ **33/1/53-10-36-50;** www.luxembourg-paris-hotel.com). $$ **Hôtel Saintonge,** 16 rue Saintonge, 3e (✆ **33/1/42-77-91-13**; www.saintonge-marais.com).

182 Straight from the Farm

Manresa

The Modernista & His Farm

Los Gatos, California

Tucked away in the brown Santa Cruz hills south of San Jose, Manresa still looks a little like the ranch-style tea room it was back in the 1940s—dark wood beams cross the low ceilings, wide casement windows run the length of the room, and the thick plaster walls are painted in solid, soothing colors like deep mustard yellow. Despite the crisp white tablecloths and pristine place settings, Manresa has the mellow patina of old Spain, or at least the California mission era.

David Kinch's cuisine has one foot in classical European cuisine (which is to say French), but the other foot is squarely in modern culinary innovation, the sort of wizardry that has made Catalonia a foodie mecca. Kinch calls it Modernista cooking, whatever that means (mosaic tile details and a curved wall in the dining room recall Barcelona's great Modernista architect

Gaudí). Since he opened Manresa in 2002, the cornerstone of Kinch's culinary philosophy has been something so radical, it sounds old-fashioned: Use lots of vegetables, biodynamic if possible. To make sure you have a ready supply, cut an exclusive deal with a like-minded local farmer—in this case, nearby Love Apple Farm.

Naturally, the daily menu depends on what Love Apple has harvested that morning. Depending on the season, you may find dishes such as delicate stuffed squash blossoms with a squash-blossom *velouté*, served with robust dark bread croquant and duck ham; a summery Gold Dust peach and basil salad with almonds and soft shell crab; marinated shellfish with golden raspberries; or a roast lamb with garden squashes with preserved Meyer lemon and beet tartare. Like the Catalan innovators (read Ferran Adrià),

At Manresa, in Los Gatos, California, David Kinch calls his cuisine *modernista*.

Kinch goes for small portions that deconstruct a dish's elements; in some of them, foams and liquids concentrate the garden flavors in surprising new forms. But Kinch's great sense of northern California *terroir* inspires every dish, and no less a locavore

fanatic than French chef Alain Passard (see ⑱) has visited Los Gatos just for the privilege of cooking with him.

You'd hardly expect to find a Michelin two-star restaurant here in out-of-the-way Los Gatos—though the software millionaires of nearby Silicon Valley certainly find their way here. For Kinch, however, the rewards of being close to his agricultural sources make it worthwhile. Open Wednesday through Sunday for dinner only, this is a destination restaurant rather than a local hangout. The tasting menu is expensive, but if you came all the way here, you'll want to sample as many of Kinch's superlative dishes as possible.

ⓘ 320 Village Lane (⌀ **408/354-4330;** www.manresarestaurant.com).

✈ San Francisco International (40 miles/64km).

🛏 $$$ **Toll House,** 140 S. Santa Cruz Ave., Los Gatos (⌀ **408/395-7070;** www. tollhousehotel.com). $$ **Garden Inn Hotel,** 46 E. Main St., Los Gatos (⌀ **408/ 354-6446;** www.gardeninn.us).

Straight from the Farm 183

Blue Hill at Stone Barns

The Field House

Pocantico Hills, New York

One fateful night, David Rockefeller had dinner at the unassuming Greenwich Village bistro Blue Hill, named after the family farm in the Berkshires where chef Dan Barber and his brother and co-owner, David, grew up. Little did the Barbers know that their customer that night was in the process of setting up the Stone Barns Center for Food and Agriculture on his family estate in Westchester County. One meal at Blue Hill and Rockefeller knew he had found the team he needed to run Stone Barns.

It was an ideal match of public-minded philanthropist and passionate, gifted chef. The Barber brothers, along with David's wife, Laureen, now split their time between their Manhattan bistro **Blue Hill** (75 Washington St.; ⌀ **212/539-1776;** www.blue hillnyc.com) and this country outpost, opened in 2004 in a simply decorated converted dairy barn of mellow golden stone, surrounded by a huge 80-acre (32-hectare) working organic farm. While the farm also trucks produce down to the city restaurant, it only takes a few minutes for vegetables and fruit to get from field to kitchen up in Westchester. Dan Barber's cooking is energized by produce so fresh the soil is still clinging moistly to its roots, the leaves still warm from the sun. As a cook, he has always favored gentle poaching and braising, methods ideally suited to expressing the deepest essence of vegetables. Many diners walk out raving over the ingredients, not realizing what skill it took to make such seemingly simple dishes soar.

Dan Barber goes way beyond the typical locavore cruising a farmer's market for daily produce. He's free to plant unusual varieties of vegetables—the sort that are bred for flavor rather than for shelf life and transportability—and raise heirloom breeds of poultry, sheep, and pigs (free-range, of course). He has become quite the activist chef, in fact, writing op-ed pieces for the *New York Times* and serving on several advisory boards including Slow Food USA.

It's impossible to predict what you'll find on the restaurant's five-course tasting menu or the even longer Farm Feast sampler. If spring peas are at their height, you may find peas everywhere on the menu— in a crisp gazpacho, in creamy cannelloni, and mixed into a seafood risotto. When it's time for beets, parsnips, and fennel in autumn, you'll find them in dizzying profusion—julienned, pureed, layered, minced, roasted whole—alongside perfectly poached fish, amazingly flavorful turkey, or deeply savory pork. Summer is an especially lovely time of year to come, not only because you'll be at the height of the growing season, but because late summer sunsets give you more daylight to enjoy the view of meadows and fields from the dining room's large windows.

The center itself (www.stonebarns center.org) hosts several weekly tours, workshops, and lectures. Monthly wine

Dan Barber's farm-to-table cuisine at Blue Hill at Stone Barns.

dinners and special holiday feasts give diners even more of a reason to take that easy train ride from Manhattan. Reservations are taken 1 month in advance for dinner Wednesday through Sunday or for Sunday brunch.

ⓘ 630 Bedford Rd., Pocantico Hills (✆ **914/366-9600;** www.bluehillstone barns.com).

✈ John F. Kennedy International (38 miles/61km); Newark Liberty International (44 miles/71km); LaGuardia (29 miles/47km).

🛏 $$ **The Lucerne,** 201 W. 79th St., New York NY (✆ **800/492-8122** or 212/875-1000; www.thelucernehotel.com). $ **Milburn Hotel,** 242 W. 76th St., New York NY (✆ **800/833-9622** or 212/362-1006; www.milburnhotel.com).

Outstanding in the Field

Jim Denevan's Moveable Feast

Around the World

Talk about farm-to-table fresh: How about a table-on-farm feast? When Jim Denevan sets up his long white linen-draped table in a farmer's field, shaded by huge white parasols, the lucky guests know they are in for an experience like no other. It's way beyond a picnic—a high-end five-course al fresco dinner cooked on-site by an invited guest chef who uses only the most local ingredients, most of them grown on the ground right under the table.

Author of the cookbook *Outstanding in the Field*, Denevan has been putting together these moveable feasts since 1999. They begin around 4pm with a tour of the host farm (or ranch, or vineyard), then progress to a 3- or 4-hour dinner served family style with paired wines. It's a prix-fixe, set menu affair, with proper crystal glasses and cutlery, linen napkins, cut flowers in little vases, and a wonderful set of mismatched vintage china. Later in the year, when the sun sets earlier, there may even be candlelight. The table seats 130 people, and the guest list always includes local farmers, winemakers, and other producers—the butcher, the baker, and perhaps the goat-cheese maker whose food you'll be eating. Menu? You'll just have to trust the guest chef—it all depends on the season, the local climate, and of course what crops the host farmer decided to plant this year.

What began as informal outdoor dinners on small organic farms around Denevan's hometown of Santa Cruz, California, gradually morphed into a sophisticated catering operation. At first, Denevan himself was the usual chef, but as the word spread, more and more local chefs begged for the chance to show off their chops. (Guest chefs in the past have included well-known cooks like Justin Severino, Melissa Kelly, Gabrielle Hamilton, Dan Barber, Traci des Jardins, Kathy Cary, David Kinch, Eric Tucker, Paul Kahan, and Bill Telepan—it makes a great day out for a working restaurant chef.) Though only 14 of these classy farm dinners took place in 2007, by the 2008 season Denevan's unique program had gained word-of-mouth excitement, and 37 dinners were a sold-out success. All across North America, the staff cruised from site to site on a red-and-white 1950s-vintage tour bus. Check the website for this season's schedule—they run from early June into November, when the last crops are available. Whether you're dining on roast suckling pig, barbecued beef, fish grilled right on the beach, tender asparagus, flash-boiled corn on the cob, a salad of heirloom tomatoes still sun-warmed from the vine, or a cobber of fresh-picked berries swimming in freshly churned cream, it will be an evening you'll never forget.

ⓘ **Outstanding in the Field,** P.O. Box 2413, Santa Cruz, CA 95063-2413 (www.outstandinginthefield.com).

Das Wirtshaus zum Herrmannsdorfer Schweinsbräu

Home of the Happy Pigs

Glonn, Germany

In Europe, they tend to call it biofood, short for biologically responsible. That's the mantra at the organic Herrmannsdorfer farm, sprawling outward from a red-roofed traditional agricultural cooperative about half an hour southeast of Munich. About 70 organic growers are involved in this cooperative, but the chief crop is pigs. And not just any pigs, but *glücklichen schweinen,* or "happy pigs," with a free-range lifestyle and organic diet. While you're dining here, stop in to visit the black-and-pink floppy eared Schwäbisch-Hällisches pigs in their pigpen, and you'll see just how happy they are.

Chef Thomas Thielemann believes that happy pigs produce better meat, and the fare at the Herrmannsdorfer Tavern may convince you he's right. The full menu draws ingredients from various producers in the co-op—fruit, vegetables, and meat, as well as organic breads from the Herrmannsdorfer baker, organic hand-made cheeses from the dairy, and hearty ales from the organic microbrewery. This isn't just a country barbecue, by any means; Thielemann is a skilled gourmet cook, who also turns out menu items like marinated sashimi tuna, or a wild duck breast with speck, cabbage, and potato pancakes. And you'll pay gourmet prices as well, upwards of 50€ per person with drinks. But the pork seems to work its way into a number of dishes, either in the form of sausages, cured meats like speck and ham, refined pork cutlets, a particularly spicy stuffed pig's foot, the juicy, tender *schweinebraten,* or roast pork, with its crispy outer crust, which is Thielemann's house specialty. The silky firmness of Herrmannsdorfer pork is much more like milk-fed veal than your usual mass-produced pork; many top Munich restaurants procure their meats from Herrmannsdorfer. How much better to relish it here in the country air, paired with the fresh vegetables plucked that morning from the nearby field, served in a light-flooded former barn with scrubbed-bare wide-plank floors and simple, sturdy wood tables.

Everywhere you look, there are pigs—in paintings, sculptures, wooden cutouts, trivets—there's even a glamorous porker on the labels of the local beer. On your way out, stock up on Herrmannsdorfer products at the village market, which sells fresh produce, breads, cheeses, sausages, preserves, and pates. You'll be buying it straight from the source.

ⓘ Herrmannsdorf 7 (✆ **49/80/9390-9445;** www.schweinsbraeu.de).

✈ Munich (57km/35 miles).

🛏 $$ **Hotel St. Paul,** St-Paul-Strasse 7 (✆ **49/89/5440-7800;** www.hotel-stpaul.de). $ **Am Markt,** Heiliggeistrasse 6 (✆ **49/89/22-50-14;** www.hotelinmunich.de).

Bordeaux Quay

The Ever Green Cook

Bristol, England

Barny Houghton is a bit of a fanatic and has been for years. When he first set up his sustainable restaurant Rocinantes in 1988, its ideals seemed far-fetched: source all ingredients from within a 81km (50-mile) radius of Bristol, make it all organic if possible, and then run the restaurant in the most environmentally efficient way. Mind you, the West Country surrounding Bristol is agriculturally rich, and it has enough seacoast to ensure there would always be plenty of local fish available. The food turned out to be so good at Rocinantes it prospered, eventually adopting the even greener name **Quartier Vert** (85 Whiteladies Rd., Clifton; ℭ **44/117/973-4482;** www.quartiervert.co.uk). Along the way, some 40 young chefs trained in Houghton's green philosophy.

His new baby, Bordeaux Quay, is an even grander statement. Instead of being out in a suburban neighborhood, it's right in the heart of Bristol's harbor, facing the docks where cross-Channel ships used to unload their cargoes of wine from France. This streamlined white Art Deco–era warehouse has been completely overhauled into a stark, stunning modern development that's as sustainable as possible, from the solar heating panels to the rooftop tanks collecting rainwater for the toilets. The complex contains a slew of catering venues—a restaurant, a brasserie, a bar, a takeout deli, a bakery, and a not-for-profit cookery school where Barny can spread his gospel.

The restaurant is a spare yet spectacular white space designed around a central atrium, with a great wall of windows letting in natural light. Black banquettes and deep purple chairs provide splashes of contrast and color to the white walls and tablecloths, a strikingly simple effect that deflects the focus onto the food itself. The menu here is a little less Continental than what Houghton serves at Quartier Vert—there's a very English ring to such dishes as smoked eel with horseradish, crème fraîche, and pickled vegetables; a game terrine with pear-and-cranberry chutney; hare ravioli with walnut sauce; grilled Cornish mackerel with crushed spring onion potato, spinach, and black olive tapenade; pot roast chicken with cabbage, carrots, and chive-sprinkled mashed potatoes; roast rump of lamb with beets and a white-bean puree; and a classic rhubarb crumble for dessert. It's wholesome and elegant, which makes for a winning combination.

Houghton also oversees the more casual brasserie, a breezy, white-walled waterfront spot that serves a short but appealing menu of pastas, soups, salads, and risottos.

ⓘ V Shed, Canon's Way (ℭ **44/117/906-5550** or 44/117/9431200 for reservations; www.bordeaux-quay.co.uk).

✈ Bristol (14km/8¹/₂ miles).

🛏 $$$ **Hotel Du Vin,** Narrow Lewins Mead (ℭ **44/1179/255577;** www.hotel duvin.com). $ **Tyndall's Park Hotel,** 4 Tyndall's Park Rd., Clifton (ℭ **44/117/9735407;** www.tyndallsparkhotel.co.uk).

Konstam at the Prince Albert

King of the Ring Road

London, England

If you think it's hard sourcing all your food from local growers when you're in Berkeley or Bristol, just try doing it when you're in King's Cross, the heart of London town.

That was Oliver Rowe's challenge on the 2006 BBC television series *The Urban Chef*. At the time, he had been running the scroungy little bare-bones Café Konstam in this former red-light district for 2 years, and he was in the process of opening Konstam at the Prince Albert, converting an old pub into a smart locavore bistro. The TV cameras followed him as he buzzed around London, generally via the Underground, visiting his eccentric collection of only-in-London suppliers—a mushroom grower in East Ham, a lamb and pig farm at Amersham, a flour miller in Ponders End, a beekeeper in Tower Hill, an ostrich breeder in southwest London. He even convinced his own grandmother to let him pick mulberries from the tree in her back garden—anything that lay within the M25 ring road was fair game.

Now that the bigger restaurant is up and running, the reviews are in: Rowe's methods may sound gimmicky, but the food is delicious. Rowe does give himself a bit of a break—only 85% of the ingredients he uses have to be from his designated area. It's true, you do find a few unusual foraged ingredients on the plate—dandelion greens, wild garlic, knotweed, landcress, mushrooms—but he doesn't restrict himself to a limited basket of local produce when it's time to cook.

Konstam has an almost discolike look—blond wood tabletops seem to float in an otherwise monochromatic blue-green room, with suspended light fixtures draped in metallic bead chains. It seems the antithesis of Rowe's whole-earth approach to cooking, but it's a magnet for the young and hip, like Rowe himself. Having trained at the trendy African-inspired restaurant Moro in Clerkenwell (where there's a very hot restaurant scene these days), he's an old hand at mixing and matching unusual flavors, even if he is only in his mid-30s.

In the end, the blend of intensely local ingredients somehow lead to deeply British menu items—dishes like a crisp-skinned roast chicken with roast potatoes and a sage-and-onion sauce; mutton chops with capers and chervil; pork belly slow-cooked in London Porter ale with braised cabbage shoots; charcoal-grilled pigeon breast with roast-onion-and-hazelnut salad and beet dressing; and of course a classic Dover sole. No cocoa beans grow within the M25 radius, so desserts include such simple sweets as a lavender ice cream with ginger snaps; and bread pudding with double cream and lemon zest. Rowe's experiment is a daring one, but it works.

ⓘ Konstam at the Prince Albert, 2 Acton St. (✆ **44/20/7833-5040;** www.konstam. co.uk).

✈ Heathrow (24km/15 miles) or Gatwick (40km/25 miles).

🛏 $$$ **22 Jermyn St.,** 22 Jermyn St., St. James (✆ **800/682-7808** in the U.S., or 44/20/7734-2353; www.22jermyn.com). $$ **Vicarage Private Hotel,** 10 Vicarage Gate, South Kensington (✆ **44/20/7229-4030;** www.londonvicaragehotel.com).

Au Pied du Cochon
Meat Me in Montreal
Montreal, Canada

In the Plateau Mont-Royal neighborhood, this storefront restaurant doesn't look all that special. It used to be a pizzeria, and with its white tile walls, honey-colored wood trim, stainless steel counter, and refrigerated case, you could still easily mistake it for one. But no pizzeria could generate the kind of buzz that pervades this place. It's packed to the walls every night (except Mon, when it's closed) with giddy Montrealers eager to delve into some of the most satisfying old-style French-Canadian food around.

Chef Martin Picard's unabashed love of meat, especially foie gras, is all over the menu; give him half a chance and he's likely to pour maple syrup on top too. Game meats like bison, venison, duck, and guinea hen seem to have displaced tame beef and chicken, and like the early settlers, Picard doesn't seem to believe in wasting any parts of the animals—there's an entire section of offal items listed. (The only pizza on the whole menu is a tripe pizza.) Sure, there are a few obligatory salads among the appetizers, even a classic French onion soup *gratiné*, but somehow what you find yourself salivating over are items like duck carpaccio, bison tartare, and roast suckling pig.

When the pizzeria owners moved out, they left behind a brick oven, and Picard uses it to roast his meats until they are ready to fall off the bone. The namesake *pied de cochon* (pig's foot) comes in two versions, with and without foie gras; the *pot au feu,* served in a portion for two, is a savory combo of boiled beef, bone marrow, vegetables, foie gras, prairie oysters, and Guinea hen. Picard also serves the Québecois comfort food *poutine,* a yummy mess of french fries, gravy, and cheese curds, on top of which he'll also throw foie gras if you'd like. Perhaps the most Canadian dish of all is the ridiculously delicious *Plogue à Champlain,* a slab of foie gras topped with a buckwheat pancake, bacon, onions, potatoes, and maple syrup.

Reserve as far in advance as you can (phone works better than e-mail, so you can negotiate a time and date). Even with a reservation, you may find yourself hustled along once you've eaten; someone else is sure to be waiting for your table. The joint is exuberantly noisy and crowded, and when you stand up after your meal, you'll probably take up more space than you did an hour earlier. Blame it on the foie gras, eh?

Chef Martin Picard's Au Pied du Cochon.

ⓘ 536 Duluth St. (✆ **514/281-1114;** www.restaurantaupieddecochon.ca).

✈ Aéroport International Pierre-Elliot-Trudeau de Montréal (14km/8³/₄ miles).

🛏 $$$ **Hôtel Le St-James,** 355 rue St-Jacques oust (✆ **866/841-3111** or 514/841-3111; www.hotellestjames.com). $$ **Auberge Bonaparte,** 447 rue St-François-Xavier (✆ **514/844-1448;** www.bonaparte.com).

Fonda El Refugio

The Folk Art of Food

Mexico City, Mexico

This Zona Rosa reliable is hardly a secret. In fact, this popular little side-street spot with its bright *folklórico* blue facade has been around so long, and is so resolutely old-style, that gourmets often bypass it for trendier places. But as a primer on Mexico's many regional cooking styles, Fonda El Refugio can't be beat.

Meaning "country inn of refuge," Fonda El Refugio is as unassuming as its name promises, with white-washed brick walls, ladder-back black chairs, small white-clothed tables tucked into niches, and a yawning fireplace hung with gleaming copper pots and pans. The atmosphere is pleasantly informal and unhurried, with respectful service and genuine congeniality; it's the sort of place where families gather to celebrate birthdays and anniversaries and other special occasions, and you'll find as many locals as tourists here.

When folk-art collector Judith Martinez Ortega first opened the restaurant in 1954, she already had an encyclopedic collection of recipes gathered from her travels around the country; her family still runs the restaurant, and those recipes are the backbone of the menu. You'll find dishes from each region of Mexico—mostly hearty country dishes like *arroz con plátanos* (rice with fried bananas), *albóndigas chipotle* (meatballs laced with spicy chili), or *enchiladas con mole poblano,* topped with the rich, thick, spicy chocolate sauce of Puebla. Chiles stuffed with ground beef or cheese are particularly popular, as is the *chicharón* with salsa verde (deep-fried pork rinds in a spicy green sauce) and the pig's trotter marinated in vinegar (*manitas de cerdo en vinegre*). Daily specials are just about always worth trying. You might find tasty seasonal specialties like red snapper cooked Veracruz-style (in onions, tomatoes, and olives); stuffed peppers in walnut sauce with pomegranate seeds; zucchini blossom quesadillas; or a special mole sauce made with pumpkin seeds. For dessert have some coconut candy, mouthwatering flan, or the Saturday night special, *huevas reales*—baked eggs glazed with sweet syrup.

Baskets of freshly handmade tortillas land on your table like magic; refreshing drinks include some excellent fruit juices and potent, delicious margaritas. El Refugio is very popular, especially on Saturday night, so make a reservation, and get here early.

ⓘ Liverpool 166 (✆ **55/5207-2732** or 55/5525-8128; www.fondaelrefugio.com. mx).

✈ Mexico City (9.2km/5³/₄ miles).

🛏 $$ **Best Western Hotel Majestic,** Av. Madero 73 (✆ **52/55/5521-8600;** www.majestic.com.mx). $ **Hotel Catedral,** Calle Donceles 95 (✆ **52/55/5521-6183;** www.hotelcatedral.com).

3 Frakkar

The Puffin Place

Reykjavik, Iceland

Dinner at this cozy little corner restaurant in the residential heart of Reykjavik can be an adventure, provided you're willing to keep an open mind. Seafood is the heart of the menu, but it's seafood like you've never had it before. Chef Úlfar Eysteinsson set out to make his restaurant a showcase for Iceland's more unusual delicacies, and this may be the best place in town to try them.

Specialties include *plokkfiskur,* hashed fish accompanied by traditional, cakey Icelandic brown bread; *smjörsteikt lúðu-flök,* a fantastic butter-fried halibut that comes with lobster and lobster sauce; or pan-fried *saltfiskur* (salted cod fillet) with pine nuts, raisins, tomato, and apple. While you may blanch at trying the whale sashimi or whale pepper steak, you can rest assured that Eysteinsson only uses meat from nonendangered minke whales, which turns out to have a delicious taste that's like a cross between tuna and beef. It would be a shame not to try the smoked lake trout caught up near Thingvellir, the ancient Icelandic parliament; the reindeer pâté is quite a delicacy as well, with a gamy taste not unlike venison.

Granted, you may be too soft-hearted to try certain dishes on the menu here—the smoked puffin breast (served with mustard sauce), cormorant, or *guillemot.* But if you do give it a try, you'll find that the half-fish, half-poultry taste of seabirds is intriguing, and Eysteinsson knows how to cook it just right (it helps that he only

Chef Úlfar Eysteinsson's salt cod with pine nuts, raisins, tomato, and apple.

offers it in season). Another beloved delicacy that may be an acquired taste is the fried cod chins, tender walnut-sized nuggets surrounded by a fatty membrane, much prized for their savory taste. But it's easy to fall in love with the famous Icelandic dessert called *skyr*, a kind of whipped whey that tastes like a cross between yogurt, crème fraîche, cream cheese, and soft-serve ice cream.

This is hardly a luxury dining experience; the tables are packed cozily together, and the walls are cluttered with nautical kitsch. Presentation and the wine list are afterthoughts, but service is fast, and the price is a pleasant surprise.

ⓘ Baldursgata 14 (✆ **354/552-3939;** www.3frakkar.com).

✈ Keflavik International (96km/60 miles).

🛏 $$ **Hotel Bjork,** Brautarholt 22-24 (✆ **354/511-3777;** www.keahotels/is). $$$ **Hotel Loftleidir,** Hlidarfótur (✆ **354/444-4500;** www.icehotels.is).

---

191 Global Traditions

F. Cooke's Pie & Mash Shop
'Ello, Guv'nor
London, England

It's like a set from *Sweeney Todd*—the gold-lettered name painted on a dark green board above the door, the marble counter and tabletops inside, simple wooden benches, gleaming yellow tiled walls, sawdust on the floor. F. Cooke's (the F stands for Frederick) has been an East End fixture since 1910, serving working-class Londoners the most iconic Cockney food there is: a crusty rectangular meat-filled pie, served next to a mound of creamy mashed potatoes in a pool of luridly green parsley "liquor."

The Cooke's chain doesn't have as many branches as it did in its heyday (the same is true of its longtime competitor, Manze's, founded in 1902, which you can find at 87 Tower Bridge Rd.; ✆ **44/20/7407-2985**). And this branch isn't the original, though it's still plenty atmospheric. Yet as the East End has increasingly gentrified, a new audience is discovering these vintage shops, still run by descendants of the original Fred Cooke. Along with the pie and mash, they also sell eels, another cheap Cockney staple. Cooke's does a brisk business in chopped eels, cut into half-inch chunks, sold both hot (stewed) or cold (chilled in a plastic tub of their own gelled juice); you can even see vats of live eels, waiting to be stewed, in the front window. Aficionados say they taste like picked herrings, but heartier.

Unlike other shops, Cooke's fills its pies with chunks of steak and kidney instead of minced beef; their golden pastry is also graced with a touch of old-fashioned suet for extra savory flavor. Although the food at Cooke's is incredibly low priced, the family refuses to take shortcuts—they take pride in serving only the freshest eels, mash made from fresh potatoes, and that weirdly tasty, nonalcoholic green "liquor" made from the water the eels were stewed in and loads of fresh parsley.

Pie-and-mash and jellied eels are such a nostalgic treat, even Gordon Ramsay has added them to the menu at his new line of gastropubs. Still, why not head to the East End to scout out the original? The chain's flagship shop is in Hackney, just south of London Fields, on a street that fills on

Saturdays with a farmer's market. Forget fish and chips shops; this is the quintessential London street grub.

ⓘ 9 Broadway Market (✆ **44/20/7254-6458**).

✈ Heathrow (24km/15 miles); Gatwick (40km/25 miles).

🛏 $$$ **Covent Garden Hotel,** 10 Monmouth St., Covent Garden (✆ **800/553-6674** in the U.S., or 44/20/7806-1000; www.firmdale.com). $$ **B + B Belgravia,** 64-66 Ebury St., Belgravia (✆ **800/682-7808** in the U.S., or 44/20/7734-2353; www.bb-belgravia.com).

Sama Sabo

Setting the Rice Table

Amsterdam, The Netherlands

Oddly enough, one of the most characteristic meals you can have in Amsterdam isn't Dutch at all—it's the Indonesian-inspired *rijsttafel,* a dining custom developed in Holland as a sampler of the exotic dishes that Dutch planters brought back from 3 centuries of rule in Indonesia. The name means "rice table"—your dining table will be covered with small dishes, each with a portion of a spicy Indonesian dish, arrayed around a central platter of steamed or fried rice. At its best it's a festive profusion of tastes—more food than anyone could eat at one sitting (though all too often people do).

Every Amsterdammer has his or her own favorite *rijsttafel* place, but Sama Sebo, located close to the Rijksmuseum, is a widespread favorite. Decorated with rush mats, panels of bamboo, traditional wood carvings, and bright hand-printed batik textiles, it sets the mood for an Indonesian feast. Sama Sebo's 23-plate *rijsttafel* will include *babi ketjap* (meat in soy sauce), various *satehs* (grilled meats on skewers with peanut sauce), *krupuk* (shrimp toast), *gado-gado* (vegetables with peanut sauce), *sambals* (various types of spicy relishes), *serundeng* (fried coconut), *rudjak manis* (fruit in sweet sauce); and *pisang goreng* (fried banana). The names are almost beside the point; the fun lies in being adventurous

and relying on your own taste buds to tell you what you like, letting the sweetness of coconut milk meld with the bite of chili peppers and the mellow earthiness of peanut sauce. You begin by scooping a mound of rice into a soup bowl, then add dollops of various side dishes around it, as well as a dab of spicy *sambal* at the edge to add a little fire. The trick is to eat it in alternating bites, rather than diluting the side dishes' flavors by mixing rice into them. Some items are indeed spicy-hot, but in general, the memorable effect comes from effectively blending spices and sauces, not just amping up the firepower.

Can't get into Sama Sebo on your desired date? Other good choices in town include **Puri Mas** (Lange Leidsedwarsstraat 37-41; ✆ **31/20/408-0664;** www.purimas.nl) and **Kantjil & de Tijger** (Spuistraat 291-293; ✆ **31/20/620-0994;** www.kantjil.nl).

ⓘ Pieter Cornelisz Hooftstraat 27 (✆ **31/20/662-8146;** www.samasebo.nl).

✈ Amsterdam Schipohl (13km/8 miles).

🛏 $$ **Estheréa,** Single 305 (✆ **31/20/624-5146;** www.estherea.nl). $ **Amstel Botel,** Oosterdokskade 2–4 (✆ **31/20/626-4247;** www.amstelbotel.com).

Au Pied du Cochon

We Never Close

Paris, France

The Les Halles meat market may not be here anymore, but that doesn't stop Parisian nightbirds from making their traditional late night stop for Au Pied du Cochon's famous onion soup. Back in the days when market workers needed a late-night meal, this is where they ate; these days, it's more likely to be frequented in the wee hours by chefs who drop in to schmooze over comfort food once they've closed the doors at their haute cuisine palaces.

Opened in 1946, right after the war, this restaurant hasn't closed its doors since sometime in 1947; it's brightly lit and buzzing 24 hours a day. (Reserve in advance to be sure of a table, and insist on sitting in the main dining room.) The vintage Parisian café look is straight out of the movies—wood trim, shiny brass fittings, yellow walls stenciled with Art Nouveau designs, red leather banquettes, and small tables set close together. Perhaps it's not genuinely a dive anymore—it's too famous for that—but the ambience is reliably authentic. Service can be slow at peak times, but then this isn't fast food, is it?

Besides that deep-flavored onion soup gratiné, the other classic item to order is the restaurant's namesake, grilled pigs' feet with béarnaise sauce. (You can also get the pig's foot stuffed with foie gras.) Seafood is another specialty—there are a dozen different varieties of oysters available, and the seafood platter comes highly recommended. Several items on the menu are reminiscent of the days when meat market workers congregated here to chow down on plebeian leftovers from the butchers' stalls, things like *andouillettes* (chitterling sausages) and a *jarret* (shin) of pork, caramelized in honey and served on a bed of sauerkraut. They all come together in *La temptation de St-Antoine*, a platter named after St. Anthony, who in medieval times was considered the patron saint of sausage makers: it's a lusty pile of grilled pig's tail, pig's snout, and half a pig's foot, all served with béarnaise and french fries. Despite the fatty richness of such fare, many diners still manage to find room for the restaurant's renowned *baba au rhum* for dessert.

ⓘ 6 rue Coquilliere, 1e (✆ **33/1/40-13-77-00;** www.pieddecochon.com).

✈ De Gaulle (23km/14 miles); Orly (14km/8²/₃ miles).

🛏 $$ **La Tour Notre Dame,** 20 rue du Sommerard, 5e (✆ **33/1/43-54-47-60;** www.la-tour-notre-dame.com). $ **Hotel de la Place des Vosges,** 12 rue de Birague, 4e (✆ **33/1/42-72-60-46;** www.hotelplacedesvosges.com).

Casa Lucio
The Soul of Old Madrid
Madrid, Spain

This place looks like it has been around forever—a cozy cellar haunt with rounded brown brick arches, whitewashed plaster walls, copper lanterns casting a yellow glow, a line of cured hams hanging over the bar, and a warren of small dining rooms with close-set simple tables. In fact, Lucio Blázquez opened his antique-looking *tasca* on this narrow street as recently as 1974, but his talent for schmoozing has made his namesake restaurant an neighborhood fixture where movers and shakers love to relax over a meal of deeply traditional Castilian food. You may still spot Blázquez circulating around the tables, genially greeting his guests, who have included the king of Spain himself.

Service is so deft you won't even notice it, and the menu strikes a great balance between interesting regional specialties and a reliable list of old Spanish classics like suckling pig, tripe, Jabugo ham with broad beans, shrimp in garlic sauce, hake with green sauce, several types of roasted lamb, the chickpea-and-sausage stew called *cochido,* and a thick steak called *churrasco de la casa,* served sizzling hot on a heated platter. The restaurant's most famous dish, however, is something surprisingly modest: *huevos estrellados,* literally "broken eggs" mixed with fried potatoes, a sloppy and utterly soul-satisfying meal. Simple as it seems, it's almost impossible for anyone to make it quite as good as Casa Lucio, though cooks all over Madrid have tried.

Laid back as it seems, unshowy as the food is, Casa Lucio still isn't cheap, not by any means. This is one of Madrid's most sought-after dining spots, and you'll pay

Dining at Casa Lucio in Madrid is a quintessentially Spanish experience.

for the privilege of dining here. But for top-quality ingredients expertly cooked, recipes that have stood the test of time, and the reassuring sense of well-being this place instills in you, it's worth it. Like a lot of things in conservative Madrid, it's more about tradition than trendiness, and more about substance than show. You may also want to check out the tapas across the street at the casual sister restaurant **Taberna los Huevos de Lucio** (Cava Baja 30; ✆ **34/91/366-2984**); next door there's also

Viejo Madrid (Cava Baja 32; 34/91/366-3838), an even more rustic-looking wood-beamed sort of inn that serves many of the same dishes as its mother restaurant.

Cava Baja 35 (34/91/365-8217 or 34/91/365-3252; www.casalucio.es).

Madrid (3.8km/2½ miles).

$$$ **Santo Mauro Hotel,** Calle Zurbano 36 (34/91/319-6900; www.ac-hoteles.com/ac_stomauro.htm). $$ **Hotel Opera,** Cuesta de Santo Domingo 2 (34/91/541-2800; www.hotelopera.com).

Trattoria Sostanza

Lining Up at the Trough

Florence, Italy

Amid Florence's Renaissance treasures, a neighborhood restaurant that first opened in 1869 may not seem all that old. But in restaurant terms, any place that has been able to survive for nearly a century and a half must be doing something right.

Trattoria Sostanza is wonderfully unpretentious—a long narrow room with communal tables stretching along each white-tiled side wall. Diners sit on hard benches (along the wall) or stools (along the center aisle) and tuck into heaping portions of Tuscan peasant food. Nicknamed "Il Troia" (The Trough) for its continual flow of hearty food, it's a clangorous, friendly atmosphere, and plenty of locals still elbow their way in here alongside visitors looking for the quintessential Florentine dining experience.

You may want to start out with the tortellini in brodo (robust meat-stuffed pasta in a nicely salty chicken broth), crostini thickly spread with chicken liver, or the flavorful zuppa alla paesana vegetable soup; artichoke pie is another favorite local dish. From there you go on to your choice of pastas, with either butter or meat sauce. For main courses, the Florentines like their meats simply grilled—alla fiorentina—with just a few herbs and a touch of olive oil; you

can choose between trippa alla fiorentina (tripe), a juicy veal chop, or a majestically thick steak (the classic bistecca alla fiorentina), although it may be hard to pass up the house specialty petti di pollo al burro (thick chicken breasts fried in butter). Accompaniments such as the spinach, sautéed in loads of butter and garlic, or the Tuscan white beans and roasted potatoes, are cooked to marvelous perfection. Even a simple omelet can be a rich revelation, cooked with utterly fresh natural eggs in real butter.

The trattoria keeps homey hours. Though it serves lunch and dinner, but closes throughout the afternoon. It's also closed Saturday and Sunday and the whole month of August. It also doesn't take credit cards. It does, however, take reservations—and surely you'll need one.

Via Porcellana 25r (39/55/212-691).

Florence (5km/3 miles).

$$$ **Hotel Monna Lisa,** Borgo Pinti 27 (39/55/247-9751; www.monnalisa.it). $ **Hotel Abaco,** Via dei Banchi 1 (39/55-238-1919; www.abaco-hotel.it).

Archaion Gefsis

Plate O' Plato

Athens, Greece

On one level it's kitschy—deeply kitschy, with plaster columns, flickering torches, and waiters in scarlet togas—the whole theme-park-like routine. On another level, though, it's a brilliant idea: Re-create a bunch of recipes from the days of ancient Greece, as recorded by the classical poets, and serve them to modern diners.

It's Greek food, yes, but so different from modern-day Greek cuisine that even the locals come here for a novel experience. Research confirms that the citizens of ancient Athens lived mostly on meat, vegetables, fish, coarsely ground barley, and honey; staples of the modern Greek diet such as potatoes, tomatoes, rice, lemon, and sugar, were completely unknown in ancient times. Within those parameters, the chefs here have been very creative, concocting smoked eel with asparagus; fried perch with mashed chickpeas and beets; pork roast stuffed with plums, artichokes, and mashed peas; cuttlefish in ink with pine nuts; wild-boar cutlets, and goat leg with mashed vegetables. Give the chef a few days advance notice, and you can have a special roast suckling pig stuffed with wild game, cheese, fried liver, eggs, apples, chestnuts, pine-kernels, raisins, and spices.

Set in an imposing manor of rough-cast stone, with a classical pediment over the door, the dining rooms have wood-beamed ceilings, tile floors, and classical-style statuary in brick niches. In warm weather, you may also eat outside in a flagstone-paved garden dotted with palm trees; it's wonderfully pleasant and romantic at night (just don't face in certain directions and you'll never notice the modern skyscrapers poking up over the walls). Food is served on wooden trenchers and crude pottery platters; honey-wine is drunk from terra-cotta tumblers. Diners are given a spoon and a knife but no fork, since the ancient Greeks didn't use them. Even the music is historically re-created, with live musicians playing on replicas of classical pipes and lyres, and dancing girls are brought in to make the evenings even more festive.

If you really want to get into the experience, book a private party for up to seven people in the special Symposium parlor, where you'll recline on individual couches, wear robes and sandals, even have a wreath of ivy placed on your heads as you eruditely discuss art, politics, and philosophy over dinner. Drink enough of that honey-wine and you'll think you sound erudite, anyway.

(i) 22 Kodratou St. ((C) **210/523-9661;** www.thematic-dining.gr/arxaion).

✈ Athens International Airport Eleftherios Venizelos (36km/23 miles).

🛏 $$ **Athens Art Hotel,** 27 Marni ((C) **30/210/524-0501;** www.arthotel athens.gr). $$ **Hermes Hotel,** 19 Appollonos St. ((C) **30/210/323-5514;** www. hermes-athens.com).

Thiptara

Down by the Riverside

Bangkok, Thailand

Most of Bangkok's top luxury hotels have a Thai-food option, many of them in gorgeous riverside garden settings. But there's something extra special about the Peninsula's highly regarded Thiptara, where you can sit in an open-air wooden pavilion nestled amid gardens along the banks of the Chao Phraya River, dining on authentic Thai cooking by the light of flaming torches.

Thai cooking in Thailand may be quite different from the sauce-laden food you've had at Thai restaurants back home. Restaurants like Thiptara boast of offering "Thai-style home cooking" to underscore the fact that the food is simple and flavorful rather than highly wrought. Dining by the water seems appropriate, given that seafood is a staple of authentic Thai cuisine; even when there is meat, it's added only in small chunks. The big hotel restaurants invariably tone down their flavorings for Westerners (advise your waiter if you'd like things more fully spiced). Remember that it's not all about heat though—authentic Thai food relies on herbs more than spices, so that even the hottest curries don't burn your mouth for long.

Thiptara's set menu includes nine courses, a wide sampling of different Thai flavors. You may begin with an appetizer of crispy shrimp pancakes or chicken-and-mushroom tartlets; then go on to a salad (the fried morning glory and prawn salad is particularly good); followed by a spicy, warming soup, usually featuring some kind of seafood and either lemon grass or coconut. If you've been dying to try authentic pad thai noodles but have been uneasy about eating from street stalls in the city, you can get an excellent *pad thai goong sod* here. Among the entrees, the duck curry is particularly good, as is the deep-fried sweet-and-sour snow fish. For dessert, you might enjoy mango and sticky rice, or the more unusual *pollamai nampheung,* a two-person dessert of Thai fruits roasted in honey with splashes of chili and vanilla, served with a refreshing lemon sorbet.

The pavilions, with their steep curling roofs, are genuine, shipped from the ancient capital of Ayutthaya and reassembled here on expansive teak decks shaded by banyan trees. Only two tables are set in each open-sided pavilion, making them very private and quiet; there are other open-air tables as well, set right on the riverbank. The hotel is downriver from central Bangkok, in Thonburi; you can get there via the Peninsula Hotel's free shuttle, either from Saphan Taksin BTS or from the hotel's own private pier next to the Shangri-La Hotel.

ⓘ 333 Charoen Nakhorn Rd. (🕾 **66/2/861-2888;** www.peninsula.com).

✈ Bangkok International.

🛏 $$$ **Peninsula Hotel,** 333 Charoen Nakhorn Rd. (🕾 **800/262-9467** or 66/2/861-2888; www.peninsula.com). $$ **Chakrabongse Villas,** 396 Maharat Rd. (🕾 **66/2/224-6686;** www.thaivillas.com).

Hyotei

The Zen Art of Kaiseki

Kyoto

Of course there are restaurants in Tokyo that are happy to oblige you with a formal kaiseki meal. But if you seek the ultimate kaiseki experience, head for Kyoto, Japan's beautiful and gracious former capital. It's where you'll find the most traditional kaiseki restaurants, the ones that raised tea-ceremony dining to an art form. Of all the kaiseki spots in Kyoto, none is more venerable than Hyotei. Founded over 300 years ago as a teahouse for pilgrims visiting Nanzenji Temple, it has become a veritable shrine itself, serving a meal that's well worth the thousands of yen it will cost you.

Originally, kaiseki meals were supposed to be simple vegetarian repasts, served before the austere rituals of the tea ceremony. But over the centuries, Kyoto's aristocratic classes began to elaborate on this meal, adding more and more elements of court ritual, until kaiseki became an intricate procession of dishes, each with its own special vessel, to be presented in a certain manner. While the forms of kaiseki are tightly prescribed by custom, within those boundaries kaiseki cooks are challenged to be creative, using only the most seasonal ingredients and coming up with ever more artful ways to garnish, sculpt, and arrange each portion.

When you arrive for your kaiseki meal, you'll be led to one of several separate tiny houses set around a beautiful formal garden with a pond, maple trees, and bushes. (The oldest of these houses is more than 3 centuries old.) You'll dine seated on a tatami floor in a private room, where kimono-clad women will bring the food to you. You may be surprised to see how small each portion is, for kaiseki isn't about gorging yourself. It's about the beauty of how each dish is presented, and about subtle preparations that make you experience food with all your senses—fragrant soups, silky sashimi, grilled or sizzled morsels of meat and fish, crisply steamed nuggets of vegetable or tofu, tangy pickled vegetables, a perfectly ripe mouthful of fruit. You'll find yourself drawn into the ritual, watching eagerly as each lidded bowl or lacquered box is presented to you like a precious gift.

Reservations are required; the kaiseki lunches are slightly less expensive than the dinners, though both have price tags over $200. Hyotei also has an annex, or *bekkan,* serving seasonal obento lunches, served in traditional lacquered boxes in a communal tatami room with views of a garden. Those are a wonderful experience too, but they're nowhere as extraordinary as the kaiseki.

(i) 35 Kusakawa-cho, Nanzenji (✆ **81/75/771-4116;** www.igougo.com/dining-reviews-b109337-Kyoto-Hyotei.html).

🚆 Kyoto, 2 ¹/₂ hr. from Tokyo, 75 min. from Kansai International Airport.

🛏 $$$ **ANA Hotel Kyoto,** Nijojo-mae, Horikawa Dori, Nakagyo-ku (✆ **800/ANA-HOTELS** in the U.S. and Canada, or 81/75/231-1155; www.anahotels.com). $ **Matsubaya Ryokan,** Higashinotouin Nishi, Kamijuzuyamachi Dori, Shimogyo-ku (✆ **61/75/351-3727** or 61/75/351-4268; www.matsubayainn.com).

4 On the Road in America

Carhops still deliver the orders, as they have for decades, at Superdawg Drive-In.

Buffalo Wings

Watch Out for Flying Buffalos

Buffalo, New York

Nowadays, all sorts of foods that have been deep-fried and sauced up with cayenne pepper are called "buffalo-style" this and "buffalo-style" that, playing on the association with Buffalo hot wings. In Buffalo, New York, though, nobody refers to their most famous local dish as Buffalo anything—they're just hot chicken wings, or hot wings, or wings. How else *would* a chicken wing be prepared around here?

The birthplace of Buffalo-style chicken wings is generally acknowledged to be the **Anchor Bar.** Run by Frank and Teresa Bellisimo, this watering hole on the edge of downtown first opened in 1935. It wasn't until a late Friday night in October 1964, however, that Teresa first threw together this hot bar snack. In desperation, she grabbed some chicken wings she'd been saving for stock, chopped them into easy-to-hold halves (drumettes and bows), then threw them in a deep-fryer and coated them in a buttery hot pepper sauce. That zesty sauce was just right for awakening the taste buds after midnight, especially contrasted with the cool creamy blue-cheese dressing Teresa serves on the side, along with a few palate-cleansing stalks of crunchy celery. And of course it didn't hurt that the wings soon made customers thirsty enough to order another round of beers.

Anchor soon became famous for its hot wings—which were, of course, then copied all over town, supplanting Buffalo's previous favorite bar food, beef on weck. (This delicious sandwich—thin-shaved rare roast beef piled on a hard roll spattered with salt crystals and caraway seeds and served au jus—is also on the Anchor's menu, of course.) But while beef on weck remains a treat exclusive to Buffalo, in the 1980s Buffalo hot wings began to appear on menus all over the nation, including some later incarnations in which the wings were breaded before deep-frying—heresy to Buffalo wing purists.

There's something about a Buffalo winter that makes the heat of hot wings particularly inviting here, where they were invented. Behind its blank brick facade, the Anchor Bar still looks like the boozy wood-trimmed hangout it always was, except for a clutter of framed clippings and celebrity photos and the wall full of license plates donated by visitors from all over the country. Teresa's and Frank's son Dominic still tends bar here. The rest of the menu includes sandwiches, pizzas, and a few Italian standards, but wings remain Anchor Bar's claim to fame. Theirs are meaty, unbreaded (of course), and sheathed in that special slick chili sauce, which Anchor now sells by the bottle. You can usually catch visiting sports stars, in town to play the Bills football team or the Sabres hockey team, chowing down at the Anchor Bar the night before their games—those wings are too tempting to resist.

ⓘ 1047 Main St. (🕾 **716/886-8920;** www.buffalowings.com).

✈ Buffalo International (9⅓ miles/15km).

🛏 $$$ **The Mansion on Delaware,** 414 Delaware Ave. (🕾 **716/886-3300;** www.mansionondelaware.com). $$ **Comfort Suites Downtown,** 601 Main St. (🕾 **800/424-6423** or 716/854-5500; www.choicehotels.com).

Philly Cheese Steak

Wit' Whiz or Witout

Philadelphia, Pennsylvania

In Philadelphia, of course, they never call it "Philly" cheese steak—it's just a cheese steak, and it's the most iconic local specialty of a city that *really loves* its local specialties. You can order it without cheese, but that's a steak sandwich; you can order it with mozzarella and tomato sauce, which is a pizza cheese steak. But those are sacrilegious variations to cheese steak purists, who allow only two options—"wit" (with fried onions) or "witout" (hold the onions, please).

Most historians credit brothers Pat and Harry Olivieri for making the first steak sandwiches, one slow afternoon in 1933 at their hot dog stand near the Italian Market. They thin-sliced a bit of cheap steak, fried it up with some onions, and shoveled the whole mess onto a hot dog roll. Customers loved the new sandwich so much, the Olivieris soon renamed their stand **Pat's**

King of Steaks. Still run by members of the Olivieri family, Pat's remains at the original South Philly location, in a ramshackle turreted corner building at 9th Street and Passyunk Avenue, easily identified by the lines running down the sidewalk—especially late at night, since Pat's is open 24 hours a day. Service is strictly walk-up, seating is limited, and they take cash only. After all these years, it's still quite a scene.

While competition sprang up all over town throughout the 1940s and 1950s, Pat's biggest rival is right across the intersection: **Geno's Steaks,** which opened with a gaudy blaze of neon in 1966. (Talk about taking on your rival *mano a mano*.) Geno's is also open 24/7, also cash-only, and also has long lines, though they move fast—read the signs on the photo-cluttered walls to nail down the complicated protocol

One wit' everything at Pat's—home of the original South Philly steak sandwich.

of ordering once you get to the counter. The most vexing choice for a first-timer may be to decide which cheese you want on top. Traditionally, Geno's supporters hold out for provolone (or, in a pinch, American cheese), while the Pat's camp goes for a gooey layer of Cheez Whiz. Both places serve all three kinds of cheese—just don't ask for Swiss.

Although Pat's and Geno's are the most famous, there are many other cheese steak joints around town. It doesn't take much to get a Philadelphian going on the subject of which is best, and Pat's and Geno's take a lot of flak from cheese steak snobs for being touristy and overpriced. Still, when judging cheese steak quality, you've got to accept that it is, above all, street food: An authentic cheese steak

needs the cheapest cuts of meat, the greasiest onions, the airiest rolls, and yes, that plastic taste of Cheez Whiz to come out just right.

ⓘ **Pat's,** 1237 E. Passyunk Ave. (© **215/468-1456;** www.patskingofsteaks.com). **Geno's,** 1219 S. 9th St. (© **215/389-0659;** www.genosteaks.com).

✈ Philadelphia International (11 miles/17km).

🛏 $$$ **Rittenhouse 1715,** 1715 Rittenhouse Sq. (© **877/791-6500** or 215/546-6500; www.rittenhouse1715.com). $$ **Penn's View Hotel,** 14 N. Front St. (© **800/331-7634** or 215/922-7600; www.pennsviewhotel.com).

Hometown Dish

201

Crab Cakes

Singing the Chesapeake Blues

Eastern Maryland

For most Marylanders, summer just isn't summer until they've tucked into a plate of crab cakes, molded out of succulent fresh crabmeat, coated with moist golden breading, and fried to sizzling perfection. Though blue crabs live all along the Atlantic Coast, the ones in the Chesapeake Bay just seem to be meatier, sweeter, and all-around tastier, especially if you're lucky enough to eat them the same day they were caught. Of course, to do that you've got to come here between May and October—but if you do, here's a road trip that should satisfy your crab cake cravings.

What you're looking for is crab cakes made with little or no filler, and from Maryland blue crabs only (sadly, as the Chesapeake's yield is drastically diminishing, some Maryland restaurants actually serve crabs flown in from North Carolina, Florida,

or Texas). Starting in Baltimore, head for the historic district of Fells Point and **Obrycki's** (1727 E. Pratt St.; © **410/732-6399;** www.obryckis.com), which puts an upscale gloss on the traditional brick-walled crab house look—though the gleaming wood tables are still covered with paper, so customers can crack open their steamed crabs with wood mallets. Obrycki's has been making its crab cakes the same way since 1944—a mix of back-fin and lump crabmeat, bound with just a whisper of eggs and seasoned bread crumbs.

Then head south to Annapolis, where waterfront **Cantler's Riverside Inn** (458 Forest Beach Rd.; © **410/757-1311;** www.cantlers.com) trundles in crabs by conveyor belt straight from the pier. In summer you'll sit outside at long communal picnic tables, watching fellow patrons tie up their boats at the restaurant's dock. Cantler's crab cakes are known for being big and meaty; go for the more expensive ones made from lump crabmeat, the choicest cut. A few minutes' drive southwest from Annapolis, **Mike's Crab House** (3030 Riva Rd., Riva; ✆ **410/956-2784;** www.mikescrabhouse.com) is another casual waterside spot, with a wood-beamed dining room and a big outdoor deck where you can overlook the South River as you feast on crab cakes made of lump crabmeat, served either broiled or pan-fried.

From Annapolis, take Rte. 50 across the Chesapeake Bay Bridge and then south along the inlet-fringed Eastern Shore, prime crab cake territory. Stop off in Easton to sample the legendary cream of crab soup at the lively pub **Legal Spirits** (42 E. Dover St.; ✆ **410/820-0765**). Then head down Rte. 13 to Crisfield to sample the outstanding crab cakes at **Captain's Galley** (1021 W. Main St.; ✆ **410/968-0544**), a simple, modern restaurant with a fine view over Tangier Sound. It may not have that ramshackle crab-shack look, but the crab meat in their meaty, lightly seasoned crab cakes is guaranteed to come from the Bay, and they're infallibly delicious.

✈ Baltimore-Washington International (10 miles/16km).

A mound of fresh crabs awaits the mallet at Obrycki's in Baltimore.

🛏 $$ **Brookshire Suites,** 120 E. Lombard St., Baltimore (✆ **866/583-4162** or 410/625-1300; www.harbormagic.com). $$ **1908 William Page Inn,** 8 Martin St., Annapolis (✆ **800/364-4160** or 410/626-1506; www.1908-williampageinn.com).

202 Hometown Dish

Soul Food, D.C.-Style
Shaw's Diner Classics
Washington, D.C.

Watch the TV news, and you'd think that Washington, D.C., is a city populated only by suave politicians operating out of white-domed and –columned seats of power. But the truth is, D.C. is a largely black city with a complex cultural history. For every expense-account dinner ordered at the swanky restaurants of Georgetown and K Street, up northwest in the Shaw district there's a tasty fried-chicken platter or bowl of chili being served.

Named an American classic by the James Beard Foundation, Ben's Chili Bowl has been a hub in Washington, D.C.'s U Street Corridor for decades.

Bill Cosby hung out at **Ben's Chili Bowl** in the early 1960s when he was an aspiring comedian, playing at one of the nearby clubs that earned U Street the nickname "Black Broadway." In 1985, when *The Cosby Show* hit number one in the TV ratings, where did Cos stage his press conference? At Ben's. Named an America's Classics restaurant by the James Beard Foundation, Ben's is still run by the Ali family. Their celebrated chili half-smokes—spicy chili ladled onto a snappy smoked sausage that's half pork, half beef—haven't changed much since they first opened the joint in 1958, in a former pool hall next to the Lincoln Theater. The neighborhood around it has endured riots, urban renewal, and the building of a subway line, but the cheerfully efficient folks behind the counter at Ben's (the original

Formica-topped counter and stools, of course) continue to throw that delectable beef or veggie chili onto just about anything—hot dogs, hamburgers, french fries—heck, they'll even serve it to you for breakfast if you want. Brightly lit into the wee hours (they don't close until 2am most nights, 4am Fri–Sat), it's a well-loved anchor of this traditionally African-American neighborhood—though the clientele is much more racially mixed these days, as white hipsters have made it a late-night haven.

Three blocks north, the **Florida Avenue Grill** offers a more extensive soul-food menu, from fried pork chops and country ham with red-eye gravy (made from ham drippings and coffee) to collard greens, glazed yams, mac-and-cheese—there's even chitterlings and pigs' feet, for those who are so inclined. Breakfast is the big attraction here, drawing lines out the door for creamy grits and gravy, thin hotcakes, delicious scrapple, or deep-flavored corned beef hash. This funky corner diner has been around since 1944, and its walls are hung with photos of the movers and shakers who've wedged into its cramped booths or hunkered down at the long pink Formica counter over the years. Service is down-home friendly (though also down-home pokey at times). If you find pools of grease on your plate—and you will—just sop them up with a flaky buttermilk biscuit or hunk of sweet cornbread, and wash it down with your third glass of sweet tea.

ⓘ **Ben's Chili Bowl,** 1213 U St. (✆ **202/ 667-0909;** www.benschilibowl.com). **Florida Avenue Grill,** 1200 Florida Ave. (✆ **202/ 265-1586**).

✈ Reagan National (3 miles/5km); Dulles International (26 miles/41km); Baltimore-Washington International (35 miles/56km).

🛏 $$ **Four Points by Sheraton,** 1201 K St. NW (✆ **202/289-7600;** www.four points.com/washingtondcdowntown). $$ **Georgetown Suites,** 1111 30th St. NW (✆ **202/298-1600;** www.georgetown suites.com).

Cincinnati Chili

5-Way on a Coney

Cincinnati, Ohio

When it comes to chili, Cincinnatians speak their own language. Around here, chili comes served over spaghetti or a hot dog (a "coney"); you can order a 3-Way (with shredded cheddar cheese), a 4-Way (with cheese and diced onions), or a 5-Way (with cheese, onions, and red beans and a side of oyster crackers—the works). But however they order it, Cincinnatians consume more chili per capita than any other city in the country.

Cincinnati style chili isn't chili con carne like you'd get in Texas—it's its own special dish, a thin but savory stew of finely ground beef spiced with aromatic ingredients such as chocolate and cinnamon rather than hot peppers. That's not surprising once you learn that Cincinnati chili was refined at diners owned by Greek and Macedonian immigrants—it's really an adaptation of Mediterranean peasant recipes. The first classic chili parlor, **Empress Chili,** opened downtown on Vine Street in 1922; chili chefs from Empress eventually started their own chili restaurants with slightly different recipes: **Dixie Chili** (opened in 1929 south across the river in Kentucky) and **Skyline Chili** (opened in 1949). The other major force in town, **Gold Star Chili,** opened in 1965. All these diners have spawned chains—Skyline and Gold Star, in fact, each have more than 100 locations, all over Ohio, Indiana, and northern Kentucky. Each has its own zealously guarded "secret" chili recipe, and though they look like fast-food joints, the chili is generally superb (Gold Star's tends to be a little thicker and chunkier). To compare them, head to the Hartwell section on the north side, where you'll find an **Empress Chili** at 8340 Vine St. (℄ 513/761-5599), a **Gold Star Chili** around the corner at 21 E. Galbraith Rd. (℄ **513/761-8633**), and a **Skyline Chili** a few blocks east in Arlington Heights, just north of Galbraith at 8506 Reading Rd. (℄ **513/821-1800**).

Still, there's no way a chain can compete with the quality of chili served at small independent restaurants. **Camp Washington Chili** (3005 Colerain Ave.; ℄ **513/541-0061**; www.campwashington chili.com) has been around since 1940, in its original building until 2000, when it moved across the street. Like the chains, it's run by a Greek immigrant family; unlike the chains, it's been cited by the James

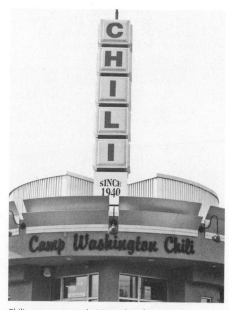

Chili comes on spaghetti or a hot dog at Camp Washington Chili in Cincinnati.

Beard Foundation as an American regional classic restaurant. Its beef is fresh ground every morning and the cheddar that's shredded for the 3-Way is real aged cheddar. With its generic diner decor, it's anything but a posh hangout, but a cadre of devoted customers swear by it. Then there are those who vote for **Price Hill Chili** (4920 Glenway Ave. # 2; 🕾**513/471-9507;** www.pricehillchili.com), a vintage coffee shop in West Cincinnati founded in 1962; it's known for its meatier, mellower take on the classic chili, as well as its great breakfasts and deli sandwiches.

➤ Cincinnati/Northern Kentucky International (24 miles/38km).

🛏 $$ **Millennium Hotel Cincinnati,** 150 W. 5th St. (🕾 **800/876-2100** or 513/352-2100; www.millennium-hotels.com). $$ **The Cincinnatian Hotel,** 601 Vine St. (🕾 **800/942-9000** or 513/381-3000; www.cincinnatianhotel.com).

Hometown Dish 204

Country-Style Fried Chicken
A Southern Classic
Atlanta, Georgia

Everybody's got a different vision of what perfect fried chicken should taste like—and it's probably based on the way your mother made it (or your grandmother, or whoever in your family was the fried-chicken whiz). Unless, of course, no one in your family could cook fried chicken, in which case you really need to visit Atlanta to find out how it's done.

Let's start with the classic: **Mary Mac's Tea Room** (224 Ponce de Leon Ave. NE; 🕾 **404/876-1800;** www.marymacs.com), a bastion of traditional southern cuisine that has been around since 1945 (Jimmy Carter was known to lunch in this cheery yellow-walled dining room when he was governor). Mary Mac's makes its famous fried chicken dredged in buttermilk and flour, with a double batter that comes out of the deep fryer curly and crisp. The thick giblet gravy is essential, and the list of possible sides is endless, including black-eyed peas, fried green tomatoes, whipped potatoes, fried okra, macaroni and cheese, sweet-potato soufflé, and more.

Just down the road from Mary Mac's, the **Watershed** (406 W. Ponce de Leon Ave., Decatur; 🕾404/378-4900; www.watershedrestaurant.com), a hip sandwich shop/wine bar located in a former gas station, has only been in business for a couple of years. But the chef, Scott Peacock, learned his craft from the great lady of southern cooking, Edna Lewis—they wrote a cookbook together, *The Gift of Southern Cooking*—and his fried chicken wins raves from foodies all over the South. Peacock brines his chicken first to make it moist, then soaks it in buttermilk for tanginess, and finally fries it in a mix of lard and sweet butter for crunchy crispness. There's just one catch—Peacock only fries chicken once a week, every Tuesday (it's too labor-intensive to keep on the daily menu). They only take reservations for large parties, so show up early and expect a wait—everyone wants a piece of Peacock's fried chicken.

A few blocks west, toward downtown, you'll find **Gladys Knight and Ron Winans' Chicken & Waffles** (529 Peachtree St. NE.; 🕾 **404/874-9393;** www.gladysandron.net), where the crispy golden fried chicken seasoning has a little more kick and comes served with sweet fluffy waffles (a vintage Harlem soul-food pairing). Founded by the veteran soul singers Gladys Knight and the late Ron Winans, the wood-paneled dining room features comfy leather booths and walls loaded with music memorabilia.

Finally, head north to the **Colonnade** (1879 Cheshire Bridge Rd. NE.; © **404/874-5642**) to find the ultimate southern cooking throwback, an unpretentious rambling restaurant that's been here since 1927. Don't let the coffee-shoppish 1950s-vintage decor fool you: The fried-chicken is superb, crisply battered yet juicy inside, and it's served with pepper-flecked cream gravy. Fried chicken livers are another

treat you won't find on too many menus these days, and be sure not to miss the divinely soft yeast rolls.

 Atlanta International (12 miles/20km).

$$$ **The Georgian Terrace Hotel,** 659 Peachtree St. (© **800/651-2316** or 404/897-1991; www.thegeorgianterrace. com). $$ **Hotel Indigo,** 683 Peachtree St. (© **404/874-9200;** www.hotelindigo.com).

205 Hometown Dish

That Catfish Place

Something Fishy at the Taylor Grocery

Taylor, Mississippi

The battered storefront, with the faded tin Coke sign over the porch, a rusted gas pump out front, and the scuffed screen door propped open, looks more like something out of *Deliverance* than one of Mississippi's top seafood restaurants. Looks can be deceiving, though; this century-old general store in the sleepy southern hamlet of Taylor, 8 miles (13km) south of Oxford in the hills of northern Mississippi, morphed into a restaurant in the 1970s. Since then it has grown famous for serving some of the best catfish in Mississippi, the epicenter of catfish cuisine. Though its famous cook Mary Katherine Hudson is no longer at the fryer, under new owners—Taylor native Lynn Hewlett and his wife, Debbie—the roadhouse is cracking along just as good as ever.

The catfish at Taylor Grocery is all locally pond-raised (wild catfish being harder to come by), and though it's briefly frozen to prevent spoilage, it still has a meaty fresh-caught flavor. It comes all sorts of ways—filleted or served whole on the bone; battered-fried, blackened Mississippi-style (spicy), or simply grilled. The fried version is a little spicier than typical fried catfish—it's

soaked in eggs, milk, Worcestershire, and hot sauce before being dipped in cornmeal batter, then fried at a slightly lower temperature so the batter remains delicately golden, and the fish inside is still flaky and moist. The menu lists steaks, shrimp, chicken, and pork tenderloin as well, but most people go for the catfish, often as an all-you-can-eat blowout. A side of hush puppies—deep-fried balls of cornmeal dough—is a given. The decor is Vintage Roadhouse, with cluttered wood-paneled walls, red-checkered tablecloths, and graffiti scribbled absolutely everywhere.

Taylor Grocery follows its own idiosyncratic rhythm—lunch buffet only, Monday through Friday, with dinners added Thursday through Sunday. That lunch buffet serves meat and veggies only; you'll have to wait until Thursday for the catfish. On weekends, there's usually live music as well, a rotating mix of bluegrass and blues. There's generally a line, but hanging around the rickety porch waiting for your table is a memorable experience in itself. ***Note:*** Taylor is a dry town, so the restaurant doesn't serve alcohol. ***Note carefully:*** Most of the patrons arrive carrying their own Styrofoam cups of various anonymous beverages. Draw your own conclusions.

✈ Memphis International (65 miles/105km).

ⓘ 4 County Rd., 338 # A (✆ **662/236-1716;** www.taylorgrocery.com).

🛏 $$ **Oliver-Britt House Inn,** 512 Van Buren Ave., Oxford (✆ **662/234-8043;** www.oliverbritthouse.com). $ **Comfort Inn,** 1808 Jackson Ave. S., Oxford (✆ **662/234-6000;** www.comfortinns.com).

Hometown Dish **206**

Nashville Hot Chicken

Feel the Burn

Nashville, Tennessee

Fried chicken? Strictly for wimps if you're a Nashville hot chicken addict. And addicting it can be—that all-hell-breaks-loose kick and I'm-still-here afterburn of such supremely spicy bird. It's not a question of slathering on hot sauce, as with hot wings, or even of throwing pepper into the batter, but of seasoning the bird deeply before it's fried, so the spiciness goes all the way to the bone. (Of course, the orange-tinted dark crust is fiery as well—why stop now?) Done right—which includes being fried in a cast-iron skillet—the chicken meat is still juicy and tender. The whole experience is a sensory roller coaster ride, and for certain culinary thrill seekers, it's irresistible.

The premier place to get it, without a doubt, is **Prince's Hot Chicken,** a funky spot on the north end of town, with a hand-painted glass front, a few wooden booths, garish turquoise walls, worn checkered linoleum on the floor, and a rickety-looking wooden counter. You can order your chicken—ask for either a breast quarter, a leg quarter, or a half—in four levels of hotness: Even the so-called mild can clear your sinuses, medium will make you break out in a sweat, and hot evokes visions of Vesuvius. You really need weeks of conditioning before trying the extra-hot—even hot-sauce junkies will admit that their mouths aren't asbestos-coated enough for the extra-hot. *Be forewarned:*

Service can be rude, the place is dirty, it's in a sketchy part of town, and you'll have to wait up to 45 minutes at busy times for your food. Oh, and they don't serve drinks (though there is a vending machine). For hot-chicken addicts, of course, all of that only whets the appetite.

Despite the many other hot chicken joints in town, aficionados claim that only **Bolton's Spicy Chicken & Fish** can compete with Prince's. Closer to the center of town, in a gray cinder block shack in East Nashville, Bolton's is mostly a takeout place—there are just a couple of tables in the tiny pink-walled "dining room"—but the service is friendlier than at Prince's and you won't have to wait so long for your food. Bolton's doesn't go quite as far up the heat index as Prince's does, but crunch through the spicy-enough crust and you'll find the interior chicken meat richly flavored. What's more, you can also try a filet of catfish spiced up the same way. Bolton's has a bigger choice of side dishes, including some excellent greens, mac-and-cheese, and cornbread.

Prince's is closed Sunday and Monday; Bolton's is closed Mondays.

ⓘ **Prince's Hot Chicken Shack,** 123 Ewing Dr. (✆ **615/226-9442**). **Bolton's Spicy Chicken & Fish,** 624 Main St. (✆ **615/254-8015**).

Nashville International (12 miles/19km). $$$ **The Hermitage Hotel,** 231 6th Ave. N (© **888/888-9414** or 615/244-3121; www.thehermitagehotel.com). $$ **Wyndham Union Station,** 1001 Broadway (© **615/248-3554;** www.wyndham.com).

207 Hometown Dish

Burgoo

All in a Stew

Owensboro, Kentucky

Where that strange name came from is anybody's guess; just as mysterious is the source of the original recipe. A quintessential frontier food, burgoo may have evolved from Irish stew, or from hearty soups introduced by Welsh coal-mining immigrants. But in the hardscrabble early 1800s, when Kentucky was first settled, nobody got too picky about what meat should go into the pot—anything from squirrel to possum would do.

Nowadays, hardly anybody outside of Kentucky knows about burgoo—and sadly, as chain restaurants and ethnic cuisines proliferate, it's becoming harder to find this down-home comfort food even in Kentucky. But burgoo is still alive and well in Owensboro, a western Kentucky riverfront town that prides itself on being a barbecue capital. (The International Bar-B-Q Festival held here every May is well worth scheduling a trip around; see the Calendar of Food Fairs & Festivals chapter for more information.)

Barbecue and burgoo are natural menumates; like barbecue, burgoo gets better the longer and slower it is cooked. At Owensboro's top barbecue restaurant, **Moonlite Barbecue,** it's made with mutton—the same meat that's traditionally used in Kentucky barbecue (western Kentucky is a big sheep-raising region)—along with some chicken and a bounty of vegetables. The slight gaminess of mutton balances out the snap of red pepper and tomatoes; cooking over an open hickory-wood-stoked pit adds a special smokiness.

It's cooked for hours in a heavy iron pot (30 hr. is typical), which allows the starchy ingredients like corn, onion, and potatoes to thicken the stew naturally—thickening it until, tradition says, you can stand a spoon up in it. Moonlite makes 35 to 70 gallons of the soul-satisfying stuff every day.

Run by the Bosley family since 1963, Moonlite is consistently voted Owensboro's top barbecue restaurant. You'll find it on the western edge of town, in a low-slung, functional brick building surrounded by black asphalt; you can smell the hickory smoke of the open pit already from the parking lot. Inside, its warmly lit wood-trimmed dining room is centered around stainless-steel buffet tables, loaded up with burgoo, hickory-smoked, fork-tender barbecue (mostly mutton, of course, but also pork, beef, and chicken), and side dishes like cheesy broccoli casserole, macaroni and cheese, creamed corn niblets, ham and beans, and butter-drizzled mashed potatoes—and of course a raft of homemade pies.

ⓘ 2840 W. Parrish Ave. (© **270/684-8143;** www.moonlite.com).

✈ Louisville (80 miles/129km).

$$ **Comfort Suites,** 230 Salem Dr. (© **270/926-7675;** www.comfortsuites. com). $$ **Holiday Inn Express Owensboro,** 3220 W. Parrish Ave. (© **270/685-2433;** www.ichotels.com).

Chicken-Fried Steak

The Taste of West Texas

Strawn, Texas

Like many regional specialties, chicken-fried steak (CFS) was born out of necessity—and in this case, the challenge was to make an inferior hunk of beef worthy of a Sunday ranch dinner. Historians speculate that the solution came from the Germans who settled large parts of Texas: Pound the meat into submission, bread or batter it like a Wiener schnitzel, and slap in into a sizzling cast-iron skillet (West Texas) or deep-fryer (South Texas). When it's done right, the meat turns astonishingly juicy and tender, playing off against the flaky, crisp crust in every bite. With a side of mashed potatoes and topped with spicy cream gravy, it's a country taste that's hard to beat.

Folks in Dallas praise the CFS at the aptly named **All Good Café** in the Deep Ellum neighborhood (2934 Main St., Dallas; © **214/742-5362**), while Houstonians are partial to the **Barbecue Inn's** (116 W. Crosstimbers St., Houston; © **713/695-8112**). But for the most part, the art of making chicken-fried steak—also known as "country-fried steak," for obvious reasons—thrives away from the big cities, in small-town cafes across the hill country and on north.

No other town is as blessed in this regard as tiny Strawn, a *Last Picture Show* sort of West Texas town about halfway between Abilene and Fort Worth, just north of I-20. In deer hunting season, you'll notice a host of pickup trucks in the gravel lot outside a converted service station, now **Mary's Café** (119 Grant Ave.; © **254/672-5741**); on weekends, it's just as likely to be a flock of Harleys. That's the sort of unpretentious spot this is, a much-added-onto series of simply furnished dining rooms with plenty of space between the tables and neon beer signs on the walls. Portions are legendarily huge—order a medium-size steak unless you're absolutely ravenous. Owner Mary Tretter cooks her pounded-thin steaks the West Texas way: dredged in seasoned flour (a secret recipe) and fried on a flat-iron griddle; don't expect fast service, because every order is cooked from scratch.

Yet while the crowds pack into Mary's, right across the street is another cafe where, locals insist, the chicken-fried steak is equally good—**Flossie's** (120 Grant Ave.; © **254/672-9201**). When Mary's started up in 1986, in fact, its business was largely overflow from Flossie's, which was already famous for its CFS. Like Mary's, it's got lots of Mexican specialties on the menu, including a superb Frito pie, but it's smaller and homier, and it's also known for its hand-cut french fries and juicy hamburgers. Only trouble is, meals at both cafes are so hearty, you can't sample both in a day.

✈ Dallas-Fort Worth International (85 miles/137km).

🛏 $$$ **Stockyards Hotel,** 109 W. Exchange Ave., Fort Worth (© **800/423-8471** or 817/625-6427; www.stockyards hotel.com). $$ **Etta's Place,** 200 W. 3rd St., Fort Worth (© **866/355-5760** or 817/255-5760; www.ettas-place.com).

Green Chili Burgers
The Battle of San Antonio
San Antonio, New Mexico

It's a keynote of southwestern culinary philosophy—the idea that any food can be improved by throwing in green chili peppers. Sometimes that leads to disaster, but not when it comes to hamburgers. With the ground beef itself given an extra zing of garlic and ground chili powder, the patty is then loaded with cheese, slices of sweet onion and ripe red tomato, and chopped green chilies—an inspired interplay of flavor and texture.

New Mexico is the heart of Green Chili Burger (GCB) Land, and some claim that Santa Fe—with both **Bobcat Bite** and **Bert's Burger Bowl** (see "7 Places to Eat in Santa Fe," p. 98)—is the inner chamber. But to fully comprehend how New Mexico worships the green chili burger, head 90 miles (145km) south of Albuquerque on I-25 to the tiny, scruffy desert town of San Antonio, New Mexico, where there's hardly anything on the main street except two dingy bars—both of which serve GCBs rated among the best in the nation.

The more famous spot is the **Owl Tavern,** where the green chili burgers (lauded in 2003 by epicurious.com as one of the top-10 burgers in the nation) have been beloved for more than 60 years, since scientists working on atomic bomb tests at the nearby White Sands missile range used to stop in for drinks and burgers in the 1940s. The Owl is, just as the name says, a tavern, darkly lit inside with a clutter of memorabilia on the walls. (Note the beautiful hardwood bar in the front room—a relic of the first Hilton hotel, run by San Antonio native Conrad Hilton.) Service is fast and friendly, and the chopped green chilies that top the Owl's crusty, hand-formed beef patties are fiery hot, at least by non–New Mexicans' standards.

But just a block down the street, in an atmospheric pink adobe shack with a cast-iron stag over the entrance, the **Buckhorn**—also founded in the 1940s—serves up its own green chili burger (this one received top-10 ranking from *GQ* in a 2005 nationwide burger survey). Manny's GCB also uses pungent hot chilies and creamy melted cheese, but it piles them on more generously, and the underlying burger, ground fresh that morning, is bigger than the Owl's these days. According to green chili burger aficionados, the competition between the two bars—which the Owl Tavern seemed to be winning just a few

Bert's Burger Bowl claims to have invented the green chili burger.

195

7 Places to Eat Along . . . Route 66

Long before the Eisenhower administration sanitized coast-to-coast car travel with its network of cookie-cutter interstate highways, there was Route 66. Running from Chicago to Los Angeles, this two-lane blacktop ribbon cut through existentially lonely swaths of the still-undeveloped American West, building its own mythic aura as the miles ticked past. There've been pop songs about it (Nat King Cole's 1946 hit "Get Your Kicks On Route 66") and even an early 1960s TV series starring George Chakiris and Martin Milner as two drifters in a jazzy sports car. Even though the road was long ago disbanded and the famous signs torn down, its iconic status persists, with guidebooks still tracing the route. In the summer of 2008, no less a fan than Paul McCartney drove it in a red Ford pickup. Driving Route 66 is a spunky adventure in blue-highway travel, with plenty of mom-and-pop motels and cafes.

Pop's roadside icon east of Oklahoma City on Route 66.

Just east of Oklahoma City, Route 66's romantic Dust Bowl vibe is startlingly interrupted by ⑳ Pops (660 W. Hwy. 66, Arcadia; ℂ 877/266-7677; www.pops66. com), a brand-new diner/gas station that looks like a futuristic spaceport set down on the site of an old gas station. At heart, however, Pops has a nostalgic streak a mile wide. Owner Aubrey McClendon stocks over 500 brands of soda pop from all over the world, championing quirky independent brands over the mass-marketed nationals. You'll know you're there when you see a 66-ft.-high (20m) neon soda bottle rising like a beacon over the wheat fields. Head west through Oklahoma City, catching State Road 66 again on the far side, to find El Reno, Oklahoma, and vintage ㉑ Jobe's Drive-In (1220 Sunset Dr.; ℂ 405/262-0194). Intercoms at each parking space let you order a classic Oklahoma-style onion burger (not listed as such—*all* burgers here come with onions smashed into the meat); carhops bring the food out on a tray that gets clipped to your car window.

Crossing the state line into Texas, Route 66 parallels I-40 as a series of unnumbered roads; halfway through, in Amarillo—a town that lovingly preserves its Route 66 heritage—stop off at the red-brick storefront ㉒ Golden Light Café (2908 W. 6th St.; ℂ 806/374-9237) for a cowboy-style burger, superlative thin-cut french fries, and frosty mugs of local beer.

In New Mexico, the original Route 66 angled north to Las Vegas; follow that route up U.S. 84 to parallel I-25, and you'll pass through Santa Fe, where an old adobe trading post was converted in 1953 into **213** **Bobcat Bite** (420 Old Las Vegas Hwy.; ☎ **505/983-5319;** http://bobcatbite.com). Many locals swear Bobcat beats in-town **214** **Bert's Burger Bowl** (see **209**) for the tangiest green chili cheeseburgers in town. (Note that Bobcat is closed Sun–Tues.) Route 66 was rerouted in 1937, however, to run through Albuquerque; follow that option to check out **215** **The Frontier** (2400 Central Ave. SE; ☎ **505/266-0550;** www.frontierrestaurant.com), a gigantic, student-friendly hangout right across from the University of New Mexico campus. Though it opened in 1971, long after Route 66 vanished, the Frontier has that *On the Road* spirit down pat, with speedy counter service, round-the-clock hours, and delicious cheap food, from breakfast burritos in the morning to green-chili stew in the evening.

Pop's stocks 500 brands of soda from around the globe.

Over in Arizona, just past the Painted Desert in Holbrook, **216** **Joe & Aggie's Café** (120 W. Hopi Dr.; ☎ **928/524-6540**) is a cheery little pink-adobe storefront dating from 1946. It's a great stop for enchiladas, chicken-fried steak, and puffy *sopapillas* (fried bread). On the other side of Flagstaff, along the last section of Route 66 to finally be bypassed, cozy wood-paneled **217** **Old Smoky's** (624 W. Bill Williams Ave., Williams AZ; ☎ **928/635-2091**) has been serving stacks of hot fluffy pancakes to Grand Canyon–bound tourists since 1946.

🛏 $ **Best Western Saddleback Inn,** 4300 SW 3rd St. (☎ **800/228-3903** or 405/947-7000; www.bestwestern.com/saddlebackinn). $ **Santa Fe Motel and Inn,** 510 Cerrillos Rd. (☎ **800/930-5002** or 505/982-1039; www.santafemotel.com). $ **Wigwam Village Motel,** 811 W. Hopi Dr., Holbrook AZ (☎ **928/524-3048;** www.wigwam-motel-arizona.com).

The green chili burger at the Buckhorn in San Antonio, NM.

years ago—has recently swung back in Manny's favor. Come here, sample both, and judge for yourself.

ⓘ**Owl Tavern,** 77 Hwy. 380 (ⓒ**505/835-9946**). **Manny's Buckhorn Tavern,** 68 Hwy. 380 (ⓒ**505/835-4423**).

✈ Albuquerque (90 miles/145km).

🛏 $$$ **Los Poblanos Inn,** 4803 Rio Grande Blvd., NW, Albuquerque (ⓒ**886/344-9297** or 505/344-9297; www.lospoblanos.com). $$ **Hacienda Antigua,** 6708 Tierra Dr. NW (ⓒ **800/201-2986** or 505/345-5399; www.haciendantigua.com).

Hometown Dish **218**

Fish Tacos
The Sea in a Tortilla
San Diego, California

Surfers wolf down fish tacos after churning up an appetite on the waves all day. Padres baseball fans clutch fish tacos instead of ballpark hot dogs as they cheer their team to victory. Doctors and lawyers and accountants unwrap takeout fish tacos at their desks; Mexican day laborers eat fish tacos at hole-in-the-wall *taquerías* where Spanish only is spoken. They're the hometown taste of San Diego, a refreshing twist on Mexican

food that surfed up the Pacific coast from Baja California and never left.

It's a simple concept—a warm tortilla envelops small pieces of fried fish in a golden, tempura-like batter (Japanese fishermen traditionally worked the waters off Baja's coast). The fish is then slathered with a variety of condiments, including tomato salsa, green chili salsa, some kind of white sauce (anything from tartarlike mayo sauce to cool and tangy Mexican *crema*), and shredded cabbage—which, unlike the lettuce on a Tex-Mex taco, won't wilt in the heat. Some restaurants also add cheddar topping, or grill the fish instead of frying it—tasty variations, but sacrilege to fish taco purists.

The place that launched the craze is **Rubio's** (4504 E. Mission Bay Dr.; ✆ **858/272-2801;** www.rubios.com), an unpretentious walk-up stand opened in 1983 across from Mission Bay Park, which has since spread into a five-state chain of casual sit-down restaurants. Its basic beer-battered fish taco is still a decent option; other taco choices on Rubio's oft-expanded menu include mahimahi and shrimp. Closer to the ocean, the quick and affordable **Taco Surf Taco Shop** (4657 Mission Blvd., Pacific Beach; ✆ **858/272-3877**) has a no-frills surfboard decor, dependable classic fish tacos, and daily specials featuring premium fish.

But some of San Diego's most authentic fish tacos are found inland, in residential neighborhoods where tourists rarely venture. Up in University Heights, small and cozy **El Zarape** (4642 Park Blvd; ✆ **619/692-1652**) sells one of the cheapest fish tacos in town, which is also tasty and authentic.

In the Hillcrest neighborhood, **Mama Testa** (1417A University Ave.; ✆ **619/298-8226;** www.mamatestataqueria.com) is like a seminar in Mexican cooking, plying tacos from every region (corn tortillas only—flour tortillas aren't authentic, they claim), including well-executed catfish, shrimp, and scallop tacos. In the Logan Heights area of town, **Mariscos German** (2802 Ocean View Blvd; ✆ **619/239-3782**) isn't German at all, but a quirky Mexican seafood restaurant—a little slice of San Felipe transported north of the border, decorated in hanging fishnets and under-the-sea murals. Its long list of fish taco options includes exotic alternatives like octopus, shrimp, or marlin. They also operate two taco trucks in the neighborhood—how authentic is that?

✈ San Diego International (7¾ miles/ 12km).

⌨ $$$ **Catamaran Resort Hotel,** 3999 Mission Blvd., San Diego (✆ **800/422-8386** or 858/488-1081; www.catamaran resort.com). $ **Park Manor Suites,** 525 Spruce St. (✆ **800/874-2649** or 619/291-0999; www.parkmanorsuites.com).

Mama Testa's corn tacos come stuffed with catfish, shrimp, scallops, and more.

New York's Pizzeria Classics
A Coal-Fired Family Tree
New York, New York

In New York City—where it often seems there's a pizzeria on every corner—locals can't even agree on who is the oldest pizza maker in town, let alone which one is best. Granted, New Yorkers love nothing better than an argument, so the debate may never be settled. The basic template is a thin-crust pizza with smooth tomato sauce and melted mozzarella, but beyond that, the esoteric shades of distinction are endless.

One important factor is having a coal-fired brick oven, which turns a thin crust into a crisp, slightly charred wonder. Since Manhattan stopped issuing permits for new coal-fired ovens, only the old-timers have that edge—places like **Lombardi's** in SoHo/Little Italy, at 32 Spring St. (☎**212/941-7994**), **John's Pizzeria** in west Greenwich Village at 278 Bleecker St. (☎ **212/243-1680**), or **Patsy's,** in East Harlem at 2287 1st Ave. (☎**212/534-9783**). Lombardi's claims to be the city's oldest pizzeria, citing Italian grocer Gennaro Lombardi's 1905 license to sell his original tomato pies; however, the original Lombardi's closed in 1984, to be reopened by a grandson 10 years later in a new brick-walled location down the street (snagging an existing coal oven from a defunct neighborhood bakery). Lombardi's pizzas are excellent, especially the red clam pie, but that gap in time makes John's, which opened in 1929 in this traditionally Italian part of the Village, qualify as the oldest *continuously operating* pizzeria in Manhattan. John's famously doesn't make deliveries, doesn't sell slices, and takes cash only, which allows this no-frills spot with scarred wooden booths and Formica-topped tables to keep its focus on making excellent blistered-crust pies. Patsy's is the baby of the bunch, dating only from 1932, when

Pasquale Lancieri—who was trained by Gennaro Lombardi—opened his pizzeria in Manhattan's third Little Italy, in northern Manhattan. Though the neighborhood is now Spanish Harlem, devotees still crowd into the retro dining room—replete with checkered tablecloths and pressed tin ceilings—for delicious thin-crust pizza.

One way to get around the Manhattan permit issues, of course, is to build your coal-fired oven in Brooklyn, which is what Lancieri's nephew Patsy Grimaldi did at **Grimaldi's** (19 Old Fulton St., Brooklyn Heights; ☎**718/858-4300**). There are usually lines down the street to get into this cramped, cash-only spot, but at least you get dynamite Manhattan skyline views while you wait.

And speaking of Brooklyn, the last entrant in that oldest-NYC-pizza contest is **Totonno's Pizzeria Napoletano,** which first fired up its coal ovens in 1924 in Brooklyn's then-popular Coney Island, at 1524 Neptune Ave. (☎ **718/372-8606;** www.totonnos.com). Despite Coney Island's current decrepitude, family-run Totonno's still draws customers to its unpretentious original storefront. Nevertheless, Totonno's has wisely expanded into Manhattan, with two modern branches (1544 Second Ave. in the Upper East Side; 462 Second Ave. in Murray Hill) that hold up the family tradition surprisingly well. You'll also see several Patsy's locations around town, but be aware that a franchise merely licensed the name from Lancieri; their pizzas and pastas are perfectly fine, but hardly classics. Then there is John's huge, snazzy offspring in a deconsecrated church near Times Square (244 W. 44th St.; ☎**212/391-7560;** www.johns pizzerianyc.com); while it lacks the original's old-school charm, its wood-fired brick oven pizzas are a superb theater district alternative (with long no-reservations lines to prove it).

✈ John F. Kennedy International (15 miles/24km); Newark Liberty International (16 miles/27km); LaGuardia (8 miles/13km).

🛏 $$$ **Carlton Hotel** on Madison Avenue, 88 Madison Ave. (✆ **212/532-4100;** www.carltonhotelny.com). $$ **Washington Square Hotel,** 103 Waverly Place (✆ **800/222-0418** or 212/777-9515; www.washingtonsquarehotel.com).

220 Pizzerias

Pepe's Versus Sally's
You Say Pizza, I Say Apizza
New Haven, Connecticut

New Haven's rich legacy of pizza—or "apizza," as it's generally spelled in south-central Connecticut, for reasons no one remembers—began in the late 19th century with an influx of Italian immigrant factory workers, hungry for the tastes of the old country. Wooster Street, the heart of New Haven's Little Italy, was a natural place for former street seller Frank Pepe to open his Neopolitan-style pizzeria in a modest brick storefront in 1925. And 13 years later, it was only natural for Frank's nephew, Sal Consiglio, to open his own restaurant, Sally's Apizza, in a similar building a block down the street.

But after that, the situation curdled into one of the longest-running rivalries in American gastronomy. Pepe's and Sally's are both still run by their founding families, and they're fiercely competitive. Yet both serve basically the same menu—nothing but pizza—and it's the same New Haven–style variation: thin-crust pizza, topped with tomato sauce, garlic, and hard cheeses (unlike the mozzarella that's standard on most American pies). At both restaurants, there's almost always a line down the street to get in.

Pizza connoisseurs regard both Pepe's and Sally's as two of the country's finest classic pizzerias, with their hand-formed pies baked in vintage coal-fired brick ovens until the cheese and tomato sauce bubble and blister temptingly, and the crusts char ever so slightly at the edge. So what's the difference between the two? Well, at Pepe's the white and red clam pizzas, made with freshly shucked clams, are the signature dish, while Sally's shines most with its vegetable pizzas, like the "white" potato-and-rosemary pizza. It's generally agreed that Sally's crust is a little thinner and lighter; service tends to be friendlier and faster at Pepe's. The long wooden booth–lined dining room at Pepe's is a little more smartly kept up, while Sally's maintains an atmospheric 1960s-throw-back decor of vinyl booths and scarred wood paneling. Sally's is closed on Mondays and doesn't open until 5pm, while Pepe's is open 7 days a week for lunch as well as dinner. Sally's is cash-only; Pepe's accepts credit cards. Frank Sinatra signed a photo on the wall at Sally's, but he hung out more at Pepe's. And so on and so forth.

But there is one major difference—Pepe's recently opened branches in Manchester and Fairfield, Connecticut, and is planning to open more. Will expansion ruin the handmade, small-scale quality of Pepe's pizzas, or will they be able to replicate the Wooster Street magic elsewhere? Pizza fans watch anxiously—and their cousins down at Sally's are probably watching most anxiously of all.

ⓘ **Frank Pepe Pizzeria Napoletana,** 157 Wooster St. (☎ **203/865-5762;** www.pepespizzeria.com). **Sally's Apizza,** 237 Wooster St. (☎ **203/624-5271;** www.sallysapizza.net).

New Haven (1½ hr. from New York City, 3 hr. from Boston).

$$ **Omni New Haven,** 155 Temple St. (☎ **800/THE-OMNI** [800/843-6664] or 203/772-6664; www.omnihotels.com).

Pizzerias

221

Pizzeria Uno & Due
Get the Dish on Deep-Dish
Chicago, Illinois

Those who have grown up with Chicago deep-dish pizza just don't get why other pizzas are so wimpy. They demand full-bodied pizza—not just its thick, cracker-edged, buttery crust, but the chunky tomato sauce, the globs of creamy mozzarella cheese, the hearty nuggets of sausage and onion and other vegetables. It's all about delivering toppings, really—a plain deep-dish pizza is heresy.

That was the intention of Ike Sewell, a nationally known University of Texas football star, when in 1943 he opened his pizza restaurant in a red-brick townhouse at the corner of Ohio Street and Wabash Avenue in Chicago's Near North neighborhood. To most Americans at the time, pizza was an exotic snack, but Ike envisioned it as a stick-to-your-ribs meal, satisfying even a football player's appetite. He and his head cook, Rudy Malnati, cooked their pizza in a deep-sided round pan, with the deep underlayer of dough parbaked before toppings were added, to prevent sogginess; reversing the New York–style order of ingredients, they laid on the mozzarella first (to melt into the dough), then other toppings, and finished off with tangy tomato sauce on top. With such a robust crust, they could increase the toppings, to the point where you'd really need a knife and fork to eat it. Sewell called his restaurant **Pizzeria Uno,** and it was such a smash hit that in 1955 he added **Pizzeria Due** in a gray-brick Victorian house nearby at Wabash and Ontario Street.

The cloning of Pizzeria Uno into a nationwide chain in the 1980s was a shame; those franchises bear no resemblance to the original, where the pizza is still hearty, fresh, and flavorful. The original location, however, now attracts hordes of tourists, who wait outside for up to an hour to squeeze into its dingy cluttered basement. (There's also outdoor patio seating in good weather.) Pizza takes an hour to make, but if you order when they put your name on the waiting list, it may be ready soon after you're seated. No matter what local

Pizzeria Uno and Due—home of Chicago's original deep dish pizza.

pizza snobs say, the pies here can still be outstanding—good enough to justify the wait and the harried service. The menu is exactly the same at Pizzeria Due, but its dining room is a little more inviting, and the service somewhat more sympathetic, though you should still expect an hour's wait for your pie.

If the lines seem too long, scoot down Ontario to popular **Gino's East** (633 N. Wells St.; ☎ **312/943-1124**), a cavernous stucco-walled pizzeria with graffiti-laden wooden booths that has been around since 1966. The pizzas still take 45 minutes to arrive (there's no avoiding that), but you may at least be seated sooner. Work up a good appetite beforehand so you can handle the supreme, with its layers of cheese, sausage, onions, green pepper, and mushrooms. Another great option in the area is **Lou Malnati's** (439 N. Wells St.; ☎ **312/828-9800**), the River North outpost of a small local chain started in 1971 by the son of Uno's original pizza chef.

ⓘ **Pizzeria Uno,** 29 E. Ohio St. (☎ **312/321-1000**). **Pizzeria Due,** 619 N. Wabash St. (☎ **312/943-2400**).

✈ O'Hare International (18 miles/28km).

🛏 $$ **Homewood Suites,** 40 E. Grand St., Chicago (☎ **800/CALL-HOME** [800/225-4663] or 312/644-2222; www.homewoodsuiteschicago.com). $$ **Hotel Allegro Chicago,** 171 N. Randolph St., Chicago (☎ **800/643-1500** or 312/236-0123; www.allegrochicago.com).

222 Pizzerias

Pizzeria Bianco

Phoenix Rising

Phoenix, Arizona

It's rare indeed for pizza-heads and finicky gourmets to agree—but both seem to be of the same mind when talking about Chris Bianco and the artisanal pizzas he has been whipping up since 1993 in, of all places, Phoenix, Arizona.

There's usually a line waiting to get in to this small red-brick restaurant—it seats only 43 diners—in Phoenix's historic Heritage Square Park district. The menu is limited, and the prices are relatively modest. The decor is softly lit and minimalist, with diners sitting at long, plain communal tables, a few tasteful paintings hanging on the brick walls, and Bianco working his wood-fired ovens behind a counter at the far end. That all suits the food, of course, which evolves naturally from Bianco's aesthetic of straightforward techniques, rustic preparations, and organic, high-quality ingredients. He offers a nightly salad of whatever looked good that morning at the farmer's market. He has his tomatoes custom-grown on a local farm; the oregano, basil, and rosemary come from his herb garden out back; and he makes his own mozzarella.

As a Bronx native, Bianco knows from pizza. He's not seeking fancy designer innovations, just interpreting the Neapolitan classic pizza according to the ingredients he's working with. Bianco comes at pizza from a bread-baker's perspective—he has also opened a spin-off café serving sandwiches made on his own artisanal bread—and he's in the kitchen every night, turning out pizza dough by hand (notice the blissfully ragged, imperfect circles of his crusts). Then he tops the pies simply; there are only six basic pizzas on his menu, plus 10 various add-on ingredients such as fennel sausage, roasted crimini mushrooms, or anchovies and mortadella imported from Italy. The ovens are kept blazing at high temperatures of 800°F or 900°F to achieve

Pizzeria Bianco's lively bar scene in Phoenix.

just the right amount of blister and char on the crust.

Pizzeria Bianco opens at 5pm for dinner only; it's closed Sunday and Monday, and they take off for 2 weeks at the end of every summer. But the reason Chris Bianco's name hangs over the door is that this is pretty much a one-man show; Pizzeria Bianco *is* Chris Bianco. And even an artisan needs a little vacation.

(i) 623 East Adams St. (© **602/258-8300;** www.pizzeriabianco.com).

✈ Phoenix Sky Harbor International (4¾ miles/7.5km).

🛏 $$$ **Sheraton Wild Horse Pass Resort,** 5594 W. Wild Horse Pass Blvd. (© **888/218-8989** or 602/225-0100; www. wildhorsepassresort.com). $$ **Fiesta Inn Resort,** 2100 S. Priest Dr. (© **800/528-6481** or 480/967-1441; www.fiestainn resort.com).

Pizzerias **223**

Pizzeria Mozza

The New Designer Pizza

Los Angeles, California

During the 1980s, Austrian chef Wolfgang Puck touched off a minirevolution in American culinary circles when he introduced his "designer pizzas" to the menu at his trendy West Hollywood restaurant, Spago. Despite the casual decor, the place had more celebrity-studded glamour than it knew how to handle; the idea that pizzas belonged on a dinner menu alongside porcini-crusted sweetbreads seemed brash and downright cheeky. How Californian was that?

But now the Sunset Strip Spago has closed, and pizza only survives on the lunch menu at Puck's new **Spago Beverly Hills** (176 N. Cañon Dr.; 310/385-0880). Favorites such as the pesto shrimp pizza, the duck sausage pizza, and spicy chicken and caramelized sweet corn pizza are still there, but not featured prominently; it's as if Puck preferred to leave his often-caricatured signature dish behind. (Not that Puck himself does much cooking these days.)

But never fear: There's a new pizza star in Hollywood. In 2007, the team of Nancy Silverton, Mario Batali, and Joseph Bastianich opened **Pizzeria Mozza** at 641 N. Highland Ave. (323/297-0101; www. mozza-la.com). It's really Silverton's baby: Having moved on from the La Brea Bakery where she made her name, she has turned her artisanal bread-baking passion toward refining the perfect Neapolitan-style pizza crust, while chef Batali, who knows a thing or two about Italian food, helped refine the pizza toppings.

The decor is entirely unpretentious—the plain, high-ceilinged space houses about a dozen tables, some counter seating, and an open kitchen where Nancy usually presides. The pizza list runs to about 15 different combinations of ingredients such as house-made fennel sausage with panna and red onion; Gorgonzola dolce with fingerling potatoes, radicchio, and rosemary; or rapini with black olives, cherry tomatoes, and anchovy—not your usual pizzeria classics, but still in the Neapolitan ballpark (though there are a few more daring experiments, like the speck, pineapple, jalapeño, mozzarella, and tomato pizza). At Pizzeria Mozza—much as at its sister restaurant, **Osteria Mozza,** around the corner at 6602 Melrose Ave. (**323/297-0100**), where the most coveted seat is at the mozzarella bar—it's all about quality ingredients and letting the flavors shine through. And of course, these days, it's as

Pizzeria Mozza—with toppings designed by Mario Batali and crusts by Nancy Silverton.

hard to get a reservation at Pizzeria Mozza as it ever was at Spago.

✈ Los Angeles International (15 miles/25km).

🛏 $$$ **Peninsula Beverly Hills,** 9882 S. Santa Monica Blvd. (📞 **800/462-7899** or 310/551-2888; www.peninsula.com). $ **Best Western Marina Pacific Hotel,** 1697 Pacific Ave., Venice (📞 **800/786-7789** or 310/452-1111; www.mphotel.com).

Barbecue Heavens **224**

Skylight Inn
Going the Whole Hog
Ayden, North Carolina

It's tempting to think that they named Pitt County, North Carolina, in honor of its world-class barbecue pits. Even though legendary pit master Pete Jones has passed on, the famous Skylight Inn he opened in 1947 in tiny Ayden, North Carolina, still shines as one of the top barbecue spots in the Carolinas—no, make that America.

The gimcrack replica of the U.S. Capitol dome that tops the squat brick Skylight Inn is testament to the high opinion folks have of this bare-bones place—it considers itself the capital of barbecue, and with good reason. Given the location, on the coastal plains of eastern North Carolina, barbecued pork (it's *always* pork in these parts) is served with a tangy red vinegar-based sauce, though most customers don't even bother with the squeeze bottles of sauce. And like other eastern North Carolina barbecue spots, Skyline splays an entire hog onto the grate, not just selected cuts. Thirteen or 14 hours later, when the hog is done cooking, they chop up those meltingly tender hunks of pork with lethally sharp cleavers into a fine mince, mixing in all the crispy bits of sizzled fat (the "outside brown") that add an extra zing of smoky moist flavor. The chopper seems to work nonstop, *thunk-thunk-thunk*, on a huge wood block hollowed out by years of cleaver-work.

Pete Jones's son Bruce and nephew Jeff carry on the family tradition—still using those time-tested Jones clan recipes, which they claim stretch back over 2 centuries of slow pig-roasting over oak embers. ("If it's not cooked with wood, it's not Bar-B-Q," the Skylight's hand-painted billboard declares.) The focus is totally on the meat here, which comes as either a sandwich or a pulled-pork dinner—"dinner" meaning a pile of loose chopped meat loaded onto a red-and-white cardboard boat with coleslaw and crusty cornbread, the only available sides. The Skylight Inn is only open until 7pm, and it's closed on Sundays—plan your pilgrimage accordingly.

ⓘ 4618 South Lee St. (old Hwy. 11) (📞 **252/746-4113**).

✈ Greenville (15 miles/24km).

🛏 $$$ **City Hotel and Bistro,** 203 W. Greenville Blvd., Greenville (📞 **877/271-2616** or 252/355-8300; www.cityhotelandbistro.com). $$ **Jameson Inn,** 920 Crosswinds St., Greenville (📞 **800/526-3766** or 252/752-7382; www.jamesoninn.com).

Lexington Barbecue
Where the Piedmont Porks Out
Lexington, North Carolina

Up in the Piedmont, they've got some different ideas about barbecue. For one thing, they don't bother with the whole pig, only the dark meat of the shoulder—which means they only have to smoke their meat for about 9 hours to get it tender enough to fall apart. Then there's the question of the sauce—why not throw in a little ketchup for tomato-ey goodness?

If there's any town in western North Carolina that cares about barbecue, it's Lexington. It's another of those communities that bills itself as "The Barbecue Capitol of the World," but considering their per-capita distribution of barbecue restaurants—some 20 of them for a town of only 20,000 residents—they may be justified. Lexington's annual October barbecue festival draws more than 100,000 people to this small town just 20 miles (32km) south of Winston-Salem.

You can—and probably should—eat your way around Lexington, trying several 'cue joints and judging for yourself which is best. But the best place to start is **Lexington Barbecue,** on 10 Hwy. 29–70 S. (© **336/249-9814**). Opened in 1962 by Wayne "Honey" Monk, generally regarded as the dean of all Lexington's pit masters, it's hard to miss from the road: Just look for a series of weird conical chimneys rising above the roof of an otherwise undistinguished warehouselike brick building.

The piles of hickory wood stacked in the shed out back are your next clue—though really, if you're that close to the place, the aroma of blue wood smoke and roasting meat is the dead giveaway. Inside, it's a little more decorated than the Skylight Inn (see ⓬ above), though of course that's not saying much—a little knotty-pine paneling, a few booths, even a couple of paintings of bucolic farms on the wall. Like the Skylight Inn, its takeout business is much bigger than its eat-in business anyway.

You can order either a sandwich or a dinner platter, and you can also specify which part of the meat you prefer—the tender interior or the smokier outsides (it's all shredded and chopped before it's served). The sides here include some pretty tasty french fries and hush puppies, but be sure not to miss the red slaw (western Carolina slaw is dressed with nothing much but vinegar and black pepper, to let the sweet crunch of the cabbage come through).

✈ Winston-Salem (20 miles/32km)

🛏 $$ **Augustus T. Zevely Inn,** 803 S. Main St. (© **800/928-9299** or 336/748-9299; www.winston-salem-inn.com). $$ **The Brookstown Inn,** 200 Brookstown Ave. (© **800/845-4262** or 336/725-1120; www.brookstowninn.com).

Bob Sykes Bar-B-Q

'Bama Barbecue 101

Bessemer, Alabama

Bob Sykes Bar-B-Q doesn't have to fret about barbecue orthodoxy, given that it's in Alabama—that is to say, neither in North Carolina nor Texas. It can serve pulled pork like the Carolinians, ribs like folks up in Memphis, and beef brisket like the Texans. What really matters is that the meat is cooked slow, for 8 or 10 hours at least, in an open pit over green hickory wood. The result, of course, is so reliably delicious that Sykes now ships packages to barbecue-craving southerners all over the country.

If anything, the barbecue style here is Tennessean—Bob Sykes grew up near Clarksville, and it was the country pit-roasted meats of his childhood that he was yearning to replicate when he added barbecue to the menu of his little Birmingham drive-in in the late 1950s. The 'cue proved such a hit, Bob Sykes changed the drive-in's name and soon was opening branches all over Alabama and Tennessee. But shortly after 1968, when the flagship was moved to the nearby steel town of Bessemer, overworked Bob suffered a stroke. His wife, Maxine, and their cook, Dot, made a shrewd decision: Shut down all the other branches and throw their hearts into making one great restaurant.

Those two determined southern ladies knew what they were doing; nowadays people drive from miles around to get a heaping plate of Sykes's barbecue. Settled in this location in 1977—the large, bright dining room has a sort of '70s fern-bar look—Bob Sykes is now run by Sykes's son Van, who was barely a toddler when the original drive-in opened. They still serve delectable pork shoulder meat, spareribs, brisket, and chicken, smoked in the brick pit you can see just beside the order counter. "Dinners" (though you can order these platters at lunch, too) are served with a full range of sides, like baked beans and creamy coleslaw and potato salad, using the same crowd-pleasing recipes that Dot developed years ago—not to mention her signature dessert, fluffy lemon-meringue pies. After a full meal of smoky, salty richness, a sweet-tart jolt of lemon meringue is just about the perfect conclusion.

(i) 1794 Ninth Ave. (📞 **205/426-1400;** www.bobsykes.com).

✈ Birmingham (15 miles/24km).

🛏 $$ **The Redmont**, 2101 Fifth Ave. N. (📞 **877/536-2085** or 205/324-2101; www.theredmont.com). $$ **The Tutwiler**, 2021 Park Place N. (📞 **800/876-3426** or 205/322-2100; www.thetutwilerhotel.com).

A Ribs Tour of Memphis
Aye, There's the (Dry) Rub
Memphis, Tennessee

With more than 100 barbecue restaurants in town, Memphis has a pretty good basis for claiming to be (yes, you guessed it) the barbecue capital of the world. They love barbecue so much, they even throw bologna and spaghetti on the grate.

If nothing else, Memphis *is* the world capital of barbecued ribs—that's the part of the pig that Memphis barbecuers really pride themselves on. The local 'cue tradition calls for rubbing a rack of ribs with dry seasoning and smoking them over hickory wood, adding sauce only as a side when it's served. Down an alley across from the Peabody Hotel, the **Rendezvous** (52 S 2nd St.; © **901/523-2746;** www.hogsfly.com), a downtown institution since 1948, has a well-deserved reputation for the best hickory-smoked dry ribs in town. As you walk into this huge but cozy cluttered cellar (upstairs is a bar), you can see the food being prepared in an old open kitchen, where owner Charles Vergos first set up his pit in an old coal chute. Be sure to ask your server if they still have any of their delicious red beans and rice—that deeply Southern side dish is served nightly, but only until the pot is empty. In midtown, the Robinson family has been serving up some equally fine dry ribs for over 25 years at the counter of cheery, no-frills **Cozy Corner** (745 North Parkway; © **901/527-9158;** www.cozycornerbbq.com); try their barbecued Cornish game hen, too.

Good-natured, boisterous **Corky's** in East Memphis (5259 Poplar Ave; © **901/ 685-9744;** www.corkysbbq.com) pretty much leads the pack when it comes to smoky-sweet pork shoulder, topped with tangy coleslaw, in a re-created roadhouse setting with vintage rock 'n' roll piped in. And when it comes to delectable pulled-pork sandwiches topped with a tangy coleslaw, locals head for a weathered old gas station down near Graceland, where Emily Payne has pretty much perfected the pork sandwich at **Payne's Bar-B-Q** (1393 Elvis Presley Blvd.; © **901/942-7433**).

Memphis even has its own barbecue dynasty, founded by Jim Neely at **Interstate Barbecue** (just off I-55 at 2265 S. 3rd St.; © **901/775-2304;** www.interstate barbecue.com) and continued by his nephews at **Neely's Bar-B-Q** (downtown at 670 Jefferson Ave.; © **901/521-9798;** and in East Memphis at 5700 Mt. Moriah Rd.; © **901/795-4177**). Just about everything is good at these bright, friendly, casual restaurants: the ribs, the pulled pork sandwiches, even—why not give it a try?—barbecued spaghetti and barbecued bologna.

✈ Memphis International (20km/13 miles).

🛏 $$$ **The Peabody Memphis,** 149 Union Ave. (© **901/529-3677;** www.pea bodymemphis.com). $$ **Wyndham Gardens Hotel,** 300 N. 2nd St. (© **901/525-1800;** www.wyndham.com).

Hill Country Barbecue

The Meat Market Connection

Lockhart, Texas

Who'd expect to find such a barbecue hot spot in the middle of Texas hill country? But here's Lockhart, Texas, about halfway between Austin and San Antonio, with a phenomenal cluster of top-notch barbecue joints evolved from a long-standing German tradition of smoked meats and sausage.

First and foremost is **Kreuz Market** (619 N. Colorado; © **512/398-2361;** www.kreuz market.com), established over 100 years ago, originally as an eating area tacked on beside a German meat market. You'll eat at long communal tables; they don't chain the knives to the table like they used to when the tables were set right by the pits, but they do provide a roll of paper towels at each table—and you'll need it with meat this juicy and tender. You'll order at the counter (no table service), and your choices will be mostly beef—brisket, prime rib, sausage—or pork chops. Sides originally were just white bread and saltines, but Kreuz (pronounced "krites") has recently added a few other options, like beans, potato salad, and sauerkraut (the heritage is German, after all). And Kreuz staunchly holds true to Central Texas's barbecue orthodoxy—if the pit master has done his job right, barbecue doesn't need sauce, and you won't find a drop of it here.

When Kreuz decamped to its modern new digs, the old store was renamed **Smitty's Market** (208 S. Commerce; © **512/ 398-9344;** www.smittysmarket.com) and is now run by various offspring of Kreuz's late longtime owner Edgar Schmidt. (The family feud that split up the Kreuz-Schmidt dynasty still simmers, much like their barbecue pits.) While the menu is much the same as at Kreuz—a few more side dish options, a slightly spicier sausage—where Smitty's excels is with its brisket, meltingly tender and served on a piece of butcher paper. The bare-bones dining room has communal tables, just like Kreuz; they do offer forks, but forget cutlery—you'll eat this barbecue with your fingers, and lick them afterward.

If you insist on having sauce with your 'cue, head for **Black's BBQ** (215 N. Main St.; © **512/398-2712;** www.blacksbbq. com), continuously family-owned since it first opened in 1949 as—yes, that's right— a meat-market annex. Today it's a proper cafeteria, with mounted animal heads and historic photos on the walls; there are even more side dishes here, and the oak-smoked barbecue options include chicken and pork ribs as well as beef brisket. The sausage ring at Black's is especially popular, a piquant ring of beef-and-pork sausage that's a great antidote to the juicy subtlety of the brisket and pork loin. Breaking with Lockhart tradition, Norma Black first whipped up a tangy, bright-orange barbecue sauce to serve sauce-addicted customers from the North, enticed here by Black's hard-to-miss billboards scattered around town. Whether or not you use it, that's up to you.

✈ San Antonio (65 miles/105km); Austin (30 miles/48km).

🛏 $$ **Havana Riverwalk Inn,** 1015 Navarro, San Antonio (© **888/224-2008** or 210/222-2008; www.havanariverwalk inn.com). $ **Austin Motel,** 1220 S. Congress St. (© **512/441-1157;** www.austin motel.com).

Sonny Bryan's & Angelo's
Cowtown Classics
Dallas/Fort Worth, Texas

By the time you get to Dallas, you're in the land of cowboy barbecue, where beef is king and sauces are thick and zesty. Barbecue is such serious business here, barroom brawls have been known to break out over whose smoke and sauce are the best.

Just about all Dallasites agree that legendary **Sonny Bryan's Smokehouse** sets the standard by which all others are measured; it's the one classic barbecue spot you've got to visit before you leave Dallas. Opened in 1958 by William Jennings Bryan, Jr.—the son and grandson of two other Dallas barbecue masters, whose own smoke shacks were opened respectively in 1910 and 1935—the ramshackle

Sonny Bryan's Smokehouse is a requisite stop in Dallas.

little building in a humble section of Oak Lawn is so popular that even on 100°F (38°C) days, you'll see businesspeople with their sleeves rolled up, leaning against their cars, trying in vain not to get barbecue sauce all over themselves. (There are branches all over the metroplex, but the Inwood original has all the atmosphere.) Inside the smoke shack, you'll order at the counter, then carry your 'cue to eat at tiny one-armed school desks (or outside in the parking lot). Offerings include hickory-smoked brisket, meaty ribs, pulled pork, chicken, turkey, sausage, or ham, but the definitive dish is the beef sandwich—chopped or sliced—along with juicy handmade onion rings. Come early, though, Sonny's is open only until the food runs out, which is apt to happen before the stated closing time.

Just north of the Cultural District over in Fort Worth, **Angelo's** opened the same year as Sonny Bryan's—1958—in what looks like a large Texas Jaycees convention hall, with an almost kitschy decor of barn wood paneling, mounted deer and buffalo heads, metal ceiling fans, and Formica tables. Angelo George's son Skeet still runs the business, and his son Jason is the current pit master, turning out fantastic hickory-smoked dry-rubbed barbecue. The sliced beef sandwich and beef brisket plates are the standard, though you can also detour toward salami, ham, turkey, and Polish sausage; chicken and pork ribs are served all day "while they last," though hickory-smoked beef ribs don't make an appearance until the table service kicks in after 3:30pm. Angelo's also prides itself on serving frosty steins of draft beer, the perfect 'cue accompaniment.

(i) **Sonny Bryan's,** 2202 Inwood Rd., Dallas (© **214/357-7120;** www.sonnybryans.com). **Angelo's,** 2533 White Settlement Rd., Fort Worth (© **817/332-0357;** www.angelosbbq.com).

✈ Dallas-Fort Worth International (85 miles/137km).

🚃 $$$ **The Melrose Hotel Dallas,** 3015 Oak Lawn Ave., Dallas (© **800/MELROSE** [800/635-7653] or **214/521-5151;** www.melrosehoteldallas.com). $$ **Etta's Place,** 200 W. 3rd St., Fort Worth (© **866/355-5760** or 817/255-5760; www.ettas-place.com).

Seafood Shacks **230**

Route 1's Roadside Seafood
Lobster Rolls to Go
Kittery, Maine

Maine dining is practically synonymous with lobsters—there's even a lobster on the state's license plates. Elsewhere in the country, lobster is a fine-dining entree; but here on the Maine coast, you get it at a lobster pound. And luckily, as soon as you enter the state from the south, you can hit **Chauncey's Creek Lobster Pier,** one of the best lobster pounds in the state.

What is a "lobster pound," you may ask? Well, if you have to ask, you're not from Maine. A lobster pound is a specific Maine term for any casual seafood eatery where live lobsters are kept in a saltwater holding pen until they're ready to be cooked (talk about fresh!). Chauncey's may be a little off the beaten path—between Kittery Point and York, just off Rte. 103—but then the whole point of a lobster pound is being close to the ocean. The Spinney family has been selling lobsters in this low-slung, red-roofed riverside restaurant since the 1950s. You reach the pound by walking down a wooden ramp to a broad wooden deck set over a lapping tidal inlet, where some 42 festively painted picnic tables await. Lobster is the specialty, of course, either boiled lobster priced by the pound or that great New England classic, the lobster roll sandwich. Steamed mussels (in wine and garlic)

and clams are also available, as well as raw oysters on the half shell and cherrystone clams. If you want a drink, though, you'll have to bring your own.

Sometimes you've just gotta have that seafood fried—in which case you can stop off in Kittery, where, tucked in among the outlet malls, behind a white picket fence, you'll find **Bob's Clam Hut.** In business since 1956, blue-shingled Bob's has slowly expanded over the years, adding an ice-cream shop and an indoor dining area, though in summer it's always more fun to sit outside at the picnic tables. The Fryolator goes strong all summer, serving up heaps of fried clams, scallops, butterflied shrimp, haddock filets, french fries, and particularly yummy onion rings, the fare is surprisingly light, cooked in cholesterol-free vegetable oil. The creamy New England clam chowder's pretty good too, and naturally there's a divinely sweet lobster roll. The procedure is simple: Order at the front window, get a soda from a vending machine, then stake out a table inside or on the deck with a Rte. 1 view, waiting for your number to be called. Oh, and leave room for the handmade ice cream.

This being Maine, these places are seasonal; Chauncey's closes entirely from

Columbus Day to Mother's Day, while Bob's keeps varied hours (call ahead) after Labor Day until the next spring's Memorial Day.

ⓘ **Chauncey's,** 16 Chauncey Creek Rd. (ⓒ **207/439-1030;** www.chaunceycreek. com).

Bob's Clam Hut, 74 State Rd. (Rte. 1) (ⓒ **207/439-4233;** www.bobsclamhut.com).

✈ Portland International (45 miles/72km); Boston Logan International (50 miles/81km).

🛏 $$ **Dockside Guest Quarters,** Harris Island, York (ⓒ **207/363-2868;** www. docksidegq.com).

Clam Alley

Getting Fat on the Ipswich Flats

Essex/Ipswich, Massachusetts

Clam fans know all about the Ipswich flats—a tidal stretch of the Atlantic off the rocky Cape Ann peninsula just north of Boston. The very fattest and tastiest clams seem to hang out here in the nutrient-rich mud, just yearning to be dug up, pried out of their shells, battered, and deep-fried. Crazy as it sounds, there must be some explanation for why so many superlative clam shacks have sprung up along this part of the North Shore.

These joints attract summertime crowds from all over the Boston area, as well as vacationers heading north to the Maine coast or Lake Winnipesaukee, or south to Cape Cod. For many travelers, a stop off in Essex is an annual vacation ritual. Dining here, of course, is "in the rough," which means you order from a window and carry it to your oceanview table, either inside or outside.

The oldest is **Woodman's of Essex** (121 Main St., Essex; ⓒ **978/768-6057;** www.woodmans.com), which has been around since 1914. It's still run by the Woodman family, which claims that founder Lawrence "Chubby" Woodman invented the fried clam. Housed in a New England-y white clapboard building, Woodman's generally draws the most traffic. Besides "Chubby's" classic fried clams, scallops,

and shrimp (still fried in old-fashioned lard, and damn the cholesterol), Woodman's serves boiled lobsters, steamed clams, lobster rolls, and clam-strip rolls.

Along Eastern Avenue (otherwise known as Rte. 133), you'll find two other superb clam shacks: the pleasantly ramshackle **Essex Seafood** (143R Eastern Ave.; ⓒ **978/768-7233**) and **J. T. Farnham's** (88 Eastern Ave.; ⓒ **978/768-6643**), housed in a nondescript marsh-side cottage with serene views from its deck. Both serve heartier portions than Woodman's does; loyalists claim their fried clams are less greasy as well (though others prefer Woodmans's lardy slickness). Don't miss Farnham's generous seafood chowder. If you're here out of season, it's good to know that Essex is open year-round.

Locals, however, tend to end up at **The Clam Box** (246 High St., Ipswich; ⓒ **978/356-9707;** www.ipswichma.com/clambox). Built in 1938 by Dick Greenleaf, it's hard to miss—it looks exactly like a giant gray clapboard box with the flaps folded open at the top. The menu here sticks to the fried classics—clams, clam strips, scallops, shrimp, haddock, oyster, calamari (plus chicken for landlubbers), served with or without fries, onion rings, and coleslaw. If you like your clams especially plump (not everyone

The Clam Box is a landmark on High Street in Ipswich, Massachusetts.

does), you can request big-belly clams here. Note that they close between lunch and dinner, to clean out the fryers, so your post-beach clams will be just as golden sweet as the ones you had for lunch.

Boston Logan International (39 miles/63km).

$$$ **Emerson Inn by the Sea,** 1 Cathedral Ave., Rockport (800/964-5550; www.emersoninnbythesea.com). $$ **Atlantis Oceanfront Motor Inn,** 125 Atlantic Rd., Gloucester (800/732-6313 or 978/283-0014; www.atlantismotorinn. com). $$$ **Bass Rocks Ocean Inn,** 107 Atlantic Rd., Gloucester (888-802-7666 or 978/283-7600; www.bassrocksocean inn.com).

Seafood Shacks

232

Rhode Island Road Trip

The Briny Taste of Narragansett Bay

Narragansett Bay, Rhode Island

One look at the map and you'll see how Narragansett Bay eats into the tiny state of Rhode Island. Its ragged shores with little muddy inlets are perfect for harboring clams. Narragansett clams may not be as legendary as those of the Ipswich/Essex

flats, but that may just be because the locals like to keep them a secret.

The grandmamma of them all is **Aunt Carrie's** (1240 Ocean Rd., Narragansett; 401/783-7930; www.auntcarriesri. com), operating on Point Judith, near the mouth of the Bay, since 1920. It's named after the founder's aunt, Carrie Cooper, the originator of Rhode Island clam cakes—deep-fried breaded patties of clam-infused dough. Naturally, clam cakes are featured on the menu, but the classic thing to order here is a full shore dinner: clam chowder, clam cakes, a brothy bowl of steamer clams, batter-fried filet of sole (served with corn on the cob and french fries), a whole boiled lobster, and warm Indian pudding for dessert. Note that Rhode Island chowder is distinct from New England or Manhattan chowders; it's a clear clam-broth soup with bacon. The lace-curtained dining room is a little more formal than your usual clam shack; there's table service, and the food is actually served on china plates.

Although Carrie's invented the clam cake, these days it's even better up north of Newport, at **Flo's Clam Shack** (Park Avenue, Portsmouth; ℂ **401/847-8141;** www.flosclamshack.com). Though Flo's has been in operation since 1936, its exposed seawall location made it a target of four successive hurricanes over the years (a post outside shows high-water marks from each). The current shingled shack is new, but still bares-bones casual (there's a more upscale location closer to

Newport at 4 Wave Ave, Middletown; ℂ **401/847-8141**). Their "stuffies" (baked stuffed quahogs) are particularly spicy, the fried whole clams full of briny juice. You've got to love a place that lists "lobsta" and "chowda" on the menu and hands you a painted rock to keep track of your order.

For a real pretty waterside location, though, head a few miles farther north along Rte. 138 to Tiverton, for **Evelyn's Drive-In** (2335 Main Rd., Tiverton; ℂ **401/624-3100;** www.evelynsdrivein.com). This summers-only mom-and-pop red chowder house with picnic tables is set right on Nanaquaket Pond (you can also eat inside in the air-conditioned dining room). The menu is extensive, but to capitalize on that waterside setting, stick to the classics Evelyn's has been serving for 40 years: plump fried clams, clam cakes, steamer clams and steamed mussels, "stuffies," and Rhode Island clam chowder.

✈ Providence International (28 miles/ 45km).

🛏 $$$ **Mill Street Inn,** 75 Mill St., Newport (ℂ **401/782-2220;** www.millstreetinn.com). $$ **Village Inn,** 1 Beach Rd., Narragansett (ℂ **401/782-2220;** www.v-inn.com).

Abbott's in the Rough
Lobster Al Fresco
Noank, Connecticut

Few summer pleasures are more congenial than tucking into a lobster dinner on the outdoor deck at Abbott's, as the waters of Fisher's Island Sound gently slap the pilings beneath you. Come at weekend mealtimes, though, and you may have to settle for a picnic table on the lawn, for Abbott's draws crowds from all over the Northeast. There are more tables under a

red-and-white-striped tent (the place to be when it rains). For some, visiting the most southeastern corner of Connecticut is about seeing the old restored ships at Mystic Seaport or cavorting whales and dolphins at the Mystic Aquarium; for lobster lovers, though, it's about dining on lobsters fresh off the boat in a clambake-casual waterside setting.

7 Places to Eat in . . . Providence, Rhode Island

Over the past 40 years, Providence has become a sort of Cinderella city. A showcase of effective urban revival, it's also a burgeoning culinary hotspot, and the two renaissances have come hand in hand.

Al Forno helped launch a culinary renaissance in Providence.

Just as Providence's long-forsaken downtown began transforming in the late 1970s, the groundbreaking restaurant ➋➌➍ Al Forno (577 S. Main St.; ✆ **401/273-9760;** www.alforno.com) opened in 1980 in a nearly 200-year-old iron warehouse on the fringes of downtown. Though Johanne Killeen and George Germon's casual-dining menu carried an Italian stamp, featuring wood-fired pizzas and open-grilled meats, it had so much more verve and sophistication than the traditional red-sauce restaurants of Federal Hill's immigrant Italian neighborhood, it touched off a dining revolution in a city spoiling for change.

In the decades since, Providence's dining scene has become one of the most vital in the nation, even as the cityscape has been resurrected. When Al Forno moved in 1990 to more spacious digs in the revived Main Street warehouse district (where there's still a wait for tables, such is Al Forno's popularity), Killeen and Germon helped Bruce Tillinghast open ➋➌➎ New Rivers (7 Steeple St.; ✆ **401/751-0350;** www.newriversrestaurant.com) in Al Forno's old site, serving a bold and inventive multicultural cuisine in that intimate 40-seat space. The name references the global mix-and-match of Tillinghast's menu, as well as the uncovering of Providence's long-buried rivers in the late 1980s, set off in 1994 by the stunning downtown Riverwalk development. Right on Riverwalk, ➋➌➏ Café Nuovo (One Citizens Plaza; ✆ **401/421-2525;** www.cafenuovo.com/cafe nuovo) offers white-linen fine dining; chef Tim Kelly turns out exquisitely presented plates of creative fusion cuisine using top-dollar ingredients sourced from all over the globe. It's a particularly elegant place to dine during **WaterFire,** festive nights (frequently on summer Saturdays) when the winding Providence river glows with bon-fires and luminarias gliding along the water on silent black gondolas. And as the down-town renaissance solidified, longtime Federal Hill favorite 237 Gracie's (194 Washington St.; ✆ **401/272-7811;** www.graciesprov.com) moved to a refined industrial-chic set-ting across from the Trinity Rep Theater, where chef Joe Hafner wows diners with deceptively simple preparations that showcase his market-fresh ingredients; his meticulous tasting menus change daily, reflecting what's in season.

Meanwhile, in the College Hill district close to both Brown University and the Rhode Island School of Design, gentrifying urban pioneers saved block after block of rundown colonial- and Federal-era townhouses from the wrecking ball through the 1980s and 1990s. A set of smart neighborhood bistros soon followed, such as the French-inspired brasserie 238 Red Stripe (465 Angell St.; ✆ **401/437-6950;** http://redstriperestaurants.com), a cheery wainscoted spot with black-and-white tiled floors and an open kitchen known for its hanger steaks, omelets, oven-roasted tomato soup, and grilled cheese with prosciutto, pear, and basil. At 239 Chez Pascal (960 Hope St.; ✆ **401/421-4422;** www.chez-pascal.com), with walls warmly painted in oranges and reds, Matthew Gennuso reinterprets French classics like cassoulets, confits, and bouillabaisses with local ingredients. On their six-course Tomato Dinner, for example, each course does something different with tomatoes grown on a nearby organic farm.

Yet amid all the trendy rehab, the gutsy spirit of old Providence hangs on in one beloved institution: the 240 Haven Bros. food truck (✆ **401/861-7777**), a beat-up aluminum-sided truck that pulls into a parking space in Kennedy Plaza next to City Hall every afternoon between 4pm and 5pm and stays there until well past midnight. There are only six stools at the counter, but the burgers and fries are excellent, and regular customers include a full cross-section of Providence society, from janitors to politicians, reporters to car mechanics, nightclub-hoppers to cops.

✈ T. F. Green Providence Airport (11miles/18km).

🛏 $$$ **Hotel Providence,** 311 Westminster St. (✆ **800/861-8990** or 401/861-8000; www.thehotelprovidence.com). $$ **Courtyard by Marriott,** 32 Exchange Terrace (✆ **800/321-2211** or 401/272-1191; www.courtyard.com).

On Fisher's Island Sound in CT, Abbott's is open only during lobster season.

Set on a quiet promontory south of downtown Mystic, Abbott's feels suitably off the beaten track. You wind around several neighborhood streets to get here (that is, unless you arrive by boat). After you turn into the gravel parking lot, look for Abbott's trademark, a huge greenish lobster painted on a weathered-gray side wall (remember, lobsters don't turn that bright orangey-red until they are cooked). If you're lucky, you won't find a line at the counter—service is strictly takeout, and every lobster is cooked to order, so you can expect a wait. Abbott's claim to fame is the size of its lobsters—some as big as 10 pounds. A chalkboard by the counter tells you current prices, which are not cheap for the jumbo monsters that have significant hunks of meat even in the hard-to-reach legs. Luckily, they give you a paper bib to protect your clothes from sweet dripping juices and the melted butter you dip your succulent morsels into. If dismembering a giant crustacean isn't your idea of fun, order the hot lobster roll, a quarter-pound of nothing but lobster meat, heaped on a lightly toasted bun.

While you're waiting, you may want to try the Rhode Island–style clam chowder, steamed mussels, or stuffed clams. Usual sides are coleslaw, roast corn-on-the-cob, or Abbott's own brand of potato chips. The place doesn't even own a deep-fryer; if someone in your party is hankering for fried clam strips, you'll have to go to their satellite restaurant up the road in Noank Shipyard, **Costello's Clam Shack** (☎ 860/572-2779), which also sells small Abbott's lobsters.

Dining is BYOB, and those in the know bring a six-pack or a bottle of wine (even champagne). Seasoned Abbott's-goers even bring their own tablecloths to cover the rough wooden tables. Naturally, Abbott's is open only during lobster season—full-time Memorial Day to Labor Day, weekends only in May, September, and early October. Reservations? You must be kidding.

ⓘ 117 Pearl St., Noank CT (☎ **860/536-7719;** www.abbotts-lobster.com).

✈ Providence (45 miles/73km).

🛏 $$ **Hilton Mystic,** 20 Coogan Blvd. (☎ **800/445-8667** or 860/572-0731; www.hiltonmystic.com).

Bowen's Island Restaurant
The World's Their Oyster
Charleston, South Carolina

If you never got down to the original Bowen's Island Restaurant, you really missed something. This rambling cinderblock shack set on a marshy inlet, at the end of a dirt road on the way to Folly Beach, far from downtown Charleston—well, it didn't look like destination dining. Inside, every wall was covered with graffiti, the tables were covered in newspapers, dead television sets stared blankly from the walls. Inside the "oyster room"—where you couldn't sit unless you were ordering the all-you-can-eat roast oysters—a cook at the far end sweated over a huge oyster pit fireplace, where local oysters, fresh-picked that day, were roasted under wet burlap sacks (the restaurant has its own oyster-catchers who haul in their fresh catch daily, dug from the tidal mud just past the dock). When their ridged shells cracked open, they were shoveled up—yes, with a shovel—and deposited on the tables. Hungry customers, armed with a knife, a rag, and some cocktail sauce, attacked the bivalves with gusto, dropping their empty shells in a bucket, washing it all down perhaps with ice-cold beer.

But this quirky little restaurant—founded as a fish camp in the mid-1940s by May and Jimmy Bowen and run today by May's grandson Robert Barber—burned to the ground in 2006, ironically only a few month after it was honored with an America's Classic citation from the James Beard Foundation. Robert Barber has reopened the place, though so far it's just the covered deck area; the original oyster room is next to be rebuilt. All the favorite dishes are back—the roasted oysters, the fabulous fried shrimp, the shrimp and grits, the Frogmore Stew (a Lowcountry specialty, a seafood boil of corn, potatoes, sausage, and shrimp)—along with the hush puppies and french fries and coleslaw, the inevitable accompaniments to every entree. They serve dinner only, it's closed Sunday and Monday, and they don't take plastic. For these prices (currently $20 for the oyster pig-out), you can probably manage the cash.

If oysters are what you plan to order (and you should), be sure to go during oyster season, September through April. Oh, and don't forget to tip the oyster cook.

(i) 1870 Bowen's Island Rd., Charleston (© **843/795-2757;** www.bowensisland restaurant.com).

✈ Charlestown International (10 miles/16km).

🛏 $$$ **Planter's Inn,** 112 N. Market St. (© **800/845-7082** or 843/722-2345; www. plantersinn.com). $$ **The Rutledge Victorian Guest House,** 114 Rutledge Ave. (© **888/722-7553** or 843/722-7551; www. charlestonvictorian.com).

Middendorf's
Through Thick & Thin
Pass Manchac, Louisiana

The long white shack with its red-and-white-striped awnings looks quite respectable amid the bait shops and railroad tracks of this commercial strip south of Ponchatoula, where Hwy. 55 stands elevated above the bayous. But don't expect fine dining—inside Middendorf's cozy wood-paneled dining room things are casual, take-us-as-you-find-us, even a little raucous on a Saturday night. (Service is friendly, too.) There's bound to be a line for weekend dinner, even though they've built a second restaurant next door to handle overflow crowds (with food this good so close to New Orleans, a line is inevitable). Be prepared to wait, and hope that you'll time it right to get that sensational sunset view across the bayou. You're only a 45-minute drive out of town, on the far side of Lake Pontchartrain (it's only a stone's throw from Lake Maurepas), but that's all it takes to feel like you're in the heart of Cajun country.

At Middendorf's—which has been here since the Depression—catfish is the main attraction; reportedly the owners buy two tons of it a week. Whether you order it thick or thin is just a question of your desired ratio of meaty fish to crisp golden batter crust. It's the thin fillets, though, that seem to earn the most rave reviews—they're so exquisitely thin, they come out of the fryer delicately curled and seem to dissolve in your mouth.

The restaurant also dishes up a host of southern Louisiana specialties, like shrimp-and-crab gumbo, boiled crawfish, crawfish cakes, po' boys, shrimp rémoulade, frog legs, and turtle soup. As you'd expect in Cajun land, many dishes come topped with barbecue sauce, but Middendorf's doesn't overwhelm customers with fiery spices—all the better to let the flavor of the fresh-caught Louisiana fish shine through. Closed Monday and Tuesday.

ⓘ 30160 Hwy. 51 (ⓒ **985/386-6666**).

✈ Louis Armstrong New Orleans International (15 miles/24km).

🛏 $$$ **Omni Royal Orleans,** 621 St. Louis St. (ⓒ **800/THE-OMNI** [800/843-6664] or 504/529-5333; www.omniroyal orleans.com). $$ **Hotel Monteleone** (ⓒ **800/535-9595** or 504/523-3341; www. hotelmonteleone.com).

New York Deli Classics
Lotsa Matzoh
New York, New York

The term "New York–style deli" seems redundant. The deli restaurant was *invented* in New York, so how could any proper deli be anything *but* New York–style?

Downtown on the Lower East Side, where America's first delicatessens sprouted in the 19th-century Jewish slums, **Katz's Delicatessen** (205 E. Houston St.;

212/254-2246; www.katzdeli.com) is a stalwart time warp relic, holding its own against the neighborhood's recently arrived hip restaurants and clubs. Founded by Russian immigrants in 1888, it almost looks like a movie set—with cheap wood paneling, Formica-topped tables, photos all over the walls, salamis hanging in the front window. Or maybe it's just familiar from movies, from *Donnie Brasco* to *When Harry Met Sally*. Their salami is justly famous, as is the divinely tender beef brisket. Potato latkes and cheese blintzes are two other musttry dishes here.

In Midtown, you can sample the world's most famous matzoh ball soup at the newest incarnation of the **Second Avenue Deli** (162 E. 33rd St.; 212/689-9000). Originally located in the East Village, on a stretch of lower Second Avenue nicknamed the Yiddish Broadway for all the Yiddish theaters nearby, the Second Avenue Deli moved uptown after the double-whammy of a rent dispute and the murder of its founder, Holocaust survivor Abe Lebewohl. But the smaller Midtown spot, run by Lebewohl's nephew Jeremy, carries on the tradition surprisingly well; it still sports the tiled coffee shop look of its predecessor and stays open 24 hours a day. Try the famous chopped liver or the luscious pastrami—it's all certified kosher (though, unlike most kosher restaurants, it is open on Sat).

In west Midtown, near the theater district, the **Carnegie Deli** (854 Seventh Ave.; 800/334-5606 or 212/757-2245; www. carnegiedeli.com), opened in 1937, is *sui generis*—a slightly grubby, cramped, defiantly unslick restaurant that has become an institution for its grumpy waiters and

Carnegie Deli's daunting pastrami sandwich.

enormous, wittily named sandwiches. Prices are tourist gouging, but it's an experience everyone should have at least once. The corned beef and pastrami, cured onsite, really are fantastic, as are the wonderfully authentic free pickles on the table. The **Stage Deli** just down the street (834 Seventh Ave.; 212/245-7850; www.stagedeli.com) is more of the same, though much jollier, with the added attraction of sandwiches name for celebrities and lots of autographed glossy headshots on the wall.

The time warp is more genuine, and the pace less hectic, uptown at **Barney Greengrass, the Sturgeon King** (541 Amsterdam Ave.; 212/724-4707) on the once heavily Jewish Upper West Side. Open daytimes only, this unassuming old-school Kosher deli has become legendary for its high-quality salmon (sable, gravlax, Nova Scotia, kippered, lox, pastrami—you choose), whitefish, and sturgeon (of course). The dining room looks like it hasn't been redecorated since it opened in 1929—the fly-specked wallpaper, the warped linoleum—but hey, if it was good enough for customers like Groucho Marx, Al Jolson, and Irving Berlin, why change?

✈ John F. Kennedy International (15 miles/ 24km); Newark Liberty International (16 miles/27km); LaGuardia (8 miles/13km).

🛏 $$ **The Lucerne,** 201 W. 79th St. (800/492-8122 or 212/875-1000; www. thelucernehotel.com). $ **Milburn Hotel,** 242 W. 76th St. (800/833-9622 or 212/ 362-1006; www.milburnhotel.com).

Manny's

Pass the Pastrami

Chicago, Illinois

It took another Russian immigrant to successfully bring the deli idea west to Chicago. When Jack Raskin opened his cafeteria-style deli in 1942, he didn't have enough money to change the existing sign, which advertised the former tenant, Sunny's Restaurant. By naming his new enterprise Manny's, after his son Emanuel, he only had to buy two new letters. It was a shrewd cost-cutting move—and who knew the place would still be going strong under that name more than 65 years later?

Manny's moved a few times in its early years, but it settled into this South Loop location, in what was once a predominantly Jewish neighborhood, in 1964. Current owner Ken Raskin is the grandson of founder Jack Raskin, and the son of the eponymous Manny Raskin. Like the old-style New York delis it was modeled after, Manny's serves its customers cafeteria-style from behind a long stainless-steel counter at the front of the store. Portions tend to be hefty, so don't over-order. You then take your tray back to a huge dining area, where the decor consists mostly of Formica tables, waist-high wood paneling, and framed press clippings and historic photos covering Manny's long history. Hang onto your receipt—you pay as you leave. (That makes it way too easy to change your mind and go back for a slice of cheesecake after all.)

The menu is huge and has a lot of rotating specials, but the regulars—and Manny's has a lot of devoted regulars, from politicos to police officers—swear by the crisp potato pancakes, stuffed cabbage, and *kreplach*. The pastrami is worthy of the best New York delis, though in Chicago, with its large Irish-American population, the tender corned beef is even more popular. And here's the mark of a genuine deli: They serve kosher brand Dr. Brown's sodas, with flavors like cel-ray and black cherry, well off the Coca-Cola company's radar.

Manny's is closed Sundays, and though it opens early (5am) it shuts at 8pm. Come here early if you want your knishes for dinner.

ⓘ 1141 S. Jefferson (✆ **312/939-2855;** www.mannysdeli.com).

✈ O'Hare International (18 miles/29km).

🛏 $$ **Homewood Suites,** 40 E. Grand St., Chicago (✆ **800/CALL-HOME** [800/225-4663] or 312/644-2222; www.homewood suiteschicago.com). $$ **Hotel Allegro Chicago,** 171 N. Randolph St., Chicago (✆ **800/643-1500** or 312/236-0123; www.allegro chicago.com).

Chez Schwartz's Charcuterie Hébraïque de Montréal
Time for a Smoke
Montreal, Canada

It's the oldest deli in Canada—or, as the French street sign describes it, a Charcuterie Hébraïque. That distinction actually means something: Montreal's Jewish population was quite sizeable in 1928, when Schwartz's was founded by Romanian immigrant Reuben Schwartz. And those Eastern European Jewish immigrants, they knew how to smoke meat like nobody's business.

Schwartz's is the great survivor of a whole generation of old Montreal delis, still smoking its meats in the traditional way (no chemicals, only a patient 10-day wait for the marinating spices to work their magic). The emphasis here is much greater on the "charcuterie" than the "hébraïque." The menu is refreshingly straightforward, featuring steaks, chicken, liver, and a few reasonably sized sandwiches of turkey, veal, chicken, salami, and Schwartz's claim to fame, smoked meat (aka *viande fume*). This smoky, bright-red brisket is a close cousin of pastrami, but with different spices; it comes in sandwiches or entrée platters with different levels of blubber—"lean," "medium," and "fatty." Just remember, the melting fat is a crucial part of what makes Schwartz's smoked meat tender and flavorful.

You'll get a good look at (and whiff of) this luscious stuff as you pass the carving counters when you first walk in, after you've worked your way up the inevitable line to enter. Customers sit at long communal wooden tables in a simple, fluorescent-lit, white-tiled room. The noise level can be crazy, as it's just about always crowded. Schwartz's french fries are especially noteworthy, perfectly crisp to complement the sweet succulence of the meat, but you may also want the tang of huge garlicky dill pickles or coleslaw to set off the savory richness of that unforgettable *viande fume*.

Only one thing remains to complete your Montreal deli experience: a stop at **St-Viateur Bagels** (1127 av. Mont-Royal est; ✆ **514/528-6361;** www.stviateurbagel.com). If you don't believe there are any decent bagels made outside of New York, St-Viateur will change your mind—'nuff said.

ⓘ 3895 Saint-Laurent Blvd. (✆ **514/842-4813;** www.schwartzsdeli.com).

✈ Aéroport International Pierre-Elliot-Trudeau de Montréal (19km/11 miles).

🛏 $$$ **Hôtel Le St-James,** 355 rue St-Jacques oust (✆ **866/841-3111** or 514/841-3111; www.hotellestjames.com).$$ **Auberge Bonaparte,** 447 rue St-François-Xavier (✆ **514/844-1448;** www.bonaparte.com).

L.A.'s Deli Wars

Left Coast Lox

Los Angeles, California

The transplanted New York Jews who founded the movie industry in Los Angeles may have been the first patrons of L.A.'s classic delis. But by now those places are such institutions, even native Angelinos are hooked on the pastrami, the seeded rye breads, the whitefish salads, and gefilte fish.

The great original is **Canter's Deli** (419 N. Fairfax Ave.; © **323/651-2030;** www.cantersdeli.com), a business that started in 1924 in Jersey City and moved to the West Coast in 1931. (The only thing older in this Miracle Mile neighborhood seems to be the saber-toothed fossils at the nearby La Brea Tar Pits.) The current location, opened in 1953, has weathered neon signs outside and a great Googie-style interior. Open 24 hours a day, it attracts a lot of hipster nighthawks (it helps that the attached Kibitz Room hosts live music acts every night). Canter's bakery section is famous, offering superb breads, including an iconic seeded rye, and Eastern European–style pastries. One look at the list of appetizers for dinner—kasha varnishkas, chopped liver, gelfilte fish, pickled herring—tells you that Canter's has stuck to its roots all those years.

L.A. deli lovers are willing to drive quite a distance to get to their favorites—which is why **Langer's** (704 S. Alvarado St.; © **213/483-8050;** www.langersdeli.com) continues to thrive in its original location across from the MacArthur Park neighborhood, even though the neighborhood is now heavily Latino. Founded in 1947 by the late Al Langer, it's now run by his son Norm, who's enough of an L.A. icon that he has appeared on the TV satire *Curb Your Enthusiasm*. Nora Ephron calls Langer's number-one specialty, its peppery, smoky pastrami sandwiches, "a work of art"; their matzoh-ball soup has a surprising number of fans as well. With its tufted leather banquettes and brass chandeliers, Langer's exudes a sort of Rat Pack cool; the only catch is that it closes at 4pm in the afternoon and all day Sunday.

Canter's and Langer's win, hands-down, in terms of colorful deli ambience, but if it's just an excellent overstuffed sandwich you're after, or perhaps a bagel and lox, you can get those at any one of a score of newer contenders: **Art's Deli** in Studio City (12224 Ventura Blvd.; © **818/762-1221;** www.artsdeli.com), opened in 1957; **Brent's** out in Northridge (19565 North Parthenia St.; © **818/886-5679**), opened in 1967; or **Izzy's** in Santa Monica (1433 Wilshire Blvd.; © **310/394-1131;** www.izzysdeli.com), opened in 1973. These are all large, friendly coffee-shop-style restaurants offering giant portions and encyclopedic menus; you'll find a few Jewish specialties tucked in among the burgers and steaks (Art's has the most).

Now here's a bit of culture shock—the vintage New York deli **Barney Greengrass** (see 243 above) has opened its first branch ever on the fifth floor of the Barneys New York department store in Beverly Hills (9570 Wilshire Blvd.; © **310/777-5877**), serving the same smoked sturgeon and silky Nova Scotia salmon as the original, minus the grimy retro decor. A Barney inside a Barneys? Bizarre.

✈ Los Angeles International.

🛏 $$$ **Peninsula Beverly Hills,** 9882 S. Santa Monica Blvd. (© **800/462-7899** or 310/551-2888; www.peninsula.com). $ **Best Western Marina Pacific Hotel,** 1697 Pacific Ave., Venice (© **800/786-7789** or 310/452-1111; www.mphotel.com).

The El Paso Two-Step

Tex-Mex Classics

El Paso, Texas

No city in the Lone Star State seems more Texan than El Paso—nestled between two mountain ranges on the banks of the Rio Grande, in the sun-swept, mountainous desert of Texas's westernmost corner. In its day it has been prime territory for American Indians, 16th-century Spanish explorers, 17th-century Catholic missionaries, railroad moguls, brothel-keepers, and gunfighters. And being just across the Rio Grande from Ciudad Juárez, El Paso segues almost effortlessly between Mexican and American traditions—which makes it a natural breeding ground for some of the world's most authentic Tex-Mex cuisine.

An El Paso landmark since it opened its doors in 1927, the **L&J Café** (3622 E. Missouri St.; ✆ **915/566-8418**) is still owned and operated by the Duran family, its original owners, and they offer some of the best Tex-Mex food you'll find anywhere. Nicknamed "The Old Place by the Graveyard"—it's right by the Concordia Cemetery—during Prohibition the L&J was a casino and speakeasy, later turned legitimate restaurant. The chicken enchiladas, overflowing with tender white meat and buried under chunky green chili and Jack cheese, approach perfection; the chili con queso and *caldillo* (beef and potato stew with a green chili and garlic kick) are intensely flavorful and fresh. The salsa is spicy, the beer is cold, and the service is quick and friendly, even when the place is filled to capacity—as it is most of the time.

In the past few years, however, the L&J's dominance has been challenged by a newcomer—located in a car wash, of all things. **H&H Car Wash and Restaurant** (701 E. Yandell Dr.; ✆ **915/533-1144**) is a well-worn little coffee shop straight out of the 1960s. It's not much to look at, but this noisy joint is packed from open to close with locals scarfing down such inexpensive Tex-Mex specialties as *carne picada* (diced sirloin with jalapeños, tomatoes, and onions), *huevos rancheros*, and *chiles rellenos*, which can be kicked up to four-alarm spiciness if you want. Sit at the counter so you can watch the cooks peeling the tomatoes, pulling tortillas from the griddle, stirring pots of refried beans, and chopping up green chilies for the house salsa. Owner Kenneth Haddad uses only the freshest ingredients and sticks with tradition. And in case your car's dirty, well, the car wash is pretty good too.

✈ El Paso International (4¾ miles/ 7.7km).

🛏 $$ **Camino Real Hotel,** 101 S. El Paso St. (✆ **800/769-4300** or 915/534-3000; www.caminoreal.com). $$ **Artisan Hotel,** 325 Kansas St. (✆ **915/225-0050;** www.artisanelpaso.com).

Joe T. Garcia's

Keeping the Tex in Tex-Mex

Fort Worth, Texas

Fort Worth is indeed the western half of the Dallas–Fort Worth metroplex, with its historic stockyards and cowboy vibe. Let Dallas dabble in fancy fusion cuisines: Just south of the Stockyards Hotel, you'll find a pioneer in the only kind of fusion Fort Worth cares about—that Texas take on Mexican cooking known as Tex-Mex, which was practically invented at Joe T. Garcia's Mexican Restaurant.

Joe T. Garcia's has been around since 1935, and by now all the locals know the drill here. The place doesn't have menus, only two dinner dishes are offered, and they only take cash or checks. It's a simple template that allows Joe T.'s (which is still run by the Garcia family) to turn out a lot of meals efficiently and focus on the fresh, handmade quality of its few menu items. Over the past 60-odd years, this green-trimmed white house, which from the front looks like a pretty Mexican hacienda, has been added to time and again until today it's large enough to seat 1,000 hungry guests. Yet it never feels overwhelming—it's more like a series of comfortable and relaxed little nooks and courtyards. The place to be, if you can swing it, is on the lush outdoor patio set around a stone pool.

Ordering couldn't be simpler: Choose between a heaping plate of succulently grilled chicken or beef fajitas or a big family-style dinner with tacos and enchiladas. At lunch your choices are *chiles rellenos,* tamales, and chicken *flautas*. The Mexican-style brunch served on Saturdays and Sundays includes *migas* (eggs scrambled with shredded tortillas), *menudo* (tripe stew), and *huevos rancheros*. These are full meals, the food sticks to your ribs, and the accompaniments are especially enticing—homemade guacamole, lively *pico de gallo* sauce, and fresh tortillas. Service can be a little erratic, though it's frequently lightning fast, and portions are gigantic, so come with an appetite. Joe T.'s is also a virtual margarita factory, spitting out thousands of margaritas on the rocks and frozen. Order a pitcher and kick back your cowboy boots.

ⓘ 2201 N Commerce St. (✆ **817/626-4356**).

✈ Dallas–Fort Worth International (85 miles/137km).

🛏 $$$ **Stockyards Hotel,** 109 W. Exchange Ave., Fort Worth (✆ **800/423-8471** or 817/625-6427; www.stockyards hotel.com). $$ **Etta's Place,** 200 W. 3rd St., Fort Worth (✆ **866/355-5760** or 817/255-5760; www.ettas-place.com).

249

Tex-Mex

Mi Tierra

Tex-Mex on the Square

San Antonio, Texas

Forget the Alamo—San Antonio has always been one of Texas's most cosmopolitan cities, one of the first settlements to welcome Spanish missionaries and host a 19th-century influx of Germans (at one time more German was spoken here than Spanish or English). But the south-of-the-border connection is still strong, as you can see any day on colorful Market Square. In the 19th century, Market Square's first restaurants were makeshift stalls where a bunch of Mexican-American women dubbed the Chili Queens sold chili con carne and tamales to a raffish crowd of cafe crawlers. Nowadays the square's indoor El Mercado bustles with craft stalls, and the Farmer's Market Plaza is peppered on weekends with stands selling *gorditas* (chubby corn cakes topped with a variety of goodies) or funnel cakes (fried dough sprinkled with powdered sugar).

Right on this historic square, the Cortez family has been serving Tex-Mex food in its lively, casual Mi Tierra cafe since 1941. This isn't fusion Tex-Mex or Mexican regional cooking; it's the enchiladas and flautas that first translated Mexican cuisine for American palates years ago, but with fresh ingredients and hearty portions that remind you of what Tex-Mex once was before Taco Bell took over. Many a lesser joint has copied the look of this place, with its brown tile floors and adobe walls hung with year-round Christmas lights (though few can also afford to provide the strolling *trovadores* singing Mexican *canciones*). Don't

get sidetracked by the *mole* or the fine cuts of steak—that's not why you're here. Start with the *botanas* platter, which offers a good smattering of dishes, such as flautas and mini tostadas, then move on to the classic Tex-Mex enchiladas bathed in chili gravy, with refried beans on the side. Mi Tierra is also known for its traditional *panadería* bakery (the same baker has been in charge since 1957), which produces wonderful Mexican *pan dulce*. Try one of their sugary *polvorones* cookies along with a cup of coffee or Mexican-style hot chocolate.

Sure, you do see plenty of out-of-towners dining at Mi Tierra—the location couldn't be more tourist-friendly—but you see a lot more locals, especially late at night (it's open 24/7). You may pay a couple of dollars more here than you would at a Tex-Mex joint on San Pedro, but it's well worth it. Come here for breakfast and get your cheese enchilada and chili gravy with a fried egg on top—that'll get your day off to the right start.

ⓘ 218 Produce Row (© **210/225-1262; www.mitierracafe.com**).

✈ San Antonio (9⅔ miles/15km).

⊨ $$$ **Emily Morgan,** 705 E. Houston St. (© **800/824-6674** or 210/225-5100; www.emilymorganhotel.com). $$ **Havana Riverwalk Inn,** 1015 Navarro (© **888/224-2008** or 210/222-2008; www.havanariverwalkinn.com).

Loma Linda
Puff the Magic Taco
Houston, Texas

Loma Linda means "beautiful hill" in Spanish. And though this unpretentious little restaurant in the funky East End doesn't have a picture-window view of rolling hills, the puffed-up bubbles of the handmade tortillas served here are beautiful hills indeed for those who love old-fashioned Tex-Mex food.

Set in a pink block building trimmed with wrought-iron window bars, Loma Linda's nothing fancy. In fact, it began its restaurant life as a simple East End lunch counter. In the mid-1980s, however, owners Thad and Joyce Gilliam saw that their favorite Mexican restaurant was closing down (part of a small local chain called Loma Linda—a Houston landmark as one of the very first Mexican restaurants in town). Before the whole chain died, they bought the recipes and equipment and converted their cafe to a reincarnation of Loma Linda here on Telephone Road.

By design, the Gilliamses' re-created Loma Linda harks back to an earlier age, before the rise of the fajita made Tex-Mex trendy. The tortillas are freshly made on an onsite vintage 1930s tortilla maker—just the right equipment to make old-school puffy tortillas. They start out with an incredibly thin tortilla base that balloons beautifully when it hits the deep-fryer—then presto, there's your puffy tortilla. It only works with superfresh *masa* (corn dough)—a finicky detail most newer Tex-Mex restaurants can't be bothered with. Add to that the Velveeta-like ooze of cheese, the savory smoothness of the pale brown chili gravy and refried beans, and the mix melds together in a subtle way that's pure retro Tex-Mex—the result when Mexican cooks toned down their pepper quotient for gringo palates long ago.

The dishes to order here are, of course, the puffy chili con queso for an appetizer and the puffy beef tacos, the perfectly seasoned Texas-style enchiladas with chili gravy, and the combination dinners. Along with the tried-and-true dishes, however, you'll also find some more unusual items such as *carne guisada*, chicken *mole*, and *chili dulce* (stuffed bell peppers). For dessert, their *sopapillas* are especially sweet and flaky.

ⓘ 2111 Telephone Rd. (✆ **713/924-6074**).

✈ George Bush Intercontinental (37 miles/60km).

🛏 $$$ **Hilton University of Houston,** 4800 Calhoun Rd. (✆ **800/HOTEL-UH** [800/468-3584] or 713/741-2447; www.hilton.com). $$ **Best Western Downtown Inn and Suites,** 915 W. Dallas St. (✆ **800/780-7234** or 713/571-7733; www.bestwestern.com).

Louis' Lunch

Birthplace of the Burger

New Haven, Connecticut

Even if the sign on top didn't say so, you might guess that this squat brick building dated from 1895, in view of those arched red-shuttered windows with their diamond-shaped panes. The story is a bit more complicated, though: In 1895, Louis' was just a lunch wagon, serving New Haven's booming population of European immigrant factory workers. And though Louis Lassen eventually moved his business into this converted tannery shed in 1917, it has moved twice since then (a victim of urban renewal), the last time in 1975 to this quiet street behind the quadrangles of Yale University. In any case, Louis' Lunch is the granddaddy of hamburger restaurants.

Though there are other contenders, Louis' Lunch stakes a pretty good claim to being the birthplace of the hamburger sandwich in 1900, when Louis Lassen stuck a patty of broiled ground beef scraps between two slices of bread to make a convenient lunch-to-go for customers on the run. Louis' reserves the right to make its burgers the same way they've been making them for over a century. You won't get a hamburger bun here; the patty is served on white toast only, toasted in a vintage 1920s vertical toaster. They'll put cheese or tomato or grilled onions on it, but never any ketchup, mustard, or mayonnaise (condiments just cloak the meat's taste, claim the Lassens, who still run the joint today). The meat has been upgraded since 1900 to a special mix of five different cuts of beef ground fresh every morning— the exact proportions are a carefully guarded secret. But the patties are still hand formed—no frozen machine-cut abominations here—and they're broiled on the same century-old antique broilers Louis' has been using for years.

Sit at the scarred wooden counter and you can get a good view of the vintage broilers: The patties are pressed into a flat two-sided metal basket and slid into vertical slots in three ornate towers, where gas flames lap from both sides. The grease drips down during cooking and drains away so that the burger is firm and juicy but never greasy.

Louis' is home to the original "hamburger sandwich"—still cooked in the original gas broilers.

Louis' doesn't serve much besides hamburgers, pies for dessert, and beverages (including old-fashioned birch beer and black cherry soda). Thursday through Saturday, when Louis' stays open until 2am, they also serve hot dogs and steak sandwiches. And on Friday they serve tuna sandwiches, a vestige of the days when Roman Catholics didn't eat meat on Fridays. So who's in any hurry to change?

ⓘ 261–263 Crown St. (ⓒ **203/562-5507; www.louislunch.com**).

🚆 New Haven (1½ hr. from New York City; 3 hr. from Boston).

🛏 $$ **Omni New Haven,** 155 Temple St. (ⓒ **800/THE-OMNI** [800/843-6664] or 203/772-6664; www.omnihotels.com).

Prime Burger

The Coffee Shop Time Forgot

New York, New York

Smack dab in the middle of glamorous, clamorous Midtown Manhattan sits an amazing little relic of prewar New York—Prime Burger. Stepping through the glass door of this narrow midblock coffee shop, you'll feel as if you've come unstuck in time.

The term "retro" doesn't even apply—Prime Burger is too straightforward, totally irony free; it's not an homage to the 1940s, it really *is* a coffee shop from the 1940s. It has been here since 1938, an offshoot of the defunct local Hamburger Heaven chain, and the DiMicelo family members who have run it all these years just never got around to redecorating it or gussying it up in any way. They've kept the space-agey crystal light fixtures, the laminate wood-grained wall paneling, the veteran waiters in white jackets, the long Formica-topped lunch counter with its spinning red-leather stools—not to mention a unique pewlike section of wooden seats with flip-out trays attached to the arms, for customers dining solo. (That alone belongs in the Smithsonian Museum.) And to go with it, there's a throwback menu with items like canned peaches with cottage cheese, a tomato stuffed with tuna-fish salad, cream of tomato soup, or a baked apple or Jell-O with whipped cream for dessert.

And now here's the crowning touch—the burgers are actually delish. While uptown restaurants serve gourmet burgers laced with truffles and foie gras, at Prime Burger they deliver the definitive American classic: a sensibly sized 4-ounce patty of freshly ground top-grade chuck, broiled on an old-fashioned flame broiler and centered neatly on a serviceable bun. It isn't piled high with tomatoes and onions and lettuce and pickles you didn't ask for; even if you order a cheeseburger or a bacon burger, it won't come overloaded. For some folks, that's a bummer; for others, it's a relief from food-wasting excess. The simple onion rings and the steak fries are also well done; desserts, such as the luscious apple crumb pie, are made on premises.

Prices aren't exactly from the Eisenhower era, but they're surprisingly low for Manhattan. Prime Burger doesn't take credit cards, it's closed Sundays, and the doors close at 7pm—the end of the working day for Manhattan's office-bound masses.

ⓘ 5 E. 51st St. (✆ **212/759-4729**; www. primeburger.com).

✈ John F. Kennedy International (15 miles/24km); Newark Liberty International (16 miles/27km); LaGuardia (8 miles/ 13km).

🛏 $$$ **Carlton Hotel on Madison Avenue,** 88 Madison Ave. (✆ **212/532-4100;** www.carltonhotelny.com). $$ **Washington Square Hotel,** 103 Waverly Place (✆ **800/222-0418** or 212/777-9515; www.washingtonsquarehotel.com).

White Manna

There's No Place Like Chrome

Hackensack, New Jersey

Even seasoned New Jerseyites sometimes confuse the White Manna in Hackensack with the White Mana diner in Jersey City. For burger hounds, however, that would be sacrilege—there's no comparison between the two, they exclaim.

It's true, these two vintage Art Deco chrome-trimmed gems were opened by the same owner, Louis Bridges. The octagonal Jersey City diner actually came first, built around 1938 and displayed as a "diner of the future" at the 1939 New York World's Fair. The Hackensack version was purchased soon after, as Bridges sought to capitalize on the World's Fair fame with a chain of these streamlined eateries around northern New Jersey. The White Manna (the original name—the other diner's sign was a later typo) was eventually moved here to the corner of River and Passaic streets in Hackensack in 1946.

But these days it's the two-N Manna that rules supreme with its juicy, onion-rich sliders—originally modeled after White Castle's, but a far superior version. Sitting at its narrow U-shaped counter (the only place you *can* sit in this pocket-sized diner), you can watch the grill cooks at work, slinging lumps of ground beef onto the sizzling griddle, topping them with a fistful of shaved onions, then smashing them flat with a spatula and flipping them, onions and all. Scooped onto a soft potato roll and wrapped in wax paper to go, they're misshapen, moist, and flavorful to the max. And *messy.*

The blazing red-and-white neon sign on top nearly overpowers this dinky little dive, a rounded-off cube with glass-brick corners and white steel walls, which seats barely more than a dozen customers at once. The menu is limited—burgers, sodas, a few breakfast items (it's certainly an atmospheric place for that morning cup o' joe)—but at lunch- and dinnertimes, there's often a wait before you can grab a seat on one of those counter stools. That 9:30pm closing time is a shame; those mouthwatering little burgers would taste divine at 2am after a night on the town.

ⓘ 358 River St. (✆ **201/342-0914**).

✈ Newark International (22 miles/35km).

🛏 $$ **Best Western Oritani Hotel,** 414 Hackensack Ave. (✆ **201/488-8900;** www.bestwesternnewjersey.com).

Lankford Grocery

Burger Star of the Lone Star State

Houston, Texas

Sure, it looks like a dump from the outside, a dilapidated white frame house with red-and-white-striped tin awnings on a residential Midtown side street. Step inside, and you're all the more convinced it *is* a dump—look at the mismatched tables and chairs, the dowdy floral tablecloths, the battered upholstered booths, the scratched wood paneling, the dangerously sloping floor. Coffee is served in a random collection of souvenir mugs; regular customers know to shuffle over to the pot and get their own refills.

But the burgers at Lankford Grocery make it all worthwhile. These are fat, handmade patties grilled with just a slight crunch on the outside, oozing juice from inside. (Instead of paper napkins, the waitresses just hand you a roll of paper towels—and for good reason.) You can order a double or even a triple, but you'll probably end up having to get it wrapped to go—even a single burger requires two hands to eat. And if it's not spicy enough—down here in Houston, spiciness is always a factor—ask to have it topped with fried jalapeños or the firehouse sauce, a hot mustard that earns its name honestly. The Firehouse Burger goes even further, with the peppers worked into the ground beef before it's thrown on the grill, and a little hot salsa thrown on for good measure. Another popular variation is the soldier burger, a cheeseburger topped with a sweetly runny fried egg. Sides? The onion rings are succulently greasy and not overbattered; the tater nuggets crunchy on the outside, soft inside; but regulars insist on the Tex-Mex, a fried mess of slivered jalapeños and onions that wakes up your taste buds. Expect an extralong wait for a table on Thursdays, when the daily special is Lankford's acclaimed chicken-fried steak.

Eydie Prior converted her parents' vintage grocery store, opened in 1939, into a full-fledged restaurant in 1977. They'd been serving hamburgers informally to their customers anyway for years, so the conversion was really more a matter of surrendering to destiny. Some might call it a dump, but for others, it's a home away from home.

(i) 88 Dennis St. ((C) **713/522-9555**).

✈ George Bush Intercontinental (37 miles/60km).

⊨ $$$ **Hilton University of Houston,** 4800 Calhoun Rd. ((C) **800/HOTEL-UH** [800/468-3584] or 713/741-2447; www.hilton.com). $$ **Best Western Downtown Inn and Suites,** 915 W. Dallas St. ((C) **800/780-7234** or 713/571-7733; www.bestwestern.com).

Taghkanic Diner
Underneath the Neon Sign
Ancram, New York

You can't miss that sign as you're whizzing along the scenic Taconic Parkway, 2 hours north of Manhattan—an American Indian chief in full-feathered headdress, silhouetted in red neon, above the name WEST TAGHKANIC DINER. It's the sort of place you notice only after you've shot past the exit turn, seeing it glow eerily against the dark trees late at night, or through the dismal gloom of an upstate winter drizzle. Maybe you vow to yourself to stop in next time. Maybe you never make it back.

But if you keep your vow, you'll be glad you did. Alongside that landmark neon sign is an equally classic 1953 chrome diner, its sleek streamlined panels maintained in tiptop condition. Inside, it's a retro vision of stainless-steel counters and cabinets, spinning counter stools, diamond-patterned terrazzo floors, Formica table tops, and blue vinyl booths (up close, you'll even see a little glitter embedded in the vinyl). Expansive curtained windows look out on the wooded Columbia County landscape bordering Lake Taghkanic State Park.

Given what an architectural showpiece this is, you might expect that the food would be merely routine—but you'd be wrong. Although the huge menu lists what looks like a standard lineup of diner fare (the only exotic items are the ostrich steak and ostrich burger), the kitchen here

The Taghkanic serves classic diner fare in a chrome setting from the 1950s.

233

ON THE ROAD IN AMERICA

seems to take pride in doing things well—they don't skimp on either quality or quantity. It's an art to turn out a classic patty melt, Yankee pot roast, corned beef hash, or a mound of half-crisp, half-fluffy savory home fries. Breakfast is served all day, and, oddly enough, on Saturdays after 2pm they offer a competent (though merely so) Mexican menu of various burritos, quesadillas, and fajitas alongside the gringo diner food.

ⓘ 1016 Rte. 82 at the Taconic Pkwy. (✆ **518/851-7117;** www.taghkanicdiner.com).

✈ Albany (50 miles/81km).

🛏 $$$ **The Country Squire B&B,** 251 Allen St., Hudson (✆ **518/822-9229;** www.countrysquireny.com). $$ **The Inn at Green River,** 9 Nobletown Rd., Hillsdale (✆ **518/325-7248;** www.innatgreenriver.com).

Blue Benn Diner
The Heart & Soul of a Diner
Bennington, Vermont

Don't look for neon above this 1948-vintage chrome diner—the artsy college town of Bennington, Vermont, made them take that garish thing down years ago. And with various additions over the years, the stainless-steel panels on its sides aren't so easy to see anymore. But though it may not be a pristine architectural example from the outside, from the inside the Blue Benn looks just like what it is—a classic hometown diner.

Underneath its low, curved, cream-colored ceiling, handwritten signs flutter from every available inch of turquoise wall and stainless-steel shelving, advertising the day's specials (who knew there could be so many varieties of omelets and pancakes?). Customers perch on stools at the long, well-worn lunch counter or crowd into the cramped wooden booths by the windows, where they can flip through the eclectic catalog offered on the wall-mounted jukeboxes. You'll probably have to wait for a seat, at least from July through October, when summer vacationers and leaf peepers flood through town, but the

friendly yet efficient service helps keep things moving.

As you'd expect from such a local institution, breakfasts are a great gathering time—the coffeepots start brewing around 6am—when you can savor a stack of pancakes or French toast topped with genuine Vermont maple syrup. In fact, the breakfast fare is so good, they serve it all day long. Places like the Blue Benn often coast by on standard diner fare—and the Blue Benn executes quite respectable blue-plate specials such as pot roast, hot turkey sandwiches, meatloaf, and creamed chipped beef, served in generous helpings. But it also caters to a more modern audience with a number of vegetarian dishes like nut burgers, vegetarian enchiladas, or grilled portobello mushroom on sourdough bread. Sonny Monroe, who has owned the place since 1974, seems to like mixing up the menu, using locally grown ingredients whenever possible. The fresh-baked pies and doughnuts are renowned; the Indian pudding dessert is a rich cornmeal-and-molasses treat. Get here earlier rather than later, because it's not really a dinner place—most days of the week, it closes by 5pm.

ⓘ 314 North St. (Rte. 7; ☎ **802/442-5140**).

✈ Albany International (32 miles/52km).

🛏 $$ **South Shire Inn,** 124 Elm St. (☎ **802/447-3839;** www.southshire.com). $ **Paradise Motor Inn,** 141 W. Main St. (☎ **802/442-8351;** www.theparadisemotor inn.com).

Sonny's Grill

Blue Ridge Country Biscuits

Blowing Rock, North Carolina

Just a few minutes' drive off the Blue Ridge Parkway, Blowing Rock has been a popular mountain resort ever since the mid–19th century, attracting nature lovers who come to admire the panoramic 4,000-foot-high (1,200m) namesake promontory just outside of town, known for its stiff updrafts (in winter, snow sometimes actually falls upward here). But lately, Blowing Rock has been increasingly inundated with antique-filled B&Bs, chichi art galleries, and trendy bistros like Crippen's (famed for its chocolate-infused beef tenderloin) or the Storie Street Grille (with its signature eggplant napoleon). And as all these new developments sprout, you can be sure the regulars at Sonny's Grill are discussing them over coffee at the eight-stool counter or one of the three tiny tables in this quintessential Main Street cafe—a stalwart relic of Blowing Rock's small-town charm.

In classic Main Street cafe style, breakfast is the main event here. The outstanding highlight of the breakfast menu—the thing Sonny's advertises in hand-painted lettering on its front window—is a perfectly simple southern dish: two flaky buttermilk biscuits sandwiched around thin slices of grilled locally cured country ham. Sweet-potato pancakes are another breakfast specialty (top them with maple syrup), with their savory-sweet taste and pumpkiny aroma. Then there's the liver mush,

which is just what it sounds like—mush made out of fried pig liver. Chances are you must have been born a Tar Heel to fully appreciate that dish. But at a place like Sonny's, that's reason enough to keep it on the menu.

The lunchtime burger and cheeseburger are also popular, though the restaurant can get crowded midday, especially during foliage season, and the small friendly staff sometimes has trouble keeping up with the flow. The ham biscuits you can order any time of day.

Sonny Klutz opened the unassuming cinder-block cafe among Main Street's quaint Victorian edifices in 1954; his son Tommy has carried on since Sonny's death in 1999. For regular visitors to the High Country, an annual stop at Sonny's provides stability in an ever-changing world—or at least reassurance that Blowing Rock isn't getting prettified out of control.

ⓘ 1119 Main St. (☎ **828/295-7577**).

✈ Asheville (90 miles/145km).

🛏 $$$ **Chetola Resort at Blowing Rock,** N. Main St. (☎ **800/243-8652** or 828/295-5500; www.chetola.com). $$ **The Green Park Inn,** 9239 Valley Blvd. (☎ **800/852-2462** or 828/295-3141; www.green parkinn.com).

Don's Drive-In

Baby, You Can Drive My Car

Traverse City, Michigan

Though it's 242 miles (390km) from Detroit—way up at the top of Lower Michigan's mitten—Don's Drive-In is still a love song to the American automobile. You can see it everywhere, from the tail-finned sedan pictured on its brash neon road sign to the car-shaped cardboard containers that the kids' meals are delivered in.

It's not as if Traverse City doesn't have plenty of its own attractions—it does, from boutique shopping, wineries, and a vibrant arts scene to spectacular Lake Michigan beaches and the justly famous local cherries (Don's does feature Traverse City cherries in its thick creamy milkshakes). But when Don's first opened on this lakeshore highway in 1958, America was infatuated with the burgeoning car culture and dazzled by the promise of Eisenhower's new interstate highway system; this hot-pink roadside restaurant still reflects that moment in time.

Don's is one of the few drive-ins in America that still has carhop service, right down to the post speakers mounted by each parking spot where drivers can phone in their order to the kitchen. Carhops deliver the food on vintage trays that hook onto your car window. The inside dining room is somewhat more self-consciously retro, with hubcaps and vinyl records slapped on the walls, a gigantic jukebox against one wall, black-and-white tiled floors, red vinyl booths, and cherry-red swirled Formica topping the tables.

Don't expect a sparkling Johnny Rockets–style rehab, though—this half-century-old drive-in sometimes shows its age around the edges.

There's nothing cutesy about the house specialty, the Big D Burger—a half-pounder consisting of hand-shaped patties of fresh ground beef broiled to a sizzled crust and topped with all the mustard, onions, mushrooms, bacon, and cheese you desire. (That kind of gustatory excess would have been unheard-of in 1958.) But where Don's really shines is with its utterly delectable milkshakes, which come in a range of flavors with chunks of real fruit.

"Quaint" is an odd adjective to apply to a busy, bright place like Don's, especially given the unabashedly greasy nature of its fast-food offerings: Onion rings and french fries and foot-long chili dogs don't belong at a "quaint" eatery. No, Don's just is what it is—a local institution that has been feeding folks, and feeding them well, for a very long time.

ⓘ 2030 U.S. 31 North (☏ **231/938-1860**).

✈ Cherry Capital Airport, Traverse City (7 miles/11km).

🛏 $$$ **Tamarack Lodge,** 2035 U.S. 31 N (☏ **877/938-9744;** www.tamarack lodgetc.com). $$ **Traverse Bay Inn,** 2300 U.S. 31 N (☏ **800/968-2646** or 231/938-2646; www.traversebayhotels.com).

Ardy & Ed's Drive-In

Rock 'n' Roll on Skates

Oshkosh, Wisconsin

On a summer evening, cruising into Ardy and Ed's for a hot beef sandwich and a root beer float—with vintage rock 'n' roll blasting from the loudspeakers and carhops roller skating from car to car—is a scene right out of *American Graffiti*. True, the roller-skating carhops aren't a 1950s holdover—that tradition didn't start until 1983, when Ardy decided to pave over the gravel parking lot because the teenage girls working the curbside service thought it would be fun to do it on skates. Several generations of carhops later, they still think it's fun.

Yes, there really is an Ardy, and there really was an Ed. The restaurant was founded in 1948, though it wasn't called Ardy and Ed's then—It was the South Side A&W, part of a chain of root-beer restaurants throughout the Midwest. (It's still painted in the orange-and-brown A&W colors, though you can hardly see that under all the signs loaded around the eaves of the compact little building.) Edward Timm bought it in 1960—his wife, Ardy, had been working there—and in 1972 they took it independent, renaming it Ardy and Ed's. Though Ed has passed on, Ardy still owns it with her second husband, Steve Davis—who himself has been working at the restaurant, making root beer, since he was 15. That's the kind of small-town fixture this drive-in is.

The menu is driven by standard drive-in fare, but with plenty of local touches: Fried fish items feature butterflied lake perch; one of the hot-dog options is a Chicago-style hot dog; alongside the hamburgers you can also find a bratwurst patty (the Drive-In Double combines a hamburger with a bratwurst patty). The Tall Boy hamburgers feature Ardy and Ed's own tangy special sauce, and they also make a signature Pizza Burger, which has melted mozzarella worked into the patty. The draft root beer is made on premises daily, and the malted milkshakes use real malt and local Cedar Crest ice cream. Then of course there's the hot beef sandwich, a longtime favorite made with thin-shaved roast beef on a seeded Kaiser roll—a distant cousin of the French dip that puts the ones at the Arby's chain to shame.

Though there are a few seats at a counter inside, most people use the carhop service and eat in their cars. It's a seasonal joint, open March through September, sitting right across the street from the Lake Winnebago shore. You may have to cruise up and down the road a while, waiting for a parking slot to open at Ardy and Ed's. But hey, it's summer at the lake—who's in a hurry?

ⓘ 2413 S. Main St. (✆ **920/231-5455;** www.foodspot.com/ardyandeds).

✈ Milwaukee (75 miles/121km).

🛏 $$ **CopperLeaf Hotel,** 300 W. College Ave., Appleton (✆ **877/303-0303** or 920/749-0303; www.copperleafhotel.com). $$ **Hawthorn Inn & Suites,** 3105 S. Washburn St., Oshkosh (✆ **800/527-1133** or 920/303-1133; www.hawthorn.com).

The Varsity

Home of Yankee Dogs & Naked Steaks

Atlanta, Georgia

Billing itself as the world's largest drive-in restaurant, the Varsity sprawls over two full blocks of Atlanta real estate, close to the Georgia Tech campus. From the nearby highway intersection known as The Connection, that gigantic red neon V is a glowing nighttime landmark, along with the neon-zipped contours of its drive-in carport.

Founded in 1928, the Varsity—originally named the Yellow Jacket, after the Georgia Tech mascot—really came into its own in the drive-in era, when its zippy service, cheap prices, and quick-cooked menu items made it a natural for college students and other diners in a hurry. In fact, the Varsity still offers carhop curbside service at the main location. It has four smaller branches around the Atlanta metro area, as well as one near the University of Georgia campus in Athens (1000 Broad St.; © **706/548-6325**), though the drive-in section isn't really the giant part.

Most people eat inside this Art Deco-ish hulk faced in crimson and beige, with its front marquee resembling a vintage movie house. That's where the real scene is, anyway. You line up to place your order at a 150-foot-long (45m) stainless-steel counter, where workers in bright red shirts bawl out

Occupying 2 full city blocks in Atlanta, the Varsity claims to be the world's largest drive-in restaurant.

the restaurant's signature request: "What'll ya have?" Over the years, the Varsity has trained its customers to respond with its own unique lingo: a "PC" is a chocolate milk; an "FO" is a creamy frosted orange drink (sublime); "walk a dog" is a hot dog to go; "glorified steak" is a hamburger with lettuce, mayonnaise, and tomato; "rings" are onion rings; "strings" are french fries; "bag of rags" is potato chips; and on and on (for newbies, the menu prints translations). Be ready by the time you reach the front of the line, because they take those orders at lightning speed.

Hot dogs are the Varsity's top-selling menu item, and among the many variations, chili dogs win out (the Varsity claims it serves 2 miles of hot dogs and 300 gallons of chili a day), although slaw dogs—a surprisingly satisfying combo—run a close second. You'll certainly know you're in the South when you see items like barbecued pork, pimiento cheese sandwiches, deviled-egg sandwiches, and a hypercaloric

fried peach pie listed on the menu boards over the counter.

The Varsity is still a fast-food restaurant: The dining areas are strictly bare-bones, with glaring lighting and blaring TV sets on the walls; the food is intensely flavored but greasy. But eaten in that tailgate-party atmosphere, it's quite a trip; it may be the best place for people-watching in all Atlanta. You can't really say you've been to Hot Lanta without making a stop at the Varsity—order a "Sally Rand in the Garden" and an FO, and surrender to the experience.

ⓘ 61 North Ave. (✆ **404/881-1706;** www. thevarsity.com).

✈ Atlanta International (12 miles/20km).

🛏 **$$$ The Georgian Terrace Hotel,** 659 Peachtree St. (✆ **800/651-2316** or 404/897-1991;www.thegeorgianterrace. com). $$ **Hotel Indigo,** 683 Peachtree St. (✆ **404/874-9200;** www.hotelindigo.com).

261 Diners & Drive-Ins

Pink's Hot Dogs

Wieners of the Stars

Hollywood, California

Some days, all the glamour in Hollywood can't compete with the pleasure of walking up to the counter at this iconic hot-dog stand and ordering a sublime chili dog.

Of course, being in Hollywood, Pink's isn't any old hot-dog stand; it has its own idiosyncratic cachet. Name another hot-dog stand with its own valet, who darts around parking the stream of Rolls-Royces and Mercedes that pull up regularly. And because it's open into the wee hours, Pink's attracts a colorful late-night crowd (half-hour-wait lines usually spill out the door even at midnight). It has been here at the corner of La Brea and Melrose since 1939, when the late Paul and Betty Pink

began selling 10¢ wieners from their secondhand hot-dog cart in what was then practically the country. Run nowadays by three of their grown children, the current building—a one-story white shack topped with a clutter of mismatched signs—isn't a whole lot fancier (it's still a cheap meal, too), though the area has become thickly developed. Pink's has worked its way deep into movie-land history over all those years: Urban legend claims that Bruce Willis proposed to Demi Moore in the parking lot of Pink's, and here the maverick actor/director Orson Welles set a record by downing 18 Pink's links at one go.

7 Places to Eat in . . . Kansas City

It was never hard to find an excellent steak in Kansas City. What's changed in the past few years, however, is that talented homegrown chefs are actually returning here, once they've finished traveling and cooking abroad, to interpret KC's heart-of-the-country honesty in refreshing new ways.

For more than 25 years, the city could boast one outstanding special-occasion restaurant: 262 **The American Restaurant** (200 E. 25th St., Kansas City, Missouri; ✆ **816/545-8001;** www.theamericankc.com), in Hallmark Cards' centerpiece-of-downtown headquarters, Crown Center, has an impressive wine cellar and a regional-fare menu originally developed by James Beard and Joe Baum. The American not only has a stunning glass-walled skyline view, it has kept its prix-fixe menu worthy of that view, with dishes such as olive-oil poached halibut, lamb T-bone, or crispy veal breast complemented by seasonal sides like heirloom tomatoes, micro-greens, artichoke puree, or locally made prosciutto or foie gras. But talk about soap operas! When chef Debbie Gold left with her husband, Michael Smith, to open a vibrant new place called 40 Sardines, the American was given worthy competition at last. The couple divorced in 2007, and 40 Sardines closed. Now Gold is back cooking up a storm at The American—while her ex, Michael Smith, competes with his own upscale bistro in the Crossroads arts district, 263 **Michael Smith** (1900 Main St., Kansas City, Missouri; ✆ **816-842-2202;** http://michaelsmithkc.com). Smith's key-note rustic style goes for hearty, more casual food with chunky textures and deep flavors, like his "8-hour" pork roast with green onion risotto or his homemade boudin blanc sausage. Meanwhile, in 2004 a third expensive fine-dining option opened south of downtown in Westport—casually elegant 264 **Bluestem** (900 Westport Rd., Kansas City, Missouri; ✆ **816/561-1101;** www.kansascitymenus.com/bluestem), where chef Colby Garrelts—a Kansas City native who trained all over the country—spins out marvelous prix-fixe multicourse New American menus. From the Wagyu beef tartare to the brown-butter gnocchi to the pork loin with lentils, spiced plums, golden raisin, and pecans, Garrelts's cooking is imaginative indeed.

You'd hardly expect a French bistro in Kansas City to be as authentic as 265 **Le Fou Frog** (400 E. 5th St, Kansas City, Missouri; ✆ **816/474-6060**); it makes sense, how-ever, when you learn that chef Mano Rafael (the crazy frog himself) hails from Mar-seilles. From the steak au poivre to the bouillabaisse to the escargots, it's a Gallic flashback—but it's also one of the liveliest and most fun restaurants downtown, with friendly service and a gorgeous 1920s-vintage front bar. Kansas Citians hungry for the next best thing have also been traveling out of town lately, 20 miles (32km) north to Smithville, to sample the locavore cooking of Jonathan Justus at his chic minimalist diner 266 **Justus Drugstore** (106 W. Main St., Smithville, Missouri; ✆ **816/532-2300;** www.drugstorerestaurant.com). Justus's passion for local sources inspires dishes such as goat cheese piped into squash blossoms, heritage pork rib-eye, or roast

Campo Lindo chicken sprinkled with fennel pollen from his own garden. (He won't ship in seafood, though freshwater fish do make it onto the menu.)

Kansas City dining has another side, however—wood-smoked and slathered with sauce. The most famous barbecue joint in town, **Arthur Bryant's** (1727 Brooklyn Ave., Kansas City, Missouri; **816/231-1123;** www.arthurbryantsbbq.com) still occupies the same no-frills brick storefront it has been in since the 1950s. Loads of tangy, sweet sauce is what makes Kansas City barbecue different from spice-rubbed Memphis barbecue, and Bryant's offers three different kinds to spread over your luscious beef brisket, pulled pork, turkey, or slab of pork ribs. But if you're over in Kansas, compare it with upstart **Oklahoma Joe's** (3002 W. 47th Ave., Kansas City, Kansas; **913/722-3366;** www.oklahomajoesbbq.com), founded in 1996—a bright and busy coffee-shop-style joint set in an old gas station. They serve incredibly tender Carolina-style brisket, pulled pork, chicken, turkey, and ribs.

✈ Kansas City International (22 miles/36km).

🛏 $$$ **Hotel Phillips,** 106 W. 12th St. (**800/433-1426** or 816/221-7000; www.hotel phillips.com). $ **The Quarterage Hotel Westport,** 560 Westport Rd. (**800/942-4233** or 816/931-0001; www.quarteragehotel.com).

Chef Colby Garrelts' rare beef at Bluestem in Kansas City.

Part of the secret of Pink's success is the lean all-beef hot dogs, custom-made by Hoffy's meatpackers to Pink's specifications; they have hardly any filler and a natural casing gives them that special snap-and-gush when you bite into them. The secret-recipe chili sauce, a fine balance of spiciness and savor developed long ago by Betty Pink herself, is another draw. The menu lists only hot dogs, hamburgers, and a few chicken breast and Mexican items, but the number of mix-and-match variations is intriguing. Several of the specialty dogs are named after the celebrities who've ordered them, like the Rosie O'Donnell (a 10-inch dog with mustard, onions, chili, and sauerkraut) or the Martha Stewart (a 10-incher with relish, onions, bacon, chopped tomatoes, sauerkraut, and sour cream).

Pink's is hardly a posh hangout, even with all those head shots of celebrity customers that line one wall of the small dining area, with its tiny tables and metal chairs. (Chances are the celebs themselves took their chili dogs to go.) But it's a scene nevertheless—and one you'd encounter only in Hollywood.

ⓘ 709 N. La Brea Blvd. (✆ **323/931-4223;** www.pinkshollywood.com).

✈ Los Angeles International (13 miles/ 21km).

🚃 $$$ **Peninsula Beverly Hills,** 9882 S. Santa Monica Blvd. (✆ **800/462-7899** or 310/551-2888; www.peninsula.com). $ **Best Western Marina Pacific Hotel,** 1697 Pacific Ave., Venice (✆ **800/786-7789** or 310/452-1111; www.mphotel.com).

Chinatowns 269

The Great American Chinatown

Chopsticks by the Bay

San Francisco, California

San Francisco has had a Chinatown almost as long as it has been any sort of a city at all. The first Chinese immigrants arrived as servants in the early 1800s; by 1850, some 25,000 Chinese had flooded into California, fleeing famine and the Opium Wars to find their fortunes in the "Gold Mountain." What they found instead was hard labor and low wages, first in the gold mines and later on railroad construction crews; they faced such virulent prejudice (a strict Chinese Exclusion Act prevailed from 1882 to 1943) that Chinese Americans couldn't even buy homes outside the Chinatown ghetto until the 1950s.

Shameful as that chapter of American history was, it did keep San Francisco's Chinatown a vital neighborhood where Chinese traditions were intently preserved. Even today, more than 80,000 people live in Chinatown, and other Chinese Americans check in regularly from their new neighborhoods (the Richmond and Sunset districts in particular). Of course tourists flock here too, to snap photos of the ornate gilded gateway at Grant Avenue and Bush Street, to peer into the three Buddhist temples along Waverly Place, to wander past the food shops and noodle parlors on Stockton Street, or to gawk at locals playing mah-jongg and chess in Portsmouth Square. But there's one place where tourists and locals happily coexist: at Chinatown's myriad restaurants, several of which remain remarkably true to Chinese culinary standards—unlike the network of by-the-numbers Chinese restaurants that crisscrosses the U. S.

There's almost always a wait for a table at tiny **House of Nanking** (919 Kearny St.;

415/421-1429), where the Shanghai-style cuisine includes traditional pot stickers, green-onion-and-shrimp pancakes, and a long menu of entrees; ask the waiter to recommend a daily special. Despite its obscure second-floor location, **Oriental Pearl** (760 Clay St.; ✆ **415/433-1817**) is usually packed; among its Chiu Chow dishes (a regional variant of Cantonese), the best are the house special chicken meatball, the *pei pa* tofu with shrimp, and the spicy braised prawns. Fish tanks line the walls at **Great Eastern** (649 Jackson St.; ✆ **415/986-2500**), a popular Hong Kong–style seafood house. Things are always hopping at the three-story **R&G Lounge** (631 Kearny St.; ✆ 415/982-7877; www.rnglounge.com), known for its deep-fried salt-and-pepper crab, the chicken with black-bean sauce, or the R&G Special Beef that melts in your mouth.

For spicy Hunan food, two great options are **Hunan Home's** (622 Jackson St.; ✆ **415/982-2844**) for great hot-and-sour soup, prawns with walnuts, and Hunan style scallops; or **Brandy Ho's Hunan Food** (217 Columbus Ave., ✆ **415/788-7527;** www.brandyhos.com) for excellent fried dumplings, fish ball soup, or the Three Delicacies (scallops, shrimp, and chicken served with black-bean sauce). For a classic dim sum lunch, there's cavernous, cacophonous **Gold Mountain** (664 Broadway; ✆ **415/296-7733;** dim sum until 3pm). And though it's a bit of a dive, **Sam Wo** (813 Washington St.; ✆ **415/982-0596**) is a beloved standby for the ultimate Chinese comfort food, *jook* (or *congee*, as it's called in Hong Kong)—a thick rice gruel flavored with fish, shrimp, chicken, beef, or pork.

✈ San Francisco International (14 miles/23km).

🛏 $$$ **Hotel Adagio,** 550 Geary St. (✆ **800/228-8830** or 415/775-5000; www.thehoteladagion.com). $ **Hotel des Arts,** 447 Bush St. (✆ **800/956-4322** or 415/956-3232; www.sfhoteldesarts.com).

Manhattan Goes Chinese

A Little More Mott Street

New York, New York

It's one of those secrets that New Yorkers like to keep under their hats: Manhattan's historic Little Italy is a tourist fiction by now, a strip of restaurants preserved just for out-of-towners, while all around it the side streets have been taken over by a booming Chinatown that long ago spilled over its traditional Canal Street boundary. And it still can't contain all the city's Asian immigrants, who have also moved out to Queens's Flushing neighborhood, where you can find yet more authentic restaurants and shops.

In the 1870s, when no other immigrant groups would live in these marshlands northeast of City Hall, a wave of Chinese workers migrating eastward from San Francisco moved in and made the area their own. Today, Chinatown—which is really a Pan-Asian conglomeration, with Vietnamese and Thai immigrants adding their own flavor—is a feast for the senses, with street signs bearing Chinese characters, banks and fast-food restaurants gussied up with pagoda-style roofs, and a perpetual din in the narrow streets, where sidewalk bins display piles of silvery fish and exotic fruits and vegetables, and bright-red roast ducks hang in steamed-up shop windows.

While New York has neighborhood Chinese takeouts all over town, locals still head down to the Manhattan Chinatown for the evocative dining experience. **Big Wong King** (67 Mott St.; © **212/964-0540**) is one lively favorite, with communal tables loaded with steaming bowls of *congee*, plates of stir-fried vegetables, and platters of roast pork and duck. The no-frills **New York Noodletown** (28½ Bowery; © **212/349-0923**) wins raves for its seafood-based noodle soups, salt-baked shrimp, and chopped roast pork platters. For seafood, head for **Oriental Garden** (14 Elizabeth St.; © **212/619-0085**), where the Cantonese-style seafood dishes are drawn from immense fish tanks set throughout the restaurant. The always bustling **HSF Restaurant** (46 Bowery; © **212/374-1319**) is perhaps the city's best-known spot for Hong Kong–style dim sum, with a continual parade of carts trundling past your table and dispensing small servings of various delicacies. **Joe's Shanghai** (9 Pell St.; © **212/233-8888**) and its offshoot **Joe's Ginger Restaurant** (25 Pell St.; © **212/285-0999**) excel in Shanghai-style dishes such as steamed soup dumplings, braised duck, and spicy yellow fish. **Wo Hop** (17 Mott St., btw. Worth and Mosco sts.; © **212/267-2536**), is a longtime favorite for cheap and deliciously filling Cantonese standards like chow fun and chop suey. If it's full, pop down the street to the similar **Hop Kee** (21 Mott St.; © **212/964-836**).

Top among the many Vietnamese restaurants that have infiltrated Chinatown, **Pho Viet Huong** (73 Mulberry St.; © **212/233-8988**) offers some amazing soups like beef-based *pho* and the hot and sour *canh* soup; barbecued beef wrapped in grape leaves is another specialty. The tiki hut-style Malaysian restaurant **Nyonya** (194 Grand St.; © **212/334-3669**) wows diners with its *roti canai* (an Indian pancake with a curry-chicken dipping sauce) and hearty, spicy *prawn mee* noodle soup.

For dessert, head to the **Chinatown Ice Cream Factory** (65 Bayard St., btw. Mott and Elizabeth sts.; © **212/608-4170**), where the ice cream comes in Asian flavors such as almond cookie, litchi, and an incredible green tea.

✈ John F. Kennedy International (15 miles/24km); Newark Liberty International (16 miles/27km); LaGuardia (8 miles/13km).

🛏 $$$ **Carlton Hotel on Madison Avenue,** 88 Madison Ave. (© **212/532-4100;** www.carltonhotelny.com). $$ **Washington Square Hotel,** 103 Waverly Place (© **800/222-0418** or 212/777-9515; www.washingtonsquarehotel.com).

Chinatowns   271

Canadian Chow Mein
The Canton of Canada
Toronto, Ontario

Toronto is known as a multiethnic city, but its Chinatown is nonetheless impressive—the world's third largest outside of China, with 350,000 Chinese Canadians and counting.

Not only is it big, Toronto's thriving Chinatown—centered along Dundas Street and Spadina Avenue—is one of North America's most vital immigrant neighborhoods, with a special sort of urban energy. Walk through it at night and you can easily be mesmerized by the bustling sidewalks, the shimmer of neon lights, windows hung with rows of glossy-brown cooked ducks, record stores blaring tracks from top-10 Chinese records, and trading companies filled with Asian produce. At the corner of Spadina and Dundas, the very heart of Chinatown, the sprawling **Dragon City** shopping mall gives you a quick shot of its flavor, with stores selling Chinese preserves (cuttlefish, lemon ginger, whole mango, ginseng, and antler) and other food; the food court here features a full Pan-Asian spectrum of Korean, Indonesian, Chinese, and Japanese cuisine.

If finding a good meal in this Chinatown is a daunting task, it's only because there are too many choices. (Add the more recent Vietnamese and Thai contenders and you may be more bewildered than ever.) Despite the sometimes-kitschy plastic Buddha decor, **Happy Seven** (358 Spadina Ave.; 416/971-9820) is widely acknowledged as one of the best kitchens in Chinatown—and as you'd guess from the number of fish tanks around the dining room, seafood dishes are its specialty. Portions are extremely generous. Seafood is also prominent on the Cantonese-style menu down the street at the veteran **Lee Garden** (331 Spadina Ave.; 416/593-9524), but they

also serve some brilliant tofu dishes, and the signature dish is fork-tender "grandfather- smoked" chicken with honey and sesame seeds. There are always long queues out in front of **Sang Ho** (536 Dundas St.; 416/596-1685), where the lovely dining room has several teeming aquariums; check out the daily specials on the wall-mounted boards.

If casual, cheap eateries are more your target, try **Goldstone Noodle House** (266 Spadina Ave.; 416/596-9053). It may look like a hole in the wall, but for flavorful classics like fried rice, salted fish, barbecue pork, and noodle soups, it's a winner. For wonderful authentic northern Chinese buns, noodles, and dumplings, the tiny basement-level cafe **Mother's Dumplings** (79 Huron St.; 416/217-2008) can't be beat.

Toronto International (30km/19 miles).

$$$ **Le Royal Meridien King Edward,** 37 King St. E (800/543-4300 or 416/863 9700; www.starwoodhotels.com). $$ **The Drake Hotel,** 1150 Queen St. W (416/531-5042; www.thedrakehotel.ca).

5 Vintage Journeys

Locanda dell'Amorosa, a working inn, restaurant, and vineyard in Sinalunga, Italy (see 78).

Stag's Leap Wine Cellars
The Giant Step Forward
Napa Valley, California

In 1976, English wine merchant Stephen Spurrier decided to conduct a blind tasting at his wine store in Paris. Intrigued by wines he'd tasted on a recent trip to California (dramatized in the 2008 film *Bottle Shock*), he gathered the best of French and California wine and invited the most prestigious French critics to taste and rate them. The results shocked the wine world: American wines fared well against the French. One particular bottle came out on top—Stag's Leap Wine Cellars' Cabernet Sauvignon.

What became known as the "Judgment of Paris" ended in a flurry of recriminations and accusations of cheating from the embarrassed French. No longer could French wine be presumed to be the world's best. Upstart California wines had become a force to be reckoned with.

Even more surprising, the winning Cabernet Sauvignon came from 3-year-old vines from a 4-year old winery in an area long deemed unsuitable for growing such a grape. The winemaker was Warren Winiarski, a political science professor from the University of California. Winiarski happens to be Polish for "winemaker's son," and in the 1960s, he decided to take his name seriously and learn the trade from Robert Mondavi (see 274). A lover of Cabernet Sauvignon, Winiarski then scoured California looking for the right terrain. In 1969 he tried a homemade wine from a particular area in Napa Valley called Stag's Leap, and he knew at once that he had found his sweet spot. The rest is history.

Today Stag's Leap Wine Cellars is arguably the most prestigious winery in the United States. Because Stag's Leap is a separate valley within Napa Valley, other wineries have taken the same name hoping to cash in on Winiarski's success. The

The 1976 blind tasting that awakened the world to California wines rated a Stag's Leap Cab above its French counterpart.

original Stag's Leap Wine Cellars is easy to miss, however; look for a large barrel-top sign sitting in a bed of flowers at its entrance, on a road known as the Silverado Trail, 7 miles (11km) north of Napa. The building is small and unassuming, with cream-colored walls and arched doorways. Its low-key tasting room feels somewhat cramped and dark, but on sunny days they open the large doors onto a pretty patio, which brightens the place up enormously. The tasting includes the winery's lower bracket wines. To try the good stuff—the SLV Cabernet Sauvignon that went down so well in France—you will have to buy the bottle. The Cask 23 Cabernet Sauvignon is the very best, produced only in good years and originally kept in a special barrel numbered 23. Recently the winery opened up its cave complex, a series of austere domed cellars that lead to a round room with a fascinating Foucault's pendulum.

This apparatus, invented by a Frenchman to prove the rotation of the earth, is somewhat fitting in a winery that tilted the world of wine firmly toward the west.

ⓘ **Stag's Leap Wine Cellars,** 5766 Silverado Trail, Napa (📞 **866/422-7523;** www.cask23.com).

✈ San Francisco International (54 miles/ 87km).

🛏 $$$ **Harvest Inn,** One Main St., St. Helena (📞 **707/963-9463;** www.harvest inn.com). $$$ **Yountville Inn,** 6462 Washington St., Yountville (📞 **707/944-5600;** www.yountvilleinn.com).

The Hess Collection Winery

The Artist's Palate

Napa Valley, California

Donald Hess nurtures his artists like a winemaker nurtures his wine. Just as a winemaker may have a sleepless night during harvest worrying about his grapes,

The Hess Collection Winery doubles as exhibition space for the owner's art collection.

Hess is known to toss and turn and wake up in a fever declaring "I must have that piece!" He then adopts an artist and supports his or her work throughout a lifetime, nudging and encouraging the creative process toward greatness—much as he does with his wine.

This Swiss beer heir, who went on to make his own second fortune in mineral water and hotels, could have done what every rich retiree does—play golf and sail his yacht into the sunset. Instead, he developed a healthy obsession with both art and wine. Pursuing those passions, he has been building wineries and galleries in the most unlikely of places.

One such place is the Hess Collection Winery on Mount Veeder, in a secluded part of Napa Valley. This is no small detour from the Rte. 29 merry-go-round; to get here, you must take a winding road that travels over rolling hills with no end in sight. It's a beautiful drive, though, and well worth the time, for the destination is a pretty ivy-covered visitor center that resembles an old country manor. Headless statues stand in groups, contemplating a lily pond that would not look out of place on the top of a box of luxury chocolates.

Inside, however, it's no chocolate box. You'll be viewing a serious collection of modern art, covering all mediums, in a purpose-built gallery with three light-filled floors of white walls and bare rafters. Oil paintings, bronzes, video displays, digital art, interactive installations—there is enough here to absorb at least 2 hours of your time, and that's before you have even started on the winery.

A thorough tour of the winemaking operations takes you through the crushing facility, the barrel room, the labs, and the bottling facility. It ends in a tasting (described as a "tour of the palate") where you basically treat your mouth like an art gallery, exploring every sensory corner between tongue and nose. Wines like their Dry Creek Zinfandel or late harvest Chardonnay will kick life into taste buds you never knew you had, and have you declaring "I want that wine!"

(i) **Hess Collection Winery,** 4411 Redwood Rd., Napa (© **707/255-1144;** www.hesscollection.com).

✈ San Francisco International Airport (67 miles/107km).

🛏 $$$ **Harvest Inn,** One Main St., St. Helena (© **707/963-9463;** www.harvestinn.com). $$$ **Yountville Inn,** 6462 Washington St., Yountville (© **707/944-5600;** www.yountvilleinn.com).

Robert Mondavi Winery
A Man with a Mission
Napa Valley, California

Robert Mondavi is a legend in California winemaking. His life reads like a Napa Valley saga, a vineyard version of the American dream: The grandson of Italian sharecroppers, he revolutionized the wine industry, built a multibillion-dollar empire, and teamed up with European aristocrats to make wine that created hysteria and sold at $24,000 a case.

They say all good wine starts in the vineyard, and the same could be said of Mondavi's life (he died in 2008). He came from a family of grape growers. His father cleverly dodged Prohibition by selling home-brew wine kits direct to the amateur winemaker, who was allowed a 200-gallon wine limit. It was assumed that Robert and his brother Peter would also work in the wine industry, and they subsequently took over the Charles Krug winery in the early sixties. However, business differences and a sibling rivalry—one that could match the best soap-opera plot of *Falcon Crest*—resulted in a famous fistfight between the two brothers over a mink coat. Robert left the company in 1965 to start out on his own.

Hardworking, charismatic, and tough, Robert Mondavi introduced pioneering winemaking methods that are now taken for granted. Inspired by the cleanliness of the dairy industry, he introduced stainless-steel tanks and insisted on new French oak barrels and cold fermentation. With a flair for marketing, he pushed the concept of single varietal wine that would so intrigue the consumer and confuse the traditionalists who always presumed a wine should be named after place of origin rather than grape varietal.

Nowadays Mondavi's legacy reaches far and wide, but it begins in a beautiful mission-style winery that has become a Napa Valley landmark. The immaculate building, complete with bell tower, has a wide, arched entrance and ample grounds adorned with statues and fountains, surrounded by green hills and vineyards that

A tasting at Robert Mondavi Winery in Napa.

slope over the horizon. The complex has a variety of tasting venues, staffed by a troop of wine educators who take the wine novice by the hand and demonstrate how it is done. There is even a mini-vineyard with grape varietals to illustrate their differences. Inside you'll find a long, vaulted wine cellar with wine-striped barrels and an ample tasting room that serves wine between nibbles of risotto balls, bread, and cheese. It is worth paying for the "Pleasure in a Glass" tour. Though a little steep at $55, it includes five-star treatment and the chance to taste the winery's top Reserve and Spotlight labels.

The huge crowds and scripted tours may make you feel as if you have taken a wrong turn and entered a Disneyland of wine. Yet even the most cynical wine snob will find it hard not to enjoy relaxing in front of the open fire, or wandering the

beautiful grounds, or just sitting back with a glass of Reserve Cabernet to people-watch. While touring the facility, you will come face to face with a poster of the man himself, wearing a suit of corks—a fitting tribute to someone who was both flamboyant and unstoppable.

ⓘ **Robert Mondavi Winery,** 7801 St. Helena Hwy., Oakville (✆ **707/259-9463;** www.robertmondaviwinery.com).

✈ San Francisco International (71 miles/114km).

🛏 $$$ **Napa Valley Lodge,** 2230 Madison St., Yountville (✆ **707/944-2468;** www.NapaValleyLodge.com). $$$ **Maison Fleurie,** 6529 Yount St., Yountville (✆ **707/944-2056;** www.foursisters.com).

Domaine Carneros

It's Good to be the King

Napa Valley, California

Put yourself in the worst mood before visiting this winery. Prepare yourself for all the Napa Valley clichés about pretentious surroundings and McWinery architecture—this is, after all, a fake château built in 1987, with a faux Louis XV–style interior. What is a French champagne house doing in California anyway? Undoubtedly it will be full of tourists who know nothing about wine. You are determined not to like it. You will not be seduced.

You storm past a pair of very pretty wrought-iron gates and up toward this impressive mansion on a hill. The building is huge, with cream-colored stonework and red brick trim. Steep, dramatic steps sweep up through an immaculate hedge garden fringed with flowers and vines. You stop to catch your breath on the large, spacious terrace on top, and take in spectacular views of the corduroy hills of the wine country below. You momentarily regret not bringing your camera—but then you spot the doorman in topcoat and are about to remark to yourself, "How tacky"—until he flashes you a welcoming smile.

You enter a room of tall windows, high ceilings, and blue cushioned wicker chairs. The piped music reminds you of a hotel lobby, but you must admit the room looks marvelous and welcoming. A friendly guide approaches and says you are just in time for the champagne tour. You want to say no, but before you know it you have a flute of sparkling in your hand and are being whisked out into the vineyard.

The guide is surprisingly upbeat and knowledgeable. You learn that the winery belongs to the Taittinger family, the blue-bloods of the Champagne region in France. The building is an exact replica of their historical Château de la Marquettere in France, once home to a philosopher called Cazotte (beheaded in the French Revolution), later Marshall Joffre's command center during World War I, and now the headquarters of the Taittinger sparkling wine empire.

Inside the American replica, you sit down in the elegant tasting room and enjoy flights of champagne paired with platters of brie, cashew nuts, and dried pears. The service is outstanding and the champagne great. You decide on another flight of wines, this time served with caviar. You note the fireplace in the private tasting room and think how cozy that will be in winter.

But it is sunny today, so you step outside and soak up the majestic view. You sip your Pinot Noir and think: "It's good to be the king."

ⓘ **Domaine Carneros,** 1240 Duhig Rd., Napa (✆ **800/716-2788;** www.domaine-carneros.com).

✈ San Francisco International (59 miles/95km).

🛏 $$$ **Napa Valley Lodge,** 2230 Madison St., Yountville (✆ **800/368-2468** or 707/944-2468; www.napavalleylodge.com). $$$ **Napa River Inn,** 500 Main St., Napa (✆ **877/251-8500** or 707/251-8500; www.napariverinn.com).

Beringer Vineyards

Welcome to Napa!

Napa Valley, California

An elm-lined avenue carries you through a 215-acre (87-hectare) estate of sculpted gardens, manicured lawns, and elaborate fountains, up to an ornate Victorian mansion. Slated roof turrets crown magnificent stonework, which in turn frames beautiful stained-glass windows. "Clark Gable graced these gables!" enthuses the guide—and you can well believe it. With its walnut furniture and Art Nouveau wood paneling inside, the mansion exudes old-world charm, fit for a star of the silver screen.

Situated more than halfway up lush green Napa Valley, this classic winery is the oldest and most historical, and arguably the most beautiful, estate in the region. It attracts huge crowds, and is even besieged from above by hot-air balloonists. You cannot help wishing you had the place to yourself. You cannot help wishing you owned it.

Beringer was founded by two German brothers in 1868, and it's easy to assume that these lucky fellows were simply in the right place at the right time. But the winery's history is as rocky as its vineyard soil; its splendid existence today was never assured. A 19th-century wine glut and problems with transport set the winery off to a shaky start; next came negative perceptions about American wine, along with the vine root disease phylloxera. In the 1920s, Prohibition seemed the final nail in the coffin.

But Beringer survived and thrived (they sidestepped the alcohol ban by producing sacramental wine). A gravity-driven facility was created, with 1,200 feet (360m) of hand-chiseled tunnels extending into the hillside to contain much of the industrial portion of the concern. No longer a family affair, the Beringer business now includes 20 wineries; there are two main visitor buildings on the sprawling estate, as well as a reconstructed carriage house and a culinary arts center.

Always a leader, Beringer was the first in Napa Valley to conduct tours (way back in 1934) and tastings (in 1956). Visitors can choose between a free, self-guided tour that is somewhat restricted, or a more expensive tour that takes you into the caves and cellars; the pricier tour includes a private tasting in a beautiful upstairs room, which is much more relaxing than the crowded barlike tasting room down below. Barrel tastings are also offered, as are wine and cheese pairings. If you are feeling adventurous, try the white Zinfandel. Or for a taste of the wine that has made the vineyard famous try the highly regarded Private Reserve Chardonnay.

Beringer is such a popular winery for visitors, you may have to contend with crowds and screaming babies—but never fear, the place is so big, there is always plenty of room for escape. Wandering around those lawns, under those shade trees—that's the most memorable part of this winery tour.

ⓘ **Beringer,** 2000 Main St., St. Helena (✆ **707/967-4412;** www.beringer.com).

✈ San Francisco International (77 miles/124km).

🛏 $$$ **Meadowood Napa Valley,** 900 Meadowood Lane, St. Helena (✆ **707/963-3646;** www.meadowood.com). $$$ **Harvest Inn,** 1 Main St., St. Helena (✆ **707/963-9463;** www.harvestinn.com).

Beringer Vineyards in St. Helena, Napa County.

Sterling Vineyards

An Englishman in Napa

Napa Valley, California

Peter Newton embodied all the peculiarities associated with an English gentleman living abroad. It might not seem eccentric now to own a winery in Napa Valley, but it was back in 1964, when there were only 25 in the whole valley, as opposed to the current bounty of more than 300—those famous hills were more used to grazing cattle than blazing vineyards. And then the winery Newton built was hardly conventional. Inspired by the white hilltop villages on the Greek island Mykonos, the Oxford-educated paper broker constructed a monastic-style edifice on top of a volcanic hill, complete with brilliant, whitewashed ramparts and simple bell towers guarding a sun-drenched roof terrace. Church bells transplanted from a bombed-out London chapel chime every 30 minutes; lush foliage surrounds the buildings (a passionate gardener, Newton later started another venture call Newton Vineyard in St. Helen, which showcases 13 stunning theme landscapes).

And while there is a beautifully landscaped driveway that goes to the top, visitors to Sterling Vineyards are instead ferried upwards from the parking lot on an aerial tram, gliding over sculpted gardens to reach the winery entrance at 300 feet (90m). Prince Charles made an even more dramatic arrival in 1977 while visiting "our

7 Places to Eat in . . . Napa Valley

Along a 35-mile (56km) stretch of Hwy. 29 north of San Francisco, the hillsides look precisely grooved with slope-hugging vineyards that produce some of the world's finest wines. The heart of California's wine country, Napa Valley is a beautiful stretch of rolling countryside—witness all those hot-air balloons overhead, with tourists sipping champagne as they gawk at the views. With its abundance of vineyard tours, wine tastings, luxury inns, and spas—it's only to be expected that sybaritic Napa Valley would also have superb food.

Ubuntu dishes are made with vegetables from the restaurant's biodynamic garden.

At the southern end of the valley in Napa, the region's gateway town, the wine-country culinary scene starts off on a wholesome, organic note with 278 Ubuntu (1140 Main St.; © **707/251-5656;** www.ubuntunapa. com). Ubuntu describes itself as a vegetable restaurant, rather than just a vegetarian restaurant. Chef Jeremy Fox is staunchly committed to cooking with local farm produce, much of it from Ubuntu's own biodynamic garden. With creative dishes such as poblano stuffed with smoked corn and chèvre, or French bean and grilled *panzanella,* even meat-eaters leave satisfied. The restaurant itself—which is attached to a yoga studio—looks sleek and contemporary, though it's completely made from recycled wood and reclaimed furnishings, reducing Ubuntu's carbon footprint.

The next town up the valley, Yountville rose to culinary fame years ago with Thomas Keller's spectacular The French Laundry (see 141). Not everyone can swing a French Laundry reservation, but you can also sample Thomas Keller's food at his more casual brasserie 279 Bouchon (6534 Washington St.; © **707/944-8037;** www. bouchonbistro.com). Expect superb renditions of French onion soup, steak *frites,* steamed mussels, croque madame, and other French classics (try the expensive and rich foie gras pâté, made on-site). The former chef at nearby Auberge de Soleil (see 70), Richard Reddington now presides over his own stunning restaurant, 280 Redd (6480 Washington St.; © **707/944-2222;** www.reddnapavalley.com). The pristine minimalist decor of the dining room sets off memorable dishes based on local produce, such as sashimi hamachi with edamame, cucumber, ginger, and sticky rice, or glazed pork belly with apple purée, burdock, and soy caramel. On the grounds of the Domaine Chandon winery, 281 Etoile (1 California Dr.; © **800/736-2892** or 707/204-7529; www.chandon.com) is the wave of the future. Etoile hold its own with any stand-alone restaurant in town, with dishes such as tuna tartare with sous-vide yolk, pink lady apple, and Persian cucumber, or a Madeira-braised veal with sweetbreads, sorrel, and red mustard, served in a casually elegant glass-enclosed dining room under a barrel-vaulted wood ceiling. All dishes are carefully paired with Chandon wines, of course.

A short drive farther north, St. Helena brims with small-town charm, great shopping, and fine food. At high-end 282 **Terra** (1345 Railroad Ave.; © **707/963-8931;** www.terrarestaurant.com), East meets West in a romantic fieldstone-walled dining room where Japanese chef Hiro Sone serves Asian-inspired dishes featuring California's agricultural bounty: broiled sake-marinated cod with shrimp dumplings and shiso broth, or grilled quail with bacon bread pudding, sautéed foie gras, figs, and *vin cotto* sauce. On a humbler scale, the gourmet burger shack 283 **Taylor's Automatic Refresher** (933 Main St.; © **707/963-3486;** www.taylorsrefresher.com) has been around since 1949. Taylor's updated diner menu—ahi tuna burgers, tacos, salads, and classic shakes—draws huge lines of tourists, who love ordering at the counter or feasting alfresco at picnic tables.

At the top of the valley, the hot-springs spa town Calistoga still has a sort of scroungy Wild West appeal. Right on the main street, the 284 **All Seasons Café** (1400 Lincoln Ave.; © **707/942-9111;** www.allseasonsnapavalley.net) maintains the laid-back aura of a wine bar. Dishes include crispy skin chicken with black truffle chicken *jus* or cornmeal-crusted diver scallops with summer vegetable succotash. The wine shop next door supports the bistro's wine list, which is impressive—because, after all, this *is* Napa Valley.

✈ San Francisco International (75 miles/121km).

🛏 $$$ **Cedar Gables Inn,** 486 Coombs St., Napa (© **800/309-7969** or 707/224-7969; www.cedargablesinn.com). $$ **Calistoga Spa Hot Springs,** 1006 Washington St., Calistoga (© **866/822-5772** or 707/942-6269; www.calistogaspa.com).

Thomas Keller's French Laundry is a destination unto itself.

man in Napa": He landed by helicopter on the grassy knoll, coincidentally known as Charlie's Hill.

Located close to the quaint and laid-back town of Calistoga, this winery is picturesque and popular. Upon disembarking from the grape gondola, you can take a self-guided tour of the immaculate facility, starting in the foyer where a refreshing glass of Pinot Gris is served. Plaques and flatscreen TVs guide you through several exhibit rooms that explicate the winery's history and the winemaking process. Eventually you exit onto that sunny roof terrace, where you can enjoy a glass of Chardonnay and spectacular views of the valley. Next you'll visit the barrel room, where a video explains the bottling process, and then you'll enter an adjoining building to find a tiny wine store and tasting lounge. Here you can sit down and sip a Cabernet Sauvignon and a delicious dessert wine.

The experience can be somewhat eerie if the winery is empty, and robotic when it is crowded, which is more common. But everything is meticulously well done, right down to the strategically placed children's crayon books in the tasting room. The wine is not bad either. And then there is the view—you really feel as if you are tasting on top of the world.

ⓘ **Sterling Vineyards,** 1111 Dunaweal Lane, Calistoga (✆ **707/942-3344;** www. sterlingvineyards.com).

✈ San Francisco International (84 miles/ 134km).

🛏 $$$ **Hideaway Cottages,** 1412 Fairway, Calistoga (✆ **707/942-4108**). $$ **EuroSpa & Inn,** 1202 Pine St., Calistoga (✆ **707/942-6829;** www.eurospa.com).

West Coast U.S. **285**

Clos Pegase

Art in a Glass

Napa Valley, California

Clos Pegase winery has the most expensive guides in the world. A Henry Moore greets visitors at the entrance; a Salvador Dalí ushers them along to the barrel cellar; and a Francis Bacon joins them for a drink in the tasting room. As visitors stroll around this templelike complex, a team of the greatest modern artists are constantly at hand, eager to sketch out, portray, and illustrate that winemaking is not an exact science but is in fact a very fine, weird, and wonderful art.

Many wineries look the same, but not this one. As soon as you enter the grounds of Clos Pegase you know you are in for something different. A black 6-foot (1.8m) thumb protrudes from the vineyard ground, prompting queues of visitors to pose for a photo with their own thumbs-up—interactive art indeed. The Italianate sculpture

garden with some very colorful pieces leads to a long building that looks like a block of ice cream from your favorite childhood memory: yellow and pink with a blue stripe down the middle. Is this a winery, or a chocolate factory owned by a guy called Charlie?

Inside, things become a little more solemn. An attractive reception room leads to endless vaulted underground chambers with back-lit niches and alcoves displaying ancient relics and artifacts. Bacchus raises his leering head in several guises, accompanied by wine-themed cupids telling you "art inspires, evokes . . . ponders, just like wine."

This marriage of grape and canvas can be traced from the wedding of Jan and Mitsuko Shrem. The Israeli-born UCLA graduate met his artist wife while on vacation in

Japan; he hung around the land of the rising sun long enough to raise a fortune, and then promptly retired to Bordeaux to study winemaking. But 30 years of art collecting left Jan and Shrem with a problem: Where to put it? They ended up indulging both passions by building this art gallery-cum-concept winery on 450 acres (182 hectares) of vineyards a couple of miles south of Calistoga. Building the winery into the side of the hill, they installed 20,000 feet (6,000m) of cave cellars and a visitor center.

Because the winery is at the northern end of the Napa wine circuit, it does not get too crowded. You can sit and eat in an elegant dining room with crystal chandeliers, marble floors, and mahogany paneling; in the bright tasting room, there are tall windows and arresting pieces of art.

The wine is arresting too—a nice, dry, oaky Chardonnay served along with an interesting port called *hommage*. Often cheese and other nibbles are available. The lawn, lined with Italian cypress trees, just begs to be picnicked on.

ⓘ **Clos Pegase,** 1060 Dunaweal Lane, Calistoga (✆ **707/942-4981;** www.clos pegase.com).

✈ San Francisco International Airport (84 miles/135km).

🛏 $$$ **Hideaway Cottages,** 1412 Fair Way, Calistoga (✆ **707/942-4108**). $$$ **Cottage Grove Inn,** 1711 Lincoln Ave., Calistoga (✆ **707/942-8400;** www.cottage grove.com).

286 West Coast U.S.

Arrowood Vineyards

The Perfectionists

Sonoma, California

When Richard Arrowood wrote off 60% of his 1989 vintage, it was like committing commercial suicide. In business only 3 years, he could not have created a bigger setback for his winery if he had doused his barrel room in gasoline and put a match to it. Yet the fact was, his "vintage from hell" had produced an inferior fruit, and he was loath to put his name to it. That's the sort of integrity that has made Arrowood one of California's most renowned and venerable winemakers today, with his classic varietal wines coveted by the most fanatical and knowledgeable oenophiles.

Arrowood first made his name during his 40-year career at Chateau St. Jean, where he created seven different Chardonnays in 1 year and became a pioneer of single-vineyard wines. He then started his own winery in 1986 with his wife, Alis. The couple's approach is very hands-on—the Arrowoods are not afraid to push

up their shirt sleeves and personally oversee the entire process, from the hand-picked harvest to the crush and the fermentation. They're great believers in winemaking restraint, always choosing methods that simply let the wine express its own *terroir*.

The winery is in the eastern hills of Sonoma County, a beautiful wine-growing region in the northern San Francisco Bay area, to the west of Napa Valley. Sonoma tends to attract wine lovers eager to avoid the madness of Napa; Sonoma is more laid back, rural, and casual, with less traffic (and the added bonus of beaches). The Arrowoods's winery consists of two New England–style farmhouses set at the end of a short driveway on a gentle slope. One is the production facility and the other a bright and airy visitor's center, graced by a wraparound veranda. The tasting room has a country-kitchen feel and a welcoming simplicity; a map collection hangs on the wall and a stone fireplace takes the chill out of the autumn air. However, the main attraction is tasting wine while seated in wicker chairs on the veranda—make sure to bring a camera to capture the view. You'll see a flower garden in the foreground, hillsides of well-combed organic vineyards, and hawks and turkey buzzards circling overhead. A glass of delicious merlot completes the picture.

Say cheese.

Snap.

Perfect.

ⓘ **Arrowood Vineyards,** 14347 Sonoma Hwy., Glen Ellen (✆ **707/935-2600;** www.arrowoodvineyards.com).

✈ San Francisco International (71 miles/114km).

🛏 $$$ **MacArthur Place,** 29 E. MacArthur St., Sonoma (✆ **707/938-2929;** www.macarthurplace.com). $$ **Relais du Soleil,** 1210 Nuns Canyon Rd., Glen Ellen (✆ **707/833-6264;** www.relaisdusoleil.com).

West Coast U.S.

287

Benziger Family Winery
The Biodynamic Bandwagon
Sonoma, California

A big red tractor pulls you on an open carriage through tidy roads that meander between gorgeous vineyards. Up and over idyllic green hills it carries you, with wildflowers bordering wooden fences on either side. Nature is let run in all its glory. The 45-minute ride is embracing and exhilarating (blankets are supplied in the chilly winter months); it may even tempt you to give up the city job and take up farming. Benziger Family Winery is in fact a working farm, set in a sprawling estate in a pastoral paradise. It is serene, tranquil, and unpretentious.

In recent years a quiet revolution has been taking place in California wine country. Vineyards have always looked beautiful from a distance, but conventional wisdom dictated they should be a controlled, barren monoculture. Unpleasant chemicals such as pesticides, insecticides, and fungicides were used to keep nature at arms' length. Unfortunately, this played havoc

with the natural ecosystem, encouraging soil erosion and water waste. The organic movement wagged a green finger at these bad practices, and many winemakers began experimenting with sustainable vineyard management. They realized that there was a better way of doing things—and guess what? It results in better wine.

Benziger is at the forefront of this green revolution. As you tour the 85-acre (34-hectare) estate in Glen Ellen, the guide points out that weeds, flowers, and birds are actually encouraged. Unwanted insects are fended off with wasps and owls. Wetlands have been constructed to save water and encourage biodiversity. Solar-powered pumps and parking lights keep down carbon emissions, as does the biofuel that runs the red tractor.

When you enter Benziger's tasting room, you will see the fruit of their labor. A trellised walkway leads to a beautiful white clapboard house with gray shutters,

All the wines are biodynamic at Benziger in Glen Ellen, Sonoma County.

besieged by flowers and plants. A shaded patio with wooden seating overlooks the hills and vines. Peacocks vie for your attention, and there's a children's playground close by to occupy those too young to sample the wine. You sip your glass of Benziger Tribute, which scored 90-plus points with Robert Parker and *Wine Spectator,* and you feel good, you feel excited, you feel . . . biodynamic.

ⓘ **Benziger Family Winery,** 1883 London Ranch Rd., Glen Ellen (**800/989-8890** or 707/935-3000; www.benziger. com).

✈ San Francisco International (70 miles/112km).

⊨ $$$ **Ledson Hotel**, 480 First St. E, Sonoma (**707/996-9779;** www.ledson hotel.com). $$ **Inn at Sonoma,** 630 Broadway, Sonoma (**707/939-1340;** www.innatsonoma.com).

288 West Coast U.S.

Martinelli Winery

Serendipity

Sonoma, California

The story of Martinelli rings like a tale of happy accidents, good fortune, and hard work. It all began when 19-year-old Giuseppe Martinelli set eyes on 16-year-old Luisa Vellutin in Tuscany in 1897. The love-struck teenagers eloped to America and worked as farmhands in Forrestville, California. Borrowing money from a wood-cutter, they bought a plot of land on a steep hill. Giuseppe, who knew a little about winemaking, decided to plant some Zinfandel grapes as well as grow apples.

The family prospered and became expert fruit growers. When Giuseppe passed away in 1918, Luisa was left with four children, the youngest being 12-year-old Leno. He decided he wanted to continue farming, much to the derision of his brothers—they said only a jackass would work that steep hill.

Fast-forward 80 years. The Martinellis have done well from growing grapes, although they themselves never made wine; they own some of the best vineyards in Sonoma, including the impossibly inclined Jackass Hill, upon which tractors habitually tip over. Leno's son Lee is walking some land he has recently purchased, and ahead he spots a couple having a picnic. They strike up a conversation over the fence. It turns out that his new neighbor, the woman, is winemaker Helen Turley. Sonoma's greatest grape grower had just bumped into one of California's greatest winemakers. The meeting turned out to be a fortunate coincidence; a friendship began, and the Martinellis soon decided to start making wine, with Turley as their consultant.

Fast forward another 20 years. Martinelli is now one of the most prestigious wineries in the United States; its wine is in such high demand that you have to go on a waiting list to purchase the top labels. Jackass Hill Zinfandel—named after that famous hill—is a sought-after California cult wine, rated by Robert Parker as "one of the best." Yet it is still very much a family operation; the owners have not lost sight of their humble origins, housing their winery in a down-to-earth old red hop barn set on a picturesque hill in the Russian River Valley. Here you enter a country store–style tasting room packed with gifts and gourmet local products. The tasting is generous—the winery often slips in one of its top wines to try for free.

The hillside behind the winery is an ideal spot for a picnic, but be careful. You never know whom you might meet.

ⓘ **Martinelli Winery,** 3360 River Rd., Windsor (✆ **800/346-1627;** www.martinelli winery.com).

✈ San Francisco International (83 miles/ 133km).

🛏 $$$ **Ledson Hotel,** 480 First St. E., Sonoma (✆ **707/996-9779;** www.ledson hotel.com). $$ **El Pueblo Inn,** 896 W. Napa St., Sonoma (✆ **707/996-3651;** www.elpuebloinn.com).

West Coast U.S. **289**

Langtry Estate Vineyards

The Wild, Wild West

Lake County, California

Lillie Langtry was a Victorian society beauty who was anything but a repressed Victorian. This flamboyant British actress went through lovers like her winery went through grapes—among others, she counted the future King of England, Edward II, as a pillow mate. She turned heads and caused scandal wherever she went (much like her friend Oscar Wilde), and when England found her too hot to handle, she crossed the Atlantic and took America by storm. The male public was obsessed by Langtry; Judge Roy Bean named a town in Texas after her when he spotted her portrait on the wrapping of a bar of soap.

In 1888, Lillie bought a vineyard estate in California, sight unseen, and arrived at St. Helena in a lavish private railroad car. A fleet of stagecoaches carried her and her entourage to the Guenoc Valley, in Lake County, north of Napa Valley. There she set up shop, determined to make "the greatest claret in the country."

Lake County—named after Clear Lake, the largest lake in California—nowadays is a farming community of rolling green hills, with only the occasional vineyard, but in

Langtry Estate Vineyards, founded in 1888 by the actress Lillie Langtry.

the early 20th century it had the reputation of making the best American wine, and it was dotted with vine plantations. Prohibition put a stop to this, however; the vines were ripped up and replaced with walnut trees and pear orchards. But vineyards have now returned, and the Langtry estate is one of the biggest and most historical—it's so big, the 35-square-mile (56 sq. km) property has its own appellation.

With its large meadows of wildflowers, the sprawling estate is more ranch land than wine country. Rivers meander through a pastoral paradise that has a rural, untouched charm. It is definitely out of the way and off the beaten wine-lover's path, 90 miles (145km) north of San Francisco. Various buildings are scattered around the property, including a grandiose plantation-style mansion and a spectacular long ivy-covered walkway, where creepers entwine thick wooden posts towards an explosion of flowers and foliage above, shading a long line of picnic tables below. The winery itself is a meticulously reconstructed barn, long, dark, and low, with enchanting views of a lake known as the Detert Reservoir, home to heron, egret, ducks, and geese. In the handsome tasting room, you can try the winery's extensive list of wines, its best being a refreshing Sauvignon Blanc and un-oaked Chardonnay.

The setting's peace and tranquillity belie the estate's glamorous beginnings. As for Lilly, she did make some of the best claret in the country, but the social scene must have bored her. She sold up in 1906 and moved to Monaco.

ⓘ **Langtry Estate Vineyards,** 21000 Butts Canyon Rd., Middletown (ⓒ **707/987-2385;** www.langtryestate.com).

✈ San Francisco International (99 miles/159km).

🛏 $$$ **Calistoga Ranch,** 580 Lommel Rd., Calistoga (ⓒ **707/254-2800;** www.calistogaranch.com). $$$ **Hideaway Cottages,** 1412 Fair Way, Calistoga (ⓒ **707/942-4108**).

Concannon Vineyard

Thank God for Sacramental Wine

Livermore Valley, California

It's a long way from the windswept rocky Irish island of Inishmaan to the red canyons and ridges of Livermore Valley in California, lying just east of the San Francisco Bay area. Jim Concannon made that long trip way back in 1865, traveling across the western wilderness of the United States in a covered wagon with his wife and 10 children. Once he reached San Francisco, he became a successful businessman, yet he remained forever restless. After a conversation with the local archbishop, who bemoaned the lack of good sacramental wine, Jim—being a good Roman Catholic—decided the clergy should suffer no more. He bought 40 rocky acres (16 hectares) near Livermore and enrolled in UC Davis to study winemaking. In 1883 he produced his first vintage. The priests seemed to like it—God was happy and so was Jim.

One hundred and twenty-five years later, grandson Jim Concannon is still making God happy—not to mention scores of wine drinkers who don't have to wait for communion to enjoy Concannon's Bordeaux- and Rhone-style wines. The family's 200-acre (81-hectare) vineyard is now one of the most famous in the country, attracting thousand of visitors every year to its historical winery. Entering through an impressive stone gateway, you'll travel upward through a field of vines set snugly between orange hills and canyons. The winery itself is a neat, ivy-covered building with brick gables and wood sidings; there is a bell set into a niche in the wall and an antique wine-press out front. A trellised walkway passes sculpted hedges and wrought-iron seating toward a warm, inviting tasting room, with floor-to-ceiling woodwork and a Turkish carpet rolled down the middle of the floor. Two large bar counters and brass chandeliers give the room a laid-back, cozy atmosphere.

After a tour of the vineyards and cellars, visitors gather here to try an excellent Reserve Syrah and a grape called Petite Sirah that the winery is famous for. Cheese is served, as well as chocolate fudge with dessert wine. You learn from the guide that not only does the winery boast the first Irish winemaker, but in the 1950s it also had the first female winemaker, a Hungarian ballet dancer called Katherine Vajdawho. Another milestone for Concannon Vineyard.

ⓘ **Concannon Vineyard,** 4590 Tesla Rd., Livermore (☎ **925/456-2505;** www.concannonvineyard.com).

✈ San Francisco International (50 miles/80km).

🛏 $$$ **Hyatt Summerfield Suites,** 4545 Chabot Dr., Pleasanton (☎ **925/730-0070;** www.hyattsummerfieldsuites.com). $$ **Rose Hotel,** 807 Main St., Pleasanton (☎ **925/846-8802;** www.rosehotel.net).

Wente Vineyards
The Chardonnay Clone
Livermore Valley, California

We all have to start somewhere. The story of this winery begins with a stormy transatlantic voyage in 1912.

An unnamed nephew of California winemaker Carl Wente was on a mission. He carried with him a delicate cutting clipped from a Chardonnay vine at Montpellier University, from the south of France, as requested by his uncle. Not only did he have to brave the icebergs of the North Atlantic (this was the year the *Titanic* went down, after all), but then he had to negotiate the bustle of New York and catch a train across the States, all the while ensuring that the tender shoot survived. It did. That California Chardonnay you have in your hand now is most likely a direct descendant of this plant—what became known as the Wente Clone is responsible for 80% of all Chardonnay in the United States.

The winery, just like the plant clipping, is a survivor (it was one of the few to live through Prohibition, by making vinegar) and what started as 25 acres is now a 3,000-acre (1,214-hectare) grape empire situated in the Livermore Valley in Northern California. The Small Lot Eric's Chardonnay comes from a carefully tended small vineyard on the estate, as does the Small Lot Syrah. There are two tasting rooms, a restaurant, an events center, and a vineyard golf course. The Mission-style architecture has been named a historical landmark; it's now surrounded by beautiful landscaped gardens, Technicolor flower beds, and sycamore groves. That romantic setting in a picturesque canyon has made it particularly popular with wedding parties, and in the summer months the grounds host live concerts, showcasing mostly '80s nostalgia bands that attract a genteel crowd. The mosh pit becomes a nosh pit where diners sit at round tables in front of the stage and toss their salads to the rhythm of UB40.

A 45-minute drive east of San Francisco, Wente is the last stop on the winery circuit in that area but is certainly worth the scenic drive. Not one to sit on its laurels (in this case vines), the winery has some innovative attractions to stimulate even the most world-weary wine tourist—events like a delicious mustard tasting that would bring any jaded palate back to life (try the smoky garlic), or movie nights in the barrel room, showing (of course) everybody's favorite film: *Titanic*.

ⓘ **Wente Vineyards,** 5565 Tesla Rd., Livermore (ⓒ **925/456-2305;** www.wente vineyards.com).

✈ San Francisco International (49 miles/79km).

🛏 $$$ **Hyatt Summerfield Suites,** 4545 Chabot Dr., Pleasanton (ⓒ **925/730-0070;** www.hyattsummerfieldsuites.com). $$$ **Rose Hotel,** 807 Main St., Pleasanton (ⓒ **925/846-8802;** www.rosehotel.net).

Ridge Vineyards

The Philosopher's Stone

Santa Cruz Mountains, California

Nobody said the Holy Grail would be easy to find. A twisting and narrow road climbs along steep canyons and quarries, with huge boulders upheaved by earthquakes threatening to block your way. The rugged terrain is punctuated by oak woods and redwood forests. There are shimmering views of Silicon Valley below.

Suddenly a winery appears tucked in a mountain fold, perched atop a ridge. Winery? It looks more like a roadside barn, the large brown sash windows just hinting that it may be something more. Inside you'll find a long L-shaped bar in a white-walled main room with a sloping ceiling. Big ceiling fans circle above; what passes for decor is simply a shabby carpet and some old barrels. Is this it? Is this Ridge Vineyards? The Holy Grail of California Cabernet Sauvignon and Zinfandel?

Wine has been blamed for many an accidental pregnancy, so it's amusing to note that this winery was founded in the 1960s by the same Stanford scientists who invented the birth control pill. Yet the winery was not truly born until 1969, when professor of philosophy and winemaking legend Paul Draper joined. Famous for giving California wine "a sense of place," by the mid-'70s Draper was raising eyebrows and flaring the nostrils of wine lovers all around the world. He shocked French wine critics when his Cabernet Sauvignon rivaled the best of France at the now-infamous Judgement of Paris blind tasting in 1976, coming in second right after the Stag's Leap Cabernet (see 272). What's more, at a 30th-anniversary repetition of the tasting event, that same 1971 vintage Cabernet from Ridge took first place.

Thus was born a California superstar wine. And yet the winery is so *not* Hollywood—it is hardy, small, and unpretentious, much like the area surrounding it. The unassuming tasting room leads to some lovely grounds with picnic tables affording a great view of San Francisco Bay and the terraced vineyard slopes. It is mellow, laid back, and casual—the only thing that comes across as serious is the wine itself. Even the bottles' labels are stark and minimalist, listing on the back exact percentages of each grape and a detailed summary of the particular process that went into this particular wine. There is no mention of what you should taste, no gushing adjectives describing red fruit and boysenberries. That is for you to decide. That is your Holy Grail.

ⓘ **Ridge Vineyards,** 17100 Montebello Rd., Cupertino, CA (✆ **408/867-3233;** www.ridgewine.com).

✈ San Francisco International (37 miles/59km).

🚌 $$$ **Hilton Garden Inn Cupertino,** 10741 N. Wolfe Rd., Cupertino (✆ **408/777-8787;** www.hiltongardeninn.com). $$$ **Cypress Hotel,** 10050 S. De Anza Blvd., Cupertino (✆ **800/499-1408** or 408/253-8900; www.thecypresshotel.com).

Bonny Doon

The Rhone Ranger

Santa Cruz Mountains, California

Where else can you sit in a room decorated with Ralph Steadman–designed posters and wine labels, where your friendly guide pours you a drink of sweet port in a molded chocolate cup that you devour immediately afterwards? Welcome to Bonny Doon, one of the world's most unconventional wineries. It's one of the few places in the United States where you can taste such exotic grapes as Mourvedre and Nebbiolo in one place. And it's great value—for $5 you get seven generous pours without a drop of condescension in sight.

Bonny Doon's tasting room is a quaint and rickety log cabin flanked by redwoods in a secluded part of the Santa Cruz valley. The old screen door bangs shut behind you as you enter a rustic tasting area with eclectic decor and tabby cats snoozing in the sun. "Welcome to the Dooniverse!" a young, laid-back guide greets you.

Charismatic owner Randall Graham—known as the "Rhone Ranger" for his love of the French wine region—sold off his share in the well-known Big House winery and is now pouring his energy instead into this alternative-style boutique operation, where he can indulge his sense of humor and an addiction to weird grapes. Graham's wine Cigar Volant, for example, is a winking reference to the 1950s French paranoia about UFOs landing and destroying their vineyards (flying saucers are known as flying cigars in France).

Graham has now made biodynamic wine his specialty. As organic farming becomes the norm, many winemakers now accept, for instance, that harvesting with the moon cycle does mean better wines—but a visit to Bonny Doon will expose you to some of the more "out there" theories of sustainable farming, such as crystal readings and ley energy lines. Graham also advocates planting stone menhirs in certain parts of the vineyards to "wake up the plant"—something he describes as a sort of viticultural acupuncture.

The winery makes for a great picnic spot, with its sunny back patio overlooking a dreamy mountain view. Despite its seclusion, the winery gets busy on weekends—many people flock here for its fun atmosphere and relaxed, quirky approach. It makes a fascinating contrast to the slick operations of Napa Valley and even Sonoma. The wine list is eclectic, to say the least, including a rosé made from Grenache Blanc. Sipping these wines just may win you over to these wacky biodynamic theories.

ⓘ **Bonny Doon Winery,** 10 Pine Flat Rd., Santa Cruz (✆ **831/425-4518;** www.bonny doonvineyard.com).

✈ San Francisco International (67 miles/107km).

🛏 $$$ **Hilton Santa Cruz,** 6001 La Madrona Dr., Scotts Valley (✆ **831/440-1000;** www1.hilton.com). $$ **Ocean Pacific Lodge,** 301 Pacific Ave., Santa Cruz (✆ **831/457-1234;** www.theocean pacificlodge.com).

David Bruce Winery

The Naked Winemaker

Santa Cruz Mountains, California

Pioneering winemaker David Bruce likes to get his hands dirty—not to mention other parts of his anatomy. This self-taught professor of Pinot once had an epiphany at 3am in the morning, while thrashing around naked in a tub full of grapes: He realized that the human body is the best grape crusher in the world. Soft, gentle, thorough, and dexterous, it beats any machine hands-down; even traditional foot-stomping can't compare.

As that episode abundantly proves, Bruce began making wine because he regarded it as "having fun." A practicing dermatologist, he was one of the first people in the 1960s to take a crazy chance and carve out by hand some terraces from the dusty, yellow clay of the Santa Cruz mountains. Those were the heady days of experimentation, when even French oak was considered a novelty. People thought Bruce had to be crazy to be wasting his weekends in an area of old orchards, jutting peaks, and sheer vertical cliffs, planting the most fickle grape of all—Pinot Noir. (Is it any coincidence that a dermatologist should choose a grape notorious for its thin, sensitive skin?)

The gamble paid off, though, as Bruce discovered a Pinot-friendly mountainside cooled by the sea breeze of Monterey Bay. Along the way he also discovered his own hidden talent for winemaking, and suddenly people started turning up at the winery to sample what is now a famous California wine.

Granted, Bruce's winery is not the easiest place to find. The 16-acre (6-hectare) operation is nestled amid redwoods on a windy narrow road 2,200 feet (670m) above sea level. Even when you get there, you're not sure you've found it—the main building's plain gray facade is unassuming, and the tasting room itself is somewhat sterile and bare inside. Out back, though, you'll marvel at the rustic picnic area's beautiful views of the rugged valley and the Pacific Ocean.

Don't come expecting a trendy boutique vineyard: The David Bruce Winery is very much a wine-lover's winery. The very basic visitor facilities are completely overshadowed by the wine itself—and, of course, the view. It must be said, however, that the view does not include any nudity these days—Bruce's workers do use waders when they're crushing.

ⓘ **David Bruce Winery,** 21439 Bear Creek Rd., Los Gatos (✆ **408/354-4214;** www.davidbrucewinery.com).

✈ San Francisco International (48 miles/77km).

🛏 $$$ **Toll House,** 140 S. Santa Cruz Ave., Los Gatos (✆ **408/395-7070;** www.tollhousehotel.com). $$ **Garden Inn Hotel,** 46 E. Main St., Los Gatos (✆ **408/354-6446;** www.gardeninn.us).

Archery Summit
The Heartbreak Grape
Willamette Valley, Oregon

Pinot Noir is so notoriously difficult to cultivate, it's known among winemakers as "the heartbreak grape." Its thin, delicate skin means it is easily damaged by too much sun or hail, and vulnerable to attack by birds, insects, and disease. It is particularly finicky regarding where it grows; Pinot vines will resolutely refuse to take hold on a certain hill or vineyard plain. In the winery, it is supersensitive to oxygen and oxidizes quickly. It does not like to be overhandled and it is no friend of oak—meaning its faults cannot be masked with a touch of wood.

David Lett was told he was crazy to be planting such a capricious grape in the red hills of Dundee, Oregon, in 1966. Even the wine experts at the wine university at UC Davis told him it was unwise to plant such a difficult varietal in an untested area that had only been making wine for 40 years. Why not go for a hardy Cabernet Sauvignon instead?

But Lett had a hunch that Oregon's mild, temperate climate would be very suitable for Pinot. He persisted, planting narrow rows on steep slopes with the grapes grown close to the soil. The canopy was handled carefully with leaf thinning and harvesting done by hand. The winery called Archery Summit was 100% gravity flow with no pumping. Such attention to detail paid off—the vines flourished and made exceptional wine. Lett had discovered the first land in the United States that could come to grips with temperamental Pinot.

Located 1 hour from Portland, the winery is set amid rolling hills and dirt tracks that now hide 30 other wineries. A long, winding gravel road leads to a large modern structure of cream-colored brick and gray slate that looks like a large, windowless warehouse with a bungalow attached. There are vineyards everywhere, fringed with rose bushes and the occasional deer. Long, barrel-lined tunnels burrow deep into the hill; on one underground wall, a bare patch reveals a shiny, wet, and flaky cross-section of the vineyard soil to demonstrate why it works so well. Back on top, a bright, modern tasting room with a small bar leads to a canopied terrace with lovely views of the Willamette Valley and breathtaking Mt. Jefferson. Here you can do a tasting of what is now Oregon's signature wine—a phenomenally popular Pinot Noir that is complex, big, and powerful. Mr. Lett's hunch paid off.

ⓘ **Archery Summit Winery,** 18599 NE Archery Summit Rd., Dayton (© **503/864-4300;** www.archerysummit.com).

✈ Portland International (40 miles/64km).

🛏 $$$ **Black Walnut Inn,** 9600 NE Worden Hill Rd., Dundee (© **866/429-4114;** www.blackwalnut_inn.com). $$ **Dundee Manor Bed & Breakfast,** 8380 NE Wordenhill Rd., Dundee (© **503/554-1945;** www.dundeemanor.com).

7 Places to Eat in . . . Portland, Oregon

Portland seems to have it all—a vigorous local wine industry, great microbreweries, local farmers committed to sustainable agriculture, and a critical mass of talented chefs who love Portland's laidback lifestyle too much to be lured elsewhere. It just isn't fair.

Portland's leading restaurants were well ahead of the curve in America when it came to cooking with local, seasonal ingredients. Even restaurants that have been around for more than a decade hardly seem to fit the label "old guard." They certainly aren't stuffy—just look at downtown's 296 **Higgins** (1239 SW Broadway; © **503/222-9070;** www.higgins.ypguides.net), where the tri-level layout and open kitchen nicely loosen up the clubby wood-paneled decor. Whipping out a constantly changing menu from that open kitchen, chef-owner Greg Higgins brings subtle new flavors into play with familiar classics, as in a honey-and-chili-glazed pork loin; a saffron-and-fennel stew of prawns, mussels, calamari, and halibut; or the "whole pig plate" composed of various pork cuts, roasted or braised, served with sausage, baked beans, and braised greens. Another top choice is 297 **Paley's Place** (1204 NW 21st Ave.; © **503/243-2403;** www.paleysplace.net), a small, bustling dining room in Nob Hill, in a charming Victorian house with a front porch often stacked with baskets of local organic produce. Chef-owner Vitaly Paley uses them to interject fresh accents into traditional bistro fare such as spit-roasted suckling pig, corn-and-crab risotto, or superb sweetbreads with Paley's crisp signature fries. The standout Italian restaurant in Portland has long been discreetly elegant 298 **Genoa** (2832 SE Belmont St.; © **503/238-1464;** www.genoarestaurant.com), where the handful of linen-draped tables are much

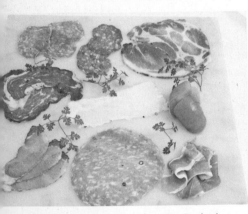

Cured meats from Higgins in downtown Portland.

in demand for romantic occasions. Service is attentive, and while the prix-fixe menu changes every 3 weeks, you can count on an intriguing interplay of robust flavors: sweet onion and Gorgonzola ravioli with walnut pesto and African pepper; grilled ono with Taggiasca olives, potatoes, and orange; or duck breast with a port wine-and-peppercorn sauce.

Younger Portland chefs are bringing their A-game to the table, too. In southeast Portland, right across the Willamette from downtown, 299 **Le Pigeon** (738 E. Burnside

St.; ✆ **503/243-2403;** www.lepigeon.com) is a casual brick-walled bistro with a mismatched clutter of furniture. Inspired by farmers' market offerings, chef-owner Gabriel Rucker likes to mix things up on the menu too, trying out fresh combinations such as hanger steak with tomatoes, feta cheese, and pancakes, or a rabbit appetizer with prosciutto, peaches, and truffles. In the northeast part of town, **300 Toro Bravo** (120 NE Russell St.; ✆ **503/281-4464;** www.torobravopdx.com) offers creative Spanish-inflected tapas, such as manchego-and-paprika fritters with spicy *salsa roja,* griddle-cooked bacon-wrapped dates, or *sous-vide* suckling pig with sherry cream potatoes and truffle *jus.* The dining room is boldly colored and bright, and trendy communal tables encourage diners to mingle.

Portlanders are happy to put aside trendiness, though, when it comes to breakfast. Every weekend morning downtown, you'll find lines down the street waiting to get into brunch at **301 Mother's Bistro** (212 SW Stark St.; ✆ **503/464-1122;** www.mothersbistro. com). Crowds pour in for satisfying repasts like the buttermilk biscuits topped with sausage gravy and eggs, crunchy French toast, or *migas* (eggs scrambled with

Marrow bones at Paley's Place, in an old Victorian house on Nob Hill.

jack cheese, onions, peppers, and bits of crispy tortillas). Chef Lisa Schroeder's comfort-food lunches and dinners are pretty fine as well—think meatloaf, mac 'n' cheese, pierogis, and long-braised pot roasts. Everyone in town seems to be there—everyone, that is, except the hordes who've driven out to the **302 Original Pancake House** (8601 SW 24th St.; ✆ **503/246-9007**) instead. This white-frame local landmark really is the original, having been around for nearly half a century. In a homey dining room that looks like someone's vintage lake cabin, they serve 20 different flavors of pancakes in steaming stacks from 7am until afternoon. If that doesn't start your day off right, nothing will.

✈ Portland International.

🚪 $$$ **RiverPlace Hotel,** 1510 SW Harbor Way (✆ **800/227-1333** or 503/228-3233; www.riverplacehotel.com). $$ **Silver Cloud Inn Portland Downtown,** 2426 NW Vaughn St. (✆ **800/205-6939** or 503/242-2400; www.silvercloud.com).

King Estates
Making Hay in Oregon
Eugene, Oregon

When farmer Ed King III went looking to buy some hay in 1991, he got a little bit more than he bargained for—a 600-acre (242-hectare) ranch and eventually a multi-million-dollar winery. Tucked between the Umpqua and Willamette valleys, the original rambling fruit farm struck him as the ideal place to grow grapes. Ed teamed up with his father, retired electronics entrepreneur and wine fanatic Ed King, Jr., and they planted 100 acres (40 hectares) with Pinot Noir and Pinot Gris. Within 10 years the two wines would become flagship Pinots for the state of Oregon and firmly place the region on every Pinotphile's must-visit list. King Estates has also led the way in sustainable vineyard management, and to reinforce its assertion that every bottle is a team effort, the entire winery staff signs each case of its top wine.

The brand-new winery the Kings built is stunning. It is part monastic château, part mission house fortress. Set on a hill, the huge imposing structure of cream-colored stone and red tiles houses a winery, restaurant, wine bar, art gallery, and conference center. The interiors are slick, with heavy timber frames, handcrafted cabinets, and copper-fitted bathrooms divided by arched hallways and backlit ceilings. The barrel rooms are impressive pillared halls, the reception area adorned with soapstone fireplaces. On an ample terrace overlooking a green, majestic landscape, you can enjoy the crisp and citric Pinot Gris while nibbling on toasted hazelnuts and bread dipped in balsamic vinegar. The wine store even sells a neat line of cookbooks based around both Pinot grapes.

It's a scenic half-hour drive from the university town of Eugene, Oregon's second biggest city, so fiercely independent it has earned the sobriquet "the People's Republic of Eugene." You'll wind through gentle hills that are especially beautiful in the fall. The climate is crisp and fresh—you can expect all seasons to occur in 1 day. King Estates is increasingly popular with visitors but never feels crowded, because it is such a big facility. It's a winery-rich area, with more than 300 wineries, concentrated in the Willamette Valley to the north; with King Estate leading the way, the region is becoming so well regarded for wine, it may soon become known as "the People's Republic of Pinot."

ⓘ **King Estates,** 80854 Territorial Rd. (✆ **800/884-4441;** www.kingestate.com).

✈ Eugene (21 miles/33km).

🛏 $$ **Hampton Inn Eugene,** 3780 W. 11th Ave. (✆ **541/431-1225;** www.hamptoninn.com). $$ **The Valley River Inn,** 1000 Valley River Way (✆ **800/543-8266** or 541/743-1000; www.valleyriverinn.com).

Chateau Ste. Michelle
A Midsummer Night's Dream
Woodinville, Washington

The balmy scent of fresh grass and oak trees wafts across the giant lawn at sunset. You lie there in your low deck chair as Elvis Costello croons live from a nearby stage. A laid-back audience relaxes with picnic coolers in a natural amphitheater; the sultry evening is alive with music, people, and atmosphere. As the orange sky grows ever darker, the "Spirit of Washington" dinner train shuttles by in the distance.

But for that glass of cool Riesling in your hand, you might forget you are in a winery. That large French-style mansion in the background also gives it away: You are in fact at Chateau Ste. Michelle, one of Washington state's leading wineries.

Woodinville must be one of the most unusual wine regions in America. For one thing, there are no vineyards—here you'll find gorgeous woodlands of beech trees, spruce bushes, and red oaks without a vine in sight. A dozen wineries have located themselves in this picturesque farming and logging community because of its proximity to Seattle, 30 minutes away, but the actual grapes are grown in the much drier climes across the Cascade Mountains in eastern Washington state. Chateau Ste. Michelle is the big boy among these bucolic vintners. Set in 87 acres (35 hectares) of verdant countryside, the estate is the former hunting ground of a lumber baron, with a mock château built in 1976, complete with tall windows and gray shutters. The tasting terrace overlooks manicured lawns; vigilant mallards patrol trout ponds with the dappled colors of maple and cherry trees in the distance. It's a plum picnic spot.

"The Chateau," as it's known locally, can trace its history from 1934. Over the years, it has been creating very good

Riesling and swallowing up neighboring wineries; it now owns a total of 3,400 acres (1,375 hectares) of vineyards and produces one million cases of wine a year, which makes it the biggest producer of Riesling in the country. The attractive visitor's center receives 200,000 people annually, not to mention thousands more who attend the phenomenally popular summer concerts.

Wine tours are free and include tours of the atmospheric and aromatic cellars. The tasting room, with its long welcoming bar, offers a range of tastings. If you can afford

The grounds of Chateau Ste. Michelle in Woodinville, Washington.

it, pip for the $50 private tour and tasting, which is much more thorough and educating. Chateau Ste. Michelle produces a wide spectrum of wines, everything from inexpensive grocery-store wine to top-notch boutique labels—and that's music to everybody's ears.

ⓘ **Chateau Ste. Michelle,** 14111 NE 145th St., Woodinville (✆ **800/267-6793** or 425/488-1133; www.ste-michelle.com).

✈ Seattle-Tacoma International (26 miles/ 41km).

🛏 $$$ **Willows Lodge,** 14580 NE 145th St., Woodinville (✆ **877/424-3930** or 425/424-3930; www.willowslodge.com).

East Coast U.S.

305

Bedell Cellars

A Cab from Long Island

Cutchogue, New York

Take the wrong turn coming out of Kennedy airport and you are in for a surprise. If you keep going long enough, the noise and bustle of the world's greatest city will fade behind; instead you will find a gentle coastal plain punctuated by clapboard houses, tall white churches, and seemingly endless vineyards. Yes, vineyards in metropolitan New York. As you cruise into the east end of Long Island, the Big Apple becomes the Big Grape.

Kip Bedell was one of the first pioneers in the area to recognize its potential for producing excellent wine. He began making wine in an old potato barn in 1985. Now Bedell's cellars have become a high-tech, gravity-based winery with a growing legion of fans. Long Island has come a long way too, with more than 50 wineries, mostly clustered along a 20-mile (32km) stretch on the North Fork of Long Island, and over a million visitors per year flocking to the area to tour them.

Bedell Cellars leads the way in style and comfort. The renovated farmhouse and barn has a breezy summer feel, with a wrap-around veranda surrounded by lush borders of flowers. The house has bright stylish interiors with white walls, big windows, and dark wood floors and furniture; a beautiful covered walkway crosses the garden, entwined with vines and creepers. The pavilion-style tasting room has a large platform overlooking the flat vineyards, where soldierly vines stretch out before you, as if ready to invade Manhattan. But the tasting bar leaves the old world behind—it is slick and minimalist, with a silver bar counter and soaring black bottle shelves. Cutting-edge art hangs on the walls.

Not only have the Bordeaux-style blends of Bedell earned some especially high scores from the wine critics, Long Island in general has lately been producing some remarkable wines. Reds like Cabernet Sauvignon, Cabernet Franc, and Merlot can compete favorably with the best of the West Coast; the area's whites are noted for being intense and elegant, and Long Island rosés are praised as both subtle and complex. Though it is still hard to find a New York wine in New York—the trendy restaurants of Manhattan have yet to accept that there can be a prestigious wine region right on its doorstep—surely it's only a matter of time before they too are catching a Cab from Long Island.

306 East Coast U.S.

Lamoreaux Landing Wine Cellars
The Fall in the Finger Lakes
Lodi, New York

Upstate New York is beautiful in the fall, with autumn colors of red, purple, and orange forming a blazing backdrop that attracts lovers of the outdoors. The Finger Lakes—a cluster of seven long, narrow, and deep lakes (on a map they look like a line of tadpoles gravitating north towards Lake Ontario)—are particularly attractive, especially since this region has the added twist of tangy grape aromas in the air.

The Finger Lakes area is the country's second biggest wine-producing area after Napa Valley, with more than 100 wineries dotted amid rolling hills, lakes, and wheat fields 6 hours north of Manhattan. The wineries here are a beehive of activity in the fall, as harvest is underway. The facilities are thronged with workers unloading grapes and tripping over wine hoses. Wine lovers are tripping over themselves in the

The grounds of Lamoreaux Landing Wine Cellars on Lake Seneca in upstate New York.

273

tasting rooms too, eager to try the cool-climate whites this area specializes in, as well as some hardy reds such as Cabernet Franc.

Lake Seneca is ringed with 40 such wineries, taking advantage of the water's cooling effects in summer and warming effect in winter. An enjoyable wine trail around the lake is marked with grape-adorned signs indicating possible spots to stop off and taste. One of the most famous wineries is Lamoreaux Landing Wine Cellars, a name referring to a now-defunct steamboat pier on the eastern lakeshore. In a region where every third town seems to have a classical name, it's not surprising that the building has tall, Greek-style architecture on its hillside setting. A sloped footpath leads you to an imposing entrance of square pillars topped by a monumental rectangular cornice. Inside, it has one of the most attractive tasting rooms on the East Coast. Tall windows light up a magnificent room of wood-paneled walls and a polished counter bar; needless to say it has stunning views of the lake and the clear blue skies. This is a serious operation making excellent wines.

The Finger Lakes region has been making wine since the mid-1800s, but the industry was practically wiped out by Prohibition. It only began to recover in 1976, when a law was passed allowing grape producers to make and sell their own wine; Lamoreaux is one of the pioneers that introduced fine European grapes to the region. After visiting templelike Lamoreaux, visit some of its neighbors as well, small farmer operations that depend on cellar door sales—where you can depend on a friendly welcome.

(i) **Lamoreaux Landing Wine Cellars,** 9224 State Rte. 414, Lodi (✆ **607/582-6011;** www.lamoreauxwine.com).

✈ Syracuse Hancock Airport (69 miles/ 111km).

🛏 $$ **The Fox & the Grapes Bed & Breakfast,** 9496 State Rte. 414 (✆ **607/582-7528;** www.thefoxandthegrapes. com). $$ **Wine Country Cabins Bed and Breakfast,** 8744 Lower Lake Spur (✆ **607/582-7025;** www.winecountrycabins.com).

East Coast U.S. 307

Linden Vineyard

Getting Vertical in Virginia

Blue Ridge Mountains, Virginia

You don't have to be standing up to do a vertical wine tasting. You can be sitting down, lying down, or on your side while trying the same wine from different vintages. Vertical tastings are the way to go in the atmospheric cellar of Linden Vineyard in Virginia. Candles dot the aromatic room, illuminating a tidy space stacked with oak barrels. A plank sitting across two barrels serves as your tasting table. A pourer guides you through different vintages; you can compare, for example, a 1999 Cabernet Sauvignon with a 2005. The difference

is startling, and you begin to understand why wine lovers put so much stock in aging wine. You may also get to try a sweet wine paired with a delicious ball of Gorgonzola cheese, while the guide talks you through the three different vineyards that supply this winery, set in the bucolic hills of the Blue Ridge Mountains.

Virginia is very much a new wine region, and Linden Vineyard is a pioneer. Set up by winemaker Jim Law in 1987 on a rustic piece of land known as hardscrabble, Linden is easily the best winery in the area.

It's famous for producing consistently good, handcrafted wines. The building itself is a warm and welcoming wooden construction perched on a hill overlooking vineyards, forests, and rocky outcrops. The 1-hour drive from Washington, D.C., is scenic and pastoral, as you pass rock walls and ponds and small woodlands. The location is quiet, beautiful, and serene. It makes for a great picnic stop.

Linden very much believes in balance and harmony. You'll notice this not only in its excellent wines, but also in the way it conducts winery visits. Large groups are discouraged, and only those who buy a case are treated to the famous deck, and all-glass indoor patio that's a wonderful spot

for some afternoon idling. The cozy fireplace and panoramic view of the valley persuade you to linger. Perhaps the best way to do a vertical tasting is to get horizontal.

ⓘ **Linden Vineyard,** 3708 Harrels Corner Rd., Linden (ⓒ **540/364-4997;** www.lindenvineyards.com).

✈ Washington Dulles Airport (53 miles/85km).

🛏 $$ **Courtyard by Marriott Harrisonburg,** Evelyn Byrd Ave., Harrisonburg (ⓒ **540/432-3031;** www.marriott.com). $ **The Village Inn,** 4979 South Valley Pike, Harrisonburg (www.thevillageinn.travel).

308 Canada

Hainle Vineyards

Jack Frost

Okanagan, British Columbia, Canada

The year 1972 looked like a bad one for Walter Hainle. A winemaker's worst nightmare had come to pass: An early frost had wiped out his entire crop of grapes. To salvage something from nothing, he picked the frozen grapes anyway. His German heritage informed him that it was still possible to make a sweet wine called *eiswein* that he could keep for personal use, helping him through what would be a lean year. But the 40 liters (10 gallons) he salvaged proved marvelous, with a clean, refreshing sweetness and high acidity that normal late-harvest dessert wines lack. Hainle mused that the Canadian climate was perfect for ice wine. And then he began wondering—could he sell it?

Little did Hainle realize that he had hit upon a multimillion-dollar industry—he had produced the first Canadian ice wine, a product that the country would become famous for. A bottle of his first commercial vintage in 1978 is now priceless; the two

remaining bottles belonging to the winery are kept in the local bank vault in Peachland, a lakeside town on the western slopes of Lake Okanagan.

Okanagan Valley is the most unpretentious wine country in the world. The entire area has a pioneer feel that betrays its fur-trapper history. Recently it has become popular with vacationers and retirees who like the outdoor life, but also with wine lovers who wish to visit the 40 or so wineries that have replaced fruit orchards with vines.

Hainle Vineyards is a low building of dark wooden posts holding up a wrap-around balcony with flower baskets hanging from the banisters. A stack of barrels sits out front. The short driveway leads to a complex that holds a traditional winery with vaulted cellars, a wonderful cluttered restaurant, and a cooking school. The tasting room is bright and homey (the garish local art on the wall makes it all the more endearing); outside there is a beautiful patio popular for wedding parties and other events. The restaurant, which is popular with both locals and visitors, has panoramic views of the vines running down to the lakeside shore, as well as an exhibition kitchen where you can sit down in front of the chef and watch him cook your meal. The food is excellent, but go easy on the starter and main course. This is one place where you will definitely want dessert—of the liquid kind.

ⓘ **Hainle Vineyards,** 5355 Trepanier Bench Rd., Peachland (✆ **250/767-2525;** www.hainle.com).

✈ Kelowna (36km/22 miles).

▭ $$ **KeriGlen's Lakeview Bed & Breakfast,** 3404 W. Bench Dr., Penticton (✆ **250/276-9370;** www.keriglen.ca). $$ **Accounting for Taste B & B,** 1108 Menu Rd., Kelowna (✆ **250/769-2836;** www. accountingfortaste.ca).

Canada 309

Cave Spring Cellars
A Rendezvous with Riesling
Jordan, Ontario

Could you have picked a more romantic setting? The mammoth Niagara Falls is a suitably grand backdrop to meet the love of your life—no wonder it is so popular with honeymooners. Lake Ontario lies to the north and Lake Erie to the south as you travel up the peninsula, away from New York State towards the mellow town of Jordan, a historic village brimming with charming cafes and antique stores. Among them, an ordinary storefront with banners flapping in the wind announces Cave Spring Cellars. You enter and find a trendy wine bar with dark granite counter and elegant decor, exuding sophistication—ideal for a little romance. You are a little early for your rendezvous, so you take the guide up on his offer to go on a short tour of the cellars.

You listen, slightly distracted and looking back at the bar, as he tells you the story of Cave Spring Cellars. The vineyards are located away from the building on the legendary Niagara Escarpment, part of the cliff over which the Niagara river plunges. It was here in 1972 that an 18-year-old geography student called Leonardo Pennachetti noted the unique microclimate with vine-growing potential. The Lake Ontario breeze is kind to grapes—it delays early budding and prevents severe winters. His father and grandfather were amateur winemakers, and they all decided to take the plunge and buy a plot of land on which to plant some grapes. The vines took hold so well, at least 20 wineries followed in its wake.

At last you take your seat and rub your knees with anticipation. What you have been waiting for is just about to arrive. First you'll prolong the anticipation by trying the excellent sparkling Cave Spring Brut. You follow up with a rich, vibrant Cabernet Franc/Cabernet Sauvignon blend known as La Penna—an unusual wine, since the Cabernet Sauvignon is fermented in the Amarone style, by drying the grapes before crushing. But at last your date arrives, and the reason you are here is placed before you: the Riesling Dolomite, one of the best examples of the white grape in the Americas. It has great minerality, aromas of peach, and a long, lingering finish.

You savor the moment and decide you are in love. You want to marry this wine—which is just as well, for it can keep for up to 10 years. You sit back and plan the evening ahead: dinner in the lovely winery restaurant and then a night in its luxury hotel across the road, Inn on the Twenty. What do you say?

ⓘ **Cave Spring Cellars,** 3836 Main St., Jordan (Ⓒ **905/562-3581;** www.cavespring cellars.com).

✈ Toronto (134km/83 miles).

🛏 $$$ **Inn on the Twenty,** 3845 Main St. (Ⓒ **905/562-8728;** www.innonthe twenty.com). $$ **Jordan House,** 3751 Main St. (Ⓒ **905/562-1607;** www.jordan house.ca).

Canada

Inniskillin

Breaking the Ice

Niagara-on-the-Lake, Ontario, Canada

Inniskillin Icewine is a modern marketing phenomenon. The best-selling wine product in duty-free stores around the world, it outsells champagne and port as the most desired wine gift. Everybody wants to get his hands on this intensely sweet and complex wine—it is a luxury good that rolls off shelves like water rolls off those famous falls 20 minutes from the winery. It sells from New York to Beijing; in fact, it's so popular in Asia that this Canadian winery is one of the few in the world that conducts daily tours in Japanese. Such is its popularity that counterfeiters have muscled in and now pass off an inferior product as the real thing with alarming regularity—in markets such as Taiwan, it is calculated that 50% of all Canadian ice wine sold is fake.

Imitation is the best form of flattery. Other signature wines, such as Australian Shiraz or Oregon Pinot Noir, do not have the same problem with pirate winemakers working from dingy backstreet garages. Indeed, the issue has become a major headache for the Canadian wine industry, for it affects its sales and tarnishes its quality image.

Ice wine grapes from Inniskillin, in Niagara-on-the-Lake, Ontario.

Inniskillin helped put ice wine on the map.

tion of putting up nets, it was prosecuted by animal rights organizations for trapping birds using grapes as bait.) It was not until the mid-'80s that the wineries finally mastered the art of using frost to freeze out unwanted water from the grape and produce a delicious sweet wine with tongue-tingling acidity.

Inniskillin winery is actually a 1920s barn with low walls and a tall imposing roof. Little would you guess that 300,000 people pass through its doors every year. This rustic-style visitor and tour center also has a wine boutique and demonstration kitchen. The winery is very much geared up for visitors, and it has the added attraction of being just as interesting to visit in the winter as in summer. Every January, a 10-day Icewine Festival draws thousands to enjoy tastings on a 7m-long (23 ft.) wine bar that is actually a 7,000-kilo (15,000-lb.) block of ice. Hundreds of ice carvers gather to partake in ice sculpture competitions. Come springtime it all melts away—but it's reassuring to know that the wine itself will last for decades.

What is remarkable about Canadian ice wine is that 30 years ago it did not exist. Hainle winery in British Colombia (see 308) was the first to produce a commercial vintage, but it was Inniskillin in Ontario that put the wine on the map. That's not to say it was easy going. In 1983 Inniskillin lost its entire crop to birds. (When neighboring Pelee Island Vineyards took the precau-

ⓘ **Inniskillin,** 1499 Line 3, Niagara Pkwy., Niagara-on-the-Lake, Ontario (ⓒ **905/468-2187;** www.inniskillin.com).

✈ Toronto (164km/102 miles).

🛏 $$$ **The Shaw Club,** 92 Picton St., Niagara-on-the-Lake (ⓒ **905/468-5711;** www.shawclub.com). $$ **The Charles Inn,** 209 Queen St., Niagara-on-the-Lake (ⓒ **905/468-4588;** www.charlesinn.ca).

France **311**

Domaine Henri Bourgeois
Getting Lost in the Loire
Sancerre, Loire Valley, France

An early morning stroll in the central vineyards of the Loire valley is embracing. Duck out of your hotel after a hearty breakfast and head for the hills, following whatever road takes you upward and away from the town. Keep walking and try not to look back—not yet, anyhow. Do not worry about getting lost, because you will anyway, whether you have a map or a portable GPS. The landscape will open up before you, sweeping hills with a textured patchwork of vine rows, wheat fields, and prairies of sunflowers. When you reach a crest, turn around and soak up the wonder. The mist still lies heavy on the valley, but the walled medieval town of Sancerre towers above the wispy haze. Its steep hills run into other gentler slopes, with the occasional village and hamlet showing its rooftops.

The narrow river Loire meanders by. It continues west as far as the Atlantic, creating a beautiful valley referred to as the "garden of France." Though it's usually regarded as one area, the Loire Valley is in fact one very long and lush horizontal shelf that has its own very distinctive personality. Sancerre, in the eastern end of the valley, is very much rural and unassuming—here you don't find the grand châteaux and cathedrals that the western valley is famous for. The Loire Valley was famous as the summer playground of the French nobility, but Sancerre is much more humble, and such purity is reflected in its wine. Sancerre lends its name to a crisp and elegant Sauvignon Blanc that the whole world tries to imitate.

The 300-odd wineries around here are all small and modest, hidden in the hills. One such place is Domaine Henri Bourgeois. A family affair that goes back 10 generations, the winery is located in the hamlet of Chavignol. Its worn vaulted cellar has intricately carved oak vats (the most recent barrels were made from a historic 400-year-old oak tree that was felled in a storm—and, this being France, its chopping-up was nationally televised). The grapes come from the forbidding hill known as Mont Damneé—literally "damn mountain," because its steep incline means backbreaking work for the harvesters. Here you can try the famous white, paired with another national treasure, the locally made, creamy goat cheese known as Crottin de Chavignol.

Sancerre itself is a town of narrow streets tightly packed with tall 17th-century stone houses. On the summit there is a tower that affords 180-degree panoramic views of the area. Numerous "caves" offer wine tastings; the tourist office provides a list of other wineries to visit on foot or on bicycle. Out there in the hills, your French will be sorely tested—and also your sense of direction.

(i) **Domaine Henri Bourgeois,** Chavignol (© **33/2/4878-5320;** www.bourgeois-sancerre.com).

✈ Tours Airport (173km/107 miles).

🛏 $$$ **Chateau de Beaujeu,** 18300 Sens Beaujeu, Bourges (© **33/2/4879-0507;** www.chateau-de-beaujeu.com). $$ **Hotel Le Panoramic,** Rempart des Augustins, Sancerre (© **33/2/4854-2244;** www. panoramicotel.com).

G. H. Mumm

Mumm's the Word

Champagne, France

France's northeastern region of Champagne has been famous for its wine since the 3rd century, but it was only in the 18th century that the region developed its namesake effervescent sparkling white. It was some happy monks who learned, sheerly by accident, how to put fizz in their wine. When bottles of supposedly still wine started unexpectedly exploding in the cellar, they salvaged one to try. It was like "tasting the stars." Years of trial and error followed; only with the introduction of stronger bottles and corks did the monks finally succeed in controlling the second fermentation in the bottle and thus the bubbles. The first champagne house opened in 1729, and its product became instantly popular with European royalty. Many years later, we now associate the word "champagne" less with the region and more with the liquid that has popped and fizzed its way through 2 centuries of parties, and doused many a jubilant Grand Prix race winner.

The Formula One of champagne has to be G. H. Mumm. This gorgeous winery is situated in the old Roman city of Reims, 4 blocks from the famous cathedral where French kings were crowned. Giant golden letters declare the winery's name on a tidy set of railings in front of a palatial mansion. A chic, classical courtyard with stone benches and sculpted hedges leads to immaculate reception rooms with marble walls, elegant wood paneling, and red leather sofas. The champagne house undoubtedly offers the best tours in the region, starting in the mammoth system of tunnels that burrow through the region's distinguishing chalk clay. Some of the caves are big enough to hold a banquet (and often do). One wide underground thoroughfare houses a pristine museum with illuminated display cases and ancient winemaking instruments. Farther into the bowels of the complex are vaulted walkways holding 25 million bottles, many still on the racks with their bottoms pointed upward as they go through the meticulous process of turning and settling.

You have a choice of three different tours, which are all basically the same— except that the best one ends in a triple tasting of Mumm's distinctive red-striped label Cordon Rouge. The facility is a major draw during the summer high season; you'll probably find yourself rubbing shoulders with other curious tourists unless you visit in the cold winter months. The champagne process is fascinating to learn about, and the guides here are very knowledgeable. You'll learn, for example, that you judge bubbly by the size of its bubbles, and those that stick to the side of a flute are a sign of dirty glassware—an interesting fact to know for your next dinner party.

ⓘ **G. H. Mumm,** 34 rue de Champ de Mars (Ⓒ **33/3/2649-5970;** www.mumm.com).

✈ Reims (29km/18 miles).

🛏 $$$ **Château Les Crayeres,** 64 blvd. Henry Vasnier (Ⓒ **33/3/2682-8080;** www.lescrayeres.com). $$$ **Best Western Hôtel de la Paix,** 9 rue Buirette (Ⓒ **33/3/2640-0408;** www.bestwestern-lapaix-reims.com).

France **313**

Taittinger

Enlightenment

Champagne, France

The history of the Taittinger family unfurls like a well-played game of chess. One of France's foremost business dynasties, they originally hailed from Lorraine but had to beat a hasty retreat after the Franco-Prussian war in 1870. The Taittingers sacrificed a castle and took refuge in Paris, where they entered the wine trade. A tumultuous 19th century saw the family adapt defensive tactics to ward off revolution, riots, and vine disease. Miraculously they dodged the onslaught and captured a couple of pieces themselves, including a 13th-century abbey in Reims that had been pulled down during the French Revolution.

They turned Caves Taittinger into one of the oldest wine cellars in the world and one of the most frequently visited. Crumbling white caves date from the 4th century, when they were actually Gallo-Roman chalk mines. You get a suffocating sense of history standing in these uneven tunnels, with ancient relics sitting in dusty nooks and crannies. Elsewhere the tunnels turn into dramatic vaulted rooms of brick and stone, stacked with literally millions of bottles of some of the world's best champagne.

In the 20th century the family went on the attack and became one of the most famous champagne houses in the world. The breakthrough came in the 1920s, when Pierre Charles Taittinger gambled that Chardonnay would play a greater role in 20th-century wine taste and invested heavily by planting the grape in the winery's many properties. The winery outmaneuvered other champagne houses by anticipating that Chardonnay would become the queen of white wine, and also part of the classic Chardonnay–Pinot Noir champagne blend. Another brilliant move was to forfeit the traditional French reserve towards advertising: As far back as the 1960s, the winery was one of the first in France to begin pushing their products. The gambit paid off and sales boomed.

Just when it seemed the endgame was in sight and Taittinger had the wine world in perpetual check, disaster struck. A hostile bid in 2006 caught the winery in a corporate move. It looked like all was lost—the family found itself without its prize. Yet this being France and Taittinger being Taittinger, the family used all its influence and a white knight came to the rescue, in the form of a French bank. The king was saved.

Taittinger headquarters is now the historic Chateau de la Marquellarie in Epernay, 26km (16 miles) south of Reims. Though it's closed to the public, this famous house from the age of the enlightenment is surrounded by rolling vineyards that are definitely worth a visit after you've checked out the caves in Reims. Unusually, they are planted with white Chardonnay vines cross-hatched in the same fields with dark Pinot Noir. Just before the harvest, the fields take on a black-and-white tile pattern—not unlike a chessboard. Suddenly it all makes sense.

ⓘ **Caves Taittinger,** 9 Place Saint-Nicaise, Reims (✆ **33/3/26 85 84 33;** www.taittinger.com).

✈ Reims (29km/18 miles).

🛏 $$$ **Mercure Reims Cathédrale,** 31 bd. Paul Doumer, Reims (✆ **33/3/26 84 49 49;** www.mercure.com). $$ **Le Clos Raymi,** 3 rue Joseph de Venoge, Epernay (✆ **33/3/26 51 00 58;** www.closraymi-hotel.com).

---

314 France

Moët & Chandon

The Blind Taster

Champagne, France

If myths are to be believed, Dom Perignon was a blind monk who invented champagne, uttering the famous words to his fellow brothers: "Come quickly! I am drinking the stars!"

Unfortunately, the reality is a little more complicated. The 17th-century cellar master at the Capuchin Abbey of Hautvillers did not invent champagne. Instead he perfected the art of refermenting in the bottle without creating a dangerous liquid explosive device. It was Dom Perignon who introduced the dark grape Pinot Noir, which he discovered was less volatile than white grapes (the juice is immediately separated from the skins to prevent coloring). He also advocated early morning harvesting, aggressive pruning, and smaller yields, all accepted practice today in what has become know as the *champenoise method*. Furthermore, he was not blind, but rather prone to blind tasting—testing grapes and wine without knowing which vineyard they came from, so as not to influence his judgment. As for the famous quote? Well that was just good, old-fashioned advertising.

Dom Perignon is now one of the best-selling labels of arguably the world's greatest champagne house. When Moët & Chandon bought the Abbey of Hautvillers in 1792, they promptly put the monk on the label to sell more wine. The champagne house's palatial headquarters can be visited in Epernay, the Champagne town 170km (105 miles) northeast of Paris. Dark wrought-iron gates enclose a French classical facade, behind which is an expansive courtyard of white pebble stones with a beautiful flower bed at its center. A 1-hour tour takes you deep inside the dungeonlike cellars and back to the time of Napoleon and the revolution. Established in 1743 by Claude Moët, the winery was selling 2.5 million bottles by 1880. Its client list reads like a roll call of European high society: Madame Pompadour, Charles VII, Czar Alexander II, the Duke of Wellington, Queen Victoria. Yet the winery also looked after its own and was one of the first to introduce a form of social security for its workers. Its 19th-century employee list included cellar masters, cork cutters, clerks, coopers, vineyard farmers, tinsmiths, needlewomen, basket makers, firemen, packers, wheelwrights, and stable boys. Such a list somewhat explains the high price of its magnums.

The 20th century saw a period of massive growth for the winery, branching out into nonwine pursuits and opening operations in far-flung places such as California

The Moët cellars in Epernay, France.

and Argentina. It is now part of LVMH, Louis Vuitton—Moët Hennessy, the largest luxury goods company in the world, a corporation with an annual turnover that eclipses the GDP of several good-size countries. Its wine and spirits list alone includes names such as Krug, Hennessy, Glenmorangie, Cloudy Bay, and Cheval des Andes. That is quite a drinks cabinet—one any drinker would like to get the keys to, whether blind or not.

ⓘ **Moët et Chandon,** 20 ave. de Champagne, Epernay (ⓒ **33/3/26 51 20 20;** www. moet.com).

✈ Reims (29km/18 miles).

🛏 $$$ **Hotel Castel Jeanson,** 24 rue Jeanson, Ay (ⓒ **33/3/26 54 21 75;** www. casteljeanson.fr). $$ **Le Clos Raymi,** 3 rue Joseph de Venoge, Epernay (ⓒ **33/3/26 51 00 58;** www.closraymi-hotel.com).

Benoit Gouez, Moët & Chandon's *chef de cave*.

315 France

Domaine Weinbach
How to Pronounce "Gewürztraminer"
Alsace, France

Alsace may be France's smallest wine region, but it is also the most fought over. France and Germany have torn each other's eyes out in an often vicious tug of war for this pastoral paradise in the far northeastern corner of France. The European Union has put a stop to such bickering, but German influence is still strong here—note the tall, flute-shaped bottles used in Alsatian wineries, similar to those employed along the Rhine.

The grapes are German too, predominantly whites such as Riesling and the tongue-twister Gewürztraminer.

A hundred wineries dot the landscape, from the towers and footbridges of Strasbourg to the main wine town Colmar. Domaine Weinbach is one of the most

prominent, situated in the quaint village of Kaysersberg, 5km (3 miles) north of Colmar. The town is a marvelous mix of cobblestones and rickety wood-frame houses that are the region's signature buildings. Tall, spindly roofs shaped like witches' hats sit atop flower-decked balconies that hang over arched entranceways. As you stroll out to the winery, you'll notice that every vineyard is fringed with a line of roses. They're not there just for beauty's sake—the roses also serve to warn the winemakers early if any diseases are about to strike the vine.

Domaine Weinbach begins as a long wall enclosing the winery grounds bearing the name Domaine Faller—the family of women who run the operation. Colette and her two gracious daughters, Catherine and Laurence, are often in attendance to show you around. Set in the foothills of the Schlossberg mountains, the winery has a small stream running through the vineyards (*weinbach* means wine brook). Originally an old Capuchin monastery confiscated during the revolution, it was parceled out to the locals, but the lovely French farmhouse you'll find at the end of the long country laneway shows no hint of its monkish past. The surrounding vineyards are all biodynamic, producing pure and vibrant whites that are stored in old casks in an atmospheric cellar. The tasting room has a delightful old-world theme with antique furniture and old photographs. Here you can try the winery's bewildering selection of wines, including a Tokay Pinot Gris.

Eventually the Gewürztraminer is put before you. Pronounced Guh-*verts*-tra-mee-ner, the word means "spicy grape"—and don't worry, it gets easier to say after a couple of delicious glasses.

ⓘ **Domaine Weinbach,** 25 route du Vin, Kaysersberg (ⓒ **33/3/89 47 13 21;** www. domaineweinbach.com).

✈ Strasbourg (66km/41 miles).

🛏 $$ **Le Chambard Kaysersberg,** 9–13 rue du Général de Gaulle, Kaysersberg (ⓒ **33/3/89 47 10 17;** www. le-chambard-kaysersberg.federal-hotel.com). $$ **Hotel les Remparts,** 4 rue de la Flieh, Kaysersberg (ⓒ **33/3/89 47 12 12;** www.lesremparts. com).

France **316**

Château de Chassagne-Montrachet
Holy Terroir
Burgundy, France

Terroir is the new buzzword in wine marketing. It gets printed on wine labels, extolled by winemakers, and repeated by winery guides all around the world. The concept, however—a sense of place—is an old one that originated in the gentle hills of Burgundy—in particular, the area known as Chassagne-Montrachet. It was here that medieval monks distinguished the different tastes in wine, noting how it differed from field to field, hedgerow to hedgerow, and how certain grapes suited a certain slope or meadow. They scoured the land, marking out every corner and hillock with stone walls that can still be seen to this day. They even went as far as to taste the clay.

Nowadays nobody requires you to eat dirt while touring Burgundy. Yet if you are looking for a sense of place, you could do no better than visiting Château de Chassagne-Montrachet. Equal parts classical

château, medieval wine cellar, and designer hotel, the winery is an enlightening stop if you're touring the area. The building itself is solid, wide, and impressive, yet strikingly simple compared to the more baroque châteaux in this region. But once you get inside, things get wacky. The interior design is a mixture of classical and modern chic. The most convoluted bookshelf you have ever seen is built in the shape of a giant purple scribble; a beautiful curved staircase matches a spindle-shaped lampshade; minimalist chrome coffee tables sit beside overstuffed red armchairs; elegant white wall paneling holds up abstract art, while polished parquet floors lead to illuminated display cases. The dining room has a fireplace hidden behind a sliding door mounted with a large bronze butterfly. The designer bedrooms feature altarlike bathrooms and see-through Perspex furniture. It all makes sense once you learn that Philippe Starck was the designer, and it contrasts with the gleaming, functional winery and dungeon-like cellars.

When you go downstairs, you leave the 21st century behind. These atmospheric 12th-century tunnels are large enough to hold gala dinners and events; the older ones are the most narrow and claustrophobic of all. Stacked barrels sit behind metal gates, and you wish you had the key—for here are the wines this area is famous for, the legendary Burgundy whites, rich Chardonnays with a thick viscosity, crisp acidity, and complex minerality. These are wines that live forever, the true essence of Burgundy's *terroir*.

(i) **Château de Chassagne-Montrachet,** 5 rue du Château, Chassagne-Montrachet (✆ **33/3/8021-9857;** www.michelpicard.com).

✈ Dijon (55km/34 miles).

🛏 $$$ **La Maison d'Olivier Leflaive,** Place du Monument, Puligny-Montrachet (✆ **33/3/8021-3765;** www.olivierleflaive.com). $$ **Hôtel de la Paix,** 45 rue Faubourg Madeleine, Beaune (✆ **33/3/8024-7808;** www.hotelpaix.corn).

317 France

Albert Bichot

Burgundy Group Therapy

Burgundy, France

"I bore people senseless. I bore myself. Sometimes I talk so much about wine I see their eyes glaze over and I realize I've crossed over from a casual interest to a complete and utter obsession".

So remarks Sarah, the guide at a wine tasting in a cave in Burgundy. The location is the historic cellar of Albert Bichot in the tidy town of Beaune, center of the legendary Côte d'Or, or *golden ridge*. The caves have an austere, atmospheric feel, not unlike a dungeon.

Bichot is one of Burgundy's oldest wine merchants, a family business that has been in operation since 1831. The headquarters in Beaune was established in 1912, after Bichot acquired many other wine houses in the wake of the phyloxera blight. It is only one of Bichot's many estates around France, but it is an ideal place to get a handle on the famous Burgundy wines. Though Beaune is in many ways a modern city, its medieval town center is thronged with Burgundy fanatics in the summer. Many start or end their day tours with a visit to Bichot or one of the town's many other cellar tasting rooms.

Burgundy is a typical French wine region, in the sense that there are no huge flagship wineries to visit, but rather a multitude of mom-and-pop operations, little more than a cellar beneath a farmhouse. Because of French inheritance laws, land is evenly divided among offspring, which means that each generation sees the land divvied up more and more, until one person might own two rows of vineyard and little more. Bichot serves an important role in this system: The firm buys up each year's harvest of wine or grapes from several of these small producers, then markets it all under its own venerable label as genuine Burgundy.

The country lanes that spread out from the city make up the *routes de grand crus,* passing towns with such venerable names as Nuits-Saint Georges and Vosne Romanée. Here you will see gangs of Burgundy lovers poring over maps and pointing excitedly at different plots and appellations, which vary remarkably in wine quality depending on soil, slope, and shade. A vineyard of *premier cru* and *grand cru* vines is greeted with hushed silence—this is the pinnacle of Burgundy wine, according to the old French ranking system. The wine crew has come to worship the *grand cru*.

ⓘ **Bichot,** 6 bis bd. Jacques Copeau, Beaune (◎ **33/3/80 24 37 37;** www.bichot. com).

✈ Dijon (39km/24 miles).

🛏 $$ **Hotel Le Cep,** 27 rue Maufoux, Beaune (◎ **33/3/80 22 35 48;** www.hotel-cep-beaune.com). $$ **Hôtel Château de Challanges,** Rue des Templiers, Beaune (◎ **33/3/80 26 32 62;** www.chateaude challanges.com).

Château du Clos de Vougeot

Knights of the Round Tasting Table

Burgundy, France

The Confrérie des Chevaliers du Tastevin don't quite cut such dashing figures as, say, the Three Musketeers. Burgundy's "knights of wine tasting" are usually a little plump and middle-aged. Their red velvet ceremonial cloaks and cardinal hats match their rosy cheeks and purple noses; instead of swords hanging from their waists, silver wine-tasting saucers dangle from their necks. They exist to defend the honor of Burgundy's wines, and they do so by holding elaborate dinners, tastings, and wine auctions. They are rather a raucous lot, prone to blowing on brass horns, linking arms, and having a good old-fashioned singalong whenever the opportunity arises. But they are also true gentlemen, ensuring that every wine they endorse has a label in Braille for those who have bad eyesight.

The center of operations for this group is their sprawling historical complex, known as Château du Clos de Vougeot. This Cistercian abbey dates from the 12th century and has a large central courtyard with Renaissance-style doorways that lead to vat rooms, banquet halls, and a medieval winery. The 16th-century reception rooms have scarlet walls illuminated by candelabras. Thick colorful tapestries hang between tall French windows, and two intricate stone fireplaces are bordered by beautiful wood paneling and a handsome ceiling. Chunky oak grape crushers lead to ancient barrel rooms and a banquet room that would not look out of place as the set for an Errol Flynn swashbuckler. Deep in the building recesses is a tiny, romantic courtyard with a statue of a harvester surrounded by ivy-covered walls.

The winery is very much a museum piece and national monument. While they make no wine here and conduct no tastings, it is a great place to visit and soak up Burgundy's ancient wine heritage. It is also the venue for the Chevaliers' wine-drenched banquets, where they ceremoniously enthrone new members to the order. An invitation to such an event should never be missed. In the large central hall stands an ornate podium with a banner reading the motto of these modern Knights of wine: *Jamais en vain, toujours en vin* (Never in vain, forever in wine!).

ⓘ **Château du Clos de Vougeot,** off rue du Vieux Château, Vougeot (◎ **33/3/80-62-86-09;** www.tastevin-bourgogne.com).

✈ Dijon (18km/11 miles).

🛏 $$$ **Château de Gilly,** rue de Vieux Château, Vougeot (◎ **33/844/414-2842;** www.hotel-chateau-de-gilly-vougeot.federal-hotel.com). $$ **Hotel de Vougeot,** 18 rue du Vieux Château, Vougeot (◎ **33/3/80-62-01-15;** www.hotel-vougeot.com).

Duboeuf en Beaujolais
Don't Believe the Hype
Burgundy, France

Green laser beams bounce off a golden Bacchus statue next to a monastic barrel room, which leads to a toy-town model of a Beaujolais village. Pretty French roof eaves and flowerpot windows compete with wooden puppets mimicking vineyard workers. Debouef Wine Park in the heart of Beaujolais is a little bit too much, but then again so is its wine. To understand this cross between a winery and a theme park, you must first understand Beaujolais, and in particular Beaujolais Nouveau.

Every November the world of wine experiences a minimarketing frenzy, not unlike the release of a major Hollywood blockbuster. Colorful posters appear in wine stores from Baltimore to Bangalore declaring *"Le Beaujolais Nouveau est arrivé."* Millions of bottles roll out, destined by plane, train, or automobile— sometimes even hot-air balloon or elephant—for anxious wine consumers eager to get their hands on the wine before its official date of birth: midnight on the third Thursday of every November. Remarkably, this wine was still grape only weeks earlier. It had hardly touched the sides of a steel tank before it was whipped out, bottled, and shipped—faster than you could say "sugar turns to alcohol."

Such excitement belies the fact that Beaujolais Nouveau is cheap, light-bodied, and absolutely forgettable wine. The breathless release of Beaujolais Nouveau is a triumph of marketing and promotion that can be put down to one man— Georges Duboeuf, the king of Beaujolais. A sprightly 75-year-old with a tidy shock of silver hair, Duboeuf was turning the grape crusher by the age of 6 at his family's small vineyard. His teenage years were spent on

a bike selling wine to restaurants. By middle age he had a wine empire that shifted 25 million cases of year. He single-handedly put Beaujolais on the map.

Critics accuse Duboeuf of giving the region a bad name, misleading consumers into associating Beaujolais with Duboeuf's fast-food version. Such allegations of tackiness and bad taste were confirmed in 1997, when Duboeuf decided to open a "Disneyland of Wine" at his base in the village of Romaneche-Thorins, 56km (34 miles) north of Lyon. What you actually find is a beautifully laid-out wine complex that exudes French charm with just a sprinkling of kitsch and good old-fashioned bad taste. Wine snobs hate it. The child inside all of us loves it.

The entrance is a tidy plaza in front of the village train station. You enter the Gare de Lyons–style ticket booth and take a 90-minute self-guided tour through 15 rooms that cover the entire story, culture, and making of wine. A replica of a Roman boat carrying amphoras stands next to soil samples from all over France. Each room has a theme, be it cork, cooperage, or glassmaking. Computer technology is combined with slide shows to tell the story of wine. Tack meets kitsch meets 3-D wizardry, and the only consistent theme seems to be wine itself. Of course it all ends in the inevitable gift store, where Duboeuf's distinctive color-splashed labels are in abundance. Here you will learn that not all Beaujolais is nouveau, and that the region has its own high-class cru that could smack lips with the best of Burgundy and win.

Allow yourself the guilty pleasure of visiting Dubouef. It might not have the steepled turrets we usually associate with French châteaux (turrets that, ironically, you can see in Euro Disney), but it is fun, frivolous, and absolutely engaging.

ⓘ **Duboeuf en Beaujolais,** La Gare, Romaneche Thorins (ⓒ **33/3/85 35 22 22;** www.hameauduvin.com).

✈ Lyon (67km/41 miles).

🛏 $$$ **Radisson SAS Hotel,** rue 129 Servient, Lyon (ⓒ **33/4/78 63 55 00;** www.radissonsas.com). $$ **Grand Hotel-Boscolo Hotels,** rue Groleé 11, Lyon (ⓒ **33/ 4/7240-4545;** www.boscolohotels.com).

France **320**

Guigal

From the Terraces

Rhone Valley, France

The vineyards of the Côte Rôtie are startling. Steep hills are carved with lines of rock wall and vines in what resembles the multiple tiers of a bucolic wedding cake. Called "the roasted slope" because of its ample sunlight, the appellation is centered around the town of Ampuis in the northern Rhone, 55km (34 miles) south of Lyon. The region is unusual in that it allows the white grape Viognier to be blended with the red grape Syrah, resulting in a wine that is both meaty and floral. The region itself is split into two subregions, a blonde and a brunette known as Côte Blonde and Côte Brune, apparently after an ancient landlord divided his property between his two daughters.

Côte Rotie is now famous around the world, and such recognition can be put down to one man—Marcel Guigal, owner of E. Guigal, the biggest exporter of Côte Rotie wine. Often a winery's success results from one person's force of personality, and this is the case with Marcel Guigal. When Guigal inherited his father's vineyard in 1961 at the age of 17, it was a small operation that made little money. The postwar years had been tough; few people could afford such prestigious wine. Little can you tell from the cramped offices he shares with his wife and son that it is now the headquarters of a global wine

empire that ships $50 million worth of wine a year.

Guigal was an innovator who fought to push forgotten winemaking methods through France's legendary wine bureaucracy. His introduction of new oak barrels in the early days met stiff resistance; it was even labeled illegal. He persevered, however, and now it's accepted practice to store wine in new oak barrels to mature. He also fought town planners who schemed to rip up the sacred vines and build houses. He frowned upon the excessive use of weed killer, and was one of the earliest proponents of organic farming, again accepted practice today.

The winery itself is a delightful surprise. From the outside it looks unassuming; a cream-colored townhouse on a tidy village street. You immediately know you are in for something different, though, when you find yourself in a light-filled conservatory overlooking a pretty courtyard of low buildings with terra-cotta-tiled roofs and arched walkways. Inside, it gets high-tech—the winemaker's control panel would not look out of place in the cockpit of the Starship *Enterprise*. Just when you think you have seen enough of huge vaulted cellars and rooms crammed with gleaming stainless steel tanks, the extensive property opens up into delightful gardens with lily ponds

Casks of Guigal champagne in Ampuis, amid the steep vineyards of the Côte Rôtie.

and a luminous blue swimming pool. In the distance are the famous amphitheater-style vineyards that produce such famous labels as La Mouline and La Turque.

ⓘ **Guigal Winery,** Ampuis (☎ **33/4/7456-1876;** www.guigal.com).

✈ Lyon (37km/22 miles).

🛏 $$$ **La Pyramide,** 14 bd. Fernand Point, Vienne (☎ **44/4/7453-0196;** www.lapyramide.com). $$ **Campanile Lyon Centre Forum Part-Dieu,** 31 rue Maurice Flandin, Lyon (☎ **33/4/7236-3100;** www.campanile.com).

321 France

Château de Beaucastel
Strange Encounters
Rhone Valley, France

French vineyard owners are very protective of their appellations, and nowhere more so than in the southern Rhone Valley wine area known as Châteauneuf-du-Pape. Fraudsters, disease, inferior wine, and poor grapes are all kept at bay with strict controls that ensure that the world-famous name retains its prestige and reputation for excellent wines.

So in 1954, when a new threat appeared, an emergency meeting of the town council was called: A new law was decreed, declaring it illegal for flying saucers to fly over, land, or take off from the vineyards.

If any such UFOs were caught damaging or interfering with the vines, they were to be immediately apprehended by the village policeman and the aircraft confiscated by the municipal authorities. This law remains in force to this day. So far such astute civil defense has worked—the only aliens wandering this hot and dusty area just north of the Mediterranean come in rented cars, armed with wine maps and tasting notes.

Châteauneuf-du-Pape is a tiny medieval village dominated by the ruins of a fortress-like castle—the "Pope's New Castle" of the title. It was the summer house of Pope John XXII when the Holy Roman Empire was not so Roman, after shifting its capital temporarily to Avignon, 10km (6 miles) to the south. More accustomed to drinking wine from Burgundy and Provence, the pope thought he would try some local fare and ordered several barrels from Châteauneuf-du-Pape. He liked it so much, he built a vacation home there.

The first thing that strikes you about the soil here is that it is not soil—it is rock (and not in the slightest way suitable for landing spacecraft). Vines here grow in bush form on a bed of smooth, fat pebbles, which apparently is good for retaining heat and moisture, highly beneficial to the 13 grape varieties that are allowed to grow here. The most dominant are Grenache Noir and Syrah, but one winery uses all 13 grapes in its blends: Château de Beaucastel. As you visit, you'll find a simple French farmhouse with white walls and blue shuttered windows, leading to a beautiful inner garden with a round spring well in the middle. Wooden doors braced with wrought-iron hinges hide a beautiful vaulted cellar, packed with bottles and barrels. Tastings are held in the garden, where you can sit in the shade and try a range of wines lined up on a wine barrel. Château de Beaucastel is an earnest champion of organic winemaking, meaning that you'll find very few foreign bodies in the wine—never mind aliens in the vineyards.

ⓘ **Château de Beaucastel,** Chemin de Beaucastel, Courthezon (☏ **33/4/90-70-41-00;** www.beaucastel.com).

✈ Avignon (18km/11 miles).

🛏 $$ **Bristol Hotel,** 44 Cours Jean Jaurès, Avignon (☏ **33/4/90-16-48-48;** www.bristol-avignon.com). $ **La Garbure,** 3 rue Joseph Ducos, Châteauneuf-du-Pape (☏ **33/4/90-83-75-08;** www.la-garbure.com).

France 322

Domaine Tempier
Everything's Coming Up Rosé
Provence, France

Officially France's sunniest province, the hilly wine region of Provence—famous for its rolling fields of lavender—is the gateway to the glamorous resorts of the Côte d'Azur, the French Riviera, and indeed Monaco and Italy if you are going that far. But on the way, be sure to stop off in Bandol, a tiny coastal wine region tucked between Marseille and Toulon. This rustic paradise of hilltop villages, down-to-earth wineries, and glorious beaches has been producing wine for 2 millennia, although until very recently, it didn't register on the wine-lover's radar. That's not to say it never went unappreciated—King Louis XV was once asked what was the secret of his youth and the son of the Sun King replied: "The wines of Bandol."

The main grape here is an obscure, dark, smoky varietal called Mourvedre.

Provence's generous sunshine and the warm blast of the famous Mistral wind make the vines here healthy and vigorous, producing powerful red wines, as well as the world's best rosé. All too often rosé gets short shrift from wine lovers, who regard it as a one-dimensional byproduct of winemaking. That is not the case with Bandol rosé; crisp, spicy, and herbaceous, it restores your faith in rosé. And Bandol's best rosé comes from a small, unassuming winery a stone's throw from the Mediterranean called Domaine Tempier.

A tree-lined country lane leads to Domaine Tempier's old two-story country house of pink, uneven walls, sky-blue window shutters, and a shady, casual courtyard. Rickety doors hold up an arched doorway that leads to a rustic facility of stained concrete floors and huge circular wooden vats. The tasting is done on a barrel top, in an atmosphere that's more barnyard than winery.

This family-owned winery has been in operation since 1834. In the early 20th century, when the vine disease phylloxera almost wiped out the fine wine industry here, Domaine Tempier was one of the few survivors; it is credited with reviving the nearly extinct grape Mourvedre. Lucien Peynaud, who married into the family in the 1930s, was astounded by an old wine served by his father-in-law at his wedding; when he took over the vineyard, he almost single-handedly put Bandol back on the wine map. Strict local rules like one bottle per vine and maturing wines for a minimum 18 months in oak resulted in better and better wines, as noted in gushing reviews from wine critics.

Despite its newfound fame, Bandol will never take on the glamour of its coastal neighbors such as St-Tropez. This is a relaxed and down-to-earth place, where many wineries have a SONNEZ sign at their gate, meaning that if you ring the bell you will eventually be welcomed by the farmer/winemaker or his wife. Domaine Tempier shares this old-world casualness, but just in case, always call ahead to reserve your spot on the wine barrel.

ⓘ **Domaine Tempier,** Le Plan du Castellet (**33/4/9498-7021;** www.domaine-tempier.com).

✈ Marseille (46km/28 miles).

⊨ $$ **Mas de la Tourette,** 505 Chemin des Bernard, Le Pradet (**33/4/9408-1591;** www.masdelatourette.iowners.net). $$ **Mas Carol,** 448 Chemin de la Calade, Le Pradet, (**33/4/9431-3697;** www.mascarol.fr).

Château Lynch-Bages

Bordeaux Opens Up

Bordeaux, France

As the gray-brown Gironde estuary snakes southward toward Bordeaux city in the northwestern corner of France, it splits in two a wine region with some 7,000 wineries and a winemaking tradition that dates from medieval times. The Medoc, which sits on the left bank of the estuary, looks flat and featureless compared to more picturesque parts of the province. Yet this is ground zero for winemaking, an area dotted with huge, castle-style châteaux bearing such venerable names as Lafite, Latour, and Mouton—wineries that leave aficionados speechless. It should be a natural mecca for the wine tourist, but when that very same wine lover turns up to check out the gorgeous architecture and even more gorgeous wines, the gates are firmly shut—no visits allowed without 2 weeks notice and a letter of introduction from your wine importer and his mother. Medieval indeed.

One winery that has opened its shutters and polished off some wineglasses is the phenomenally successful Château Lynch-Bages. Situated at the gates of the port town of Pauillac, this handsome château has 90 hectares (223 acres) of vineyards on a gentle slope lapped by the tides of the river estuary. Away from the main building, a photogenic small 18th-century structure with a double roof sits amid the vines. In a charming 19th-century vat room, huge oak vats sit on white plinths in a wooden-framed store room. Bare timber rafters and beams morph into a sturdy modern structure with stainless-steel tanks sitting on brick foundations. But as you take a thorough tour of the bottling line and bottle-stacked cellars, you realize that the classical facade hides a modern, high-tech operation. And the winery is refurbishing the quaint, abandoned hamlet of Bages nearby, installing a brasserie, boulangerie, and wine store.

In the winery's tasting room, friendly pourers guide you through a sampling of their excellent Cabernet Sauvignon and Merlot blends. The winery also houses a wine school, which conducts fascinating classes on blending and the region's various *terroirs*. There is an art gallery to wander through while sipping your wine; special events have been planned, such as a Christmas-season tasting of roasted chestnuts and mulled wine.

Perhaps inspired by Château Lynch-Bages, other châteaux are now following suit and receiving visitors (contact the tourism office in Bordeaux for a list). The town of Pauillac's tourism center conducts free tastings, and Bordeaux's fascinating Musée des Chartrons museum celebrates the region's wine merchants.

You swirl your glass and muse that Bordeaux, just like this wine, is finally opening up.

ⓘ **Château Lynch-Bages,** Pauillac (✆ **33/5/5673-2400;** www.lynchbages.com).

✈ Bordeaux-Mérignac Airport (42km/26 miles).

🛏 $$ **Hotel Château Beau Jardin,** 50 Route de Soulac, Gaillan-en-Medoc (✆ **33/5/5641-2683;** www.chateaubeaujardin.com). $ **Hotel de France,** 7 rue Franklin, Bordeaux City (✆ **33/5/5648-2411;** www.hotel-france-bordeaux.fr).

The Château Lynch-Bages in Bordeaux welcomes visitors—a rare custom in the region.

Château Lascombes

Crush on You

Bordeaux, France

Is it possible to fall in love with a winery? It is only brick and mortar, after all. But what brick and mortar!

The Château Lascombes winery is a château in every sense of the word—tall and Gothic with a narrow roof turret up front that looks like a witch's hat. Attic windows sprout from the roof, as do narrow chimneys and a dome-capped circular tower in back. Tall white window frames only add to the uplifting effect, and to cap it all off, every bit of brickwork is covered in thick green foliage. It puts you in a good mood just to look at it.

Around the back, the production facility occupies a huge hangarlike building with giant gray doors; inside is a warehouse with all the modern necessities of winemaking—steel tanks, huge oak vats, grape hoppers, destemmers, a conveyor belt. Visitors walk right over the underground vats, with pumps and hoses snaking around the floor; industrial walkways lead upstairs to a large attic-style room where the grapes are dumped in maceration tanks and cooled down with dry ice. But the real surprise is downstairs in the basement, where the long barrel room is dramatically lit with blue fluorescent lighting, almost like a disco.

Heading back to the tasting room, you can get a panorama of the estate's expansive gardens and vines, punctuated by roses and flower beds (if you're lucky, the guide may let you have a peek inside the castle itself, which is surprisingly homey,

with striped curtains, large lamps, and doilies—domestic bliss). In the tasting room, the guide explains that the winery was first founded by a French knight, Antoine de Lascombes, in the mid–17th century. In 1885 it was declared a second-growth winery, a French winery rating that makes it one of the most prestigious in the country. Unfortunately, the winery was mistreated by a series of proprietors throughout the 20th century—absentee landlords, a corporate brewer—it was even used as a military headquarters by Allied troops in the Second World War. Amid such uncertainty, the winery underperformed. Then in 2001 Michel Rolland stepped in, a modern knight in shining armor who, under new owners, has overseen a huge improvement in the wines. Their 2004 blend is superb—dark, perfumed, and seductive. At last, Château Lascombes once again has a wine that lives up to its architecture.

ⓘ **Château Lascombes,** 1 Cours de Verdun, Margaux (🕿 **33/5/5578-89743;** www.chateau-lascombes.com).

✈ Bordeaux-Mérignac Airport (31km/19 miles).

🛏 $$$ **Relais de Margaux,** 5 Route de L'Ile Vincent (🕿 **33/5/5578-83830;** www.relais-margaux.fr). $$ **Le Pavillon de Margaux,** 3 rue Georges Mandel (🕿 **33/5/5578-87754;** www.pavillonmargaux.com).

Château Smith Haut-Lafitte

Sour Grapes

Bordeaux, France

It must be confusing to be a grape, especially if you are growing on the gentle vineyards of Château Smith Haut-Lafitte. You spend the entire spring and summer being nurtured and spoiled on the vine; come harvest time you are carefully hand-picked and laid in especially small trays to prevent damage. You are then carried to the truck in Sherpa-inspired hods, ergonomically designed and detachable so you can be gently rolled into the load. In the winery, grapes are hand-selected and cleaned of any foreign particles.

But then what happens after such five-star treatment? They crush you. To add insult to injury, you may even find yourself smeared across a stranger's face, or floating in a bath with a naked human, as part of a recent phenomenon known as wine therapy.

Château Smith Haut-Lafitte is as grand as the name implies. It is a sprawling complex of square turrets and cupolas, some dating from the 16th century. Lichen-stained statues of lions, cupids, and Bacchus dot an ivy-covered property that exudes aristocratic charm. Fork-tongued flags flap from medieval weather vanes, and a grand stone staircase inside leads to a large banquet hall overlooking the vineyards. Below in the cellar, a spectacular vaulted room contains some 1,300 barrels, backlit with spotlights and the company logo.

Apparently this was all a crumbling mess before it was acquired by ski professionals and sport retailers Daniel and Florence Cathiard. Not only have they breathed new life into an historic building, the wine itself has undergone a renaissance. The classic blends of Merlot, Cabernet Sauvignon, and Cabernet Franc are fresh and rich.

Nearby is the beautiful luxury hotel **Les Sources de Caidale,** a grand mansion with a garden lake and swans. The hotel's wine-therapy spa lets you literally immerse yourself in the stuff—apparently a grape face-wrap has wonderful anti-aging qualities, brimming with antioxidants (Madonna is a big fan of the winery's beauty products). Its Michelin-starred restaurant attracts foodies; a leather-clad cigar room draws lovers of tobacco; and a 15,000-bottle cellar gratifies the wine lover. The hotel is a destination in itself—let's just hope they pamper their guests even better than their grapes.

(i) **Château Smith Haut-Lafitte,** Martillac (© **33/5/5738-1122;** www.smith-haut-lafitte.com).

✈ Bordeaux-Mérignac Airport (27km/16 miles).

🛏 $$$ **Hotel Bordeaux Continental,** 10 rue Montesquieu, Bordeaux (© **33/5/5652-6600;** www.hotel-le-continental.com). $$ **Hotel Majestic,** 2 rue Condé, Bordeaux (© **33/5/5652-6044;** www.hotel-majestic.com).

Villa Cafaggio

Classic Chianti

Greve, Tuscany, Italy

The rolling drive is breathtaking, twisting and turning through Tuscany's majestic hills, passing olive groves, crop fields, and, of course, vineyards. Lines of vines follow the contours of the slopes like a draftsman's sketch. You reach a beautiful woodland of cypress trees, framing a tiny, picturesque chapel worthy of a postcard. The road becomes a dirt track, and as you turn a curve, a captivating vista unfurls before you—the legendary *conca de oro* or "golden hollow," a sweet piece of vineyard terrain that produces some of Tuscany's finest Chianti, wine so good somebody had to christen it "Super Tuscan."

The lucky owner is a winery called Villa Cafaggio, housed in a typical Tuscan building of brown stone and terra-cotta tiles. Wine has been made in this area for centuries, including a medieval period when Benedictine monks worshipped God by making some great wine (and then drinking it, of course). But then the area went through tumultuous times. When the Farkas family took over Villa Cafaggio in the 1960s, they found it in a sorry estate—neglected vineyards, poor varietals, and derelict buildings. Son Stefano Farkas rebuilt the winery and in turn built a reputation as one of Italy's more talented and forward-thinking winemakers. He restored the buildings, planted new vineyards, and even injected new life into the winery's olive oil operation. It wasn't easy going—because the market had collapsed, the winery often found itself with excess grapes, nowhere to store them, and no grape buyers. But times have changed, and now wine lovers cannot get enough of Villa Cafaggio wines; their top vintages earn top scores from all the critics.

The facilities are surprisingly high-tech. Take, for example, a newfangled bottling machine that leaves a vacuum in the bottle top, thus eliminating wine's greatest enemy, oxygen. Yet there is enough old-world charm here to warm the heart of die-hard romantics—a fragrant cellar room with casks made from Slovakian oak, or the upstairs terrace where the winery throws the occasional sun-drenched luncheon or star-sparkled dinner with seasonal treats such as roasted chestnuts in November. The winery tour includes a vineyard walk followed by a tasting within the winery. Super people, super wine, super Tuscany.

ⓘ **Villa Cafaggio,** Via San Martino in Cecione 5, Panzano (✆ **39/55/54-9094; www.villacafaggio.it).

✈ Florence Airport (40km/24 miles).

🛏 $$$ **Villa Bordón,** Via San Cresci 31/32, Loc. Mezzuola (✆ **39/55/88-40005; www.villabordoni.com). $$ **Castello Vicchiomaggio,** Via Vicchiomaggio 4 (✆ **39/55/85-4079; www.vicchiomaggio.it).

Places to Eat in . . . Rome

Like any major European capital, Rome has its share of three-star gourmet shrines and trendy bistros, but the essence of Roman cuisine is the sort of simple, robust peasant fare that doesn't necessarily register on the foodie radar. With Rome's multifaceted cultural and historical offerings, few people come here exclusively for the food. Many restaurants can coast on the tourist trade and turn a profit despite mediocre fare, rude service, and jacked-up prices, and so it can be tricky to find genuine *cucina Romana*—though the real deal is soul-satisfying indeed.

Checchino dal 1887 has been serving visceral Roman cuisine for more than a century.

Hunt around in the narrow street behind the Trevi Fountain for ⬤ **Al Moro** (Vicolo delle Bollette 131; ℂ **39/6-6783495**), a slightly dowdy family trattoria that has drawn discriminating locals, including Frederico Fellini and his *compagnos,* since 1929. It's worth enduring the gruff *patrone* and exclusive regulars to sample such authentic specialties as the crispy roast baby goat flavored with fresh rosemary, the spaghetti Al Moro (aka carbonara, which they claim to have invented here), or a fork-tender milk-fed lamb stewed with fresh tomatoes. On a secluded square in the historic Jewish ghetto area, the classic place to enjoy a deep-fried artichoke (referred to as *carciofi alla Giudeca,* or artichokes Jewish-style) is family owned ⬤ **Piperno** (Via Monte de'Cenci 9; ℂ **39/6/68806629;** www.ristorantepiperno.com), a mellow taverna that has been around since 1856. Along with the crispy fried artichokes and the *fritto misto vegetariano* (a sampler of Jewish-style artichokes, cheese-and-rice croquettes, mozzarella, and stuffed squash blossoms), Piperno serves delicious hearty pastas (the mellow *gnocchetti alla matriciana* is a specialty), seafood, and veal dishes.

Near Piazza Navona, acclaimed ⬤ **Il Convivio** (Vicolo dei Soldati 31; ℂ **39/6/6869432;** www.ilconviviotroiani.com), a chic white dining room in a beautiful 16th-century building, is known for its market-inspired modern cooking. Seasonally changing menu items might include caramelized tuna with chestnut honey, ginger, green pepper, rosemary, and green apple purée, or tagliatelle with a white pork ragout, wild asparagus, and ginger. Yet even at this high-end restaurant you can find some touches of classic *cucina Romana,* like the salt cod with tomato confit, olives, and artichokes. For a more casual and less expensive meal in the same area, there's always ⬤ **Pizzeria Baffetto** (Via del Governo Vecchio 114; ℂ **39/6/6861617**), a bustling, eternally popular no-frills spot in a scruffy-looking corner building (you'll recognize it by the lines of people outside waiting for a table). These pizzas are typically Roman style with a crisp, thin crust; the house special is generously topped with tomato sauce, mozzarella, mushrooms, onions, sausages, roasted peppers, and eggs. (If Baffetto's full, pop around the corner to La Montecarlo at Vicolo Savelli 12, run by the daughter of Baffeto's owner.)

Down in the rapidly gentrifying working-class neighborhood of Testaccio, more and more trendy bistros and bars are opening up in old converted warehouses. Yet close to the outdoor food market in Piazza Testaccio—already an essential stop for anyone who loves food—traditional *cucina Romana* is alive and well at 331 Da Felice (Via Mastro Giorgio 29; © **39/6/574-6800**), a spiffed-up neighborhood trattoria serving time-honored favorites such as *tonnarelli cacao e pepe,* chunky egg-rich pasta tossed with crumbled sheep's cheese and black pepper; or bucatini *all'amatriciana,* hollow spaghetti in a sauce of tomatoes, onion, pancetta, and pecorino cheese. The cozy, whitewashed cellar of 332 Checchino dal 1887 (Via di Monte Testaccio 30; © **39/6/5743816;** www.checchinodal1887.com) began serving workers from the area's former slaughterhouses in 1887, and the menu still features succulent butcher's leftovers—dishes such as *rigatoni con pajata* (pasta with small intestines), *coda alla vaccinara* (oxtail stew), *fagioli e cotiche* (beans with intestinal fat), and, in winter, a tender wild boar slow-braised with prunes and red wine.

Across the Tiber in bohemian Trastevere, 333 Sabatini (Piazza Santa Maria 13; © **39/06-5812026**) is a welcoming neighborhood trattoria with homey beamed ceilings and stenciled walls. It's a great place for seafood (spaghetti with seafood sauce, grilled scampi), delicious pastas, chicken and veal dishes (try *pollo con peperoni,* chicken with red and green peppers) and, of course, oxtail stew—the mark of any bona fide *ristorante cucina Romana.*

✈ Leonardo da Vinci International Airport (Fiumicino; 30km/19 miles).

🛏 **$$$ Hotel de Russie,** Via del Babuino 9 (© **800/ 323-7500** in the U.S. and Canada, or 39/6/328881; www. roccofortehotels.com). $ **Hotel Grifo,** Via del Boschetto 144 (© **39/6/4871395;** www.hotelgrifo.com).

Al Moro in Rome claims to have invented carbonara.

Castello Banfi

A Touch of Glass

Brunello, Tuscany, Italy

Castello Banfi appears on the horizon like a pink hilltop castle straight out of a fairy tale. A tall, slender Rapunzel-style tower overlooks a huge estate that reaches as far as the nearby Mediterranean. Within this authentic medieval fortress lies a cozy courtyard; outside lies a cluster of stone cottages with narrow vine-covered streets, a hamlet that clung to the castle walls in the dark ages. The estate holds vines, olive groves, wheat fields, plum orchards, and woodlands; within those same forests live wild boar, deer, pheasant, even truffles.

But unlike many European winery castles, this place is no fortress when it comes to visitors. It has two restaurants, one of which has a Michelin star. It has a gorgeous wine store with spacious ceramic flooring, handsome dark wood rafters, and attractive display shelves. The winery facilities with their endless rows of barrels are immaculate, as are the 14 guest rooms located in the surrounding stone cottages. The winery even has its own onsite cooperage, where the best oak planks from France and Slavonia are custom made into barrels.

If this isn't quite enough, what surely marks this winery out as a must-see in southern Tuscany is its intriguing Glass Museum, six rooms displaying glass from the present day all the way back to the 15th century B.C. Egyptian urns sit beside Babylonian vases beside ancient Roman ampules and goblets; present-day examples include

The grounds of Castello Banfi encompass a Michelin-star restaurant, accommodations in stone cottages, and a Glass Museum.

decorative crystal by some guys called Picasso, Cocteau, and Dalí. It focuses your mind temporarily away from the wine onto the see-through object that holds it.

Such rich, historic splendor has its genesis in the most unlikely of places—Long Island, New York. This is where owner John F. Mariani's father started out with an Italian wine importer called Banfi in 1919. His timing could not have been worse—Prohibition came a year later. He limped through those dry years selling wine for "medicinal purposes," then wasted no time importing the very best from Italy when the law was finally lifted. Business boomed, and over the years Banfi introduced the finest of Italian wines to the American market, including Lambrusco and Chianti.

The winery itself has put its faith in Sangiovese; vineyards teeming with the grape now besiege the castle walls. While the whole complex has a somewhat polished, corporate feel, rest assured that this is no Disneyland of wine—it's the genuine article.

ⓘ **Castello Banfi,** Montalcino (☎ **39/577/840111;** www.castellobanfi.com).

✈ Florence Airport (85km/52 miles).

🛏 $$$ **Borgo Grondaie,** Strada delle Grondaie, Siena (☎ **39/577/332539;** www.borgogrondaie.com). $$ **Hotel Villa Elda,** Viale 24 Maggio, Siena (☎ **39/577/247927;** www.villeldasiena.it).

335 Italy

Allegrini

The Forgetful Winemaker

Verona, Italy

It seems the best inventions happen by accident. In the early 1950s, an unknown winemaker went about making a rich sweet wine called *recioti,* unique to the area around Verona in northern Italy. He picked the dark Corvina grapes and then laid them out on straw mats to dry for several weeks, so that the grapes could shrivel and lose their water while retaining their sugar. Next they were crushed and fermented and put away in a barrel. And then the winemaker committed his stroke of genius—he forgot about the wine. Perhaps he went skiing in the nearby Alps or took a fishing trip on beautiful Lake Garda; perhaps a new romance had him wining and dining around the ancient city of Verona, showing his new beau the city's beguiling Roman ruins, medieval walls, and Renaissance churches. Whatever it was, the wine remained in the barrel for way too long.

By the time our absent-minded winemaker got around to checking it, his sweet *recioti* wine was ruined. There was no sugar left—it had all fermented—and what he got instead was a dry, powerful red. It was slightly bitter yet completely drinkable—in fact, it had a lush raisin taste with lots of body. The wine became known as *amarone* (literally "the big bitter") and it has since proved a hit among wine aficionados the world over, its style satisfying the shift in taste to more concentrated wines. Soon every winery in the region was making it.

Allegrini has established its name as one of the finest makers of *amarone.* Located just north of Verona in Fumane de Valpolicello, it's run by a family that has owned vineyards in the area for hundreds of years, but only recently won accolades for its winemaking. The vineyards are particularly beautiful, sitting as they do on terraced slopes, buttressed by white rock walls and bordered by tall slender cypress trees. Snowcapped Alps sit in the distance, and the vineyard slopes are embellished with the occasional stone statue. The dark intense berries grown from these slopes are placed in special drying houses for 100 days before being moved to large red-rimmed casks in the winery's brick vaulted cellars. They keep the wines 5 years before releasing them.

Allegrini conduct tours of the facility with the emphasis on good old-fashioned Italian hospitality. They host cellar tastings and vineyard tours, even cookery classes conducted by Marilisa Allegrini at the nearby Villa Giona, a gorgeous Italianate villa of arched windows. The Villa surrounds an expansive lawn with wicker chairs and the occasional Renaissance statue; inside you'll find period artworks, antique furniture, and colorful frescos. Tastings are conducted in the medieval tower, and eight luxury bedrooms welcome guests.

ⓘ **Allegrini Winery,** Via Giare 9/11, Fumane di Valpolicella (☎ **39/45/6832011;** www.allegrini.it).

✈ Airport Catullo, Verona (15km/9 miles).

🛏 $$$ **Ai Capitani Hotel,** Via Castelletto 2/4, Peschiera del Garda (☎ **39/45/6400782;** www.aicapitani.com). $$ **Al Quadrifoglio Bed and Breakfast,** Via 24, Maggio 6, Verona (☎ **39/338/2253681;** www.alquadrifoglio.it).

Italy
336

Ruffino

The Chianti Effect

Tuscany, Italy

It is called the "Chianti effect." It happens when wine lovers visit a beautiful winery and are so carried away with the utter charm of their surroundings, they proclaim the wine the best they have ever tasted—when in fact it is rustic grape glop.

It is easy to understand why people get so carried away and delusional in Chianti, Tuscany. Italy's oldest wine appellation is an enchanting set of rolling green hills punctuated by lonely clusters of tall cypress trees. The area lends its name to a famous red wine that unfortunately people now associate with checkered table cloths, pizzas, and straw-covered wine jars. Though Renaissance poets called it the wine of Bacchus, Chianti's excellent reputation faded in the 20th century, after strict controls went lax and winemakers began mixing the rich, earthy, floral Sangiovese grape with other wines including (unforgivably) white wine. America's most popular Italian wine became regarded as cheap and light-bodied, not worth storing. Then a scandal erupted questioning the authenticity of Chianti. Other wines appeared on the scene that rivaled and outbid Chianti, most notably the Super Tuscans. When Hannibal Lecter famously declared the wine perfect to drink with the liver of a dead census taker in the movie *Silence of the Lambs,* he nearly sealed its fate.

But now Chianti is back. New controls insist that the wine cannot be called Chianti unless it contains 80% Sangiovese grapes; adding white wine is forbidden. This has yielded a marked rise in quality, and Chianti is once again making poets wax lyrical.

Leading the charge is one of Italy's most important wineries, Ruffino, a name that has become practically synonymous with high-class Chianti. This 130-year-old winery has seven properties spread across Tuscany; one of the most beautiful is Poggio Casciano Estate, just outside historic Florence. Here you can visit a beautiful Tuscan mansion surrounded by random patches of vineyard of every shape and size. Pink walls hold shuttered windows and a roof cluttered with old terracotta tiles. Bright archways overlook an ample courtyard with a central fountain. Inside, wide circular tunnels are lined with barrels and paved with cobblestones; beautiful antique cellars lead to a large airy room with polished parquet floors and a collection of antique prints, showing Bacchus in all his Bacchanalian glory down through the centuries. It seems even the god of wine was not immune to the Chianti effect.

ⓘ **Ruffino,** Via Poggio, Cappanuccia, San Polo, Chianti (✆ **39/55/649-9703;** www. ruffino.it).

✈ Amerigo Vespucci Florence (37km/22 miles).

🛏 $$$ **Hotel Davanzati,** Via Porta Rossa no. 5, Florence (✆ **39/55/286-666;** www.hoteldavanzati.it). $$ **Hotel Vecchio Asilo,** Via delle Torri 4, Ulignano San Gimignano (✆ **39/57/795-0032;** www. vecchioasilo.it).

337 Italy

Cerretto Winery
Save the Truffle
Piedmont, Italy

It must be the toughest wine tour in the world—to rise when it is still dark and traipse in rubber boots over foggy hills and through freezing forests, with a bunch of dogs sniffing at trees, looking for the famous Piedmont white truffle. A dog barks and the *trifolai,* or truffle hunter, runs to the spot where the dog has unearthed a small dirty nugget that looks like a wrinkled potato.

Truffles are a mysterious delicacy. They are neither mushroom nor vegetable, and how they grow remains a complete mystery. Despite extensive research, scientists have failed to domesticate it; nobody knows why it only grows in certain places (in the case of Italy, only in the Piedmont and Tuscany), usually in the exact same spot year after year. What is known is that the *tuber magnatum pico* is highly sensitive to the environment, and truffle fields have been shrinking as forests slowly disappear. The high price of white truffles, which may reach $1,600 a pound, has spurred a huge increase in the number of hunters, pursuing what used to be a gentle countryside pastime. Rivalry has seen jealous hunters go so far as to poison other hunter's dogs, and there have been calls to regulate the industry.

The Cerreto winery conducts truffle hunts, however, not to make money but to let wine visitors explore the fascinating art of truffle hunting. After all, truffles are a natural accompaniment to Barolo wine, and Cerretto is looked upon as the master of this wine. Cerretto is situated close to the wine town of Alba in the northwestern region of Piedmont; Barolo is the best-known wine from this region, a red made from the Nebbiolo grape. Cerretto's owners Bruno and Marcello Cerretto are known the world over as the Barolo Brothers.

The Cerretto winery is a surprising mix of old, new, and downright funky. The usual vaulted cellars are there, but so too is a surprising sculpture in the winery gardens, a huge glass cube that sits like a giant dice rolling through the grounds. With its sharp corners, this bizarre little structure is meant to symbolize the sharp robustness of the Cerretto wines. Elsewhere in the vineyards sits a delightful multicolored chapel that looks like a children's playground castle. The whole effect is utterly charming.

In the tasting room you can sample the perfumed and velvety Barolo wines, while truffles reappear as thin slivers placed over fried eggs. The smell is distinctive and arresting, pungent and earthy, and they taste like a mixture of garlic and mushroom. You learn that truffles are also considered an aphrodisiac—all the more reason to enjoy them with such a sensuous wine.

ⓘ **Cerretto,** Strada Provincial Alba/Barolo, Localita San Cassiano 34, Alba (✆ **39/173/282-582;** www.ceretto.com).

✈ Turin (82km/52 miles).

🛏 $$$ **Hotel Castello di Sinio,** 1 Vicolo del Castello, Sinio (✆ **39/173/263-889;** www.hotelcastellodisinio.com). $$ **Ca del Lupo,** Via Ballerina 15, Montelupo Albese, (✆ **39/173/617-045;** www.cadellupo.it).

Italy 338

Fontanafredda
The King of Grapes
Piedmont, Italy

The lifespan of a vine is very much like a human being's. At less than 10 years old, it is too young to be taken seriously but requires lots of love, care, and attention. In the teenage years, it is young and robust but not fully formed, producing wine that is shy and awkward. Then it hits its prime as it reaches 30—rounded, enthusiastic, and full of energy. This is the age when a vine creates grapes that pair well with another grape in a harmonious blend. After 40 the vine slowly mellows, its grapes becoming more complex and sophisticated. After 60, it loses some abilities but remains an expert in others—it produces less wine but it is rich and concentrated and full of wisdom.

King Victor Emmanuel II may have been the first king of Italy, but he also regarded himself as lord and master of a rather large population of grapes. His 100-hectare (247-acre) estate called Fontannafredda is a private Piedmont village populated with every grape age bracket. This beautiful hamlet is now one of Italy's most famous wineries. It appears on a hilltop like a magical castle, surrounded by a picturesque wine country of contoured hills and rounded ridges. Tall mansions with trellised eaves hold wrought-iron balconies overlooking cobbled streets. Here the King built opulent Villa Contessa Rosa for his mistress; modern-day guests can sleep in its simple, comfortable rooms and immerse themselves completely in the world of royal wine.

Guests have the run of this beautiful estate, which has its own church, park, and lake. Below ground, long narrow tunnels lead to cathedral-like cellars with giant casks.

The surrounding countryside is perfect for wandering, dropping into numerous caves and cellars to try the local wine. Piedmont itself is a foodie's paradise with the aromas of local delicacies such as white truffle and veal roast wafting from the regions finest restaurants.

Around 500 growers in the area still contribute their grapes to the estate's wine in a tradition that goes back to the time of the king. Grapes such as Nebbiolo and Barbera, ingredients of the famous

Barolo wine, pour in through the winery's gates every harvest time—a loyal line of *grapeful* subjects, so to speak.

ⓘ **Fontanafredda,** Via Alba 15, Serralunga d'Alba (☎ **39/173/626-111;** www.fontanafredda.it).

✈ Turín (82km/52 miles).

🛏 $$$ **Hotel Castello di Sinio,** 1 Vicolo del Castello, Sinio (☎ **39/173/263-889;** www.hotelcastellodisinio.com). $$ **Ca del Lupo,** Via Ballerina 15, Montelupo Albese (☎ **39/173/617-045;** www.cadellupo.it).

339 Italy

Florio

Perpetual Wine

Marsala, Sicily, Italy

John Woodhouse was somewhat annoyed when a storm forced him to sail into the sleepy, anonymous village of Marsala on the western coast of Sicily in 1773. The English merchant was on his way south to pick up a cargo of soda water. Dejected, he decided to drown his sorrows in a waterfront tavern where he was served the local wine, *vino perpetuo*—so called because the cask never empties, as it is periodically topped up with a new vintage. Woodhouse took one sip and forgot about his soda water.

Woodhouse liked the wine so much he bought up every drop he could find—some 5,000 imperial liters—and shipped it off to England. He had a hunch that the wine could compete with Madeira port, which was all the rage in London at the time.

His hunch was correct. By the end of the 18th century, Woodhouse had built up a wine empire. Lord Nelson liked the new *marsala* so much, he declared it the wine of the Royal British Navy and signed up Woodhouse as its sole purveyor. Marsala became a thriving port, with Sicilian wineries—known as *bagli*—popping up all along the waterfront. The port expanded as it became thronged with ships picking up barrels to carry to northern Europe and the Americas.

Marsala the town had become a wine, all because of the weather.

These days Marsala has reverted to its sleepier incarnation, a sun-kissed village on the Mediterranean with roots in the Roman Empire (as a restored Carthaginian ship in the town museum proves). Woodhouse's firm was eventually taken over by Cinzano and continues under the name Florio. Its beautiful, bleached-white *baglio* is the heart of an enormous winery complex, including an Art Nouveau villa surrounded by handsome old warehouses. The cellar is a double row of barrels lined up for 150m (500 ft.). The winery museum contains fascinating mementoes, including examples of Florio's Marsala Tonic, a "medicine" available in the United States during Prohibition. (The label reads, in thick red print, "a small glassful twice a day.")

A change in tastes and fashion means Marsala wine is no longer as popular as it once was, best known these days perhaps only as an ingredient for cooking veal scaloppine. Yet nobody should write it off just yet. Florio's top-of-the-line Marsala Vergine is a powerful and delicious port. Often the best samples, though, are only found directly in the wineries—a wonderful excuse for an island holiday.

ⓘ **Florio,** 1 Via Vincenzo Florio, Marsala (📞 **39/923/781-111;** www.cantineflorio.it).

✈ Palermo (72km/44 miles).

🛏 $$$ **New Hotel Palace,** Via Lungo-mare Mediterraneo, Marsala (📞 **39/923/ 719-492;** www.newhotelpalace.com). $$ **Hotel Carmine,** Piazza Carmine, Marsala (📞 **39/923/717-574;** www.hotelcarmine.it).

Europe **340**

Lopez de Heredia
A Big Splash
La Rioja, Spain

Try not to arrive in Haro, the medieval capital of La Rioja, on June 29. As soon as you step on the street, complete strangers will douse you in buckets of wine, all the while cackling with glee. You have inadvertently walked into the town's famous Wine Battle, an annual orgy of wine-throwing that makes a cafeteria food fight look like child's play. Thousands gather on the city's streets armed with buckets, basins, trash cans, giant water pistols, and even back-mounted crop sprayers, all with the firm intention of drowning each other in wine.

Every year, the good folks of Haro apparently go through 13,000 gallons on this one festival day. Everybody is dressed in white, but they don't stay that way for long. Soon the teeming, screaming masses of people are covered head to toe in purple, with sticky hair and stinging eyes. More savvy veterans cover their cars' seats with plastic and their cameras with cling film; some even wear goggles. The whole affair is accompanied by brass bands and tractor-drawn floats, and culminates in a nighttime fiesta on the town plaza, complete with fireworks and more wine ducking.

Just down the road from all this madness sits the top source of Haro's wine, Lopez de Heredia, one of Spain's most historical and prestigious wineries. Lopez de Heredia is a family-owned operation originally established back in 1877. The winery itself appears as somewhat of a surprise—architecturally it resembles an old English railway station more than a Spanish villa, with its tidy stone walls, carved roof eaves, and solid gables pierced by little round windows. In fact, as you'll soon discover on your winery tour, the winery was actually a train station at one point, complete with its own platform, so that Lopez de Heredia could dispatch wine to all corners of the country and farther afield.

Within the bowels of the building, you'll find an impressive vaulted cellar lined with ancient casks. Like a lot of traditional Rioja wineries, Heredia is known for aging its wines, sometimes for up to 8 years, in barrels. This practice is slowly changing to meet the tastes of modern consumers, who increasingly prefer their wine young and fruity, perhaps containing just one varietal. Here in Rioja, however, the custom is to blend the rich and fruity Tempranillo grape with the darker, more alcoholic Grenache. The Lopez de Heredia Reserva is a heavy, lush wine that will jolt your palate into life. This is one wine you won't waste by throwing it in a stranger's face.

ⓘ **Lopez de Heredia,** Avda. de Vizcaya 3, Haro (📞 **34/941/310-244;** www.lopez deheredia.com).

✈ Logroño Airport (60km/37 miles).

🛏 $$ **Casa de Lgarda,** Briñas (📞 **34/ 941/312-134;** www.casadelegarda.com). $$ **El Hotel Rural Villa de Abalos,** Plaza Fermin Gurnino No. 2, Abalos (📞 **34/941/ 33-4302;** www.hotelvilladeabalos.com).

Marques de Riscal

The Drunken Winery

La Rioja, Spain

This winery seems to dance on the horizon like a madman—just look at that metallic roof, made with strands of pink, gold, and silver titanium. It seems to jump around like a tangled ball of ribbons, with no sense of shape but sheer exuberance to compensate. Inside and out, the building is loud, outrageous, and flamboyant. With its zigzag walls and angular windows, it is illogical, ridiculous, and enthralling.

Welcome to the "City of Wine," designed by star architect Frank Gehry. The new complex—opened with great fanfare in 2006 by King Juan Carlos of Spain himself—is located 1 hour from Gehry's more famous creation, the shiny and (by comparison) sober Guggenheim Museum in Bilbao. This fanciful winery complex is all the more astonishing for its contrasting surroundings: It is set against a background of a beautiful dusty mountain range, the Sierra de Cantabria, and in the middle of a traditional Spanish winery of sandstone brick and red earth in the medieval village of Elciego—which, ironically enough, translates as "the blind man." In the older part of the winery, you'll find a historical cellar with narrow, winding flagstone tunnels draped in cobwebs. What a contrast that makes to the brand-spanking-new wine cellar of 150,000 bottles called "the Cathedral to Wine." Inside the complex, you'll also find a 43-room designer inn called the **Marqués de Riscal Hotel** (© **34/945/180-880;** www.starwoodhotels.com) linked by glass walkway to a wine therapy spa—luxury indeed.

At first it may seem perplexing to find such radical stuff at one of Spain's most historical wineries. Famous for its rich, dense reds, which may be aged in a bottle for more than 100 years, the winery will often keep a wine for up to 40 years before releasing it. Yet the juxtaposition makes more sense when you learn that the winery's founder, Marques de Riscal, was not just a winemaker but a famous 19th-century diplomat, journalist, and freethinker. This is a winery that appreciates the old, but has never been afraid of the new.

To commemorate the winery's new extension, the auction house Sotheby's recently held a gala dinner of ancient wines. Among those served was a 1900 Tempranillo from Marques de Riscal that was so old, it could not be uncorked—each bottle had to be decapitated with giant hot tongs.

The madness continues.

ⓘ **Marques de Riscal,** C/ Torrea 1, Elciego (© **34/945/606-000;** www.marquesderiscal.com).

✈ Logroño airport (33km/20 miles).

🛏 $$ **Gran Hotel AC La Rioja,** C/ Madre de Dios 21, Logroño (© **34/941/272-350;** www.ac-hotels.com). $$ **Antigua Bodega De Don Cosme Palacio,** Ctra. El Ciego s/n, Laguardia (© **34/945/621-195;** www.habarcelo.es).

Cavas Freixenet

New Beginnings

Barcelona, Spain

Halfway through the 19th century, the European wine industry was almost wiped out by a disease called phylloxera, a small yellow bug from North America that took a liking to the roots of the noble European grapes and literally sucked the life out of them. It caused devastation across the continent, destroying 90% of all vineyards and forcing millions off the land and into the cities. Thanks to this root lice, waves of immigrants from Italy, Spain, and France went west to Ellis Island to escape poverty and starvation.

The wineries tried everything to combat the plague—dousing the vineyards in nasty chemicals, or flooding the fields (the bug apparently could not swim); the more superstitious even tried planting a dead toad under each vine. None of this worked. In the end, vineyards had to completely replant their vines, grafting their varietals onto American roots that were bug-resistant—a method that horrified the French, but in the end proved the only solution. To this day, all fine wines have an American root.

Like most catastrophes, phylloxera brought a new beginning. Among other things, it created a modern wine phenomenon called Spanish Cava: sparkling wine from the Iberian peninsula that has gained more fizz than champagne. When the Sala family began to dig up disease-ridden vines on their 13th-century estate, La Freixenada, in the Mediterranean region of Penedes, they decided to replant the red grapes with white varietals such as Macabeo, Xarel, and Parellada, vines that were more suited to the dry rocky area than what had been planted there before. They then decided to make sparkling wine

using the traditional *champenoise* method, inducing a second fermentation in the bottle. Within 100 years, the winery was the biggest producer of sparkling in the world, and the word *cava* has become synonymous with high-quality bubbly.

The winery itself is a rambling spread of handsome limestone buildings, just west of Barcelona. An ample courtyard is graced with vintage motorcars and a magnificent fountain; the words *Cavas Freixenet* are framed by ivy, above a classical-style facade. Inside, however, is a slick, modern operation—reception rooms have designer box sofas and backlit vaulted ceilings, glass doors swing between rock walls, a receptionist sits at a hotel-like counter. Past that you'll see a massive industrial operation, a huge bottle-stacked cellar, and a massive wine store. The fascinating tour goes into messy detail about how the winemakers get sediment out of the bottle without losing the bubbles; walls of bottles stand behind net protection in case one should explode and drown a tourist.

Speaking of drowning, Cava is traditionally the wine used at Catalonian church christenings. As numerous bottles are popped open, even the newborn gets his or her first sip. New beginnings, indeed.

ⓘ **Cavas Freixenet,** Joan Sala 2, Sant Sadurni d'Anoia (✆ **34/93/891-7000;** www.freixenet.es).

✈ Barcelona (44km/27 miles).

🛏 $$$ **Hotel Villa Emilia,** Calábria 115-117 (✆ **34/93/252-5285;** www.hotelvillaemilia.com). $$ **Hostal L'Antic Espai,** Gran Via de les Cortes Catalane 660 (✆ **34/93/304-1945;** www.lanticespai).

Taylor's Port

War & Peace

Vila Nova de Gaia, Oporto, Portugal

The story of port is one of war, accident, tenacity—and patience. In the Douro Valley, a wild and mountainous region in the north of Portugal, the locals have been making wine since Roman times, carving out terraces from the dry sandy soil and shoring up the hardscrabble earth with rambling rock walls. The whole area is a monument to human doggedness, to the determination to wrest something from such unyielding soil. For centuries they crushed the grapes by standing in line and linking arms while treading the fruit in long concrete troughs. The wine was then transported down a treacherous river of rapids 200km (124 miles) to the town of Aporto, where it stayed, to be enjoyed by the locals.

That was until the English came along. Unending wars with France and Spain in the 17th century meant the British had to look elsewhere for their wine, and so they looked instead to unknown Portugal. They enjoyed the robust wines of the Douro valley, but transportation was a problem. In response, winemakers began adding brandy or grape spirit to fortify the wine and preserve it for the Atlantic voyage. The almost pure alcohol stopped fermentation in its tracks, and the wine retained a sweetness that the English loved. Thus port was born, the favorite after-dinner tipple of the aristocracy.

British companies began setting up wine aging lodges in the riverside town of Villa Nova de Gaia, a steep hillside settlement on the river Douro facing Oporto. One of the first companies to do so was Taylor's in 1692. This family-owned port house is now one of the most prestigious

in the world. (A 1992 vintage Taylor's port was awarded a perfect 100 points by Robert Parker, Jr., which is about as good as you can get.)

Taylor's estate, farther up the valley, is full of vines that are older than your grandmother. The free tour of their ancient lodge is fascinating—as well as the usual arched cellars and giant wooden vats, there is a stately library full of leather-bound volumes and polished wood paneling where tastings are held at the end of the tour. There is also an on-site restaurant, and a gorgeous lawn terrace with lovely views of the river and Aporto.

During the tour you discover that the area, which now has some 85,000 growers, is going through a renaissance, and gaining a name for fine table wines as well. Port may be steeped in history, but Taylor's is investing heavily in technology and releasing new types of port, including a white variety. Although workers still tread the grape by foot, they have also invented an ingenious device called a "port toes"— a stainless-steel wine tank equipped with an internal system of pistons that replicate the human foot.

ⓘ **Taylor's Port,** Rua do Choupelo 250, Vila Nova de Gaia (✆ **351/22/374-2800;**www.taylor.pt).

✈ Oporto Airport (15km/9 miles).

🛏 $$ **Tiara Park Atlantic Oporto,** Av. da Boavista 1466, Oporto (✆ **351/22/607-2500;** www.tiara-hotels.com). $ **Andarilho Oporto Hostel,** Rua da Firmeza 364, Oporto (✆ **351/22/201-2073;** www.andarilhohostel.com).

Madeira Wine Company

Dessert Island

Madeira Island, Portugal

Everything about Madeira wine is exotic. To begin with, it originates on a shimmering tropical island 643km (400 miles) off the coast of Africa, often called the "pearl of the Atlantic." This tiny Portuguese colony seems overrun with green vegetation, covered in multicolored flowers and fruit gardens. Beautiful terraced vineyards are carved out of steep slopes, surrounded by a bright blue sea. The island's capital, picturesque Funchal, sits on a hillside overlooking a wide bay, with high sea cliffs looming in the distance. It is a sleepy, laid-back paradise for wine lovers.

Grapes don't normally take hold on a tropical island—the humidity and rich soil usually mean poor quality and disease. Yet Madeira is blessed with certain unique factors. Its volcanic soil is perfect for hardy, exotic, strangely named grapes like Bastardo and Strangled Dog. Over the years, the island's inventive winemakers discovered that if they fortified their local wine with alcohol they could produce a rich, sweet or dry port that would last for literally centuries. Geographic location also blessed Madeira, for it could handily supply the New World with wine; the heat it endured on such journeys only improved its taste. (That heat is now simulated in ovenlike lofts on the island.)

And Madeira became the most famous wine in the world. In 1478, when the Duke of Clarence faced execution for treason in the Tower of London, he chose to drown himself in a tub of Madeira rather than face the axe. Shakespeare referred to it in his plays (in *Henry II,* the Prince of Wales is accused of selling his soul for a glass of Madeira and a chicken leg), and Madeira was the wine used to toast the American Declaration of Independence (George Washington reputedly could not get by without a pint a day).

Madeira wine is currently going through a renaissance, led by the island's main winery, the Madeira Wine Company. Better quality control and labeling means that wine lovers are rediscovering this long-lasting wine, exploring its complex tastes of dried fruits, nut, and caramel, depending on the varietal. The island itself has become a much-visited holiday spot, with the Madeira Wine Company's headquarters a popular stop-off (call it a "port" of call).

The winery's quaint white townhouse, surrounding a tropical cobbled courtyard, features creaky aging lofts piled high with oak, mahogany, and satinwood casks, as well as an atmospheric wood-raftered tasting room where dark wooden shelves hold ancient bottles of port. Here you'll find 100-year-old wine—captured sunlight from Victorian times.

(i) **Madeira Wine Company,** Av. Arriaga 28, Funchal ((C) **351/291/740-110;** www.madeirawinecompany.com).

✈ Funchal Airport (15km/9 miles).

🛏 $$$ **Quinta Casa Branca,** Rua da Casa Branca 7, Funchal ((C) **351/291/700-770;** www.quintacasabranca.pt). $$ **Albergaria Dias,** Funchal ((C) **351/291/206-680;** www.albergariadias.com).

Schloss Vollrads

Kaiser Riesling

The Rheingau, Germany

The wide, majestic Rhine flows for 1,000km (620 miles) north through the heart of Europe, starting in the Swiss Alps and skirting the borders of Austria, Germany, France, Luxembourg, and the Netherlands. Within Germany it runs into the dark forested summits of the Taunus mountain range, takes a sharp turn, and continues west for 30km (18 miles) before resuming its flow northward toward the North Sea. On the map it looks like a brief kink in the river's course—but this accidental diversion creates a tiny wine region, the Rheingau, that is regarded as one of Germany's best. Sunny south-facing vineyards gently ascend toward the thickly wooded northern slopes; the area is dotted with castles, fortresses, and villages, with a network of footpaths and cycle trails that make it a wine wanderer's paradise.

The Rheingau is the homeland of Germany's noblest grape, Riesling. Often regarded as the Cinderella of white grapes (with Chardonnay and Sauvignon Blanc playing the ugly but more favored stepsisters), Riesling turns into a pure, fresh wine with very German characteristics: blondness, iron minerality, and sharp acidity. Often regarded as the wine-lover's favorite white, Riesling has gained an obsessive cult following around the world, only now becoming more generally fashionable. Some call it the new "It" wine—and if so, its favorite catwalk is the winery Schloss Vollrads.

Schloss Vollrads claims to be the oldest winery in the world, with vineyard deeds that date from 850 and wine sales first recorded in 1211. It is regarded as a German national treasure, and it's easy to understand why. The sprawling estate is home to magnificent mansions with historic towers; one castlelike manor is even surrounded by a romantic moat and only accessible by bridge. (With typical German understatement, Goethe described its grandiose 14th-century tower as "interesting.") The gateway and farm buildings are adorned with armorial designs; the palatial cavalier's house has sumptuous interiors with baroque flourishes; the cellar holds bottles dating from 1857.

Schloss Vollrads produces 100% Riesling—this grape is unsuitable for blending with others and is best left alone. It also rarely comes with oak, as the wood would only mask its startling freshness. Yet with its racy acidity, it can be aged for up to 10 years or more. The best Riesling attains a weird faint aroma of gasoline and diesel as it ages, but the taste is sublime.

Schloss Vollrads's on-site restaurant, Guts (an unappetizing name in English, but in German *gut* means "good"), has a lovely terrace overlooking the ample, manicured grounds and a three-story glass structure called the Orangerie. Here you can try exquisite German cuisine accompanied by the estate's famous Riesling—the dry, sweet Cinderella wine that's the new "It."

ⓘ **Schloss Vollrads,** Oestrich-Winkel (✆ **49/6723/660;** www.schlossvollrads.de).

✈ Frankfurt (54km/33 miles).

🛏 $$ **Akzent Waldhotel Rheingau,** Marienthaler Str. 20, Geisenheim-Marienthal (✆ **49/6722/99600;** www.waldhotelgietz.de). $$ **Zum Baeren Restaurant & Hotel,** Hohnerstrasse 25, Trossingen (✆ **49/7425/6007;** www.trossingenhotelbaeren.de).

Royal Tokaji

The Noble Rot

Mád, Tokaji, Hungary

The sleepy hills and quaint villages of northern Hungary have seen their fair share of war and revolution. One of those wars created a wine—and one of those revolutions nearly killed it.

The story begins in the 13th century. One year, the vineyard workers had to abandon their harvest—the Turks had once again decided to invade, and help was needed to fight them off. By the time the farmers returned, the white grapes not only grew old and shriveled on the vines, they were covered in an unpleasant fungus called botrytis. The workers picked the grapes anyway, leaving them piled in a heap. Soon they noticed a rich, honey-colored syrup oozing from the bunches. Mixed with the previous year's white wine, it tasted surprisingly good.

Thus was born the famous Tokaji Aszu wine. The fungus—which became known as "the noble rot"—produced an intense, sweet wine so rich, each plant can only produce a glassful. It became the favorite drink of royalty all across the continent; kings, popes, queens, and emperors clashed to own the wine region. The grapes literally became worth their weight in gold; to touch them was punishable by death. (Catherine the Great of Russia went so far as to place a permanent sentry around the area.) The vineyards became the first classified wine region in the world in 1772 (a mere 150 years before Bordeaux was classified), with a secret network of hidden caves built to hide the wine from marauders.

Nowadays the only marauders are tourists, and those very same moldy underground complexes can be toured and tasted in. The 3-hour train ride from romantic Budapest takes you through picturesque towns with red onion-shaped church towers, and past bucolic hills divided by two great rivers called the Tisza and Bodrog. In the morning, the vineyards lie covered in a heavy mist that encourages the noble rot.

The Royal Tokaji is probably Hungary's most famous winery. Located in a small yellow-fronted house in the town of Mád, it has a charming underground cellar and tasting room. You learn from the guide that the sweet wine Tokaji Aszu nearly disappeared during the Cold War; this winery only reopened its doors in 1989. Just as royalty coveted the wine, communism dismissed it as manna for the bourgeoisie, and when the Iron Curtain came down, so did the bar counter. During the communist era, private vineyards became one big state collective, and all the juice went into one big pot, so to speak. Since the fall of the Soviet Union, however, the region has experienced a renaissance in its wines. The rot has become noble once again.

ⓘ **Royal Tokaji,** Rakoczi Ut 35, Mád (✆ **36/ 47/548-500;** www.royal-tokaji.com).

✈ Budapest (173km/107 miles).

🛏 $$$ **Mamaison Residence Izabella,** Izabella u. 61, Budapest (✆ **36/47/ 55-900;** www.residence-izabella.com). $$ **Millennium Hotel,** Bajcsy-Zs. út 34, Tokaj (✆ **36/47/352-247;** www.tokajmillennium. hu).

Boutari Fantaxometoho

Dionysus on a Motorbike

Crete, Greece

What is the first thing you do when you arrive on the island of Crete? Hire a scooter in the sun-kissed capital of Heraklion and head for the hills. Zoom by the 16th-century Venetian fortress that dominates the skyline, pounded on all sides by a dark blue sea. Mountains beckon in the distance, some tipped with snow. Green villages dot the rugged landscape, surrounded by vineyards and olive groves. As you zip up and down the twisting roads, mountain goats scamper from the roadside and farmers can be seen in the distance herding their sheep. You glide past meadows of wildflowers and fields of chamomile, punctuated with ancient Minoan ruins.

Eventually you reach a long, gently sloping driveway leading to a low glass-fronted building. This is Boutari Fantaxometoho, headquarters of a 122-year-old group that owns eight vineyards across the country. Crete's showcase winery, it announces to the world that the island will no longer be known only for murky brown local wine, now that it's producing quality wines that can compete with the best.

Boutari means "the haunted house," referring to a legend about an old winemaker who, tired of local youths stealing his wine, cleverly invented a dramatic story about a terrifying ghost haunting his house. This supernatural security guard kept the superstitious locals away. The name stuck.

But there is nothing ghostly about the modern Boutari—it is slick and stylish, with its curved glass facade overlooking the vineyards. The tasting room is cool in every sense of the word, with air-conditioning and subtle lighting. Gracious staff present wines with unpronounceable names as well as more conventional varietals such as Syrah and Chardonnay. Several charming buildings lead to gorgeous flower-decked courtyards, and the original "haunted" house is a rickety little cottage framed with flowers—an appealing mix of old and new.

Crete's wine tradition goes back millennia, but its recent history has been as patchy as the landscape. In the Middle Ages, Venetian traders set up wineries, the ruins of which can still be seen today on rocky outcrops. But when the Turks invaded, they frowned upon alcohol, and the vineyards gave way to olive trees. Modern Greek wine focused on low-quality grapes, and a brief renaissance in the '70s was stopped in its tracks by a phylloxera outbreak. Only recently has industry gotten back on its feet, with the sunny island now producing one-fifth of Greece's wine.

After sampling wine in the gorgeous tasting room, get on your feet and climb the hill behind the winery buildings. At the top, the island stretches before you (it is a marvelous view at sunset). Below you lies an ancient winemaking land, the same land that produced Europe's first wine—a pleasant reminder that Dionysus, god of wine and ecstasy, was Greek.

ⓘ **Boutari Fantaxometoho,** Heraklion (☏ **30/210/660-5200;** www.boutari.gr).

✈ Heraklion (15km/9 miles).

🛏 $$$ **Lato Boutique Hotel,** 15 Epimendou St., Heraklion (☏ **30/2810/228103;** www.lato.gr). $$ **Nymphes Luxury Apartments,** Aglia Pelagia, Heraklion (☏ **30/2810/371605;** www.nymphes-apts. gr).

Ruca Malen

A Room with a View

Mendoza, Argentina

When you sit on the balcony of Ruca Malen winery, you get an idea of just how vast Mendoza province is. A huge plain of scrubland, punctuated by the odd boxy modernist winery, rolls out before you. It would all be rather flat and boring if not for the sweeping wall of ice and rock on the horizon, otherwise known as the Andes. The longest mountain range in the world, the Andes feed this desert plain with melted snow, irrigating everything, including the beautiful garden city of Mendoza 30 minutes to the north.

Mendoza province is one of the biggest wine-producing regions in the world, with more than 1,000 wineries. Yet only 6% of the province is actually cultivated and lived upon—the rest is barren mountains or desolate desert, with just the occasional nodding-donkey oil well working silently. Mendoza doesn't just have red gold, it has black gold too.

Ruca Malen is alive with noise. Below the long, beautiful hardwood balcony is a small restaurant that is always busy, especially in summer. The building itself is warm and modern with red brick walls and gray-framed windows; the winemaking facilities are clean and functional, their only unusual feature a huge experimental tank that looks like a giant coffee plunger.

Owner Jean Pierre Thibauld is a Franco Argentine who grew up surrounded by wine. His father stored many valuable bottles in the cellar of their country house on the outskirts of Buenos Aires. One day, the butler announced that the cellar was flooded and the bottles had lost their labels. For the next 20 years, the family drank the finest wine without knowing exactly what was what.

Thibauld grew up to be the chairman of the Argentine branch of Chandon, the famous French winery, which has been operating here since the early 1960s. (As the story goes, when French Chandon's president Robert Jean de Vogue first visited Argentina in 1955, he noted the locals imbibing prodigious amounts of wine topped off with ice cubes and soda water, and observed, "This country is ready for champagne!")

Chandon Argentina became the French château's most profitable arm, and it was Thibauld who helped steer it through the boom time of the Menem presidency, an era nicknamed the "pizza and champagne years."

When Thibauld finally retired from Chandon in 1998, he decided to start his own winery. He chose the name Ruca Malen for his new venture, a term from local Mapuche legend meaning "the girl's house." Along with informative and entertaining guided tours, the bodega offers the best winery lunch in Mendoza—a five-course spectacular where each dish is paired with a particular wine. Guests get to try the winery's full range, while soaking up the amazing view.

ⓘ **Ruca Malen,** Ruta Nacional 7, Mendoza (ⓒ **54/11/4807-1671;** www.bodegaruca malen.com).

✈ Mendoza City (30km/18 miles).

🛏 $$$ **Finca Adalgisa,** Pueyrredon 2222, Chacras de Coria (ⓒ **54/261/496-0713;** www.fincaadalgisa.com.ar). $$ **Hotel Argentino,** Espejo 455, Mendoza City (ⓒ **54/261/405-6300;** www.hotel-argentino.com).

Achaval Ferrer
The Wine Thieves
Mendoza, Argentina

A tall, beautiful Argentine woman stands in a modern cellar room that is fragrant with oak aromas of chocolate and vanilla. She has in her hand a long metal object known in the trade as a "wine thief." With it she extracts dark red wine from one of the barrels, explaining that this is a Malbec, one of the four grape varietals that go into the delicious blend Achaval Ferrer Altamira—the highest-scoring Argentine wine in the world.

Altamira is not just any old wine, and Achaval Ferrer is not just any old winery. The most prestigious Argentine bodega in the world, it occupies a modern, practical-looking building situated close to the wide dry river bed known as the Río Mendoza, 30 minutes south of Mendoza city.

Its founders, Santiago Achaval and Manuel Ferrer, were two industrialists from the Argentine cement industry who made an alchemist-like career change because they wanted to do something "that didn't involve wearing a tie." They persuaded Italian winemakers Roberto Cipresso and Tiziano Siviero that the eastern slopes of the Argentine Andes were the new frontier in millennial winemaking. The result was the sensational 1999 Gran Malbec Finca Altamira, a wine made with a rich ratio of three plants for every bottle. Their next step was to build a winery in Lujan de Cuyo, with a dramatic Andean backdrop. From there they produce wines that continue to astound wine critics both at home and abroad. When the Finca Altamira 2003 was awarded a lofty 96 points by *Wine Spectator*, it confirmed Achaval Ferrer as undisputed kings of fine wine from Argentina.

So how do they do it? Any winemaker will tell you it starts and ends with the grape, and Achaval Ferrer ensured they sourced the very best. Cipresso and Siviero pay almost obsessive attention to every detail. Attached to every wine tank, for example, is a giant fan that blows on the wine as it's passing through, to lower the taste-masking alcohol content of what's already a hot, fruity wine.

Considering the owners' background in cement, it's interesting to note that they have chosen to use old-fashioned concrete wine chambers, which went out of fashion in Argentina in the drive to improve winemaking methods. After replacing them with steel tanks, many wineries knocked doorways into their old concrete wine chambers and started using them as cellars and storage rooms. But in recent years cement has made a comeback, largely due to Cipresso's belief that the old system had certain advantages over steel—better heat retention, for example, and more controlled maceration. Suddenly new wineries were installing concrete tanks in their state-of-the-art wineries, keeping them small for better control. The result is a richer, more concentrated wine.

The winery guide uses the wine thief to inject a splash of inky wine—an almost perfect wine, awarded 98 points by wine critic Robert Parker, Jr.—into each visitor's glass. Amazingly, Achaval Ferrer does a barrel tasting for every curious visitor who passes their door. It makes you feel honored, privileged—like a wine thief.

(i) **Achaval Ferrer,** Calle Cobos 2601, Perdriel (© **54/261/488-1131;** www.achaval-ferrer.com).

✈ Mendoza City (25km/15 miles).

📖 $$$ **Club Tapiz,** Lujan de Cuyo (© **54/11/4005-0050;** www.fincaspatagonicas.com). $$ **Premium Tower Suite Mendoza,** Av. España 948, Mendoza City (© **54/261/425-3533;** www.hotelpremiumtower.com.ar).

O. Fournier

The Velvet Underground

Mendoza, Argentina

In the late '90s, when Spaniard José Ortega decided to buy vineyards in Mendoza, he chose the stunning Valle de Uco, 2 hours south of Mendoza city. This high-altitude valley—a barren, rural plain in the foothills of the Andes—is regarded as the new frontier in Argentine wine. It wasn't just anywhere in the valley he wanted, though; it was the subregion of La Consulta, where some Malbec vines were planted during the era when tango was as controversial as gangster rap is today.

As he crisscrossed the dusty dirt tracks in search of the perfect vine, Ortega had difficulty persuading landowners that he wanted quality over quantity. On one such trip between grape-heavy *fincas,* he passed through a derelict vineyard. The vines were overgrown and unkempt and had obviously been neglected for several years. When he asked his agent, the man shrugged dismissively and said it was a vineyard abandoned for various reasons. They stopped to take a look. Beneath the jungle of tangled climbers and leaves they found ancient vines with small clusters of grapes, few in number but sweet and highly concentrated. "This is what I want!" declared Ortega.

Ten years later, Ortega owns what must be the weirdest and most wonderful winery in South America. The building itself resembles an airport tower sliced by a flying saucer. Huge Herculean pillars suspend cubicles of glass. The giant underground cellar looks like a subterranean football field of concrete, with prisonlike walkways above endless rows of oak barrels. If Darth Vader owned a winery, this is what it would look like.

Yet unlike many concept wineries, O. Fournier avoids seeming like a ridiculous vanity project. The building is purely functional—those Herculean pillars are actually tanks, the sweeping arch a ramp for the harvest trucks, the glass cubicles air-conditioned labs and tasting rooms. Even the strange sloping tanks inside were designed to ease the winemaking process. The fact that everything starts at the top means there is little need for pumping. And guess what? They make great wine.

O. Fournier specializes in the silky, concentrated Spanish grape Tempranillo, as well as the famously fruity Malbec. All can be tried in the winery's snazzy restaurant, which sits on a serene pond and has panoramic views of the Andes. Ortega chose his site well; the proof is in the wine.

(i) **O.Fournier,** Calle Los Indios s/n, La Consulta (© **54/2622-451579;** www.ofournier.com).

✈ Mendoza City (91km/56 miles).

📖 $$$ **Cavas Wine Lodge,** Costaflores s/n, Alto Agrelo (© **54/261/410-6927;** www.cavaswinelodge.com). $$$ **Park Hyatt** Mendoza, Chile 1124, Mendoza City (© **54/261/441-1234;** www.mendoza.park.hyatt.com).

Benegas Lynch

Head Poncho

Mendoza, Argentina

When Federico Benegas Lynch decided to renovate his beautiful 100-year-old winery, he had trouble making the plaster stick. "You just cannot get the adobe-skilled workers anymore," explained the wiry ex-banker with gray flecked hair, "and I truly wanted to keep this winery in the traditional style."

He seems to have made an excellent job of it. This winery, 20 minutes south of the city, has to be one of the most gorgeous boutique bodegas in Mendoza, combining tradition with modern flair and style. The plaster problem was solved with an old Mexican recipe of cactus juice. Now, warm cappuccino-colored walls are topped with arched windows and hedged with lines of vines in an ample courtyard. You'll notice, however, an unusual number of doors in the low, stablelike buildings—in this earthquake-prone area, traditional architecture always provided lots of exits so people could get out fast when the tremors came.

The winery itself is immaculate. Blood-colored concrete tanks stand in a neat row, their polished steel doors betraying the high-tech winemaking that takes place here. The cellar is an atmospheric corridor of tall square pillars, dividing neat lines of new oak barrels. The aesthetic is at once monastic and romantic, conventlike, and cool.

The larger building has an attractive central salon with two long white sofas on either side, showered with a multitude of cushions. A large stainless-steel hood gleams in the corner, covering an indoor grill used for the famous Argentine *asado* (barbecue). A long, dark, polished table of oak stands in the center. Thick, luxurious ponchos hang from the walls, their rich, colorful fiber contrasting with the stark

brick and adobe walls. "I'm a collector," Benegas Lynch explains. "Here you see ponchos that once belonged to great Indian chiefs, gifted to my great grandfather Tiburcio Benegas Lynch."

The Lynch name stems from an exodus of the Irish tribe that fled religious persecution in 1702. They spread across the world and left their mark in many places, not least of all Bordeaux, where the Château Lynch-Bages (see 323) produces wines to this day. The Argentine contingent became successful merchants in Buenos Aires. They continued an aristocratic line that digressed In many directions—as far as Cuba, in the case of one who went by the name of Che Guevara Lynch.

Tiburcio ended up in Mendoza in the late 19th century and started his own revolution in wine by founding Trapiche, currently Argentina's biggest winery. He is regarded as one of the great pioneers who

The tasting room at Benegas Lynch in Mendoza, Argentina.

introduced fine winemaking to the Americas. Now his great-grandson is concentrating on making high-quality boutique wines—earthquakes notwithstanding.

ⓘ **Bodega Benegas Lynch,** Carril Ardoz and Ruta 60, Lujan de Cuyo (☏ **54/261/496-0794;** www.bodegabenegas.com).

✈ Mendoza (18km/11 miles).

🛏 $$ **Le Terrada Suites,** Calle Terrada 1668, Perdriel, Lujan de Cuyo (☏ **54/261/154-31136;** www.terradasuites.com). $$ **Club Tapiz,** Ruta 60, Lujan de Cuyo (☏ **54/11/4005-0050;** www.tapiz.com.ar).

South America 352

Familia Schroeder

Dungeons & Dragons

Neuquén, Patagonia, Argentina

The winery Familia Schroeder has a lot of things going for it. For one thing, it is in Argentina, one of the rising stars of winemaking in the New World. This nation has been making wine for 200 years, and lots of it—it's the sixth biggest producer in the world. Until the 1990s, however, most of it was drunk by porteños (residents of Buenos Aires), most of whom are of Mediterranean background and partial to a drop of *vino*. Now that Argentine wineries are exporting their excellent-value wines, booming sales are being led by a grape called Malbec, the country's signature varietal.

But Familia Schroeder isn't just in Argentina, it's in Patagonia—a romantic name that conjures up images of desolate beauty, glaciers, Alpine lakes and forests, and end-of-the-world remoteness. Just to place the name on a wine label invites you to try it. The winery is in fact a long way from the southern toe of Argentina, being halfway up this long wedge-shaped country, near the northern Patagonian city of Neuquen. But the landscape does not disappoint. The winery is set on an austere, windy plain in a brand-new winemaking region called San Patricio del Chañar. The ice-tipped Andes tower far in the distance, acting as a huge umbrella that shelters the land from any coastal dampness. Dry air equals healthy grapes, though they are watered well by melted snow, carried by pipe to each individual plant in a system known as drip irrigation.

Familia Schroeder suits its surroundings. A stark gray monolith, snuggled into the side of a slope, hides five stories of tanks, barrels, and cellars designed with a gravity system that ensures the juice requires little pumping. The elegant winery restaurant serves gourmet food with a big sky view.

Yet it is in the cellar that the winery hides its prize possession. Sure, there are stacks of Malbec and Chardonnay stored amid immaculate brick-lined corridors with designer spot lighting. There's Schroeder's Pinot Noir, reputedly the finest in South America. Yet what makes visitors gasp is a simple pile of bones: Embedded in the walls are 75-million-year-old dinosaur fossils, dug up by accident when the winery was planting its first vineyards. They're some of the oldest dinosaur fossils in the world, commemorated in the name of Schroeder's top wines, Saurus.

You suddenly realize why Familia Schroeder is different from every other winery. They may all have dungeons, but no others have dragons.

ⓘ **Familia Schroeder,** Calle 7 Norte, San Patricio del Chañar, Neuquén (☏ **54/299/489-9600;** www.saurus.com.ar).

Neuquén (53km/32 miles).

$$ **Hotel del Comahue,** Avda Argentina 377, Neuquén (© **54/299/443-2040;** www.hoteldelcomahue.com). $$ **Hotel**

Costa Limay, Baschman 269, Plottier (© **54/299/493-6832;** www.hotelcosta limay.com.ar).

Colomé

Cactus & Vineyards

Salta, Argentina

The tiny wine town of Cafayate has its own distinct colors—pink dust, red hills, and olive-green mountains. Corn-yellow sand gathers along the curbstones of this sun-kissed village, while gray donkeys graze on the central plaza. Heaps of unlocked bicycles stand outside schools and the coffee-colored cathedral. Add to this some lovely baronial wineries, luxury lodges, excellent arts and crafts, and stunning vineyard country producing the aromatic white Torrontes grape—and you can see why this area is becoming known as the Tuscany of Argentina.

Colomé is the newest edition to Salta's ever-increasing list of wineries. Located 4 hours over bumpy, unpaved roads from either Cafayate or Salta city, it fits in nicely with owner Donald Hess's penchant for building art-gallery wineries in far-flung, isolated places. The scenery is spectacular, with giant cacti giving a three-fingered salute amid vineyards and multicolored mountains. As you approach the winery, you pass the ancient village of Molinos, which has been virtually adopted by the winery—Hess not only employs the local population, he has built the village a new church and community center.

Neat, stone-lined roads lead to a low cream-colored colonial-style building with a long gallery of arches, an upscale lodge and restaurant catering to guests who want to escape from it all. (In fact, getting here requires such a long dusty drive, it's best to stay overnight in the area.) The restaurant produces some of Argentina's best cuisine—no small achievement considering the excellent restaurants of Buenos Aires. There is a helicopter pad for high rollers, and talk of a private landing strip for airplanes.

These are biodynamic vineyards, producing high-octane Malbec and Torrontes grapes. At over 2,000m (6,500 ft.) altitude, they are also some of the highest in the world. The winery itself—designed to be totally energy efficient—is situated away from the main lodge complex, in a stark, modern building with a stylish design that fits well with the owner's collection of thought-provoking art.

Some people might think it strange that a world-class art collection should be gathered in such an isolated place, in a region that looks and feels more like Bolivia than any other part of Argentina. Yet with the backdrop of that dazzling scenery, an award-winning art gallery may be just what it needs. It certainly has breathed life into a community.

ⓘ **Bodega Colomé,** Ruta Provincial 53, Molinos (© **54/3868-494044;** www.bodega colome.com).

✈ Salta (222km/138 miles).

$$$ **Patios de Cafayate,** Ruta Nacional 40 at Ruta Provincial 68, Cafayate (© **54/3868/421747;** www.luxurycollection. com/Cafayate). $$ **Hostal Killa,** Colon 47, Cafayate (© **54/3868/422-254;** www. hostalkillacafayate.nortevirtual.com).

Viña Montes

The Full Monte

Colchagua Valley, Chile

When Chilean winemaker Aurelio Montes first scouted a rocky, forested hillside in Chile's Colchagua Valley in the 1980s and suggested planting it with Syrah vines, he was told he was crazy. Chile had a well-established wine industry, but it was mostly centered closer to the capital, Santiago, and focused on mass-market table wines. Colchagua, however, is a dry valley 160km south (100 miles), tucked between the Pacific and the towering Andes. On these narrow plains, a few winemakers grew Cabernet Sauvignon vines, irrigating them with open water channels. To plant Syrah on a steep incline and water it with expensive piped irrigation seemed pure folly.

Montes went ahead anyway. In recognition of his critics, he even called his new wine Montes Folly. Of course, it astounded the naysaying critics, earning an unprecedented 92 points from Robert Parker, Jr., for its second vintage. Montes had not only put Colchagua on the map, he had also launched Chile and South America into the ranks of the world's elite wine-making regions.

Montes had a point to prove and he proved it beautifully. Chile *was* capable of producing more than mediocre supermarket wines. The winery started out as a four-man partnership and $65,000 investment back in 1988; it now produces more than three million bottles a year and exports to 76 countries around the world.

It is regarded as Chile's flagship fine-wine operation.

The winery itself is a modern glass structure tucked away in the dusty folds of this dry valley. At the forefront of developing wine tourism in Chile, Viña Montes delivers an excellent winery experience. Guides are knowledgeable, and tours are exhilarating, rumbling guests along hard yellow dust paths in the back of white pickup trucks, crisscrossing the spread-out estate. Tours include an excursion up a steep mountain path, where a sunny lookout platform affords commanding views of the surrounding area. Here you can sample some of Chile's famous seafood, paired with wines such as Merlot, Cabernet Sauvignon, and the local favorite Carménère. Back at the winery, the dramatic circular barrel room reminds you of a Shakespearean theater—except that here you'll find no folly, farce, or tragedy. Just pure joy.

ⓘ **Viña Montes,** Parcela 15, Millahue de Apalta, Santa Cruz (✆ **56/72/825417;** www.monteswines.com).

✈ Santiago de Chile (164km/102 miles).

🛏 $$$ **Casa Lapostolle Winery Lodge,** Clos Apalta Winery, Santa Cruz (✆ **56/72/321-803;** www.casalapostolle.com). $$$ **Hotel Santa Cruz Plaza,** Plaza de Armas 286, Santa Cruz (✆ **56/72/209-600;** www.hotelsantacruzplaza.cl).

Viu Manent

The Chile Express

Colchagua Valley, Chile

An aproned steward serves you the best Chilean wine as you sit back on Merlot-colored velvet seats and take in the Andean peaks rolling by. You are sitting on the San Fernandez–Santa Cruz wine train, a steam-operated railway that travels 42km (26 miles) into the heart of Chile's finest wine country, Colchagua Valley. This is no graffiti-covered commuter subway, but a sleek set of restored rail carriages with polished brass fittings, elegant curtains, and white cloth-laid tables with wine glasses sprouting immaculate napkins. It gently rattles past a valley of vines with the odd farmyard and terra-cotta-topped house. It is the best way to arrive in style at the bright yellow railway station of the valley's main port of call, the laid-back wine town of Santa Cruz.

Santa Cruz is the jumping-off point to visit one of Chile's most beautiful wineries, Viu Manent. The heart of the winery is a 19th-century hacienda that exudes class and colonial grandeur. Your tour begins with a horse-and-carriage ride through the vineyards, where you learn that this is one of the few places on earth that evaded the vine disease phylloxera, which nearly wiped out the fine-wine industry at the turn of the 20th century. Because of Colchagua's relative isolation, its vines escaped the devastating root lice that caused havoc in the rest of the world. The vines you are looking at have venerable lineage indeed, especially the Cabernet Sauvignons, Malbecs, and Merlots that were among the area's first cultivated vines.

Back at the tasting center, you'll find white adobe buildings surrounding a picturesque garden with a central fountain. Pyramids of old oak barrels stand in a bright, stylish tasting room bedecked with red walls and colorful art. There is also a charming restaurant, graced with a sweeping landscape painting of the valley that runs along an entire wall. Elsewhere, back-lit wooden vats sit amid easy chairs in a room of bare wooden rafters and beams. It is at once old and modern, quaint and stylish.

The owners of this family-run winery still live close at hand, in a gorgeous Spanish-style villa, where they can personally oversee the winemaking operations. It all

The vineyards of Viu Manent.

Transporting the harvest at Viu Manent.

harks back to an earlier era, except for the wines. You'll find no sleepy bottled throw-backs here—just Colchagua Valley's fin-est, most up-to-date vintages.

ⓘ **Viu Manent,** Av. Antonio Varas 2740, Santiago (✆ **56/2/379-0020;** www.viu manent.cl).

✈ Santiago de Chile (152km/95 miles).

🛏 $$$ **Hotel Santa Cruz Plaza,** Plaza de Armas 286, Santa Cruz (✆ **56/72/209-600;** www.hotelsantacruzplaza.cl). $$$ **Casa Silva,** Hijuela Norte s/n, San Fernando (✆ **56/2/710-180;** www.casasilva.cl).

South America **356**

Viña Indómita
Operation Indómita
Casablanca, Chile

You work for the French Secret Service. You have been sent on an urgent mission to discover the high-tech underground lair of a company intent on world wine domi-nation. Intelligence and satellite imagery have located the winery in the coastal region of Casablanca in Chile. This is not surprising—the valley is fast becoming the heartland for some of the most prestigious white wines to come out of South Amer-ica. A Pacific breeze coupled with intense afternoon sunshine is creating an army of grapes that threatens the Old World order. Further investigations and discreet inquiries at the tourist office in Santiago de Chile reveal that your quarry is located 80km (49 miles) from the capital. Its name: Vina Indomita.

Penetrating vineyard security is your next challenge. You go disguised as a tourist, armed with a digital camera and SPF 30 sunscreen. The winery is a gleaming, churchlike structure on top of a hill overlooking hundreds of acres of vineyards. Huge white arches sweep in front of a mirrored-glass facade that leads to a tall round tower. The fact that you made a telephone appointment gets you safely past reception, and suddenly you are in the heart of a gleaming, hangarlike winery crammed with tanks and the latest winemaking wizardry. It is huge, spacious, and well designed. The network of pipes that feed the stainless-steel vats is operated by an invincible energy source—gravity. The impression is startling—it looks unnervingly like the showroom for a secret weapon.

You go below, skillfully dodging a busy platoon of men on forklifts. Built into the side of the hill, the cellar room is cool and dark. Tidy rows of barrels line the long cellar floor. You surreptitiously join a tour group and successfully infiltrate the wine-tasting rooms. The hostess pours you an Indomita Sauvignon Blanc, golden and fragrant. You are speechless.

Dangerous thoughts of defecting enter your head. You could hide out in the nearby Pacific resort of Viña del Mar, you begin to plot resourcefully. To buy time, you decide to have lunch in the winery restaurant, an elegant space of curved windows, designer lamps, and polished floors. Desperately trying to maintain your cover, you order some wine from the winery's vineyards in Maipo Valley, a region just south of Santiago with some of the oldest vineyards in South America. You sip the delicious Carménère.

You panic.

You see the future, and it says Indómita. The French are doomed. You envision huge lakes of European wine, unwanted Beaujolais poured down drains. You must go and report to HQ as soon as possible, but wait. First let's try that nice bottle of Cabernet Sauvignon. . . .

ⓘ **Viña Indómita,** Casablanca Valley (✆ **56/32/275-4400;** www.indomita.cl).

✈ Santiago de Chile (72km/44 miles).

🛏 $$$ **Hotel Casablanca Valle,** Ruta 68, Tapihue, Casablanca (✆ **56/32/274-2711;** www.hotelrutadelvino.cl). $$ **Hotel Thomas Somerscales,** San Enrique 446, Cerro Alegre, Valparaíso (✆ **56/32/233-1006;** www.hotelsomerscales.cl).

357 South America

Casa Madero

A Mexican Revolution

Coahuila, Mexico

Think Mexican wine is a new phenomenon? Think again. Founded in 1597, Casa Madero is the oldest winery in the Western Hemisphere, an intriguing mix of Spanish colonial splendor and ancient winemaking heritage.

Walking around the winery grounds, you realize that there is a lot more to Mexican beverages than tequila and beer. Take, for example, the copper still on a narrow brick pedestal—it looks like a giant magic lantern, except that in this case, the genie in the bottle is brandy. The steel tank room that holds surprisingly good Chardonnay is actually an outside courtyard dappled in sunlight with a long vine-covered pergola providing shade. Elsewhere, old shuttered windows lead to silent cellars with dark oak casks. At your tastings, looks for the Cabernet Sauvignons and Shirazes that have won the winery so many medals lately.

The Maderos are one of Mexico's oldest families, with a heritage that goes back centuries. They are members of the landed gentry, with a range of business interests that include gold and silver mines and TV channels; their ancestors include assassinated presidents. But the Maderos certainly know how to throw a fiesta: Every year they hold a family reunion on the sprawling estate and invite every relative, all 5,000 of them. Private jets ferry guests onto their personal airstrip, and the festivities include bullfighting and good old-fashioned horsemanship, not to mention lots of food and wine.

Casa Madero's owners have decided to extend further this typical Mexican hospitality by opening a wine lodge for guests (groups only). The 25-room **Posada Casa Grande** is a long, white adobe building draped in purple bougainvillea, complete with a splendid wide lawn, serene shaded courtyards, and an immaculate blue swimming pool. The decor is deeply Old World—16th-century art and ancient tapestries on the walls, hand-carved wooden

furniture in every room. The whole beautiful complex is set in its own lush valley of vines surrounded by dry crumpled hills.

The resurgence in Mexican wine is happening mostly in Baja California; Madero is much farther east, 210km (130 miles) west of Monterey, close to a quaint colonial town called Parras. But the name Parras means "vines" in Spanish, and the city has been trying to raise its wine profile, holding a spectacular wine festival every August and hosting outside consultants, who have jump-started a marked increase in the region's wine quality. After all, it has dry desert soil, constant sunshine, and spring-irrigated vineyards—a perfect wine-making climate.

Beautiful, gracious Casa Madero is definitely off the beaten track, but it is worth an adventurous road trip. After all, how many 400-year-old wineries are there?

ⓘ **Casa Madero,** Emilio Carranza Sur 732, Parras, Coahuila (✆ **52/8/390-0936;** www.madero.com.mx).

✈ Torreon Airport (124km/77 miles).

🛏 $$ **Hampton Inn Torreon Coahuila,** Perif Raul Lopez Sanchez 10995, Torreon (✆ **52/871/705-1550;** www.hamptoninn.hilton.com). $$ **Howard Johnson Torreon Coahuila,** Hidalgo 1353 Poniente C.P., Torreon (✆ **800/446-4656;** www.hojo.com).

Vergelegen

The Cape of Good Hope

Stellenbosch, Western Cape, South Africa

Standing beside the fat trunks of 300-year-old camphor trees, you begin to question the concept of New World and old-world wines. Surely this South African winery has more claim to the badge of heritage and tradition than, say, a modern day

garagista working out of a steel-framed corrugated warehouse in Bordeaux.

After all, wines were first made here in the Western Cape in the 17th century, when Jan Van Riebeeck first saw the potential for vine-growing in these sweeping valleys of dry orange soil. He pestered his superiors back in Europe to send him some vine cuttings. His bosses at the Dutch East India Company must have thought him crazy. African wine? How ridiculous! They eventually relented, however, and sent him some sprigs. Seven years later, on February 2, 1659, he noted in his diary "Today, so praise be to God, wine was pressed from Cape grapes for the first time."

There are no tasting notes to tell us how it went, but soon South African wine became favored by European aristocrats, deprived of French wine during the Napoleonic wars. Ironically, years later Napoleon himself drank it liberally to drown his sorrows while brooding in exile at Elba.

These ancient camphor trees were planted by Van Riebeeck's successor, Governor Willem Adrian van der Stel. In 6 short years he transformed a barren valley west of Cape Town into lush orchards, orange groves, vineyards, and cattle farms by installing an irrigation system. Amid gardens and vineyards he built a majestic homestead that can be visited today. But after Willem Adrian was expelled from the colony, the property was broken up and the estate fell into disrepair—as did the South African wine industry. Its low point was probably the dark days of apartheid, when wine from this region became about as politically correct as whale oil.

New owners in 1987 went about reviving the Vergelegen vineyards. Just as Nelson Mandela ushered in a new era in South African politics, Vergelegen has become the country's flagship winery. It produces a dark and elegant Shiraz and a complex, spicy Cabernet Sauvignon. The winery is a fascinating mix of old and new: Its magnificent mansion is surrounded by an octagonal wall enclosing beautiful grounds with petal-strewn lawns and delightful lily ponds. This eight-sided motif is repeated with the octagonal hilltop winery, built with space-age winemaking facilities and cellars arranged around a gravity system. With its onsite restaurant and hill walking tour, the entire experience feels like a glossy photo shoot for *Homes & Gardens*.

Standing on the winery's minimalist roof garden, enjoying a 360-degree view of mountains and blue bay, you again question the logic of labeling wine regions Old World and New World. The answer is obvious. Vergelegen is neither Old World nor New World—it is Other World.

ⓘ **Vergelegen,** Somerset West (☎ **27/ 21/847-1334;** www.vergelegen.co.za).

✈ Cape Town Airport (25km/15 miles).

🛏 $$$ **Arabella Western Cape Hotel & Spa,** R 44 Kleinmond, Overberg (☎ **27/ 28/284-0000;** www.westerncapehotel andspa.co.za). $$ **Best Western Cape Suites Hotel,** De Villiers and Constitution streets, Cape Town (☎ **27/21/461-0727;** www.capesuites.co.za).

359 Southern Hemisphere

Penfolds

Shiraz Conquers the World

Adelaide, Australia

If the grape is called Syrah, why do so many wineries these days call their Syrah wines Shiraz? The answer lies Down Under, in a dynamic South Australian winery named Penfolds.

In 1844, a visionary English doctor, Christopher Rawson Penfold, planted some French cuttings around his humble cottage called "the Grange" outside of Adelaide, to make fortified wine for his patients. Within 20 years it was producing 500,000 liters (132,000 gal.) a year. By the 1920s, half of all bottles of wine sold in Australia were from Penfolds, which had by then expanded to include extensive property in the Barossa Valley. In 1955 came a major turning point: Penfolds produced Australia's first fine wine, a Syrah (or "shiraz" in Australia-speak) called Penfolds Grange. It went on to win 50 gold medals around the world; wine writer Hugh Johnson called it "the only `first growth´ of the southern hemisphere" (a reference to France's most elite ranking system), while wine critic Robert Parker, Jr., called it "the world's most exotic and concentrated wine." The wine became so influential, other wineries around the world began to mimic the Australian word Shiraz to describe Syrah, even though their wines were made with Syrah grapes.

Australian wine has conquered the world, with Penfolds leading the charge. Its flagship operation, The Grange, is located 15 minutes outside Adelaide, the sunny capital of South Australia. You cannot miss the winery's tall white chimney-stack, with "Penfolds" written large and vertical. Here you'll find 60-year-old Shiraz vineyards surrounding the original stone cottage, as well as a rock-walled winery trimmed in red brick. Inside are the usual tunnels and cellars, along with a port barrel so huge you could throw a party in it. Around the back is an ultra-modern glass-fronted restaurant. The old still house holds Penfolds' award-winning tasting room, the Cellar Door.

Penfold's other main facility is 1 hour north of Adelaide in the Barossa Valley, the huge dusty, heart of Australian wine. Here kangaroos jump old bush vines and the hilly landscape of vineyards and long dry grass is punctuated with German architecture and restaurants. Penfolds Barossa is a huge building first constructed in 1911 with many extensions, including reputedly the biggest cellar room in the Southern Hemisphere.

The Barossa valley facility offers a special blending tour—a tour of the vineyards and winery, followed by a session in the winery laboratory. You don a white coat and listen to the instructor talk of the fascinating art of blending, then make your own blend, which is then bottled for you to take home. The label will have your name on it, beside the title "Assistant Wine-maker." Will you come out knowing the difference between Syrah and Shiraz? That's for you to find out.

ⓘ **Penfolds,** 78 Penfold Rd., Magill (✆ **61/ 8/8301-5569;** www.penfolds.com.au).

✈ Adelaide International (17km/10 miles).

🛏 $$$ **Majestic Roof Garden Hotel,** 55 Frome St., Adelaide (✆ **61/8/8100-4400;** www.majestichotels.com.au). $$$ **Quality Hotel Old Adelaide,** 160 O'Connell St., North Adelaide (✆ **61/8/8267-5066;** www. oldadelaideinn.com.au).

Southern Hemisphere 360

Seppelt Winery
Old Skool Winery
Barossa Valley, Australia

Everything about Seppelt Winery is eccentric. Polish immigrant Joseph Seppelt founded it in 1851, making it one of Australia's most historic wineries. His son Benno was fond of galloping around the estate on a white horse with a violin strapped to his back and an umbrella over his head. When the winery went through a rough patch in the late 19th century, rather than lay off workers, Benno, who was now in charge, had them plant as many trees as they could to keep them busy. (They obviously had a lot of time on their hands—the 150-year old winery is now surrounded by 2,000 palm trees.) Then Benno had the marvelous idea to age his fortified wine for 100 years. The winery now has port older than Portugal's; a bottle of its rich syrupy Para Liquer Port sells for $1,000 a bottle. Needless to say, this wine is not offered in the usual tasting sessions.

The winery itself, located 1 hour from Adelaide, is like something from Charles Dickens's *Old Curiosity Shop.* To enter the winery, you pass the charming family home and over a little bridge through a lush, tropical garden. The winery building is something of a shock—long and box-like, it looks like a sunken steamboat. This is the original gravity winery, built long before the current fad for all things Newtonian. While modern winemakers let gravity have its way, rather than use machines to pump the wine from tank to vat to barrel—they claim that pumping "stresses" the juice—old Seppelt built his winery with good old-fashioned practicality in mind: Lacking electricity, he built the winery atop a set of terraces, where the grapes could go in one end and have their juice flow through the crushers and tanks to casks at the other end. Beyond the winery is a massive warehouse with 9 million liters (2.3 million gal.) of maturing wine, stacked in pyramids in ancient barrels.

The winery is a living museum to how things used to be done on an industrial scale. A set of old steam-powered engines sits in pristine condition, surrounded by pulleys and chain drives. Back near the entrance, you'll find an intriguing museum with grape crushers that date from the 1890s. All sorts of oddities lie around the room, including ancient sales rep kits and well-thumbed accounts ledgers. A few brandy pot stills remind you that in the past the winery produced other products besides wine, including vinegar and sherry. Turn the corner and you'll find another cellar with 3 million liters (800,000 gal.) of wine gently aging (watched over by a ghost, or so the tour guides tell you).

In the tasting room, a series of rich and concentrated ports are laid before you—a tribute to old Seppelt's vision. As you sip and enjoy, you can almost imagine you hear the plaintive strains of his ghost's violin echoing from the cellar.

ⓘ **Seppelt Winery,** Seppeltsfield (✆ **61/8/8568-6217;** www.seppelt.com.au).

✈ Adelaide (77km/47 miles).

🛏 $$$ **The Lodge Country House,** RSD 120, Seppeltsfield (✆ **61/8/8562-8277;** www.thelodgecountryhouse.com.au). $$ **Barossa Motor Lodge,** 182 Murray St., Tanunda (✆ **61/8/8563-298;** www.barossamotorlodge.com.au).

361 Southern Hemisphere

Stonier's Winery

The Peninsula

Mornington Peninsula, Victoria, Australia

Start the day with a bracing walk up to Arthur's Seat, a 300m-high (980-ft.) granite hill that provides sweeping views of Mornington Peninsula and the distant Melbourne skyline. Seabirds swoop down on yacht-spangled Port Phillip Bay. The coastal road runs before you, passing pale sandy beaches with colorful vacation huts and shaggy dunes leading to golf links. Surfers ride the morning waves, and the cool wind brushes through fruit orchards, pine trees, and vineyards.

Places to Eat in . . . Sydney, Australia

For lack of a better term, cuisine in Australia's most cosmopolitan city has been labeled Mod Oz—a melding of local ingredients with an international grab bag of culinary traditions, the birthright of this polyglot nation of immigrants. Even though it's hardly a new phenomenon—the first Mod Oz menus appeared in the early 1990s—its spirit still energizes the dining scene in this Pacific port, where ambitious young chefs become celebrities overnight.

Rockpool's chef Neil Perry sources all his ingredients locally.

Of course the pioneer Mod Oz restaurants are still outstanding and breaking new ground. The serene setting of elegant ⟨362⟩ **Tetsuya's** (529 Kent St.; ✆ **61/2/9267 2900;** www.tetsuyas.com)—two starkly contemporary dining rooms overlooking a traditional Japanese garden—is a metaphor for Tetsuya Wakada's brilliant cooking, which is a paradoxical blend of Japanese delicacy and maverick imagination. The only option here is the pricey, precisely choreographed 10-course tasting menu: Dishes might include a shot of pea soup with bitter chocolate sorbet, a leek-and-crab custard, a confit of seaweed-crusted Tasmanian ocean trout on a bed of daikon radish and fennel, or grilled Wagyu beef with wasabi and lime. Book 4 weeks in advance, and prepare to be wowed. Tetsuya's colleague Neil Perry at ⟨363⟩ **Rockpool** (109 George St.; ✆ **61/2/9252 1888;** www.rockpool.com) is fanatical about sourcing, whether it be sustainable local seafood, his award-winning wine list, or his select cheese board. But what vaults this gleaming wood-burnished restaurant to the top is his globe-trotting range of preparations—dishes such as grilled king prawns with goat-cheese tortellini, pine nuts, and raisins; a whole john dory pan-fried with Indian spices and served with tomato, braised silverbeet (Swiss chard), and cardamom sauce; or sautéed bass grouper with *vongole,* cabbage, serrano ham, tea-smoked potato, and herb butter sauce.

The city's most dazzling panoramic view, day or night, is at ⟨364⟩ **Quay** (Upper level, Overseas Passenger Terminal, Circular Quay West; ✆ **61/2/9251 5600;** www.quay.com.au), with its wall of windows overlooking the harbor, Opera House, and Sydney skyline. But chef Peter Gilmore's subtle, playful cooking, with vegetables and herbs from Quay's own farm in the Blue Mountains, more than lives up to that view. Signature items include poached rock lobster with lobster-and-tapioca dumplings, crisp pig-belly confit with a braise of abalone and soft curds of handmade tofu, or his wondrous "sea pearls"—tiny opalescent globes of sturgeon roe, abalone, tuna, scallops, octopus, eel, mud crab, and oyster pearl meat. The floor-to-ceiling harbor views at sleek 🔵 **Aria** (1 Macquarie St.; ☎ **61/2/9252 2555;** www.ariarestaurant. com.au) are similarly eclipsed by Matthew Moran's intricate preparations—dishes such as pan-fried jewfish fillets with globe artichokes and potato chips, a sweet pork loin with black pudding and apple-and-elderflower purée, or a lamb loin roasted with basil, ratatouille, and fennel. (It's worth forfeiting the view to book a seat in the kitchen at Moran's chef's table.) Set above a swimming club on the cliffs overlooking Bondi Beach, trendy 🔵 **Icebergs** (1 Notts Ave.; ☎ **61/2/9365 9000;** www.irdb.com) has its own breathtaking ocean view and a cool airy dining room with ice-blue frosted-glass dividers and crisp white table linens. Somehow that view makes you long for *frutti di mare,* and the menu obliges, with superb haute-Italian preparations such as risotto with coral trout and oregano or savory Ancona-style fish stew.

Coming down several notches on the price scale, take a CityRail train out to student-y Newtown, where the tiny black-and-white cafe 🔵 **Oscillate Wildly** (275 Australia Dr.; ☎ **61/2/9517 4700**) has a history of hiring daring young future-star chefs. The latest, Karl Firla, started in January 2009. Molecular gastronomy experiments here include salmon roe on a dollop of pureed cauliflower and white chocolate; or beef cheek with watermelon foam and turtle bean. Need a break from kitchen wizardry? Go "down the loo"—out to Woolloomooloo—to 🔵 **Harry's Café de Wheels** (Cowper Wharf Rd.; ☎ **2/9357 3074;** www.harryscafedewheels.com.au). Now an officially decreed landmark, this food truck has been serving hearty meat pies since 1938. Even the hippest of Sydneysiders can't resist an occasional late-night stop at Harry's for a meat pie topped with mashed potatoes, peas, and gravy.

✈ Sydney International.

🛏 **$$ Ravesi's On Bondi Beach,** Corner of Hall St. and Campbell Parade, Bondi Beach (☎ **61/2/9365 1481;** www.ravesis. com.au). $$ **The Russell,** 143A George St., The Rocks (☎ **61/2/ 9241 3543;** www.the russell.com.au).

The view at Quay takes in Sydney's harbor, opera house, and skyline.

There are no fewer than 60 wineries on Mornington Peninsula, and undoubtedly one of the foremost is Stonier's. In 1978, when there was no wine industry to speak of down here, Brian Stonier bought a plot of land in the area, hoping to do something special for his daughter's wedding by making his own sparkling wine. On his new land he planted the classic champagne varietals Chardonnay and Pinot Noir (it was obviously a long engagement). By lucky chance, Mornington's cool maritime climate proved perfect for producing wines with vibrant acidity, and Stonier's varietal wines were soon winning awards around the world. (His Pinot Noir in particular has been declared the best on the planet by several critics.) Stonier himself is now regarded as one of Australia's preeminent winemakers. He's gone well beyond wedding bubbly.

Stonier's new winery, built in 2001, is a startling arrangement of gray and white corrugated walls and sharp angular open roofing. Here winery staff members conduct excellent and informative tours; their wine tastings also include food platters that showcase the rich produce of the peninsula.

Mornington Peninsula has its own charms, well worth the excursion from Melbourne. Traditionally an agricultural zone and weekend getaway, "the peninsula" (as locals call it) has undergone a recent renaissance. Weekenders and tourists still come for the Mediterranean-style beaches, but they are also flocking here to check out the region's wineries and a new wave of olive farms. Known as the fruit basket of Victoria, the peninsula has several farmer's markets, with everything from apricots to asparagus in bountiful display. Artists have set up shop, and antique dealers are open to catch the wandering tourist. There is a national park to hike around in the toe of the peninsula, and long piers where you can stroll down into the sunset.

But whatever you do, don't forget the champagne.

ⓘ **Stoniers,** Frankston Flinders Rd. and Thompsons Lane, Merricks (✆ **61/3/5989-8300;** www.stoniers.com.au).

✈ Melbourne airport (114km/70 miles).

🛏 $$ **Crown Promenade Hotel,** 8 Whiteman St., Southbank (✆ **61/3/9292-6688;** www.crownpromenade.com.au). $$$ **Lindenderry,** 142 Arthurs Seat Rd., Red Hill (✆ **61/3/5989-2933;** www.lindenderry.com.au).

McWilliams Mount Pleasant Estate
Getting High on Mount Pleasant
Hunter Valley, Australia

In 1962 locals in the Hunter Valley noticed a new type of weed growing along ditches and embankments in this river valley 2 hours north of Sydney. The tenacious green plant soon began appearing everywhere, along streams and rivers, ditches and irrigation canals. When the Department of Agriculture and Fisheries was called in, they identified it as cannabis, causing a sensation in the press (and excitement in college circles). The police promised to wipe it out in one summer. They failed.

The rampant weed soon covered 30 sq. km (18 sq. miles) and had overtaken entire fields, some as large as 8 hectares (19 acres). A cat-and-mouse game began between law enforcement and cannabis lovers, with the latter making midnight raids and harvesting the weed buds for drying and distribution in Sydney. In the end, the authorities had to bring in crop-dusting aircraft and powerful chemicals to beat the infestation. It ended up taking 9 years to eradicate.

Fortunately Hunter Valley is more famous for another type of intoxicating substance called wine. The oldest wine region in Australia, established as early as 1830, it contains almost 200 wineries, most of them in the Lower Hunter Valley. This open, picturesque landscape, with gentle hills and fertile plains, makes a popular day trip from Sydney—most wineries are open to visitors, and they run the gamut from large and high-tech to small and rustic.

One of the most famous Hunter Valley wineries, McWilliams was founded in 1921 by legendary winemaker Maurice O'Shea, one of the first pioneers to recognize the fine-wine promise in Australian *terroir*. The winery is particularly well known for its single-vineyard Semillon, often called the best in the world. Visiting McWilliams, you'll admire its grand, pioneer-style homestead with its wraparound veranda overlooking the vineyards. Well-clipped hedges border a tidy lawn, and steps lead to a large courtyard with fountain. Inside the house are large salons with bare, raftered ceilings and a fascinating photographic display detailing a 60-year history of winemaking.

The on-site restaurant, Elizabeth's, comes highly recommended for its special tapas-style menu, where each morsel of food is paired with a particular wine.

The actual winery itself is a gigantic warehouse behind the homestead, where McWilliams's excellent, well-trained staffers conduct informative tours and tastings. Seeing the modern, somewhat industrial facilities, you can believe that this is the largest family-owned winery in Australia. Don't miss tasting the Semillon—it is excellent, strong and full-bodied. As you swirl it around you can understand why it is one of the few white wines that can be successfully aged. Just be sure it is not a wine from the sixties—that might give new meaning to the term "a grassy taste."

ⓘ **McWilliams,** Marrowbone Rd., Pokolbin (✆ **61/2/4998-7505;** www.mountpleasantwines.com.au).

✈ Sydney International (173km/107 miles).

🛏 $$ **The Kirketon Hotel,** 229 Darlinghurst Rd., Darlinghurst (✆ **61/2/9332-2011;** www.kirketon.com). $$$ **Patrick Plains Estate,** 647 Hermitage Rd., Pokolbin, NSW (✆ **61/2/6574-7071;** www.patrickplains.com).

370 Southern Hemisphere

Vasse Felix

Walkabout in Margaret River

Margaret River, Australia

The neighbors must have thought him mad. Dr. Tom Cullity would rise at 3am every Saturday morning and drive 3 hours south from Perth to Margaret River. He would spend the weekend wandering the forested land, hand-boring the clay with an auger, and sleeping in a metal shed at night. It seemed like a modern reincarnation of the Aborigine ritual known as *walkabout*.

Cullity did this for over a year before he found what he was looking for—gravely soil, which he had read was essential for growing vines. This was in the 1960s, when Margaret River was an inhospitable Western Australia backwater with just a few hardy farmers and some brave surfers. The Australian government had tried to encourage settlement there in the 1920s, but with dismal results. The land was just not suitable for dairy farming. Nobody thought about growing vines, except Dr. Cullity.

Eventually finding his patch of suitable soil, Cullity bought 3.2 hectares (8 acres) at $75 an acre. His first vintage in 1972 was a disaster, but Cullity was learning as he was going along, and his learning curve was steep. (One mistake he made: spraying the vines with veterinary medicine.) Yet by 1974, his Riesling and Cabernet Sauvignon were winning awards and people started to take notice. Soon the big wineries out east were sending scouts to test Margaret River's air, and the price of land shot up. Margaret River now has 100 wineries producing 20% of Australia's premium wine; it's one of the fastest-growing economic regions in Australia, all because of the booming wine industry.

As you enter rustic, pastoral Vasse Felix, you'll notice the hawk blazoned on its stone entrance pillars—birds of prey were once used to deter grape-eating Silvereye birds. A long, tree-lined driveway leads to woodlands and streams surrounded by vineyards. The tasting room is a rock-and-wood cottage with a publike chalkboard on the large doorway advertising the price list. Part of the winery is a large hangarlike art gallery; there's also a pleasant restaurant with a wooden deck overlooking the vines.

As you taste some the winery's excellent reds, muse on the fact that so many of Australia's most famous wineries were started by medical doctors (others include Penfolds, Cullen, and Lindeman). There must be some link between wine and health. Or, as one local put it succinctly when trying Vasse Felix wine back in 1974: "It was," the humble builder said, "like pouring racing fuel into a bulldozer."

ⓘ **Vasse Felix,** Caves Rd. and Harmans Rd. S., Margaret River (✆ **61/897/565000**).

✈ Perth (282km/175 miles).

🛏 $$$ **Basildene Manor,** Wallcliffe Rd., Margaret River (✆ **61/897/573140;** www.basildene.com.au). $$ **Adamson's Riverside,** 71 Bussell Hwy., Margaret River, (✆ **61/897/572013;** www.adamsonsriverside.net.au).

Southern Hemisphere 371

Stony Ridge

Paradise Island

Waiheke Island, New Zealand

"Christ on a bike!" exclaims the tall stranger in shorts and flip-flops. He has just tasted the famous Stony Ridge Larose, and judging by the expression on his face, he likes it.

"That's golden, mate, I give you the word," he elaborates, before draining his glass completely.

Such praise is well deserved. Stony Ridge produces a Bordeaux-style blend that has more kick than the entire squad of the famous New Zealand rugby team, the All Blacks. The wine regularly outrates the best from Europe and California; it is even listed on the menus of Michelin-starred restaurants in Paris. The powerful red has become a collector's favorite, and like many other New Zealand wines, it gets a much better price on foreign wine shelves than alternatives from other countries.

It used to be that the only round and full-bodied thing to come from New Zealand was sheep. This green, verdant island nation is still very much agricultural, but as it diversifies its domestic product, it has entered the gourmet's paradise of fruit, vegetables, nuts, olive oil, and, most notably wine—particularly a zingy and herbaceous Sauvignon Blanc that has become the country's signature grape.

Vineyards have popped up the length and breadth of the country, on both the North Island and South Island, including wine regions with exotic Maori names such as Wairarapa, Aawatere, and Otago. The cool maritime climate with plentiful sun means the country can produce both reds and whites with lots of flavor and punch.

Stony Ridge is located on Waiheke Island, a tiny green collection of hillocks 40 minutes by ferry from the country's biggest city, Auckland. Sailboats sit on mirrorlike waters, as gentle green hills roll upward toward a lonely tree or a patch of the white netting that protects vines from birds. The island used to be a hippy haunt, full of individuals seeking an alternative lifestyle from the modern bustle of the city. Now it is a popular weekend retreat with 20-odd wineries to visit, excellent restaurants with great seafood, and lovely beach walks to help visitors digest that same food.

Stony Ridge evokes the Mediterranean with its faded pink walls and sky blue window frames. The giant silver tank along the side betrays the main pastime here. Out back, a charming, rickety veranda of green fencing and roof eaves holds a sunny terrace restaurant that overlooks the undulating vineyards. The Mediterranean cuisine is ideal to accompany Stony Ridge's deeply delicious reds—like the stranger said, that's golden, mate.

ⓘ **Stony Ridge,** 80 Onetangi Rd., Waiheke Island (✆ **64/9/372-8822;** www.stonyridge.co.nz).

✈ Auckland Airport (55km/34 miles).

🛏 $$ **Villa Pacifica,** Half Moon Bay, Waiheke Island (✆ **64/9/372-6326;** www.villapacifica.co.nz) $$ **Waiheke Midway Motel,** 1 Whakarite Rd., Ostend, Waiheke Island (✆ **64/9/372-8023;** www.waihekemotel.co.nz).

Craggy Range Winery

Where the World Is Your Oyster

Hawkes Bay, New Zealand

Steve Smith is obsessed with dirt. He is particularly concerned with the dark clay that nourishes his Hawkes Bay vineyard. He is annoyed that it is not a bit more like the famous clay of Bordeaux, which is peppered with light-colored stones that reflect the heat upwards. Smith even considered putting reflective fabric along the ground to get the same effect, but in the end he settled for something much more practical: crushed oyster shells from the nearby sea. They now act as fertilizer and heat reflector, bathing the canopy with sunlight and producing a more velvety wine.

Smith is a single-minded winemaker in a winery that produces single-vineyard wines. Craggy Range has been waking the world up to the fact that this far-off corner of the wine world is making not just great Sauvignon Blanc, but superb reds too. Smith's meticulous attention to detail is creating Pinot Noir, Merlot, and Bordeaux-style blends that outpunch their Australian neighbors and far-off rivals in Europe.

The winery complex—named the Giant's Winery, after a local Maori legend—is just as ambitious. Its stark design is Bordeaux-medieval meets New Zealand–barn house, held up with good old-fashioned steel and glass. This sprawling lakeshore complex of tall warehouse-style buildings ends in an imposing limestone roundhouse, site of the winery's restaurant, Terroir; in the distant vineyards there is a luxury lodge for guests. Suffice to say, it is impressive. In the distance lies a rocky line of mountains, the

The peaks from which Craggy Range Winery takes its name.

craggy range of the winery's title. Looming above them all is Te Mato Peak, a sacred Maori mountain regarded as powerful and serene.

Anchored by the lovely Art Deco town of Napier, the Hawkes Bay region stretches along the eastern coast of the North Island, known as the "garden of New Zealand." Not only does it boast some 30 wineries to visit, it's famous for its rich wholesome food, much of it organically farmed. Much of that local food ends up on the menu at Terroir, where it is cooked on an open fire in front of diners. The menu is strong on meat and seafood, including—you've guessed it—oysters. Steve Smith has to get his oyster shells from somewhere.

ⓘ **Craggy Range,** 253 Waimarama Rd., Havelock North (☏ **64/6/8730143;** www.craggyrange.com).

✈ Wellington (304km/188 miles).

🛏 $$ **Pebble Beach Motor Inn,** 445 Marine Parade, Napier, Hawkes Bay (☏ **64/6/835-7496;** www.pebblebeach.co.nz). $$ **Motel de la Mer,** 321 Marine Parade, Napier, (☏ **64/6/8356-7001;** www.moteldelamer.co.nz).

Southern Hemisphere

373

Montana Winery

A Whale of a Time

Marlborough, New Zealand

In the wine industry, big is not beautiful. Usually, the larger a winery is, the less well regarded is its wine. Big, industrial operations find it difficult to persuade the consumer that their wines are just as good as mollycoddled juice from a boutique, low-production winery with a lone and passionate winemaker.

Montana Winery, however, proves the exception to the rule. New Zealand's biggest winery used to be a big fish in a small pond; even now that the country's wines have become so popular, Montana has grown to become the country's champion brand. Its wines have achieved cult status around the world, particularly its herbal and aromatic Sauvignon Blanc.

Montana still produces 70% of New Zealand's output; it has vineyards dotted around the country, including Gisborne and Hawkes Bay. The heart of its operation, however, is in the verdant nucleus of Kiwi winemaking, coastal Wairau Valley on the South Island's northern end. Along the calm blue waters of Marlborough Sound, popular with sailors and vacationers, white foamy tides buff low cliffs crowned with green hedges and vineyards. The vast green plain of Wairau Valley spreads west of the region's laid-back town of Blenheim.

Traditionally farmland, in the past 30 years this area has replaced sheep and cow pastures with tidy lines of vineyards veiled with white silklike bird netting. Montana resembles a rustic French château more than a New World winery, with its tall, steep roof and tower covering a handsome cream-colored building facing onto an expansive lawn. Yet as you approach it from the stone gateway, you realize that this is a very modern operation. Inside you'll find a slick visitor center with tasting rooms, a wine store, and a small theater; the on-site restaurant serves excellent seafood, such as mussels and salmon farmed along the coast. There is even a wine-themed children's playground.

Open fireplaces built with river stones are scattered about to warm your toes in the cold season.

Speaking of cold, Montana has a big problem with frost. A late freeze in spring can destroy the harvest before it has even begun. Giant wind machines dot the landscape to create wind circulation that can raise the temperature and save the vine. On very cold nights, wineries in the area hire up to 100 helicopters to fly over the vines and beat off Jack Frost. Such high-tech winemaking is reflected in the winery, with its ultramodern *coquard* press. The only instrument of its kind in the Southern Hemisphere, this specially designed French grape crusher ensures a cleaner, fruitier juice. Montana also has invested in novel grape tipper tanks that you will not see anywhere else.

Montana is a popular stop on the tourist circuit, so expect crowds, especially in the high season. While you're here, try a little whale-watching in Marlborough Bay—that way you can see two big fish in one pond.

ⓘ **Montana Winery,** RD4, Blenheim (**64/9/3368300;** www.montana.co.nz).

✈ Christchurch (311km/193 miles).

🛏 $$ **Marlborough Vintners Hotel,** 190 Rapaura Rd. (**64/3/572-5094;** www. mvh.co.nz). $$ **Château Marlborough,** High and Henry Sts. (**64/3/578-0064;** www.marlboroughnz.co.nz).

374 Southern Hemisphere

Two Paddocks

Hidden Drama

Central Otago, New Zealand

Central Otago's landscape is certainly dramatic—dark forests and imposing moors, surrounded by snowcapped mountains and jagged creeks. Famous for old hiking trails, ski resorts, and abandoned gold mines, this part of the South Island is the last place you'd expect to find wine country. All the same, there are some 80 wineries in the area, all producing first-class Pinot Noir.

On first glance, though, Two Paddocks is one of the area's least dramatic wineries. A simple but attractive gray shed sits surrounded by lavender beds in a bucolic setting. A tall wood-framed porch leads to a barn-style facility with offices and a tasting room that looks like somebody's minimalist kitchen. The buildings blend in with the environment, the two paddocks referring to the surrounding vineyard.

This low-key, down-to-earth winery gives you no reason to guess that it's owned by one of New Zealand's most famous names—actor Sam Neill, star of movies such as *Jurassic Park* and *The Piano*. Call it his way of getting back to his own New Zealand roots. Neill started out making wine in 1997 for his family and friends. Soon he realized that it was good enough to sell—and, frankly, too good for his friends, who "would just drink anything." He proceeded to set up this beautiful winery in Central Otago, one of New Zealand's most noteworthy wine regions. By keeping his own star power out of the spotlight, he allows the wines themselves to shine.

Winemaking in Central Otago is a relatively recent phenomenon. A Frenchman called Jean Desire Feraud actually produced award-winning Pinot Noir here in 1895, but when he could not persuade the local miners to give up hard liquor, his enterprise failed. The land returned to sheep and rabbits. It was only in the 1980s that vineyards started popping up again. Now the Pinot Noir here is regarded as one of the best in the world, riding the crest of popularity this subtle wine has enjoyed of late.

Neill's low-key operation does not run formal tours, but visitors who make the long track to the winery are enthusiastically welcomed. The wine is as rich and ebullient as the winery's owner, who declares on his website: "Triumphs and calamities, scandals and dispatches, heroes and hornswogglers, dimwits and halfwits, mountebanks and masterminds . . . Welcome!"

ⓘ **Two Paddocks,** Clyde (✆ **64/3449/ 2756;** www.twopaddocks.com).

✈ Queenstown (80km/50 miles).

🛏 $$$ **The Glebe,** 2 Beetham St., Queenstown (✆ **64/3441/0310;** www. theglebe.co.nz). $$ **Crowne Plaza Queenstown,** Beach St., Queenstown (✆ **64/800/444-9944;** www.crowneplaza. com).

6 Good Spirits

Bourbon from Woodford Reserve, Kentucky's oldest distillery.

A Pilsener Pilgrimage

Czech It Out

From Prague to Plzen, Czech Republic

Brewing industry statistics show that Czechs drink more beer per capita than any other people—on average, 320 pints of brew a year (compared to 190 pints for Americans). But once you've drunk Czech beer, it all makes perfect sense: The golden ale that the Czechs call *pivo* is what the rest of the world's brewers only hope to imitate.

Start your tour in the Bohemian forest, in the birthplace of beer (*zde se narodilo piv*): the town of Plzen (88km/55 miles southwest of Prague). It has been a brewing center since the 14th century, thanks to a royal grant of brewing rights from King Václav II. But its moment of glory came in 1842, when the town's brewers joined forces to develop a new brewing process: the Pilsener method, which involves bottom-fermenting and brewing over direct heat in copper kettles. Sadly ravaged in World War II, Plzen is a an unlovely industrial town today, but what you're here for is a clutter of stone buildings just west of the Radbuza River: **Plzenský Pivovary** (U Prazdroje 7; (C) **420/377/ 062-888;** www.pilsnerurquell.com), where the famous lager Pilsener Urquell ("authentic Pilzn") is brewed, as well as the popular domestic brand Gambrinus. Built in 1869, the factory (now owned by SABMiller) has barely changed since then; the hour-long tour includes visits to cool sandstone fermentation cellars and copper-kettled brewing rooms, as well as a tasting of freshly brewed beer with that special smooth texture that only the alkaline Plzen water produces. Just inside the sculpture-topped arches of the brewery gates, the **Na Spilce** restaurant serves good schnitzels, goulash, and *svíčková na smetane* (pork tenderloin in cream sauce). There's also a charming beer museum in an old pub nearby, the **Pivovarské muzeum** (Veleslavínova 6; (C) **420/377/235-574;** www.prazdroj.cz).

Head southeast 116km (72 miles) on the E49 to Ceské Budejovice, home of the original Budweiser beer, first brewed in 1895: **Budejovický Budvar** (Karolíny Svetlé 4; (C) **420/387/705-341;** www. budvar.cz). The brewery is still government-owned to protect it from Anheuser-Busch, which has been fighting over the name for years. Compared to U.S. Bud, the delicate, semisweet Budvar lager—made with Moravian malt, water from artesian wells, and heavy Budvar yeast—is an entirely different brew, deemed vastly superior by most drinkers. Phone ahead to arrange an hour-long tour of the gleaming, modern plant. Although most of the tour is a multimedia presentation, a fine beer tasting takes place at the end. Follow up your visit with a meal at the recently restored **Masné Krámy** restaurant (Krajinská 13; (C) **420/603/154 649**), where they serve unpasteurized Budvar on tap.

Another 147km (91 miles) north on the E55, you'll reach the Czech capital, Prague, and your last brewery visit: the venerable **U Fleku** (Kremencova 11; (C) **420/224/934-019;** www.ufleku.cz). Although U Fleku was originally founded in 1499, the current facility only dates from the early 1900s. Its stacked cooling vats and massive oak wood fermenters still look quaintly historic. Don't miss the attached brewery museum in an old malt house, which includes a replica of a Renaissance-era malt-drying room. Stop in the connected pub for more tastes of U Fleku's only brew, an unfiltered dark lager with an incredibly strong and complex flavor. Also visit the

Novoměstský Pivovar brewpub (Vodičkova 20; ☏ **420/222/232-448;** www.npivovar.cz), where you can dine and drink in smartly restored cellars right by the brewing apparatus. When it opened in 1993, it was the first new brewery in Prague for nearly a century, though a whole new generation of microbreweries has blossomed since then. Novoměstský serves two superb lagers, both of them unfiltered—one dark and one light (though even the light one is more amber than

golden). As the Czechs like to say, "There's no beer like beer."

✈ Ruzyně Airport, Prague (45km/28 miles).

🛏 $$$ **Hotel Pariz,** U Obecního domu 1, Prague (☏ **420/222/195-195;** www.hotel-pariz.cz). $$ **Hotel Malý Pivovar,** Ulice Karla IV 8-10, Ceske Budejovice (☏ **420/386/360-471;** www.malypivovar.cz). $ **Pension K,** Bezrucova 13, Plzen (☏ **420/377/329-683**).

376 Breweries

A Black Forest Beer Tour
Raising a Fine Stein
Baden-Württemberg, Germany

While the Bavarian brewers get all the Oktoberfest attention, some of the best beer in Germany today is brewed in southwestern Baden-Württemberg, where both the Neckar and the Danube rivers begin in the high Swabian plain. A host of 19th-century breweries here still pour out a range of excellent beer—not only pilsener-type lagers but also regional specialties like strong dark *doppelbock,* malty dark Dunkel beers, and the effervescent pale wheat ale called Weissbeer.

Start out in the region's most beautiful landscape—the thickly wooded mountains of the Black Forest, and the lovely medieval market town of Freiburg im Breisgau. Founded in 1865, the handsome pale-yellow plant of family owned **Brauerei Ganter** (Schwarzwaldstrasse 43; ☏ **49/761/21850;** www.ganter.com) can be toured by appointment, and in summer, major outdoor music concerts take place in the cobblestoned courtyard. Like most of these breweries, Ganter produces several beers, but the best are its golden pilsener lager and its aromatic dark wheat beer, Badisch Weizen Hefedunkel. Also in town, **Hausbrauerei Feierling** (Gerberau

46; ☏ **49/761/243-480;** www.feierling.de) is a modern reincarnation of an 1877 brewery across the street. Since 1999, the new operation has gone organic, with a leisurely 6-day fermentation and four week-long lagering process. You can tour this brewery by appointment, or just enjoy its wonderfully complex Inselhof house brew, along with German specialties like Inselschnitzel or Rostbratwurst with sauerkraut. Visitors dine in a cozy wood-paneled pub or, in fair weather, out in the beer garden.

You'll have a beautiful drive east from Freiburg through the Black Forest, along Rte. 31 and then Rte. 500, for 58km (36 miles) to the historic Renaissance town of Donaueschingen, source of the Danube river. The fief of the Fürstenberg princes for centuries, it's home to their ancestral brewery, **Fürstlich Fürstenbergische Brauerei** (Postplatz 1-4; ☏ **49/771-860;** www.furstenberg.de), founded in 1283. Fürstenberg's dark Salvator beer was the favorite of 19th-century chancellor Otto Von Bismarck, while Kaiser Wilhelm preferred its hoppy golden pilsener. Although Heineken bought the brewery in 2004, the many premium beers produced here are still full of regional character. Book in advance for daily tours of the state-of-the-art brewery, which of course include a tasting session. There's also a sizeable museum of historic brewing equipment, and you can eat and drink heartily on-site at Braüstüble restaurant.

So what makes these southern German beers so delicious? Beer lovers claim it's because of the local "noble hops," grown on the plains just north of the jewel-like waters of Bodensee, known in Switzerland as Lake Constance. Drive southeast 111km (69 miles) on A81 and then A98 from Donaueschingen to Tettnang, capital of this hop-growing hotspot. You can eat, drink, and stay overnight at the cheery red **Brauerei & Gasthof Zur Krone** (Bärenplatz 7; ✆ **49/7542/7452;** www.krone-tettnang.de). This marvelous little artisanal craft brewery, founded in 1847, is still family owned and produces a range of beers,

some of them organic. There are regular Saturday afternoon tours with brew master Franz Tauscher; other times are available by appointment. Though the guestrooms are surprisingly white and modern, the heart of the place is its old pub, full of intricate dark wood carving. The menu features robust Swabian specialties like beer bacon soup with dumplings, fried whitefish from the nearby lake, sour lentils with Saiten-würstle and *spätzle,* or a beef roast with onions and handmade noodles—perfect beer-drinking accompaniments.

✈ Stuttgart (207km/128 miles).

⊨ $$ **Zum Roten Bären,** Oberlinden 12, Freiburg im Breisgau (✆ **49/761/387870;** www.roter-baeren.de). $$ **Brauerei & Gasthof Zur Krone,** Bärenplatz 7 (✆ **49/7542/7452;** www.krone-tettnang. de).

Breweries 377

Abbaye de Notre Dame de Scourmont
The Shrine of Belgian Beer
Chimay, Belgium

Since the Middle Ages, the tiny bourgeois nation of Belgium has raised the craft of brewing to a high art; its outsized reputation in the world of beer is completely disproportionate to its size. Today it produces around 450 different brews, from golden pilseners such as Stella Artois, to light and effervescent lambics, to dark and strong double bocks and triple bocks. For many aficionados, however, the quintessential Belgian beers are the rich, complex dark brews made by reclusive Trappist monks at six Belgian monasteries: Orval, Rochefort, Sint-Benedictus of Achel, Westmalle, Westvleteren, and, the best-known of them all, the Abbaye de Notre Dame de Scourmont at Chimay.

Manual labor is considered a form of meditation by these monks, and they take great pride in their time-honored methods, zealously guarding their recipes and special strains of yeast. Brewing operations are a major source of income, helping the monasteries fund their charitable activities. Because they're such strict religious communities, the breweries themselves aren't open to the public—but with a little ingenuity, you can get close to the source.

On your way from Brussels toward Chimay in southern Belgium, just west of Namur you can glimpse medieval monastic life at the 12th-century Cistercian **Abbey de**

Floreffe (7 rue du Séminaire, Floreffe; ✆ **32/81/44 53 03;** www.abbaye-de-floreffe.be). After touring the abbey—which belongs to a less strict order than the Trappists—you can sample some of the traditional beers still made at the Abbey in an old mill on the grounds. With that monastic model in mind, work your way south on N92 to explore more artisanal Belgian beers. In the picturesque Ardennes village of Purnode (take N937 east), tour the 19th-century family-owned brewery **Brasserie du Bocq** (rue de la Brasserie 4, Purnode; ✆ **32/82/61 07 90;** www.bocq.be); their white wheat beers and blond Triple Moine are especially fine. In Falmignoul (take the N95 and N96 south), check out **Brasserie Caracole** (Côte Marie-Thérèse 86; ✆ **32/82/74 40 80;** www.brasserie-caracole.be; call ahead for a tour), housed in a rustic 18th-century stone building; their Troublette white wheat beer and Nostradamus dark strong ale are complex and delicious.

From there, it's about an hour's drive east on N99 to the highlight of your visit, the **Abbaye de Notre-Dame de Scourmont,** where the monks have been brewing Chimay beer since 1862. Though you can't tour the brewery, drink in the serene, contemplative atmosphere by strolling through the abbey gardens and church. Then head to **L'Auberge de Poteaupre,** an old school that the monks converted to a restaurant-hotel, with plenty of freshly brewed Chimay beers on tap.

The three Chimay beers are color-coded—the red label is a double beer (7% alcohol), the white is a triple (8% alcohol), and the blue Grand Reserve is a dark strong ale (9% alcohol). Full bodied, with creamy heads and velvety-smooth textures, these are some of the

The Abbaye de Notre Dame de Scourmont, where monks have been brewing Chimay ale since 1862.

world's great beers—drinking them so close to their holy source may feel like a religious experience.

ⓘ **Abbaye de Notre-Dame de Scourmont,** Route de Rond Point 294, Chimay-Forges (✆ **32/60/21 30 63;** www.chimay.be).

✈ Brussels (138km/86 miles).

🛏 $$ **Auberge de Poteaupré,** Rue de Poteaupré 5, Bourlers (✆ **32/60/21 14 33;** www.chimay.be). $ **L'Auberge des Bouvignes,** Rue Fétis 112, Dinant (✆ **32/82/61-16-00;** www.aubergedebouvignes.be).

At L'Auberge de Poteaupre restaurant in Chimay, Belgium, visitors can sample the town's namesake ale.

Carlsberg Brewery

The Elephant Never Forgets

Copenhagen, Denmark

Though it's the flagship plant of the world's fifth largest beer company, somehow Copenhagen's Carlsberg Brewery still has the warmhearted spirit of its 19th-century founder, J. C. Jacobsen. An avid philanthropist and art collector, he also founded the city's preeminent art museum, the **Ny Carlsberg Glyptotek** (Dantes Plads 7; © **45/33/41-81-41**). An immense Victorian-era industrial site, the sooty brick structure, built in 1847, has its own imposing grace, with neoclassical arched windows and two stately square smokestacks rising high over its roofs. There's a sort of Danish whimsy about its trademark Elephant Gate, an entrance building graced by four huge elephant statues. Note the swastikas on the elephants' armored regalia. The swastika was Carlsberg's trademark symbol long before Hitler adopted it, although after the Nazi era, the company quickly stopped using it and put the emphasis on the elephants themselves. (Carlsberg's signature Elephant Beer— *Stærk som en elefant!*, meaning strong as an elephant!—was first brewed in 1959.) Architectural landmark as it is, this is still a working plant, turning out at least three million bottles of beer a day.

Now that both Guinness in Dublin and Heineken in Amsterdam have turned their brewery tours into mere multimedia simulations (the Guinness Storehouse and the Heineken Experience, respectively), Copenhagen's Carlsberg Brewery is the last of the big commercial European breweries that you can actually visit. True, you'll only be able to glimpse the operations from the brew house's glass-walled observation gallery, but it still feels accessible, especially since this 2005 addition is where the company is returning to its artisanal roots, making four new "affiliated" microbrews marketed under the brand name of Jacobsen. In the visitor's center, a series of video screens and informational plaques, all translated into English, outline the brewing process step by step and narrate the background of the company's two historic beers, Tyborg and Carlsberg.

You'll also see a copy of Copenhagen harbor's famous Little Mermaid statue (a 1913 gift to the city from J. C. Jacobsen) and the dizzying array of the world's largest bottle collection, with more than 16,600 different kinds of beer bottles. Of course there's a free beer at the end— your choice of the company's various brews. If you'd like to go on drinking, you can do so in the on-site pub. Don't pass up the chance to order the Elephant Beer, a strong dark bock that's only available here in Denmark.

ⓘ 11 Gamle Carlsberg Vej (© **45/33/27 13 14;** www.visitcarlsberg.dk).

✈ Copenhagen Kastrup Airport.

⊨ $$$ **Kong Frederik,** Vester Voldgade 25 (© **800/448-8355** in the U.S., or 45/33/12-59-02; www.remmen. dk). $ **Copenhagen Crown Hotel,** Vesterbrogade 41 (© **45/33/21-21-66;** www. profilhotels.dk).

Black Sheep & Theakston Breweries
All in the Family
Masham, Yorkshire, England

Tramp around the dramatic rolling landscape of the Yorkshire Dales, laced with tumbling streams and precipitous little waterfalls, and you'll understand why Dales water is so pure and clear. Thanks to that water and a little help from fine English hops, North Yorkshire yields some outstanding traditional ales. Not one but two of the best are brewed right here, in the picturesque Georgian market town of Masham.

It's no coincidence, actually—there's quite a tale behind the two firms, one worthy of a Trollope novel. It all began in 1827 when Robert Theakston leased the Black Bull Inn and brew house in Masham and began to develop a superb line of traditionally brewed ales. In 1875 his son, Thomas, built a full-scale brewery in an area of Masham known as Paradise Fields. This is the rough-cast stone brewery you can tour today, **T&R Theakston** (Red Lane; ⊘ **44/1765/680 000;** www.theakstons.co.uk), an evocative old tower-style plant of steep stairs and narrow walkways, where gravity pulls the beer from one stage of the process down to the next. It's one of the few breweries that still make its own oak casks; you may even see a coopering demonstration during your tour. Best known for its classic dark ale Old Peculier and full-bodied ruby-colored XB ale, Theakston grew over the years, acquiring several smaller local breweries, until it itself was taken over in 1987 by the Scottish & Newcastle conglomerate. This rancorous takeover battle ended when the Theakston family finally regained control in 2004.

Luckily, Theakston ales remained high-quality brews throughout it all. But before the truce, in 1992, brewery scion Paul Theakston decided to start his own traditional craft brewery right in Masham. Rather than stoop to accept a job with the S&N conglomerate-owned Theakston, he decided to go head-to-head with them. He bought a neglected Victorian-era malting house from a defunct brewery his grandfather had taken over years ago, and he rigged it with odds and ends of old-fashioned equipment, rescued from several breweries that were going out of business. It's now the award-winning **Black Sheep Brewery** (Wellgarth, Masham; ⊘ **44/1765/680 100;** www.blacksheep.co.uk), a name that refers not only to Masham's historic sheep markets but to Paul's rebellion against the family business. From the very start, brewery tours and an attached brewpub/bistro were part of the Black Sheep business plan; hour-long tours of the plant, with its hilltop setting above the Ure River, should be booked in advance. You'll walk past the brew house's immense copper brewing kettles, the oak-sided mash vats, and a set of deep square fermenting vessels. (Because Black Sheep's beers, like Theakston's, are ales rather than lagers, they are fermented with the yeast on the top.) You can even climb to the top of the rooftop conditioning tanks for a stupendous view of the Dales. At the tour's end, settle into the mellow brewery pub and savor Black Sheep's best bitter, and you may agree—Theakston's loss was the beer world's gain.

ⓘ www.visitmasham.com.

✈ Leeds-Bradford International (52km/32 miles).

⊨ $$ **Kings Head Hotel,** Market Place (⊘ **44/1765/689295;** www.kingshead masham.co.uk). $$ **White Bear Hotel,** Wellgarth (⊘ **44/1765/689319**).

Places to Eat in . . . Copenhagen, Denmark

Long known as the "fun capital of Scandinavia," Copenhagen has always been a place where people take joy in food. But a culinary explosion in the past few years has made dining out the hippest game in town, and the wave of new restaurants is exciting architecturally as well as gastronomically.

Set in an antique, stone-sided warehouse in Christianshavn,  **380 Noma** (Strandgade 93; © **45/32/96-32-97;** www.noma.dk) champions the cuisine of the cold North Atlantic (the name of the place is short for *nordatlantiskl mad,* or North Atlantic food). Importing ultrafresh fish and shellfish three times a week from Greenland, Iceland, and the Faroe Islands, they poach, grill, pickle, smoke, and even salt it according to old Nordic traditions. Chef Rene Redzepi's French Laundry training comes through in his lapidary plate presentations; having also spent time at El Bulli, he's not above throwing in a little intensely flavored foam as well. Inside, Noma looks spare and white as an Atlantic ice floe. In contrast, there's the warm-colored cozy clutter of **381 MR** (5 Kultorvet, © **45/33/91-09-49;** www.mr-restaurant.dk), named after the initials of chef/owner Mads Reflund. He's been generating loads of buzz with his ever-changing set menus (four or seven courses), featuring dishes like scallops and duck tongue with *cèpes* and onions, or langoustine in milk skin with woodruff and elderberries. The French-inflected cooking of Kristian Møller and Rune Jochumsen is anything but simple, though the name of their minimalist chic cafe translates to "basic formula": **382 Formel B.** (Vesterbrogade 182, © **45/33/25-10-66;** www.formel-b.dk). They're fanatical about fresh ingredients—vegetables from a farm in Lammefjorden, *cèpes* and chanterelles from their own mushroom grower, dairy products from Grambogård—and they transform them into seasonal menu items such as monkfish with lemon chutney, glazed quail with chanterelles, or rack of veal with foie gras and fresh cherries.

Noma's name derives from *nordatlantiskl mad,* Danish for North Atlantic food.

While venerable Michelin-starred places like Kong Hans Kælder and Kommandanten still wow the expense-account crowd, lately they've been getting competition from a brash new rival, **383 The Paul** (Vesterbrogade 3; © **54/33/75-07-75),** located in the greenhouselike Glassalen in the quaintly historic Tivoli Gardens amusement park. British-born chef Paul Cunningham's sense of whimsy is expressed not only in the restaurant's quirky postmodern decor but in the chatty, offbeat service here; seats at Cunningham's chef's table (Denmark's first) are highly coveted. His exuberant mix of traditions and ingredients yields dishes like a Bornholm free-range chicken served with a confit of veal sweetbreads, or a baked turbot with smoked beef marrow, celeriac, and chives.

When the park is closed, October through April, Cunningham travels the world gathering new ideas.

For a much more down-to-earth Tivoli experience, try the hearty Danish fare at 384 **Færgekroen Bryghus** (Vesterbrogade 3; ✆ **45/33/12-94-12;** www.faergekroen. dk), a pink half-timbered cottage in a lakeside setting.

Even here there's innovation, with two fine house beers produced in the gleaming vats of a new on-site micro-brewery. The food is what you might expect from a local farm—Wiener schnitzel, braised lamb shank, fried plaice with melted butter, and a range of *smørrebrød* open-faced sandwiches—served in a convivial setting with live music most evenings. If beer is your thing, also head out to the Nørrebro district's 385 **Nørrebro Bryghus** (Ryesgade 3; ✆ **45/35/30-05-30;** www.norrebro bryghus.dk), which sprawls over two floors of a converted 19th-century metal foundry. You can sample 10 different beers brewed on premises as well as several dishes braised, fried, or stewed in beer—things like crisp-fried whitefish served with roasted fennel in Pacific Pale Ale, or poached filet of beef served with snow peas, baby carrots, and green beans, under a sage sauce flavored with La Granja Stout. Reserve a seat at the "brew master's table" for a special set menu.

Noma's vegetable field with malt soil and herbs.

You can't leave Copenhagen without trying some *smørrebrød*—but the open-faced sandwiches at designer-sleek 386 **Aamanns** (Oster Farimagsgade 10, ✆ **45/35/55-33-44;** www.aamanns.dk) are *smørrebrød* as you've never known it before. You can scarcely get a seat in this small, hip cafe at mealtime, where crowds dine on these miniature works of art—smoked fish and meat precisely sliced onto superbly fresh rye bread, then topped with creamy medallions of cheese and crisp, flavorful vegetables. Luckily, they also do takeout.

✈ Copenhagen Kastrup Airport (70km/43miles).

🛏 $$$ **Kong Frederik,** Vester Voldgade 25 (✆ **800/448-8355** in the U.S., or 45/33/12-59-02; www.remmen.dk). $ **Copenhagen Crown Hotel,** Vesterbrogade 41 (✆ **45/33/21-21-66;** www.profilhotels.dk).

Fuller's Brewery

London's Pride

London, England

You'll spot it from the car window as you're driving into London from the West along the A4—a hulking complex of dull brick Victorian-era factory buildings along the bank of the Thames, with the name FULLER'S running up the slim smokestacks. Although it's not quaint, this Griffin Brewery represents a historic ale-brewing tradition, as the last traditional family brewery left in London (look for the gold griffin figure on every beer label). With so many other historic British brands—Bass, Whitbread, Courage, Worthington—swallowed up by multinational conglomerates, Fuller's very survival gives it nostalgic cachet.

Since the days of Oliver Cromwell, beer has been brewed on this site, originally as a private operation in the garden of Bedford House, when Chiswick was a pastoral country retreat for the aristocracy. The original Fuller, John Fuller, joined the Griffin Brewery business in 1829; by 1845, when this factory was built, it had become Fuller, Smith, & Turner, which is still its name. Although it became a limited company in 1929, members of all three families are still involved—which is why they call it a "family company," even though it's technically no longer family owned.

Fuller's also owns more than 350 "tied" pubs and bars around the country, which primarily sell its brands of ales, both in bottles and in casks (cask-conditioned ales are designed to finish their fermentation in a pub cellar rather than at the brewery). Fuller's most famous brand is probably the rich, mahogany-colored London Pride, the U.K.'s leading premium cask ale; it's also known for award-winning ales such as Chiswick Bitter, ESB (which stands for Extra Special Bitter), and their dark, rich, hoppy London Porter, often rated as the world's best porter beer. Their chief export to the United States is Fuller's IPA, a delicately amber-colored India Pale Ale that's only seasonally available in the U.K. They also make several other seasonal beers and a specially boxed Vintage Ale that comes out in a new recipe every Christmas.

Daily tours of the Griffin Brewery fill up fast—be sure to book in advance. It's definitely a major industrial site, full of massive pipes and rattling conveyor belts and loud pumping machinery. Nevertheless it's a rare experience to walk around the brew house; the fermentation rooms, which are warm, unlike the cold cellars lager requires; the bottling section; and the immense cask racks. With so much territory to cover, the tours last nearly 2 hours, though of course that also includes a full tasting session in the brewery's on-site pub, the Mawson Arms.

ⓘ **Fuller's Griffin Brewery,** Chiswick Lane South (✆ **44/20/8996-2048;** www. fullers.co.uk).

✈ Heathrow (24km/15miles); Gatwick (40km/25miles).

🛏 $$$ **22 Jermyn St.,** 22 Jermyn St., St. James (✆ **800/682-7808** in the U.S., or 44/20/7734-2353; www.22jermyn.com). $$ **Vicarage Private Hotel,** 10 Vicarage Gate, South Kensington (✆ **44/20/7229-4030;** www.londonvicaragehotel.com).

Traquair House Brewery

Those Thrifty Scots

Interleithen, Scotland

It must have been a pretty amazing moment of discovery. When Peter Maxwell—aka the 20th laird of Traquair—discovered an entire set of 18th-century brewing equipment, tucked away in a wing of his ancient castle in the Scottish Borders, he glimpsed a once-in-a-lifetime opportunity. By a stroke of good luck, Peter himself had been an executive at the Haig whiskey distillery before coming into his title; he knew just how to turn that jumble of old junk into a profit-making enterprise to fund desperately needed repairs on the rundown family castle.

Today the Traquair House Brewery turns out 600 to 700 barrels of traditional ale every year, using that same vintage gear that the 18th-century household used to make beer for its domestic staff. The ale is even fermented in the original oak casks. (Now there's old-fashioned workmanship for you.) Traquair's ale is made with the simplest high-quality ingredients—Munton's malted barley from Suffolk, Golding's hops from East Kent, and fresh clear water from an underground spring discovered right on the estate. If you tour the old-fashioned brewery, you'll see old-fashioned production methods, including an infusion mashing process, oak-cask fermentation for at least a week, and a long period of maturing in cold storage tanks. (There are no regularly scheduled tours, but special arrangements can be made.) Traquair uses no preservatives or stabilizing enzymes—what you taste is practically the same thing that Maxwell's 18th-century ancestors would have tasted. While much of the output is sold in casks for draft beer, they also put up 200,000 bottles' worth, in suitably chunky, dark-brown glass bottles. As Traquair has expanded, it now produces three ales: the malty amber Bear Ale; the rich, dark, oaky Traquair House Ale; and the strongest of them all, spicy, chocolatey, bittersweet Traquair Jacobite Ale.

The brewery's success allowed Maxwell and his wife to bring the rest of the estate into top-notch condition as well. Traquair House is said to be Scotland's oldest inhabited house—a royal hunting lodge dating from 1107, later a hideout for Catholic priests during Protestant persecution. Rebuilt and fortified many times over those tumultuous years, today it's a graceful white manor with a pitched gray roof and tiny corner turrets, set on 41 hectares (100 acres) of woodlands and lawns, including a forest maze, some of the oldest yew trees in Scotland, and an old walled garden—site of a pleasant restaurant, where of course Traquair ales are served. Peacocks strut around the lawns, and swans glide around the ponds. Not only is the house itself fascinating to tour, three bedrooms are available as bed-and-breakfast accommodations. Beer for breakfast is strictly optional.

ⓘ **Traquair House,** off the B709, Innerleithen (© **44/1896/830323;** www.traquair.co.uk; closed Dec–Feb).

✈ Edinburgh Airport (47km/29 miles).

🛏 $$$ **Traquair House,** Interleithen (© **44/1896/830323;** www.traquair.co.uk). $$ **Traquair Arms Hotel,** Traquair Rd., Interleithen (© **44/1896/830229;** www.traquairarmshotel.co.uk).

Popping Cork

All About Stout

Cork, Ireland

The Irish call it *leann dubh*—"black ale"—as good a name as any for this iconic Irish drink. Originally it was just another name for English porter—"stout" meant a strong variant of porter—but over the years Irish stout has developed its own personality: toasty, less sweet, and surprisingly lower in alcoholic content than other beers. For many years, Dublin's Guinness brand has dominated the market, both at home and abroad. But Cork, true to its traditional rebel nature, steadfastly prefers its home-town brands: Walk into any pub and order a "home and away," and you'll be given one pint of Guinness and one of either Murphy's or Beamish.

The future of Cork stout, however, may be in peril. In 1993, Heineken bought Murphy's and changed the name of Murphy's historic Lady's Well Brewery, founded in 1856, to Heineken Ireland. The taste of Murphy's remains the same, touted as having a less bitter taste than Guinness, but both Murphy's Stout and popular Murphy's Irish Red ale are now brewed at other plants as well. Creamy-headed, smooth Beamish Stout is brewed only in Cork with pure Cork water by the **Beamish & Crawford** brewery (South Main St.; © **353/21/4911 100;** www.beamish.ie). After a long series of corporate acquisitions, however, Heineken bought Beamish too in 2008, and it remains to be seen whether the Dutch giant will go on brewing two rival stouts in the same town. Founded in 1791, on the site of an earlier 17th-century brewery, Beamish occupies a garish mock-Tudor building that's a kitschy local landmark. The actual beer making takes place across the road in a monstrous 1960s-vintage cluster of huge steel tanks and vats. Contact the brewery to arrange a tour, and pay special attention

to the production step that makes stout different from other ales: The malt barley is roasted before brewing. After your Beamish tour, stop in across the street to raise a pint at **An Spailpin Fanac** (28–29 S. Main St.; © **353/21/427-7949**), a lovely 18th-century pub with low-beamed ceilings, flagstone floors, and open fireplaces, where traditional Irish music is played most nights.

Thanks to a 2005 tax break initiative, the future of Cork's brewing culture may rest instead with small independent microbreweries like the **Franciscan Well Brewery** (North Mall, Cork; © **353/21/421-0130;** www.franciscanwellbrewery.com), launched in 1998 on the site of an old 13th-century monastery. They don't offer tours of the brew house, but you can sit in the flagstoned outdoor courtyard and look right into the brewing operation while you down your pint. The monks also brewed here, using a well said to have curative powers; today's brew masters use that same well to make the brewpub's award-winning beers: Rebel lager (made with German and Czech hops), Rebel Red amber ale, straw-colored Blarney Blonde, creamy-headed Shandon Stout, and Friar Weisse, a German-style unfiltered wheat beer. What's interesting is the cosmopolitan range of beers that Franciscan Well offers. Could Irish drinkers at last be giving up their stout?

✈ Cork Airport (100km/76 miles south of Shannon International).

🛏 $$$ **Hayfield Manor Hotel,** Perrott Ave. (© **800/525-4800** or 353/21/431-5600; www.hayfieldmanor.ie). $$ **The Gresham Metropole,** MacCurtain St., Tivoli (© **353/21/450-8122**).

Biddy Early's Brewery

The Crafty Brewers of County Clare

Ennis, County Clare, Ireland

This is the Ireland most tourists picture—misty green countryside, winding roads, flocks of sheep in craggy pastures, tidy little villages, and of course a cheery wood-paneled village pub with polished pine floors, open stone fireplaces, and perhaps some twinkly eyed gent in a nubby sweater pulling the taps.

Yet as much as it conforms to this postcard image, the Biddy Early's Brewery in Inagh (15km/10 miles northwest of the county town of Ennis on the N85) isn't any old village pub; it's the first brewpub opened in Ireland in years. No doubt Biddy Early's benefits from proximity to major visitor attractions such as the awesome ocean views at the Cliffs of Moher and the spectacularly weird stony landscape of the Burren. But even if it weren't on that sightseeing circuit, beer lovers would seek it out for its award-winning brews: a rich, fruity Irish-style stout (Black Biddy), a ruddy herb-flavored traditional Celtic ale (Red Biddy), a hoppy red cask-conditioned ale (Real Biddy), a crisp golden pilsener lager (Blonde Biddy) for those whose beer taste is more continental, and various seasonal and specialty beers.

Founded in 1995 by industrial chemist Dr. Peadar Garvey, whose family still runs the pub, Biddy Early's produces small batches of artisanal beer without preservatives, enzymes, or artificial additives. The ingredients are as local as possible—Irish-grown barley, local carrageen moss to help refine the beer, bog myrtle for flavoring, and carefully selected hops from abroad (hops don't grow well in Ireland's damp climate). You can look right into the brew kitchen from the adjoining bar and see the gleaming stainless-steel vats and copper kettles used for milling, mashing, boiling, and refining the grain into liquor. Fermentation and maturation vats are in an adjacent building. Top-fermented stout and ale take about 4 days, while bottom-fermented lager takes 1 to 2 weeks. In yet another area, the beer is poured into either casks or bottles, where the final conditioning takes place.

The attached visitor center explains the process before you embark on a tour of the small plant, followed by a beer tasting. (Prebook to make sure there's room on the daily tour.) With all of Ireland's big breweries now owned by foreign conglomerates, craft breweries like Biddy Early's may be the wave of the future for Irish beer. In terms of the charm factor alone, there's no competition.

ⓘ Ennis Rd., Inagh (📞 **353/65/683-6742;** www.beb.ie).

✈ Shannon (32km/52 miles).

🛏 $$$ **Old Ground Hotel,** O'Connell St. (📞 **353/65/682-8127;** www.flynn hotels.com). $$ **Cill Eoin House,** Killady-sert Cross, Clare Rd. (📞 **65/6841668;** www.euroka.com/cilleoin).

The Microbrews of Melbourne

The Flip Side of Foster's

Melbourne, Australia

Considering Australians' reputation as world-class beer drinkers, it's surprising they have been so slow to jump on the microbrewery bandwagon. But in Melbourne—home of the behemoth Foster's brewery, which brews mainstream best-sellers Victoria Bitter, Carlton Draught, and Melbourne Bitter—a spunky crew of independent little operations have begun to preach the real ale gospel Down Under.

Wednesday and Friday evenings, head for the inner suburb of Richmond to check out kegging sessions at the **Mountain Goat Beer** brewery (North and Clark sts.; 61/3/9428 1180; www.goatbeer.com.au). Opened in an old tannery building in 2004 (although they've been brewing since 1997), this environmentally minded craft brewery has won a slew of prizes for its two year-round all-natural ales, their Pale Ale (a dry, grassy Australian-style ale), and Hightail Ale (a malty, full-bodied English-style ale), as well as robust Surefoot Stout in winter and 100% organic India Pale Ale in summer. At those biweekly brewery nights you can also sample some intriguing single-batch experiments. On the nights Mountain Goat isn't open, pop around the corner to the **Royston Hotel** (12 River St.; 61/3/9421 5000; www.royston.com.au), a mellow old workingman's local (in Australia, "hotel" is a common term for a neighborhood bar), where the tannery workers used to congregate after work; now it's a homey pub devoted to microbrews, with at least a couple of Mountain Goat brews always on tap.

In the northern suburb of Thornbury, the **Three Ravens Brewing Co.** (1 Theobald St.; 61/3/8480 1046; www.3ravens.com.au) set up shop in 2003, brewing top-fermented, unpasteurized, cask-conditioned ale. Even their bottled beers are bottle-conditioned—the antithesis of watery commercial lager. Every Friday afternoon they open the brewery for an extended sampling session of their five award-winning beers: White *(witbier)*, Blond *(altbier)*, Bronze (pale ale), Black (stout), Dark (smoke beer), and 55 (a full-bodied American-style pale ale). In South Melbourne, the city's oldest microbrewery started in 1988 at **Bell's Hotel** (157 Moray St.; 61/3/9690 4511; www.bellshotel.com.au), a roomy, rambling corner hangout with no fewer than four different bars in a Victorian-era corniced stone building. Bell's boutique brewery produces five traditional slow-vat, full-mash ales. Favorites include their flagship all-grain Hell's Bells bitter and refreshingly crisp Black Ban Bitter pale ale.

Downtown at the renovated Portland Hotel, the upscale **James Squire Brewhouse** (115 Russell St.; 61/3/9810 0064; www.maltshovelbrewery.com.au) is tied to the Malt Shovel craft brewery in Camperdown, Sydney. It has a working brewery on-site that produces small batches of Malt Shovel beers. The real draw here is the excellent food, like beer-battered sea bream or beer-braised kangaroo and beef sirloin served in a crusty baked bread loaf. Another James Squire Brewhouse recently opened in the Waterfront City development in Melbourne's Docklands.

Now that the microbrewery gospel has spread, there's even a tour operator specializing in visits to craft brewers far- ther afield in Victoria. Contact **Scruffy Bunch Tours** (☎ **61/3/9859 4932;** www. scruffybunch.com.au) and leave the driv- ing to them.

✈ Melbourne (23km/14 miles).

🛏 $$$ **The Como Melbourne,** 630 Chapel St., South Yarra (☎ **1800/033 400** in Australia, or 800/552-6844 in the U.S. and Canada; www.mirvachotels.com.au). $$ **Fountain Terrace,** 28 Mary St., St. Kilda (☎ **61/3/9593 8123;** www.fountain terrace.com.au).

392 Breweries

Maine's Microbrew Capital
From Pale Ales to Porters
Portland, Maine

Everyone expects Portland, Oregon, to have fine microbreweries to complement its excellent wineries and cutting-edge restaurants. But back on the East Coast, it's the other Portland—Portland, Maine— that sustains one of the country's most vital craft brewery scenes. Their secret? Maybe it's the waters of cold, clear Sebago Lake, which has an ideal pH for beer mak- ing. Just as likely it's the critical mass of skilled brew masters catering to an ever more discerning local clientele.

First on the scene was the first micro- brewery in New England—the **D. L. Geary Brewing Co.** (38 Evergreen Dr.; ☎ **207/ 878-2337;** www.gearybrewing.com; tours by appointment), which opened in 1986. Mentored by Peter Maxwell Stuart of Traquair House Brewery (see 388), David Geary developed his signature British-style pale ale, followed by a hoppy Hampshire- style ale and a dark London porter that has been rated the world's best. In 1988, Grit- ty's Portland Brew Pub (since renamed **Gritty McDuff's,** 396 Fore St.; ☎ **207/772- BREW** [207/772-2739]; www.grittys.com), opened down in the historic Old Port area. Gritty's brews its own fine British-style ales on premises to serve alongside a casual menu of burgers, sandwiches, and other pub grub. You can view the vats and kettles from a seat at the copper-topped bar in this cozy wood-beams-and-brick hangout.

In 1994, **Shipyard Brewing Co.** (86 Newbury St.; ☎ **800/273-9253;** www. shipyard.com) came on the scene, operat- ing out of an old foundry in the downtown waterfront. Under its British brew master, Alan Pugsley, it's now Maine's largest brewery, and Pugsley now mentors many American craft brewers. Shipyard makes 12 prized varieties of English-style real ale, including a stout, a brown ale, an India pale ale, and its flagship, the full-bodied golden Export Ale. They don't offer a full- fledged tour, but if you visit the plant you can view a video, observe the bottling line, and have a tasting session—the real point of visiting here.

Around the corner from D. F. Geary, **Allagash Brewing Company** (50 Indus- trial Way; ☎ **800/330-5385;** www. allagash.com) started up in 1995, intro- ducing something new to the American craft brewery movement—beers based on a Belgian model rather than a British one. Under brew master Rob Tod, they have developed an intriguing range of beers, from their flagship Allagash White, a pale wheat beer, to Black, a Trappist- style stout. Half-hour tours take place reg- ularly on weekdays and include tastings. Meanwhile, neighboring **Casco Bay Brewing Co** (57 Industrial Way; ☎ **207/ 797-2020;** www.cascobaybrewing.com; tours available by appointment) didn't hit its stride until 1998, when brew master Bryan Smith introduced a line of lager-style beers. Smith began as a humble bottling-line worker but quickly developed a passion for the craft. His cheeky little operation is best known for its flagship Irish-style Riptide Red Ale and Carrabassett Pale Ale, which is more a West-Coast-style beer than a European imitator. Around the same time, Casco Bay's buddies at **Stone Coast Brewing** (14 York St.; © **207/773-BEER** [207/773-2337]; www.stonecoast.com) broke the mold themselves by introducing German-style beers like Sunday River Lager and Sunday River

Alt, as well as their 420 IPA pale ale and a robust Black Bear Porter, kicked up with a little rock-and-roll spirit.

In sum, Portland is a great town for serious beer drinking—drain it to the last drop.

✈ Portland (4¹/₃ miles/7km).

🛏 $$$ **Portland Harbor Hotel,** 468 Fore St. (© **888/798-9090** or 207/775-9090; www.portlandharborhotel.com). $$ **Inn at ParkSpring,** 135 Spring St. (© **800/437-8511** or 207/774-1059; www.innatparkspring.com).

Breweries **393**

Samuel Adams Brewery
Brewing Up a Revolution
Boston, Massachusetts

In the dark days of the early 1980s, beer drinkers had little choice when it came to their brew. Major manufacturers like Miller and Anheuser-Busch dominated the market with beer that was tepid compared to their full-bodied European counterparts. Those who wanted a heartier beer had scant options, save for a few imports like Beck's.

That began to change in 1985, when Jim Koch ditched a career in management counseling to restart the family business of beer making. The son of a fifth-generation brewer, Koch believed that if you offered people a better beer, they'd choose it. Armed with recipes stored in the trunk of an attic, he set out with partner Rhonda Kallman to revolutionize the beer market. Koch filled his old briefcase with bottles of his handmade brew and made the rounds of Boston bars and restaurants with samples of Samuel Adams Boston Lager.

By April 1985, the beer—named after a Boston revolutionary whose father was also a master brewer—debuted in roughly 24 bars and restaurants in the Boston

area. By the end of the year, they had reached 500 barrels and expanded distribution to the rest of Massachusetts, Connecticut, and, as a real testament to the quality of their product, West Germany. Soon after, new varieties followed, including a line of seasonal beers. Samuel Adams Lager became an inspiration to other brewers and changed forever the way American consumers viewed beer.

Samuel Adams continues to innovate with different styles of beer, including "extreme" brews with the greatest complexity. There are breweries in Boston; Cincinnati; Rochester, New York; and Eden, North Carolina. Tours of the Boston brewery are given on a first-come, first-served basis Monday through Saturday (the day tours are popular, so arrive early in the day). The tours take about 1 hour and include a visit to the beer museum and gift shop.

ⓘ 30 Germania St., Boston (© **617/368-5080;** www.samueladams.com).

✈ Boston Logan International (8 miles/ 13km).

🛏 $$ **Harborside Inn,** 185 State St., Boston (✆ **617/670-6015;** www.harbor sideinnboston.com). $$$ **The Charles Hotel,** 1 Bennett St., Cambridge (✆ **800/ 882-1818** or 617/864-1200; www.charles hotel.com).

Saranac Brewery
Time-Honored Regional Brew
Utica, New York

While most microbreweries are young upstarts, the Saranac Brewery has been producing beer since 1888, when F. X. Matt I, a German-born immigrant, founded a brewery in the foothills of the Adirondack Mountains of New York. Today, Saranac produces a wide variety of beer and soft drinks, including Utica Club, the first beer that the government permitted for sale after Prohibition. It remains a popular mainstay and, like all Saranac beers, it is made from high-quality, natural ingredients, right down to the locally harvested grains and pure water that flows from the Adirondacks. Safeguarding the tradition of brewing with only the freshest ingredients, a Matt family member has been at the helm of the Matt Brewing Company for four generations.

Like most small breweries, Saranac offers a wide variety of brews throughout the year, with limited editions and seasonal brews on tap at various times. Saranac Imperial Stout is part of a line of beers rich in complexity, flavor, and—as should be noted—alcoholic content. These are beers to sip, rather than gulp. Most aficionados stick with the excellent ales and lagers (Three Stooges Ale being the wackiest). Saranac's line of sodas includes favorites such as root beer along with more unusual offerings like Shirley Temple and orange cream.

Although Saranac is an old brewery, its commitment to recycling and the environment is thoroughly up to date. They sell used grain to farmers as cow feed and recycle all materials used in brewing and packaging, including aluminum, glass, plastic straps, and cartons. The brewery itself employs a system to cut down on energy during peak times and has eliminated air-conditioning and other nonessential energy consumption in the company offices (when you're lucky enough to be working in these deliciously cool north woods, air-conditioning is decidedly optional).

Tours are available June through August, 7 days a week; September through May, tours are available on Fridays and Saturdays. Set aside 2 hours to take the tour and visit the gift shop and tavern. Naturally, two samples of either beer or soda are offered at the conclusion of the tour.

ⓘ 830 Varick St., Utica, New York (✆ **800/765-6288** or 315/732-0032; www. saranac.com).

✈ Syracuse Hancock Intl (58 miles/ 93km).

🛏 $$ **Hotel Utica,** 102 Lafayette St. (✆ **877/906-1912** or 315/724-7829; www. hotelutica.com).

Great Lakes Brewing Co.

Ecofriendly Brewing

Cleveland, Ohio

When brothers Patrick and Daniel Conway founded the Great Lakes Brewing Company, they wanted to make the freshest beer possible while creating a company that was environmentally respectful. Since 1988, they have made hand-crafted brews in what was once the center of Cleveland's brewing industry. The brewpub is, in fact, two historic buildings that have been merged; one of them was notorious as the chief watering hole for Eliot Ness, the Prohibition agent known for pursuing 1920s gangster Al Capone and his gang of bootleggers. Today, you can cool down with a glass of Eliot Ness Amber Lager while sitting at Cleveland's oldest bar, or enjoy a meal at the Beer Garden, an ecofriendly restaurant dedicated to serving food as fresh as the handmade beer.

Patrick Conway's interest in beer began when he worked as a bartender to make money for graduate school. After a trip to Europe that included tours of several breweries, he was so taken with the European-style beers that he'd sampled, he joined forces with his brother, a commercial banker with a shared appreciation of traditional brews. There began their dream of establishing Ohio's first microbrewery.

Early on, however, they adopted a mission statement that deemed social consciousness as important as making great beer. The brewery's commitment to the environment is evident: They only use vehicles fueled by vegetable oil from the restaurant, and they conserve energy so thoroughly, they keep heating costs for the restaurant down to less than $8 a day.

Great Lakes' beers include stouts, ales, and an IPA, as well as the Edmund Fitzgerald Porter, a complex brew with a bittersweet, chocolate-coffee taste. Seasonal beers are also available. Even if you can't make it to Cleveland, you can find Great Lakes beer throughout Illinois, Indiana, Kentucky, Michigan, New York, Pennsylvania, West Virginia, and Wisconsin.

Free public tours are available on Fridays and Saturdays, and private tours by arrangement.

ⓘ 2516 Market Ave. (✆ **216/771-4404;** www.greatlakesbrewing.com).

✈ Cleveland International (10 miles/ 17km).

🛏 $$ **Radisson Hotel Cleveland Gateway,** 651 Huron Rd. (✆ **800/333-3333** or 216/377-9000; www.radisson.com). $$ **Glidden House,** 1901 Ford Dr. (✆ **800/ 759-8358** or 216/231-8900; www.glidden house.com).

The long bar at the Great Lakes Brewing Company in Cleveland, Ohio.

Sprecher Brewing Company & Lake Front Brewery

The Beers That Keep Milwaukee Famous

Milwaukee, Wisconsin

When most people think of Milwaukee, they think of beer, and rightfully so. In the 1800s, thanks to its German immigrant heritage, the city was home to more than 100 breweries, including giants like Miller, Pabst, Blatz, and Schlitz. It was not by accident that the 1970s sitcom *Laverne & Shirley* cast its two Milwaukee heroines as brewery workers. Today only a few big commercial breweries remain—Miller's the only biggie left—but Milwaukee is undergoing a renaissance with a number of fine microbreweries. By definition, a microbrewery produces less than 15,000 barrels a year (compared to the 20–40 million barrels produced by major corporate breweries). The emphasis on quality over quantity is apparent at first quaff.

One operation, in particular, has been gaining renown and awards for both its beer and designer sodas. The **Sprecher Brewing Company** (701 W Glendale Ave. Glendale; *C* **414/964-2739;** www.sprecher brewery.com) was founded in 1985 by Randall Sprecher, a former brewing supervisor for Pabst. Sprecher began making his distinctive European and traditional brews in the Walker Point neighborhood, though as demand grew, he had to move 10 years later to a larger facility in the nearby suburb of Glendale. The varieties of beer increased along with demand. As a small operation, Sprecher can produce small batches for almost any event; specialty brews include Irish

Oktoberfest lager from Sprecher.

Stout, brewed for Milwaukee's yearly Irish Fest. Tours (every weekday in summer, Fri the rest of the year) include a visit to a museum full of brewing memorabilia, the brew house, and a large cellar graced by Bavarian murals, as well as a tasting session in an outdoor tent. After your tour, stop at the indoor beer garden which features oompah music to go with the house drink.

Milwaukee's innovative **Lake Front Brewery** (1872 N. Commerce St., Milwaukee; *C* **800/328-7275;** www.lakefront brewery.com) began as a rivalry between Russ Klisch and his brother Jim over who could make the best homemade brew. After prompting by their family, the brothers went public in 1988 with a small brewery on the site of a pizza bakery. As business grew, they moved to their current location, which features a Palm Garden that hosts a Friday night fish fry. Lake Front's beers include ales, lagers, and specialty beers like their award-winning Pumpkin Ale. The Klisch brothers think out of the box: In order to make gluten-free beer for people who are intolerant to wheat, they successfully challenged a government requirement that all beer be made with 25% malted barley. Their brewery tours (call ahead for times) are also unorthodox. For one thing, they start right off with the tasting session, rather than waiting until the end to offer the goods.

✈ Milwaukee International (15 miles/24km).

🛏 $$$ **Pfister Hotel,** 424 E. Wisconsin Ave. (*C* **800/472-4403** or 414/273-8222; www.thepfisterhotel.com). $$ **Ambassador Hotel,** 2308 W. Wisconsin Ave. (*C* **888/322-3326** or 414/345-5000; www.ambassadormilwaukee.com).

7 Places to Eat in . . . The Twin Cities

Facing off across a loopy, not-yet-mighty northern stretch of the Mississippi River, Minneapolis and St. Paul still carry on like rivals. St. Paulites are proud of their adherence to traditions, while Minneapolitans take pride in edginess and verve. But this cosmopolitan oasis at the intersection of the Great Plains and the North Country is united on one score: the white-hot synergy of its culinary scene, with several buzz-worthy chefs drawing inspiration from a bounty of Midwestern ingredients. The dishes they're concocting stray far beyond the prime steaks, Scandinavian home cooking, and German comfort foods that used to signify dining out around here.

The first place most serious food folk mention is ③⑨⑦ La Belle Vie (510 Groveland Ave., Minneapolis; ✆ 612/874-6440; www.labellevie.us), out near Loring Park. The muted elegance of the dining room—with its pale wainscoted walls, dark woods and leathers, and white-linen table settings—gives center stage to Tim McKee's French Mediterranean-inspired cooking. The five- or eight-course tasting menus are the best way to sample the full range of what he can do with dishes such as roasted poussin with caramelized pork belly, broccoli rabe, and eggplant, or grilled beef tenderloin with chanterelle mushrooms and artichokes. (McKee's other restaurant, Solera, is another Minneapolis favorite.) La Belle Vie first opened in 1998; the next year, Alex Roberts opened ③⑨⑧ Restaurant Alma (528 University Ave. SE, Minneapolis; ✆ 612/ 379-4909; www.restaurantalma.com), with an equally refined New American menu. The blond woods and simple lines of this restaurant make it look more casual, but there's nothing offhanded about Roberts' fixed-price menu, which focuses on

The elegant interior of Tim McKee's La Belle Vie in Minneapolis.

organic, sustainably farmed seasonal ingredients. For each of three courses, you choose among four or five options such as grilled swordfish with glazed fennel, or a pan-roasted duck breast with sautéed swiss chard, lentils, and glazed figs.

As the dining scene in the Twin Cities has ripened, second-generation stars have risen such as ❸❾❾ 112 Eatery (112 N. 3rd St., Minneapolis; ✆ 612/343-7696; www. 112eatery.com), the brick-walled downtown bistro opened in 2005 in the night-clubbing warehouse district. After polishing his reputation at two other esteemed kitchens in town (D'Amico Cucina and Café Lurcat), chef/owner Isaac Becker brings flair to every cafe item, like his sirloin steak crusted with nori, tagliatelle with foie gras meatballs, and even a bacon-and-egg sandwich spiked with hot harissa sauce. Then there's long, sleek ❹❶❶ Spoonriver (750 S. 2nd St., Minneapolis; ✆ 612/436-2236; www.spoonriverrestaurant.com), opened in a riverfront plaza across from the Guthrie Theater in 2006. Chef Brenda Langton reprises the fresh and healthy locavore fare of her acclaimed former cafe, Brenda. Her menu is somehow upscale and homey at the same time, with lots of artful salads, charcuterie, pates and terrines, and vegetarian specials. Over in St. Paul, Lenny Russo—who earned his stars at longtime St. Paul favorite W. A. Frost & Co.—opened ❹❶❶ Heartland (1806 St. Clair Ave., St. Paul; ✆ 651/699-3536; www.heartlandrestaurant.com) in 2002. The Prairie-Style decor of Heartland suits its Midwestern farmer's market-inspired menu. The daily changing roster of entrees includes roasted rabbit, braised elk chops, pan-fried trout, salt-cured Lake Superior smelt, bison bratwurst, or duck prosciutto.

Locavores flock to Spoonriver on the banks of the Mississippi.

The scene is so hot even nationally celebrated chefs are trying to muscle their way in. Wolfgang Puck recently opened ❹❶❷ 20.21 as the house cafe of the superb Walker Art Center (1750 Hennepin Ave., Minneapolis; ✆ 612/253-3410; www.wolfgangpuck.com). Several menu items, including some fancifully sculptural desserts, are designed specifically to complement the Walker's 20th- and 21st-century art. Modern artworks also line the walls at ❹❶❸ Chambers Kitchen, Jean Georges Vongerichten's hip hotel restaurant in the Chambers Hotel (901 Hennepin Ave., Minneapolis; ✆ 612/767-6979; www.chambersminneapolis.com), which features Vongerichten's trademark Asian-accented rustic French cooking in a sleekly minimalist informal space with an open kitchen.

🛪 Minneapolis/St. Paul International (10 miles/16km).

🛏 $$$ **Graves 601 Hotel,** 601 First Ave. N., Minneapolis (✆ **866/523-1100** or 612/677-1100; www.graves601hotel.com). $$ **Saint Paul Hotel,** 350 Market St., St. Paul (✆ **800/292-9292** or 651/292-9292; www.stpaulhotel.com).

Anchor Brewing

From the Gold Rush to Amber Ale

San Francisco, California

Don't let that beautiful streamlined brewing plant from the 1930s fool you. Anchor Brewery has been around a lot longer than that—all the way back to California's second Gold Rush. The first batch of Anchor Steam was brewed to slake the thirst of all the newcomers to rough-and-tumble San Francisco's myriad taverns and saloons in 1896. No one really knows the meaning of the term "steam beer," although most likely it refers to the time when beer was brewed without the benefit of ice. At any rate, its deep amber color and full taste resemble traditional European beers.

But while Anchor's fine lagers have a wonderfully smooth taste, its history has been anything but smooth. In 1906, the fire that followed the great San Francisco earthquake consumed the original brewery. The next year, a new building was constructed and the business enjoyed a brief period of success until Prohibition came along in 1920. Many breweries stayed afloat during those years by making soda, but Anchor remained dark until 1933, when Prohibition was lifted. Brewing resumed, but the business was hard-hit by the public's taste for lighter, mass-produced beer. In 1959, the brewery shut down again.

In 1960, a new owner rescued the Anchor brand by reopening the brewery at another location. Business stumbled along until 1965, when Fritz Maytag took the helm, saving it from bankruptcy and bringing it back to solvency. In 1971, a revamped business plan finally put Anchor Steam into bottles instead of just kegs, and added four more brews to the lineup.

Although it's such a long-established brand, Anchor fits right into the ethos of the craft brewery revolution. Its brews are handmade from an all-malt mash, and its gleaming copper-kettled brew house still follows traditional German brewing techniques. Along with its original mainstay, Anchor Steam Beer, the company makes several ales, a rich bock, and seasonal beers like Christmas Ale and the light, wheat-based Summer Beer, believed to be the first wheat beer brewed in America since Prohibition. Because it works in relatively small batches, Anchor can also produce limited edition beers, like its Liberty Ale, first brewed in 1975 to commemorate the bicentennial of Paul Revere's ride. Public tours and tastings are offered weekday afternoons by reservation only; call as early as a month in advance to reserve a spot.

ⓘ 1705 Mariposa St. (✆ **415/863-8350;** www.anchorbrewing.com).

✈ San Francisco International (14 miles/ 23km).

🛏 $$$ **Hotel Adagio,** 550 Geary St. (✆ **800/228-8830** or 415/775-5000; www. thehoteladagion.com). $ **Hotel des Arts,** 447 Bush St. (✆ **800/956-4322** or 415/956-3232; www.sfhoteldesarts.com).

Hopping Around in San Diego
Brews by the Beach
San Diego, California

Let Northern California have its wine industry. Down south in beachy, casual San Diego, beer's the drink that warrants gourmet attention, with a whole crop of talented local craft brewers scooping up prizes every year at events such as the World Beer Cup and Great American Beer Festival.

San Diego has a longer brewing history than you might expect, starting in 1896 with the huge **San Diego Brewing Company.** Although the original company closed down during World War II, the label was revived in 1993 as a craft brewery, located in a strip mall near Qualcomm Stadium (10450-L Friars Rd.; © **619/284-2739;** www.sandiegobrewing.com). Seven small-batch beers are brewed on premises; the bestseller is the coppery San Diego Amber, though the Friars IPA and Old Town Nut Brown are also remarkable. Windows in the convivial bar afford a great view of the brewing apparatus; fresh beer flows directly from the vats into the bar taps. With 50 taps operating, the brewpub also features a host of interesting "guest beers."

San Diego's best-known brewery is a half-hour's drive up I-15, in the North County suburb of Escondido. Founded in 1996, **Stone Brewery** (1999 Citracado Pkwy., Escondido; © **760/471-4999;** www.stone brew.com) offers tours and tastings at its new state-of-the-art, solar-powered, 55,000-sq.-ft. (5,110 sq. m) brewing plant. The adjacent **World Bistro and Gardens** is a cavernous, lively indoor brewpub with a rambling garden strewn with boulders. The bistro's adventurous menu, founded on Slow Food philosophy, garners mixed reviews. But there's no quibbling about the quality of the craft beers, including varieties such as Arrogant Bastard Ale and Stone Ruination IPA. They serve a huge menu of draft and bottled beers from local competitors as well, not to mention an impressive range of imported brews.

Southern California's largest distributing microbrewery, the **Karl Strauss Brewing Company** (www.karlstrauss.com) was founded in 1989 by two college friends, Chris Kramer and Matt Rattner. Chris signed on his uncle, a skilled German brew master (the eponymous Karl Strauss) to oversee the brewing process. Though Strauss's seven signature beers are on tap at many local bars, the best place to enjoy the label is at the company's four San Diego brewpubs—1157 Columbia St., downtown (© **619/234-2739**); 1044 Wall St., La Jolla (© **858/551-2739**); 9675 Scranton Rd., Sorrento Mesa (© **858/587-2739**); and 5801 Armada Dr., Carlsbad (© **760/431-2739**). Try to stop in on the first Thursday of every month, when they tap a keg of special cask-conditioned real ale.

Across the majestic Coronado Bridge on the resortlike Coronado Island, family-friendly **Coronado Brewing Company** (170 Orange Ave., Coronado; © **619/437-4452;** www.coronadobrewingcompany. com) serves an eclectic range of its own brews—golden pilseners, nutty brown ales, robust dark porters and stouts, unfiltered wheat beers, sweet malty red ales, and intriguing seasonal specialties. Wood-fired pizzas, burgers, and of course San Diego fish tacos are all on the pub-grub menu.

Two other local microbreweries are superlative. **AleSmith Brewing** (9368 Cabot Dr.; © **858/549-9888;** www.ale smith.com), led by acclaimed brew master Peter Zien, has won over 400 awards for unpasteurized, handcrafted European-style ales. Tours of the refreshingly small-scale brewery take place the last Saturday of every month. **Ballast Point Brewing** (5401 Linda Vista Rd., Ⓒ **619/298-2337;** and 10051 Old Grove Rd., Ⓒ **858/695-2739,** www.ballastpoint.com) conducts daily tastings of its multiple prize-winning German and Belgian-style beers. Even if you can't make it to the plants, you can sample both companies' beers on tap all over town.

✈ San Diego (15 miles/24km).

🛏 $$$ **Catamaran Resort Hotel,** 3999 Mission Blvd., San Diego (Ⓒ **800/422-8386** or 858/488-1081; www.catamaran resort.com). $ **Park Manor Suites,** 525 Spruce St. (Ⓒ **800/874-2649** or 619/291-0999; www.parkmanorsuites.com).

Bavarian Biergärtens
Raising a Stein
Munich, Germany

Bavaria is the birthplace of the *biergärten,* open-air establishments where drinkers— and often entire families—relax in the summer at simple tables, traditionally set on gravel and shaded by chestnut trees. In a classic beer garden, customers bring their own food, though most beer gardens also serve hearty regional specialties. Münchners—who hold the world's record for beer consumption per capita (280 liters/73 gal. a year)—treasure these establishments so much they protested in the streets against a 1995 proposal to shorten the hours of a popular beer garden. You don't need to wait for Oktoberfest to raise a stein with a Münchner; all summer long you can experience the soul of Bavaria's capital at one of these *gemütlich* watering holes.

The biggest tourist draws are the big cheery beer garden at the heart of Munich's central Viktualienmarkt, which sells only beers brewed within the city limits, and the immense **Hirschgarten** (Hirschgarten 1; Ⓒ **49/89/179 99 117**) out west in Neuhausen, which can seat 10,000 customers. It's so big it even has its own deer park. Also in Neuhausen, the **Augustinerkeller** (Arnulfstrasse 52; Ⓒ **49/89/59 43 93**) is a more relaxed choice, where patrons sit under linden trees drinking draft Augustiner beer, one of the few brews still served from wooden casks.

Or head for the Englischer Garten, Munich's largest park, which has a number of beer gardens to choose from, including a popular one around the base of the **Chinese Tower** ornamental pagoda (Englisher Garten 3; Ⓒ **49/89/39 50 28**). The **Biergarten Chinesischer Turm** (Englischer Garten 3; Ⓒ **089/383 87 30**), adjacent to the artsy Schwabing neighborhood, is a particular favorite for its homemade dumplings and sausages, as well as a succulent sauerbraten made the Bavarian way, with pork instead of beef. There's also the shady **Aumeister** in the north end of the park (Sondermeierstrasse 1; Ⓒ **49/89/32 52 24**); the laid-back **Hirschau** (Gysslingstrasse 15; Ⓒ **49/89/322 10 80**), known for its live jazz; and the often crowded lakeside **Seehaus** (Kleinhesselohe 3; Ⓒ **49/89/381 61 30**).

Near the park in Schwabing, **Max Emanuel** (Adalbertstrasse 33; Ⓒ **49/89/2715158**) is a small but friendly beer garden that feels wonderfully secluded on summer evenings; Löwenbrau and Franziskaner are the house beers.

✈ Franz-Josef-Strauss International (29km/18 miles).

🛏 $$ **Hotel St. Paul,** St-Paul-Strasse 7 (Ⓒ **49/89/5440-7800;** www.hotel-stpaul. de). $ **Am Markt,** Heiliggeiststrasse 6 (Ⓒ **49/89/22 50 14;** www.hotelinmunich.de).

A Bourbon Tour of Bluegrass Country
The Whiskey Rebellion
Lexington, Kentucky

It was the Whiskey Rebellion that did it. That 1791 excise tax on whiskey sent droves of spirit-makers from the Northeast into the frontier territory of Kentucky to escape the tax. When they tasted the first whiskies made with Kentucky's clear limestone waters, mashed from its native corn, rye, and barley, and aged through its distinct cycle of seasons—well, they never budged again. Most of the territory at that time was called Bourbon County, named after the French dynasty. When Kentucky whiskey was rafted down the Ohio River to the Mississippi and on south, it got called "Bourbon whiskey," and the name stuck. (By a weird twist of history, the much smaller modern-day Bourbon County is

"dry," meaning alcohol can't be served in public or sold.)

Several of America's finest distilleries are tucked around the bucolic rolling landscape between Lexington and Louisville, also revered for its Thoroughbred horse farms. Though distances are short, visiting them all would take a couple of days; bring a designated driver if you plan to indulge in the tasting sessions. Take U.S 60 about 10 miles (16km) west of Lexington to visit the state's oldest distillery, **Woodford Reserve** (7855 McCracken Pike, Versailles; © **859/879-1812;** www.woodfordreserve. com; closed Mon, closed Sun Nov–Mar). This picturesque distillery, a National Historic Landmark dating back to 1812, is a

Casks of bourbon at Woodford Reserve.

The Wild Turkey distillery in Lawrenceburg, Kentucky.

the same divine drink he'd served on their last turkey hunt. Though the Wild Turkey plant (now owned by Pernod) is more industrial-looking than Woodford's, it's still fascinating to see and smell its immense copper stills, gigantic steel vats of fermenting mash, and tens of thousands of racked-up white-oak barrels, slightly charred to give the whiskey its smoky-sweetness and reddish hue.

Go south to pick up the scenic Blue Grass Parkway and zip west about 40 miles (64km) to the turnoff for state road 49, which leads south to Loretto, home of another great small-batch bourbon, **Maker's Mark** (3350 Burks Spring Rd., Loretto; 270/865-2099; www.makersmark.com; closed Sun Jan–Feb). A rambling set of 19th-century clapboard buildings centered around an 1805 grist mill, this distillery has a great backwoods atmosphere, with its antique grain rollers and cypress-wood fermenting vats. Even in peak years, this boutique distillery doesn't turn out more than 38 barrels, so tasting a sample of this silky-smooth bourbon is quite a treat.

Heading back up toward Louisville, the bourbon-obsessed may also want to stop off to visit the more slickly packaged tours at **Heaven Hill Distilleries** (1064 Loretto Rd., Bardstown; 502/348-3921; www.heaven-hill.com), the producers of Evan Williams bourbon, and the **Jim Beam Distillery** (149 Happy Hollow Rd., Shepherdsville; 502/543-9877; www.jimbeam.com). Cheers!

cluster of rustic century-old stone buildings on the banks of a churning limestone creek. A handcrafted small-batch premium bourbon, Woodford Reserve is so prestigious it's the official whiskey of the Kentucky Derby. The in-depth tour here is especially informative, a great crash course in the fine art of bourbon-making. Take U.S. 62 another 10 miles (16km) west to Lawrenceburg to visit the **Wild Turkey Distillery** (1525 Tyrone Rd., Lawrenceburg; 502/839-4544; www.wildturkeybourbon.com; closed Sun). Founded in 1869, the Austin Nichols distillery rechristened its top whiskey in 1940, when a distillery executive's hunting buddies begged him to bring along

Blue Grass Airport, Lexington (17 miles/28km).

$$$ **Gratz Park Inn,** 120 W. Second St., Lexington (800/752-4166 or 859/231-1777; www.gratzparkinn.com). $$ **Camberley Brown,** 4th St. and West Broadway, Louisville (502/583-1234; www.thebrownhotel.com).

Jack Daniels Distillery
A Mash Note From Mr. Jack
Lynchburg, Tennessee

One of the things that makes bourbon taste so different from European whiskies is that the mash—that stewing vatful of ground corn, barley, and rye—is kicked up with a dose of already-soured slop mash from a previous distillation. It's that "sour mash" that gives bourbon its bracing acidic bite, a pleasing astringency that lingers on throughout distillation and oak-barrel aging. Though this technique was first introduced at the Old Oscar Pepper Distillery (nowadays known as Woodford Reserve, see **407**), all straight bourbons today use this process, and none more effectively than Jack Daniels.

Setting up shop in Tennessee, the next state south from Kentucky, Jack Daniels couldn't properly call his product "Bourbon" whiskey when he distilled his first batch in 1866, right after the Civil War. Even today, you'll notice the old-fashioned black-and-white label refers to it as Tennessee Sour Mash Whiskey. But what Mr. Jack (as the locals called him) distilled was pretty much the same thing as his Kentucky colleagues made, except for two factors: the pure, iron-free water of the cave spring feeding the distillery, and the sugar-maple charcoal through which he filtered the distilled spirit. Both are still part of whiskey production down here, and they give the whiskey a mellow, earthy taste that's instantly recognizable.

The distillery is only an hour's drive southeast of Nashville, in tiny Lynchburg,

Tennessee, with a population less than 400. Free tours of the distillery grounds run frequently; expect to do a lot of walking as you traipse around this verdant hollow from the fermenting house to the still to the barrel-crammed warehouse. After touring the distillery, you can glance in at the office used by Mr. Jack and see the battered iron safe that broke his toe in 1911, eventually leading to his death via blood poisoning. One can only hope that regular doses of Tennessee sippin' whiskey helped ease the pain of his last days.

While you're here, you may also want to dig into some southern home cooking at the century-old white clapboard **Miss Mary Bobo's Boarding House** (call for reservations, ✆ **931/759-7394**). If you want to take home a bottle of Jack Daniels, you can purchase it here at the distillery, but there are no tastings. Lynchburg is in tiny Moore County, one of Tennessee's many "dry" counties that don't permit the serving or sale of alcohol.

ⓘ 280 Lynchburg Hwy. (TN 55), Lynchburg (✆ **931/759-4221;** www.jackdaniels.com).

✈ Nashville (89miles/142km).

🛏 $$$ **The Hermitage Hotel,** 231 6th Ave. N (✆ **888/888-9414** or 615/244-3121; www.thehermitagehotel.com). $$ **Wyndham Union Station,** 1001 Broadway (✆ **615/248-3554;** www.wyndham.com).

The Malt Whisky Trail

Single-Minded About Whisky

Speyside, Scotland

Some people come to Scotland to play golf. Some come to explore romantic castles. Others come to shop for nubby sweaters, thick tweed jackets, and kilts. But then there are those who visit Scotland simply to indulge in the smooth, peaty taste of Scotch whisky—preferably premium single-malt whiskies, with their complex, deep, and distinct tastes. While blended whiskies are cheaper, often smoother, and go better with mixers, there's no comparison for aficionados.

East of Inverness in the heart of the Scottish Highlands, half the malt distilleries in Scotland are sprinkled through the valley of the River Spey. The tourist board markets it as the **Malt Whisky Trail,** a route 113km (70 miles) long through the glens of Speyside, connecting several fine distilleries that accept visitors, usually from March through October.

Begin in Keith with the oldest operating distillery in the Highlands, the **Strathisla Distillery** (Seafield Ave.; © **44/1542/783-044;** www.chivas.com), dating from 1786. With its twin pagoda-like kiln chimneys in front, this cozy stone distillery may be the most picturesque on the trail. Most of its whisky is spirited off to be blended into Chivas Regal, but the small amount of single-malt it does bottle is excellent, slightly sweet and fruity.

Just off the A941 in Craigellachie, the **Macallan Distillery** (© **44/1340/872-280;** www.themacallan.com) is built around a Jacobean manor house on a dramatic hilltop

The grounds of the Balvenie single malt distillery in Dufftown, Scotland.

Glenfiddich was the first single malt exported from Scotland.

overlooking the Spey; it's surrounded by its own golden barley fields and a pure mountain spring on site. Guided tours (prebooking essential) let you see the unusually small stills and hand-crafted oak barrels that give The Macallan its extraordinary complex and full-bodied smoothness— which of course you'll be able to savor in post-tour tasting sessions.

The epicenter of the whisky universe seems to be down the A941 in Dufftown, which has no fewer than seven distilleries. The best-known is **Glenfiddich** (A941; ✆ **44/1340/820-373;** www.glenfiddich. com), still owned by the Grant family who founded it in 1887. Glenfiddich was the first single malt to be exported out of Scotland; today nearly 90% of its whisky is sold as single-malt. With its white silos and smokestacks, it's not as picturesque as the others, but the kilted guides run an informative tour, and the tasting at tour's end gives you a satisfying dram of mellow, golden whisky. The Grant family's other excellent Dufftown distillery, **The Balvenie** (✆ **44/1340/820-373;** www.balvenie. com) now runs a limited number of in-depth

tours of its century-old maltings, mash house, cooperage, and still rooms. They're pricey, but well worth it. Tours depart from the Glenfiddich plant; advance booking is essential.

A great place to end your tour is south of A95 at the **Glenlivet Distillery** (B9008, 16km/10 miles north of Tomintoul; ✆ **44/1340/821-720;** www.glenlivet.com). Set near the River Livet, a Spey tributary, this distillery was founded in 1824. The current low-slung, rustic stone buildings date only from 1958, however, replacing an earlier plant that burned down. Madly popular worldwide, Glenlivet has a sweet, rounded taste with intriguing hints of bitterness. The distillery's wind-scoured moorland setting will take your breath away.

✈ Inverness (66km/41 miles).

🛏 $$$ **Minmore House Hotel,** Glenlivet (✆ **44/1807/590-378;** www.minmore househotel.com). $$ **Grange House,** Grange (near Keith; ✆ **44/1542/870-206;** www.aboutscotland.com/banff/grange house.html).

Islay Malts
For Peat's Sake
Isle of Islay, Scotland

Hugging Scotland's ragged western coast, the Hebrides Islands have that impossibly wild and romantic look down pat. Dubbed the "Queen of the Hebrides," Islay (pronounced "eye-la") lies a mere 26km (16 miles) from the Kintyre peninsula, but that's enough distance to preserve its remote, isolated charm. It's an unspoiled island of moors, salmon-filled lochs, ruined castles, mossy Celtic crosses, and wild rocky cliffs pocked with caves where whisky smugglers of yore hid their liquid booty.

Laphroaig distillery on the rocky shore of a cove on the Isle of Islay.

Yes, whisky, for this windswept island is fiercely devoted to its single malts. Far from the mainland's tax officers, Islay's renegade distillers did quite a business in freebooting whisky in the 18th century; once the excise tax was lifted, the island was perfectly poised to become a whisky powerhouse. Islay's brown peaty water infuses the local malts with its earthy tang; hints of briny salt air and even a little mossy seaweed can be detected as well. It's a strong flavor, further concentrated by the antiquated pot-still methods used by the island's distilleries. Some whisky drinkers are put off by the taste; others consider it the finest and truest expression of malt whisky.

Since tourism is Islay's other main industry, nearly all of Islay's distilleries run tours year-round, Mondays through Fridays; be sure to call ahead for an appointment. Begin down south in Port Ellen, with **Laphroaig** (1.6km/1 mile east of Port Ellen; ⓒ **44/1496/302-418;** www.laphroaig. com), a neat whitewashed plant perched on the rocky shore of a tiny cove. Since 1994 Laphroaig has carried the crest of a royal warrant from Prince Charles, though illegal stills operated on the Johnston farm for years before the distillery was officially founded in 1815. Its sweet, smoky flavor results in part from aging in recycled American bourbon casks (most other malts use sherry casks). A few minutes' drive east, Laphroaig's longtime rival, **Lagavulin** (3km/2 miles east of Port Ellen; ⓒ **44/1496/302-730;** www.malts.com), looks virtually the same and turned legitimate nearly the same time, in 1816. Using unique pear-shaped stills, Lagavulin's distillers add extra time to the process at every stage—distilling, fermenting, aging—to give this dark, peaty whisky an especially deep, rounded flavor. Up the coast another mile or so, 19th-century **Ardbeg** (Ardbeg; © **44/1496/302-244;** www.ardbeg.com) went out of business in the 1980s but was revived in 1997 by Glenmorangie, which painstakingly replicated and restored old stills, copper-topped kilns, and mash tuns to produce a classic peaty Islay malt.

Deep in the crook of Loch Indaal on the west coast of Islay, **Bowmore Distillery** (School St., Bowmore; © **44/1496/810-671;** www.morrisonbowmore.com) is the island's oldest, founded in 1779; here you'll see one of the country's last old-fashioned malting floors, where a malt man gently hand-turns the malting barley with a wooden shovel. That malt gives Bowmore a hint of toffee beneath the peatiness; it's also distilled to be lighter than Laphroaig or Lagavulin. Across the loch, small privately owned **Bruichladdich** (© **44/1496/850-190;** www.bruichladdich.com) is another

revived artisanal 19th-century distillery. With its old-fashioned narrow-necked copper still out front, this feisty newcomer makes a clearer and more delicate malt, using unpeated barley and clear spring water. On the northwest coast, also visit **Bunnahabhain** (5km/3 miles north of Port Askaig; © **44/1496/840-646;** www.bunnahabhain.com), known for its gentle Islay malt.

✈ Islay Airport, Port Ellen (11km/6³/₄ miles).

Ferry: Port Ellen or Port Askaig (2 hr. from West Tarbert, Kintyre, via MacBrayne steamers; © **44/1880/730-253;** www.calmac.co.uk).

🛏 $$$ **Harbour Inn,** The Square, Bowmore (© **44/1496/810-330;** www.harbour-inn.com). $$ **Bridgend Hotel,** Bridgend (© **44/1496/810-212;** www.bridgend-hotel.com).

411 Distilleries

Talisker Distillery
The King O' Drinks
Isle of Skye, Scotland

As Robert Louis Stevenson once wrote: "The king o' drinks, as I conceive it, Talisker, Islay or Glenlivit . . ." He wasn't specific about which Islay malt he was talking about, and probably only threw in Glenlivet for the rhyme. But Talisker—yes, there's a whisky a Scotsman like Stevenson was bound to be partial to.

While the Isle of Islay is peppered with distilleries, there's only one on the magnificent Isle of Skye, which lies farther up Scotland's west coast. The largest of the Inner Hebrides, since 1995 Skye has finally been connected to the mainland by bridge. Whether or not this improves life on Skye is a hotly contested issue, but it certainly makes it easier for visitors to wend their way up the island's rugged seaward coast

to the tiny town of Carbost, lying in the shadow of the jagged black Cuillin Hills mountain range. Here, on the shore of Loch Harport, the Talisker Distillery has been brewing single-malt whisky since 1830. Talisker has had its business ups and downs ever since it first opened, and it's now owned by the multinational conglomerate Diageo (which also owns Johnny Walker blended whisky—a brand that includes a strain of Talisker to give the blend a bracing shot of peat). Throughout all its changes in ownership, however, the whisky has remained superlative.

Talisker draws the water for its whisky from peaty springs that rise up in nearby Hawks Hill (look for peregrines circling overhead). The result is a uniquely smoky, spicy whisky that tastes like the essence of the Highlands. After a disastrous 1960 fire, the simple whitewashed plant was largely rebuilt, with replicas made of the five old-fashioned stills—two wash stills for the first distillation, and three spirit stills for a second distillation (until 1928 Talisker even distilled the spirit a costly third time). You'll also notice on your tour that while most of the whisky is aging in reused American bourbon casks, some of the older vintages are still mellowing in sherry casks, which was for years the industry standard.

When you call ahead to book a spot on a tour, consider the afternoon Connoisseur's

Tour, which includes an extended tasting session. There's no other distillery to rush on to next—take time to savor the taste of Skye.

ⓘ Carbost (✆ **44/1478/614-308;** www. malts.com).

✈ Inverness (129km/80 miles).

🛏 $$ **Sligachan Hotel,** Sligachan (✆ **44/1478/650-204;** www.sligachan.co. uk). $$$ **The Cuillin Hills Hotel,** Portree (✆ **44/1478/612-003;** www.cuillinhills. demon.co.uk).

Distilleries 412

Jameson Whiskey Distilleries

It's All Still History

Dublin/Midleton, Ireland

Though they're both tied to Ireland's most famous whiskey, Jameson's, these two attractions present the whiskey tourist with a devil of a choice. Which do you tour—the snazzy refurbished space in Dublin where John Jameson actually began producing whiskey in 1780, or the beautiful historic section of the plant in rural Cork where Jameson's is made today?

If you're the sort of traveler who needs to stand on the very ground where important events happened, opt for the Dublin attraction, officially titled the **Old Jameson Distillery.** Whiskey isn't made here anymore, but the brick-walled, wood-beamed building just north of the Liffey is the same plant where John Jameson began making whiskey in 1780. Back then, Dublin was the greatest whiskey-producing city in the world, and by 1805, Jameson's was the world's number-one brand. Over the next 2 centuries, it managed to survive the Irish temperance movement, the rise of cheaper blended Scotch whiskey, Irish wars of independence, and finally Prohibition in

America. (On the other hand, it benefited greatly from the late-19th-century phylloxera epidemic, which arrested European wine-drinking for several years.) As you stroll through the "experience," Jameson's history and traditional production methods are illuminated in videos, dioramas, and replicas of old equipment. Though it's a bit Disneyland-ish (you almost expect the molded figures to start singing), the guides are engaging and, of course, there's a generous tasting session afterwards.

If you're the sort of traveler, however, who likes to enter an authentic setting that evokes a dreamy sense of the past, head for Midleton, a short drive east from Cork city, for a guided tour of The **Old Midleton Distillery/Jameson Heritage Center.** After Jameson's joined forces with its chief Irish rivals in 1966, forming the Irish Distillers Group (now owned by Pernod), Jameson's shifted operations to a new modern distillery nearby; this series of rustic stone buildings in the lush Cork countryside was that distillery's 1825 precursor. You'll stand next to the giant waterwheel that powered the distillery's mill, see the cooper's shop where aging barrels were made, and visit a typical cottage where the distiller lived. Dray horses rattle into the courtyard pulling wagons piled with sacks of Irish barley, some of which is malted and the rest left green to produce Jameson's distinctively complex flavor. In the brew house you can see Jameson's original huge gleaming copper pot still, the largest in the world. Of course this tour ends with—you guessed it—a generous tasting session.

Hmmm . . . come to think of it, why not do both tours?

ⓘ **The Old Jameson Distillery,** Bow St., Smithfield Village (✆ **353/1/807-2355;** www.jamesonwhiskey.com). **Jameson Heritage Center,** Distillery Rd., Midleton (✆ **3353/21/461-3594;** www.jameson whiskey.com).

✈ Dublin/Cork (11km/7 miles).

⊨ $ **Abbott Lodge,** 87–88 Lower Gardiner St., Dublin (✆ **1/836-5548;** www. abbott-lodge.com). $$$ **Hayfield Manor Hotel,** Perrott Ave., Cork (✆ **800/525-4800** or 353/21/431-5600; www.hayfield manor.ie).

413 Distilleries

Cruzan Rum Distillery
Yo Ho Ho & a Barrel of Rum
St. Croix, Virgin Islands

It's no accident that most Caribbean resorts welcome guests with a refreshing glass of planter's punch, that delicious concoction of tropical fruit juices and rum. For better or worse, the history of the Caribbean is spiked with rum. When the islands' early European settlers discovered that their plantation slaves were enjoying a potent drink made from fermented molasses, the dregs of the sugar cane refining process, they spied a new commercial opportunity. Distilling that drink into a liquor, they sold it all over the world (for years the British Royal Navy seemed powered largely by ship's grog). The booming sugar trade created a need for more African slaves, pirates arrived to prey on lucrative slave and rum cargoes, and the tropical islands' culture was changed forever.

The site of Columbus's first landfall in the New World, St. Croix had many different rulers over the years—the Spanish, the Dutch, the English, the French, even the

Knights of Malta—but after the Danish took over in 1733, St. Croix really boomed. Sugar cane was its claim to fame (only Barbados produced more sugar) and at one point, some 150 St. Croix plantations had factories for making molasses and rum.

The sole survivor today is the Cruzan distillery (pronounced *cru*-cian, the nickname for St. Croix residents), founded in 1760 on the island's lush western end. Still owned by the Nelthorpp family, Cruzan has grown into one of the world's most respected brands, producing a variety of dark and light rums. Its finest, the 12-year Cruzan Single Barrel, has won the title of world's best rum in various competitions.

Exploring the property on a half-hour guided tour, you'll see remnants of the Estate Diamond plantation's original buildings—the manorial green wooden great house, a 19th-century square stone chimney, the ruined base of an old windmill (St. Croix was once thickly dotted with windmills). As you tour the small plant, you'll discover some of the factors that make this rum so good. The slight licorice taste of Cruzan is characteristic of St. Croix sugarcane, you'll learn, and the alcohol gets an extra smoothness from being blended with pure island rainwater. The stills they use have five stainless-steel columns, to refine the liquor five times. (The distillate comes out crystal-clear; the rum's amber color comes from the white oak barrels it's aged in.) The sugary aroma throughout the plant is intoxicating. Despite the industrial environment, it's not hard to imagine that the laid-back islanders working here impart some of their own mellowness to the drink.

All this and a tasting session too—you'll be glad you interrupted your beach lounging for half a day.

(i) Estate Diamond 3 (© **340/692-2280;** www.cruzanrum.com).

✈ St. Croix (7km/4¹/₃ miles).

🛏 $$$ **The Buccaneer,** Gallows Bay (© **800/255-3881** or 340/773-2100; www. thebuccaneer.com). $ **Pink Fancy,** 27 Prince St., Christiansted (© **800/524-2045** in the U.S., or 340/773-8460; www.pink fancy.com).

Distilleries **414**

A Taste of Tequila

From Aztec to High-Tech

Tequila, Mexico

No, it doesn't come with a worm in the bottle—that's mescal you're thinking of, Mexico's other wickedly potent distilled beverage. (And even mescal doesn't really have a worm in the bottle anymore, just a plastic caterpillar.) Smooth, sweetish, fiery-tasting, this heady liquor first drunk by the ancient Aztecs is Mexico's alcoholic ambassador to the world, consumed now in many more forms than that old standby, the margarita cocktail. Mexico has conferred tequila with controlled appellation status, meaning that no liquor can be labeled tequila if it isn't distilled in the state of Jalisco—better yet, in its traditional source, a town called (you guessed it) Tequila.

Just an hour outside of Guadalajara, this small colonial town has built its tourism industry around tours of its many tequila distilleries. On your drive there, you'll notice the spiky blue agaves growing in vast fields as far as the eye can see. Tequila is made from the heart of the agave's *piña,* or pineapple, which is cooked to a pulp and crushed to remove its juices; the juices are then fermented, distilled, and aged in stacked wooden casks (it's the length of aging that gives tequila its range of colors, from the harsh clear *blanco* to the mellow long-aged golden *añejo*).

In the center of town, the biggest draws are **Mundo Cuervo** (75 Calle José Cuervo; © **52/374/742-2170;** www.mundocuervo. com) and **Sauzo** (80 Francisco Javier Sauza; © **866/510-2250** or 52/374/742-4140; www.sauzatequila.com). Mundo Cuervo makes the famous José Cuervo brand, dating from 1795, and its slick well-run tours offer snazzy audiovisuals, a cafe, and an art gallery (featuring several statues of the distillery's namesake black crow). Sauzo, founded in 1873, was the first company to export tequila beyond Mexico. Its tours have an Old Mexico aura—fountained courtyard, colorful murals, tasting sessions in a pleasant garden—and lead off with a walk around real agave fields. Although it isn't a factory tour, the **Sauza Family Museum** (Vicente Albino

Rojas #22; 52/374/372-0247) makes an interesting stop. It displays historical photos and old tools in what was once the family home, followed by a tasting of Tequila Los Abuelos, the artisanal tequila that Guillermo Erickson Sauza began making after the family sold its big operation in 1988 (in the U.S. it's marketed as Fortaleza). In town, there's also a small **Museo Nacional de Tequila** (Ramón Corona 34; 52/374/742-0012) full of photos, artwork, and artifacts about the history of the drink.

On the outskirts of town, **La Cofradia** (Calle La Cofradia; 52/374/742-1015; www.tequilacofradia.com), makers of Casa Noble tequila, feels more like a rural estate. Visitors mingle with factory workers as they tour the distillery, cellar, onsite museum, and art gallery. An even more rural setting is at **Hacienda San José del Refugio** (800/710-9868 or 52/333/942-3900; www.herradura.com), in Amatitan, just 27km (17 miles) from

Guadalajara. Run by the makers of Herradura tequila, it has preserved several crumbling adobe rooms from its original distilling plant, so you can compare old-fashioned methods with today's up-to-date distillery process. Tours are 90 minutes with a tasting session; book in advance.

Whichever tour you take, at the tasting sessions be aware that Mexicans don't mess around with licking salt off their hands and sucking a slice of lime after a shot of tequila. That elaborate ritual is purely an American invention. Kinda like the worm.

Guadalajara (954km/593 miles).

$$ **Old Guadalajara,** Belén 236, Guadalajara (33/3613-9958; www. oldguadalajara.com). $$$ **Villa Ganz,** López Cotilla 1739, Guadalajara (800/ 728-9098 in the U.S. or 866/818-8342 in Canada; www.villaganz.com).

Traditional high tea service.

Bramah Museum of Tea & Coffee

Have a Cuppa

London, England

Here in the land of high tea service, it's only fitting that you'd find the world's first museum devoted entirely to the history of tea and coffee. Founded in 1992 by the late Edward Bramah, a globe-trotting tea planter and coffee broker, it's an obsessive's delight—a comprehensive look at the history of tea and coffee.

Granted, England is more often associated with tea—after all, it was the price of tea that finally drove its North American colonists to rebel. But coffee has also had its day in Great Britain, from the Restoration era of the mid-1700s, when coffeehouses were essential hangouts for writers, politicians, and intellectuals (the famous insurance company Lloyd's of London had its humble beginnings in a coffeehouse) down to the trendy espresso bars of 1950s Soho and modern-day Internet cafes. China tea sets, complicated coffee brewing machines, ancient maps, bills of lading, painted canisters, engravings of clipper ships, vintage advertising images—all tell the story of how the British Empire spread around the globe to India, Ceylon, Africa, and China in pursuit of tea and coffee. The museum isn't large—after all, this is a pretty specialized collection—but its displays do an admirable job of covering a 4-century-long sweep of commercial and social history.

Naturally, there's a refined pink tearoom, where the pots of tea are steeped from leaves instead of teabags, and the coffee is brewed by the traditional jug method. Cucumber sandwiches, crumpets, and traditional cream teas—with clotted cream, jam, and scones—are also available. The adjacent shop also sells Bramah's own brands of leaf tea and ground coffee from around the world. The museum is handily located on the south bank of the Thames, in a neighborhood of converted warehouses near Butler's Wharf, where the great tea ships once unloaded their cargoes; it's conveniently close to the Borough Market and to the **George Inn** (77 Borough High St.; **20 7407 2056**), an old coaching inn which has preserved its original 17th-century coffee room, a favored haunt of Charles Dickens.

ⓘ 40 Southwark St. (**44/20/7403 5650;** www.teaandcoffeemuseum.co.uk).

✈ Heathrow (24km/15 miles); Gatwick (40km/25 miles).

🛏 $$$ **Covent Garden Hotel,** 10 Monmouth St., Covent Garden (**800/553-6674** in the U.S., or 44/20/7806-1000; www.firmdale.com). $$ **B + B Belgravia,** 64–66 Ebury St., Belgravia (**800/682-7808** in the U.S., or 44/20/7734-2353; www.bb-belgravia.com).

Coffee **416**

Johann Jacobs Museum

Where Kaffekultur Is King

Zurich, Switzerland

Even if you're not a java junkie, this smart lakefront museum will eventually seduce you into sharing its coffee-centric view of the world. Every year, a different in-depth exhibit explores some aspect of coffee's cultural history—no matter how arcane the topic sounds, they'll manage to make it fascinating.

One of Johann Jacobs' many novelty coffee vessels.

Open since 1984, the Jacobs Museum (named after a 19th-c. coffee merchant from Bremen, Germany) focuses less on science than on the social dimensions of coffee—how the coffee trade influenced global economic development; how coffeehouse culture differed from country to country, class to class, and gender to gender; the complicated rituals associated with brewing, serving, and packaging coffee; and popular images of coffee from generation to generation.

The museum develops these exhibits from its own extensive collection of coffee-related art, literature, and artifacts—which includes everything from porcelain figurines to all shapes of silver coffee jugs, illustrated 17th-centry travelogues, and 19th-century medical treatises on the horrors of imbibing coffee. The museum's art collection is particularly comprehensive, with prints and paintings by a range of artists including William Hogarth, Henri Toulouse-Lautrec, and Roy Lichtenstein—all them with some tangential relation to coffee and coffee-drinking. It's a pity, really, that only a portion is on public display at any one time.

The setting in itself is worth a visit—a baroque sandstone villa built in 1913 with an elegant marble entrance hall and a fine view over Lake Zürich. The upstairs coffee room charges for a premium selection of brews from around the world (Johann Jacobs's business eventually grew into a major German coffee importer, now owned by Phillip Morris), but the downstairs bar serves free coffee in a sort of Internet cafe that also features informative videos and photo displays.

Les Amateurs de Café.

An illustration from the Johann Jacobs Museum, devoted to the history of coffee.

ⓘ Seefeldquai 17 (✆ **41/44/388 61 51;** www.johann-jacobs-museum.ch).

Zurich International (17km/10 miles).

$$$ **Hotel Ambassador**, Falkenstrasse 6 (℃ **41/44/258-98-98;** www. ambassadorhotel.ch). $$ **Lady's First,** Mainaustrasse 24 (℃ **41/44/380-80-10;** www.ladysfirst.ch).

417 Coffee

Don Juan Coffee Plantation

The Golden Bean

Monteverde, Costa Rica

The very name Costa Rica means "rich coast," and anyone looking at the dense jungles of this Central American nation should have guessed that its rich volcanic soil would be a planter's dream—if only the right crop could be found. In 1748, the first cuttings of Arabica coffee plants brought from Cuba were planted on high cloud-forest slopes, where temperatures were moderate and the climate moist—and it became clear at once that coffee (or as Costa Ricans call it, "the golden bean") had found a fitting home.

Costa Rican coffee—prized for its smooth taste, much like Colombian—has become one of the world's premier coffees. That may have something to do with the fact that nearly three-quarters of the country's crop is raised on small family-run farms that can afford the labor-intensive practices that yield high-quality beans, such as contour planting and hand-picking.

Until world coffee prices began to fall in 1990, coffee was Costa Rica's chief source of income. It has since been replaced by tourism, although coffee tourism is a budding trend. While half a million tourists have learned about Costa Rica's coffee industry from the slickly packaged tour at **Café Britt** (℃ **800/GO-BRITT** [800/462-7488]; www.cafebritt.com), in the San Jose suburb San Rafael de Heredia, diehard coffee lovers will get much more out of a trip to Monteverde to the **Don Juan Coffee Estate.** This organic, fair-trade plantation will initiate visitors into the mysteries of coffee growing, and the Monteverde Biological Cloud Forest Preserve is nearby.

At the Don Juan plantation, visitors ride a gaudily painted ox-drawn cart around the orchards planted with coffee bushes of various sizes, from seedlings to 30-year-old veterans. (If you come in the winter during harvest season, you'll see workers meticulously examining the red coffee cherries to see which are ready to be picked.) You then walk through the on-site mill, or *beneficio*, where the husk is removed, the raw bean soaked in water, and then beans are sorted in a long water-filled trough (inferior beans float to the surface; premium beans sink). You'll peek into a greenhouse, where beans lie drying for 6 weeks—it takes longer in this supermoist climate—and end up in the mill where they are finally shelled and roasted.

Although larger operations have more machines and shortcuts, the Don Juan operation, which has been here since the 1950s, follows time-honored methods, as the bilingual guides explain. It's amazing how crude most of the machines in the *beneficio* look—but they get the job done. The tour takes about 2 hours and ends at the plantation's cafe, where you'll appreciate every drop of your sample cup of Don Juan coffee.

ⓘ 2km (1¼ miles) outside Santa Elena (℃ **506/2645-7100;** www.donjuancoffeetour.com).

Juan Santamaria International, San José (161km/100 miles).

$$ **Monteverde Lodge** (℃ **257-0766** in San José or 645-5057 in Monteverde; www.costaricaexpeditions.com). $$ **Hotel El Establo** (℃ **645-5110;** www. hotelelestablo.com).

The Panama Plantations

Wear Your Panama Hat

Boquete, Panama

Boquete, in Panama—a charming colonial mountain town with flowers spilling from window boxes everywhere—is no longer off the beaten track, now that it has been rated one of the best places in the world to retire. But for coffee lovers, it's worth traveling here for another reason: Some of the finest Arabica beans in the world are grown in the western highlands right around Boquete.

On the rich volcanic slopes of Volcán Barú, Panama's highest mountain, coffee orchards are still planted the traditional way—combined with shade trees, a technique that not only prevents soil exhaustion but allows rare shade-loving varieties such as typica and geisha to thrive. Touring the plantations, you'll also notice that the workers are generally indigenous nomads, the Ngöbe Buglé people, who for generations have tended the crops up here and hand-picked their red coffee berries. It's a perfect model of sustainability, proving that the old ways sometimes are the best.

Three top-notch local producers offer excellent tours of their plantations and processing plants. **Café Ruiz** (507/720-1000; www.caferuiz-boquete.com), family owned for three generations, runs tours beginning from its roadside shop just north of downtown Boquete in Palmira; the tours go into special depth on their processing plant, which also processes coffee for more than 300 smaller farmers in the area. Three

times in the past decade, Café Ruiz has won international awards for the world's best coffee. And in years when it doesn't win, **Kotowa Coffee Estate** (in Palo Alto, east of Boquete; **507/720 3852;** www.kotowacoffee.com) takes the prize instead. Kotowa's comprehensive plantation tour shores up the contrast between the original 100-year-old mill and the state-of-the-art processing plant (with all the latest environmentally friendly adaptations). **Finca Lérida,** in Alto Quiel northwest of town, offers the most deluxe tour—a day-long jaunt up the mountainside to the Collins family's ranch house, where a ramble through the orchards and processing plant is followed by a lunch of Panamanian local dishes. You can stay overnight at Finca Lérida's ecolodge (see Lodging below), an option that's also available in bungalows nestled in the orange grove at Barry and Jane Robbins's coffee farm (**The Coffee Estate Inn,** see Lodging, below). Bring your binoculars; both places also happen to offer spectacular bird-watching. That's what eco-friendly coffee planting will do for you.

David (45 min. from Boquete).

$$ **La Montaña Y El Valle/Coffee Estate Inn,** Jaramillo Arriba (**507/720-2211;** www.coffeeestateinn.com). $$ **Finca Lerida,** Alto Quiel (**507/720-2285;** www.fincalerida.com).

Filadelfia Coffee Estate
Wake Up & Smell the Coffee
Antigua, Guatemala

Here's a novel twist: You don't just tour this coffee plantation, you actually stay there overnight, waking in the morning to the intoxicating smell of coffee roasting in the mill nearby.

Just outside the old colonial city of Antigua, this small luxury country hideaway is on a 360-hectare (900-acre)working plantation owned for four generations by the family of Don Roberto Dalton, with smoky blue views of the Agua Volcano in the near distance. (Remember, volcanic soils equal premium coffee beans.) Built in a rustic fieldstone style with traditional red-tiled roofs, this isn't just a converted bunkhouse but a resort with five-star amenities: a restaurant, an outdoor pool and tennis courts, horseback riding, arrangements with a nearby golf course and spa, even Pratesi linen sheets and Wi-Fi in all the rooms. So you don't forget where you are, green coffee bushes cover the hillsides, and coffee beans dry in the sun on large patios just past the hotel buildings, raked into geometric designs that have a Zen garden quality to them.

If you don't stay at the resort, you can still take the 2-hour tour of the plantation and its *beneficio*, tracing the various stages of the coffee chain from tender green seedlings to roasted bean. Filadelfia's award-winning coffee is made from Arabica beans, transplanted from the nursery to upland slopes at an elevation of 1,950m (6,500 ft.; high altitudes equal premium coffee beans too), which tour participants reach via mule or jeep. The tour ends with a cupping session in the plantation's "coffee laboratory," where guests learn how to distinguish among different types of coffee.

Don Roberto's brainstorm—adding a hotel to his ancestral estate—enabled him to remain in the coffee business even as world coffee prices have plummeted. His longtime workers remain employed too, so it's a win-win-win situation.

✈ Guatemala City (47km/29 miles).

🛏 $$$ **Filadelfia Coffee Resort & Spa,** San Felipe de Jesus, Antigua (✆ **502/ 7728-0800;** www.filadelfiaresort.com).

The Kona Coast
The Land of Kona Gold
Big Island, Hawaii

Driving along the Big Island's southwest coast, on a breathtakingly beautiful 20-mile (32km) stretch of the Mamalahoa Highway, you can't help but notice the lush green plantations carpeting the steep slopes on either side. Those aren't just any orchards; they grow America's only domestically grown coffee—Kona, a strain of Arabica that originally came from Ethiopia, via Brazil and then Oahu. While Maui has recently revived its coffee farming too, it's Kona's rich volcanic soil—you're actually on the lower slopes of Mauna Loa—that has consistently produced Hawaii's finest beans.

Kona's coffee industry began in 1828, launched by American missionary Samuel Ruggles. At first a few large growers dominated the area, but after they switched to more lucrative sugar crops in the early 1900s, several small tenant farmers took over (principally the Japanese immigrants who'd already been working the large farms for years). Some 600 coffee farms are crowded along this coast nowadays; most are small, family-run operations. (For many years, local schools ran from Dec–Aug so that children could be free during the Sept coffee harvest.) Springtime is lovely here, with the hillsides spangled with white blossoms ("Kona snow"), but autumn is the best time to visit, as the scent of roasting coffee beans permeates the air along the coast.

Several estates offer guided tours and coffee tastings to drop-in visitors (with the expectation, of course, that you'll then buy some pricey, farm-fresh Kona beans to take home). If you've tasted Kona coffee and weren't too impressed, don't dismiss it: Coffee is often labeled "Kona" even if it contains only 10% genuine Kona beans. The taste of unblended premium Kona coffee should restore your faith, especially if you drink it right on the lush coast where it's grown.

Just south of Lailua-Kona in the small town of Holualoa, one of the largest estates, the 400-acre (160-hectare) **Kona Blue Sky Coffee Company** (76-973A Hualalai Rd.; © **808/322-1700**) is just off Hwy. 180; the same owners run the Holualoa Coffee Company's **Kona Lea Plantation** (77-6261 Mamalahoa Hwy./

Hwy 180; © **808/322-9937**), where you can tour organically farmed coffee orchards as well as a mill and roasting operation that serves 100 other local farms.

Farther south in Kealakekua, after Mamalahoa Hwy. merges with Hwy. 11, you can tour the 35-acre (14-hectare) **Greenwell Farms** (81-6581 Mamalahoa Hwy.; © **808/323-2862**), still operated by descendants of Henry Nicholas Greenwell, an early pioneer in Kona coffee exporting. For more historical perspective, continue south to the village of Captain Cook and the **Kona Coffee Living History Farm** (82-6199 Mamalahoa Hwy.; © **808/323-2006;** www.konahistorical.org), a 5½-acre (2.2-hectare) homestead where costumed guides lead tours of a 1920s-era farmhouse, century-old coffee and macadamia nut orchards, the *kuriba* (processing mill), *hoshidana* (drying roofs), and a traditional Japanese bathhouse. Attached to one of the larger mills, the **Royal Kona Coffee Museum** (83-5427 Mamalahoa Hwy.; © **808/328-2511**) is little more than a gallery displaying photos of the old plantations, but free samples of Kona coffee and rum cake are offered. Before you leave Captain Cook, branch off on impossibly squiggly Napoopoo Road, which leads down to Kealakekua Bay, to try roasting beans yourself at the Ueshima Coffee Company's **Espresso Bar and Roastery** (82-5810 Napoopoo Rd.).

✈ Kona (9½ miles/15km).

🛏 $$$ **Holualoa Inn,** 76-5932 Mamalahoa Hwy. (© **800/392-1812** or 808/324-1121; www.holualoainn.com). $$ **Areca Palms Estate Bed & Breakfast,** off Hwy. 11, South Kona (© **800/545-4390** or 808/323-2276; www.konabedandbreakfast.com).

421 Coffee

Paradisa Plantation Retreat

A Spicy Bit of Paradise

Kerala, India

Paradise, indeed. Set on the jungle-shrouded hillsides of a coffee and spice plantation in the Cardamom Hills of south-western India, this peaceful lodge takes some travel to reach, but once you're there, you feel as if you're in another world.

The word "retreat" in the title couldn't be more apt, either. Guests stay in individual teak villas, built in traditional Kerala-style architecture and adorned with antique columns and intricate rosewood carvings. Each roomy villa has its own private setting and a stupendous view of the dense green hills overlooking a maharajah's former hunting grounds. You can swim in a footprint-shaped pool on a mountainside terrace, take yoga classes and ayurvedic treatments, play golf at a historic planter's club nearby, spot wild

elephants and perhaps even tigers at the Periyar Wildlife Sanctuary just over the hills. Or just stroll around the lush plantation grounds, where orchids bloom, monkeys chatter, and the scent of wild spices hangs alluringly in the air (they don't call these the Cardamom Hills for nothing). Watch the harvesting of coffee, cloves, and pepper, visit the nearby plant where cardamom is processed, or swing up to Munnar to see the Tata tea factory and museum.

Breakfast is served on a lovely terrace, and even if you're not a regular coffee drinker, the smell of fresh-brewed coffee—organically grown right here—can be intoxicating. On the open-air stone pavilion of the central dining area, host Simon Paulose makes every meal into a

The Paradisa Plantation Retreat in the Cardamom Hills of southwestern India.

7 Places to Eat in . . . Istanbul, Turkey

Straddling Asia and Europe across the Bosporus strait, the great, glorious hodge-podge of cultures that is Istanbul by all rights should be one of the great dining cities of the world. Yet too many visitors remain stuck in the Sultanahmet area, hewing close to the Topkapi Palace, the Blue Mosque, the Ayasofya museum, and the Grand Bazaar; compelling as those attractions are, the cafes in that area seem bent on gouging tourists with high prices, aggressive come-ons, and mediocre food. It's a shame, really, because once you venture farther afield, you'll discover all the savory nuances that make Turkish food so delicious.

Out in the foothills of Edirnekapi, next to the St. Saviour in Chora church, the Kariye Hotel's ④²² Asitane (Kariye Camii Sok. 18; ℭ 90/212/534-8414; www.asitane restaurant.com) features one of the world's earliest fusion menus—painstakingly researched recipes that were once served at the Ottoman court to sultans like Mehmet the Conqueror and Suleiman the Magnificent. This imperial blending of Arabic, Greek, Persian, and North African influences results in luscious dishes like eggplant stuffed with grilled quail; spring chicken stewed with almonds, dried apricots, grapes, honey, and cinnamon; or *nirbach,* a diced lamb, meatball, carrot, and walnut stew spiced with coriander, ginger, cinnamon, and pomegranate syrup. Don't expect hokey faux-historic decor—Asitane's tasteful gold-and-white look is restrained and modern, throwing the emphasis squarely where it should be: on the food itself. Similar recipes have been updated at ④²³ Feriye (Çiragan Cad.

Stuffed quince and *mutanjene* at Asitane.

124; ⓒ **90/212/227-2216**), with its stunning location in Ortaköy in a stately 19th-century neoclassical building overlooking the Bosporus. In summers you can eat outside on a seaside terrace—an ideal setting for seafood dishes such as grilled turbot with saffron, courgette balls, and raspberry purée, or medallions of sword-fish topped with seafood ragout. Classic Ottoman meat dishes include *pastırma,* spicy cured beef wrapped in vine leaves.

Meat is an essential element of traditional Turkish food, and the meat's especially fine at the stylish modern steakhouse ⟨424⟩ Dükkan (Fatih Sultan Mehmet Mah, Atatürk Cad. 4; ⓒ **90/212/277-8860;** www.dukkanistanbul.com), just north of the E-80 belt-way in the Armutlu neighborhood. You know the dry-aged steaks and superb hand-made sausages are fresh, because it's just down the street from its own specialty butcher shop. Out by the fish market in Samatya, not far from the airport, the flag-ship cafe of ⟨425⟩ Develi (Gümüşyüzük Sok. 7; ⓒ **90/212/529-0833**) raises the bar on *köftes,* a variety of highly seasoned ground meats from southeastern Turkey—juicy, savory morsels like *çig köfte* (incredibly spicy raw beef meatballs wrapped in a let-tuce leaf), *findik lahmacun* (Turkish-style thin-crust pizza), or the lamb sausage and pistachio *kebap.* Its outdoor terrace is a glorious place to sit in warm weather.

In Beyoglu, where many locals live and eat, you'll find a number of cozy *meyhanes,* or taverns, serving cold shots of the potent grape-and-aniseed spirit *raki* along with a succession of *mezes,* the Turkish equivalent of tapas—a series of small dishes developed, legend has it, so that the sultan's tasters could test his food for poison. On a popular restaurant street near the bustling fish market, one of your best bets is ⟨426⟩ Boncuk (Nevizade Sok. 19; ⓒ **90/212/243-1219**), a usually jam-packed no-frills spot featuring delicacies like *kizir* (spicy bulgur-and-tomato salad); fried calamari; grape leaves stuffed with fish, pine nuts, and currants; or *topik,* a savory Armenian specialty of mashed chickpeas, onions, and currants. Within the fish market itself, hunt for the civilized oasis of ⟨427⟩ Degustasyon Lokantasi (Balikpazari, Beyoglu; ⓒ **90/212/292-0667**), where the huge selection of inventive *mezes* include Armenian and Turkish recipes like fava-bean loaf and a perfectly seasoned eggplant purée.

If hunger does strike while you're sightseeing in Sultanahmet, avoid the tourist traps and head for ⟨428⟩ Tarihi Meshur Sultanahmet Koftecisi (DivanYolu 12A; ⓒ **90/212/513-1438**). Unprepossessing as it may look from the street, this clean, cheap, genial little storefront has been serving reliably delicious *köfte* meatballs since the 1920s.

✈ Atatürk Intl, Istanbul (12km/7½ miles).

🛏 $$$ **Çirağán Palace Hotel Kempinski Istanbul,** Çirağán Cad. 84 (ⓒ **800/426-3135** in the U.S., or 90/212/258-3377 in Istanbul; www.ciraganpalace.com). $$ **Mavi Ev (Blue House),** Dalbastı Sok. 14 (ⓒ **90/212/638-9010;** www.bluehouse.com.tr).

Organically grown coffee beans from the Paradisa Plantation.

social occasion; with only 12 units on the property, the number of guests at any one time is equivalent to a gracious dinner party. And the meals are unbelievably delicious, superb examples of refined Keralan cuisine, which some say is the best in south India: crispy-thin *dosa* pancakes, abundant seafood, the pervasive richness of coconut milk, and deeply spiced stews and curries.

Seeing where the spices grow and then tasting them in your dinner is its own sort of farm-to-table experience, of the most exotic and luxurious variety. If you're intrigued by this extraordinary combination of flavors, you can arrange a cooking class with the chef, who will teach you how to re-create any dish on the menu. It's one way to take home a little piece of paradise.

ⓘ Off the Kottayam-Kumily Rd., Murinjapuzha (**91/469/270-1311** for reservations, 91/4869/288-119, or 0944/7088-119; www.paradisaretreat.com).

✈ Kochi International Airport (140km/87 miles).

🚃 Kottayam (70km/43 miles).

Coffee 429

The Turkish Kahvehane

Brewed on the Bosporus

Istanbul, Turkey

If it hadn't been for Turkey, the Western world might never have gotten hooked on coffee. There are apocryphal accounts of a coffee shop in Constantinople (modern-day Istanbul) from as far back as 1475; whether or not that's true, it is certain that by the mid-1500s Constantinople had coffee houses (*kahvehanes*, in Turkish) serving the bitter black brew adopted from neighboring Arab lands. From there, the habit spread to Constantinople's frequent trading partner, Venice, from where it disseminated to England and Germany. In 1683 Turkish invaders brought their favorite drink with them when they swept into Vienna, and the rest, as they say, was history.

In the heyday of the Ottoman Empire, coffeehouses were essential gathering places, where customers (men, of course) reclined on kilims, gazed onto a panoramic view or a reflecting pool, smoked water pipes *(narghiles)*, played backgammon, and discussed affairs of the day. A complicated brewing ritual evolved—for each individual serving, beans are hand-roasted on a metal tray, then ground with mortar and pestle into a superfine powder, mixed with cold water and sugar (and sometimes cardamom) in a specially designed copper pot (an *ibrik*), and boiled several times until the froth on top is just right. It's then poured carefully into a tiny handleless cup and served with a glass of cold water. The drinker waits a minute or two for the coffee grounds to settle, then savors it in small sips. The bitter sludge of grounds left at the bottom of the cup may be poured into a saucer for a fortune-teller to read.

Traditional Turkish coffee houses, however, are an endangered species these days, as modern Turks have turned to drinking flavored teas and (sad to say) instant coffee. Most of the remaining *kahvehanes* are out in residential neighborhoods, where locals can indulge after a day at work. If you're lucky enough to know a regular at one of these, be a good friend, because it's your best entry into this unique culture. **Les Arts Turcs** (90/212/527 68 59; www.bazaarturkey.com) runs half-day Turkish coffee- and tea-tasting tours that offer insight into the *kahvehane*.

If you're not lucky enough to have a local "in," you can still taste authentic Turkish coffee at the famous **Pierre Loti Cafe** (Gümüşsuyu Balmumcu Sok. 1; 90/212/581 26 96). The waiters even wear 19th-century costumes at this cozy historic cafe on a hilltop above the Eyup Sultan Cemetery, near the landmark Eyup Mosque. Its dazzling view of the Bosporus and the Istanbul skyline makes it a must-see experience, well worth the arduous climb. If you're wandering around the Grand Bazaar—which can be an exhausting and disorienting experience—try the good, traditional coffee at **Fez Café** (Halıcılar Cad. 62; 90/212/527-3684) or **Café Ist** (Tarakçılar Caddesi; 90/212/527-9353). Traditional coffee is a specialty at **Fazil Bey's Turkish Coffee House,** one of the oldest stores in the Kadiköy bazaar, on the Asian side of Istanbul. Even though the decor is spruced up and modern (it has recently been turned into a chain), Fazil Bey's takes pride in serving Turkish coffee the old-fashioned way, right down to that telltale muddy residue in every cup.

✈ Atatürk International, Istanbul (1.4km/¾ miles).

🛏 $$$ **Çirağan Palace Hotel Kempinski Istanbul,** Çirağan Cad. 84 (**800/426-3135** in the U.S., or 90/212/258-3377 in Istanbul; www.ciraganpalace.com). $$ **Mavi Ev (Blue House),** Dalbastı Sok. 14 (**90/212/638-9010;** www.bluehouse.com.tr).

430 Coffee

The *Qahwas* of Cairo

Hookah Up

Cairo, Egypt

The big attraction in Egyptian *qawhas* (coffee shops) is not the coffee and various teas served but the *sheesha* or hookah pipe. Serving as traditional neighborhood hangouts, the sidewalk tables of *qahwas* are male bastions where Egyptian men can escape their crowded households, discuss politics and religion (in Egypt, the two are interchangeable), play chess or dominos, and puff away on water pipes. Female customers are liable to attract unnerving attention, though less so if they're with a man (better yet, an Egyptian). The coffee served is invariably strong, sludgy, Turkish-style coffee (sometimes flavored with tamarind), served at ridiculously low prices.

Unless you're hanging around with Cairo natives, you'll probably be more comfortable visiting certain coffeehouses that are known to welcome outsiders. Close to Islamic Cairo's bustling Khan al-Khalili market, **Al Fishawi's** has been around since 1772, open 24 hours a day (except during Ramadan), in an alleyway just off Midan Hussein. Your fellow tourists will definitely be there too, huddled at tiny brass tables under baroque mirrors and carved wood paneling, but it's a reliable option in this sometimes bewildering part of town.

In the heart of downtown's Bab al-Luk neighborhood, the square named Midan Falaki is home to a food market, including several coffee merchants; spacious **Cafe Hurriya** on the north side of the square has been around since the 1930s. Though it looks run down, it's still a de facto club for many writers and intellectuals. The artsy crowd also hangs out at **Cafe Ta'kiba,** a short walk away on Nabrawy Street, just around the corner from the Town House Gallery contemporary art museum.

Another vintage coffeehouse downtown is the original **Groppi's,** on Midan Talaat Harb, which has been around since 1924 (notice the beautiful mosaic-tiled columns either side of the entrance). The coffee at Groppi's is not so distinctively Egyptian—as it has become a chain, the emphasis now is on European-style cappuccinos, fancy teas, exotic juices, and rich pastries, and you'll pay tourist-gouging prices. Still, it's worthwhile to spend some time lounging on Groppi's shady garden terrace, which served as an unofficial British officers' club during World War II—a different slice of Cairo history, but atmospheric in its own way.

✈ Cairo International (18km/11 miles).

🛏 $$$ **Semiramis InterContinental,** Corniche El-Nil, Cairo (☎ **888/424-6835** or 20/2/2795-7171; www.ichotelsgroup.com). $$ **The Nile Hilton,** 1113 Corniche El-Nil (☎ **800/HILTONS** [800/445-8667] or 20/2/2578-0444; www1.hilton.com).

Coffee 431

The Cafes of Paris

Brewing up Atmosphere

Paris, France

Coffee drinking is so ingrained in French culture it inspired its own restaurant genre, the cafe. Yet many visitors to Paris are surprised—horrified!—to discover how mediocre the coffee served in Parisian cafes can be, at least by the standards of Starbucks Nation.

The truth is, coffee quality is almost beside the point in a Parisian cafe; it's the ambience that counts. In modern Paris, cafes have morphed into bar/restaurants where patrons order coffee mostly because it's the cheapest way to claim a table for hours (and therefore cafe owners know they can stint on the quality of the product they buy). For Parisians, cafes are hangouts—everybody's got one—where they eat, drink, work, socialize, and, above all, people-watch. They used to smoke as well: Until a 2008 restaurant smoking ban went into effect, the peculiarly pungent scent of Gauloises and Gitanes cigarettes wafted through every Parisian cafe. What the ban will do to cafe culture remains to be seen.

The old Latin Quarter, in the 6th arrondissement, was traditionally Cafe Central, and its most famous cafes are well-known tourist lures: the lacquered upscale **Le Procope** (13 rue de l'Ancienne-Comédie), founded in 1686 and once patronized by Voltaire and Victor Hugo; or the trio of rival cafes that once hosted Left Bank intellectuals such as Jean-Paul Sartre, Camus, and Picasso— **Brasserie Lipp** (151 bd. St-Germain), founded in 1865; the **Café de Flore** (172 bd. St-Germain), founded in 1870; and **Les Deux Magots** (6 place St-Germain-des-Prés), founded in 1875. For a more local experience, head to relative newcomers **La Palette** (43 rue de Seine), with its 1930s-vintage tiled murals, or **Le Rouquet** (188 bd. St-Germain), founded in 1922, with decor from the 1950s.

In the 8th arrondissement, posh cafes along the Champs-Elysées are designed for unabashed people-watching, from tables set on extrawide terraces shaded by canopies and bordered by flower-filled planters. The chichi places to see and be seen are **Fouquet's** (99 av. des Champs-Elysées) and **Le Deauville** (75 av. des Champs-Elysées); locals go instead to the friendlier (and cheaper) **Café Le Paris** (93 av. des Champs-Elysées). Across from the Opéra, the *fin de siècle* elegance of the **Café de la Paix** (in the Grand Hotel, 12 bd. des Capucines) is another glam setting for people-watching.

On Place de la Bastille, the adjacent **Café des Phares** (7 place de la Bastille) and **Café Le Bastille** (8 place de la Bastille) have reinvented themselves as *philocafés*, where groups of people meet to argue great ideas. In the trendy Marais, **La Belle Hortense** (31 rue Vieille du Temple, 4e) has book-lined walls and regularly scheduled poetry readings. Up in Montparnasse, Ernest Hemingway's old hangout, **Closerie des Lilas** (171 bd. du Montparnasse), open since 1847, has preserved its vintage 1920s look with leather banquettes, wood tables, and cozy red lampshades. Its counterpart—barnlike **La Coupole** (102 bd. du Montparnasse), once patronized by Josephine Baker, Henry Miller, Salvador Dalí, and Samuel Beckett—has been renovated beyond recognition. In Montmartre, **Café des Deux Moulins** (15 rue Lepic, 18e; 01-42-54-90-50) preserves a 1950s look, right down to the yellowed ceilings and lace curtains (parts of the 2001 film *Amélie* were shot here).

De Gaulle (23km/14 miles); Orly (14km/8⅔miles).

$$$ **Hôtel Luxembourg Parc,** 42 rue de Vaugirard, 6e (33/1/53-10-36-50; www.luxembourg-paris-hotel.com). $$ **Hôtel Saintonge,** 16 rue Saintonge, 3e (44/1/42-77-91-13; www.saintonge marais.com).

Espresso Bars
Standing Room Only
Rome, Italy

In Paris, coffee is often just an excuse to linger for hours at a table; Italians, on the other hand, stand at a counter to down tiny shots of coffee before heading back out the door in 10 minutes. Of course, they'll dart back in to repeat the process several times a day, during which time Parisians won't have budged from their ad hoc office/living rooms in the cafe.

Perhaps that's why there's an espresso bar on nearly every corner in Rome, serving bracing doses of strong coffee to get Romans through their day. In a typical Italian espresso place, a skilled barista executes a continual dance, smartly jerking the levers and hissing spigots of his espresso machine hundreds of times a shift. The preferred look for an espresso bar is gleaming and modern, with chrome counters, neon signs, and impeccable cleanliness—forget the vintage atmospheric looks that Parisian cafes trade in. There's a limit to

Patrons drink and run in Rome's espresso bars.

the city's best: **La Tazza d'Oro** (Via Degli Orfani 85 A) and the **Sant' Eustachio** (Piazza Sant' Eustachio 82). At the Tazza d'Oro, which also roasts its own beans on premises, large bags full of Brazilian coffee are stacked up right by the counter, and regulars use them for ad hoc seating. Several other roasteries line the nearby Via di Tor Cervara, informally nicknamed Rome's Coffee Way.

In other neighborhoods, an artistic crowd hangs out at the trendy **Rosati** (Piazza del Popolo 5), at that vast public gathering spot Piazza del Populo. Across the Tiber in Trastevere, **Café-Bar di Marzio** (Piazza di Santa Maria in Trastevere 15) is a warmly inviting spot with a view of the famous fountain.

For most Romans, their favorite espresso bar is simply the most conveniently located; the coffee quality is routinely high wherever you stop in. There are many variations on the straight shot of espresso, besides just adding milk to make it a cappuccino (named after the pale brown robes of Capuchin monks). Customers may order their espressos *ristretto* (short and dense) or *lungo* (diluted); if you only want a drop of milk, ask for *macchiato*. If you want a shot of brandy or some other liquor, ask for *caffe corretto* (or "revised coffee"). Order a *caffe Americano* and you'll get a somewhat diluted brew in a larger cup. You can either sugar it yourself or have the barista sweeten it to order.

Espresso bars generally serve light food as well, but connoisseurs warn against those that offer warm food—after all, warm food equals fragrant food, and who wants any other aroma to compete with the glorious smell of coffee?

modernity, however: A genuine espresso is always served in a ceramic cup, never in cardboard or plastic "to go."

The city's oldest coffeehouse, founded in 1760, is **Antico Caffè Greco** near the Spanish Steps (Via Condotti 84; *06-6791700*). Although such notable foreigners as Stendhal, Goethe, Keats, Liszt, and Mendelssohn count among its former patrons, it hardly qualifies as an espresso bar anymore, spiffed up as it is into a romantic sit-down restaurant with marble-topped tables and red velvet chairs.

Folklore has it that the best coffee bars are near the Pantheon, because of its superior water supply, piped through an ancient Roman Empire aqueduct leading from a crystal-pure spring outside the city. Whether or not this has any basis in scientific fact, espresso bars throng that neighborhood, including two regularly cited as

✈ Leonardo da Vinci International Airport (Fiumicino; 30km/19 miles).

🛏 $$$ **Hotel de Russie,** Via del Babuino 9 (*800/323-7500* in the U.S. and Canada, or 39/6/328881; www.roccofortehotels.com). $ **Hotel Grifo,** Via del Boschetto 144 (*39/6/4871395*; www.hotelgrifo.com).

Intelligentsia Roasting Works
Celebrity Roast
Chicago, Illinois

Looking back, it's hard to believe that Americans used to drink endless cups of coffee *with no idea* which countries had produced the beans. That benighted era ended in the 1990s, when a crop of gourmet roasting operations sprang up around America. Suddenly java junkies could reinvent themselves as coffee connoisseurs, attending "cuppings" (coffee's equivalent of a wine tasting) and using insider vocabulary to describe notes, shadings, varietals, and ideal degrees of roasting.

While it's easy to mock the apparatus of coffee snobbery, boutique roasting companies rescued America from the era of percolators and freeze-dried coffee crystals. The best coffee is roasted right before it's drunk. So local roasteries import raw beans (technically called green beans, though they're more gray than green)—rather than letting preroasted beans sit around losing flavor in warehouses, cargo holds, and docks. By shortening the time between roasting and brewing, they significantly heighten the coffee's flavor and complexity.

Opened in 1995, Chicago's Intelligentsia Roasting Works is an artisanal coffee company, selling both single-origin coffees and their own custom blends. Intelligentsia's peripatetic buyers source beans from coffee-growing nations all over the world—Tanzania, Nicaragua, Honduras, Kenya, Sumatra, Colombia, El Salvador, Brazil—working as much as possible with small estate growers rather than wholesalers. The company now supplies many of the Windy City's top restaurants and operates three coffee bars in town (3123 N. Broadway in Lakeview, 53 W. Jackson Blvd., and 53 E. Randolph St. in the Loop), and another in the Silver Lake neighborhood of Los Angeles (3922 Sunset Blvd.).

As the business has grown, so has the roasting plant, and Intelligentsia now offers small guided tours of the facility one Saturday a month. While most of us have seen small roasters operating in specialty coffee stores, those are nothing like the towering cast-iron-and-steel roasters at work in Intelligentsia's plant—one 51-pound (23-kg) roasting machine and two 198-pound (90-kg) numbers, each a different bright color, all hand-crafted in the 1950s by the same German manufacturer, Gothat (the Mercedes-Benzes of coffee roasters). As you walk past, you can hear the beans crackling away inside the roasting drum, releasing that divine aroma that permeates the plant. Tour admission includes a tasting session with plenty of fresh brewed coffee or tea, plus a half-pound bag of roasted coffee to take home.

ⓘ 1850 W. Fulton St. (🕾 **312/521-7962;** www.intelligentsiacoffee.com).

✈ O'Hare International (18 miles/28km).

🛏 $$ **Homewood Suites,** 40 E. Grand St., Chicago (🕾 **800/CALL-HOME** [800/225-4663] or 312/644-2222; www.homewoodsuiteschicago.com). $$ **Hotel Allegro Chicago,** 171 N. Randolph St., Chicago (🕾 **800/643-1500** or 312/236-0123; www.allegrochicago.com).

A Seattle Coffeehouse Tour
Beyond Starbucks
Seattle, Washington

There's no better place in the United States to overdose on espresso than Seattle, Washington, the city that gave the world Starbucks, for better or worse. Seattle probably has more coffee bars per capita than any other American city, and the quality is consistently high. Seattleites generally subscribe to certain immutable tenets of 21st-century coffeehouse culture—opting for recyclable containers, unrefined sugar, and organic milk, while passionately arguing the merits of different roasts and countries of origin, and parsing the finer points of barista technique.

The original **Starbucks** store, which opened in 1971, is still in operation as a stand-up counter in the Pike Place Market (1912 Pike Place). You'll know it by the bare-breasted-mermaid sign outside—the PG version of which has appeared on millions of cardboard cups since. Seattle's oldest coffeehouse, however, is up by the University of Washington, **Café Allegro** (4214 University Way NE; © **206/633-3030**), a student favorite tucked down an alley around the corner from "the Ave," as University Way is nicknamed. (The coffee may be even better, though, at comfy **University Zoka,** nearby at 2901 NE Blakeley St.)

Seattle's best coffeehouses just keep raising the bar. David Schomer's perfectionistic

The Vashon Island Roasting Company—the original home of Seattle's Best Coffee.

The Vashon Island Roasting Company's java has a lot of horsepower.

approach to espresso has put the coffee at **Espresso Vivace** (227 Yale Ave. N) head and shoulders above most contenders, but **Victrola Coffee** (in Capitol Hill at 411 15th Ave. E or downtown at 310 E. Pike St.) has its own fierce band of partisans, who also prefer Victrola's artsy vibe. When you want a break from espresso, try the Latin coffees such as *café Cubano* and *café con leche* at the **El Diablo Coffee Co.** (1811 Queen Anne Ave. N.). That area, Upper Queen Anne, is just the sort of yuppified neighborhood where coffeehouses sprout like weeds; there's a particularly welcoming branch of the excellent local chain **Caffe Ladro** up the street at 2205 Queen Anne Ave. N. In Lower Queen Anne, you can sample the premium blends of local roaster **Caffe Vita** (813 Fifth Ave. N.), another chain worth seeking out around town.

Just a ferry ride away on laid-back Vashon Island, **The Vashon Island Roasting Company** (19529 Vashon Hwy. SW) shares premises with an organic health food store, The Minglement, in a charming century-old white frame building with a rambling front porch. Unpretentious as it looks, it's a landmark: Specialty coffee pioneer Jim Stewart first opened The Wet Whisker here in 1968, which eventually became Seattle's Best Coffee (a chain now owned by Starbucks). Fair-trade, shade-grown heirloom coffees are still the stock in trade here—as far away from Nescafé as you can get.

✈ Seattle-Tacoma International (14 miles/23km).

🛏 $$$ **Inn at the Market,** 86 Pine St. (✆ **800/446-4484** or 206/443-3600; www.innatthemarket.com). $$ **Bacon Mansion Bed & Breakfast,** 959 Broadway E (✆ **800/240-1864** or 206/329-1864; www.baconmansion.com).

High Tea Lowdown
Afternoon Delight
London, England

No trip to London is complete without a traditional English afternoon tea. The cups must be porcelain, the sugar served in lumps, and the tea brewed from loose leaves, with nary a teabag in sight. To make a proper meal of it, that pot of tea is supplemented with dainty sandwiches, scones, or a few sweet cakes. Put Devonshire double cream and jam on those scones, and you've made it a "cream tea."

Several London institutions will fulfill your fantasy of high tea: For £25 and up, you'll feel as though you've stepped into an Edwardian country-house weekend, though you must book your table weeks in advance. At **Harrods** department store (see ⑲), the fourth-floor Georgian Room is devoted to tea, as are the St. James restaurant and Fountain Room at **Fortnum & Mason's** (see ④). Most of London's large luxury hotels also offer a pricy afternoon tea service; the most lavish are at the Reading Room at **Claridge's** (55 Brook St., W1; ⓒ **44/20/7409-6307**), The **Palm Court at the Ritz Hotel** (Piccadilly, W1; ⓒ**44/20/7493-8181**), the **Palm Court at the Sheraton Park Lane Hotel** (Piccadilly, W1; ⓒ **44/20/7499-6321**), or the **Conservatory at The Lanesborough** (Hyde Park Corner, SW1; ⓒ **44/20/7259-5599**). Teatime is a bit more discreet and aristocratically dowdy at **Brown's Hotel** (30 Albemarle St., W1; ⓒ **44/20/7493-6020**).

For a more colorful, less touristy afternoon tea at a reasonable price, venture beyond snooty Mayfair and Knightsbridge. In Soho, arty locals lounge on cozy mismatched sofas at **The Blue Room** (3 Bateman St., W1; ⓒ**44/20/7437-4827**) or hunch over the tiny tables at cluttered, homey

Patisserie Valerie (44 Old Compton St.; ⓒ **44/20/7437-3466**). In Holborn, London's old financial center, **The Old Bank of England** (194 Fleet St.; ⓒ **44/20/6430-2255**) serves a quiet, intimate tea in a tapestried chamber that could easily be pompous, but isn't. Out in Chelsea, the low-key **Tearoom at the Chelsea Physic Garden** (66 Royal Hospital Rd., SW3; ⓒ **44/20/7352-5646**) is open only 4 days a week, but on those days you can sip your tea within the brick-walled confines of a shaggy garden that has been prized as a botanical laboratory since the height of the British Empire. Or head up to north London to find **High Tea of Highgate** (50 Highgate High St., N6; ⓒ**44/20/83483162**), a shabby-chic little tearoom selling organic teas and home-baked pastries.

In Kensington, you can choose between palaces—either the sprawling **Tea Palace** (175 Westbourne Grove, W11; ⓒ **44/20/7727-2600**), a serious tea emporium offering over 200 blends, or the 18th-century garden pavilion of a real palace at **The Orangery** (Kensington Palace, W8; ⓒ **44/20/7376-0239**), where you can sip a cream tea amid mossy stone urns and rows of potted orange trees.

✈ Heathrow (24km/15 miles); Gatwick (40km/25 miles)

🛏 $$$ **Covent Garden Hotel,** 10 Monmouth St., Covent Garden (ⓒ **800/553-6674** in the U.S., or 44/20/7806-1000; www.firmdale.com). $$ **B + B Belgravia,** 64-66 Ebury St., Belgravia (ⓒ **800/682-7808** in the U.S., or 44/20/7734-2353; www.bb-belgravia.com).

436 Tea

The Tea Gardens of Shizuoka
The Way of Tea
Shizuoka, Japan

China and India may have been the only places where tea grew naturally, but the Chinese and Indians regarded the plant (*Camellia sinensis*) as mere medicine. It took the Japanese to raise tea drinking to an art form.

Japan's traditional brew is green tea, a slightly different tea variety processed differently from black tea—oxidized less, so that more of the delicate juices remain in the leaf. The first green tea seeds arrived in Shizuoka province way back in 1241, when a monk named Shoichi Kokushi brought them home from his travels to Sung China. With good pure water and a cool, moist climate ideal for tea-growing, this prefecture southwest of Tokyo produces almost half of all Japan's tea today. As the breadbasket, so to speak, of Japanese tea, Shizuoka specializes in *sencha* tea, which comes from earlier harvests and is exposed to more sunlight while growing.

In Shimada, on the Makinohara tea estate—Japan's first large commercial tea plantation—the **World Tea Museum** (Ocha-no-Gou, 3053-2 Kanaya; © **81/47/ 46-5588**) is a good place to start any tea tour of Japan. It has detailed exhibits on tea, tasting rooms, tea ceremony rooms, and a restored 16th-century Japanese teahouse once used by Enshu Kobori, a great master of the tea ceremony. The tea used in classic tea ceremonies is powdered green tea, or *matcha,* brewed following a prescribed ritual and served with precisely prepared foods; tea ceremonies can last up to 4 hours and follow an intricate protocol (don't worry, in these educational sessions your hosts will lead you through each step). Even in abbreviated form, this elaborate ritual becomes an exercise in tranquillity, respect, and harmony—an essential Japanese experience.

Visitors can try picking tea in the fields before experiencing a traditional Japanese tea ceremony at the **Kaori-no-Oka Chapia** ("Fragrant Hill" Teahouse) in Fukuroi (7157-1 Okazaki; © **81/538/44-1900;** www.chiapia.net). (Picking is harder than it seems—workers are supposed to pluck only two leaves and a bud at a time.) The tea factory here demonstrates an old-fashioned manual tea process, which best preserves the delicate flavor of quality sencha.

Also nearby in the Suruga area, **Fore Nakakawane Chameikan Hall** (71-1 Mizukawa, Kawanehon-cho, Haibara-gun) is a theme park focusing on Kawane tea. While many of the attractions are more entertaining than informative (kids seem to love the *suikinkutsu,* a type of Japanese garden ornament that echoes gentle sounds), there is an exhibit that teaches classic tea-brewing technique.

Wind up your tour of Shizuoka in the town of Kakegawa, at the historic Kakegawa Castle. The castle is surrounded by beautiful gardens, where the traditional-style **Ninomaru Tearoom** is set like a jewel—a great place to sample the local tea.

🚆 Atami railway station (107km/ 66 miles SW of Tokyo).

🛏 $$$ **Taikanso,** 7-1 Hayashigaoka-cho, Atami City (© **0557/81-8137;** www.heartonhotel.com/taikanso). $$$ **Hotel Century Shizuoka,** 18-1 Minami-Cho, Suruga-Ku, Shizuoka (© **81/54/2840111;** www.centuryshizuoka.co.jp).

7 Places to Eat in . . . Tokyo, Japan

For sheer urban energy, you can't beat Tokyo—densely populated, affluent, juiced up with a thirst for whatever's new. Even if the cultural demand for corporate entertaining hadn't boosted the city's restaurant stock, one suspects that Tokyoers would find other reasons to dine out constantly. When everyone lives in such tiny apartments, what else can you do but live life intensely in public places?

In the West, we have one catch-all category for "Japanese food," but in Japan, there's a full gamut of cuisines, each satisfying a different hunger. Sushi, of course, is Japan's signature food, and Tokyo's high-end sushi bars serve sushi that's a quantum leap finer than what you'll get in other countries. One of the most esteemed is 437 **Fukuzushi** (5-7-8 Roppongi; *81/3/3402-4116;* www.roppongifukuzushi.com), in bustling Roppongi, which was founded in Hokkaido in 1917 and moved here in 1968. Past its serene traditional courtyard, you'll enter a slick black-and-red interior that makes you feel like you're inside a bento box. Set menus change seasonally to make use of the freshest ingredients—highlights include sea urchin in spring, abalone in summer, delicate *hirame* (brill) in autumn, and meltingly tender tuna belly (*otoro*) in winter.

438 **Hayashi** (2-22-5 Kabuki-cho; *81/3/3209-5672;* also 2-14-1 Akasaka; *81/3/ 3582-4078*) strikes a more rustic mood, with an interior imported intact from the

Tokyo-style sushi.

mountain region of Takayama. An oasis amid the skyscrapers of Shinjuku, this small, intimate restaurant provides a Zen-like version of the Benihana experience, as you cook your own set menu on your table's *sumiyaki* charcoal grill (kimono-clad women servers are there to help out). The cook-your-own technique is also part of the fun at cheery, efficient **Shabusen** (Core Bldg. 2F, 5-8-20 Ginza; **81/3/3571-1717**), in the heart of the Ginza shopping buzz, where diners sizzle their own paper-thin slices of meat and vegetables in a bubbling pot of seaweed-flavored broth; here you can sit either at a table or at a round counter.

A longtime favorite for *tonkatsu* (deep-fried breaded pork cutlet) is **Maisen**; while there are a couple of branches around town, the one in trendy Harajuku (4-8-5 Jingumae; **81/3/3470-0071**) is the most interesting, occupying a converted pre–World War II public bathhouse, with high ceilings and original architectural details. Maisen is especially known for its black pork, originally from China and prized for its sweet, intense flavor. For soba noodles—the ultimate Japanese comfort food—try **Matsugen** (Hagiwara Bldg., 1-3-1 Hiroo; **81/3/3444-8666**), a serenely spare restaurant amid a cluster of noodle shops in the Ebisu nightlife district. Sit at communal tables and watch the chefs roll out the buckwheat noodles by hand; eaten cold, either dipped in seasoned soy sauce or plain, the noodles' earthy, subtle flavors are a revelation.

The ultimate Japanese dining experience is a full *kaiseki* meal, a ritualized series of tiny, elaborately prepared dishes served with great ceremony as you sit on the floor in a tatami room. The intricate progression of flavors, textures, aromas, colors (even the serving vessels are prescribed by custom) raises dining to the level of art. Don't skimp on kaiseki; go to a classic place like expensive **Takamura** (3-4-27 Roppongi; **81/3/3585-6600**), in a gracious 60-year-old house secluded by gardens on a hillside at the edge of Roppongi. Similar to *kaiseki* but a little less formal (and less expensive), *kappo* meals allow an individual chef to get more creative with his precisely choreographed dishes; one of the city's most respected kappo chefs is Hiromitsu Nozaki at **Waketokuyama** (5-1-5 Minami-Azbu; **81/3/5789-3838**), near the Hiroo station in the Minato district. Try to nab one of the seats at the chef's counter for a close-up view of the intricate preparations—it's some of the best theater in town.

Narita International (66km/40 miles).

$$$ **Capitol Tokyu Hotel,** 2-10-3 Nagata-cho, Chiyoda-ku (**800/888-4747** in the U.S. and Canada, or 03/3581-4511; www.capitoltokyu.com). $$ **Park Hotel Tokyo,** 1-7-1 Higashi Shimbashi, Minato-ku, Ginza (**03/6252-1111;** www.parkhoteltokyo.com).

The Tea Heartland
Tea Capital of the World
Assam, India

India can't claim to be the birthplace of tea, but thanks to an aggressive crew of 19th-century British planters, India eventually became the world's greatest tea-growing nation, supplying a seemingly endless stream of fragrant brew to teapots all over the globe. India's tea industry faltered in the 1990s—when the Soviet Union (their biggest export market) collapsed and both Sri Lanka and Kenya stepped up tea production. But as India's tea-growers work to reclaim lost ground, they're focusing on marketing top-of-the-line teas and opening their historic estates to tourists—all of which is good news for tea connoisseurs.

Assam is where it all started, in the 1820s, when British military officers noticed local Singhos drinking restorative beverages brewed from the local *Camellia sinensis* shrub; Assam is still India's most productive tea region today. At its golden-tipped best, Assam tea is favored for its full-bodied flavor and rich brown color, which makes for a bracing breakfast tea. Much Assam tea is processed for the domestic market, using the CTC—meaning "crush, tear, and curl"—process, which produces a redder brew.

Most plantations are around Jorhat, which markets itself as Tea Capital of the World. There's a tea festival here every November, and even a special tea research institute, the Teklai Experimental Centre (in Chinnamara, 5km/3 miles from Jorhat). Driving around Jorhat, you'll notice densely planted emerald-green tea bushes on either side of the road, interspersed with shade trees (tea is a shade-loving evergreen). Workers continually harvest leaves, plucking bushes every 7 days during harvest season, late June through early October (which also happens to be monsoon season). Both the **Gatoonga** and **Sangsua** tea estates outside Jorhat have sprawling vintage "bungalows" where you can stay overnight. Teak-framed, with high ceilings, wood floors, whirring ceiling fans, and wide verandas, these bungalows seem lifted right out of a Somerset Maugham story.

About halfway between Jorhat and Guwahati, on the north bank of the Brahmaputra River near Tezpur, the Adabari Tea Estate's Victorian-era white bungalow, where the estate's manager once lived, is now open to visitors as the upscale **Wild Mahseer Lodge.** Farther up the river, the **Mancotta Chang Bungalow** near Dibrugarh is over 140 years old. A traditional "chang," or platform bungalow, it was originally built by Scottish planters but is now owned by the Jalans, one of the pioneer tea families of Assam. Raised on stilts for protection from jungle predators, including tigers and one-horned rhinos, Mancotta almost seems to float above the scrubby bright green tea bushes of the surrounding plantations.

✈ Jorhat/Dibrugarh.

🛏 $$$ **Mancotta Chang Bungalow,** 12km (7½ miles) from Dibrugarh (✆ 91/373/2301120; www.purviweb.com). $$$ **Wild Mahseer Lodge,** Balipura (✆ 91/3714/234354). $$ **Mistry Sahbi's Bungalow,** Gatoonga Tea Estate, Jorhat (✆ 91/11/46035500 for reservations; www.welcomheritagehotels.com). $$ **Burra Sahib's Bungalow,** Sangsua Tea Estate, (✆ 91/11/46035500 for reservations; www.welcomheritagehotels.com).

Tour Operator: Travel Plus, New Delhi (✆ 91/011/43436666; www.plustours.com). **NamasteTours** (✆ 91/124/4040636; www.namastetoursindia.com). **Flamingo Travels** (✆ 91/361/2454669; www.flamingotravels.com).

Darjeeling's Tea Estates
The Champagne of Teas
Darjeeling, India

Though it only accounts for 3% of India's total tea output, Darjeeling gets all the glory—and rightly so. It's a romantically remote area, for one thing, surrounding a picturesque hill station where British officers once fled to escape India's brutal summers. You can traverse its vertiginous slopes on a bright-blue steam-powered railway so cunningly tiny, it's nicknamed the Toy Train. But that evocative setting is one thing; the delicately floral, aromatic flavor of Darjeeling tea is the region's real claim to fame.

Often called "gardens," 87 estates spread across these steep, misty slopes. In March, workers (mostly ethnic Nepali women) deftly pluck Darjeeling's much-touted "first flush" harvest from the bristling green bushes; teas plucked in May and June are only slightly less superb. The most prestigious estate in the area—the one whose teas routinely fetch the world's highest prices—is **Makaibari,** just south of Kurseong (25km/16 miles south of Darjeeling), which has been run by the Banerjee family since the 1840s. Under its enterprising fourth-generation owner, Rajah Banerjee, the plantation's slope-hugging fields are now completely organic and biodynamic; he has even added bungalows and bedrooms in the vintage Stone House for tourists staying overnight. After walking the fields, you can explore the Victorian-era factory, where tea leaves are processed by the so-called "orthodox" method: withered in large troughs, rolled under steel rollers to release natural juices, left in a cool room to ferment, then baked, sorted, graded, and packed for shipping. Naturally, a tea tasting follows.

Just 6km (3½ miles) below Kurseong, you can tour another renowned organic/biodynamic/fair trade estate, **Ambootia.**

Founded in 1861, it's an inspiring example of how an old plantation, virtually farmed out by the 1990s, restored the soil with new agricultural techniques and developed a boutique brand of organic tea. To see a similar Cinderella story in progress, visit the **Happy Valley Tea Estate** just 3km (2 miles) north of Darjeeling. Established in 1854, it's now being revived by Ambootia's organic wizards.

Also in Kurseong (the name means "land of the white orchid"), the **Goomtee Tea Estate** offers accommodations in a tastefully spare planter's house, with big windows overlooking magnificent surrounding gardens. Planted in 1899, the fields at Goomtee are organically farmed, the processing factory is orthodox, and meals are totally vegetarian, which seems in keeping with the Zen-like peacefulness of the place. The uphill hike to the outlying tea fields is strenuous, but the views at the top are worth it (if necessary, they can drive you).

The **Glenburn Tea Estate** affords the region's most luxurious accommodations, an hour and a half from Darjeeling. Visitors stay in a smartly restored, century-old planter's house on the edge of a plateau, with a Shangri-La-like view across the Rangeet River Valley. This 648-hectare (1,600-acre) plantation was founded in 1860 as the Scottish Tea Company; nowadays it's run by the Prakash family and produces its own upscale brand of tea. Guests can view the fields, observe the on-site factory, enjoy a tasting session, or visit the tea-plant nursery with its own orange grove—source of the marmalade served during afternoon tea on the verandah.

Glenburn may be getting some competition with the new **Tumsong Retreat,** an upscale four-bedroom hideaway in a white verandaed planter's bungalow on the Tumsong estate near Ghoom, just south of Darjeeling (it's the highest stop on the Toy Train route). Tumsong is owned by the Chamong Tea Company, which has 13 estates in the Darjeeling district; similar lodgings are planned for four others. All stays, of course, will include a tea estate/factory tour.

In Darjeeling town, jostle your way through the thronged lower section of Darjeeling's bazaar, lined with small shops and tented stalls, where the aroma of tea hangs tantalizing in the air. Don't miss the stunning sunrise view from Tiger Hill, 13km (8 miles) from town. Watching the sun burst over the peaks of the Himalayas is the sort of transcendent experience you get very few times in life.

ⓘ ⓒ **91/34/54050**; www.wbtourism.com/darjeeling.

✈ Bagdogra Airport, Siliguri (90km/56 miles).

🛏 $ **Makaibari,** Kurseong (ⓒ **91/354/233-0181** or 91/33/2287-8560; www.makaibari.org). $$$ **Glenburn** (ⓒ **91/33/2288-5630;** www.glenburnteaestate.com). $$ **Goomtee,** Hill Cart Rd., Kurseong (ⓒ **91/354/233-5066** for reservations; www.darjeelingteas.com). $$$ **Tumsong Retreat** (ⓒ **91/33/3093 6400;** www.chiabari.com).

Tour Operator: Fair Trade Teas (ⓒ **615-335-4063;** www.fairtradeteas.com). **Help Tourism Heritage Tours** (ⓒ **91/353/2535893** or 91/33/24550917; www.helptourism.com).

Tea 446

The Plantations of Old Ceylon

A Peek at Pekoe

Nuwara Elia, Sri Lanka

Maybe the mention of Sri Lankan tea doesn't ring a bell—but call it by its colonial name, Ceylon tea, and tea drinkers around the world perk up. Check inside a Lipton teabag and what will you find? Ceylon orange pekoe.

Fifteenth-century Portuguese and Dutch traders were the first Europeans to exploit this tropical island off India's south coast. It became a British colony in 1796, but at first it was coffee the British planted on its cool, moist hills. Then came the coffee fungus of the 1840s, and Ceylon's planters desperately switched to tea, knowing that the East India Tea Company had just been shut out of China and needed new sources. Luckily, the crop thrived, and Sri Lanka—a sovereign state since 1972—is now one of the world's prime tea producers.

Just outside the atmospheric hill city of Kandy, known for its Buddhist shrines and botanical gardens, the Sri Lanka Tea Board has opened a **Tea Museum** in Hantana.

(Look for the tea board's lion logo stamped on certified Ceylon tea.) Small but comprehensive, the museum features restored tea-processing machines, and the restaurant serves several local tea varieties, also for sale in the museum shop.

Nuwara Eliya is the heart of Sri Lanka's premier tea-producing region. The sensational train ride there from Colombo climbs through jungle-clad slopes with cascading waterfalls. Soon you'll notice acres and acres of vibrantly green tea fields alongside the tracks and tea workers bending diligently over the low bushes. The steep final segment of the journey, from Nanu Oya, is accessible only by bus. Once you finally reach Nuwara Eliya, it may take you by surprise, it looks so bizarrely British. Expatriate tea-planters created a nostalgic mini-England for themselves here, with tidy hedges and lawns and Georgian-style villas, along with the requisite cricket pitch, polo field, and manicured golf course.

Just outside N'Eliya in Kandapola, the **Tea Factory** hotel is, as the name suggests, cleverly converted from an old British-era tea factory. Guests can pick their own leaves from the bushes of the Hethersett Estate and process them at the hotel's miniature tea factory. Also outside N'Eliya, follow the Ramboda road to visit the **Oliphant Tea Estate,** the region's first, where Sir Anthony Oliphant planted thirty Chinese tea plants in the 1830s. Today owned by Mabroc Teas, it's known for a particularly fine delicate green tea, rare for Ceylon. You can also visit the **Pedro Tea Estate** at Boralanda, 3km (2 miles) from town, which still uses some old-style machinery in its processing plant, or the **Labookele Tea Estate** (Kandy Rd.), which gives free factory tours and has a cafe.

Driving back to Colombo via the Hatton road, an essential rest stop is the **St. Clair's Tea Centre** in Talawakalee (150km mile marker), a century-old planter's cottage that has been refurbished as a tea room by the estate's current owners, Maskeliya Plantations. Here visitors can sample a wide range of Ceylon teas—traditional orange pekoes as well as silver tips, golden tips, and herbal teas. Besides the tea, the great attraction here is scenic views of two of Sri Lanka's most dramatic waterfalls, St. Clair's Falls and Devon Falls, named after two of the area's big tea planters.

ⓘ **Nuwara Eliya Tourism** (www.nuwaraeliya.org).

✈ Colombo (180km/111 miles).

🛏 $$$ **Grand Hotel,** Grand Hotel Rd, (✆ **94/52/2288105;** www.tangerinehotels.com/thegrandhotel/index.htm). $$$ **The Tea Factory,** Kandapola (✆ **94/52/2229600;** www.aitkenspencehotels.net).

Tour Operator: The Tea House (✆ **630/961-0877;** www.theteahouse.com).

447 Tea

Luk Yu Tea House

Dim Sum & Bo Lai

Hong Kong, China

Whether you were sealing a business deal or arbitrating a dispute, in old China you didn't go to a lawyer's office or a courthouse. All interested parties would meet together at a teahouse, where affairs could be amicably settled over a pot of tea and some dim sum. Unlike the Japanese, whose tea ceremony is elaborately formal, the Chinese respected tea-drinking as a rite of companionship. And in mercantile Hong Kong, teahouse camaraderie was treasured for the way it greased the wheels of commerce.

The classic Hong Kong teahouse is a dying breed, but you'll still see businessmen negotiating over their teapots at the Luk Yu Tea House in the bustling Central District. First opened in 1933, it's a treasured survivor, a vestige of old Hong Kong named in honor of the Tang Dynasty tea master who wrote *Cha Ching*, China's 8th-century treatise on the rituals of tea. Despite the streamlined elegance of its Art Deco decor, the restaurant is full of old-fashioned details—black ceiling fans, spittoons, individual wooden booths, marble tabletops, wood paneling, and stained-glass murals. Regulars gravitate to the upper floor dining room, where they can wheel and deal in relative calm.

The house specialty is classic Cantonese dim sum, served 7am to 5:30pm; from midmorning on, customers order not from carts but from picture menus (a recent concession to customer service—the famously rude waiters have also toned down their grumpy shtick). It's one of the best places to try a few Chinese teas, including *bo lai* (a fermented black tea, which is the most common tea in Hong Kong; also spelled bo lay), jasmine, *lung ching* (a green tea), and *sui sin* (narcissus or daffodil).

After you've sampled the classic ambiance of Luk Yu, scout out its low-rent equivalent in the more traditional Western District, the **Lin Heung Lau Tea House** (160–164 Wellington St., Sheung Wan; ✆ **2544-4556**). The dining rooms look decidedly worn, and the clientele is mostly old-timers, but the dim sum is delicious. Note that here the tea is brewed in old-style lidded cups, rather than in pots—another dying tradition in the scrum of modern Hong Kong.

ⓘ 24–26 Stanley St. (✆ **852/2523 5464**).

✈ Hong Kong International (26km/16 miles).

🛏 $$$ **Conrad International Hong Kong,** 88 Queensway, Pacific Place, Central District (✆ **800/CONRADS** [800/266-7237] in the U.S. and Canada, or 852/2521 3838; www.conradhotels.com). $$ **Stanford Hillview Hotel,** 13–17 Observatory Rd., Tsim Sha Tsui, Kowloon (✆ **852/2722 7822;** www.stanfordhillview.com).

Tea **448**

Drinking Mint Tea
Moroccan Whiskey
Marrakech, Morocco

Moroccans laughingly describe mint tea to Westerners as "Moroccan whiskey." In this predominantly Islamic country, where alcohol is officially proscribed, mint tea—*atei benna'na'*—is Morocco's national drink, and it's available anywhere, anytime.

English soldiers first introduced tea in Tangiers during the Crimean War in the mid–19th century, but Moroccans put their own spin on it almost from the start. They mixed the tea leaves with fresh mint, skipped the milk the English usually added, and went straight for the sugar—lots of sugar, ladled in large chunks. Mint tea can be found in cafes and *snak* restaurants countrywide; despite the desert heat, locals generally drink it piping hot, often accompanied by sweet Moroccan pastries dripping in sweet honey or dusted in cinnamon and sugar icing.

Mint tea makes a particularly welcome break in Marrakech, where travelers often succumb to the temptation to exhaust themselves dashing around the *medina*, ticking off the sights, bartering for souvenirs, and clicking away on their camera. It's available almost everywhere, but some of the best spots for it are the rooftop terrace of arty **Café des Épices** (place Rahba Qedima; ✆ 212/24/391770), the terrace of **Café-Restaurant Argana** on the medina's lively main square (place Jemaa el Fna; ✆ **212/24/445350**), the literary cafe-cum-art gallery **Dar Cherifa** (Derb Cherifa Lakbir, off rue Mouassine; ✆ 212/24/426463), or the air-conditioned *salon de thé* at the back of **Patisserie des Princes** (32 rue Bab Agnaou; ✆ 212/24/443033).

Locals drink the tea from glasses—never from a china cup—and brew it according to long-established ritual: They heat it slowly in a small pot, preferably over an open charcoal fire, then pour it from an arm's length height into the glass to aerate the brew. They perform this step two to three times, tasting after each pour, until the tea is considered ready to drink. The length of time and height of pour can vary, depending on your location and the inclination of your waiter or host. Expect the tea to come presweetened unless you order it *la sukka* (pronounced la *soo*-ka).

✈ Marrakech International.

🛏 $$$ **La Sultana,** 403 rue de la Kasbah (☎ **212/24/388008;** www.lasultana marrakech.com). $$ **Dar Vedra,** 3 Derb Sidi Ahmed ou Moussa (☎ **212/24/389370;** www.darvedra.com).

449 Tea

Mariage Frères
Les Gentilhommes des Thé
Paris, France

For generations, the Mariage brothers were always the go-to guys when it came to tea. Though Henri and Edouard didn't officially found their tea importing company on the rue de Bourg-Tibourg until 1854, their forbears had been trading tea and spices to the Orient since 1660, when Nicolas and Pierre Mariage worked for Louis XIV to open trading routes on behalf of the French East India Company. Now *that's* a family business.

When granddaughter Marthe finally started selling directly to the public in the 1980s, the firm catered strictly to the upscale end of the market. Though they've got a dizzying selection of some 500 teas, sourced from 35 different countries, each one is top-class. The place is fitted out like an old-fashioned apothecary. Standing in the shop, gazing along the long wall where each tea is stored in its own wooden cubbyhole can be overwhelming. Mariage Frères's buyers obsessively taste every year's crop and announce the year's new Darjeelings with all the same fanfare with which wine merchants offer up a season's nouveaux Beaujolais. They create expressive blends you'll find nowhere else, giving them evocative names like Marco Polo, Genghis Khan, Elixir of Love, or the Solitary Poet's Tea. White tea, green tea, black tea; flavored with flowers, with spices, with fruits—you never knew there could be so many variations. It's not just leaf-tea, either—they sell tea in compressed bricks, in powders, and even in tea bags made only from the finest muslin.

Tea sets and teapots sold in this shop were designed exclusively for Mariage

The tea room at Mariage Frères.

Mariage Frères has been trading tea and spices on the rue de Bourg-Tibourg since 1854.

Frères, from eggshell-thin ceramics and delicate hand-blown glass to robust Japanese cast-iron. They sell tea-flavored pastries, tea-scented candles, even a tea-flavored chocolate from a recipe developed back in 1860. The shop leads naturally into a serene tearoom, decked out in colonial rattan and potted palms, quietly animated by a murmur of conversation and the clack of white china cups. A general luncheon menu is served from noon to 3pm; afternoon tea is from 3pm to 7pm.

Now that it's on an entrepreneurial roll, Mariage Frères has expanded beyond its historic location in the Marais, launching two other shops/salons in Paris (13 rue des Grands-Augustins in the 6th arrondissement and 260 Faubourg Saint-Honoré in the posh shopping district of the 8th), as well as one in Berlin (Franzôsiche Strasse 23) and another in Tokyo (Suzuran-Dori, 5-6-7 Ginza). You can even order Mariage Frères tea on the Internet these days—but what a pale experience, compared to browsing along that Wall of Tea in Paris.

ⓘ 30 rue du Bourg-Tibourg, 4e (✆ **33/1/42 72 28 11;** www.mariagefreres.com).

✈ De Gaulle (23km/14 miles); Orly (14km/8⅔miles).

🛏 $$ **La Tour Notre Dame,** 20 rue du Sommerard, 5e (✆ **33/1/43-54-47-60;** www.la-tour-notre-dame.com). $ **Hotel de la Place des Vosges,** 12 rue de Birague, 4e (✆ **33/1/42-72-60-46;** www.hotelplacedesvosges.com).

Fortnum & Mason

Grocers to the Crown

London, England

Fortnum & Mason has been importing tea for nearly as long as the English have been drinking it. Granted, its elegant Piccadilly store has lost a good deal of its snob appeal lately—these days it's generally inundated with American and Japanese tourists. But Londoners still secretly pop in from time to time to buy three luxuries: champagne, caviar, and one-of-a-kind teas.

Setting up shop in 1707, grocers Fortnum and Mason made the most of their connections with the palace. Fortnum was a footman to Queen Anne and got in on the ground floor when the East India Tea Company was founded in the 1740s. They were never just tea merchants; the store also dealt snuff to Regency dandies, exquisitely provisioned picnic hampers to Victorian aristocrats, and exotic tinned goods to the Edwardian smart set. But tea was their first imported specialty, and quality teas have always been a backbone of their business.

There's still a certain noblesse oblige about Fortnum's seven-story red-brick building. The name is discreetly spelled out on a refined pale-green *porte cochere* and food is sumptuously displayed in a series of arched windows. The ornate mechanical clock above the door features painted figures of Mr. Fortnum and Mr. Mason popping out every hour on the hour. The ground floor is fitted out beautifully, with stately columns, chandeliers, and a sweeping marble staircase; shop attendants wear morning coats, and the house brand comestibles—chocolates, toffees, biscuits, caviar, jam, teas, coffee—are beautifully packaged, with the crest of the store's royal warrant discreetly displayed.

A good rule of thumb: If it has the Fortnum & Mason store label on it, buy it. Skip the upper floors, which are just another department store; even the fresh food selection on the upper level of the food halls can't quite match Harrods (19). But the ground floor is full of luxury comestibles you can't buy anywhere else, not even through F&M's website. With long-established connections to tea estates around the world, Fortnum's sells an impressive number of single-estate teas and exclusive blends (several named after the former monarchs who inspired them), all in beautiful embossed tins. Alongside the teas are a host of exotic

Fortnum & Mason has been supplying the queen's teas since the East India Tea Company formed in the 1740s.

399

Fortnum & Mason specializes in champagne and caviar, as well as unique teas.

preserves to grace the tea table—rose petal jam, gooseberry and elderflower preserve, lime curd, and pink grapefruit marmalade.

For years, Fortnum's Fountain restaurant was an iconic spot for afternoon tea—a charming gilded salon, tucked behind the ground floor food hall. Sadly, the tea service has moved to the fourth floor, where it merely coasts on its reputation, while Fortnum's promotes its five other full-menu restaurants stashed around the store. You have to applaud Fortnum & Mason for not cloning itself in branches all over the world. Now if they could just keep their focus on tea . . .

ⓘ 181 Piccadilly (✆ **44/20/7734-8040;** www.fortnumandmason.com).

✈ Heathrow (24km/15 miles); Gatwick (40km/25 miles).

🛏 $$$ 22 Jermyn St., St. James (✆ **800/ 682-7808** in the U.S., or 44/20/7734-2353; www.22jermyn.com). $$ **Vicarage Private Hotel,** 10 Vicarage Gate, South Kensington (✆ **44/20/7229-4030;** www.londonvicarage hotel.com).

Tea   451

Cotswolds Tearooms
Tea Cakes in the Countryside
Around Broadway, England

No part of England is more postcard picturesque than the Cotswolds, with its low rounded hills, winding leafy lanes, and tidy villages built of warm golden Cotswold stone. Because it's only a 2-hour drive from London, the Cotswolds' bucolic charm is hardly undiscovered by tourists. Come on a weekday when it's not high summer, however, and you can easily imagine life here in the 16th century, when the wool from Cotswold sheep made these villages prosperous.

It seems that every Cotswold town has its own nostalgic tea room, where those

hordes of visitors can find refreshment. Right on High Street in the market town of Broadway—the most popular base for touring this area—**Tisane's Tea Rooms** (21 The Green; ✆ **44/1386/853296;** www. tisanes-tearooms.co.uk) is set in a lovely 17th-century stone building with a bow-fronted window. (The old-fashioned delivery bicycle parked on the pavement outside is a quaint touch.) Besides serving morning coffee, light lunches, and afternoon tea, the shop sells teapots, coffee jugs, and, instead of tacky Cotswold souvenirs, a line of preserves, mustards, and spices from a specialty firm called Elizabethan England. Their wide-ranging tea list includes some 30 teas from around the globe, including a mellow blend named Cotswold Afternoon. As suggested by the shop's name—*tisanes* is French for infusions—they also ply several herbal and fruit-steeped drinks (not to be confused with herbal tea, which technically must contain tea). Solid menu items include fresh-baked pastries and granary-bread sandwiches.

Southeast of Broadway on the A44, in the smaller town of Moreton-On-Marsh you can also stop in at **Marshmallow Tearooms** (High St.; 44/1608/651536), with more of a farmhouse-cozy look. Its afternoon tea menu focuses on traditional English teatime classics such as toasted tea cakes, crumpets, scones, carrot cake, and Bakewell tart, all baked on premises. Southwest of Broadway, in the village of

Winchcombe, you'll have to book ahead for afternoon tea at **Juri's—The Old Bakery Tea Shoppe** (High St.; 44/1242/602-469; www.juris-tearoom.co.uk), open only Thursday through Sunday. The baked goods at this charming stone-walled tearoom are outstanding, and the tea list is carefully selected. Juri herself is of Japanese heritage, which accounts for the number of green teas on the menu, including tea-ceremony *matcha*.

✈ London Heathrow (136km/84 miles).

🛏 $$$ **The Lygon Arms,** High St., Broadway (44/1386/852255; www.the lygonarms.co.uk). $$ **The Falkland Arms,** Great Tew (on the B4022), near Chipping Norton (44/1608/683653; www.falkland arms.org.uk).

452 Tea

Taking Tea in Bath
Cream Tea in a Spa Town
Bath, England

Americans have a tough time pronouncing its name (it should be a broad-A "Bawth," not "bahht" like a bathtub), but the 18th-century spa town of Bath remains a perennial tourist favorite in the heart of England, with ancient Roman baths and stunning Georgian architecture. And when the bus tours begin to clear out in the midafternoon (got to check off Salisbury before dark!), Bath's elegant ambience will come to light as you dawdle over a spot of tea.

The place to see and be seen in Bath has always been the Pump Room, an exquisite neoclassical salon built in 1795 overlooking the bubbling natural hot spring. (You can still buy a glass of hot spa water from the fountain here—there are those who swear by its medical efficacy, though, frankly, it tastes pretty nasty.) The on-site tea room, **Searcy's** (Stall St.; 44/1225/444477; www.searcys.co.uk), could no

doubt coast on the fact that tourists will stream through here anyway, but instead its management strives to deliver a first-class afternoon tea—cakes, pastries, smoked salmon sandwiches, and that famous trio of scones, strawberry preserve, and clotted cream known as a cream tea. The creamy wood-paneled setting is formal, with linen tablecloths, heavy silverware, and fine china. It's a pricey experience, but isn't spending lavishly on carnal pleasures the very essence of Bath?

Around the corner, the tea experience is a little less aristocratic at **Sally Lunn's** (4 N. Parade Passage; 44/1225/461634; www.sallylunns.co.uk), which is very much on the package-tour route. Set in a narrow timber-framed building that's purportedly the oldest house in Bath (built in 1482), this business has been running since the late 17th century, when a Huguenot refugee named Sally Lunn began selling her famous briochelike buns to aristocratic households. Yeastier and sweeter than scones, Sally Lunn buns make an interesting variation on the cream tea; they're also good toasted and served with lemon curd. Even if you don't choose to cram into the tearoom, you can buy specially blended teas in the shop in the cellar.

Jane Austen enthusiasts know that the novelist lived in Bath from 1800 to 1806, and used it as a setting for her novels *Persuasion* and *Northanger Abbey*; the handsome Georgian townhouse that contains the Jane Austen Centre on its ground floor now has a teashop upstairs, the **Regency Tea Rooms** (40 Gay St.; *44/1225/442187*). Primly decorated with Wedgewood-blue walls and tiny cloth-draped tables, it offers a good range of teas, including a special Jane Austen blend. Though the menu indulges in cutesy names referring to characters in Austen novels, the food is quite good traditional teatime fare. (Where else can you order an old-fashioned *salma-gundi* salad?) One fancies Jane would approve.

🚆 Bath (.3km/¼ mile).

🛏 $$$ **The Royal Crescent Hotel,** 15–16 Royal Crescent (*888/295-4710* in the U.S., or 44/1225/823333; www.royal crescent.co.uk). $$ **Badminton Villa,** 10 Upper Oldfield Park (*44/1225/426347;* www.smoothhound.co.uk/hotels/badmin ton.html).

Tea **453**

Betty's Café

High Tea in the Yorkshire Moorland

Harrogate, England

As the story goes, a young Swiss confectioner named Frederick Belmont arrived in the lovely Georgian-era spa town of Harrogate by accident in 1918 (something about catching the wrong train in London). It turned out to be a happy accident, though; he promptly fell in love with the Alpine-like rolling landscape of the Yorkshire Dales and opened Betty's Café the next year. Though no one is really sure who Betty was, or how she fit into the picture, her namesake cafe has been in business ever since.

The selection here is a bit overwhelming—the menu lists more than 300 breads, cakes, and chocolates, as well as 50 different teas and coffees. But all the baked goods are locally made, at Betty's own Craft Bakery, which the enterprising Belmont founded in 1920. (Betty's has since opened five branches around Yorkshire, but the company is committed not to expand beyond easy delivery distance of the bakery.) The teas are all supplied by the top-drawer specialty tea company Taylor's of Harrogate, which was founded in 1886 but merged with Betty's in the 1960s. Their premium blend is Yorkshire Gold tea, a hearty blend of some 20 different tea leaves which was especially formulated to brew up well in the water of the Dales. Their broad catalogue of teas is sourced worldwide, much of it fair trade.

The Art Nouveau decor of the original Harrogate location features lots of curlicued wrought iron and an airy conservatory-like interior. Servers continuously wheel cakes and pastries past your table on trolleys, making them hard to resist. Betty's iconic pastry is the Fat Rascal—an oversized flaky scone plumped up with citrus peel, almonds, and cherries. The Yorkshire curd tart and Swiss chocolate torte are also long-standing favorites. If you order the full afternoon tea, your table will be loaded with finger sandwiches, tiny cakes, a sultana scone with all the fixings, and a pot of tea. That should hold you until dinner.

ⓘ 1 Parliament St. (ⓒ **44/1423/502746**; www.bettys.co.uk).

✈ Leeds-Bradford International (19km/12 miles)

🚆 Harrogate (15km/9⅔ miles).

🛏 $$ **Arden House Hotel,** 69–71 Franklin Rd. (ⓒ **44/1423/509224**; www.arden househotel.co.uk). $$ **Applewood House,** 55 St Georges Rd. (ⓒ **44/1423/544549**; www.applewoodhouse.co.uk).

San Francisco's World of Tearooms

Golden Gate Tea Fest

San Francisco, California

San Francisco has always been such a cultural melting pot, it's only natural it should be all over the globe when it comes to tea.

A natural place to start is in Chinatown, at the **Imperial Tea Court** (1411 Powell St.; ⓒ **800/567-5898** or 415/ 788-6080). Book ahead for a tea tasting in this wood-paneled salon, which is like taking a seminar. They may offer a few light foods, but the focus is undisputedly on what's in your cup. Their extensive tea list includes greens, oolongs, blacks, and a few whites and herbals. (The owners, Roy and Grace Fong, also have an Internet tea business, at www. imperialtea.com.) Each tea you taste will be precisely brewed at the table, either in a lidded cup (or *gaiwan*) or in a small pot (or *gongfu*), according to the method that best suits the particular tea. You may learn the difference between a floral Keemun Mao Feng and a smoky Lapsang Soulong, but more than that, you'll realize how vast the realm of tea lore can be.

In the South of Market neighborhood, the **Samovar Tea Lounge** (730 Howard St.; ⓒ **415/626-4700**; www.samovartea. com) is the sort of tea-fetishist joint that could only exist in food-centric San Francisco. On the upper terrace of Yerba Buena Gardens, the bazaarlike decor is a cozy mélange of colorful cushions and rattan chairs. (A second branch is in the Castro, at 498 Sanchez St.) The tea list is stupendously huge and exotic, including several exclusive blends and single-estate teas, with an emphasis on artisanal organic and fair-trade varieties. But the coolest thing about the Samovar is the global variety of high tea menus they've assembled: stir-fry and dumplings for China (paired with a nice oolong); a curry-and-chai pairing representing India; beets, whitefish, and rye bread to go with a Russian samovar of black tea; and so on. (Poor America, represented by a paltry egg-salad sandwich and potato chips with iced tea.)

If you're jonesing for a traditional English high tea, you can get that too, at **Lovejoy's** in Noe Valley (1351 Church St.; ⓒ **415/648-5895;** www.lovejoysrearoom. com), a warm little spot with mismatched antique furniture and shelves lined with vintage china teapots. Taylor's of Harrogate teas are featured on the 20-tea menu. You can also order with scones, crumpets, cucumber sandwiches, shepherd's pie, sausage rolls, pear-and-Stilton salad, or pasties with baked beans. It's an Anglophile's dream.

✈ San Francisco International (23km/14 miles)

🛏 $$$ **Hotel Adagio,** 550 Geary St. (ⓒ **800/228-8830** or 415/775-5000; www. thehoteladagion.com). $ **Hotel des Arts,** 447 Bush St. (ⓒ **800/956-4322** or 415/956-3232; www.sfhoteldesarts.com).

8 Just Desserts

A tart from the Macrina bakery in Seattle.

Cacao Country

Back to the Bean

Tabasco, Mexico

It all began in Mexico, really. Ages ago, the ancient Olmecs and Mayans drank a bitter chocolate beverage brewed from the beans of the local cacao tree. Devoted to their *xocolatl*—like hot chocolate but spicier—they cultivated cacao in the lowland tropical jungles of southern Mexico. That's where the Spanish conquistadors discovered the drink and promptly sent it back to Europe. And while chocolate is now grown in equatorial climates around the globe—from the Ivory Coast to Indonesia, from Cameroon to Costa Rica, from Panama to Papua New Guinea—Mexico is one of the few cacao-growing countries that still consumes most of its own homegrown chocolate. And they still mostly drink it hot, just as the ancient Mayans did.

Around the town of Comalcalco, in Tabasco, close to a haunting set of Mayan ruins, you'll find the descendants of those ancient Mayans working on cacao plantations. The 12-hectare (30-acre) **Finca Cholula,** just east of the ruins (Cardenas-Paraiso road; © **52/933/33-4-38-15;** www.finca cholula.com.mx), grows its beans by totally organic practices, which isn't always easy, considering the complex tropical ecosystem where cacao trees flourish. To keep this finicky rainforest native happy, these farmers allow it to be surrounded by the shade of a heavy tree canopy (unlike many plantations where the trees are grown in neat rows). The humid jungle vegetation helps attract midges that pollinate the white cacao flowers, which grow right on the stem of the trees. Cacao requires consistent year-round temperature and rainfall, because it has no seasons; it continuously produces fruit—the long, ridged yellow pods that contain cacao beans. Both flowers and fruit can be on the tree at the same time, and workers are always harvesting.

You can also visit the large estate of Cacep Chocolates, **Hacienda Cacaotera Jesus Maria** (Ranchería Sur 5th section, Tulipán Rd.; © **933/33-76176** or 933/32-53504; www.cacep.com), which offers tours of its nursery, plantations, and processing plant. After workers remove the beans from the pods, you'll see the boxes where they are fermented, the patio where they are spread out to dry, and then the ovens where they are roasted. Cacep has its own chocolate factory as well, where the beans are processed into cacao paste; in the hacienda there's a relic of an old-fashioned *chontal* plant for processing chocolate.

Another leading cacao estate that welcomes visitors, sprawling **Hacienda La Luz** (Blvd. Engineer Leandro Rovirosa Wade; © **52/933/334-1129**) is close to the center of town. Here visitors can browse through an informative Cacao and Chocolate Museum before touring the plantation, the processing areas, the handsome rustic-style ranch house, and beautiful botanical gardens.

✈ Villahermosa (78km/48 miles).

🛏 $$$ **Best Western Hotel Maya Tabasco,** Bulevar Ruiz Cortines 907, Villahermosa (© 800/528-1234 in the U.S. and Canada, or 52/993/358-1111, ext. 822; www.bestwestern.com). $$ **Hotel Plaza Independencia,** Independencia 123 (© **52/ 993/312-1299** or 993/312-7541; www. hotelesplaza.com.mx).

Tour Operator: Mayatabasco (www. mayatabasco.com).

Mina Street

Chocolate Avenue

Oaxaca, Mexico

Though most cacao beans grow in neighboring Chiapas and Tabasco, the gracious old city of Oaxaca has become the epicenter of chocolate in the nation that invented it, thanks to one shop-lined street of chocolate specialists: Mina Street.

Thread your way through Oaxaca's narrow colonial streets and shady plazas to find the 20 de Noviembre Market, just south of the town center. Mina Street runs along the south side of the market—you'll probably be able to find it by following the heady chocolaty aromas. The shops on Mina Street don't just sell chocolate, they make it on premises, grinding cacao beans with almonds and cinnamon into a fine powder or paste, then pressing it into bars or tablets that can then be dissolved in hot milk or water. (To the surprise of some visiting chocoholics, Oaxacans believe that chocolate is best enjoyed not as candy but in hot chocolate drinks or in *mole* sauce.) The three largest purveyors are **Chocolate Mayordomo** (corner of Mina and 20 Noviembre sts.; © **52/951/516-0246**), **Chocolate La Soledad** (Mina 212; © **52/951/516-5841**), and the slightly smaller, family-run **Guelaguetza Chocolate** (20 de Noviembre St. 605; © **52/951/516-3513**). Any of these stores will customize chocolate for you with whatever ingredients you want; nibble on the tablets of chocolate and you'll find they're grittier and sweeter than the chocolate you may be used to eating, but still delicious.

The chocolate stores also have "chocolate bars" on site, meaning a counter where customers are served hot chocolate. There are three kinds of hot chocolate drinks:

chocolate de agua (made with water), *chocolate de leche* (made with milk), and *champurrado,* a thicker drink that has corn mixed in with the cocoa. Then of course there's *tejate,* a Oaxacan delicacy once reserved only for the rulers of the Zapotec Indians; it's made from corn, roasted cacao beans, *mamey* seed, and *rosita* flowers, laboriously mixed by hand and served in a painted gourd bowl called a *jicara*. To sample *tejate,* you'll have to explore inside the market to find a food stall that serves it—look for stacks of the gourd bowls. Also inside the market are a few pottery stalls where you can buy traditionally shaped cups and spouted jugs for serving hot chocolate, as well as implements for making chocolate the old-fashioned way, with *metates* (a flat stone used to grind cacao beans) and *molinillos* (wooden whisks used to whip the beverage into a froth).

Oaxaca's other great use for chocolate is to make *mole* paste for cooking. Actually, of the seven *moles* used in Oaxacan cooking, only the black *(negro)* variety includes chocolate, but it's the best known of them all. The proprietors of **Casa Crespo** (see Lodging below) conduct an English-language cooking class centered on chocolate, which includes a guided shopping trip to the market.

✈ Oaxaca City (3.6km/2¼ miles).

🛏 $ **Chocolate Posada,** Mina 212 (© **52/951/516 5760**). $$ **Casa Crespo,** Crespo 415 (© **52/951/514 1102;** www.casacrespo.com).

457

Cacao Sampaka
Pushing the Envelope
Barcelona, Spain

We have the Spaniards to thank for bringing chocolate to Europe, so perhaps it's not surprising that one of the best chocolate shops in Europe is in Spain—or more precisely in Catalonia, in the great culinary city of Barcelona.

Stylishly sleek and minimalist, Cacao Sampaka is the flagship store of an artisanal chocolate manufacturer that sources its own cocoa beans and produces quality chocolate in its own small factory. (There are also Cacao Sampaka boutiques in Madrid, Málaga, Torrelodones, Valencia, Lisbon, and Berlin.) Their boxes of chocolates follow many different flavor themes—mixed with dried fruit and nuts, flavored with herbs and flowers, filled with liqueurs, filled with fruit, whipped into truffles, or spiced Mexican-style—as well as an exclusive line of chocolates made from the rare *criolla,* or "white" cacao bean. Browsing around the blond wood-trimmed store, you can find bins of unusual little tidbits like fried corn with bitter chocolate, orange peel coated in chocolate, salted sunflower seeds enrobed in bitter chocolate—culinary experiments that aren't always successful but certainly stir the imagination.

(You've got to give their designers credit for pushing the envelope.) Jars of all kinds of chocolate spreads and sauces are on display, as well as a wide selection of ice creams (all variations of chocolate, of course). You can only marvel at the creative combinations. Best of all, there's an entire wall of chocolate bars, in all sorts of intense designer flavors.

While there's also a shop in the historic section of town (Calle Ferran 43; ⓒ **34/93/304-1539**), it's worth going out to the main store in the Eixample neighborhood. The trendy little cafe on premises serves hot and cold chocolate drinks, mousses, pastries and cakes, and a range of chocolate desserts. The place has such an air of utter cool, it doesn't even feel like an indulgence.

ⓘ **Calle Consell de Cent 292** (ⓒ **34/93/272-0833;** www.cacaosampaka.com).

✈ El Prat (13km/8 miles).

🛏 $$$ **Montecarlo,** Les Ramblas 124 (ⓒ **34/93/412-0404;** www.montercarlo bcn.com). $$ **Duques de Bergara,** Bergara 11 (ⓒ **34/93/301-5151;** www.hoteles-catalonia.com).

458

The Capital of Chocolate
A Praline Passion
Brussels, Belgium

Belgium may be a small country, but there's nothing small about the Belgian passion for chocolate—especially for the mouthwatering little chocolate-covered confections they call pralines. According to the Belgian tourist office, this tiny nation

7 Places to Eat in . . . Puebla, Mexico

Though it's Mexico's fourth-largest city, Puebla doesn't feel like a metropolis. The Moorish Spanish flair of its colonial architecture has remained wonderfully intact, and the local lifestyle is gracious, relaxed, and welcoming to visitors. But Puebla's real ace in the hole—the thing you've probably come for—is the food: Among Mexicans, it's revered as the cradle of Mexican cuisine, the original source of such iconic spicy dishes as *mole poblano* sauce (a complex mix of ingredients including cinnamon and chocolate), *pipián* (a similar sauce based on ground toasted squash seeds), *mixiotes* (beef, pork, or lamb baked in red sauce), and *chiles en nogada* (sweet meat-stuffed poblano chilies in walnut cream sauce, a summer-only treat).

Culinary skills seem genetically imprinted here; as Anthony Bourdain revealed in *Kitchen Confidential,* thousands of Pueblans have moved north of the border (often undocumented) to cook at fine-dining restaurants all over the United States. Despite that exodus, however, the city's pool of skilled cooks shows no signs of depletion. One of the classic places to sample Pueblan regional cuisine is at 459 Fonda de Santa Clara (Calle 3 Poniente 307; © **52/222/242-2659;** www.fondadesantaclara. com), just 1½ blocks west of the *zócalo,* or central square. With its fiesta-like red-and-blue furnishings and fluttering ceiling flags, it's a bit touristy, but there's no arguing with the excellence of its robust *mole* dishes and *chiles en nogada.* Priding themselves on preserving the old ways, they also offer a number of intriguing seasonal specialties—where else in the world can you try ant eggs or *maguey* fried worms? A somewhat more refined place is the restaurant at 460 Mesón Sacristía de la Compañía (6 Sur 304, Callejón de los Sapos; © **52/222/232-4513;** www.mesones-sacristia.

Mesón Sacristía de la Compañía is a restaurant, hotel, and antiques shop.

com), a converted 18th-century mansion that's also a hotel and antiques shop (and part-time cooking school). The flagstone patio here is an especially inviting place to dine on *mole* dishes or the excellent chalupas, deep-fried tostadas topped with shredded chicken, meat, peppers, and salsa. Travel out to the nightlife strip along Avenida Juárez to find ⦿ Mi Ciudad (Av. Juárez 2507; ✆ **52/222/231-5326**), a vibrant big dining room with lively wall murals, featuring excellent *mole* and *pipián* sauces (in either green or red varieties), as well as deeply soothing cream soups like *chile atole* and *sopa poblana*.

In the hip Hotel Purificadora, a snazzy conversion of an old ice warehouse, the ⦿ Purificadora Restaurant (Callejón de la 10 Norte 802; ✆ **52/222/309-1920; www.lapurificadora.com**) showcases a nuevo-Mexicano twist, courtesy of Mexico City star chef Enrique Olvera. His recipes break the box, creatively mingling European techniques with Mexican flavors in dishes like slow-braised chicken with green *pipián*, or jumbo shrimp with chipotle hollandaise. Similar creative fusion goes on at intimate, low-ceilinged ⦿ La Conjura (Calle 9 Oriente 201; ✆ **52/222/232-9693**), where the tapas and entrees throw local Mexican ingredients into what is essentially Spanish cooking—things like *arroz negro con calamares* (rice with squid cooked in squid ink) or *huachinango en alberino* (snapper in wine sauce topped with mussels, clams, and shrimp).

Pueblan cuisine is very much based on fresh-from-the-farm ingredients; to understand that connection, stroll through the ⦿ Mercado el Carmen food market (21 Oriente between Dos Sur and Cuatro Sur). While you're here, stop by the Cemitas Poblanos stand to pick up a tortalike *cemita* sandwich, pillowy rolls traditionally stuffed with meat, poblano peppers, white cheese, lush avocado slices, and a kick of chipotles. There's an even livelier market in the small neighboring town of Cholula (site of an immense pre-Columbian ruin, the Great Pyramid), a 10-minute drive out of Puebla. The ⦿ Mercado de Cholula (Camino Real a Cholula and Calle 20 Norte) has not only loads of butchers, fishmongers, vegetable farmers, and spice sellers, it also has a few fabulous quesadilla counters toward the back, where the corn tortillas come packed with fresh cheese, earthy mushrooms, zucchini blossoms, and nuggets of fried pork skin.

✈ Puebla International (20km/12 miles).

⌦ $$$ **NH Puebla,** Calle 5 Sur 105 (✆ **888/726-0528** in the U.S., or 52/222/309-1919; www.nh-hotels.com). $ **Hotel Royalty,** Portal Hidalgo 8 (✆ **52/222/242-4740** or 01-800/638-9999 in Mexico; www.hotelr.com).

The Museum of Cocoa and Chocolate in Brussels.

Place, **Planete Chocolat** (rue du Lombard/ Lombardstraat 24; ℂ **32/2/511 07 55**) sells distinctively elegant medallions of rich chocolate, which lie meltingly flat on your tongue. There's also a cafe and a small museum here, where they run a hands-on demonstration on Saturdays (www.planete chocolate.be). Farther south, on the place du Grand Sablon (also notable for the flamboyant Gothic Notre-Dame du Sablon church), **Wittamer Chocolate** (ℂ **32/2/ 546 11 10**) sells a luscious line of hand-made pralines and, a few doors down, runs an upscale cafe and pastry shop. To the west, near the Park van Brussel, there are two superb chocolate shops to check out: petite **Chocolatier Mary** (rue Royale/ Konigstraat 73; ℂ **32/2/217-45-00**), which provides its smooth handcrafted pralines to the Belgian royal court; and **Le Choco-latier Manon** (rue du Congrès/Con-gresstraat 24; ℂ **32/2/425-26-32**), a tidy little white shop with red awnings that sells pralines so beautiful, you almost feel guilty biting into them. If you haven't overdosed yet, you can circle back to the Grand Place area to **La Maison du Chocolat Artisanal**

produces 172,000 tons of chocolate per year and has more than 2,000 chocolate shops—most of them artisanal chocolat-iers, even in the smallest towns. With such keen competition, and such a refined pub-lic palate, it's not enough for their candies to taste good—they're also expected to look like tiny works of art.

In the capital, Brussels, chocolate is so ubiquitous you almost expect the city's mascot sculpture, Mannequin Pis, to be spouting a stream of hot cocoa. Kick off your chocolate tour at the **Museum of Cocoa and Chocolate** (rue de la Tête d'Or/ Guldenhoofdstraat 9–11; ℂ **32/2/514 20 48;** www.mucc.be), a lovely little museum set in a fine old stepped-gable townhouse close to the Grand Place. Three floors of exhibitions describe the history and mak-ing of chocolate in detail, but the real draw here is the daily chocolate-making demonstrations.

After the museum, it's time to hit the streets. A few streets south of the Grand

Pralines from Le Chocolatier Manon in Brussels.

(rue Marché aux Herbes/Grasmarkt 67; *32/2/513 78 92*), a crowded, busy shop that sells a variety of pralines by top chocolate makers from all over this chocolate-loving country.

✈ Brussels (14km/9 miles).

🛏 $$$ **Le Dixseptième,** rue de la Madeleine/Magdalenastraat 25 (*32/2/502-57-44;* www.ledixseptieme.be). $$ **Mozart,** rue du Marché-aux-Fromages 23 (*32/2/502-66-61;* www.hotel-mozart.be).

A Chocolate Tour de Paris
Les Chocolats Supremes
Paris, France

The French take chocolate *seriously*. True, the French take all culinary matters seriously, but over the past few years Paris has seen a sweeping resurgence in the art of chocolate-making, led by a posse of master chocolatiers who've won rock-star-level celebrity. Using only the most refined ingredients, these *artistes du chocolat* turn out confections too exquisite to be gobbled heedlessly.

The name most aficionados breathe first is **Christian Constant** (37 rue d'Assas, 6e; *33/1/53 63 15 15*), who has been selling his delectable chocolates since 1970. It's the quality of his ingredients that draws fans to this swanky shop near the Luxembourg Gardens—velvety chocolate scented with exotic flowers or herbs, or whipped into delicacies such as raspberry ganache, *aiguillettes* of Sicilian mandarins, or toothsome truffles. While you're here, head up the street to **John-Charles Rochoux** (16 rue d'Assas, 6e; *33/1/42 84 29 45*), where luscious chocolate is crafted into amazingly intricate edible sculptures. (If the art seems too precious to eat, don't fret—you'll also find satiny chocolate squares and hand-dipped confections here.)

Superstar chocolatier Robert Linxe came along in 1977 to open **La Maison du Chocolat** (225 rue du Faubourg St. Honoré, 8e; *33/1/42 27 39 44*) in Paris's toniest shopping area. Renowned for his silky ganaches and a particularly sweet chocolate flavor (La Maison uses only 65% cacao to avoid bitterness), Linxe soared to immediate fame. Lately some chocolate fanciers complain that La Maison has overexpanded—there are branches in London, New York, and Tokyo, and six other shops around Paris—but the shop on rue François 1er (*33/1/47 23 38 25*) is also particularly worth visiting for its special tasting sessions. Head east toward the Tuileries, where the Faubourg becomes simply rue St-Honoré, and you'll find two other top-notch artisans: **Jean-Louis Hevin** (231 rue St-Honoré, 1e; *33/1/45-51-99-64*), known for surprisingly heavenly combinations of chocolate and cheese (don't scoff until you've tried it), and **Michel Cluizel** (201 rue St. Honoré, 1e; *33/1/42 44 11 66*), whose fanatical attention to processing his own carefully selected cocoa beans results in wonderfully complex yet balanced chocolate flavor. If you haven't overdosed yet, continue east to the Marais, where **Josephine Vannier** (4 rue du Pas de la Mule, 3e; *33/1/44 54 03 09*) offers fanciful gift chocolates in a little shop just off the Place des Vosges.

Back on the Left Bank, near Les Invalides, La Maison alumnus **Michel Chaudun** (149 rue de l'Université, 7e; *33/1/47 53 74 40*) is justly famous for his whimsical chocolate sculptures, though even a simple milk chocolate bar from this shop is a treat.

Head east from here to the Boulevard St-Germain, where you'll find two other chocolate must-sees—the stylish Paris outpost of **Richart** (258 bd. St-Germain, 7e; ☏ **33/ 1/45 55 66 00**), a Lyons-based chocolate maker selling spectacular gift boxes, and **Patrick Roger** (108 bd. St-Germain, 6e; ☏ **33/1/43 29 38 42**), whose audacious combinations of ingredients play off flavors and textures in poetic flights of inspiration.

✈ De Gaulle (23km/14 miles); Orly (14km/ 8⅔ miles).

🛏 $$$ **Hôtel Luxembourg Parc,** 42 rue de Vaugirard, 6e (☏ **33/1/53-10-36-50;** www.luxembourg-paris-hotel.com). $$ **Hôtel Saintonge,** 16 rue Saintonge, 3e (☏ **44/1/42-77-91-13;** www.saintonge marais.com).

Chocolate World 467

London: The Choc Walk
A Suite of Sweets
London, England

Studies show the United Kingdom ranks first in the world in per capita chocolate consumption. In a country with such a raging national sweet tooth, artisanal chocolates are almost beside the point; most Britons are perfectly content to wolf down a Mars bar or a Kit Kat or an entire Dairy Milk assortment, just so long as they get their daily fix. Perhaps that's why London's luxury chocolate boutiques have to go the extra mile, enticing customers with gorgeous packaging and over-the-top romantic flavorings.

The sentimental favorite is **Charbonnel & Walker** (28 Old Bond St., in the Royal Arcade; ☏ **44/20/7491-0939;** www. charbonnel.co.uk), which has been around since 1875 and counts the Prince of Wales as one of its first customers. Traditional hand-dipped chocolates they may be, but oh, the boxes they come in! Floral bandboxes, creamy white tins with gilt accents, gold-foil *bonbonnieres,* all display Charbonnel's Victorian-era logo and the seal of its royal warrant as chocolate maker to the royal family.

Nearby in Piccadilly, **Prestat** (14 Princes Arcade; ☏ **44/20/8896 8699**) is also an old-timer, founded in 1902, but the gaudy *fin de siècle* decor of the shop makes it look like a brash newcomer. There's a sense of fun about its packaging, with gold lettering that looks taken from an old theater poster. Under its new owners, Prestat is anything but sleepy, offering single-origin and organic chocolates as well as a line of artisanal truffles (after all, the firm's founder, Antoine Dufour, came from the French family that invented truffles).

In contrast, London's new breed of chocolatiers are making their mark with unique flavors and techniques. Down in Chelsea, **Demarquette** (285 Fulham Rd.; ☏ **44/20/7351 5467;** www.demarquette. co.uk) uses its silken chocolate as a base for conveying a wide range of flavors, from Earl Grey tea to Highland malt whisky, from Java cinnamon to Brazilian pink pepper to Provençal lavender. Check for regular tasting events, a great way to be led through this palette of flavors. Despite the French-sounding name, Marc Demarquette is London born and bred, though he learned his craft in France. At Demarquette's Chelsea rival, **L'Artisan du Chocolat** (89 Lower Sloane St.; ☏ **44/20/7824 8365;** www.artisanduchocolat.com), Irish-born chocolatier Gerard Coleman makes his chocolate from scratch, grinding premier cacao beans at the firm's manufactory (they call it an "atelier") in Ashford, Kent—where, by the way, they offer weekend tasting sessions. That refined chocolate is then used to enrobe all sorts of chocolate treats, notably salted caramels, truffles, and O's—incredibly thin chocolate discs filled with taste-bud-flooding flavors such as passion fruit, pistachio, or peppery fresh mint.

✈ Heathrow (24km/15 miles); Gatwick (40km/25 miles).

🛏 $$$ **22 Jermyn St.,** 22 Jermyn St., St. James (📞 **800/682-7808** in the U.S., or 44/20/7734-2353; www.22jermyn.com). $$ **Vicarage Private Hotel,** 10 Vicarage Gate, South Kensington (📞 **44/20/7229-4030;** www.londonvicaragehotel.com).

468 Chocolate World

The Peaks of Swiss Chocolate

Swiss Family Artisans

Zurich, Switzerland

Swiss chocolate—the very phrase conjures images of contented cows grazing in refreshing Alpine meadows and gingerbread chalets nestled beneath snow-glistening peaks. The fact that no cacao bean has ever been grown in the country is practically irrelevant.

So how did Swiss chocolate become so famous? For one thing, Sprüngli chocolates has set the bar high, ever since the business began in 1836. At one time combined with chocolate rival Lindt (they split in 1892), **Confiserie Sprüngli** (Paradeplatz; 📞 **44/224-47-11**) has remained a refined family business, operating out of its gleaming flagship store in the heart of downtown Zurich (while Lindt went the way of the multinational giant). Yes, it has 17 branches in the Zurich area, and yes, its chocolates are now manufactured 10 minutes away in Kilchberg instead of in the back of the store—but it is still admirably focused on artisanal confectionery. The store's glass cases display a stunning array of gleaming filled chocolates, rich truffles, chocolate *gaufrette* wafers, glittering marzipan fruits, and pastel-hued *luxemburgerli,* the cream-filled macaroon sandwiches that are a local passion. Adjacent to the store, you'll find a coffee shop, a small restaurant, and a room exclusively for mailing chocolate gifts to friends and family abroad.

On a narrow cobblestone street in Old Town, the small **Teuscher** store (Storchengasse 9; 📞 **41/44/211-51-53**) is the original home of this famed line of epicurean chocolates, founded in the 1930s by Swiss chocolate-maker Adolf Teuscher. Despite the old-world charm of its 17th-century half-timbered building, Teuscher has installed the biggest plate-glass windows the site can manage, the better to fill with dazzling displays. Teuscher has now expanded worldwide, particularly into the North American market, but it's still a family-run company with high quality control. Though they also make chocolate bars and pralines, velvety truffles are Teuscher's specialty; they come in milk, dark, and white chocolate, variously flavored with such exotic tastes as almond, orange, raspberry, butter crunch, caramel, kirsch, Bailey's Irish cream, champagne, and jasmine tea. Teuscher's souvenir assortments, with glossy full-color photos of Zurich and its lake on the box front, may look a little kitschy but they are perennial bestsellers. Can't wait to get home to try some of the Teuscher cocoa mix you just bought? Teuscher also serves chocolate specialties at **Café Schober**

(Napfgasse 4; ☎ **41/44/251-80-60**), located in a nearby 14th-century building.

✈ Zurich (16km/10 miles).

🛏 $$$ **Hotel Ambassador**, Falkenstrasse 6 (☎ **41/44/258-98-98;** www.ambassadorhotel.ch). $$ **Lady's First,** Mainaustrasse 24 (☎ **41/44/380-80-10;** www.ladysfirst.ch).

Chocolate Bolognese

Where Italian Chocolate Started

Bologna, Italy

Any gastronomic tour of Italy absolutely has to include Bologna, the city that gave its name to the most classic of ragout sauces, not to mention sublime *mortadella* sausage, which bears about as much resemblance to American-style bologna as chicken Marengo does to McNuggets. Italians call the city "Bologna the Fat," and for good reason; its restaurants are of a high caliber for a city of this size, and the number of excellent food specialty shops is extraordinary. Strolling through the Pescherie Vecchie, the city's market area near the landmark Due Torri, it's easy to lose all sense of time. But to satisfy your sweet tooth, wend your way past the salumerias, cheese shops, pasta factories, bakeries, and produce, and you can visit two of Italy's most venerable chocolate shops.

Near the Pescherie Vecchie, **Roccati** is a family business founded in 1909 in Trentino; the current proprietors, a husband-and-wife team, moved it to Bologna a few years ago. Roccati is still celebrated for the *gianduja* orange chocolate that their ancestors made specially for the princes of Savoy a century ago. In their smart modern shop, you'll see some amazing chocolate sculptures—books made out of chocolate, boats and cars made of chocolate, horses and birdhouses of chocolate—there's even a box of chocolate that's literally a box of chocolate. In their open-air laboratory, you can stand and watch these heavenly delights being created by hand. The only catch is that the shop closes in summer, but that's a tricky season for chocolate anyway.

A few streets farther south from the Piazza Maggiore, on Via Carbonesi, **Majani** claims to be Italy's oldest sweets shop, in business since 1796. Behind a gleaming old-fashioned wood-paneled shop, resplendent with gold letters and coats-of-arms, you'll find a wide assortment of chocolates, artisanally made with the highest-quality ingredients (though they eventually moved the chocolate-making operations out of the back room to a small plant in nearby Crespellano). Their specialties include a wonderful coruscated chocolate bark, scrumptious little tortellini-shaped ganaches, and their classic confection: melt-in-your-mouth Fiats, bite-sized cubes of layered satiny chocolate invented in 1912 to honor the Italian car of the same name.

ⓘ **Majani,** Via Carbonesi 5 (☎ **39/51/234302;** www.majani.it). **Roccati,** Via Clavature 17A (☎ **39/51/261964;** www.roccaticioccolato.com).

✈ Marconi International (6km/3¾ miles).

🛏 $$$ **Grand Hotel Baglioni,** Via dell'Indipendenza 8 (☎ **39/51/225445;** www.baglionihotels.com). $ **Albergo Della Drapperie,** Via della Drapperie 5 (☎ **39/51/223955;** www.albergodrapperie.com).

Valle di Cioccolato

Slow Food Chocolate

Tuscany, Italy

Tuscany doesn't have a long-standing tradition of chocolate-making like Bologna does; still, it has something just as vital—a Slow Food veneration for culinary artisans. Even though they can't grow cacao beans on the rounded hills of Tuscany like they grow grapes and olives, once they've imported the beans, a new generation of confectioners is now producing high-end chocolate the same way their colleagues produce wine and olive oil—in small batches with fanatical attention to ingredients.

With Florence as a starting point, you can sample products from several of these artisans at ever-crowded **Hemingway** (Piazza Piattellina 9/r; © **39/55/284-781**), a tiny cafe-bar in the heart of the historic center specializing in rich hot chocolate, indulgent fudgy cakes, and handmade pralines. The old-fashioned fine-foods shop **Procacci** (via Tornabuoni 64/r; © **39/55/211-656**), which dates from 1885, sells top-of-the-line mixed chocolates as well, on the city's swankiest shopping street. Keep a special lookout for chocolate bars and pralines with the **Amadei Chocolate** label; using beans from their own South American plantations, Amadei produces these exceptional chocolates in a small cheery atelier near Pisa in Pontedera (call © **39/587/484849** and you may be able to arrange a tour). Another chocolate haven in Florence is **Vestri** (Borgo degli Albizi 11/r; © **39/55-284-781**), which sells chocolates made at the family plant in Arezzo; their intriguing flavors range from nutmeg to chili pepper to Earl Grey tea.

But that's just the beginning: Drive the E76 highway between Pisa and Florence and you'll have to stop off every few miles to visit chocolate artisans. One absolutely essential stop is in the small town of Algiana, halfway between Prato and Pistoia, to sample the wares of **Roberto Catinari** (via Provinciale 378; © **39/574/718506;** www.robertocatinari.it), generally regarded as the godfather of this new breed of Tuscan chocolatiers. His pralines are precisely sculpted little gems, including a line of nut-flavored chocolates that uncannily resemble the nuts themselves. Also in Algiana is the chocolate laboratory **Mannori Espace** (via G Bruno 12; © **39/574/719557;** www.mannoriespace.it), where dynamic young pastry chef Luca Mannori has been venturing deeper and deeper into the art of making chocolate. Check to see if any chocolate-making classes or demonstrations are scheduled while you're here. He also has a shop in Prato, at via Lazzerini 2 (© **39/574/21628**).

In Pistoia, you can sample traditional handmade chocolates from **Corsini** (Piazza San Francesco 42; © **39/573/20138;** www.brunocorsini.com), sold in this shop since 1918. East of Pistoia, venture off the highway to find **Slitti Cioccolate e Caffé** (Via Franceso Sud 1268, Monsummano Terme; © **39/572/640-240;** www.slitti.it), where Andrea Slitti's show-stopping chocolate sculptures and fanciful pralines are made out of an exceptionally full-bodied chocolate. And once you've reached Pisa, make a beeline for **DeBondt Chocolate,** Lungarno Pacinotto 5, Pisa (© **39/50/316-0073;** www.debondtchocolate.com), where Dutch-born chocolate maker Paul DeBondt flavors his satiny chocolate with exotic tastes such as jasmine, ginger, tea, cardamom, fennel, cinnamon, and lemon-lime. Tours and tastings take place at his small laboratory-plant in Visignano, near Navacchio (Via Sant'Antioco 31; ☎ **39/50/779042**).

✈ Florence (5km/3 miles).

📧 $$$ **Hotel Monna Lisa,** Borgo Pinti 27, Florence (☎ **39/55/247-9751;** www. monnalisa.it). $ **Hotel Abaco,** Via dei Banchi 1, Florence (☎ **39/55-238-1919;** www.abaco-hotel.it).

Chocolate World **471**

Wisconsin's Candy Land
Meltaways & More
Northeast Wisconsin

Though Wisconsin is famous for its dairy herds, most of the milk is channeled into cheese; the state's German immigrant food tradition leans more towards beer and bratwurst than *schokolade*. But there's one candy-crazy corner of the state—the area around Lake Winnebago, close enough to Milwaukee to cover in one long sugar-buzz of a day trip. Here, multi-generation family businesses operate out of time-warp shops, where workers using wooden paddles stir copper kettles full of rich melted chocolate, into which they hand-dip caramels and nut clusters and cherry cordials—breathing life back into the classic American candy box.

Several towns are blessed with not just one but two premium chocolate makers. Halfway down the west shore of Lake Winnebago, Oshkosh nourishes a long-running chocolate rivalry between **Oaks Candy Corner** (1206 Oregon St.; ☎ **920/231-3660;** www.oakscandy.com) and **Hughes Homaid Chocolate Shop** (1823 Doty St.; ☎ **920/231-7232**). Oaks has been in business since 1890 in its mock-Tudor store south of the river (it now has two other locations as well, at 9 Waugoo Ave., ☎ **920/231-2323;** and at 3001 S. Washburn St., ☎ **920/230-4548**). But Hughes Homaid is no newcomer either; since 1942, it has been operating out of its white clapboard cottage near the lake, where the candy's made down in the basement. To ratchet up the rivalry even further, both shops pride themselves on the same luscious

confection—traditional Midwestern meltaway chocolates. Folks in Oshkosh are fiercely partial to whichever brand they've eaten every Christmas since childhood. Luckily, if you weren't born in Oshkosh, you're free to taste both and make up your own mind.

At the north end of the lake, in Appleton, you've got **Wilmar Chocolates** (1222 N. Superior St.; ☎ **920/733-6182;** www.wilmarchocolates.com) going head-to-head against **Vande Walle's Candies** (400 N. Mall Dr.; ☎ **920/738-7799;** www.vandewallecandies.com). Wilmar has been selling chocolates out of its charmingly dowdy corner shop since 1956, though inside it's a thoroughly sophisticated high-end operation; go around the corner to the display windows of its candy kitchen and watch the candy makers at work. The Vande Walle family business only opened in 1974, but their family recipes date from the 1920s; at Vande Walle's, you can tour the second-floor candy-making area and maybe snag a few samples. Compare the Wilmar Wilmarvel (caramel-covered cashews enrobed in chocolate) to Vande Walle's Angelfood Candy (a honeycombed center draped in chocolate, not available in summer); better yet, try the chocolate meltaways at both and see which you prefer.

Green Bay folks have to juggle a three-way rivalry—between **Kaap's Old World Chocolates** (1921 S. Webster Ave.; ☎ **920/430-9041;** www.kaapscandy.com), **Beerntsen's Green Bay** (2000 N. Broadway;

920/437-4400; www.chocolatecandies. net), and **Seroogy's Chocolates** (in the suburb of DePere, 144 N. Wisconsin St.; 920/336-1383; www.seroogys.com). They're all old-timers—Seroogy's has been around since 1899, Kaap's since 1907, Beerntsen's since 1929. Both Seroogy's and Beerntsen's still occupy their original locations, with gleaming glass cases full of hand-dipped chocolates. Of course, each claims to make the city's best

meltaways. Sounds like a blind taste test is in order—any volunteers?

✈ Milwaukee (75 miles/121km from Oshkosh;100 miles/161km from Green Bay).

🛏 $$ **CopperLeaf Hotel,** 300 W. College Ave., Appleton (877/303-0303 or 920/749-0303; www.copperleafhotel. com). $$ **Hotel Sierra Green Bay,** 333 Main St., Green Bay (888/695-7608 or 920/432-4555; www.hotel-sierra.com).

472 Chocolate World

Jin Patisserie

Artistry in Chocolate

Venice, California

The New-Agey elegance of this shop on hip Abbott Kinney Road creates its own cool oasis in funky surfer-haven Venice. It's an upscale pastry cafe, it's a soothing tea garden—but it's also the place to go for some of the most refined chocolates in the world.

Jin's owner, Kristy Choo, comes at the art of chocolate-making from a globe-hopping perspective. (At various points in her career, she worked as an international flight attendant, then as pastry chef at Raffles Hotel in multicultural Singapore; so culture-spanning comes naturally to her.) Starting with a chocolate base of exceptional smoothness and complexity, she then infuses her gift chocolates with various essences from a botanical garden of flavors—lavender, chrysanthemum, bergamot, jasmine, lemon grass, ginger, clove, rosemary, sesame, lychee, and on and on. Startling as some of these combinations may sound, she almost always pulls them off; it's not just about adding tastes, but about suffusing the chocolate with scents that play against the earthy chocolate aroma in intriguing ways. Choo then paints the top with a delicate tracery of color that somehow expresses the personality of the confection. Exquisite gift packaging in

monklike wood cartons or long beribboned silk boxes is just the icing on the cake, so to speak.

The Zen-like tranquillity of this shady little courtyard cafe puts you in the right mood to taste the subtleties of these chocolates. With the murmur of a stone fountain in the background, shaded by banana trees and tufts of reeds outside the tidy little blue bungalow, you can sit down and order dainty pastries—many of them Asian influenced or tea flavored—as well as a wide range of teas from around the world. (Regulars swear by her luscious, inventively flavored macaroons.) Though the meal may be called "afternoon tea," there's absolutely nothing dowdy about it.

ⓘ 1202 Abbott Kinney Rd., Venice (310/399-8801; www.jinpatisserie.com).

✈ Los Angeles International (6¾ miles/11km).

🛏 $$$ **Peninsula Beverly Hills,** 9882 S. Santa Monica Blvd. (800/462-7899 or 310/551-2888; www.peninsula.com). $ **Best Western Marina Pacific Hotel,** 1697 Pacific Ave., Venice (800/786-7789 or 310/452-1111; www.mphotel.com).

Bay Area Chocolate Tour

California Dreaming

San Francisco/Berkeley, California

Once upon a time, when you said San Francisco chocolate, you were probably talking about **Ghirardelli,** a venerable candy company founded in 1852 by Dominico Ghirardelli. Ghirardelli still produces an upscale American-style chocolate, but it has gone sadly downhill since its landmark 19th-century factory was transmogrified into the trilevel tourist magnet Ghirardelli Square (900 North Point St.; © **415/474-3938;** www.ghirardelli.com). Though Ghirardelli moves tons of chocolate at its ever-crowded shop and soda fountain here, the sweets are now manufactured at a giant production facility in the East Bay and have lost the gourmet cachet they once had.

Luckily, a new league of chocolate artisans has taken over, riding on San Francisco's status as a culinary capital. First, there's **Scharffen Berger** chocolate, sold only in bars and squares of a Shaker-like simplicity, available at fancy food stores all around town and a Scharffen Berger shop at the Ferry Building Marketplace (© **415/981-9150**). Launched in 1996, Scharffen Berger's approach is very Berkeley-esque—they're less concerned with making fancy confectionery than with sourcing fine, sustainable ingredients and turning them into pure chocolate with a rich full-bodied taste. It's well worth a trip out to their home base in Berkeley (914 Heinz Ave.; © **510/981-4066;** www.scharffenberger.com) for the free factory tour, where you can watch top-quality beans from around the world being transformed into chocolate right before your eyes. Beautiful vintage European-made machines take the beans through every step of the process—roasting, grinding, mixing, tempering, molding—working only in small batches for the highest quality control. No wonder those chocolate squares melt on your tongue.

At the other end of the spectrum, **Joseph Schmidt Confections** (3489 16th St.; © **800/861-8682** or 415/861-8682; www.josephschmidtconfections.com), founded in 1983 and located in the Castro district, expresses all the artistry of Schmidt's training in European-style confectionery. Customers ooh and aah over his exquisite sculptural chocolate pieces, such as long-stemmed tulips, colorful bowls, or heart-shaped boxes. They're so beautiful, you'll hesitate before biting in. Schmidt's signature egg-shaped truffles are densely luscious, many of them flavored with liqueurs; another intriguing treat are his mosaics, bite-sized chocolate confections with exquisitely painted top surfaces.

San Francisco's other top chocolate artiste, former pastry chef Michael Recchiuti, sells his chocolates exclusively through Williams-Sonoma and the tiny **Recchiuti** stall in the Ferry Building Marketplace (© **415/826-2868;** www.recchiuti.com). The Recchiuti look is refined minimalism; the drawings atop some of his gift chocolates look delicate as Japanese pen-and-ink sketches. Yet the flavor is intense: Try the ginger hearts (ginger-infused dark chocolate with a Venezuelan white chocolate glaze), *fleur de sel* caramels (actually a salty, chewy chocolate), or his divine burnt caramel truffles.

✈ San Francisco International (14 miles/ 23km).

⊨ $$$ **Hotel Adagio,** 550 Geary St. (© **800/228-8830** or 415/775-5000; www.thehoteladagion.com). $ **Hotel des Arts,** 447 Bush St. (© **800/956-4322** or 415/956-3232; www.sfhoteldesarts.com).

Sampling Sacher Torte

Princely Pastry

Vienna, Austria

In 1832, a 16-year-old Austrian pastry apprentice named Franz Sacher, covering for his sick boss, was ordered to create a special dessert for powerful Prince Metternich. The youngster threw together a dense chocolate sponge cake, layered apricot jam on top, then sheathed it in dark chocolate icing, sprinkled with shredded chocolate and served with whipped cream (*mit Schlagobers*). The prince loved it, of course; Franz Sacher's career was made.

In this pastry-obsessed nation, it's no surprise that Franz Sacher's creation, the Sacher torte, is still revered today. The elegant **Hotel Sacher Wien** (Philharmonikerstrasse 4; ☎ **01/514560;** www.sacher. com), founded by Sacher's son, prominently features Sacher torte in its brocaded jewel box of a cafe. The cakes are sold in wooden gift boxes at the pastry shop inside the hotel, as well as at the sister hotel in Salzburg (Schwarzstrasse 5–7; ☎ **43/662/88 977 0**) and in Sacher cafes in Innsbruck (Rennweg 1; ☎ 43/512/56 56 26) and Graz (Herrengasse 6; ☎ 43/316/ 8005 0). You can even order it for shipment overseas (☎ 43/1/51 456 861; www. sacher.com); a molded chocolate seal on the icing certifies an *echt* Sacher torte.

The Hotel Sacher naturally trademarked that cake, and it was embroiled for years in litigation against another Vienna landmark, the splendidly baroque **Café Demel** (Kohlmarkt 14; ☎ **43/1/5351717**), for calling its own superb version "original" Sacher torte. (They differ in the location of the apricot jam layer.) But just about every one of Vienna's classic coffeehouses and cafes serves some version of Sacher torte—always, of course, with *Schlagobers*. The bitter chocolate, the slightly dry and not overly sweet cake, often surprise those who prefer their desserts sugary and moist, but the Viennese consider it pastry perfection.

Between St. Stephen's and the State Opera, try the cake at **Gerstner** (Kärntnerstrasse 11–15, ☎ **43/1/512-49360**), one of Vienna's top confectioners since 1847. Across from the Hofburg, Sacher torte is served at **Café Central** (Herrengasse 14, ☎. **43/1/5333764**), with its grand neo-Gothic entrance and vaulted interior, a famous 19th-century hangout for Austria's intellectual elite. Opened in its prime Ring location in 1873, the well-burnished Art Nouveau **Café Landtmann** (Dr.-Karl-Lueger-Ring 4; ☎ **43/1/241000**) has served Sacher torte to a celebrity clientele since the days of Sigmund Freud. Near the MUMOK modern art museum, you can get a slice of Sacher torte at cozy wood-paneled **Café Sperl** (Gumpendorferstrasse 11; ☎ **43/1/5864158**), which hasn't changed since it opened in 1880. Or if you're out visiting Schönbrunn Castle, try the Sacher torte at nearby **Café Dommayer** (Auhofstrasse 2; ☎ **43/1/8775465**), a high-ceilinged black-and-white 18th-century salon where Johann Strauss, Jr., made his musical debut in 1844. Sacher torte may well have been served that evening too—who knows?

✈ Vienna International (22km/14 miles).

🛏 $$$ **Hotel Sacher Wien,** Philharmonikerstrasse 4 (☎ **43/1/514560;** www. sacher.com). $ **Hotel Kärntnerhof,** Grashofgasse 4 (☎ **43/1/5121923;** www. karntnerhof.com).

The Art of French Pastry

Star-Power Patisseries

Paris, France

Part of the pleasure of a Paris vacation is finding your own little divine patisseries, which lie waiting to be discovered all around the city. But there's no denying that two *patissiers* have set the bar in modern-day Paris; they are the masters whom all others either emulate or defy.

The first is the late **Gaston Lenôtre,** the legendary pastry chef who in 1957 opened his first shop in Paris at 44 rue d-Auteuil, near the Bois de Boulogne. As its success took off, Lenôtre was never shy about expanding his business; he published cookbooks, started a cooking school, opened restaurants, and cloned his Paris bakery several times. (Other more centrally located branches are at 10 rue St

Antoine, on the edge of the Marais and near the Bastille; and 35 av. de la Mot Picquet, near the Champs des Mars in the 7th arrondissement). The Lenôtre chain now has 16 sleek, stylish shops in France, plus branches around the world from Tokyo to Las Vegas. The quality of the pastries remains impeccably high, if perhaps a little too correct, and any visitor to Paris who's interested in food should stop in at one of them to view the extraordinary assortment of frilly mille-feuilles, feather-light meringues, dense chocolate mousse cakes, glossy fruit tarts, plump éclairs, jewel-like chocolates, and smooth ice creams—the craftsmanship is simply extraordinary.

As is so often the case, the master was eventually challenged by his apprentice. **Pierre Hermé** began his career at age 14 as a Lenôtre trainee, but 25 years later, in 2001, opened his own jewel box–like pastry shop in Paris, on the artsy Left Bank at 72 rue Bonaparte. Now he has a space-agey second shop at 185 rue de Vaugirard as well. The dramatic decor of these shops is quite different from the glossy corporate look of the Lenôtre shops—which is not surprising, given Hermé's avant-garde flair. He's known for surprise combinations of ingredients, for arresting sculptural effects, and for intriguing "themes" that organize each season's pastry collection almost like a couture collection. You can see this in signature items like the raspberry-layered Ispahan tart, the *trompe l'oeil* effect of his vanilla infinity tart, or the whimsical cake mosaic with its flaked pistachio topping looking like a miniature Zen garden. Visiting the Hermé shop is almost

The Pierre Hermé boutique.

like strolling through an art gallery—no wonder *Vogue* dubbed him "the Picasso of the pastry world."

Which begs the question: Whose pastries would you rather eat—Lenôtre's classic flaky delicacies or Hermés' inventive, modern take on patisserie? Why not try both and judge for yourself?

ⓘ **Lenôtre,** 44 rue d-Auteuil (metro: Michel-Ange-D'Auteuil), 16e (✆ **33/1/45 24 52 52;** www.lenotre.fr). **Hermé,** 72 Rue Bonaparte (metro: St.-Germain-des-Près), 6e (✆ **33/1/354 47 77;** www.pierre herme.fr).

✈ De Gaulle (23km/14 miles); Orly (14km/ 8⅔ miles).

🛏 $$$ **Hôtel Luxembourg Parc,** 42 rue de Vaugirard, 6e (✆ **33/1/53-10-36-50;** www.luxembourg-paris-hotel.com). $$ **Hôtel Saintonge,** 16 rue Saintonge, 3e (✆ **44/1/42-77-91-13;** www.saintonge marais.com).

Macarons from Hermé in Paris.

Espai Sucre

Where Afters Are No Afterthought

Barcelona, Spain

It's billed as the "first dessert restaurant in the world"—a grand claim, perhaps, but Espai Sucre does take its sweets very seriously. It's the brainchild of chef Jordi Butrón and confectioner Xano Saguer I Gregori, two men fired with passion about show-stopper restaurant pastries. Their adjacent cooking school acknowledges the reality that pastry-making is its own discipline; most pastry chefs follow an entirely separate track in culinary school, and many top restaurants promote their pastry chefs as stars in their own right. At Espai Sucre, they're the only stars that count.

Located in the heart of Barcelona's medieval historic core, this chic modern cafe stands out with its smoked-glass-and-marble entrance, polished wood floor, slick black tables, and taupe leather chairs, the sophisticated antithesis of a cutesy sweet shop or ice-cream parlor. More than just the school's calling card, it's quite a classy operation on its own. It's only open in the evenings (so much for those of us who'd like to gorge on sweets midafternoon), with specific seatings at 8:30 and 11pm on weekend nights (midweek, the flow's a little more casual). They offer several set menus, including an all-chocolate series of sweets; two of the tasting menus include some savory dishes as well, if you want to make a full meal. Wine pairings are suggested for all of the menus.

Espai Sucre's innovative desserts introduce surprising elements, defying expectations about what is sweet and what is savory—you'll find items like a cold soup with green apple and spicy yogurt ice cream; an olive oil cake with white peach, green olive, and cheese; vanilla cream with coffee, black cardamom, and banana; or a bread pudding with bacon ice cream and pineapple. The idea is not to seek a gluttonous sugar high but to compare and contrast delicate distinctions of flavor. Of course, Espai Sucre's desserts are spectacular presentations—precisely cut slices of dense cake stacked with an almost mathematical precision, divided by crisp glossy wafers, topped with scoops of cream or sherbet, drizzled with jewel-colored sauces, garnished with crystallized fruits or sprigs of herbs, set in dreamy pools of chocolate or butterscotch or lemon liqueur or whatever a creative patissier can dream up.

You don't just drop into Espai Sucre for a quick nibble—it's the focus of your evening, an event to be taken seriously. If you're one of those diners who regrets not being able to do proper justice to dessert after a full gourmet meal, then Espai Sucre's the place for you: Here you can skip the meal and go straight for the good stuff.

(i) C. Princesa 53 (34/93/268-1523; www.espaisucre.com).

✈ El Prat (13km/8 miles).

🛏 $$$ **Montecarlo,** Les Ramblas 124 (34/93/412-0404; www.montercarlo bcn.com). $$ **Duques de Bergara,** Bergara 11 (34/93/301-5151; www.hoteles-catalonia.com).

The Baker's Best

477

Gerbeaud Cukrászda

The Pastry Heart of Pest

Budapest, Hungary

Lit up at night, the front of this famous old cafe on one of Pest's liveliest pedestrian squares looks almost like a wedding cake, all white stone arches and sculptural swags. In days past, Gerbeaud was the coffeehouse where Budapest's elite gathered to see and be seen; it's much more democratic these days, though still pricey (don't expect to see students or ragged poets occupying the tables for hours). Sure, it's listed in just about every guidebook to the city, but Gerbeaud's is one of those tried-and-true culinary landmarks that still deserves a visit.

Founded by confectioner Henrik Kugler in 1858, the cafe moved into this stately neobaroque building in 1870; it's now named, however, after Emil Gerbeaud, a Swiss patissier who was brought in as a partner in the 1880s and propelled the cafe to prominence. By adding French elements like cream fillings and chocolate coatings to the traditional golden sponge cakes and fruit fillings of Hungarian desserts, Gerbeaud almost single-handedly transformed Budapest into one of the pastry capitals of Europe.

The excellent Viennese-style coffees come in a wide range of flavors, but the pastries are still the draw, baked on premises to Gerbeaud's recipes. It's the definitive place to sample classic Hungarian desserts such as richly layered chocolate Dobos torte, rum-soaked Punch torte, salty *pogácsa, szilvás lepény* (moist plum pies), *somloi* (sponge cake with whipped cream and chocolate), and, of course, a variety of hand-pulled strudels. If the dense, rich sweetness of Hungarian pastry is not to your taste, try the ice creams, which are also superb. The adjacent shop sells some of these treats as well as some wonderful handmade chocolates, like Gerbeaud's trademark *konyakos meggy*, a dark chocolate candy surrounding a cognac-soaked sour cherry.

During the Communist years, when the government discouraged coffeehouses, seen as potential hotbeds of dissent, Café Gerbeaud had begun to look rundown and shabby. But in the late 1990s it finally received a much-needed floor-to-ceiling renovation. Now every crystal chandelier,

gilt-framed mirror, and marble-topped table in the opulent high-ceilinged interior gleams like new. Of course, inside isn't where you want to sit; if the weather's fine, try for one of the umbrella tables in the outdoor cafe, where the people-watching is best.

ⓘ Vörösmarty Ter 7 (☎ **36/1/429-9000;** www.gerbeaud.hu).

✈ Budapest (22km/13 miles).

🛏 **$$ Hotel Erzsébet,** V. Károlyi Mihály u. 11–15, Budapest (☎ **36/1/889-3700;** www.danubiusgroup.com). $$ **Hotel Papillon,** II. Rózsahegy u. 3/b (☎ **36/1/212-4750**).

478 The Baker's Best

NYC: New York Cupcakes
Sex & the City Cupcake Wars
New York, New York

Blame *Sex and the City* for spilling the beans—Carrie and the girls were always raving about the sinfully rich red-velvet cupcakes at Greenwich Village's southern-style Magnolia Bakery (never mind that none of them looked like they *ever* indulged in baked goods). Soon enough, long lines perpetually snaked out that homey little bakery's door—so much for well-kept secrets.

The good news is that the **Magnolia Bakery** (401 Bleecker St.; ☎ **212/462-2572;** www.magnoliacupcakes.com; now also at 200 Columbus Ave.) isn't Manhattan's only cupcake source, not by a long shot. In fact, well before Magnolia arrived, you could get fine moist cupcakes topped with incredible butter-cream flowers at the endearingly shabby **Cupcake Café** (545 9th Ave.; ☎ **212/268-9975**) on West Midtown's grungy Ninth Avenue (Cupcake Café now also has a branch in chic Chelsea, at 18 W. 18th St.; ☎ **212/465-1530**). But from 1999 on, in the wake of the

Magnolia Bakery's runaway success, renegade Magnolia bakers set up rival shops all around town, offering the same oversized home-style cupcakes crowned with huge dollops of frosting, made from quality butter and sugar and flour. No preservatives needed—these cupcakes are meant to be ordered to-go and gorged on *now*.

First came the trim **Buttercup Bake Shop** (2nd Ave.; ☎ **212/350-4144;** now also at 141 W. 72nd St.), launched by Magnolia cofounder Jennifer Appel in a Midtown location convenient for lunch-hour indulgence (not to mention office-party catering). Buttercup's cupcakes emphasize frosting over cake, its glass cases full of dazzling whipped-pastel confections; a large window in the back of the shop lets you watch the bakers at work. A couple of years later, amid the art galleries of Chelsea, another Magnolia alumnus opened the retro-1940s-look **Billy's Bakery** (184 9th Ave.; ☎ **212/647-9956**), serving moist, buttery cupcakes slathered with icing that isn't overly sweet. With its friendly, nostalgic ambience, Billy's offers all sorts of classic American baked goods, including pecan pie and pineapple-upside-down cake. On the ever-more-hip Lower East Side, **Sugar Sweet Sunshine** (126 Rivington St.; © **212/995-1960;** www.sugar sweetsunshine.com), launched by two Buttercup defectors, strives for a cheery junk-shop look; cake quality is superior here (devotees claim their vanilla and pumpkin-spice flavors outdo Magnolia's). On the Upper East Side (but in the unsnooty Yorkville section), cozy **Two Little Red Hens** (1652 2nd Ave.; © **212/452-0476;** www.twolittleredhens.com) sells stunningly frosted cupcakes and a wide range of muffins and other cakes.

Crumbs Bake Shop (321 Amsterdam Ave.; © **212/712-9800;** also at 1371 3rd Ave., 43 W. 42nd St., 37 E. 8th St., 87 Beaver St.; www.crumbsbakeshop.com) rides the giant cupcake bandwagon as well, but in a coffee-shop setting where you can linger; several of their tasty cupcakes come topped with fun add-ons like crushed Oreos or M&M's. You can avoid the Magnolia lines and still get authentic southern-style cupcakes if you head up to Harlem and **Make My Cake** (121 St. Nicholas Ave.; © **212/932-0833**). And out in the low-rent hipster-chic wilds of Red Hook, Brooklyn, check out **Baked** (359 Van Brunt St.; ©**718/222-0345**), which serves wickedly rich cupcakes in a thrift-shopish Boho hangout.

✈ John F. Kennedy International (15 miles/24km); Newark Liberty International (16 miles/27km); LaGuardia (8 miles/13km).

🛏 $$$ **Carlton Hotel on Madison Avenue,** 88 Madison Ave. (© **212/532-4100;** www.carltonhotelny.com). $$ **Washington Square Hotel,** 103 Waverly Place (© **800/222-0418** or 212/777-9515; www.washingtonsquarehotel.com).

The Baker's Best **479**

Apple Pie Bakery Café

Yesterday's Desserts from Tomorrow's Top Chefs

Hyde Park, New York

For most of us, this is the closest we'll ever get to studying at the Culinary Institute of America, alma mater of such notable American chefs as Todd English, Charlie Palmer, Larry Forgione, Alfred Portale, John Besh, and Anthony Bourdain (it's no coincidence that most of the winners of TV reality shows like *Top Chef, Iron Chef,* and *Hell's Kitchen* have CIA degrees). But even if you don't harbor a secret fantasy to don a toque and sauté with the pros, this lovely little cafe in the Hudson Valley just north of Poughkeepsie is a delicious primer on the Great American Dessert.

The CIA's New York campus operates four other public restaurants at its upstate New York campus—the St. Andrew's Café (Hudson Valley locavore specialties), Ristorante Caterina de' Medici (upscale Italian), the Escoffier Restaurant (classic French), and American Bounty Restaurant (new American)—but the Apple Pie Bakery Café is the most casual, and the only one you don't need advance reservations for. It's set in the imposing Georgian red-brick Roth Hall—the central building on campus, a former Jesuit seminary overlooking the Hudson River. Inside the cafe is all brick walls, rustic tiles, country murals, and tall wood-trimmed windows. The full lunch menu includes sandwiches, soups, salads, and pizzas; CIA baking students provide the whole spectrum of breads, from ciabattas and foccacia to hoagie rolls. They also serve breakfast, with a creative assortment of croissants, muffins, brioches, scones, and filled pastries.

But the real draw is the handiwork of CIA patissiers-in-training, honing their baking skills on down-home items such as strawberry shortcake, lemon meringue pie, devil's food cupcakes, banana cream tart, and New York–style cheesecake (though, oddly enough, no apple pie). Of course, they also turn out more exotic items like vanilla panna cotta, chocolate *pots de crème,* tiramisu, a praline and caramel gâteau, and a flourless chocolate mousse cake, but those are American too in their way. Don't expect like-Mom-made simplicity—these are culinary school students, after all, and they're here to learn the shades of distinction between their crèmes frâiches and their crèmes anglaises. They're just not being turned loose yet on whimsical towers and confectionary flights of fancy. Not until they've mastered the basics.

ⓘ **Culinary Institute of America,** 1946 Campus Dr. (Rte. 9), Hyde Park (✆ **845/471-6608;** www.ciachef.edu).

✈ John F. Kennedy International / Newark Liberty International / LaGuardia (approx. 2 hr.). Albany Airport (approx. 2 hr.).

🛏 $$$ **Inn at the Falls,** 50 Red Oaks Mill Rd., Poughkeepsie (✆ **800/344-1466** or 845/462-5770; www.innatthefalls.com).

---

480 The Baker's Best

Cannolis on the Inner Harbor
The Other Little Italy
Baltimore, Maryland

Baltimore's Little Italy may not be as famous as the one up the coast in New York, but if you judge your Little Italys according to where you can get great biscotti and cannolis there—well, Baltimore stacks up with the best.

During the great early-20th-century wave of Italian immigration, Baltimore was a major intake port, and lots of immigrating Italians never got further than this waterfront neighborhood of narrow streets and brick storefronts. And unlike New York's Little Italy, Baltimore's has remained mostly Italian American. The 1980s revitalization of the nearby Inner Harbor and the gentrification of neighboring Fells Point was a windfall for Little Italy's flock of restaurants and trattorias, which line High Street and Eastern Avenue (try **Della Notte** at 801 Eastern Ave., ✆ **410/837-5500;** or **Sabatino's** at the corner of High and Fawn Street, ✆ **410/727-9414**). It's an easy water taxi ride from Federal Hill, or you can walk from the Inner Harbor across the Pratt Street and Lombard Street canal bridges.

The city's signature Italian bakery is **Vaccaro's Italian Pastry Shop,** founded in 1956 by Palermo-born Gioacchino Vaccaro and still run by the Vaccaro family. Much in demand, their specialties are the traditional Sicilian favorites—rum cake, casatta (layered sponge cake filled with cannoli cream), and, of course, cannoli itself, which you can buy either filled or unfilled, with a container of rich smooth cannoli cream so you can stuff the crispy deep-fried sweet shells yourself. The gelato and granita (Italian shaved ice) are huge draws in summer. If you just want to pick up a pastry or a box of superb Italian cookies, you can do so from Vaccaro's stands at Harborplace, at Market House in Annapolis, and at Union Station down in Washington, D.C.; expansion doesn't seem to have affected the quality one bit. But the corner location on Albemarle Street, in the heart of Little Italy, is the one with a bustling sit-down cafe, where you can enjoy your rum cake or cannoli with a frothy cappuccino—that is, after you've waited in line to get a table.

After all these years, however, Vaccaro's is getting serious competition from **Piedigrotta Bakery,** which opened in 2002 4 blocks east on Central Avenue. It's run by Carminantonio Iannaccone, a Neapolitan native who claims to having invented tiramisu in Treviso in 1969. Whether or not that's true—the origins of tiramisu are hotly debated—Iannaccone certainly turns out admirably flaky *sfogliatelle,* fluffy cream-filled *profiteroles,* and sleek éclairs, as well as fine cannoli and cookies, in this small, unassuming shop. There's no room for seats, but it's well worth a little walk to sample Iannaccone's masterful pastries. And with *two* great Italian bakeries, Baltimore's Little Italy really scores.

ⓘ **Vaccaro's,** 222 Albemarle St. (✆ **410/685-4905;** www.vaccaropastry.com). **Piedigrotta Bakery,** 319 S. Central Ave. (✆ **410/522-6900;** www.piedigrotta bakery.com).

✈ Baltimore-Washington International (10 miles/16km).

🛏 $$$ **Baltimore Marriott Waterfront Hotel,** 700 Aliceanna St., Inner Harbor East (✆ **410/385-3000;** www.baltimore marriottwaterfront.com). $$ **Brookshire Suites,** 120 E. Lombard St. (✆ **866/583-4162** or 410/625-1300; www.harbormagic. com).

The Baker's Best 481

Lucy's Sweet Surrender

When You're Hungry for Hungary

Cleveland, Ohio

Forty years ago, Cleveland had more Hungarian residents than Budapest—and those transplanted Hungarians *needed* their strudel. Lucy's Sweet Surrender came to the rescue, with feather-light strudels from a gingerbread-trimmed shop on Buckeye Road, in the thick of what was then the Hungarian immigrants' neighborhood in southeast Cleveland.

Times have changed. Lucy herself has passed on, and the Buckeye Road area is a victim of urban blight; Clevelanders are more likely to buy their pastries at a Starbucks or the bakery counter of some mega-supermarket over in upscale Shaker Heights to the east. But at Lucy's—owned now by Michael Feigenbaum, who grew up eating Lucy's strudel—the strudel is still being hand-pulled daily on wooden tables in the back kitchen, layers of flaky golden pastry dough folded around delectable fillings—apple, cherry, cheese, apricot cheese, peach apricot, even Eastern European variations like poppy seed and cabbage strudel that are nearly impossible to find anywhere else. Of course everything's baked from scratch, even though two bakers can only turn out 72 traditionally handmade strudels a day—hardly enough when holidays roll around and Clevelanders suddenly get a hankering for long-forgotten childhood treats. (Lucy's does a big business in shipping strudel to transplanted Clevelanders, too.)

There's more than strudel here—the bakery has 150 items in its repertoire: cakes, pies, dense traditional cookies, nut rolls, poppy seed rolls, Danish breakfast pastries, cinnamon rolls, sour cream pastries, European-style tortes such as Dobos torte and Sacher torte, even the exotic chocolate-and-raspberry Hungarian confection called *zserbo*. Despite the slightly dingy look of the little shop, Lucy's desserts are served at top restaurants all around the city (including its sister restaurant Café Marika, at 5601 Waterloo Rd.). There are a couple tiny tables inside in case you want to eat in—but be forewarned, the bakery closes at 4pm every afternoon (except Sun, when it's closed).

Lucy's hand-baked methods and traditional recipes fit right into the area's locavore farm market scene, where Lucy's stall is a weekly fixture. It's the sort of independent artisanal concern that Slow Food's all about. Even more, it's a little slice of Midwestern history, wrapped up in tissue-thin layers of strudel dough.

ⓘ 2516 Buckeye Rd. (✆ **216/752-0828;** www.lucyssweetsurrender.com).

✈ Cleveland International (24 miles/ 15km).

🛏 $$ **Radisson Hotel Cleveland Gateway,** 651 Huron Rd. (✆ **800/333-3333** or 216/377-9000; www.radisson.com). $$ **Glidden House,** 1901 Ford Dr. (✆ **800/759-8358** or 216/231-8900; www.gliddenhouse.com).

482 The Baker's Best

Boule Patisserie

Macaron Madness

Los Angeles, California

In body-conscious L.A., a bakery's got to offer something really special to inspire a caloric splurge. Boule Patisserie seems to have hit upon a winning formula: cutting-edge pastries with exotic flavorings that look like cunning little works of art, and *still* deliver quite a sugar rush. If they're a little pricey, all the better—that just adds to its luxury status.

The name is French, and Boule's severe pale-blue-walled decor has a certain Francophile chic, but these are anything but traditional French pastries—things like a devilishly rich chocolate torte enrobed in a thin shell of satiny chocolate, a pillow-soft cheesecake made with Cowgirl Creamery fromage blanc, or clingingly moist brown spice cake. There's a full line of tiny hand-dipped chocolates infused with all sorts of global flavors like Asian limes, habañero pepper, Lapsang souchong tea, or South American tonka beans. The glacerie section offers a rotating selection of delicate sorbets and creamy, high-fat ice creams with vivid flavors.

But the item that Boule's repeat customers seem hooked on is the European-style *macarons*—lighter-than-air almond cookies sandwiched around various flavored cream fillings, then colored in intense shades to match. (They're an entirely different thing from American double-o macaroons.) The interplay of texture and taste can be like a symphony when it works right, combining the faint snap of the crust, a slightly chewy interior, and a melt-on-your-tongue rush of sweetness. The wide choice of flavors in the glass case is a little overwhelming, a constantly changing palette of tastes like raspberry, rosewater, Venezuelan chocolate, coconut, Meyer lemon, passion fruit, apple cinnamon, lavender, or mocha. (Inevitably, as soon as you discover one you love, it won't be available the next time you visit the store.)

Boule is the elegant brainchild of award-winning pastry chef Michelle Meyers, a cofounder of Sona and Comme Ça restaurants, and it's got both its detractors and

Chocolates from Boule Patisserie in Los Angeles.

its partisans. As a pastry innovator who's very much on the foodie radar, Meyers constantly pushes the limits; not every one of her controversial taste combinations works. No matter. You've got to try Boule when you're in Los Angeles, if only so you can drop its name at the next cocktail party you go to.

ⓘ 420 N. La Cienega Blvd. (✆ **310/289-9977;** www.boulela.com). Also at 413 Bedford Rd., in Beverly Hills (✆ **310/273-4488**).

✈ Los Angeles International (12 miles/19km).

⊨ $$$ **Peninsula Beverly Hills,** 9882 S. Santa Monica Blvd. (✆ **800/462-7899** or 310/551-2888; www.peninsula.com). $ **Best Western Marina Pacific Hotel,** 1697 Pacific Ave., Venice (✆ **800/786-7789** or 310/452-1111; www.mphotel.com).

The Baker's Best **483**

Macrina Bakery
How the Cookie Crumbles
Seattle, Washington

All too often, retail bakeries overlook the humble cookie, that mainstay of American home baking. Not so the Macrina Bakery in Seattle's Belltown neighborhood.

Owner Leslie Mackie isn't just an acclaimed artisanal bread baker—though she is that. She's a passionate believer in the importance of food in creating community. Macrina's breads and baked goods whenever possible incorporate ingredients from the local region (organic and natural, it goes without saying), but they also hark back to old-world rustic traditions—the original comfort foods.

Since she opened the cafe in 1993, homey items like muffins, scones, buttermilk biscuits, and coffee cakes have been prominent on the menu. Longtime customers, though, find themselves coming

back for the cookies—hearty, quintessentially American cookies like ginger molasses, snickerdoodles, peanut butter, chocolate chip, and brown sugar shortbread cookies. If you want to get fancy, there's a chocolate oat peanut butter chip cookie, and a chocolate apricot espresso cookie. Brownies, fruit and oat bars, macaroons (the chewy coconut kind), and austere Scottish oatcakes—those are the sort of unfussy sweets that Macrina serves. In this age of mass-produced cookies loaded with transfats and preservatives, the simple pleasure of an old-fashioned, homey cookie made with the purest ingredients cannot be underestimated.

As more and more Seattlites became Macrina regulars, the Belltown location eventually expanded into more than a bakery, serving a limited menu of salads, sandwiches, and small pizzas. Smaller locations in the Queen Anne neighborhood (615 W. McGraw St.; © **206/283-5900**) and on Vashon Island (19603 Vashon Hwy. SW; © **206/567-4133**) were added as well. Now that Mackie has published a *Macrina* cookbook, and her rustic breads are available at specialty stores all over town, the place no longer feels like a neighborhood secret. Be prepared to wait up to an hour for a table at the Belltown spot; service can be slipshod.

For cookie fans, though, that's all beside the point. They sidle up to the antique pastry case near the counter, intent on today's thick, moist, chewy treat. Now just add a loaf of that divine fresh bread to your bag and you're good to go.

ⓘ 2408 First Ave. (© **206/448-4032**; www.macrinabakery.com).

✈ Seattle-Tacoma International (14 miles/23km).

🛏 $$$ **Inn at the Market,** 86 Pine St. (© **800/446-4484** or 206/443-3600; www.innatthemarket.com). $$ **Bacon Mansion Bed & Breakfast,** 959 Broadway E (© **800/240-1864** or 206/329-1864; www.baconmansion.com).

Baked goods from Macrina in Seattle.

---

484 The Baker's Best

Golden Gate Fortune Cookies Co.
A Dessert You Can Read
San Francisco, California

Touristy it may be, but this tiny factory tucked away in a Chinatown alley offers a glimpse into an intriguing byway of American food history: the fortune cookie.

Hard as it may be for most Americans to believe, fortune cookies are not the traditional end to a Chinese meal in China, but a marketing stratagem by early-20th-century Chinese immigrants to entice dessert-loving Americans into their restaurants.

(The Chinese themselves more often finish a meal with fruit.) What they came up with wasn't even Chinese, but a novelty cookie first made in Japan: a crisp sugary wafer folded into a crescent with koanlike sayings on tiny slips of paper baked inside. Transplanted to the United States, the fortune cookie industry grew, though it remained dominated by Japanese family businesses. Immigrant Japanese women

Places to Eat in . . . Brussels, Belgium

With more Michelin-star restaurants per capita than any other city in the world—yes, even more than Paris—Brussels doesn't have to take a back seat to anyplace else when it comes to food. The Bruxellois are passionate about eating, whether they're patronizing the gastronomic palaces around the Grand-Place, the ethnic eateries along narrow cobblestoned rue de Bouchers, or the humblest corner stand. Don't expect dazzling trendsetters—Brussels is a deeply traditional culinary town—but with traditions this flavorful, it can afford to be.

Eating well in Brussels doesn't have to mean booking a table at a hot restaurant-of-the-moment. It can also mean indulging in two of the most delectable street foods anywhere. Thick, square Belgian waffles, loaded with powdered sugar, are offered at waffle stands all over town; locals swear by the slightly sweeter Liege variety sold by the 485 Belgaufra chain, with several city branches. Then there are Belgian *frites*, perhaps the world's best french fries, twice-fried for an intensely crunchy crust; the city is peppered with stands selling *frites* in paper cones, typically topped with mayonnaise (though many other sauces are offered as an extra). Generally you can carry your fries into nearby bars to accompany your drinks—look for signs saying *frites acceptés*. Every local has his or her favorite, but one standout is 486 Maison Antoine, on Place Jourdanplein close to the European Parliament.

Brussels's other great local dish is steamed mussels (mussels from Brussels—it even rhymes!), served in huge bowls, typically in a white-wine-and-garlic broth. Huge, jam-packed 487 Chez Léon (rue des Bouchers 18; © **32/ 2/511-14-15;** www.chezleon.be) has been the city's top spot for mussels since 1893. Though it has spun off several branches, this noisy hall on rue de Bouchers, with its checkered paper tablecloths and open kitchen, still

Comme chez Soi is a time capsule of Art Nouveau design and classic French cooking.

serves the most flavorful mussels—fried, baked au gratin, steamed, even raw in season—not to mention wonderfully crispy frites. Its closest rival is convivial wood-paneled 488 Au Vieux Bruxelles (Rue St-Boniface 35; © 32/2/503-31-11; www.auvieuxbruxelles.com), dating from 1882, which presents a few more daring ways to serve mussels—with curry sauce, for example, or with blue cheese. Both also serve a range of other traditional Belgian dishes, such as *waterzooi* (a rustic stew) or eels in green sauce.

Every visitor to Brussels should splurge on at least one evening at one of the city's top fine-dining spots. The one reservation you should make well ahead of your arrival is for dinner at 489 Comme chez Soi (Place Rouppe 23; © 32/2/512-29-21; www.commechezsoi.be). It's not only a showpiece of Art Nouveau design (one of Brussels's architectural specialties), it also boasts one of Europe's most accomplished classic French kitchens. The menu changes often, but grilled guinea fowl with rosemary, lobster medallions with risotto, or cardamom-crusted rabbit with sweetbreads sausage are among the kind of inspired main courses to expect. Ask for a table in the kitchen, where you can watch master chef Pierre Wynants at work. Another classic French winner, 490 Le Maison du Cygne (Grand-Place 9; © 32/2/511-82-44; www.lamaisonducygne.be), has an unbeatable location right on the Grand-Place, a postcard-perfect assemblage of gabled 16th-century guildhalls, Brussels's most famous architectural view. With its polished walnut walls, bronze wall sconces, and green velvet, Le Maison de Cygne has haute cuisine written all over it, and it more than lives up to the image, with superbly executed classics like roast pheasant, beef tournedos with duck liver, oysters in champagne, and salt-crusted sea bream.

While you're in the Grand-Place area, however, don't overlook the cozy brick-arched cellar restaurant 491 't Kelderke (Grand-Place 15; © 32/2/513-73-44). For hearty, distinctly Belgian cuisine—*bloedpens* (blood sausage), *stoemp* (mashed potato and vegetable) with *boudin* (sausage), *lapin à la gueuze* (rabbit in Brussels beer), or robust *carbonnades à la flamande* (Flemish beef stew)—it can't be beat; you'll see as many Bruxellois as tourists thronging its long wooden tables.

✈ Brussels (14km/9 miles)

🛏 $$$ **Le Dixseptième,** rue de la Madeleine/Magdalenastraat 25 (© 32/2/502-57-44; www.ledixseptieme.be). $$ **Mozart,** rue du Marché-aux-Fromages 23 (© 32/2/502-66-61; www.hotel-mozart.be).

provided cheap labor for the painstaking job of swiftly hand-folding the cookies before they hardened in the cool air. (Read Jennifer 8. Lee's fascinating book *The Fortune-Cookie Chronicles* for the full history of this phenomenon.)

The factory can be hard to locate, because street numbers aren't always posted in Chinatown, but follow the scent of baking cookies and you'll find your way to this narrow, crowded little operation. In business since 1962, the Golden Gate Fortune Cookies Co. is no longer a major fortune cookie producer—it has been superseded by other companies with bigger, more automated plants that can manufacture cookies at a much greater volume. On this older machinery, however, you have a clearer view of the thin brown wafer coming off the hot cast-iron discs of the cookie press; the dexterity of the women tucking in the fortunes and folding the cookies is impressive indeed.

While there's no admission charge, there's a tacit assumption that you'll buy some cookies in return. You can purchase them in small bags or in bulk; you can even bring your own messages and watch them inserted into fresh cookies before your eyes. The cookies come in many more flavors that you'd expect—strawberry, almond, sesame, chocolate—and they taste marvelous when they're still warm and fresh. (You'll suddenly realize how stale the cookies are that you get at most Chinese restaurants.) The tour doesn't take more than a few minutes, and the factory is so small, there's no room to linger. But you'll never eat a fortune cookie again without remembering this atmospheric little workshop.

ⓘ 56 Ross Alley, between Washington and Jackson sts. (✆ **415/781-3956**).

✈ San Francisco International (14 miles/ 23km).

🛏 $$$ **Hotel Adagio,** 550 Geary St. (✆ **800/228-8830** or 415/775-5000; www. thehoteladagion.com). $ **Hotel des Arts,** 447 Bush St. (✆ **800/956-4322** or 415/956-3232; www.sfhoteldesarts.com).

Ice Creameries 492

French Vanilla & Beyond

Berthillon

Paris, France

The ice-cream machine was an afterthought when Raymond Berthillon opened a cafe in 1954 in his small hotel on the aristocratic Ile St-Louis. But when packs of local schoolchildren were seen lining up for their ice-cream cones every afternoon, soon the adults in the neighborhood began to pay attention. They discovered that the *glacés* Berthillon was whipping up—made with fresh eggs, whole milk, pure sugar, and carefully sourced flavorings—were more than just a kids' treat. Eventually, Berthillon surrendered to his destiny; he dropped the hotel business and concentrated on ice cream, branching out only by adding a line of fruit sorbets a few years later.

Fast forward half a century, and Raymond's descendants are still selling rich, creamy *glacés* at the original wood-paneled shop on this island in the Seine, just east of Notre-Dame's Ile de la Cité. A few years ago, they added a cafe next door where they serve fresh baked pastries, juice, coffee, and tea—only Mariage Fréres tea, *naturellement*. All the ice cream is still made right on premises, with milk and cream delivered fresh each morning. Although the actual flavors depend on which ingredients the ice-cream makers have been able to obtain that day, the long list of possibilities includes several variations on chocolate and caramel, as well as pistachio, hazelnut, pignoli, orange, mint, banana, melon, blood orange, mocha, cappuccino, even ice creams flavored with Grand Marnier or whiskey. Besides a dizzying number of fruit sorbets (including pink grapefruit, rhubarb, apricot, litchee) they also make some liqueur-based flavors like cassis and cocktail exotique.

Exotic as some of these flavors are—just try to imagine what praline with lemon and coriander tastes like!—even basic flavors like chocolate and vanilla are transformed when they're made with cacao butter just flown in from the Ivory Coast or vanilla pods from Madagascar. And, in the words of Raymond Berthillon, you can always tell a good ice-cream maker by the quality of his vanilla ice-cream. The proof is in the line running out the door, especially in hot weather: Berthillon's ice cream is worth waiting for.

ⓘ Rue St-Louis 29 (✆ **33/1/43 54 31 61;** www.berthillon.fr).

✈ De Gaulle (23km/14 miles); Orly (14km/ 8⅔ miles).

🛏 $$ **La Tour Notre Dame,** 20 rue du Sommerard, 5e (✆ **33/1/43-54-47-60;** www.la-tour-notre-dame.com). $ **Hotel de la Place des Vosges**, 12 rue de Birague, 4e (✆ **33/1/42-72-60-46;** www.hotelplacedes vosges.com).

---

493 Ice Creameries

Vivoli Gelato
The World Capital of Gelato
Florence, Italy

Gelato fanciers are wont to speak of Florence in hushed terms as the world capital of Gelato. Since the 16th century, when it was a favorite dessert of the ruling Medici dynasty, this fabled Renaissance city has been known for its superb gelato, made with a milk-and-egg-yolk base that renders it dense and creamy. Both the quantity and the quality of the *gelateria* in Florence today are unmatched, and every self-styled connoisseur has his or her own secret favorite. But in the end, almost everyone acknowledges one spot as Florence's foremost gelateria: Vivoli.

Founded in 1930, Vivoli still has only one shop, and an unassuming one at that, a flat stuccoed storefront with small windows and a barely noticeable orange neon sign. The store's traditional recipes, however, produce an exceptionally rich gelato, with a silky texture that feels magical on

Gelato from Vivoli in Florence.

the tongue. The chocolate gelatos are especially intense; they also serve a few whipped mousse flavors that are supremely light. Tiny chunks of real fruit or caramel may be mixed into the gelato to kick up the flavor as well. Vivoli only serves whatever gelati they've made fresh that day, so the flavor you're craving may not be available, but all the more reason to try one of their more adventurous flavors, like pear with caramel or blackcurrant mousse. Also following tradition, Vivoli serves its gelato only in cups—there isn't a cone on the premises.

Vivoli is often overrun with tourists—with that central location near Santa Croce, it's all too handy for sightseers—and with that lock on the tourist trade, they've been able to get away with higher-than-average prices and the smaller-than-usual portion sizes. In summer especially, scornful locals may retreat to **Perchè No!** (Via dei Tavolini 19/r; ✆ **39/55/ 2398969**) or **Gelateria dei Neri** (via dei Neri 20-22; ✆ **39/55/210 034**), two other excellent *gelateria* in the center of town. (How easy to be a gelato snob if you're lucky enough to live in Florence!) The solution for any right-thinking visitor, of course, is to be impartial and try them all—two or three times if possible.

ⓘ 7 via Isole delle Stinche (✆ **39/55/ 292334;** www.vivoli.it).

🛏 $$$ **Hotel Monna Lisa,** Borgo Pinti 27 (✆ **39/55/247-9751;** www.monnalisa. it). $ **Hotel Abaco,** Via dei Banchi 1 (✆ **39/ 55-238-1919;** www.abaco-hotel.it).

Ice Creameries 494

Il Gelato di San Crispino
The Art & Science of Gelato
Rome, Italy

For over a century, Rome's oldest gelateria, glossy **Giolitti** (40 via Uffici del Vicario; ✆ **39/6/6991243,** near the Piazza Navona), ruled Rome's gelato scene with an encyclopedia of inventive flavors and over-the-top sundaes served in its adjoining cafe. But that was before the Alongi brothers set up shop on the suburban Via Acacia in 1993. Inspired by the gelati they had eaten while students in Florence—especially the gelato at Vivoli (see above)—Giuseppe and Pasquale Alongi, with Giuseppe's wife Paola, decided it was time to reinvent gelato.

The Alongi brothers aren't just ice-cream artisans, they're ice-cream scientists. They're zealous not only about the purity and freshness of their ingredients but about controlling the temperature at which it is made and stored. (Because they don't use chemical preservatives or emulsifiers, freezing temperatures are essential to prevent spoilage and preserve a uniformly smooth texture.) They have developed a distinct recipe—or perhaps it should be called a formula—for each gelato flavor, with precise proportions calibrated to ensure that the texture, aroma, and balance of flavors are just right. They refuse to add dyes to color their gelato—don't expect to see the usual rainbow effect in their glass cases. And like Vivoli, they serve it in cups, not cones, on the theory that the taste of the cone alters the gelato's flavor.

San Crispino's best-known flavors include zabaglione, made with organic eggs and aged Marsala wine; the "house" flavor San Crispino, delicately made with high-grade honey; and the ever-popular hazelnut and pistachio, made with nuts freshly ground by hand. And while the summertime brings a host of heavenly fruit flavors—exotic things like pomegranate and pink grapefruit, and a simply divine pear gelato—they refuse to make them out of season when the local fruit's not ripe.

Encouraged by the raging success of the Via Acacia shop (at one point the city had to detail policemen to manage the lines outside), the Alongis opened more branches around Rome, most notably one on via della Panetteria, where tourist foot traffic from the nearby Trevi Fountain ensures a steady stream of business. They claim, however, that they will never open a branch outside of Italy, lest different local products alter their formulas or long-distance shipping admits breaches in their strict temperature regulation. With marketing flair, they have furnished the shops with a streamlined modern look that looks more like a laboratory than a gelato parlor—the servers even wear white coats.

ⓘ Via Della Panetteria (✆ **39/6/679 39 24**); Via Acaia 56 (✆ **39/6/704 504 12**); also at Via Collatina, Piazza della Maddalena; and Fiumincino airport; www.ilgelato disancrispino.it.

✈ Leonardo da Vinci International Airport (Fiumicino; 30km/19 miles).

🛏 **$$$ Hotel de Russie,** Via del Babuino 9 (✆ **800/323-7500** in North America, or 39/6/328881; www.rocco fortehotels.com). $ **Hotel Grifo,** Via del Boschetto 144 (✆ **39/6/4871395;** www. hotelgrifo.com).

---

495 Ice Creameries

La Sorbetteria Castiglione

Frozen in Time

Bologna, Italy

The third in Italy's trio of destination gelato shops is in some ways the most evocative. It's set on the southeast fringe of Bologna's historic center, a stunning panorama of sienna-colored buildings, marbled sidewalks, and arched porticos; walking here on a soft summer evening for your nightly gelato fix, you almost feel as if you're in a Merchant-Ivory movie. The deliberately old-fashioned tin street sign above **La Sorbetteria Castiglione** makes it look as if it's been here a lot longer than since 1994.

Inside the gleaming shop, you'll notice that the servers are scooping the gelato from unmarked stainless-steel containers—a good sign that the gelato is made on premises, rather than shipped in from some industrial plant in plastic tubs. You'll also notice the chunks of chocolate, fresh fruit, candied nuts, even caramelized fig mixed into the creamy egg-based gelato. And looking up at the menu posted above the counter, you'll see signature flavors charmingly named after owners Giacomo and Marina Schiavon's children (like crema Michelangelo, praline almond; crema Edoardo, mascarpone with caramelized pine nuts; or dolce Karin, white chocolate and hazelnut crunch); the menu itself is printed over black-and-white photos of the kids.

La Sorbettaria Castiglione is the sort of artisanal gelato maker you'd expect in Italy's gastronomic capital. The Schiavons also run a confectionery shop down the street (**Il Coccolato,** Via Castiglione 44/B) that sells some wonderful handmade chocolates, presumably the same chocolate that studs the sumptuously rich *straciatelle* gelato, and that turns the dark chocolate gelato into a revelatory experience. Like most Bologna gelati, La Sorbettaria's is not overly sweet, allowing the various flavors to shine through; the Schiavons don't offer as many flavors as some of their rivals do, but that allows them to focus on the flavors they do best. The fact that La Sorbetteria Castiglione is often cited as Italy's best gelato (which probably makes it the world's best gelato as well) is quite a testament to the Schiavons' passion for fresh ingredients and scrupulous hand-mixing.

Just being considered the best gelato maker in Bologna would be enough of a coup. Bologna's other top contenders are outstanding as well: **Gianni's** (via Monte Grappa 11/A, 🕓 **39/51/233 008;** via S. Stefano 14/A, 🕓 **39/51/238 949**), known for its creatively named, far-out flavors; **Stefino** (via Galliera 49/b; 🕓 **39/51/246 736**), admired for its dense chocolate gelatos; and **Gelatauro** (Via San Vitale 98; 🕓 **39/51/230 049**), which gets a special nod for using only organic produce and exotic ingredients like jasmine, bergamot, pumpkin, fennel seeds, and cinnamon. You owe it to yourself to stay in Bologna long enough to try all four.

ⓘ La Sorbetteria Castiglione, via Castiglione 44 (🕓 **39/51/233 257;** www.lasorbetteria.it).

✈ Marconi International (6km/3¾ miles).

🛏 $$$ **Grand Hotel Baglioni,** Via dell'Indipendenza 8 (🕓 **39/51/225445;** www.baglionihotels.com). $ **Albergo Della Drapperie,** Via della Drapperie 5 (🕓 **39/51/223955;** www.albergodrapperie.com).

Ice Creameries 496

Heladería Coromoto

One for the Record Books

Mérida, Venezuela

When Portuguese immigrant Manuel Da Silva Oliveira opened his ice cream shop in this picturesque colonial city in 1981, at first there was no indication that the single-story orange stucco building would become one of Mérida's chief tourist draws. Most visitors to this western Venezuelan college town were outdoorsy types, come here to ride the world's highest and longest cable car system, a breathtaking trip over cloud forest to the summit of Pico Espejo, 4,765m (15,629 ft.) high. Who knew from ice cream?

Oliveira, a construction worker and former chef, started out with just four standard flavors of decent but unremarkable ice cream. But in his spare time, Oliveira began to experiment with other flavors, starting with avocado. It was an immediate hit, and as time passed, he got bolder and bolder. Eventually Heladería Coromoto wound up in the Guinness Book of World Records, with a roster of around 900 flavor titles on slips of paper tacked up like a crazy quilt across two shop walls. (Another wall is covered with newspaper clippings and postcards from satisfied customers.) A rotation of around 75 flavors are available each day at the long glass counter; despite efficient service, lines can move slowly, as each customer struggles to choose just one or two.

Some of Coromoto's flavors, while unusual, make sweet sense, like the Coca-Cola flavored ice cream, or the pumpkin, champagne, black bean, ginger, or orange blossom varieties. But then there are outrageous flavors like garlic, smoked trout, tuna, crab, sardine, avocado, onion, squid, chili, hamburger, asparagus, or fried pork rind. Most customers sample those just for the novelty factor, then are pleasantly surprised to discover that they actually taste good. Part of Oliveira's secret is that he mixes actual bits of the foods into his ice-cream bases, rather than rely on chemical flavorings. (Well, except for the Viagra-flavored ice cream—that only contains traditional aphrodisiacs like honey and pollen, though there may be a placebo effect in the name alone.) Since you've come all this way, be aware that Coromoto's is closed on Mondays and doesn't open until 2pm.

(i) Av. 3, #28–75 (🕿 **274/252-3525**); also on Calle 29 in front of the Plaza el Llano.

✈ Mérida (25km/15 miles).

🛏 $$ **Hotel & Spa La Sevillana,** Sector Pedregosa Alta (🕿 **274/266-3227;** www.andes.net/lasevillana). $ **Posada Casa Sol,** Avenida 4 (🕿 **274/252-4164;** www.posadacasasol.com).

497 Ice Creameries

Four Seas Ice Cream

American Classic

Centerville, Massachusetts

Maybe it has something to do with how short a New England summer can be—Atlantic waters are bone-chilling cold until the end of June, and by mid-August, nights are already getting nippy again. That's why New Englanders tend to be passionate about only-in-summer pleasures like clambakes, minigolf, blueberry pies, and ice cream—especially ice cream. Why not, when you can get the ice cream from an old-fashioned roadside shack like Four Seas?

Open only mid-May through early September, Four Seas has been around since 1934, though the low-slung building it occupies—a former blacksmith shop—is even older. Cruising through Centerville on the main road from nearby Hyannis, you can't miss its vintage blue-and-white neon sign—it's a stone's-throw east of the only traffic light in town, with a mere yard of lumpy blacktop between the road and its aluminum-shuttered front. All of the ice cream is handmade on premises, and served by earnest, clean-cut local high schoolers (it's one of the most sought-after summer jobs on the Cape). There are generally a couple of dozen flavors available every day, including a few frozen yogurts and sherbets, but the ice cream here is such satisfyingly creamy full-fat stuff, regulars tend to forgo their diets for it, night after night. The lineup is mostly classic flavors like peach, banana, maple walnut, black raspberry, coconut, butter crunch, and peppermint stick—some of them so dependent on freshness and quality ingredients that they've become hard to find elsewhere.

There are a few cramped wooden booths inside, but Four Seas is generally so packed every summer evening, it's all you can do to squeeze through the swinging screen door, order your cone at the well-worn formica counter, and get out. Besides, hanging out in the rambling weed-edged gravel parking lot is an essential part of the whole experience. Summer neighbors share blow-by-blow accounts of the day's sail or round of golf, while sunburned children still in sandy bathing suits swing their bare feet from station wagon tailgates and lick trails of dribbled ice cream off their wrists. From time to time a golden retriever barks hoarsely; if you listen really close, you can hear the harsh caw of seagulls, or the clang of a buoy off nearby Craigville Beach—all the sounds of a perfect New England beach summer.

(i) 360 S. Main St. (🕿 **508/775-1394;** www.fourseasicecream.com).

✈ Hyannis (2 miles/3km).

🛏 $$$ **Centerville Corners Inn,** 1338 Craigville Beach Rd., Centerville (🕿 **800/ 242-1137** or 508/775-7223; www.centervillecorners.com). $$ **SeaCoast Inn,** 33 Ocean St., Hyannis (🕿 **800/466-4100** or 508/775-3828; www.seacoastcapecod.com).

Doumar's Barbecue

Cone Sweet Cone

Norfolk, Virginia

Let the Italian gelato shops get snooty about serving their creamy confections in cones; the classic way to enjoy American ice cream is by heaping it on top of a waffle cone. And we have a Syrian immigrant named Abe Doumar to thank for inventing that cone. Legend has it that street vendor Doumar invented the cone in a flash of inspiration, shrewdly rolling up a neighboring vendor's crisp waffle as an ad hoc way to sell ice cream without serving bowls at the 1904 St. Louis World's Fair.

Soon after his World's Fair triumph, Doumar opened an ice-cream cone stand in Norfolk's Ocean View amusement park. His brother George moved the business to this site in 1934, expanding it into a new kind of restaurant entirely—a drive-in restaurant, to capitalize on America's nascent car culture. George's son Albert, who ran the place for

years, still shows up most mornings to bake cones on the original waffle machines, though a younger generation of Doumars is in charge these days.

With its carhops and curb service, Doumar's Barbecue has a great sort of nostalgic *American Graffiti* ambience, and the burgers and pulled-pork sandwiches are local favorites. But as its historic roadside sign proclaims—the name Doumar's flanked by two giant neon ice-cream cones—ice cream is still Doumar's calling card. Inside, the look is classic soda shop, with black-and-white checkerboard floors, red leatherette booths with formica-topped tables, and cherry-red steel stripes running the length of the long counter. Doumar's still serves a lot of ice cream in waffle cones; in good weather, they even take the cone-making machine out on the

Doumar's Barbecue features car hops, curb service, and cones made on premises.

front sidewalk so kids can watch it in action. The ice cream shoveled into those cones is a particularly creamy soft-serve, in just four flavors—chocolate, vanilla, strawberry, and pecan—and as different from your standard Dairy Queen as it could be. (It also makes a fantastically thick milkshake.)

ⓘ 1919 Monticello Ave. (ⓒ **757/627-4163;** www.doumars.com).

✈ Norfolk International Airport (5⅔ miles/9km).

🛏 $$$ **Page House Inn,** 323 Fairfax Ave. (ⓒ **800/599-7659** or 757/625-5033; www.pagehouseinn.com). $$ **Tazewell Hotel & Suites,** 245 Granby St. (ⓒ **757/623-6200;** www.thetazewell.com).

499 Ice Creameries

Beantown's Creamiest
The Inside Scoop
Boston, Massachusetts

Who knows why Boston is such a great place for ice cream? It's not in a dairy state, or even in a hot climate, and yet Bostonians are blessed with an extraordinary number of world-class ice creameries, places that dish out full-fat gourmet ice cream with loads of mix-ins and exotic gourmet flavors.

Let's start our tour where it all began: **Herrell's** (15 Dunster St., Harvard Square; ⓒ 617/497-2179), run by Steve Herrell, who in 1973 invented the idea of mixing crushed cookies and candy into the superpremium ice cream at his original Somerville store, Steve's Ice Cream (since sold). Quality ingredients and small-batch production keep Herrell's at the top of ice-cream lovers' global lists. Next came **Emack & Bolio's** (290 Newbury St., ⓒ **617/536-7127;** 255 State St., ⓒ 617/367-0220; 140 Brookline Ave., ⓒ 617/262-1569; 23 White St., Cambridge, ⓒ 617/492-1907; www.emackandbolios.com), founded in 1975 by a pair of pro bono lawyers who named their shop after two homeless men who were among their clients. Trading on their countercultural hipness, E&B wooed a late-night rock-'n'-roll customer base with inventive flavors like the original Oreo Cookie ice cream; it still has that hippieish vibe, with way-out flavors like Cosmic Crunch, Deep Purple Cow, and Trippin' on Espresso.

In 1981, along came sleek **Toscanini's** in Cambridge's Central Square (899 Main St.; ⓒ **617/491-5877**), an ice-cream-and-coffee cafe conveniently close to both the Harvard and MIT campuses; it's known for soft, creamy upscale ice cream in elegant flavors like burnt caramel and black pepper bourbon. Weekend brunches at Toscanini's are justly famous. Founded the same year out in the Jamaica Plain suburb, **JP Licks Ice Cream Café** has more of a whole-earth image, emphasizing ice cream made from scratch and fair trade organic coffees. Besides the original cafe (659 Centre St., Jamaica Plain; ⓒ **617/524-6740**), it has expanded to Boston (352 Newbury St., ⓒ 617/236-1666; and 1618 Tremont St., ⓒ 617/566-6676), Cambridge (1312 Massachusetts Ave.; ⓒ 617/492-1001), and other suburbs.

It only stands to reason that a city with so many college students would be a great market for ice-cream shops, which is why so many are in student-thronged Cambridge. Besides the ones listed above, the luscious ice creams and crisp sorbets at **Christina's** (1255 Cambridge St., Inman Sq.; ⓒ 617/492-7021) push the envelope with exotic flavors such as lemon grass, cardamom, or chocolate Chinese five spices. Another up-and-coming entrant is

Lizzy's (29 Church St., near Harvard Sq.; ☎ **617/354-2911**), a slender takeout shop that prides itself on its decadent sundaes.

✈ Boston Logan International (8¾ miles/ 14km).

🛏 $$ **Harborside Inn,** 185 State St., Boston (☎ **617/670-6015;** www.harbor sideinnboston.com). $$$ **The Charles Hotel,** 1 Bennett St., Cambridge (☎ **800/ 882-1818** or 617/864-1200; www.charles hotel.com).

Woodside Farm Creamery

The Pasture-to-Cone Connection

Hockessin, Delaware

The Mitchell family has worked Woodside Farm since 1796, and until 1961, it was always a dairy farm. For the next 35 years, the Mitchells kept on farming, even as the western Wilmington suburbs gradually encroached on their pastoral acreage. Then in 1995, rather than sell the family farm, the current generation of Mitchells launched a new dairy herd, but with a whole different approach—a farm-to-table ethic. They weren't going to just milk their cows and ship the milk off to some big industrial dairy; they were going to turn that milk into small batches of natural ice cream and sell it right on the farm.

Driving out to Woodside Farm is like having a model farm visit, an artisanal manufactory tour, and an ice-cream splurge all in one. As Jim Mitchell is fond of telling customers, "A week ago that ice cream you're eating was grass," and each stage of that weeklong process happens right here. As you sit licking your cone at the picnic table outside the gray clapboard ice-cream stand (a converted farm shed), you can gaze out over the level green pastures where a herd of about 30 brown Jersey cows placidly graze free on a lush mix of alfalfa, clover, rye grass, and orchard grass. Morning and evening, the cows are steered into the milking parlor to be milked (ask if you can see the milking machines); their high-butterfat milk is then sent to a local dairy to be pasteurized and homologized, then combined with sugar and eggs to make "sweet cream." In a small building next to the milking parlor, the sweet cream is manually combined with various flavor ingredients, then frozen in small batches in a stainless-steel mixing freezer.

Along with a wide range of more traditional flavors, Woodside's cheery scoopers dish out novelty flavors like peanut butter and jelly, Fluffernutter, chocolate thunder, turtle (caramel and pecan pieces in chocolate ice cream), dirt (crushed Oreos and gummy worms in chocolate ice cream—a big hit with kids), and motor oil (which they describe as "chocolate-flavored tractor engine crankcase deposits"—but it sure tastes like coffee ice cream with fudge swirls and green-tinted caramel goo). Speaking of fudge, Woodside Farm also sells a selection of wickedly dense handmade fudge. The ice cream stand is only open from early April through October—like good farmers, they respect the rhythms of the seasons.

ⓘ 1310 Little Baltimore Rd. (☎ **302-239-9847;** www.woodsidefarmcreamery.com).

✈ New Castle County Airport, Wilmington (10 miles/16km).

🛏 $$$ **Inn at Montchanin Village,** Rte. 100 and Kirk Rd., Montchanin, Delaware (☎ **800/COWBIRD** [800/269-2473] or 302/888-2133; www.montchanin.com). $ **Fairfield Inn Wilmington Newark**, 65 Geoffrey Dr., Newark, Delaware (☎ **800/ 228-2800** or 302/292-1500; www.marriott. com).

Calendar of Food Fairs & Festivals

Ice Wine Festival   Sun Peaks, British Columbia
In the alpine-style village of the Sun Peaks ski resort, this weeklong celebration of boutique winter wines from the Okanagan Valley includes wine masters' dinners, seminars, and a gala progressive tasting.
© **800/807-3257;** www.sunpeaksresort.com

Lowcountry Oyster Festival   Mount Pleasant, South Carolina
Held on a January Sunday, the world's largest oyster roast feeds 10,000 people with 65,000 pounds of oysters on the grounds of Boone Hall Plantation. Highlights include oyster-shucking and oyster-eating contests and an oyster recipe competition.
© **843/452-6088;** www.charlestonrestaurantassociation.com/oyster_festival.php

South Beach Food & Wine Festival   Miami, Florida
Sponsored by the Food Network and *Food & Wine* magazine, this 3-day extravaganza includes tastings, seminars, cooking demonstrations, dinners, and celebrity appearances at various Miami-area hotels and outdoor locations.
© **877/762-3933** ; www.sobefest.com

Mexican National Chili Cook-Off   Ajijic, Jalisco, Mexico
This 3-day outdoor event on the shores of Lake Chalapa raises money for local charities; festivities include food stalls, mariachi bands, dancing horses, contests for best green and red chili and salsas, and an international chili competition.
www.mexicanchilicookoff.com

Le Fête du Citron (Lemon Festival)   Menton, France
One of the Riviera's most colorful winter events, this 3-week-long carnival includes an exhibition, illuminated displays in the park, monumental civic sculptures made of lemons, and daytime and nighttime parades.
© **33/4/92-41-76-76** for information, or 33/4/92-41-76-95 for tickets; www.feteducitron. com

Food and Fun   Reykjavik, Iceland
During this 4-day event, 13 international guest chefs, each assigned to a different Reykjavik restaurant, compete to create the best menu from purely Icelandic ingredients.
www.foodandfun.is

National Maple Syrup Festival   Medora, Indiana
On 2 consecutive March weekends, Burton's Maplewood Farm in the southern Indiana hills features maple syrups from across the nation. The event includes all-day pancake-eating, frontier crafts demonstrations, live music, and syrup harvesting.
© **812/966-2168;** www.nationalmaplesyrupfestival.com

Melbourne Food and Wine Festival   Melbourne, Australia
More than 150 tastings, dinners, master classes, and seminars take place over the course of 2 weeks, at venues around the state of Victoria, including the World's Longest Lunch, with more than 1,000 seats set at one long table along the Yarra River.
© **61/3/9823-6100;** www.melbournefoodandwine.com.au

Cioccolato   Turin, Italy
Turin celebrates its role as the birthplace of solid chocolate with 10 tasty days of cook-offs, demonstrations, tastings, Slow Food workshops, readings, music concerts, and some 75 stalls from top chocolate makers set up in Piazza Vittorio Veneto.
© **39/11/818-5011;** www.cioccola-to.com

APRIL

Ponchatoula Strawberry Festival   Ponchatoula, Louisiana
Louisiana's second largest event after Mardi Gras, this weekend-long event features booths, baking contests, a talent show, a running race, live entertainment, and a huge parade featuring marching bands, floats, and the strawberry queen and her court.
© **800/917-7045** or 985/370-1889; www.lastrawberryfestival.org

World Grits Fest   St. George, South Carolina
Grits-grinding demonstrations, a grits-eating contest, grits rolling, and a grits dinner are highlights of this lighthearted weekend festival outside of Charlestown, first held in 1986; there's also a parade, a midway, a running race, folk dancing, and live music.
© **843/563-8187;** www.worldgritsfestival.com

National Grits Festival   Warwick, Georgia
Since 2002, this Georgia town on Lake Blackshear has hosted its own one-day extravaganza of grits eating, grits cooking, corn shelling, and a rolling in the instant grits contest; expect lots of food vendors, live entertainment, antique cars, and a Grits Queen.
© **229/881-6297;** www.gritsfest.com

Blue Ridge Food & Wine Festival   Blowing Rock, North Carolina
Four-day celebration includes both commercial and amateur wine competitions, vintners' dinners, seminars, cooking classes, the popular Fire on the Rock chefs' challenge, and a grand wine-tasting event at Chetola Resort.
© **877/295-7965** or 828/295-7851; www.blueridgewinefestival.com

Sugar Festival   Clewiston, Florida
On the shore of Lake Okeechobee, Clewiston honors its top crop, sugar cane, with a country fair that spans 2 weekends. Top events include a parade, sugar-grinding demonstration, antique car show, rodeo, fishing contest, and confectionery cook-off.
© **863/983-7979;** www.clewiston.org

Festival de Nopales (Cactus)   San Bernardino Tlaxcalancingo, Puebla, Mexico
Honoring *nopales,* the edible trunk of the prickly pear cactus and a popular Lenten food, this weekend fair in an outlying town southwest of downtown Puebla features nopal salads, stews, stuffed nopales, and even nopal ice cream.
© **52/222/246-2044**

MAY

Artichoke Festival   Castroville, California
This 2-day outdoor fest founded in 1959 features a parade, cooking demos, fruit and vegetable art, wine tastings, a farmer's market, crafts, games, live music, tours of artichoke fields, and vendors serving artichokes grilled, deep-fried, steamed, pickled, or creamed in soup.
© **831/633-2465;** www.artichoke-festival.org

Blue Crab Festival   Little River, South Carolina
Overrunning the historic waterfront of this coastal town north of Myrtle Beach, this 2-day spring street festival features arts and crafts, food booths, live music, and family activities.
www.bluecrabfestival.org

The International Bar-B-Q Festival   Queensboro, Kentucky
Every year during the second week in May, the town of Queensboro, Kentucky, fills with the aroma of hickory-smoked barbecue, featuring regional specialities such as burgoo and roasted mutton. Events include a pie-eating contest, Miss Bar-B-Q pageant, horse-shoe pitching, and a range of live music.
www.bbqfest.com

Vegas Uncork'd   Las Vegas, Nevada
This 4-day culinary showcase sponsored by *Bon Appétit* magazine stars Las Vegas's top chefs (which means some of the world's biggest names in cooking), with workshops, competitions, tastings, and gala luncheons and dinners.
www.bavegasuncorked.com

Feria de la Piña (Pineapple Festival)   Loma Bonita, Oaxaca, Mexico
The biggest event of the year in this tropical town in northern Oaxaca, this agricultural fair devoted to the juicy local pineapples features horse racing, cock fights, folk dances, fireworks, and a parade with floats and a Pineapple Queen.
www.visitmexico.com

Stilton Cheese Rolling Festival   Stilton, England
Every May Day bank holiday, teams compete to roll wheels of Stilton cheese down the High Street of the cheese's namesake village. Festivities also include a maypole, folk dancing, costume parade, live music, and lots of food and drink.
www.stilton-about.org

Sagra dei Limoni (Lemon Festival)   Monterosso al Mare, Italy
Honoring the lemon groves of this historic seaside Ligurian town, this Saturday festival includes contests for biggest local lemon and best shop window decorations, along with food booths and live music throughout the day.
☏ **39/187/817-525** for town office; www.cinqueterre.it

JUNE

Great Wisconsin Cheese Festival   Little Chute, Wisconsin
Kicking off June Dairy Month in the state nicknamed America's Dairyland, this 3-day event at Doyle Park features cheese tasting, cheese carving, a cheesecake contest, cheese curd eating contests, live music, a carnival, the Big cheese parade, and the Big Cheese Breakfast.
☏ **920/788-7380;** www.littlechutewi.org

Georgia Peach Festival   Byron and Fort Valley, Georgia
The world's largest peach cobbler is the star of this 8-day festival in the heart of Georgia's peach-growing country, featuring fireworks, games, tours of a fruit packing plant, a pancake breakfast, live music, a parade, and an art show.
www.gapeachfestival.com

American Craft Beer Fest   Boston, Massachusetts
Held at the Seaport World Trade Center, this 2-day event sponsored by *Beer Advocate* features food booths, seminars, guest speakers—and continuous 2-ounce tastings of some 300 beers from over 75 craft breweries from all over the country.
www.beeradvocate.com/acbf

Food & Wine Classic   Aspen, Colorado
Sponsored by *Food & Wine* magazine, this premier culinary confab features celebrity-studded food and wine tastings, seminars, cooking demonstrations, chef competitions, and a grand tasting dinner prepared by the magazine's "Best New Chefs."
www.foodandwine.com/promo/classic

Shrimp Festival   Oostduinkerke, Belgium
The only place in the world where shrimp fishermen drag their nets from horseback, this seacoast town in West Flanders celebrates its unique heritage with net-dragging contests, a costumed procession, the crowning of a shrimp queen, and a shrimp feast.
© **32/58/51-29-10;** www.koksijde.be

Festa del Risotto (Rice Harvest Festival)   Villimpenta, Italy
In the heart of the Lombardy plain, this historic walled town east of Mantua celebrates the harvest of its most important crop—rice—with 3 weekends of live music concerts, and, of course, feasting on vats of risotto.
© **39/376/667-508;** www.comune.villimpenta.mn.it

JULY

Mandeville Seafood Festival   Mandeville, Louisiana
Held in Fontainebleau State Park over July Fourth weekend, this 3-day event on the Lake Pontchartrain shore features live music, arts and crafts vendors, a car show, fireworks, and a food court full of New Orleans–style cooking and fresh seafood.
www.seafoodfest.org

National Cherry Festival   Traverse City, Michigan
Held since 1926, this immense weeklong celebration includes entertainment, food, crafts, sports events, tours, gala meals, a parade, a talent show, a giant Cherryopoly game, a cherry dessert cook-off, and competitions for cherry-pit spitting and cherry pie eating.
© **800/968-3380** or 231/947-4230; www.cherryfestival.org

Yarmouth Clam Festival   Yarmouth, Maine
Get your clams fried, steamed, in crab cakes or in chowder at this coastal Maine festival; townwide weekend events include an art show, running races, canoe race, parade, battle of the bands, live music, family activities, and pancake breakfasts.
© **207/846-3984;** www.clamfestival.com

Gilroy Garlic Festival   Gilroy, California
Founded in 1979, this weekend celebration devoted to garlic serves garlic bread, garlic fries, garlic sausage sandwiches, garlic chicken stir-fry, garlic shrimp, garlic popcorn, even garlic ice cream—along with entertainment, a beauty pageant, and the hotly contested Garlic Cook-Off.
© **408/842-1625;** www.gilroygarlicfestival.com

Maine Lobster Festival   Rockland, Maine
King Neptune and the Sea Goddess rule for 5 days of carnival rides, live music, art shows, crafts and games, ship tours, seafood cooking contests, pancake breakfasts, a parade, a cod-carrying race, lobster crate races, and 20,000 pounds of lobster consumed.
© **800/LOB-CLAW** (800/562-2529) or 207/596-0376; www.mainelobsterfestival.com

Sardine Festival   Scala Kallonis, Lesvos, Greece
At the end of July or early August, nighttime festivities in the village square of this working fishing harbor on Lesvos island include free ouzo and grilled sardines, a live band, and traditional dancers.
www.lesbos.co.uk or www.lesvos.com

Sweet Corn Festival   West Point, Iowa
The Corn State's biggest corn-harvest hoedown: a 4-day celebration with carnival rides, races, arts and crafts, music, tractor pulls, horseshoe pitching, a corn queen and parade, and 17 tons of free corn-on-the-cob consumed along with barbecue chicken and pork chops.
© **319/837-6313;** www.westpointcornfestival.com

National Blueberry Festival   South Haven, Michigan
Kicking off with a blueberry pie social, this four-day event on the Lake Michigan shore features food booths, a parade, a car show, a 5K run, a sand-sculpture contest, live music, and of course daily pancake breakfasts.
© **800/SO-HAVEN** (800/764-2836) or 269/637-5252 for South Haven visitor info; www. blueberryfestival.com

Mendota Sweet Corn Festival   Mendota, Illinois
Held since 1947, this harvest festival takes over downtown Mendota with food booths, crafts and games, carnival rides, beer garden, talent contest, corn recipe competition, corn-eating contest, a parade, and loads of free buttered fresh Del Monte corn on the cob.
© **815/539-6507;** www.sweetcornfestival.com

Fisherman's Feast   Boston, Massachusetts
Dating from 1911, this 4-day Italian street fair carries on such Sicilian fishing village traditions as a Blessing of the Waters, a procession of the Madonna, and "angels" flying through a blizzard of confetti. Food booths, crafts, games, and entertainment galore.
www.fishermansfeast.com

Great Taste of the Midwest   Madison, Wisconsin
Book early (in person or by mail-order lottery) for this always-sold-out outdoor beer fest in mid-August on the shores of Lake Monona, where 5,000 lucky beer lovers get to sample brews from over 100 brewpubs and microbreweries throughout the Midwest.
www.mhtg.org

La Pourcailhade (Festival of the Pig)   Trie sur Baïse, France
Colorful 1-day event in rural Pyrenees town includes contests for best shop window painting, best sausage eating, piglet racing, and guessing a porker's weight, culminating in a contest for best imitation of pigs' cries. Over 60 booths and festive meals as well.
© **33/5/62-35-44-08;** www.pourcailhade.com

Jackson County Apple Festival   Jackson, Ohio
Founded in 1937, this 5-day apple harvest celebration in southern Ohio features a gala parade, carnival rides, food stands, games, races, and live music, as well as apple-butter making, an apple-peeling contest, and apple-pie judging.
www.jacksonapplefestival.com

Great Chowder Cook-Off   Newport, Rhode Island
Newport's historic waterfront hosts this festive daylong competition, where restaurants from across the country vie for Best Chowder and Best Clamcakes awards, while spectators down 30,000 gallons of chowder and enjoy live entertainment on three stages.
www.newportfestivals.com/chowder-cook-off

Great American Beer Festival   Denver, Colorado
This 3-day event at Colorado Convention Center hosts almost 500 breweries from across the U.S., serving nearly 3,000 beers. Over 40,000 attendees line up for tasting sessions, seminars, food-pairing sessions, dinners, and a Boulder County Brews Cruise.
© **888/822-6273** or 303/447-0816; www.beertown/events/gabf

Great British Cheese Festival   Cardiff, Wales
Held in Cardiff Castle, this huge 2-day festival follows the British Cheese Awards dinner with master classes, wine workshops, cheese-making demos, cheese tossing and cheese skittles, and a marketplace with over 100 cheese makers and related food vendors.
✆ **44/2920/872-087;** www.thecheeseweb.co.uk

Oktoberfest die München (Munich Oktoberfest)   Munich, Germany
Munich's Lord Mayor taps the first keg of the year, followed by 2 weeks of night-and-day beer quaffing in over a dozen tents set up along Theresienwiese, accompanied by parades, rides, and other festivities. First held in 1810.
✆ **49/89/232-3900** or 49/89/500-77500; www.oktoberfest.de

OCTOBER

Circleville Pumpkin Show   Circleville, Ohio
Over a century old, this 4-day agricultural fair includes seven separate parades, food booths and displays, cooking and crafts demonstrations, carnival rides, a giant pumpkin weigh-in, pumpkin sculpting, pumpkin-pie eating, and a prettiest pumpkin pageant.
✆ **740/474-7000;** www.pumpkinshow.com

World Beer Festival   Raleigh and Durham, North Carolina
Tents fill the Durham Bulls athletic park for a day, featuring beers from over 150 breweries worldwide, from Germany and Belgium to Lithuania and Sri Lanka, along with several U.S. craft brewers. Food booths and live music keep things hopping.
✆ **800/977-2337;** www.allaboutbeer.wbf

Fiera del Tartufo (Truffle Festival)   Alba, Italy
This historic Piedmontese city celebrates the white truffle with a month of festivities—tastings, cooking demonstrations, awards, concerts, a literary festival, an art show, a gourmet food marketplace, a major truffle auction, and the historic Donkey Palio.
✆ **39/173/361-051;** www.fieradeltartufo.org

Zweibelmarkt (Onion Market)   Weimar, Germany
Three-day townwide festival (first held in 1658) includes a contest for the longest braid of onions intertwined with flowers, and over 500 stalls selling crafts, sausage, cheese, and, of course, onion soup and onion cake.
✆ **49/3643/745-0;** www.weimar.de

NOVEMBER

Wurstfest   New Braunfels, Texas
This weeklong salute to East Texas's German heritage dishes up sausage, beer, and sauerkraut in Landa Park along with oompah bands, yodelers, cloggers, and kinderchoirs, plus sports events, tours, an art show, and family fun.
✆ **830/25-9167;** www.wurstfest.com

Trois Glorieuses Wine Festival   Beaune, France
One of the wine world's most prestigious events, held since 1851, this 2-day celebration includes street entertainment, tastings, and gala dinners, culminating in the annual wine auction to benefit Hopsices de Beaune.
✆ **33/3/80-26-21-30;** www.beaune-burgundy.com

Fête du Hareng Roi (King Herring Festival)   Etaples, France
Along the quay of this Brittany fishing town, this annual 2-day event has fishermen dressed in local costume demonstrating traditional fishing methods, followed by music, folk dancing, and feasting on grilled herring, baked potatoes, and mulled wine.
✆ **33/3/21-09-56-94;** www.etaples-tourisme.com.

Tamale Festival   Indio, California
The world's largest tamale is the centerpiece of this festival in downtown Indio, celebrating the area's Mexican heritage with a parade, carnival rides, folkloric dancing, a tamale-eating contest, a tamale cook-off, mariachi bands, and other live music.
© **760/391-4175;** www.tamalefestival.net

Pig's Ear Beer and Cider Festival   Hackney, London, England
"Pig's Ear" is Cockney rhyming slang for beer, and more than 100 real ales and hard ciders are served during this annual 5-day drinkathon at Ocean (270 Mare St.) in East London, run by CAMRA, the Campaign for Real Ale.
www.pigsear.org.uk

La Noche de los Rabanos (Night of the Radish)   Oaxaca, Mexico
Every December 23, Christmas festivities in Oaxaca are kicked off in the *zócalo* at this unique, century-old gathering: Townsfolk gather to display intricately carved red-and-white radishes and win cash prizes, followed by fireworks and feasting.
www.christmasinoaxaca.com

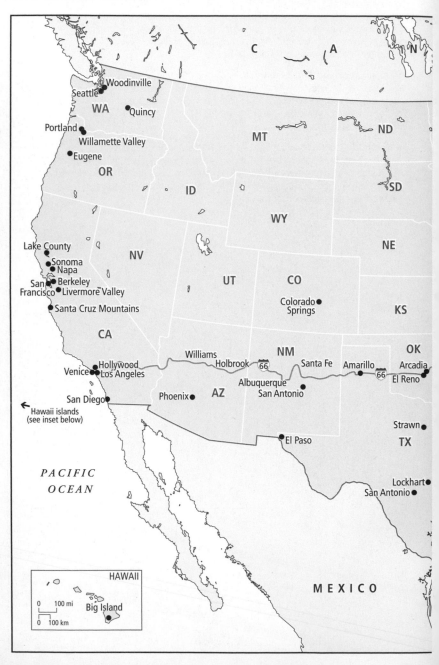

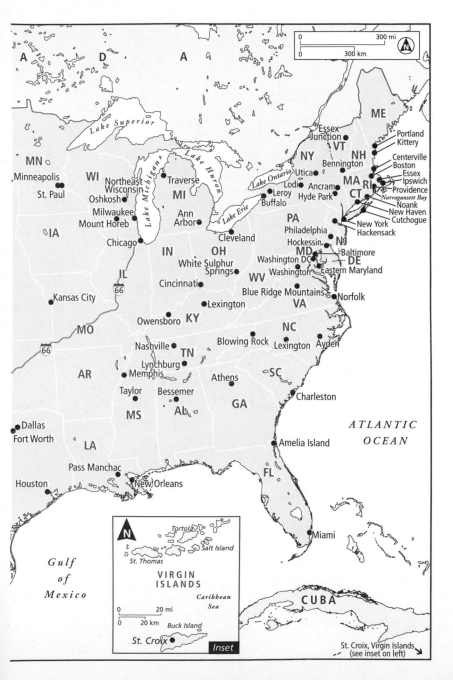

Lake Superior

A   D   A

MN
Minneapolis
St. Paul

WI
Northeast
Wisconsin
Oshkosh
Milwaukee
Mount Horeb

IA

Lake Michigan

Traverse

MI

Lake Huron

Ann
Arbor

Chicago

IN

OH

White Sulphur
Springs

Cleveland

Lake Ontario
Utica
Lodi
Leroy
Buffalo

Lake Erie

Essex
Junction

ME

VT
Bennington

NH
Portland
Kittery
Centerville
Boston
Essex
Ipswich
Providence

NY

Ancram
Hyde Park

MA   RI
CT

Narragansett Bay
Noank
New Haven
Cutchogue

New York
Hackensack

PA
Philadelphia

NJ

Hockessin
Washington DC
Washington

MD
Baltimore
DE

IL
66

Kansas City

Cincinnati

WV

Eastern Maryland

Lexington

VA

Blue Ridge Mountains
Norfolk

MO

Owensboro

KY

NC

Nashville
Lynchburg
Memphis

TN

Blowing Rock
Lexington

Ayden

66

AR

Taylor   Bessemer

Athens

SC

Charleston

MS

AL

GA

ATLANTIC
OCEAN

Dallas
Fort Worth

LA

Amelia Island

Houston

Pass Manchac
New Orleans

FL

Miami

Gulf
of
Mexico

N

Tortola
Salt Island

St. Thomas

VIRGIN
ISLANDS

Caribbean
Sea

0   20 mi
0   20 km
Buck Island

St. Croix

Inset

CUBA

St. Croix, Virgin Islands
(see inset on left)

0   300 mi
0   300 km

N

Europe

Faroe Islands

Shetland Islands

NORWAY

Orkney Islands

North Sea

Hebrides

Isle of Skye

DENMARK

Copenhagen

Edinburgh

Innerleithen

Berlin

Masham

Harrogate

Yorkshire

NETH.

Alkmaar

IRELAND

U.K.

GERMANY

Ennis

Broadway

Shanagarry

Oxford

London

The Rheingau

Cork

Bath

BELGIUM

Pizen

Brussels

English Channel

Chimay

Reims

LUX.

Baden-Württemberg

Normandy

Paris

Alsace

Munich

ATLANTIC OCEAN

Champagne

Loire Valley

Sancerre

Zurich

AUSTRIA

Burgundy

SWITZERLAND

Vevey

Bay of Biscay

FRANCE

Rhone Valley

Milan

ITALY

Verona

Piedmont

Bologna

Bordeaux

Parma

Florence

Provence

Tuscany

Greve

Sinalunga

La Rioja

ANDORRA

Brunello

Corsica

Rome

Oporto

SPAIN

Barcelona

Sardinia

Tyrrhenian Sea

PORTUGAL

Majorca

Mediterranean Sea

To Madeira Island (530 Mi)

Aracena

Marsala

Sicily

Strait of Gibraltar

Madeira

TUNISIA

MALTA

0   15mi

0   15km

MOROCCO

ALGERIA

450

SWEDEN

Gulf of Bothnia

Stockholm

Baltic Sea

Gulf of Finland

ESTONIA

Rybinsk Res.

R U S S I A

LATVIA

LITHUANIA

Moscow ●

P O L A N D

BELARUS

UKRAINE

CZECH

Vienna ●

SLOVAKIA

Mád, Tokaji ●

AUSTRIA

Budapest ●

HUNGARY

MOLDOVA

SLOVENIA

CROATIA

ROMANIA

Sea of Azov

BOSNIA
and
HERZ.

YUGOSLAVIA

BULGARIA

B l a c k   S e a

Adriatic Sea

MACEDONIA

ITALY

ALBANIA

Istanbul ■

T U R K E Y

GREECE

Aegean Sea

Lesbos

L. Tuz

Ionian Sea

Athens ●

Rhodes

Crete

Cyprus

SYRIA

M e d i t e r r a n e a n   S e a

0   250 mi

0   250 km

N

Canada

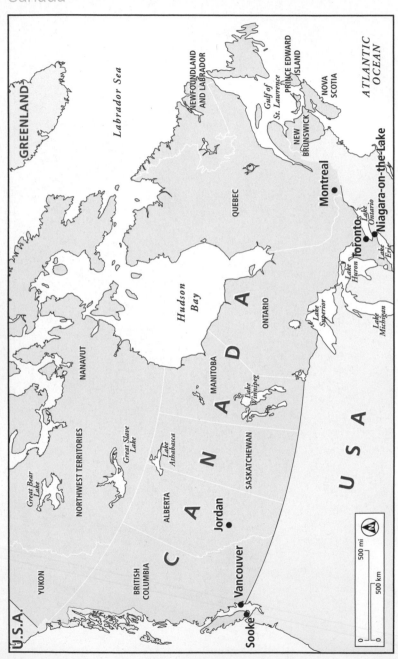

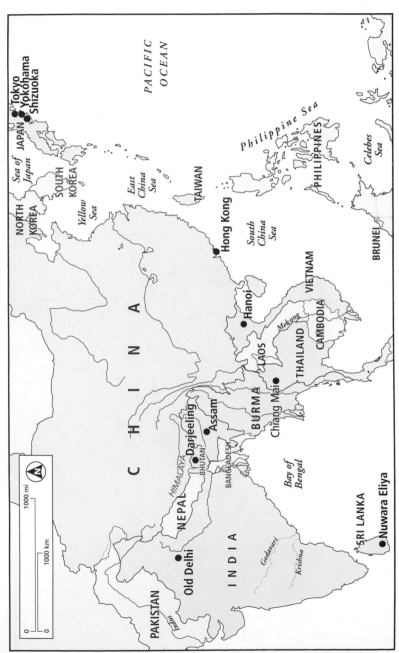

Africa

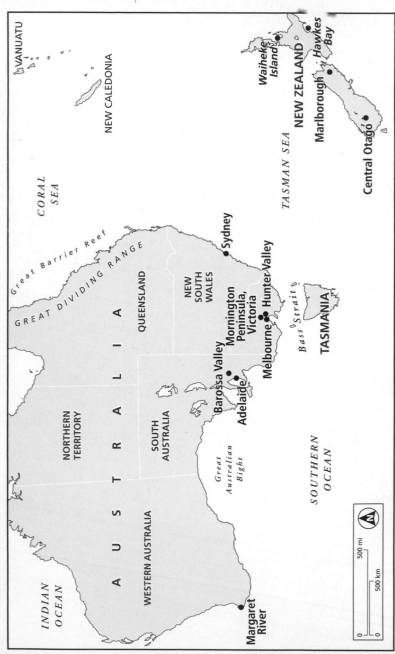

Indices

Regional Index

Alphabetical Index

Photo Credits

p. 1: © Aaron Kohr; p. 3: © Anthony Woods; p. 4: © Borough Market; p. 9: © Neil Sclecht; p. 16: © Courtesy Pike Place Market PDA; p. 18: © Gary Morgret; p. 21: © Courtesy Harrod's; p. 22: © Ethel Davies; p. 25: © Matthieu Alexandre for Poilâne; p. 27: © Courtesy Peck; p. 32: © Courtesy Zingerman's; p. 38: © Courtesy Taller de Tapas; p. 39: © Courtesy Taller de Tapas; p. 41: © Courtesy Superdawg Drive-In, Inc.; p. 42: © Dean Cambray Photography; p. 44: © Courtesy Barbara-Jo's Books to Cooks; p. 45: © Kitchen Arts & Letters; p. 46: © Chris Mason Stearns; p. 47: © John Sherlock; p. 49: © Mark Berndt; p. 56: © Shawn Colin; p. 57: © Courtesy Herbsaint; p. 60: © 2006 The Culinary Institute of America; p. 61: © Courtesy The Inn at Little Washington; p. 62: © Gordon Beall; p. 66: © Sooke Harbour House; p. 67: © Alan Donaldson; p. 69: © Courtesy Troisgros; p. 71: © Courtesy Locanda dell'Amorosa; p. 73: © Courtesy Mount Nelson Hotel; p. 80: © French Country Waterways, Ltd.; p. 81: © Courtesy Ballymaloe Cookery School; p. 85: © Davide Maestri; p. 88: © Courtesy Seasons of my Heart; p. 89: © Courtesy Chiang Mai Thai Cookery School; p. 90: © Simon Hare Photography; p. 91 bottom: © Alyssa Dragun; p. 91 top: © Courtesy Talula's; p. 94: © 2006 The Culinary Institute of America; p. 97: © Stephen Elphick; p. 98: © Addison Doty; p. 99: © Addison Doty; p. 103: © Courtesy Fairburn Farm; p. 104: © Andrei Federov; p. 106: ©Tracey Kuziewicz; p. 108: © Courtesy The Fat Duck; p. 110: Courtesy Arzak; p. 111: © Courtesy Arzak; p.112: © Patricia Niven; p.114: © Takahiko Marumoto; p. 119: © Laurence Mouton; p.122: © Matteo Piazza; p. 125: © Courtesy Nobu Restaurants; p. 126: © Deborah Jones; p. 128: © Kipling Swehla; p. 131: © Darko Zagar; p. 137: © 2008 Lara Ferroni, Plates & Packs; p. 138: © Charles Schiller; p. 141: © Natalie Ross; p. 143: © Sharon Engelstein; p. 145: © Andrea Wyner; p. 147: © Kingmond Young; p. 149: © Sean M. Hower; p. 152: © Courtesy Figueira Rubaiyat; p. 153: © Tadeu Brunelli; p. 155: © Courtesy Babbo; p. 160: © Aya Brackett; p. 166: © GoodEye Photography/Chris Schmauch; p.167: © Jen Munkvold; p. 172: © Eliane Excoffier; p. 174: © Courtesy 3 Frakkar; p. 178: © Courtesy Casa Lucio; p. 183: © Courtesy Superdawg Drive-In, Inc.; p. 185: © Courtesy Pat's; p. 187: © Obrycki's 2008; p. 188: © Nizam Ali; p. 189: © Courtesy Camp Washington Chili; p. 195: no credit; p. 196: © Courtesy Pops; p. 197: © Courtesy Pops; p. 198: © Courtesy Manny's Buckhorn Tavern; p. 199: © John E. Hall; p. 202: © Courtesy Pizzeria Uno; p. 204: © John Hall Photography; p. 205: © Barry Michlin; p. 211: © Courtesy Sonny Bryan's Smokehouse; p. 214: © Courtesy The Clam Box; p. 216: © Courtesy Al Forno; p. 218: © Courtesy Abbott's in the Rough; p. 221: © Courtesy Carnegie Deli; p. 229: © Courtesy Louis' Lunch; p. 233: © Courtesy The Taghkanic Diner; p. 238: © Courtesy The Varsity; p. 241: © Myndi Pressley/The Square Studio; p. 246: © Courtesy Locanda dell'Amorosa; p. 247: © Erhard Pfeiffer 2007; p. 248: © Courtesy The Hess Collection Winery; p. 250: © Jerry Alexander/Lonely Planet Images; p. 253: © Courtesy Beringer Vineyards; p. 254: © Scott Nugent/designthis.com; p. 255: © Deborah Jones; p. 259: © Jason Tinacci/TrellisCreative.com; p. 261: © Jay Graham; p. 268: © Courtesy Higgins; p. 269: © John Valls; p. 271: © Kevin Cruff; p. 273: © Kristian S. Reynolds; p. 277: © Courtesy Inniskillin; p. 278: © Courtesy Inniskillin; p. 282: © Courtesy Johansen Krause; p. 283: © Courtesy Moet & Chandon; p. 289: © Courtesy Guigal; p. 292: © Courtesy Château Lynch-Bages; p. 296: © Checchino Restaurant; p. 297: © Lisa Romerein/Getty Images; p. 298: © Courtesy Castello Banfi; p. 315: © Courtesy Bodega Benegas Lynch; p. 319: © Courtesy Viu Manent; p. 320: © Courtesy Viu Manent; p. 326: © Earl Carter; p. 327: © Courtesy QUAY; p. 332: © Courtesy Craggy Range Vineyards Ltd.; p. 335: © Courtesy of Woodford Reserve; p. 339 top: © Bières de Chimay; p. 339 bottom: © Bières de Chimay; p. 342: © Ditte Isager; p. 343: © Ditte Isager; p. 352: © Russell Lee; p. 353: © Courtesy Sprecher's; p. 354: © Craig Bares; p. 355: © Mette Nielsen; p. 359: © Courtesy of Woodford Reserve; p. 360: no credit; p. 362: © John Paul; p. 363: © John Paul; p. 364: © Paul Bock; p. 370: © Hollenbeck Productions; p. 372 top: